Student CD contains:

MegaStat® for Excel®
Getting Started with MegaStat® for Excel® (User's Guide)
Visual Statistics 2.0
ScreenCam Tutorials
- Excel
  - Introduction
  - Regression
- MegaStat® for Excel®
  - Introduction
  - Descriptive Statistics/Frequency Distributions
  - Regression
- Minitab
  - Introduction
  - Regression

Quizzes
Solved Problems
Data Sets
- Excel
- Minitab
- SPSS

Data Files
- Excel
- Minitab

PowerPoint
Weblinks
- Online Learning Center
- **www.exercises**
- Business Statistics Center
- ALEKS
- Homework Manager

Optional Chapters (PDF files):
- Statistical Quality Control
- Time Series and Forecasting

Basic Statistics for Business & Economics

Fifth Edition

Douglas A. Lind
Coastal Carolina University and The University of Toledo

William G. Marchal
The University of Toledo

Samuel A. Wathen
Coastal Carolina University

Boston Burr Ridge, IL Dubuque, IA Madison, WI New York San Francisco St. Louis
Bangkok Bogotá Caracas Kuala Lumpur Lisbon London Madrid Mexico City
Milan Montreal New Delhi Santiago Seoul Singapore Sydney Taipei Toronto

BASIC STATISTICS FOR BUSINESS AND ECONOMICS
Published by McGraw-Hill/Irwin, a business unit of The McGraw-Hill Companies, Inc. 1221 Avenue of the Americas, New York, NY, 10020.

This book is printed on acid-free paper.

3 4 5 6 7 8 9 0 DOW/DOW 0 9 8 7 6

ISBN-13: 978-0-07-298396-8 (student edition)
ISBN-10: 0-07-298396-5 (student edition)
ISBN-13: 978-0-07-298401-9 (instructor's edition)
ISBN-10: 0-07-298401-5 (instructor's edition)

Editorial director: *Brent Gordon*
Executive editor: *Richard T. Hercher, Jr.*
Developmental editor II: *Christina A. Sanders*
Senior marketing manager: *Douglas Reiner*
Media producer: *Greg Bates*
Project manager: *Jim Labeots*
Senior production supervisor: *Michael R. McCormick*
Senior designer: *Adam Rooke*
Photo research coordinator: *Lori Kramer*
Photo researcher: *Jennifer Blankenship*
Supplement producer: *Joyce J. Chappetto*
Senior digital content specialist: *Brian Nacik*
Cover design: *Allison Traynham*
Typeface: *9.5/11 Helvetica Neue 55*
Compositor: *Cenveo*
Printer: *R. R. Donnelley*

Library of Congress Cataloging-in-Publication Data

Lind, Douglas A.
Business statistics for business & economics / Douglas A. Lind, William G. Marchal, Samuel A. Wathen.—5th ed.
p. cm—(McGraw-Hill/Irwin series Business statistics)
Includes index.
ISBN 0-07-298396-5 (student ed. : alk. paper)—ISBN 0-07-298401-5 (instructor's ed. : alk. paper)
1. Social sciences—Statistical methods. 2. Economics—Statistical methods. 3. Industrial management—Statistical methods. 4. Commercial statistics. I. Title: Basic statistics for business and economics. II. Marchal, William G. III. Wathen, Samuel Adam. IV. Title. V. Series.

HA29.L75 2006
519.5—dc22

2004057810

www.mhhe.com

The McGraw-Hill/Irwin Titles

Business Statistics

Aczel and Sounderpandian, **Complete Business Statistics,** *Sixth Edition*

ALEKS Corp., **ALEKS for Business Statistics**

Alwan, **Statistical Process Analysis,** *First Edition*

Bowerman and O'Connell, **Business Statistics in Practice,** *Third Edition*

Bowerman and O'Connell, **Essentials of Business Statistics,** *Second Edition*

*Bryant and Smith, **Practical Data Analysis: Case Studies in Business Statistics, Volumes I and II** *Second Edition*; **Volume III,** *First Edition*

Cooper and Schindler, **Business Research Methods,** *Ninth Edition*

Delurgio, **Forecasting Principles and Applications,** *First Edition*

Doane, Mathieson, and Tracy, **Visual Statistics,** *Second Edition, 2.0*

Doane, **LearningStats CD-ROM,** *First Edition*

Gitlow, Oppenheim, Oppenheim, and Levine, **Quality Management: Tools and Methods Techniques,** *Third Edition*

Lind, Marchal, and Wathen, **Basic Statistics for Business and Economics,** *Fifth Edition*

Lind, Marchal, and Wathen, **Statistical Techniques in Business and Economics,** *Twelfth Edition*

Merchant, Goffinet, and Koehler, **Basic Statistics Using Excel for Office XP,** *Fourth Edition*

Merchant, Goffinet, and Koehler, **Basic Statistics Using Excel for Office 2000,** *Third Edition*

Kutner, Nachtsheim, Neter, and Li, **Applied Linear Statistical Models,** *Fifth Edition*

Kutner, Nachtsheim, and Neter, **Applied Linear Regression Models,** *Fourth Edition*

Sahai and Khurshid, **Pocket Dictionary of Statistics,** *First Edition*

Siegel, **Practical Business Statistics,** *Fifth Edition*

Wilson, Keating, and John Galt Solutions, Inc., **Business Forecasting,** *Fourth Edition*

Zagorsky, **Business Information,** *First Edition*

Quantitative Methods and Management Science

*Bodily, Carraway, Frey, and Pfeifer, **Quantitative Business Analysis: Text and Cases,** *First Edition*

Hillier and Hillier, **Introduction to Management Science: A Modeling and Case Studies Approach with Spreadsheets,** *Second Edition*

*Available only on Primis at www.mhhe.com/primis

To Jane, my wife and best friend, and to our sons and their wives,
Mike (Sue), Steve (Kathryn), and Mark (Sarah).
Douglas A. Lind

To Andrea, my children, and our first grandchild, Elizabeth Anne.
William G. Marchal

To my wonderful family: Isaac, Hannah, and Barb.
Samuel A. Wathen

A Note to the Student

We have tried to make this material "no more difficult than it needs to be." By that we mean we always keep the explanations practical without oversimplifying. We have used examples similar to those you will encounter in the business world or that you encounter in everyday life. When you have completed this book, you will understand how to apply statistical tools to help make business decisions. In addition, you will find that many of the topics and methods you learn can be used in other courses in your business education, and that they are consistent with what you encounter in other quantitative or statistics electives.

There is more data available to a business than there has been in previous years. People who can interpret data and convert it into useful information are not so easy to find. If you thoughtfully work through this text, you will be well prepared to contribute to the success and development of your company. Remember, as one of the authors read recently in a fortune cookie, "None of the secrets of success will work unless you do."

Learning Aids

We have designed the text to assist you in taking this course without the anxiety often associated with statistics. These learning aids are all intended to help you in your study.

Objectives Each chapter begins with a set of learning objectives. They are designed to provide focus for the chapter and to motivate learning. These objectives indicate what you should be able to do after completing the chapter. We include a photo that ties these chapter objectives to one of the exercises within the chapter.

Introduction At the start of each chapter, we review the important concepts of the previous chapter(s) and describe how they link to what the current chapter will cover.

Definitions Definitions of new terms or terms unique to the study of statistics are set apart from the text and highlighted. This allows for easy reference and review.

Formulas Whenever a formula is used for the first time, it is boxed and numbered for easy reference. In addition, a formula card that summarizes the key formulas is bound into the text. This can be removed and carried for quick reference as you do homework or review for exams.

Margin Notes There are concise notes in the margin. Each emphasizes the key concept being presented immediately adjacent to it.

Examples/Solutions We include numerous examples with solutions. These are designed to show you immediately, in detail, how the concepts can be applied to business situations.

Statistics in Action Statistics in Action articles are scattered throughout the text, usually about two per chapter. They provide unique and interesting applications and historical insights into statistics.

Self-Reviews Self-reviews are interspersed throughout the chapter and each is closely patterned after the preceding **Example/Solution.** They will help you monitor your progress and provide immediate reinforcement for that particular technique. The answers and methods of solution are located at the end of the chapter.

Exercises We include exercises within the chapter, after the **Self-Reviews,** and at the end of the chapter. The answers and method of solution for all odd-numbered exercises are at the end of the book. For most exercises with more than 20 observations, the data are on the CD-ROM in the text.

Chapter Outline As a summary, each chapter includes a chapter outline. This learning aid provides an opportunity to review material, particularly vocabulary, and to review the formulas.

Web Exercises Almost all chapters have references to the Internet for companies, government organizations, and university data sets. These sites contain interesting and relevant information to enhance the exercises at the end of the chapters.

Dataset Exercises In most chapters, the last four exercises refer to four large business data sets. A complete listing of the data is available in the back of the text and on the CD-ROM included with the text.

Supplements

The **Student CD,** packaged free with all copies of the text, features self-graded practice quizzes, software tutorials, PowerPoint slides, the data files (in MINITAB and Excel formats) for the end-of-chapter data and for exercises having 20 or more data values. Also included on the CD is an Internet link to the text website and to the websites listed in the Web exercises in the text. **MegaStat** and **Visual Statistics** are included. MegaStat provides software that enhances the power of Excel in statistical analysis. Visual Statistics is a software program designed for interactive experimentation and visualization.

A comprehensive **Study Guide,** written by Professor Walter Lange of The University of Toledo, is organized much like the textbook. Each chapter includes objectives, a brief summary of the chapter, problems and their solution, self-review exercises, and assignment problems.

The Online Learning Center includes online content for assistance and reference. The site provides chapter objectives, a summary, glossary of key terms, solved problems, downloadable data files, practice quizzes, PowerPoint, web links and much more. Visit the text website at http://www.mhhe.com/lindbasics5e.

ALEKS for Business Statistics (Assessment and Learning in Knowledge Spaces) is an artificial intelligence based system that acts much like a human tutor and can provide individualized assessment, practice, and learning. By assessing your knowledge, ALEKS focuses clearly on what you are ready to learn next and helps you master the course content more quickly and clearly. You can visit ALEKS at www.business.aleks.com.

Douglas A. Lind
William G. Marchal
Samuel A. Wathen

Preface

The objective of *Basic Statistics for Business and Economics* is to provide students majoring in management, marketing, finance, accounting, economics, and other fields of business administration with an introductory survey of the many applications of descriptive and inferential statistics. While we focus on business applications, we also use many problems and examples that are student oriented and do not require previous courses.

When Professor Robert Mason wrote the first edition of this series of texts in 1967 locating relevant business data was difficult. That has changed! Today locating data is not difficult. The number of items you purchase at the grocery store is automatically recorded at the checkout counter. Phone companies track the time of our calls, the length of calls, and the number of the person called. Credit card companies maintain information on the number, time and date, and amount of our purchases. Medical devices automatically monitor our heart rate, blood pressure, and temperature. A large amount of business information is recorded and reported almost instantly. *CNN, USA Today,* and *MSNBC,* for example, all have websites where you can track stock prices with a delay of less than twenty minutes.

Today, skills are needed to deal with the large volume of numerical information. First, we need to be critical consumers of information presented by others. Second, we need to be able to reduce large amounts of information into a concise and meaningful form to enable us to make effective interpretations, judgments, and decisions.

All students have calculators and most have either personal computers or access to personal computers in a campus lab. Statistical software, such as Microsoft Excel and MINITAB, is available on these computers. The commands necessary to achieve the software results are available in a special section at the end of each chapter. We use screen captures within the chapters, so the student becomes familiar with the nature of the software output. Because of the availability of computers and software it is no longer necessary to dwell on calculations. We have replaced many of the calculation examples with interpretative ones, to assist the student in understanding and interpreting the statistical results. In addition we now place more emphasis on the conceptual nature of the statistical topics. While making these changes, we have not moved away from presenting, as best we can, the key concepts, along with supporting examples.

The fifth edition of *Basic Statistics for Business and Economics* is the product of many people: students, colleagues, reviewers, and the staff at McGraw-Hill/Irwin. We thank them all. We wish to express our sincere gratitude to the reviewers:

Jodey Lingg
City University

Miren Ivankovic
Southern Wesleyan University

Michael Bitting
John Logan College

Vadim Shilov
Towson University

James Dulgeroff
San Bernardino Valley College

Gordon Johnson
California State University Northridge

Andrew Parkes
University of Northern Iowa

Abu Wahid
Tennessee State University

William F. Younkin
University of Miami

Michael Kazlow
Pace University

Jim Mirabella
Webster University
John Yarber, Jr.
Northeast Mississippi Community College
Stanley D. Stephenson
Texas State University-San Marcos
Hope Baker
Kennesaw State University

Their suggestions and thorough review of the previous edition and the manuscript of this edition make this a better text.

Special thanks go to a number of people. Dr. Jacquelynne Mclellan of Frostburg University and Lawrence Moore reviewed the manuscript and checked exercises for accuracy. Professor Walter Lange, of the University of Toledo, prepared the study guide. Dr. Temoleon Rousos checked the study guide for accuracy. Dr. Samuel Wathen, of Coastal Carolina University, prepared the test bank. Professor Joyce Keller, of St. Edward's University, prepared the PowerPoint Presentation. Ms. Denise Heban and the authors prepared the Instructor's Manual.

We also wish to thank the staff at McGraw-Hill/Irwin. This includes Richard T. Hercher, Jr., Executive Editor; Christina Sanders, Developmental Editor; Douglas Reiner, Marketing Manager; James Labeots, Project Manager, and others we do not know personally, but who made valuable contributions.

Brief Contents

Contents

1

What Is Statistics?

High speed conveyor belts and state-of-the-art technology efficiently move merchandise through Wal-Mart's distribution centers to keep its nearly 3,000 stores in stock. In 2004, the five largest American companies, ranked by sales were Wal-Mart, BP, Exxon Mobil, General Motors, and Ford Motor Company. (See Goal 5 and Statistics in Action box, page 4.)

GOALS

When you have completed this chapter you will be able to:

1. **Understand why we study statistics.**
2. **Explain what is meant by *descriptive statistics* and *inferential statistics.***
3. **Distinguish between a *qualitative variable* and a *quantitative variable.***
4. **Distinguish between a *discrete variable* and a *continuous variable.***
5. **Distinguish among the *nominal, ordinal, interval,* and *ratio* levels of measurement.**
6. **Define the terms *mutually exclusive* and *exhaustive.***

Introduction

More than 100 years ago H. G. Wells, an English author and historian, suggested that one day quantitative reasoning will be as necessary for effective citizenship as the ability to read. He made no mention of business because the Industrial Revolution was just beginning. Mr. Wells could not have been more correct. While "business experience," some "thoughtful guesswork," and "intuition" are key attributes of successful managers, today's business problems tend to be too complex for this type of decision making alone.

Fortunately, business managers of the twenty-first century have access to large amounts of information. Alan Greenspan, Chairman of the Federal Reserve, is well known for his ability to analyze economic data. He is well aware of the importance of statistical tools and techniques to provide accurate and timely information to make public statements that have the power to move global stock markets and influence political thinking. Dr. Greenspan, speaking before a National Skills Summit, stated: "Workers must be equipped not simply with technical know-how, but also with the ability to create, analyze, and transform information and to interact effectively with others. That is, separate the facts from opinions, and then organize these facts in an appropriate manner and analyze the information."

One of the tools used to understand information is statistics. Statistics is used not only by business people; we all also apply statistical concepts in our lives. For example, to start the day you turn on the shower and let it run for a few moments. Then you put your hand in the shower to sample the temperature and decide to add more hot water or more cold water, or you conclude that the temperature is just right and enter the shower. As a second example, suppose you are at the grocery store and wish to buy a frozen pizza. One of the pizza makers has a stand, and they offer a small wedge of their pizza. After sampling the pizza, you decide whether to purchase the pizza or not. In both the shower and pizza examples, you make a decision and select a course of action based on a sample.

Businesses face similar situations. The Kellogg Company must ensure that the mean amount of Raisin Bran in the 25.5-gram box meets label specifications. To do so, they might set a "target" weight somewhat higher than the amount specified on the label. Each box is then weighed after it is filled. The weighing machine reports a distribution of the content weights for each hour as well as the number "kicked-out" for being under the label specification during the hour. The Quality Inspection Department also randomly selects samples from the production line and checks the quality of the product and the weight of the product in the box. If the mean product weight differs significantly from the target weight or the percent of kick-outs is too large, the process is adjusted.

On a national level, a candidate for the office of President of the United States wants to know what percent of the voters in Illinois will support him in the upcoming election. There are several ways he could go about answering this question. He could have his staff call all those people in Illinois who plan to vote in the upcoming election and ask for whom they plan to vote. He could go out on a street in Chicago, stop 10 people who look to be of voting age, and ask them for whom they plan to vote. He could select a random sample of about 2,000 voters from the state, contact these voters, and, on the basis of this information, make an estimate of the percent who will vote for him in the upcoming election. In this text we will show you why the third choice is the best course of action.

Why Study Statistics?

If you look through your university catalog, you will find that statistics is required for many college programs. Why is this so? What are the differences in the statistics courses taught in the Engineering College, Psychology or Sociology Departments in the Liberal Arts College, and the College of Business? The biggest difference is the examples used. The course content is basically the same. In the College of Business we are interested in such things as profits, hours worked, and wages. In the Psychology Department they are interested in test scores, and in Engineering they may be interested in how many units are manufactured on a particular machine. However, all three are interested in what is a typical value and how much variation there is in the data. There may also be a difference in the level of mathematics required. An engineering statistics course usually requires calculus. Statistics courses in colleges of business and education usually teach the course at a more applied level. You should be able to handle the mathematics in this text if you have completed high school algebra.

Examples of why we study statistics

So why is statistics required in so many majors? The first reason is that numerical information is everywhere. Look on the internet (www.gallup.com or www.standardandpoors.com) and in the newspapers (*USA Today*), news magazines (*Time, Newsweek, U.S. News and World Report*), business magazines (*Business Week, Forbes*), or general interest magazines (*People*), women's magazines (*Home and Garden*), or sports magazines (*Sports Illustrated*, *ESPN The Magazine*), and you will be bombarded with numerical information.

Here are some examples:

- In 2002 Maryland had the highest 3-year-average median income of $55,912, Alaska was second with a median income of $55,412, and West Virginia had the lowest median income $30,072. You can check the latest information by going to www.census.gov, under *People* select *Income,* then under *Current Population Survey* select *Income in the United States: 2002,* and then move to *Median Household Income by State.*
- About 77 percent of golfers in the United States attended college, their average household income is more than $70,000 per year, 60 percent own computers, 45 percent have investments in stocks and bonds, and they spend $6.2 billion annually on golf equipment and apparel. You can find additional information about golfers at www.fcon.com/golfing/demographics.htm.

- The average cost of big Hollywood movies soared in 2003. The top seven studios spent an average of $102.8 million to make and market their films. This is an increase of 15 percent from 2002. How did this increase affect ticket prices? The average ticket price was $6.03, an increase of $0.23 from 2002. The number of admissions declined 1.574 billion or 4 percent from the previous year.
- *USA Today* prints *Snapshots* that provide interesting data. For example, newly constructed single family homes in 2003 are on average 2,320 square feet, up 40 percent from 1973. During the same time the average household size has decreased from 3.1 to 2.6. So, we have more space in the home and less people occupying the space.

Year	Home in square feet	Household size
1973	1,660	3.1
2003	2,320	2.6

Another Snapshot reported that the typical first-time bride and groom in the United States are more than four years older than they were in 1960.

Year	Man	Woman
1960	22.8 years	20.3 years
2003	26.9	25.3

You can check other Snapshots by going to www.usatoday.com and then click on *Snapshots.* You will see a selection of recent Snapshots, sorted by News, Sports, Money, and Life.

Statistics in Action

We call your attention to a feature we title *Statistics in Action.* Read each one carefully to get an appreciation of the wide application of statistics in management, economics, nursing, law enforcement, sports, and other disciplines. Following is an assortment of statistical information.

- In 2004, *Forbes* published a list of the richest Americans. William Gates, founder of Microsoft Corporation, is the richest. His net worth is estimated at $46.6 billion. (www.forbes.com)
- In 2004, the five largest American companies, ranked by sales were Wal-Mart, BP, Exxon Mobil, General Motors, and Ford Motor Company. (www.forbes.com)
- In the United States, a typical high school graduate earns $1.2 million in his or her lifetime, a typical college graduate with a bachelor's degree earns $2.1 million, and a typical college graduate with a master's degree earns $2.5 million. (usgovinfo.about.com/library/weekly/aa072602a.htm)

How are we to determine if the conclusions reported are reasonable? Was the sample large enough? How were the sampled units selected? To be an educated consumer of this information, we need to be able to read the charts and graphs and understand the discussion of the numerical information. An understanding of the concepts of basic statistics will be a big help.

A second reason for taking a statistics course is that statistical techniques are used to make decisions that affect our daily lives. That is, they affect our personal welfare. Here are a few examples:

- Insurance companies use statistical analysis to set rates for home, automobile, life, and health insurance. Tables are available showing estimates that a 20-year-old female has 60.16 years of life remaining, and that a 50-year-old man has 27.63 years remaining. On the basis of these estimates, life insurance premiums are established. These tables are available at www.ssa.gov/OACT/STATS/table4cb.html.
- The Environmental Protection Agency is interested in the water quality of Lake Erie. They periodically take water samples to establish the level of contamination and maintain the level of quality.
- Medical researchers study the cure rates for diseases using different drugs and different forms of treatment. For example, what is the effect of treating a certain type of knee injury surgically or with physical therapy? If you take an aspirin each day, does that reduce your risk of a heart attack?

A third reason for taking a statistics course is that the knowledge of statistical methods will help you understand how decisions are made and give you a better understanding of how they affect you.

No matter what line of work you select, you will find yourself faced with decisions where an understanding of data analysis is helpful. In order to make an informed decision, you will need to be able to:

1. Determine whether the existing information is adequate or additional information is required.
2. Gather additional information, if it is needed, in such a way that it does not provide misleading results.
3. Summarize the information in a useful and informative manner.
4. Analyze the available information.
5. Draw conclusions and make inferences while assessing the risk of an incorrect conclusion.

The statistical methods presented in the text will provide you with a framework for the decision-making process.

In summary, there are at least three reasons for studying statistics: (1) data are everywhere, (2) statistical techniques are used to make many decisions that affect our lives, and (3) no matter what your career, you will make professional decisions that involve data. An understanding of statistical methods will help you make these decisions more effectively.

What Is Meant by Statistics?

How do we define the word *statistics*? We encounter it frequently in our everyday language. It really has two meanings. In the more common usage, statistics refers to numerical information. Examples include the average starting salary of college graduates, the number of deaths due to alcoholism last year, the change in the Dow Jones Industrial Average from yesterday to today, and the number of home runs hit by the Chicago Cubs during the 2004 season. In these examples statistics are a value or a percentage. Other examples include:

- The typical automobile in the United States travels 11,099 miles per year, the typical bus 9,353 miles per year, and the typical truck 13,942 miles per year. In

Canada the corresponding information is 10,371 miles for automobiles, 19,823 miles for buses, and 7,001 miles for trucks.
- The mean time waiting for technical support is 17 minutes.
- The mean length of the business cycle since 1945 is 61 months.

The above are all examples of **statistics.** A collection of numerical information is called **statistics** (plural).

We often present statistical information in a graphical form. A graph is often useful for capturing reader attention and to portray a large amount of information. For example, Chart 1–1 shows Frito-Lay volume and market share for the major snack and potato chip categories in supermarkets in the United States. It requires only a quick glance to discover there were nearly 800 million pounds of potato chips sold and that Frito-Lay sold 64 percent of that total. Also note that Frito-Lay has 82 percent of the corn chip market.

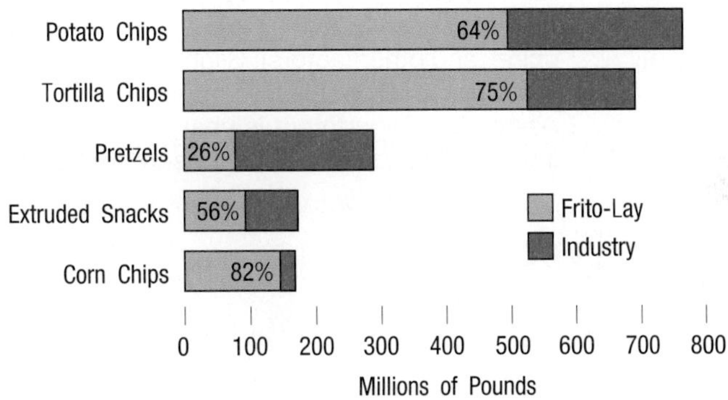

CHART 1–1 Frito-Lay Volume and Share of Major Snack Chip Categories in U.S. Supermarkets

The subject of statistics, as we will explore it in this text, has a much broader meaning than just collecting and publishing numerical information. We define statistics as:

> **STATISTICS** The science of collecting, organizing, presenting, analyzing, and interpreting data to assist in making more effective decisions.

As the definition suggests, the first step in investigating a problem is to collect relevant data. It must be organized in some way and perhaps presented in a chart, such as Chart 1–1. Only after the data have been organized are we then able to analyze and interpret it. Here are some examples of the need for data collection.

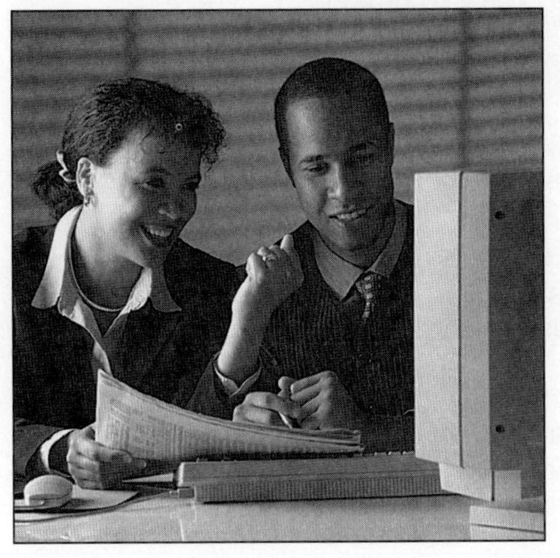

- Research analysts for Merrill Lynch evaluate many facets of a particular stock before making a "buy" or "sell" recommendation. They collect the past sales data of the company and estimate future earnings. Other factors, such as the projected worldwide demand for the company's products, the strength of the competition, and the effect of the new union management contract, are also considered before making a recommendation.
- The marketing department at Colgate-Palmolive Co., a manufacturer of soap products, has the responsibility of making recommendations regarding the potential profitability of a newly developed group of face soaps having fruit smells, such

as grape, orange, and pineapple. Before making a final decision, they will test it in several markets. That is, they may advertise and sell it in Topeka, Kansas, and Tampa, Florida. On the basis of test marketing in these two regions, Colgate-Palmolive will make a decision whether to market the soaps in the entire country.

- The United States government is concerned with the present condition of our economy and with predicting future economic trends. The government conducts a large number of surveys to determine consumer confidence and the outlook of management regarding sales and production for the next 12 months. Indexes, such as the Consumer Price Index, are constructed each month to assess inflation. Information on department store sales, housing starts, money turnover, and industrial production are just a few of the hundreds of items used to form the basis of the projections. These evaluations are used by banks to decide their prime lending rate and by the Federal Reserve Board to decide the level of control to place on the money supply.
- Management must make decisions on the quality of production. For example, automatic drill presses do not produce a perfect hole that is always 1.30 inches in diameter each time the hole is drilled (because of drill wear, vibration of the machine, and other factors). Slight tolerances are permitted, but when the hole is too small or too large, these products are defective and cannot be used. The Quality Assurance Department is charged with continually monitoring production by using sampling techniques to ensure that outgoing production meets standards.

Types of Statistics

Descriptive Statistics

The study of statistics is usually divided into two categories: descriptive statistics and inferential statistics. The definition of statistics given earlier referred to "organizing, presenting, . . . data." This facet of statistics is usually referred to as **descriptive statistics**.

DESCRIPTIVE STATISTICS Methods of organizing, summarizing, and presenting data in an informative way.

For instance, the United States government reports the population of the United States was 179,323,000 in 1960, 203,302,000 in 1970, 226,542,000 in 1980, 248,709,000 in 1990, and 265,000,000 in 2000. This information is descriptive statistics. It is descriptive statistics if we calculate the percentage growth from one decade to the next. However, it would **not** be descriptive statistics if we use these to estimate the population of the United States in the year 2010 or the percentage growth from 2000 to 2010. Why? Because these statistics are not being used to summarize past populations but to estimate future populations. The following are some other examples of descriptive statistics.

- There are a total of 42,796 miles of interstate highways in the United States. The interstate system represents only 1 percent of the nation's total roads but carries more than 20 percent of the traffic. The longest is I-90, which stretches from Boston to Seattle, a distance of 3,081 miles. The shortest is I-878 in New York City, which is 0.70 of a mile in length. Alaska does not have any interstate highways, Texas has the most interstate miles at 3,232, and New York has the most interstate routes with 28.
- According to the *Bureau of Labor Statistics,* the seasonally adjusted average hourly earnings of production workers are $15.55 for March 2004. You can review the latest information on wages and productivity of American workers by going to the Bureau of Labor Statistics website at: http://www.bls.gov and select Average hourly earnings.

Masses of unorganized data—such as the census of population, the weekly earnings of thousands of computer programmers, and the individual responses of 2,000 registered voters regarding their choice for President of the United States—are of little value as is. However, statistical techniques are available to organize this type of data into a meaningful form. Some data can be organized into a **frequency distribution.** (This procedure is covered in Chapter 2.) Various **charts** may be used to describe data; several basic chart forms are also presented in Chapter 4.

Specific measures of central location, such as the mean, describe the central value of a group of numerical data. A number of statistical measures are used to describe how closely the data cluster about an average. These measures of central location and dispersion are discussed in Chapter 3.

Inferential Statistics

Another facet of statistics is **inferential statistics**—also called **statistical inference** or **inductive statistics.** Our main concern regarding inferential statistics is finding something about a population from a sample taken from that population. For example, a recent survey showed only 46 percent of high school seniors can solve problems involving fractions, decimals, and percentages. And only 77 percent of high school seniors correctly totaled the cost of soup, a burger, fries, and a cola on a restaurant menu. Since these are inferences about a population (all high school seniors) based on sample data, they are inferential statistics.

INFERENTIAL STATISTICS The methods used to determine something about a population on the basis of a sample.

Note the words *population* and *sample* in the definition of inferential statistics. We often make reference to the population living in the United States or the 1.29 billion population of China. However, in statistics the word *population* has a broader meaning. A *population* may consist of *individuals*—such as all the students enrolled at Utah State University, all the students in Accounting 201, or all the CEOs from the Fortune 500 companies. A population may also consist of *objects,* such as all the XB-70 tires produced at Cooper Tire and Rubber Company in the Findlay, Ohio, plant; the accounts receivable at the end of October for Lorrange Plastics, Inc.; or auto claims filed in the first quarter of 2004 at the Northeast Regional Office of State Farm Insurance. The *measurement* of interest might be the scores on the first examination of all students in Accounting 201, the wall thickness of the Cooper Tires, the dollar amount of Lorrange Plastics accounts receivable, or the amount of auto insurance claims at State Farm. Thus, a population in the statistical sense does not always refer to people.

POPULATION The entire set of individuals or objects of interest or the measurements obtained from all individuals or objects of interest.

To infer something about a population, we usually take a **sample** from the population.

SAMPLE A portion, or part, of the population of interest.

Why take a sample instead of studying every member of the population? A sample of registered voters is necessary because of the prohibitive cost of contacting millions of voters before an election. Testing wheat for moisture content destroys the wheat, thus making a sample imperative. If the wine tasters tested all the wine, none would be available for sale. It would be physically impossible for a few marine biologists to capture and tag all the seals in the ocean. (These and other reasons for sampling are discussed in Chapter 8.)

Reasons for sampling

As noted, using a sample to learn something about a population is done extensively in business, agriculture, politics, and government, as cited in the following examples:

- Television networks constantly monitor the popularity of their programs by hiring Nielsen and other organizations to sample the preferences of TV viewers. For example, in a sample of 800 prime-time viewers, 320 or 40 percent indicated they watched *CSI* (*Crime Scene Investigation*) on CBS last week. These program ratings are used to set advertising rates or to cancel programs.
- Gamous and Associates, a public accounting firm, is conducting an audit of Pronto Printing Company. To begin, the accounting firm selects a random sample of 100 invoices and checks each invoice for accuracy. There is at least one error on five of the invoices; hence the accounting firm estimates that 5 percent of the population of invoices contain at least one error.
- A random sample of 1,260 marketing graduates from four-year schools showed their mean starting salary was $42,694. We therefore estimate the mean starting salary for all marketing graduates of four-year institutions to be $42,694.

The relationship between a sample and a population is portrayed below. For example, we wish to estimate the mean miles per gallon of SUVs. Six SUVs are selected from the population. The mean MPG of the six is used to estimate MPG for the population.

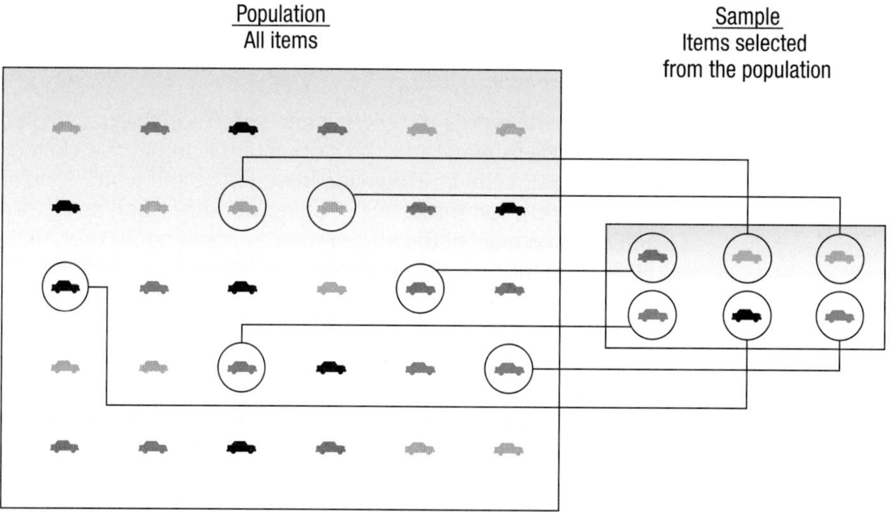

We strongly suggest you do the Self-Review exercises.

Following is a self-review problem. There are a number of them interspersed throughout each chapter. They test your comprehension of the preceding material. The answer and method of solution are given at the end of the chapter. You can find the answer to the following Self-Review on page 22. We recommend that you solve each one and then check your answer.

Self-Review 1–1

The answers are at the end of the chapter.

Chicago-based Market Facts asked a sample of 1,960 consumers to try a newly developed chicken dinner by Boston Market. Of the 1,960 sampled, 1,176 said they would purchase the dinner if it is marketed.

(a) What could Market Facts report to Boston Market regarding acceptance of the chicken dinner in the population?

(b) Is this an example of descriptive statistics or inferential statistics? Explain.

Types of Variables

Qualitative variable

There are two basic types of variables: (1) qualitative and (2) quantitative (see Chart 1–2). When the characteristic being studied is nonnumeric, it is called a **qualitative variable** or an **attribute.** Examples of qualitative variables are gender, religious affiliation, type of automobile owned, state of birth, and eye color. When the data are qualitative, we are usually interested in how many or what proportion fall in each category. For example, what percent of the population has blue eyes? How many Catholics and how many Protestants are there in the United States? What percent of the total number of cars sold last month were SUVs? Qualitative data are often summarized in charts and bar graphs (Chapter 2).

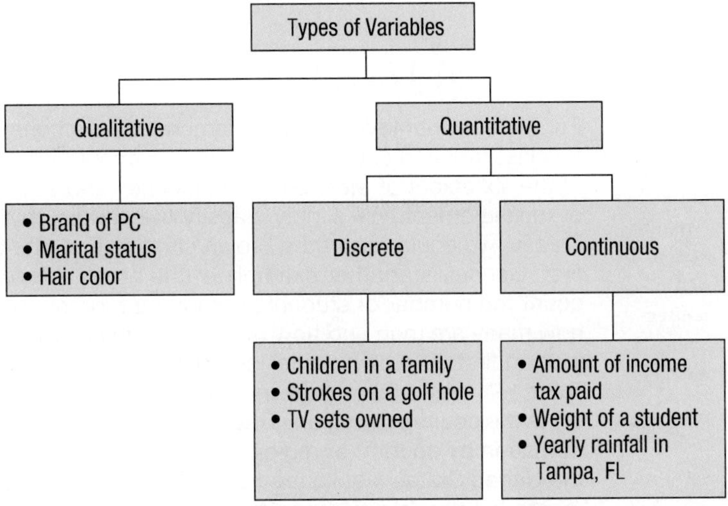

CHART 1–2 Summary of the Types of Variables

When the variable studied can be reported numerically, the variable is called a **quantitative variable.** Examples of quantitative variables are the balance in your checking account, the ages of company CEOs, the life of an automobile battery (such as 42 months), and the number of children in a family.

Quantitative variables are either discrete or continuous. **Discrete variables** can assume only certain values, and there are usually "gaps" between the values. Examples of discrete variables are the number of bedrooms in a house (1, 2, 3, 4, etc.), the number of cars arriving at Exit 25 on I-4 in Florida near Walt Disney World in an hour (326, 421, etc.), and the number of students in each section of a statistics course (25 in section A, 42 in section B, and 18 in section C). Typically, discrete variables result from counting. We count, for example, the number of cars arriving at Exit 25 on I-4, and we count the number of statistics students in each section. Notice that a home can have 3 or 4 bedrooms, but it cannot have 3.56 bedrooms. Thus, there is a "gap" between possible values.

Observations of a **continuous variable** can assume any value within a specific range. Examples of continuous variables are the air pressure in a tire and the weight of a shipment of tomatoes. Other examples are the amount of raisin bran in a box and the duration of flights from Orlando to San Diego. Typically, continuous variables result from measuring.

Levels of Measurement

Data can be classified according to levels of measurement. The level of measurement of the data often dictates the calculations that can be done to summarize and present

Statistics in Action

Where did statistics get its start? In 1662 John Graunt published an article called "Natural and Political Observations Made upon Bills of Mortality." The author's "observations" were the result of a study and analysis of a weekly church publication called "Bill of Mortality," which listed births, christenings, and deaths and their causes. Graunt realized that the Bills of Mortality represented only a fraction of all births and deaths in London. However, he used the data to reach broad conclusions about the impact of disease, such as the plague, on the general population. His logic is an example of statistical inference. His analysis and interpretation of the data are thought to mark the start of statistics.

the data. It will also determine the statistical tests that should be performed. For example, there are six colors of candies in a bag of M&M's candies. Suppose we assign brown a value of 1, yellow 2, blue 3, orange 4, green 5, and red 6. From a bag of candies, we add the assigned color values and divide by the number of candies and report that the mean color is 3.56. Does this mean that the average color is blue or orange? Of course not! As a second example, in a high school track meet there are eight competitors in the 400 meter run. We report the order of finish and that the mean finish is 4.5. What does the mean finish tell us? Nothing! In both of these instances, we have not properly used the level of measurement.

There are actually four levels of measurement: nominal, ordinal, interval, and ratio. The lowest, or the most primitive, measurement is the nominal level. The highest, or the level that gives us the most information about the observation, is the ratio level of measurement.

Nominal-Level Data

For the **nominal level** of measurement observations of a qualitative variable can only be classified and counted. There is no particular order to the labels. The classification of the six colors of M&M's milk chocolate candies is an example of the nominal level of measurement. We simply classify the candies by color. There is no natural order. That is, we could report the brown candies first, the orange first, or any of the colors first. Gender is another example of the nominal level of measurement. Suppose we count the number of students entering a football game with a student ID and report how many are men and how many are women. We could report either the men or the women first. For the nominal level the only measurement involved consists of counts. Table 1–1 shows a breakdown of the sources of world oil supply. The variable of interest is the country or region. This is a nominal-level variable because we record the information by country or region and there is no natural order. We could have reported the United States last instead of first. Do not be distracted by the fact that we summarize the variable by reporting the number of barrels produced per day.

TABLE 1–1 World Oil Supply by Country or Region

Country or Region	Millions of Barrels per Day	Percent
United States	9.05	12
Persian Gulf	18.84	25
OAPEC	19.50	26
OPEC	28.00	37
Total	75.39	100

Table 1–1 shows the essential feature of the nominal scale of measurement: there is no particular order to the categories.

The categories in the previous example are **mutually exclusive,** meaning, for example, that a particular barrel of oil cannot be produced by the United States and the Persian Gulf Region at the same time.

MUTUALLY EXCLUSIVE A property of a set of categories such that an individual or object is included in only one category.

The categories in Table 1–1 are also **exhaustive,** meaning that every member of the population or sample must appear in one of the categories. So the categories include all oil producing nations.

EXHAUSTIVE A property of a set of categories such that each individual or object must appear in a category.

In order to process data on oil production, gender, employment by industry, and so forth, the categories are often numerically coded 1, 2, 3, and so on, with 1 representing the United States, 2 representing Persian Gulf, for example. This facilitates counting by the computer. However, because we have assigned numbers to the various categories, this does not give us license to manipulate the numbers. For example, 1 + 2 does not equal 3, that is, United States + Persian Gulf does not equal OAPEC. To summarize, nominal-level data have the following properties:

1. Data categories are mutually exclusive and exhaustive.
2. Data categories have no logical order.

Ordinal-Level Data

The next higher level of data is the **ordinal level.** Table 1–2 lists the student ratings of Professor James Brunner in an Introduction to Finance course. Each student in the class answered the question "Overall how did you rate the instructor in this class?" The variable rating illustrates the use of the ordinal scale of measurement. One classification is "higher" or "better" than the next one. That is, "Superior" is better than "Good," "Good" is better than "Average," and so on. However, we are not able to distinguish the magnitude of the differences between groups. Is the difference between "Superior" and "Good" the same as the difference between "Poor" and "Inferior"? We cannot tell. If we substitute a 5 for "Superior" and a 4 for "Good," we can conclude that the rating of "Superior" is better than the rating of "Good," but we cannot add a ranking of "Superior" and a ranking of "Good," with the result being meaningful. Further we cannot conclude that a rating of "Good" (rating is 4) is necessarily twice as

TABLE 1–2 Rating of a Finance Professor

Rating	Frequency
Superior	6
Good	28
Average	25
Poor	12
Inferior	3

high as a "Poor" (rating is 2). We can only conclude that a rating of "Good" is better than a rating of "Poor." We cannot conclude how much better the rating is.

Another example of ordinal-level data is the Homeland Security Advisory System. The Department of Homeland Security publishes this information regarding the risk of terrorist activity to federal, state, and local authorities and to the American people. The five risk levels from lowest to highest including a description and color codes are:

Risk Level	Description	Color
Low	Low risk of terrorist attack	Green
Guarded	General risk of terrorist attack	Blue
Elevated	Significant risk of terrorist attack	Yellow
High	High risk of terrorist attack	Orange
Severe	Severe risk of terrorist attack	Red

This is ordinal scale data because we know the order or ranks of the risk levels—that is, orange is higher than yellow—but the amount of the difference between each of the levels is not necessarily the same. You can check the current status by going to http://www.whitehouse.gov/homeland.

In summary, the properties of ordinal-level data are:

1. The data classifications are mutually exclusive and exhaustive.
2. Data classifications are ranked or ordered according to the particular trait they possess.

Interval-Level Data

The **interval level** of measurement is the next highest level. It includes all the characteristics of the ordinal level, but in addition, the difference between values is a constant size. An example of the interval level of measurement is temperature. Suppose the high temperatures on three consecutive winter days in Boston are 28, 31, and 20 degrees Fahrenheit. These temperatures can be easily ranked, but we can also determine the difference between temperatures. This is possible because 1 degree Fahrenheit represents a constant unit of measurement. Equal differences between two temperatures are the same, regardless of their position on the scale. That is, the difference between 10 degrees Fahrenheit and 15 degrees is 5, the difference between 50 and 55 degrees is also 5 degrees. It is also important to note that 0 is just a point on the scale. It does not represent the absence of the condition. Zero degrees Fahrenheit does not represent the absence of heat, just that it is cold! In fact 0 degrees Fahrenheit is about -18 degrees on the Celsius scale.

The properties of interval-level data are:

1. Data classifications are mutually exclusive and exhaustive.
2. Data classifications are ordered according to the amount of the characteristic they possess.
3. Equal differences in the characteristic are represented by equal differences in the measurements.

There are few examples of the interval scale of measurement. Temperature, which was just cited, is one example. Others are shoe size and IQ scores.

Ratio-Level Data

Practically all quantitative data are the ratio level of measurement. The **ratio level** is the "highest" level of measurement. It has all the characteristics of the interval level, but in addition, the 0 point is meaningful and the ratio between two numbers is meaningful. Examples of the ratio scale of measurement include: wages, units of production, weight, changes in stock prices, distance between branch offices, and height. Money is a good illustration. If you have zero dollars, then you have no money. Weight is another example. If the dial on the scale of a correctly calibrated device is at zero, then there is a complete absence of weight. The ratio of two numbers is also meaningful. If Jim earns $40,000 per year selling insurance and Rob earns $80,000 per year selling cars, then Rob earns twice as much as Jim.

The difference between interval and ratio measurements can be confusing. The fundamental difference involves the definition of a true zero and the ratio between two values. If you have $50 and your friend has $100, then your friend has twice as much money as you. You may convert this money to Japanese yen or English pounds, but your friend will still have twice as much money as you. If you spend your $50, then you have no money. This is an example of a true zero. As another example, a sales representative travels 250 miles on Monday and 500 miles on Tuesday. The ratio of the distances traveled on the two days is 2/1; converting these distances to kilometers, or even inches, will not change the ratio. It is still 2/1. Suppose the sales representative works at home on Wednesday and does not travel. The distance traveled on this date is zero, and this is a meaningful value. Hence, the variable distance has a true zero point.

Let's compare the above discussion of the variables money and distance with the variable temperature. Suppose the low temperature in Phoenix, Arizona, last night was 40°F and the high today was 80°F. On the Fahrenheit scale the daytime high was twice the nighttime low. To put it another way, the ratio of the two temperatures was 2/1. However, if we convert these temperatures from the Fahrenheit scale to the Celsius scale the ratio changes. We use the formula $C = (F - 32)/1.8$ to convert the temperatures from Fahrenheit to Celsius, so the high temperature is 26.67°C and the low temperature is 4.44°C. You can see that the ratio of the two temperatures is no longer 2/1. Also, if the temperature is 0°F this does not imply that there is no temperature. Therefore, temperature is measured on an interval scale whether it is measured on the Celsius or the Fahrenheit scale.

In summary, the properties of the ratio-level data are:

1. Data classifications are mutually exclusive and exhaustive.
2. Data classifications are ordered according to the amount of the characteristics they possess.
3. Equal differences in the characteristic are represented by equal differences in the numbers assigned to the classifications.
4. The zero point is the absence of the characteristic.

Table 1–3 illustrates the use of the ratio scale of measurement. It shows the incomes of four father and son combinations.

TABLE 1–3 Father–Son Income Combinations

Name	Father	Son
Lahey	$80,000	$ 40,000
Nale	90,000	30,000
Rho	60,000	120,000
Steele	75,000	130,000

Observe that the senior Lahey earns twice as much as his son. In the Rho family the son makes twice as much as the father.

Chart 1–3 summarizes the major characteristics of the various levels of measurement.

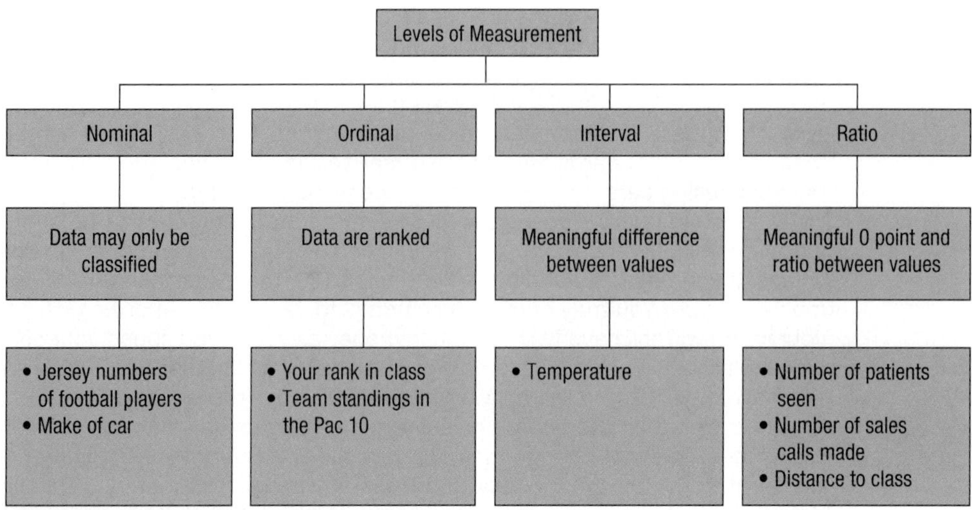

CHART 1–3 Summary of the Characteristics for Levels of Measurement

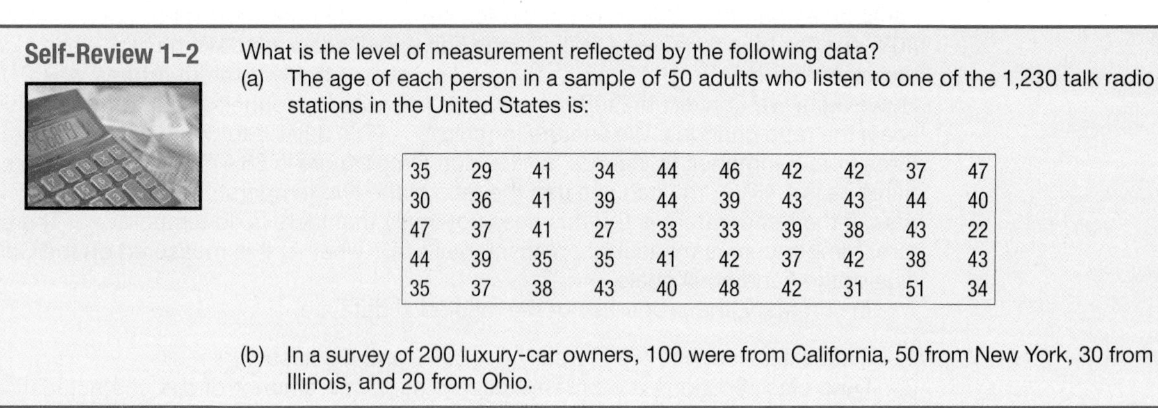

Self-Review 1–2

What is the level of measurement reflected by the following data?

(a) The age of each person in a sample of 50 adults who listen to one of the 1,230 talk radio stations in the United States is:

35	29	41	34	44	46	42	42	37	47
30	36	41	39	44	39	43	43	44	40
47	37	41	27	33	33	39	38	43	22
44	39	35	35	41	42	37	42	38	43
35	37	38	43	40	48	42	31	51	34

(b) In a survey of 200 luxury-car owners, 100 were from California, 50 from New York, 30 from Illinois, and 20 from Ohio.

Exercises

The answers to the odd-numbered exercises are at the end of the book.

1. What is the level of measurement for each of the following variables?
   a. Student IQ ratings.
   b. Distance students travel to class.
   c. Student scores on the first statistics test.
   d. A classification of students by state of birth.
   e. A ranking of students by freshman, sophomore, junior, and senior.
   f. Number of hours students study per week.
2. What is the level of measurement for these items related to the newspaper business?
   a. The number of papers sold each Sunday during 2004.
   b. The departments, such as editorial, advertising, sports, etc.
   c. A summary of the number of papers sold by county.
   d. The number of years with the paper for each employee.
3. Look in the latest edition of *USA Today* or your local newspaper and find examples of each level of measurement. Write a brief memo summarizing your findings.
4. For each of the following, determine whether the group is a sample or a population.
   a. The participants in a study of a new cholesterol drug.
   b. The drivers who received a speeding ticket in Kansas City last month.
   c. Those on welfare in Cook County (Chicago), Illinois.
   d. The 30 stocks reported as a part of the Dow Jones Industrial Average.

Statistics, Graphics, and Ethics

You have probably heard the old saying that there are three kinds of lies: lies, damn lies, and statistics. This saying is attributable to Benjamin Disraeli and is over a century old. It has also been said that "figures don't lie: liars figure." Both of these statements refer to the abuses of statistics in which data are presented in ways that are misleading. Many abusers of statistics are simply ignorant or careless, while others have an objective to mislead the reader by emphasizing data that support their position while leaving out data that may be detrimental to their position. One of our major goals in this text is to make you a more critical consumer of information. When you see charts or data in a newspaper, in a magazine, or on TV, always ask yourself: What is the person trying to tell me? Does that person have an agenda? Following are several examples of the abuses of statistical analysis.

Misleading Statistics

Several years ago, a series of TV advertisements reported that "2 out of 3 dentists surveyed indicated they would recommend Brand X toothpaste to their patients." The implication is that 67 percent of all dentists would recommend the product to their patients. What if they surveyed only three dentists? It would certainly not be an accurate representation of the real situation. The trick is that the manufacturer of the toothpaste could take *many* surveys of three dentists and report *only* the surveys of three dentists in which two dentists indicated they would recommend Brand X. This is concealing the information to mislead the public. Further, a survey of more than three dentists is needed, and it must be unbiased and representative of the population of all dentists. We discuss sampling methods in Chapter 8.

An average may not be representative of all the data.

The term *average* refers to several different measures of central location that we discuss in Chapter 3. To most people, an average is found by adding the values involved and dividing by the number of values. So if a real estate developer tells a client that the average home in a particular subdivision sold for $150,000, we assume that $150,000 is a representative selling price for all the homes. But suppose there are only five homes in the subdivision and they sold for $50,000, $50,000, $60,000, $90,000, and $500,000. We can correctly claim that the average selling price is $150,000, but does $150,000 really seem like a "typical" selling price? Would you like to also know that the same number of homes sold for more than $60,000 as less than $60,000? Or that $50,000 is the selling price that occurred most frequently? So what selling price really is the most "typical"? This example illustrates that a reported average can be misleading, because it can be one of several numbers that could be used to represent the data. There is really no objective set of criteria that states what average should be reported on each occasion. We want to educate you as a consumer of data about how a person or group might report one value that favors their position and exclude other values. We will discuss averages, or measures of central location, in Chapter 3.

Sometimes numbers themselves can be deceptive. The mean price of homes sold last month in the Tampa, Florida, area was $134,891.58. This sounds like a very precise value and may instill a high degree of confidence in its accuracy. To report that the mean selling price was $135,000 doesn't convey the same precision and accuracy. However, a statistic that is very precise and carries 5 or even 10 decimal places is not necessarily accurate.

Association Does Not Necessarily Imply Causation

Another area where there can be a misrepresentation of data is the association between variables. In statistical analysis often we find there is a strong *association* between variables. We find there is a strong negative association between outside work hours and grade point average. The more hours a student works, the lower will be his or her grade point average. Does it mean that more hours worked causes a lower grade point

Statistics in Action

There are about 700,000 physicians in the United States. Each year, according to the U.S. Dept. of Health and Human Services, there are 120,000 accidental deaths caused by physicians. In other words, there are 0.171 accidental deaths per physician, found by 120,000/700,000. Also in the United States, there are 80,000,000 gun owners and 1,500 accidental gun deaths per year (all age groups). The number of accidental deaths per gun owner is 0.0000188, found by 1,500/80,000,000. Statistically, doctors are approximately 9,000 times more dangerous than gun owners. Are doctors more dangerous than gun owners? FACT: Not everyone has a gun, but everyone has at least one doctor. This is an example of the abuse of statistics.

average? Not necessarily. It is also possible that the lower grade point average does not make the student eligible for a scholarship and therefore the student is required to engage in outside work to finance his or her education. Alternatively, both hours worked and lower GPA could be a result of the social circumstances of the student. Unless we have used an experimental design that has successfully controlled the influence of all other factors on grade point average except the hours worked, or vice versa, we are not justified in establishing any causation between variables based on statistical evidence alone. We study the association between variables in Chapters 13 and 14.

Graphs Can Be Misleading

Really, today in business, graphics are used as a visual aid for an easy interpretation. However, if they are not drawn carefully, they can lead to misinterpretation of information.

As either the preparer or the consumer of such graphics, it is useful to remember that the intention is to communicate an objective and accurate representation of reality. Neither sender nor receiver will benefit by intentional or sloppy distortions.

Examples School taxes for the Corry Area Exempted School District increased from $100 in 2000 to $200 in the year 2005 (see Chart 1–4). That is, the taxes doubled during the 5-year period. To show this change, the dollar sign on the right is twice as tall as the one on the left. However, it is also twice as wide! Therefore the area of the dollar sign on the right is 4 times (not twice) that on the left.

Chart 1–4 is misleading because visually the increase is much larger than it really is.

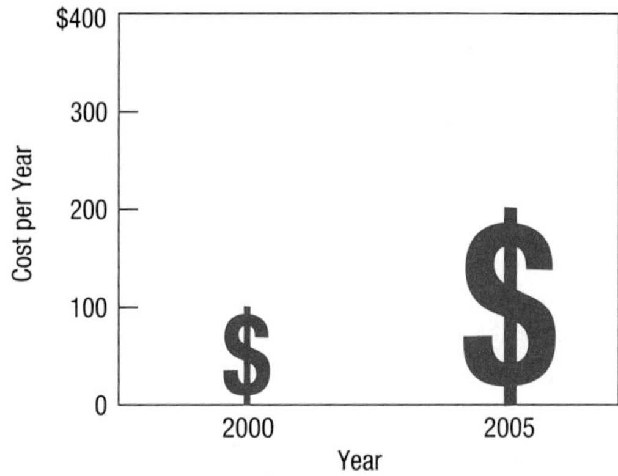

CHART 1–4 School Taxes for 2000 and 2005, Corry Exempted School District

Graphs and charts of data, such as histograms, line charts, and bar charts, can also be misleading if they are not drawn appropriately. We cover these graphs and charts in detail in the next chapter. A misleading visual interpretation in the context of charts arises often due to a presentation of only part of the data, or using the horizontal and/or vertical axis inappropriately.

Chart 1–5 is designed to show a relationship between unemployment rate (in percent) and crime rate (in thousands, per year) in Canada in three different ways based on the same data. In Chart 1–5a, we have broken the vertical axis at 2000, and thus show a strong relation between unemployment rate and crime. In Chart 1–5b, we have broken the horizontal axis at a 7-percent rate of unemployment. In this graph, we get an impression of a weaker relation between unemployment rate and crime. A more accurate depiction of the relationship can be obtained by using values near the minimum values of the variables as starting points on each axis. Thus, a break on the vertical axis at 2000 and on the horizontal axis at 7 percent will give you a more accurate picture of the relationship as shown in Chart 1–5c.

There are many graphing techniques, but there are no hard and fast rules about drawing a graph. It is therefore both a science and an art. Your aim should always be

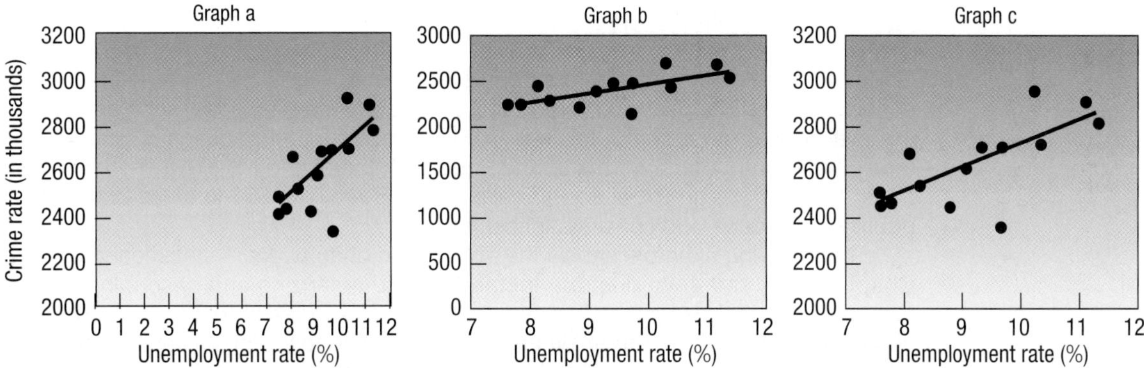

CHART 1–5 Unemployment Rate and Crime Rate in Canada

a truthful representation of the data. The objectives and the assumptions underlying the data must be kept in mind and mentioned briefly along with graphs. The visual impressions conveyed by the graphs must correspond to the underlying data. The graphs should reveal as much information as possible with the greatest precision and accuracy. *Graphical excellence is achieved when a viewer can get the most accurate and comprehensive picture of the situation underlying the data set in the shortest possible time.* In brief, a graph should act like a mirror between the numerical data and the viewer. According to a popular saying, *"Numbers speak for themselves."* This is true for small data sets. For large data sets, it may be difficult to discern any patterns by looking at numbers alone. We therefore *need accurate portrayal of data through graphs that can speak for numbers,* and can give a quick overview of the data. We discuss graphic techniques in detail in Chapters 2 and 4.

Become a Better Consumer and a Better Producer of Information

There are many other ways that statistical information can be deceiving. It may be because (1) The data are not representative of the population; (2) Appropriate statistics have not been used; (3) The data do not satisfy the assumptions required for inferences; (4) The prediction is too far out from the range of observed data; (5) Policy analysis does not meet the requirements of either data or theory or both; (6) Ignorance and/or carelessness on the part of the investigator; (7) A deliberate attempt to introduce bias has been made to mislead the consumer of information.

Entire books have been written about the subject. The most famous of these is *How to Lie with Statistics* by Darrell Huff. Understanding the art and science of statistics will make you both a better consumer of information as well as a better producer of information (statistician).

Ethics

Aside from the ethical issues raised in recent years with financial reporting from companies such as Enron and Tyco International, professional practices with statistical research and reporting is strongly encouraged by the American Statistical Association. In 1999 the ASA provided written guidelines and suggestions (see http://www.amstat.org) for professionalism and the responsibilities that apply to researchers and consultants using or conducting statistical analysis. As the guidelines state, "Clients, employers, researchers, policy makers, journalists, and the public should be urged to expect that statistical practice will be conducted in accordance with these guidelines and to object when it is not. While learning how to apply statistical theory to problems, students should be encouraged to use these guidelines whether or not their target professional specialty will be 'statistician.'"

Software Applications

Computers are now available to students at most colleges and universities. Spreadsheets, such as Microsoft Excel, and statistical software packages, such as MINITAB, are available in most computer labs. The Microsoft Excel package is bundled with many home computers. In this text we use both Excel and MINITAB for the applications. We also use an Excel add-in called MegaStat. This add-in gives Excel the capability to produce additional statistical reports.

The following example shows the application of software in statistical analysis. In Chapters 2, 3, and 4 we illustrate methods for summarizing and describing data. An example used in those chapters refers to the price reported in thousands of dollars of 80 vehicles sold last month at Whitner Autoplex. The following Excel output reveals, among other things, that (1) 80 vehicles were sold last month, (2) the mean (average) selling price was $23,218, and (3) the selling prices ranged from a minimum of $15,546 to a maximum of $35,925.

Microsoft Excel - Whitner-2003

	B	C	D
1	Price($000)	Age	Type
2	23.197	46	0
3	23.372	48	0
4	20.454	40	1
5	23.591	40	0
6	26.651	46	1
7	27.453	37	1
8	17.266	32	1
9	18.021	29	1
10	28.683	38	1
11	30.872	43	0
12	19.587	32	0
13	23.169	47	0
14	35.851	56	0
15	19.251	42	1
16	20.047	28	1
17	24.285	56	0
18	24.324	50	1
19	24.609	31	1
20	28.67	51	1
21	15.546	26	1
22	15.935	25	1
23	19.873	45	1
24	25.251	56	1

Price($000)	
Mean	23.2181625
Standard Error	0.486840947
Median	22.831
Mode	20.642
Standard Deviation	4.35443781
Sample Variance	18.96112864
Kurtosis	0.5433087
Skewness	0.72681585
Range	20.379
Minimum	15.546
Maximum	35.925
Sum	1857.453
Count	80

The following output is from the MINITAB system. It contains much of the same information.

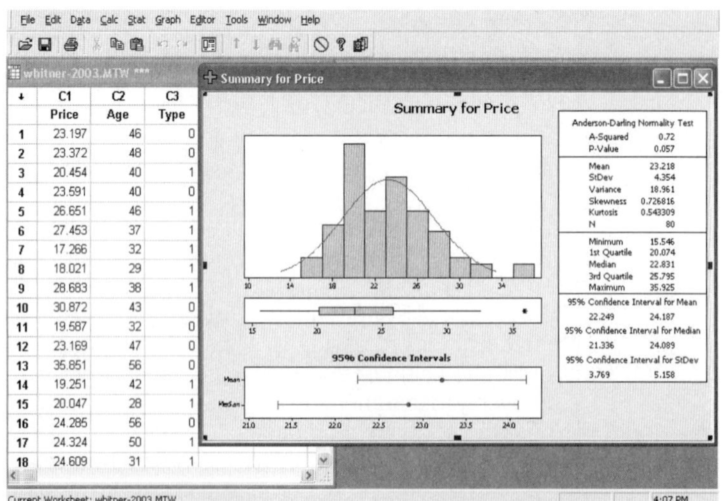

Had we used a calculator to arrive at these measures and others needed to fully analyze the selling prices, hours of calculation would have been required. The likelihood of an error in arithmetic is high when a large number of values are concerned. On the other hand, statistical software packages and spreadsheets can provide accurate information in seconds.

At the option of your instructor, and depending on the software system available, we urge you to apply a computer package to the exercises in the **Dataset Exercises** section in each chapter. It will relieve you of the tedious calculations and allow you to concentrate on data analysis.

Chapter Outline

I. Statistics is the science of collecting, organizing, presenting, analyzing, and interpreting data to assist in making more effective decisions.

II. There are two types of statistics.
- **A.** Descriptive statistics are procedures used to organize and summarize data.
- **B.** Inferential statistics involve taking a sample from a population and making estimates about a population based on the sample results.
  1. A population is an entire set of individuals or objects of interest or the measurements obtained from all individuals or objects of interest.
  2. A sample is a part of the population.

III. There are two types of variables.
- **A.** A qualitative variable is nonnumeric.
  1. Usually we are interested in the number or percent of the observations in each category.
  2. Qualitative data are usually summarized in graphs and bar charts.
- **B.** There are two types of quantitative variables and they are usually reported numerically.
  1. Discrete variables can assume only certain values, and there are usually gaps between values.
  2. A continuous variable can assume any value within a specified range.

IV. There are four levels of measurement.
- **A.** With the nominal level, the data are sorted into categories with no particular order to the categories.
  1. The categories are mutually exclusive. An individual or object appears in only one category.
  2. The categories are exhaustive. An individual or object appears in at least one of the categories.
- **B.** The ordinal level of measurement presumes that one classification is ranked higher than another.
- **C.** The interval level of measurement has the ranking characteristic of the ordinal level of measurement plus the characteristic that the distance between values is a constant size.
- **D.** The ratio level of measurement has all the characteristics of the interval level, plus there is a zero point and the ratio of two values is meaningful.

Chapter Exercises

5. Explain the difference between *qualitative* and *quantitative* variables. Give an example of qualitative and quantitative variables.
6. Explain the difference between a sample and a population.
7. List the four levels of measurement and give an example (different from those used in the book) of each level of measurement.
8. Define the term *mutually exclusive.*
9. Define the term *exhaustive.*
10. Using data from such publications as the *Statistical Abstract of the United States,* the *World Almanac, Forbes,* or your local newspaper, give examples of the nominal, ordinal, interval, and ratio levels of measurement.
11. The Struthers Wells Corporation employs more than 10,000 white collar workers in its sales offices and manufacturing facilities in the United States, Europe, and Asia. A sample of 300

of these workers revealed 120 would accept a transfer to a location outside the United States. On the basis of these findings, write a brief memo to Ms. Wanda Carter, Vice-President of Human Services, regarding all white collar workers in the firm and their willingness to relocate.

12. AVX Stereo Equipment, Inc. recently began a "no-hassles" return policy. A sample of 500 customers who had recently returned items showed 400 thought the policy was fair, 32 thought it took too long to complete the transaction, and the remainder had no opinion. On the basis of these findings, make an inference about the reaction of all customers to the new policy.

13. Explain the difference between a discrete and a continuous variable. Give an example of each not included in the text.

14. The following chart depicts sales, in thousands, of manufactured homes sold in the United States between 1990 and 2003.

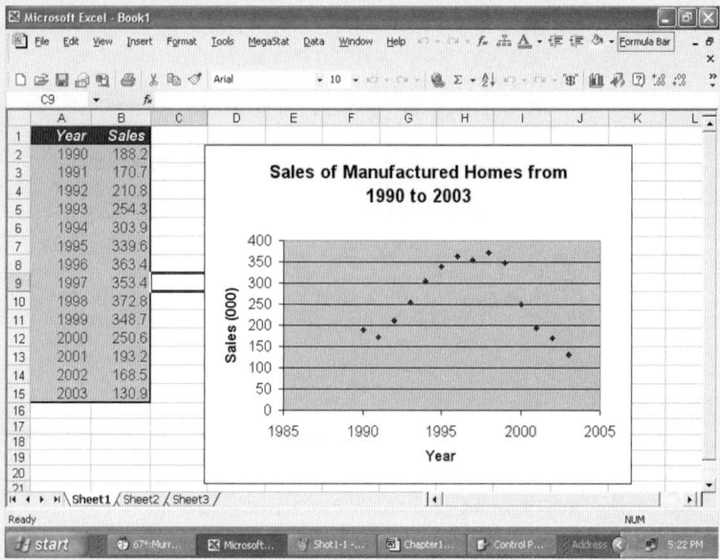

Write a brief description of the sales information. Did sales increase or decrease over the period? What was the trend of sales over the period?

exercises.com

These exercises use the World Wide Web, a rich and growing source of up-to-date information. Because of the changing nature and the continuous revision of websites, you may well see different menus, and the exact addresses, or URLs, may change. When you visit a page, be prepared to search the link.

15. Suppose you recently opened an account with AmeriTrade, Inc., an on-line broker. You decide to purchase shares of either Johnson and Johnson (a pharmaceutical company) or PepsiCo (the parent company of Pepsi and Frito Lay). For a comparison of the two companies go to http://finance.yahoo.com and in the space where it says "Enter Symbol" enter the letters JNJ and PEP, which are the respective symbols for the two companies. Click on GO and you should receive some current information about the selling price of the two stocks. To the right of this information click on More Info and then click on Research. Here you will find information from stock analysts evaluating these stocks. Brokers rate the stock a 1 if it is a strong buy and a 5 if it is a strong sell. What level of measurement is this information? Which of the stocks would you recommend?

Dataset Exercises

16. Refer to the Real Estate data at the back of the text, which reports information on homes sold in the Denver, Colorado, area last year. Consider the following variables: selling price, number of bedrooms, township, and distance from the center of the city.
a. Which of the variables are qualitative and which are quantitative?
b. Determine the level of measurement for each of the variables.

17. Refer to the Baseball 2003 data, which reports information on the 30 Major League Baseball teams for the 2003 season. Consider the following variables: number of wins, team salary, season attendance, whether the team played its home games on a grass field or an artificial surface, and the number of home runs hit.
a. Which of these variables are quantitative and which are qualitative?
b. Determine the level of measurement for each of the variables.

18. Refer to the Wage data, which reports information on annual wages for a sample of 100 workers. Also included are variables relating to industry, years of education, and gender for each worker.
a. Which of the 12 variables are qualitative and which are quantitative?
b. Determine the level of measurement for each variable.

19. Refer to the CIA data, which reports demographic and economic information on 46 countries.
a. Which of the variables are quantitative and which are qualitative?
b. Determine the level of measurement for each of the variables.

Chapter 1 Answers to Self-Review

1–1 **a.** On the basis of the sample of 1,960 consumers, we estimate that, if it is marketed, 60 percent of all consumers will purchase the chicken dinner $(1{,}176/1{,}960) \times 100 = 60$ percent.

b. Inferential statistics, because a sample was used to draw a conclusion about how all consumers in the population would react if the chicken dinner were marketed.

1–2 **a.** Age is a ratio scale variable. A 40-year-old is twice as old as someone 20 years old.

b. Nominal scale. We could arrange the states in any order.

2

Describing Data:

Frequency Distributions and Graphic Presentation

The chart on page 41 shows the hourly wages of a sample of certified welders in the Atlanta, Georgia area. What percent of the welders make less than $20.00 per hour? Refer to the chart. (See Goal 2 and Exercise 13.)

GOALS

When you have completed this chapter, you will be able to:

1 Organize data into a *frequency distribution.*

2 Portray a frequency distribution in a *histogram, frequency polygon,* and *cumulative frequency polygon.*

3 Present data using such graphical techniques as *line charts, bar charts,* and *pie charts.*

Introduction

The highly competitive automotive retailing business has changed significantly over the past 5 years, due in part to consolidation by large, publicly owned dealership groups. Traditionally, a local family owned and operated the community dealership, which might have included one or two manufacturers, like Pontiac and GMC Trucks or Chrysler and the popular Jeep line. Recently, however, skillfully managed and well-financed companies have been acquiring local dealerships across large regions of the country. As these groups acquire the local dealerships, they often bring standard selling practices, common software and hardware technology platforms, and management reporting techniques. The goal is to provide an improved buying experience for the consumer, while increasing the profitability of the larger dealership organization. In many cases, in addition to reaping the financial benefits of selling the dealership, the family is asked to continue running the dealership on a daily basis. Today, it is common for these megadealerships to employ over 10,000 people, generate several billion dollars in annual sales, own more than 100 franchises, and be traded on the New York Stock Exchange or NASDAQ.

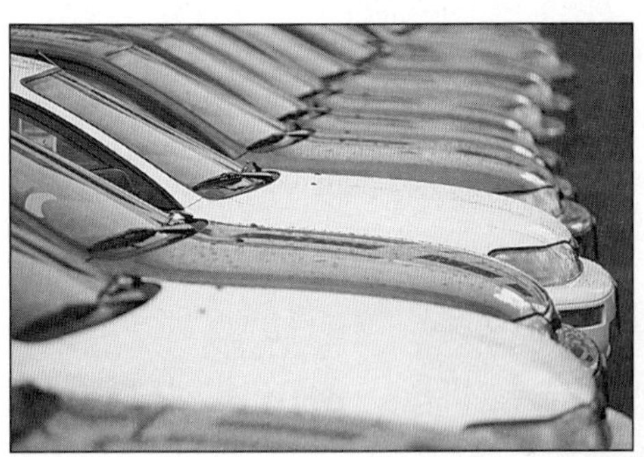

The consolidation has not come without challenges. With the acquisition of dealerships across the country, AutoUSA, one of the new megadealerships, now sells the inexpensive Korean import brands Kia and Hyundai, the high-line BMW and Mercedes Benz sedans, and a full line of Ford and Chevrolet cars and trucks.

Ms. Kathryn Ball is a member of the senior management team at AutoUSA. She is responsible for tracking and analyzing vehicle selling prices for AutoUSA. Kathryn would like to summarize vehicle selling prices with charts and graphs that she could review monthly. From these tables and charts, she wants to know the typical selling price as well as the lowest and highest prices. She is also interested in describing the demographics of the buyers. What are their ages? How many vehicles do they own? Do they want to buy or lease the vehicle?

Whitner Autoplex located in Raytown, Missouri, is one of the AutoUSA dealerships. Whitner Autoplex includes Pontiac, GMC, and Buick franchises as well as a BMW store. General Motors is actively working with its dealer body to combine at one location several of its franchises, such as Chevrolet, Pontiac, or Cadillac. Combining franchises improves the floor traffic and a dealership has product offerings for all demographics. BMW, with its premium brand and image, wants to move away from calling its locations dealerships, instead calling them stores. In keeping with the "Nordstrom's" experience, BMW wants its consumers to feel a shopping/ownership experience closer to a Nordstrom's shopping trip, not the image a trip to the dealership often creates.

Ms. Ball decided to collect data on three variables at Whitner Autoplex: selling price ($000), buyer's age, and car type (domestic, coded as 1, or foreign, coded as 0). A portion of the data set is shown in the adjacent Excel worksheet. The entire data set is available on the student CD (included with the book), at the McGraw-Hill website, and in Appendix N at the end of the text.

Microsoft Excel - Whitner-2003

	B	C	D
1	Price($000)	Age	Type
2	23.197	46	0
3	23.372	48	0
4	20.454	40	1
5	23.591	40	0
6	26.651	46	1
7	27.453	37	1
8	17.266	32	1
9	18.021	29	1
10	28.683	38	1
11	30.872	43	0
12	19.587	32	0
13	23.169	47	0
14	35.851	56	0
15	19.251	42	1
16	20.047	28	1
17	24.285	56	0
18	24.324	50	1
19	24.609	31	1
20	28.67	51	1
21	15.546	26	1
22	15.935	25	1
23	19.873	45	1
24	25.251	56	1

Output Sheet1 Sheet2 Sheet3

Constructing a Frequency Distribution

Recall from Chapter 1 that we refer to techniques used to describe a set of data as *descriptive statistics.* To put it another way, we use descriptive statistics to organize data in various ways to point out where the data values tend to concentrate and help distinguish the largest and the smallest values. The first procedure we use to describe a set of data is a **frequency distribution.**

FREQUENCY DISTRIBUTION A grouping of data into mutually exclusive classes showing the number of observations in each.

How do we develop a frequency distribution? The first step is to tally the data into a table that shows the classes and the number of observations in each class. The steps in constructing a frequency distribution are best described by using an example. Remember, our goal is to construct tables, charts, and graphs that will quickly reveal the shape of the data.

EXAMPLE

In the Introduction we described a situation where Ms. Kathryn Ball of AutoUSA wants to develop some tables, charts, and graphs to show the typical selling price on various dealer lots. Table 2–1 reports only the price of the 80 vehicles sold last month at Whitner Autoplex. What is the *typical* selling price? What is the *highest* selling price? What is the *lowest* selling price? Around what value do the selling prices tend to cluster?

TABLE 2–1 Prices of Vehicles Sold Last Month at Whitner Autoplex

$23,197	$23,372	$20,454	$23,591	$26,651	$27,453	$17,266
18,021	28,683	30,872	19,587	23,169	35,851	19,251
20,047	24,285	24,324	24,609	28,670	15,546 (Lowest)	15,935
19,873	25,251	25,277	28,034	24,533	27,443	19,889
20,004	17,357	20,155	19,688	23,657	26,613	20,895
20,203	23,765	25,783	26,661	32,277	20,642	21,981
24,052	25,799	15,794	18,263	35,925 (Highest)	17,399	17,968
20,356	21,442	21,722	19,331	22,817	19,766	20,633
20,962	22,845	26,285	27,896	29,076	32,492	18,890
21,740	22,374	24,571	25,449	28,337	20,642	23,613
24,220	30,655	22,442	17,891	20,818	26,237	20,445
21,556	21,639	24,296				

SOLUTION

We refer to the unorganized information in Table 2–1 as **raw data** or **ungrouped data.** With a little searching, we can find the lowest selling price ($15,546) and the highest selling price ($35,925), but that is about all. It is difficult to determine a typical selling price. It is also difficult to visualize where the selling prices tend to cluster. The raw data are more easily interpreted if organized into a frequency distribution.

The steps for organizing data into a frequency distribution.

Step 1: Decide on the number of classes. The goal is to use just enough groupings or **classes** to reveal the shape of the distribution. Some judgment is needed here. Too many classes or too few classes might not reveal the basic shape of the data set. In the vehicle selling price example, three classes would not give much insight into the pattern of the data (see Table 2–2).

TABLE 2–2 An Example of Too Few Classes

Vehicle Selling Price ($)	Number of Vehicles
15,000 up to 24,000	48
24,000 up to 33,000	30
33,000 up to 42,000	2
Total	80

A useful recipe to determine the number of classes (k) is the "2 to the k rule." This guide suggests you select the smallest number (k) for the number of classes such that 2^k (in words, 2 raised to the power of k) is greater than the number of observations (n).

In the Whitner Autoplex example, there were 80 vehicles sold. So $n = 80$. If we try $k = 6$, which means we would use 6 classes, then $2^6 = 64$, somewhat less than 80. Hence, 6 is not enough classes. If we let $k = 7$, then $2^7 = 128$, which is greater than 80. So the recommended number of classes is 7.

Step 2: Determine the class interval or width. Generally the class interval or width should be the same for all classes. The classes all taken together must cover at least the distance from the lowest value in the raw data up to the highest value. Expressing these words in a formula:

$$i \geq \frac{H - L}{k}$$

where i is the class interval, H is the highest observed value, L is the lowest observed value, and k is the number of classes.

In the Whitner Autoplex case, the lowest value is \$15,546 and the highest value is \$35,925. If we need 7 classes, the interval should be at least (\$35,925 − \$15,546)/7 = \$2,911. In practice this interval size is usually rounded up to some convenient number, such as a multiple of 10 or 100. The value of \$3,000 might readily be used in this case.

Unequal class intervals present problems in graphically portraying the distribution and in doing some of the computations which we will see in later chapters. Unequal class intervals, however, may be necessary in certain situations to avoid a large number of empty, or almost empty, classes. Such is the case in Table 2–3. The Internal Revenue Service used unequal-sized class intervals to report the adjusted gross income on individual tax returns. Had they used an equal-sized interval of, say, \$1,000, more than 1,000 classes would have been required to describe all the incomes. A frequency distribution with 1,000 classes would be difficult to interpret. In this case the distribution is easier to understand in spite of the unequal classes. Note also that the number of income tax returns or "frequencies" is reported in thousands in this particular table. This also makes the information easier to understand.

Step 3: Set the individual class limits. State clear class limits so you can put each observation into only one category. This means you must avoid overlapping or unclear class limits. For example, classes such as \$1,300–\$1,400 and \$1,400–\$1,500 should not be used because it is not clear whether the value \$1,400 is in the first or second class. Classes stated as \$1,300–\$1,400 and \$1,500–\$1,600 are frequently used, but may also be confusing without the additional common convention of rounding all data at or above \$1,450 up to the second class and data below \$1,450 down to the first class. In this text we will generally use the format \$1,300 up to \$1,400 and \$1,400 up to \$1,500 and so on. With this format it is clear that \$1,399 goes into the first class and \$1,400 in the second.

TABLE 2–3 Adjusted Gross Income for Individuals Filing Income Tax Returns

Adjusted Gross Income		Number of Returns (in thousands)
No adjusted gross income		178.2
$ 1 up to	$ 5,000	1,204.6
5,000 up to	10,000	2,595.5
10,000 up to	15,000	3,142.0
15,000 up to	20,000	3,191.7
20,000 up to	25,000	2,501.4
25,000 up to	30,000	1,901.6
30,000 up to	40,000	2,502.3
40,000 up to	50,000	1,426.8
50,000 up to	75,000	1,476.3
75,000 up to	100,000	338.8
100,000 up to	200,000	223.3
200,000 up to	500,000	55.2
500,000 up to	1,000,000	12.0
1,000,000 up to	2,000,000	5.1
2,000,000 up to	10,000,000	3.4
10,000,000 or more		0.6

Statistics in Action

In 1788, James Madison, John Jay, and Alexander Hamilton anonymously published a series of essays entitled *The Federalist.* These Federalist papers were an attempt to convince the people of New York that they should ratify the Constitution. In the course of history, the authorship of most of these papers became known, but 12 remained contested. Through the use of statistical analysis, and particularly the study of the frequency of the use of various words, we can now conclude that James Madison is the likely author of the 12 papers. In fact, the statistical evidence that Madison is the author is overwhelming.

Because we round the class interval up to get a convenient class size, we cover a larger than necessary range. For example, 7 classes of width $3,000 in the Whitner Autoplex case result in a range of 7($3,000) = $21,000. The actual range is $20,379, found by $35,925 − $15,546. Comparing that value to $21,000 we have an excess of $621. Because we need to cover only the distance ($H - L$), it is natural to put approximately equal amounts of the excess in each of the two tails. Of course, we should also select convenient class limits. A guideline is to make the lower limit of the first class a multiple of the class interval. Sometimes this is not possible, but the lower limit should at least be rounded. So here are the classes we could use for this data.

$15,000 up to 18,000
18,000 up to 21,000
21,000 up to 24,000
24,000 up to 27,000
27,000 up to 30,000
30,000 up to 33,000
33,000 up to 36,000

Step 4: Tally the vehicle selling prices into the classes. To begin, the selling price of the first vehicle in Table 2–1 is $23,197. It is tallied in the $21,000 up to $24,000 class. The second selling price in the first column of Table 2–1 is $18,021. It is tallied in the $18,000 up to $21,000 class. The other selling prices are tallied in a similar manner. When all the selling prices are tallied, the table would appear as:

Class	Tallies
$15,000 up to $18,000	~~IIII~~ III
$18,000 up to $21,000	~~IIII~~ ~~IIII~~ ~~IIII~~ ~~IIII~~ III
$21,000 up to $24,000	~~IIII~~ ~~IIII~~ ~~IIII~~ II
$24,000 up to $27,000	~~IIII~~ ~~IIII~~ ~~IIII~~ III
$27,000 up to $30,000	~~IIII~~ III
$30,000 up to $33,000	IIII
$33,000 up to $36,000	II

Step 5: Count the number of items in each class. The number of observations in each class is called the **class frequency.** In the $15,000 up to $18,000 class there are 8 observations, and in the $18,000 up to $21,000 class there are 23 observations. Therefore, the class frequency in the first class is 8 and the class frequency in the second class is 23. There is a total of 80 observations or frequencies in the entire set of data.

Often it is useful to express the data in thousands, or some convenient unit of measurement, rather than the actual data. Table 2–4, for example, reports the vehicle selling prices in thousands of dollars, rather than dollars.

TABLE 2–4 Frequency Distribution of Selling Prices at Whitner Autoplex Last Month

Selling Prices ($ thousands)	Frequency
15 up to 18	8
18 up to 21	23
21 up to 24	17
24 up to 27	18
27 up to 30	8
30 up to 33	4
33 up to 36	2
Total	80

Now that we have organized the data into a frequency distribution, we can summarize the pattern in the selling prices of the vehicles for the AutoUSA lot of Whitner Autoplex in Raytown, Missouri. Observe the following:

1. The selling prices range from about $15,000 up to about $36,000.
2. The selling prices are concentrated between $18,000 and $27,000. A total of 58, or 72.5 percent, of the vehicles sold within this range.
3. The largest concentration, or highest frequency, is in the $18,000 up to $21,000 class. The middle of this class is $19,500. So we say that a typical selling price is $19,500.
4. Two of the vehicles sold for $33,000 or more, and 8 sold for less than $18,000.

By presenting this information to Ms. Ball, we give her a clear picture of the distribution of selling prices for last month.

We admit that arranging the information on selling prices into a frequency distribution does result in the loss of some detailed information. That is, by organizing the data into a frequency distribution, we cannot pinpoint the exact selling price, such as $23,197 or $26,372. Further, we cannot tell that the actual selling price for the least expensive vehicle was $15,546 and for the most expensive $35,925. However, the lower limit of the first class and the upper limit of the largest class convey essentially the same meaning. Likely, Ms. Ball will make the same judgment if she knows the lowest price is about $15,000 that she will if she knows the exact price is $15,546. The advantages of condensing the data into a more understandable and organized form more than offset this disadvantage.

Self-Review 2–1

The answers are at the end of the chapter.
The commissions earned for the first quarter of last year by the 11 members of the sales staff at Master Chemical Company are:

$1,650	$1,475	$1,510	$1,670	$1,595	$1,760	$1,540	$1,495	$1,590	$1,625	$1,510

(a) What are the values such as $1,650 and $1,475 called?
(b) Using $1,400 up to $1,500 as the first class, $1,500 up to $1,600 as the second class, and so forth, organize the quarterly commissions into a frequency distribution.
(c) What are the numbers in the right column of your frequency distribution called?
(d) Describe the distribution of quarterly commissions, based on the frequency distribution. What is the largest amount of commission earned? What is the smallest? What is the typical amount earned?

Class Intervals and Class Midpoints

We will use two other terms frequently: **class midpoint** and **class interval.** The midpoint is halfway between the lower limits of two consecutive classes. It is computed by adding the lower limits of consecutive classes and dividing the result by 2. Referring to Table 2–4, for the first class the lower class limit is $15,000 and the next limit is $18,000. The class midpoint is $16,500, found by ($15,000 + $18,000)/2. The midpoint of $16,500 best represents, or is typical of, the selling price of the vehicles in that class.

To determine the class interval, subtract the lower limit of the class from the lower limit of the next class. The class interval of the vehicle selling price data is $3,000, which we find by subtracting the lower limit of the first class, $15,000, from the lower limit of the next class; that is, $18,000 − $15,000 = $3,000. You can also determine the class interval by finding the difference between consecutive midpoints. The midpoint of the first class is $16,500 and the midpoint of the second class is $19,500. The difference is $3,000.

A Software Example

As we mentioned in Chapter 1, there are many software packages that perform statistical calculations. Throughout this text we will show the output from Microsoft Excel, from MegaStat, which is an add-in to Microsoft Excel, and from MINITAB. The commands necessary to generate the outputs are given in the **Software Commands** section at the end of each chapter.

The following is a frequency distribution, produced by MegaStat, showing the prices of the 80 vehicles sold last month at the Whitner Autoplex lot in Raytown, Missouri. The form of the output is somewhat different than the frequency distribution of Table 2–4, but the overall conclusions are the same.

Self-Review 2–2

Barry Bonds of the San Francisco Giants established a new single season home run record by hitting 73 home runs during the 2001 Major League Baseball season. The longest of these home runs traveled 488 feet and the shortest 320 feet. You need to construct a frequency distribution of these home run lengths.

(a) How many classes would you use?
(b) What class interval would you suggest?
(c) What actual classes would you suggest?

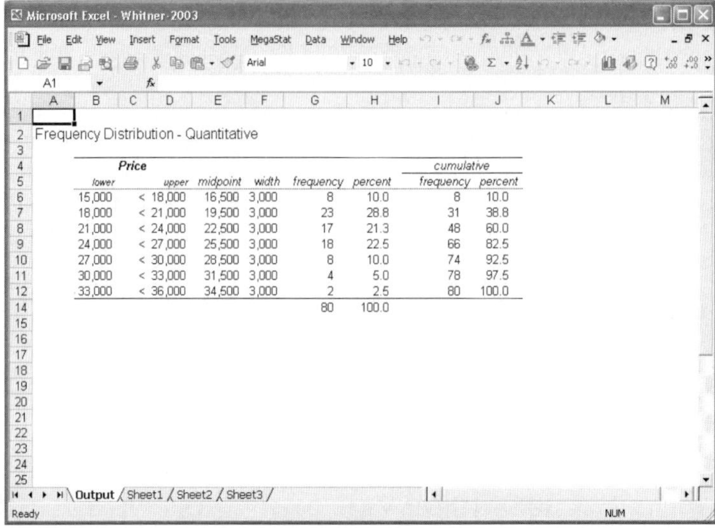

Frequency Distribution - Quantitative

Price lower	upper	midpoint	width	frequency	percent	cumulative frequency	cumulative percent
15,000	< 18,000	16,500	3,000	8	10.0	8	10.0
18,000	< 21,000	19,500	3,000	23	28.8	31	38.8
21,000	< 24,000	22,500	3,000	17	21.3	48	60.0
24,000	< 27,000	25,500	3,000	18	22.5	66	82.5
27,000	< 30,000	28,500	3,000	8	10.0	74	92.5
30,000	< 33,000	31,500	3,000	4	5.0	78	97.5
33,000	< 36,000	34,500	3,000	2	2.5	80	100.0
				80	100.0		

Relative Frequency Distribution

A relative frequency distribution converts the frequency to a percent.

It may be desirable to convert class frequencies to **relative class frequencies** to show the fraction of the total number of observations in each class. In our vehicle sales example, we may want to know what percent of the vehicle prices are in the $21,000 up to $24,000 class. In another study, we may want to know what percent of the employees used 5 up to 10 personal leave days last year.

To convert a frequency distribution to a *relative* frequency distribution, each of the class frequencies is divided by the total number of observations. From the distribution of vehicle selling prices, the relative frequency for the $15,000 up to $18,000 class is 0.10, found by dividing 8 by 80. That is, the price of 10 percent of the vehicles sold at Whitner Autoplex is between $15,000 and $18,000. The relative frequencies for the remaining classes are shown in Table 2–5.

TABLE 2–5 Relative Frequency Distribution of the Prices of Vehicles Sold Last Month at Whitner Autoplex

Selling Price ($ thousands)	Frequency	Relative Frequency	Found by
15 up to 18	8	0.1000 ←	8/80
18 up to 21	23	0.2875	23/80
21 up to 24	17	0.2125	17/80
24 up to 27	18	0.2250	18/80
27 up to 30	8	0.1000	8/80
30 up to 33	4	0.0500	4/80
33 up to 36	2	0.0250	2/80
Total	80	1.0000	

Self-Review 2–3

Refer to Table 2–5, which shows the relative frequency distribution for the vehicles sold last month at Whitner Autoplex.

(a) How many vehicles sold for $18,000 up to $21,000?
(b) What percent of the vehicles sold for a price between $18,000 and $21,000?
(c) What percent of the vehicles sold for $30,000 or more?

Exercises

The answers to the odd-numbered exercises are at the end of the book.

1. A set of data consists of 38 observations. How many classes would you recommend for the frequency distribution?
2. A set of data consists of 45 observations between $0 and $29. What size would you recommend for the class interval?
3. A set of data consists of 230 observations between $235 and $567. What class interval would you recommend?
4. A set of data contains 53 observations. The lowest value is 42 and the largest is 129. The data are to be organized into a frequency distribution.
   a. How many classes would you suggest?
   b. What would you suggest as the lower limit of the first class?
5. Wachesaw Manufacturing, Inc. produced the following number of units the last 16 days.

27	27	27	28	27	25	25	28
26	28	26	28	31	30	26	26

   The information is to be organized into a frequency distribution.
   a. How many classes would you recommend?
   b. What class interval would you suggest?
   c. What lower limit would you recommend for the first class?
   d. Organize the information into a frequency distribution and determine the relative frequency distribution.
   e. Comment on the shape of the distribution.
6. The Quick Change Oil Company has a number of outlets in the metropolitan Seattle area. The numbers of oil changes at the Oak Street outlet in the past 20 days are:

65	98	55	62	79	59	51	90	72	56
70	62	66	80	94	79	63	73	71	85

   The data are to be organized into a frequency distribution.
   a. How many classes would you recommend?
   b. What class interval would you suggest?
   c. What lower limit would you recommend for the first class?
   d. Organize the number of oil changes into a frequency distribution.
   e. Comment on the shape of the frequency distribution. Also determine the relative frequency distribution.
7. The manager of the BiLo Supermarket in Mt. Pleasant, Rhode Island, gathered the following information on the number of times a customer visits the store during a month. The responses of 51 customers were:

5	3	3	1	4	4	5	6	4	2	6	6	6	7	1
1	14	1	2	4	4	4	5	6	3	5	3	4	5	6
8	4	7	6	5	9	11	3	12	4	7	6	5	15	1
1	10	8	9	2	12									

   a. Starting with 0 as the lower limit of the first class and using a class interval of 3, organize the data into a frequency distribution.
   b. Describe the distribution. Where do the data tend to cluster?
   c. Convert the distribution to a relative frequency distribution.
8. The food services division of Cedar River Amusement Park, Inc. is studying the amount families who visit the amusement park spend per day on food and drink. A sample of 40 families who visited the park yesterday revealed they spent the following amounts.

$77	$18	$63	$84	$38	$54	$50	$59	$54	$56	$36	$26	$50	$34	$44
41	58	58	53	51	62	43	52	53	63	62	62	65	61	52
60	60	45	66	83	71	63	58	61	71					

a. Organize the data into a frequency distribution, using seven classes and 15 as the lower limit of the first class. What class interval did you select?
b. Where do the data tend to cluster?
c. Describe the distribution.
d. Determine the relative frequency distribution.

Graphic Presentation of a Frequency Distribution

Recall that a frequency distribution gives insight about the shape of the set of observations by showing them organized into a set of nonoverlapping classes. A frequency distribution is easier to understand than the initial raw or ungrouped data. For example, you can more easily determine which values are common or typical and which are extraordinary or infrequent. In this section we describe three charts that graphically portray a frequency distribution. These charts are the histogram, frequency polygon, and cumulative frequency polygon.

Histogram

One of the most common ways to portray a frequency distribution is a **histogram.**

HISTOGRAM A graph in which the classes are marked on the horizontal axis and the class frequencies on the vertical axis. The class frequencies are represented by the heights of the bars, and the bars are drawn adjacent to each other.

Thus, a histogram describes a frequency distribution using a series of adjacent rectangles, where the height of each rectangle is proportional to the frequency the class represents. The construction of a histogram is best illustrated by reintroducing the prices of the 80 vehicles sold last month at Whitner Autoplex.

EXAMPLE

Below is the frequency distribution.

Selling Prices ($ thousands)	Frequency
15 up to 18	8
18 up to 21	23
21 up to 24	17
24 up to 27	18
27 up to 30	8
30 up to 33	4
33 up to 36	2
Total	80

Construct a histogram. What conclusions can you reach based on the information presented in the histogram?

SOLUTION

The class frequencies are scaled along the vertical axis (*Y*-axis) and either the class limits or the class midpoints along the horizontal axis. To illustrate the construction of the histogram, the first three classes are shown in Chart 2–1.

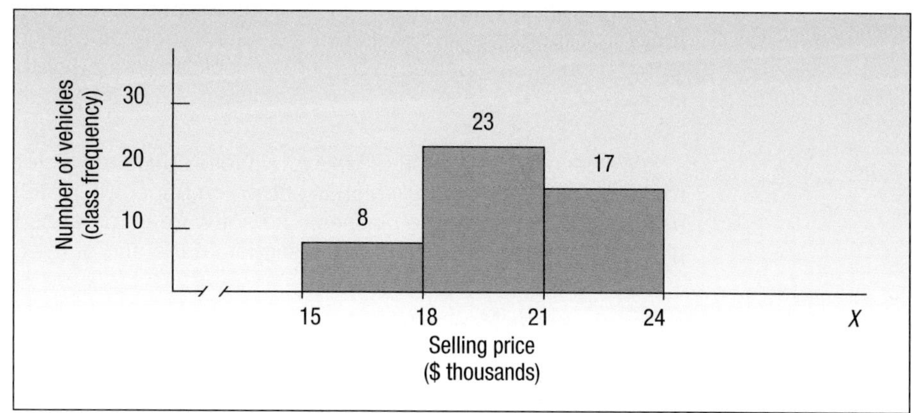

CHART 2–1 Construction of a Histogram

From Chart 2–1 we note that there are eight vehicles in the $15,000 up to $18,000 class. Therefore, the height of the column for that class is 8. There are 23 vehicles in the $18,000 up to $21,000 class. So, logically, the height of that column is 23. The height of the bar represents the number of observations in the class.

This procedure is continued for all classes. The complete histogram is shown in Chart 2–2. Note that there is no space between the bars. This is a feature of the histogram. Why is this so? Because the variable plotted on the horizontal axis selling price (in $000) is quantitative and of the interval, or in this case the ratio, scale of measurement. In bar charts, which are described in a later section, the vertical bars are separated.

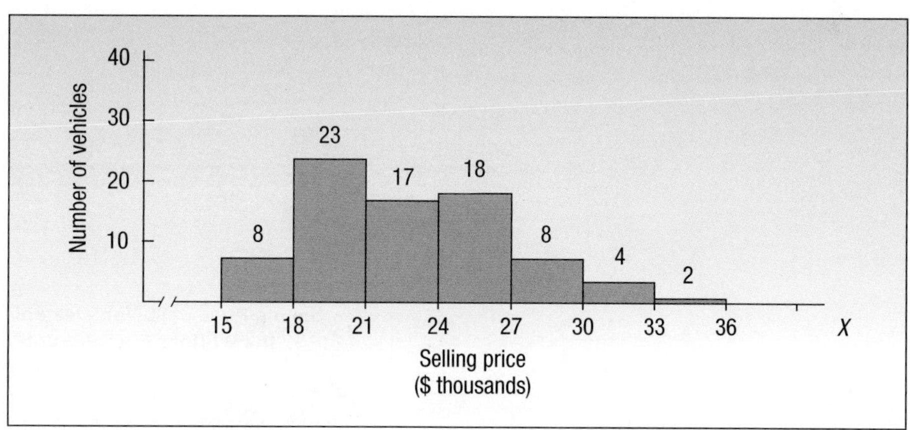

CHART 2–2 Histogram of the Selling Prices of 80 Vehicles at Whitner Autoplex

From the histogram in Chart 2–2, we conclude:

1. The lowest selling price is about $15,000, and the highest is about $36,000.
2. The largest class frequency is the $18,000 up to $21,000 class. A total of 23 of the 80 vehicles sold are within this price range.
3. Fifty-eight of the vehicles, or 72.5 percent, had a selling price between $18,000 and $27,000.

Thus, the histogram provides an easily interpreted visual representation of a frequency distribution. We should also point out that we would have reached the same conclusions and the shape of the histogram would have been the same had we used a relative frequency distribution instead of the actual frequencies. That is, if we had used the relative frequencies of Table 2–5, found on page 30, we would have had a histogram of the same shape as Chart 2–2. The only difference is that the vertical axis would have been reported in percent of vehicles instead of the number of vehicles.

We used the Microsoft Excel system to produce the histogram for the Whitner Autoplex vehicle sales data (which is shown on page 30). Note that class midpoints are used as the labels for the classes. The software commands to create this output are given in the **Software Commands** section at the end of the chapter.

Frequency Polygon

In a frequency polygon the class midpoints are connected with a line segment.

A **frequency polygon** is similar to a histogram. It consists of line segments connecting the points formed by the intersections of the class midpoints and the class frequencies. The construction of a frequency polygon is illustrated in Chart 2–3 (on page 35). We use the vehicle prices for the cars sold last month at Whitner Autoplex. The midpoint of each class is scaled on the X-axis and the class frequencies on the Y-axis. Recall that the class midpoint is the value at the center of a class and represents the values in that class. The class frequency is the number of observations in a particular class. The frequency distribution of selling prices at Whitner Autoplex are:

Selling Prices ($ thousands)	Midpoint	Frequency
15 up to 18	16.5	8
18 up to 21	19.5	23
21 up to 24	22.5	17
24 up to 27	25.5	18
27 up to 30	28.5	8
30 up to 33	31.5	4
33 up to 36	34.5	2
Total		80

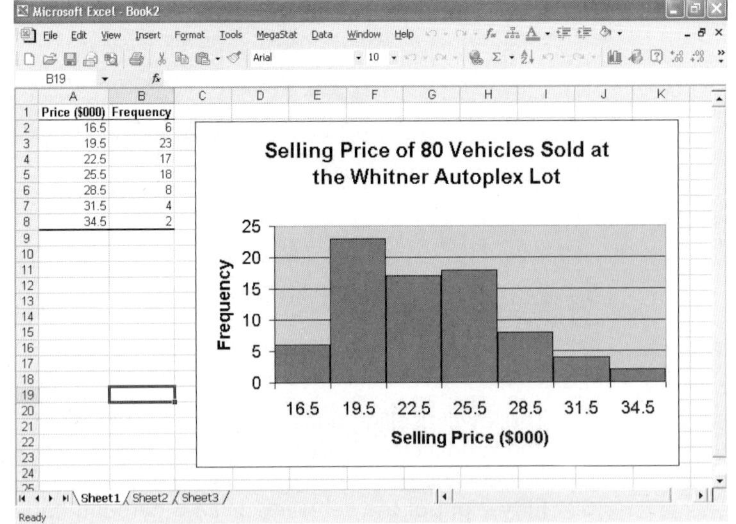

Statistics in Action

Florence Nightingale is known as the founder of the nursing profession. However, she also saved many lives by using statistical analysis. When she encountered an unsanitary condition or an undersupplied hospital, she improved the conditions and then used statistical data to document the improvement. Thus, she was able to convince others of the need for medical reform, particularly in the area of sanitation. She developed original graphs to demonstrate that, during the Crimean War, more soldiers died from unsanitary conditions than were killed in combat. The adjacent graph by Nightingale is a polar-area graph showing the relative monthly proportions of causes of death from April 1854 to March 1855.

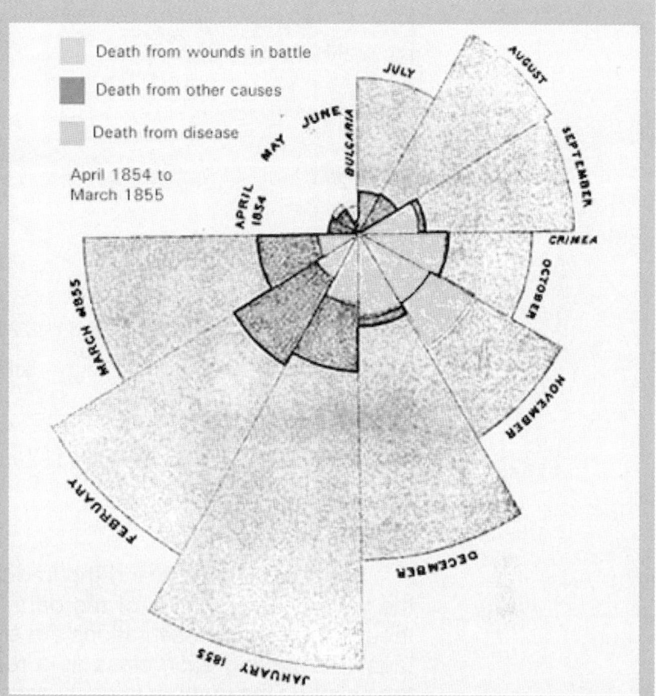

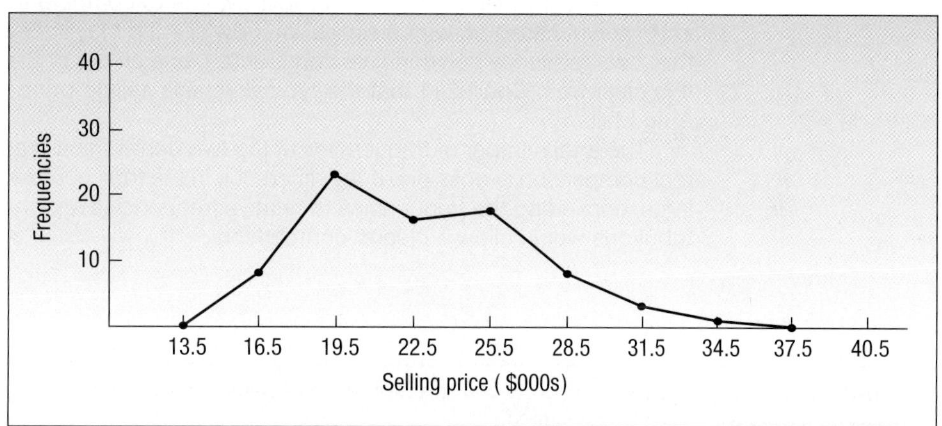

CHART 2–3 Frequency Polygon of the Selling Prices of 80 Vehicles at Whitner Autoplex

As noted previously, the $15,000 up to $18,000 class is represented by the midpoint $16,500. To construct a frequency polygon, move horizontally on the graph to the midpoint, $16.5, and then vertically to 8, the class frequency, and place a dot. The X and the Y values of this point are called the *coordinates.* The coordinates of the next point are $X = \$19.5$ and $Y = 23$. The process is continued for all classes. Then the points are connected in order. That is, the point representing the lowest class is joined to the one representing the second class and so on.

Note in Chart 2–3 that, to complete the frequency polygon, midpoints of $13.5 and $37.5 are added to the X-axis to "anchor" the polygon at zero frequencies. These two values, $13.5 and $37.5, were derived by subtracting the class interval of $3.0 from the lowest midpoint ($16.5) and by adding $3.0 to the highest midpoint ($34.5) in the frequency distribution.

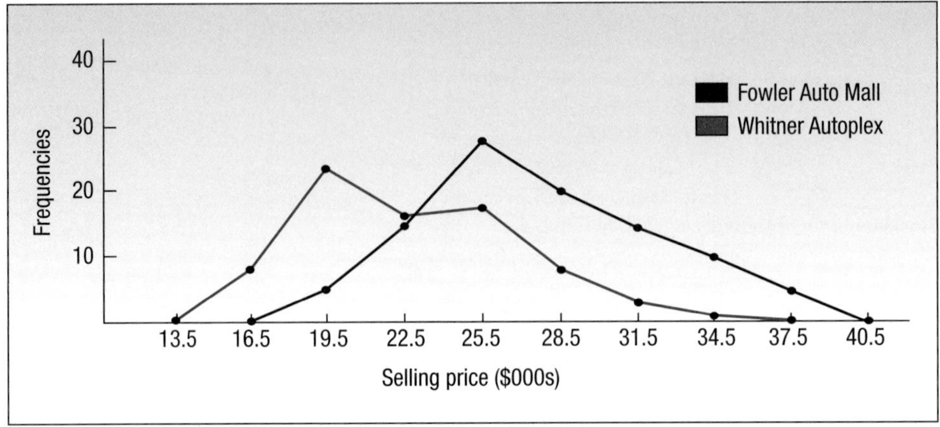

CHART 2–4 Distribution of Vehicle Selling Prices at Whitner Autoplex and Fowler Auto Mall

Both the histogram and the frequency polygon allow us to get a quick picture of the main characteristics of the data (highs, lows, points of concentration, etc.). Although the two representations are similar in purpose, the histogram has the advantage of depicting each class as a rectangle, with the height of the rectangular bar representing the number in each class. The frequency polygon, in turn, has an advantage over the histogram. It allows us to compare directly two or more frequency distributions. Suppose Ms. Ball of AutoUSA wants to compare the Whitner Autoplex lot in Raytown, Missouri, with a similar lot, Fowler Auto Mall in Grayling, Michigan. To do this, two frequency polygons are constructed, one on top of the other, as in Chart 2–4. It is clear from Chart 2–4 that the typical vehicle selling price is higher at the Fowler Auto Mall.

The total number of frequencies at the two dealerships is about the same, so a direct comparison is possible. If the difference in the total number of frequencies is quite large, converting the frequencies to relative frequencies and then plotting the two distributions would allow a clearer comparison.

Self-Review 2–4

The annual imports of a selected group of electronic suppliers are shown in the following frequency distribution.

Imports ($ millions)	Number of Suppliers
2 up to 5	6
5 up to 8	13
8 up to 11	20
11 up to 14	10
14 up to 17	1

(a) Portray the imports as a histogram.
(b) Portray the imports as a relative frequency polygon.
(c) Summarize the important facets of the distribution (such as classes with the highest and lowest frequencies).

Exercises

9. Molly's Candle Shop has several retail stores in the coastal areas of North and South Carolina. Many of Molly's customers ask her to ship their purchases. The following chart shows the number of packages shipped per day for the last 100 days.

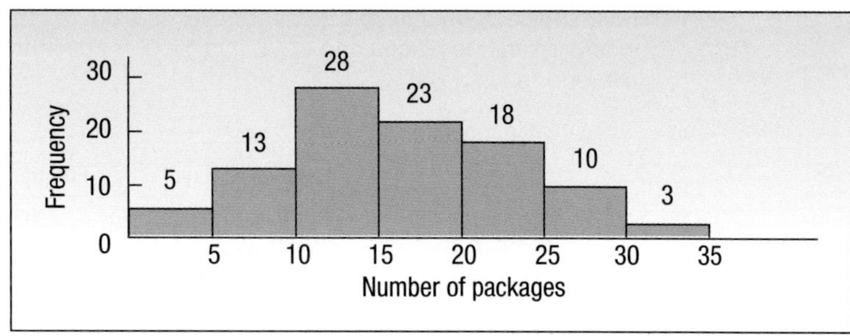

   a. What is this chart called?
   b. What is the total number of frequencies?
   c. What is the class interval?
   d. What is the class frequency for the 10 up to 15 class?
   e. What is the relative frequency of the 10 up to 15 class?
   f. What is the midpoint of the 10 up to 15 class?
   g. On how many days were there 25 or more packages shipped?

10. The audit staff of Southeast Fire and Casualty, Inc. recently completed a study of the settlement amount, in $000, of claims. The staff report included the following chart.

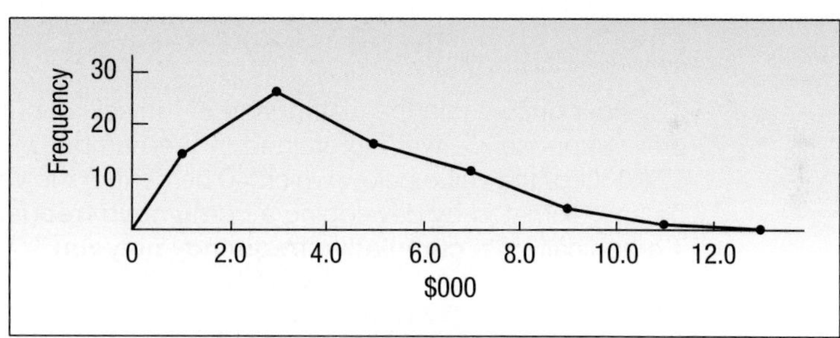

   a. What is the midpoint of the 2 up to 4 class?
   b. How many claims were in the 2.0 up to 4.0 class?
   c. Approximately how many claims were studied?
   d. What is the class interval?
   e. What is this chart called?

11. The following frequency distribution reports the number of frequent flier miles, reported in thousands, for employees of Brumley Statistical Consulting, Inc. during the first quarter of 2004.

Frequent Flier Miles (000)	Number of Employees
0 up to 3	5
3 up to 6	12
6 up to 9	23
9 up to 12	8
12 up to 15	2
Total	50

a. How many employees were studied?
b. What is the midpoint of the first class?
c. Construct a histogram.
d. A frequency polygon is to be drawn. What are the coordinates of the plot for the first class?
e. Construct a frequency polygon.
f. Interpret the frequent flier miles accumulated using the two charts.

12. Ecommerce.com, a large Internet retailer, is studying the lead time (elapsed time between when an order is placed and when it is filled) for a sample of recent orders. The lead times are reported in days.

Lead Time (days)	Frequency
0 up to 5	6
5 up to 10	7
10 up to 15	12
15 up to 20	8
20 up to 25	7
Total	40

a. How many orders were studied?
b. What is the midpoint of the first class?
c. What are the coordinates of the first class for a frequency polygon?
d. Draw a histogram.
e. Draw a frequency polygon.
f. Interpret the lead times using the two charts.

Cumulative Frequency Distributions

Consider once again the distribution of the selling prices of vehicles at Whitner Autoplex. Suppose we were interested in the number of vehicles that sold for less than $21,000, or the value below which 40 percent of the vehicles sold. These numbers can be approximated by developing a **cumulative frequency distribution** and portraying it graphically in a **cumulative frequency polygon.**

EXAMPLE

The frequency distribution of the vehicle selling prices at Whitner Autoplex is repeated from Table 2–4.

Selling Prices ($ thousands)	Frequency
15 up to 18	8
18 up to 21	23
21 up to 24	17
24 up to 27	18
27 up to 30	8
30 up to 33	4
33 up to 36	2
Total	80

Construct a cumulative frequency polygon. Fifty percent of the vehicles were sold for less than what amount? Twenty-five of the vehicles were sold for less than what amount?

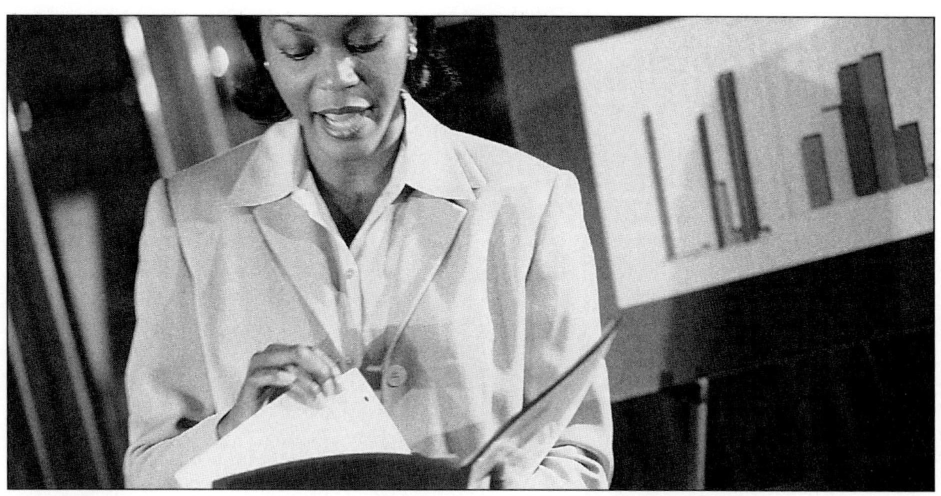

SOLUTION

As the name implies, a cumulative frequency distribution and a cumulative frequency polygon require *cumulative frequencies.* To construct a cumulative frequency distribution, refer to the preceding table and note that there were eight vehicles sold for less than $18,000. Those 8 vehicles, plus the 23 in the next higher class, for a total of 31, were sold for less than $21,000. The cumulative frequency for the next higher class is 48, found by 8 + 23 + 17. This process is continued for all the classes. All the vehicles were sold for less than $36,000. (See Table 2–6.)

TABLE 2–6 Cumulative Frequency Distribution for Vehicle Selling Price

Selling Price ($ thousands)	Frequency	Cumulative Frequency	Found by
15 up to 18	8	8	
18 up to 21	23	31 ←	8 + 23
21 up to 24	17	48	8 + 23 + 17
24 up to 27	18	66	8 + 23 + 17 + 18
27 up to 30	8	74	•
30 up to 33	4	78	•
33 up to 36	2	80	•
Total	80		

To plot a cumulative frequency distribution, scale the upper limit of each class along the *X*-axis and the corresponding cumulative frequencies along the *Y*-axis. To provide additional information, you can label the vertical axis on the left in units and the vertical axis on the right in percent. In the Whitner Autoplex example, the vertical axis on the left is labeled from 0 to 80 and on the right from 0 to 100 percent. The value of 50 percent corresponds to 40 vehicles sold.

To begin the plotting, 8 vehicles sold for less than $18,000, so the first plot is at $X = 18$ and $Y = 8$. The coordinates for the next plot are $X = 21$ and $Y = 31$. The rest of the points are plotted and then the dots connected to form the chart (see Chart 2–5).

To find the selling price below which half the cars sold, we draw a horizontal line from the 50 percent mark on the right-hand vertical axis over to the polygon, then drop down to the *X*-axis and read the selling price. The value on the *X*-axis is about 22.5, so we estimate that 50 percent of the vehicles sold for less than $22,500.

To find the price below which 25 of the vehicles sold, we locate the value of 25 on the left-hand vertical axis. Next, we draw a horizontal line from the value of 25 to the

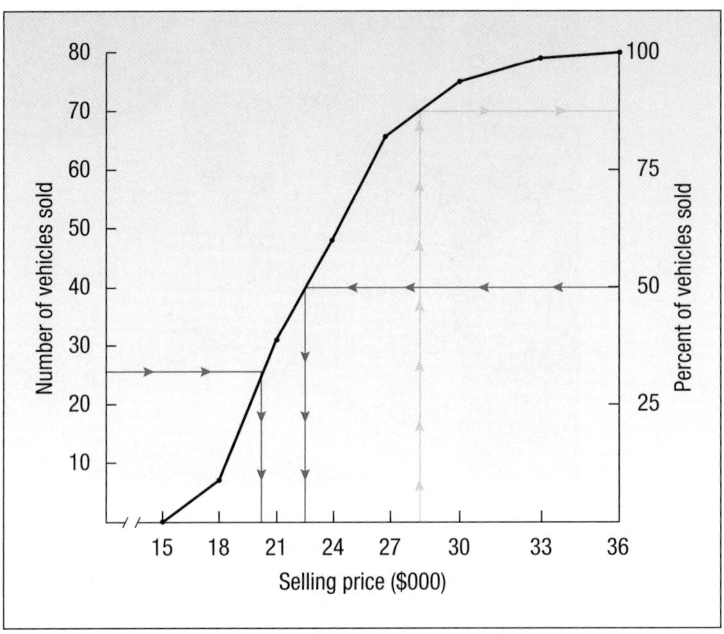

CHART 2–5 Cumulative Frequency Distribution for Vehicle Selling Price

polygon, and then drop down to the *X*-axis and read the price. It is about 20.5, so we estimate that 25 of the vehicles sold for less than $20,500. We can also make estimates of the percent of vehicles that sold for less than a particular amount. To explain, suppose we want to estimate the percent of vehicles that sold for less than $28,500. We begin by locating the value of 28.5 on the *X*-axis, move vertically to the polygon, and then horizontally to the vertical axis on the right. The value is about 87 percent, so we conclude that 87 percent of the vehicles sold for less than $28,500.

Self-Review 2–5

The hourly wages of 15 employees at the Home Depot in Brunswick, Georgia, is organized into the following table.

Hourly Wages	Number of Employees
$ 8 up to $10	3
10 up to 12	7
12 up to 14	4
14 up to 16	1

(a) What is the table called?
(b) Develop a cumulative frequency distribution and portray the distribution in a cumulative frequency polygon.
(c) On the basis of the cumulative frequency polygon, how many employees earn $11 an hour or less? Half of the employees earn an hourly wage of how much or more? Four employees earn how much or less?

Exercises

13. The following chart shows the hourly wages of a sample of certified welders in the Atlanta, Georgia, area.

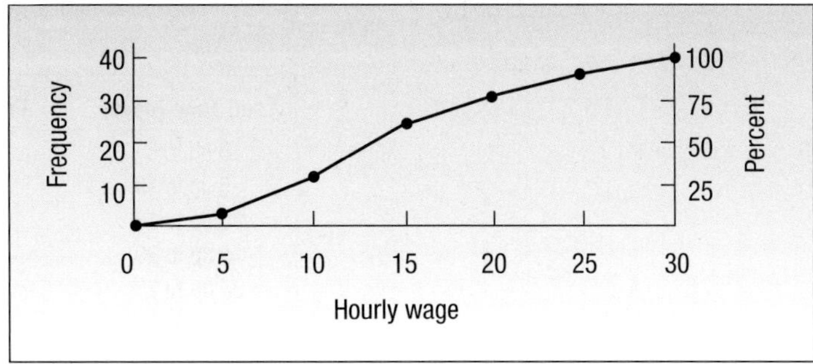

a. How many welders were studied?
b. What is the class interval?
c. About how many welders earn less than $10.00 per hour?
d. About 75 percent of the welders make less than what amount?
e. Ten of the welders studied made less than what amount?
f. What percent of the welders make less than $20.00 per hour?

14. The following chart shows the selling price ($000) of houses sold in the Billings, Montana, area.

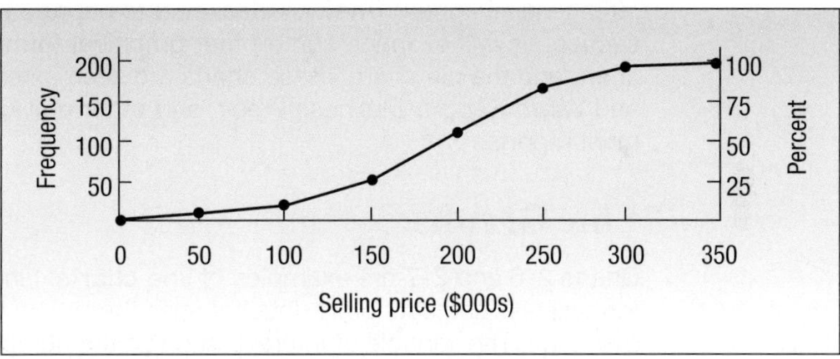

a. How many homes were studied?
b. What is the class interval?
c. One hundred homes sold for less than what amount?
d. About 75 percent of the homes sold for less than what amount?
e. Estimate the number of homes in the $150,000 up to $200,000 class.
f. About how many homes sold for less than $225,000?

15. The frequency distribution representing the number of frequent flier miles accumulated by employees at Brumley Statistical Consulting Company is repeated from Exercise 11.

Frequent Flier Miles (000)	Frequency
0 up to 3	5
3 up to 6	12
6 up to 9	23
9 up to 12	8
12 up to 15	2
Total	50

a. How many employees accumulated less than 3,000 miles?
b. Convert the frequency distribution to a cumulative frequency distribution.
c. Portray the cumulative distribution in the form of a cumulative frequency polygon.
d. Based on the cumulative frequency polygon, about 75 percent of the employees accumulated how many miles or less?

16. The frequency distribution of order lead time at Ecommerce.com from Exercise 12 is repeated below.

Lead Time (days)	Frequency
0 up to 5	6
5 up to 10	7
10 up to 15	12
15 up to 20	8
20 up to 25	7
Total	40

a. How many orders were filled in less than 10 days? In less than 15 days?
b. Convert the frequency distribution to a cumulative frequency distribution.
c. Develop a cumulative frequency polygon.
d. About 60 percent of the orders were filled in less than how many days?

Other Graphic Presentations of Data

The histogram, the frequency polygon, and the cumulative frequency polygon all have strong visual appeal. They are designed to capture the attention of the reader. In this section we will examine some other graphical forms, namely the line chart, the bar chart, and the pie chart. These charts are seen extensively in *USA Today, U.S. News and World Report, Business Week,* and other newspapers, magazines, and government reports.

Line Graphs

Charts 2–6 and 2–7 are examples of **line charts.** Line charts are particularly effective for business and economic data because they show the change or trends in a variable over time. The variable of interest, such as the number of units sold or the total value of sales, is scaled along the vertical axis and time along the horizontal axis. Chart 2–6 shows the Dow Jones Industrial Average and the NASDAQ, the two most widely reported measures of stock activity. The time of the day, beginning with the opening bell at 9:30 is shown along the horizontal axis and the value of the Dow on the vertical

CHART 2–6 Line Chart for the Dow Jones Industrial Average and the NASDAQ

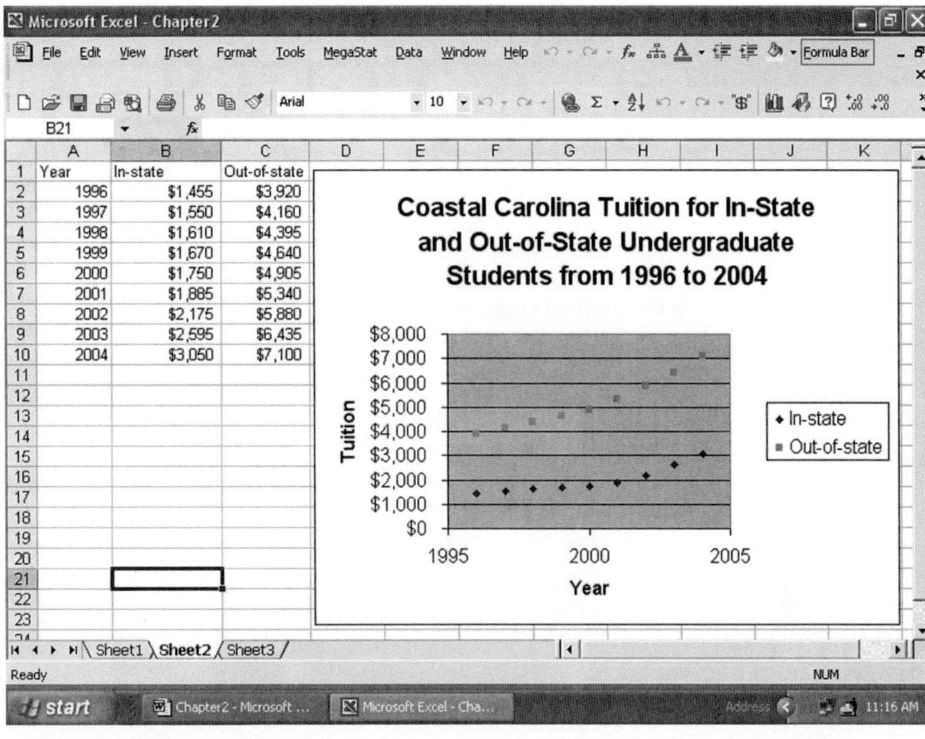

	A	B	C
1	Year	In-state	Out-of-state
2	1996	$1,455	$3,920
3	1997	$1,550	$4,160
4	1998	$1,610	$4,395
5	1999	$1,670	$4,640
6	2000	$1,750	$4,905
7	2001	$1,885	$5,340
8	2002	$2,175	$5,880
9	2003	$2,595	$6,435
10	2004	$3,050	$7,100

CHART 2–7 Tuition for In-State and Out-of-State Students at Coastal Carolina University

axis. For this day the Dow was at 8,790.44, up 5.55 points, at 12:09 PM. The NASDAQ was at 1,447.67, down .05 points, as of 12:09 PM. Line graphs are widely used by investors to support decisions to buy and sell stocks and bonds.

Chart 2–7 is also a line chart. It shows the tuition per semester for undergraduate students at Coastal Carolina University from 1996 to 2004. Note that there has been an increase each year for the period. The increase for in-state students from 2003 to 2004 was $455 or 17.5 percent. This is the largest dollar and yearly percent increase during the period. Since 1996, the overall in-state tuition increase was $1,595 or 109.6 percent.

Quite often two or more series of data are plotted on the same line chart. Thus one chart can show the trend of several different variables. This allows for the comparison of several variables over the same period of time. Chart 2–7 also shows the out-of-state tuition per semester. As might be expected for a state-supported university, such as Coastal Carolina, the out-of-state tuition is always higher. Tuition for out-of-state students increased $665 or 10.3 percent from 2003 to 2004. For the period from 1996 to 2004 tuition increased $3,180 or 81.1 percent. So tuition increased by a larger *dollar* amount for out-of-state students but a larger *percent* for in-state students.

Bar Charts

A **bar chart** can be used to depict any of the levels of measurement—nominal, ordinal, interval, or ratio. (Recall, we discussed the levels of measurement beginning on page 9 in Chapter 1.) From the Census Bureau *Current Population Reports,* the typical annual earnings for someone over the age of 18 are $22,895 if a high school diploma is the highest degree earned. With a bachelor's degree the typical earnings increase to $40,478, and with a professional or master's degree the typical amount increases to $73,165. This information is summarized in Chart 2–8. With this chart it is easy to see that a person with a bachelor's degree can expect to earn almost twice as much in a year as someone with a high school diploma. The expected earnings of someone with a master's or professional degree are nearly twice as much as someone with a bachelor's degree and three times that of someone with a high school diploma.

In Chart 2–8 the variable of interest is the level of education. The level of education is an ordinal scale variable and is reported on the horizontal axis. The bars are not adjacent. That is, there is space between the bar for the earnings of high school graduates and the bar for the earnings of those with a Bachelor's degree. This is different from Chart 2–2, which is a histogram. In a histogram, the horizontal axis refers to the ratio scale variable—vehicle selling price. This is a continuous variable; hence there is no space between the bars. Another difference between a bar chart and a histogram is the vertical scale. In a histogram the vertical axis is the frequency or number of observations. In a bar chart the vertical scale refers to an amount.

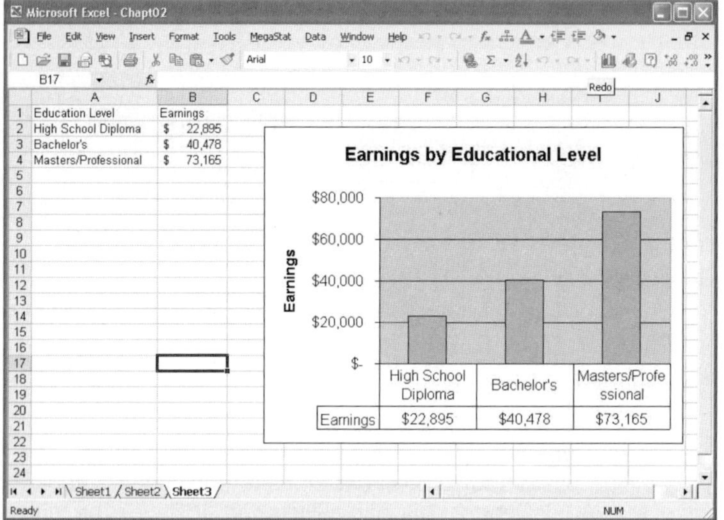

CHART 2–8 Typical Annual Earnings Based on Educational Level

Pie Charts

A **pie chart** is especially useful for illustrating nominal-level data. We explain the details of constructing a pie chart using the information in Table 2–7, which shows a breakdown of the expenses of the Ohio State Lottery for 2002.

TABLE 2–7 Ohio State Lottery Expenses in 2002

Use of Sales	Amount ($ million)	Percent of Share
Prizes	1,148.1	57
Payments to Education	635.2	32
Bonuses/Commissions	126.6	6
Operating Expenses	103.3	5
Total	2,013.2	100

The first step is to record the percentages 0, 5, 10, 15, and so on evenly around the circumference of a circle. To plot the 57 percent share awarded for prizes, draw a line from the center of the circle to 0 and another line from the center of the circle to 57 percent. The area in this "slice" represents the lottery proceeds that were awarded in prizes. Next, add the 57 percent of expenses awarded in prizes to the 32 percent payments to education; the result is 89 percent. Draw a line from the center of the circle to 89 percent, so the area between 57 percent and 89 percent depicts the payments made to education. Continuing, add the 6 percent for bonuses and commissions, which gives us a total of 95 percent. Draw a line from the center of the circle to 95, so the "slice" between 89 percent and 95 percent represents the payment of bonuses and commissions. The remaining 5 percent is for operating expenses.

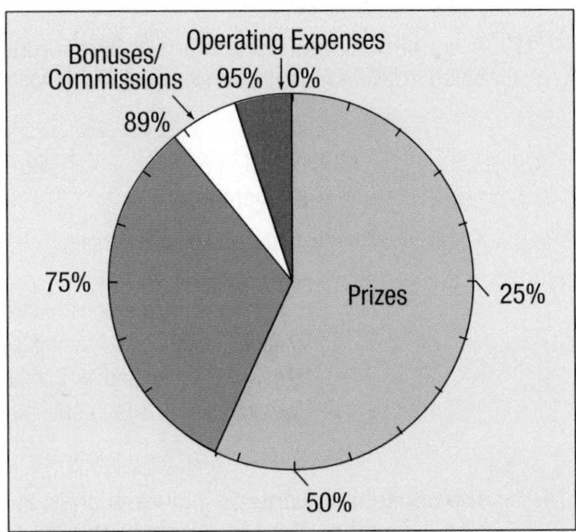

Because the area of the pie represents the relative share of each component, we can easily compare them:

- The largest expense of the Ohio Lottery is for prizes.
- About one-third of the proceeds are transferred to education.
- Operating expenses account for only 5 percent of the proceeds.

The Excel software will develop a pie chart and output the result. See the following chart for the information in Table 2–7.

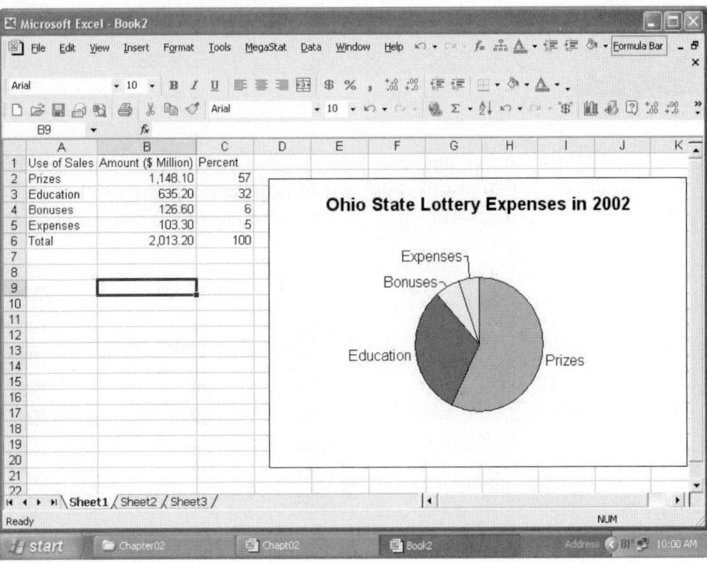

Use of Sales	Amount ($ Million)	Percent
Prizes	1,148.10	57
Education	635.20	32
Bonuses	126.60	6
Expenses	103.30	5
Total	2,013.20	100

Self-Review 2–6

The Clayton County Commissioners want to show taxpayers attending the forthcoming meeting what happens to their tax dollars. The total amount of taxes collected is $2 million. Expenditures are: $440,000 for schools, $1,160,000 for roads, $320,000 for administration, and $80,000 for supplies. A pie chart seems ideal to show the portion of each tax dollar going for schools, roads, administration, and supplies. Convert the dollar amounts to percents of the total and portray the percents in the form of a pie chart.

Exercises

17. A small business consultant is investigating the performance of several companies. The sales in 2004 (in thousands of dollars) for the selected companies were:

Corporation	Fourth-Quarter Sales ($ thousands)
Hoden Building Products	$ 1,645.2
J & R Printing, Inc.	4,757.0
Long Bay Concrete Construction	8,913.0
Mancell Electric and Plumbing	627.1
Maxwell Heating and Air Conditioning	24,612.0
Mizelle Roofing & Sheet Metals	191.9

The consultant wants to include a chart in his report comparing the sales of the six companies. Use a bar chart to compare the fourth quarter sales of these corporations and write a brief report summarizing the bar chart.

18. The Blair Corporation, located in Warren, Pennsylvania, sells fashion apparel for men and women plus a broad range of home products (http://www.blair.com). It services its customers by mail. Listed below are the net sales for Blair from 1998 through 2003. Draw a line chart depicting the net sales over the time period and write a brief report.

Year	Net Sales ($ millions)
1998	506.8
1999	522.2
2000	574.6
2001	580.7
2002	568.5
2003	581.9

19. A headline in a Toledo, Ohio, newspaper reported that crime was on the decline. Listed below are the number of homicides from 1986 to 2003. Draw a line chart to summarize the data and write a brief summary of the homicide rates for the last 18 years.

Year	Homicides	Year	Homicides
1986	21	1995	35
1987	34	1996	30
1988	26	1997	28
1989	42	1998	25
1990	37	1999	21
1991	37	2000	19
1992	44	2001	23
1993	45	2002	27
1994	40	2003	23

20. A report prepared for the governor of a western state indicated that 56 percent of the state's tax revenue went to education, 23 percent to the general fund, 10 percent to the counties, 9 percent to senior programs, and the remainder to other social programs. Develop a pie chart to show the breakdown of the budget.

21. The following table shows the population, in millions, of the United States in 5-year intervals from 1950 to 2000. Develop a line chart depicting the population growth and write a brief report summarizing your findings.

Year	Population (millions)	Year	Population (millions)
1950	152.3	1980	227.7
1955	165.9	1985	238.5
1960	180.7	1990	249.9
1965	194.3	1995	263.0
1970	205.1	2000	281.4
1975	216.0		

22. Shown below are the military and civilian personnel expenditures for the eight largest military locations in the United States. Develop a bar chart and summarize the results in a brief report.

Location	Amount Spent (millions)	Location	Amount Spent (millions)
St. Louis, MO	$6,087	Norfolk, VA	$3,228
San Diego, CA	4,747	Marietta, GA	2,828
Pico Rivera, CA	3,272	Fort Worth, TX	2,492
Arlington, VA	3,284	Washington, DC	2,347

Chapter Outline

I. A frequency distribution is a grouping of data into mutually exclusive classes showing the number of observations in each class.
  A. The steps in constructing a frequency distribution are:
    1. Decide how many classes you wish.
    2. Determine the class interval or width.
    3. Set the individual class limits.
    4. Tally the raw data into the classes.
    5. Count the number of tallies in each class.
  B. The class frequency is the number of observations in each class.
  C. The class interval is the difference between the limits of two consecutive classes.
  D. The class midpoint is halfway between the limits of two consecutive classes.

II. A relative frequency distribution shows the percent of the observations in each class.

III. There are three methods for graphically portraying a frequency distribution.
  A. A histogram portrays the number of frequencies in each class in the form of rectangles.
  B. A frequency polygon consists of line segments connecting the points formed by the intersections of the class midpoints and the class frequencies.
  C. A cumulative frequency polygon shows the number of observations below a certain value.

IV. There are many charts used in newspapers and magazines.
  A. A line chart is ideal for showing the trend of a variable such as sales or income over time.
  B. Bar charts are similar to line charts and are useful for showing changes in nominal scale data.
  C. Pie charts are useful for showing the percent that various components are of the total.

Chapter Exercises

23. A dataset consists of 83 observations. How many classes would you recommend for a frequency distribution?

24. A dataset consists of 145 observations that range from 56 to 490. What size class interval would you recommend?

25. The following is the number of minutes to commute from home to work for a sample of aerospace workers in Houston, Texas.

28	25	48	37	41	19	32	26	16	23	23	29	36
31	26	21	32	25	31	43	35	42	38	33	28	

a. How many classes would you recommend?
b. What class interval would you suggest?
c. What would you recommend as the lower limit of the first class?
d. Organize the data into a frequency distribution.
e. Comment on the shape of the frequency distribution.

26. The following data give the weekly amounts spent on groceries for a sample of households in rural Wisconsin.

$271	$363	$159	$ 76	$227	$337	$295	$319	$250
279	205	279	266	199	177	162	232	303
192	181	321	309	246	278	50	41	335
116	100	151	240	474	297	170	188	320
429	294	570	342	279	235	434	123	325

a. How many classes would you recommend?
b. What class interval would you suggest?
c. What would you recommend as the lower limit of the first class?
d. Organize the data into a frequency distribution.

27. The following histogram shows the scores on the first statistics exam.

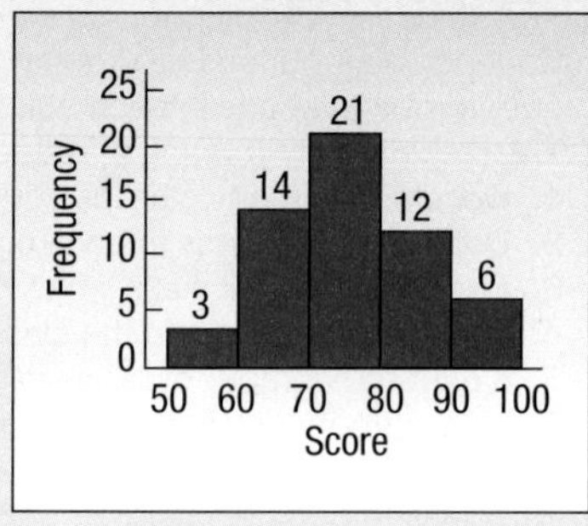

a. How many students took the exam?
b. What is the class interval?
c. What is the class midpoint for the first class?
d. How many students earned a score of less than 70?

28. The following chart summarizes the selling price of homes sold last month in the Sarasota, Florida, area.
a. What is the chart called?
b. How many homes were sold during the last month?
c. What is the class interval?
d. About 75 percent of the houses sold for less than what amount?
e. One hundred seventy-five of the homes sold for less than what amount?

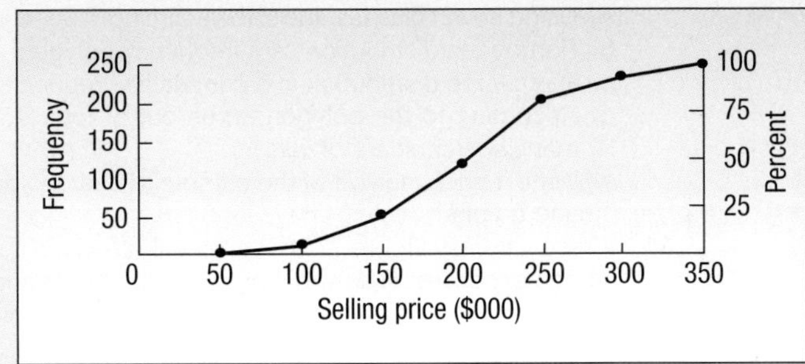

29. A chain of sport shops catering to beginning skiers, headquartered in Aspen, Colorado, plans to conduct a study of how much a beginning skier spends on his or her initial purchase of equipment and supplies. Based on these figures, they want to explore the possibility of offering combinations, such as a pair of boots and a pair of skis, to induce customers to buy more. A sample of their cash register receipts revealed these initial purchases:

$140	$ 82	$265	$168	$ 90	$114	$172	$230	$142
86	125	235	212	171	149	156	162	118
139	149	132	105	162	126	216	195	127
161	135	172	220	229	129	87	128	126
175	127	149	126	121	118	172	126	

a. Arrive at a suggested class interval. Use five classes, and let the lower limit of the first class be $80.
b. What would be a better class interval?
c. Organize the data into a frequency distribution using a lower limit of $80.
d. Interpret your findings.

30. The numbers of shareholders for a selected group of large companies (in thousands) are:

Company	Number of Shareholders (thousands)	Company	Number of Shareholders (thousands)
Southwest Airlines	144	Standard Oil (Indiana)	173
General Public Utilities	177	Home Depot	195
Occidental Petroleum	266	Detroit Edison	220
Middle South Utilities	133	Eastman Kodak	251
DaimlerChrysler	209	Dow Chemical	137
Standard Oil of California	264	Pennsylvania Power	150
Bethlehem Steel	160	American Electric Power	262
Long Island Lighting	143	Ohio Edison	158
RCA	246	Transamerica Corporation	162
Greyhound Corporation	151	Columbia Gas System	165
Pacific Gas & Electric	239	International Telephone & Telegraph	223
Niagara Mohawk Power	204	Union Electric	158
E. I. du Pont de Nemours	204	Virginia Electric and Power	162
Morris Knudsen Corporation	195	Public Service Electric & Gas	225
Union Carbide	176	Consumers Power	161
BankAmerica	175		
Northeast Utilities	200		

The numbers of shareholders are to be organized into a frequency distribution and several graphs drawn to portray the distribution.

a. Using seven classes and a lower limit of 130, construct a frequency distribution.
b. Portray the distribution as a frequency polygon.
c. Portray the distribution in a cumulative frequency polygon.
d. According to the polygon, three out of four (75 percent) of the companies have how many shareholders or less?
e. Write a brief analysis of the number of shareholders based on the frequency distribution and graphs.

31. A recent survey showed that the typical American car owner spends $2,950 per year on operating expenses. Below is a breakdown of the various expenditure items. Draw an appropriate chart to portray the data and summarize your findings in a brief report.

Expenditure Item	Amount
Fuel	$ 603
Interest on car loan	279
Repairs	930
Insurance and license	646
Depreciation	492
Total	$2,950

32. The Midland National Bank selected a sample of 40 student checking accounts. Below are their end-of-the-month balances.

$404	$ 74	$234	$149	$279	$215	$123	$ 55	$ 43	$321
87	234	68	489	57	185	141	758	72	863
703	125	350	440	37	252	27	521	302	127
968	712	503	489	327	608	358	425	303	203

a. Tally the data into a frequency distribution using $100 as a class interval and $0 as the starting point.
b. Draw a cumulative frequency polygon.
c. The bank considers any student with an ending balance of $400 or more a "preferred customer." Estimate the percentage of preferred customers.
d. The bank is also considering a service charge to the lowest 10 percent of the ending balances. What would you recommend as the cutoff point between those who have to pay a service charge and those who do not?

33. Residents of the state of South Carolina earned a total of $70.6 billion in 2003 in adjusted gross income. Seventy-three percent of the total was in wages and salaries; 11 percent in dividends, interest, and capital gains; 8 percent in IRAs and taxable pensions; 3 percent in business income pensions; 2 percent in social security, and the remaining 3 percent was from other sources. Develop a pie chart depicting the breakdown of adjusted gross income. Write a paragraph summarizing the information.

34. A recent study of home technologies reported the number of hours of personal computer usage per week for a sample of 60 persons. Excluded from the study were people who worked out of their home and used the computer as a part of their work.

9.3	5.3	6.3	8.8	6.5	0.6	5.2	6.6	9.3	4.3
6.3	2.1	2.7	0.4	3.7	3.3	1.1	2.7	6.7	6.5
4.3	9.7	7.7	5.2	1.7	8.5	4.2	5.5	5.1	5.6
5.4	4.8	2.1	10.1	1.3	5.6	2.4	2.4	4.7	1.7
2.0	6.7	1.1	6.7	2.2	2.6	9.8	6.4	4.9	5.2
4.5	9.3	7.9	4.6	4.3	4.5	9.2	8.5	6.0	8.1

a. Organize the data into a frequency distribution. How many classes would you suggest? What value would you suggest for a class interval?
b. Draw a histogram. Interpret your result.

35. Merrill Lynch recently completed a study regarding the size of on-line investment portfolios (stocks, bonds, mutual funds, and certificates of deposit) for a sample of clients in the 40- to 50-year-old age group. Listed below is the value of all the investments in $000 for the 70 participants in the study.

$669.9	$ 7.5	$ 77.2	$ 7.5	$125.7	$516.9	$219.9	$645.2
301.9	235.4	716.4	145.3	26.6	187.2	315.5	89.2
136.4	616.9	440.6	408.2	34.4	296.1	185.4	526.3
380.7	3.3	363.2	51.9	52.2	107.5	82.9	63.0
228.6	308.7	126.7	430.3	82.0	227.0	321.1	403.4
39.5	124.3	118.1	23.9	352.8	156.7	276.3	23.5
31.3	301.2	35.7	154.9	174.3	100.6	236.7	171.9
221.1	43.4	212.3	243.3	315.4	5.9	1002.2	171.7
295.7	437.0	87.8	302.1	268.1	899.5		

a. Organize the data into a frequency distribution. How many classes would you suggest? What value would you suggest for a class interval?
b. Draw a histogram. Interpret your result.

36. In May 2004, 18.5 percent of the Prime Time TV viewing audience watched shows on ABC, 25.9 percent on CBS, 18.5 percent on Fox, 18.5 percent on NBC, 7.4 percent on Warner Brothers, and 7.4 percent on UPN. You can find the latest information on TV viewing from the following website: http://tv.zap2it.com/news/ratings/. Develop a pie chart or a bar chart to depict this information. Write a paragraph summarizing the information.

37. The American Heart Association reported the following percentage breakdown of expenses. Draw a pie chart depicting the information. Interpret.

Category	Percent
Research	32.3
Public Health Education	23.5
Community Service	12.6
Fund Raising	12.1
Professional and Educational Training	10.9
Management and General	8.6

38. In their 2003 annual report Schering-Plough Corporation reported their income, in millions of dollars, for the years 1998 to 2003 as follows. Develop a line chart depicting the results and comment on your findings. Note that there was a $46 million loss in 2003.

Year	Income ($ million)
1998	1,756
1999	2,110
2000	2,423
2001	1,943
2002	1,974
2003	(46)

39. Annual revenues, by type of tax, for the state of Georgia are as follows. Develop an appropriate chart or graph and write a brief report summarizing the information.

Type of Tax	Amount (000)
Sales	$2,812,473
Income (Individual)	2,732,045
License	185,198
Corporate	525,015
Property	22,647
Death and Gift	37,326
Total	$6,314,704

40. Annual imports from selected Canadian trading partners are listed below for the year 2003. Develop an appropriate chart or graph and write a brief report summarizing the information.

Partner	Annual Imports (million)
Japan	$9,550
United Kingdom	4,556
South Korea	2,441
China	1,182
Australia	618

41. Farming has changed from the early 1900s. In the early 20th century, machinery gradually replaced animal power. For example, in 1910 U.S. farms used 24.2 million horses and mules and only about 1,000 tractors. By 1960, 4.6 million tractors were used and only 3.2 million horses and mules. In 1920 there were over 6 million farms in the United States. Today there are less than 2 million. Listed below is the number of farms, in thousands, for each of the 50 states. Write a paragraph summarizing your findings.

47	1	8	46	76	26	4	3	39	45
4	21	80	63	100	65	91	29	7	15
7	52	87	39	106	25	55	2	3	8
14	38	59	33	76	71	37	51	1	24
35	86	185	13	7	43	36	20	79	9

42. One of the most popular candies in the United States is M&M's, which are produced by the Mars Company. In the beginning M&M's were all brown; more recently they were produced in red, green, blue, orange, brown, and yellow. You can read about the history of the product, find ideas for baking, purchase the candies in the colors of your school or favorite team, and learn the percent of each color in the standard bags at http://global.mms.com/us/about/products/milkchocolate.jsp. Recently the purchase of a 14-ounce bag of M&M's Plain had 444 candies with the following breakdown by color: 130 brown, 98 yellow, 96 red, 35 orange, 52 blue, and 33 green. Develop a chart depicting this information and write a paragraph summarizing the results.

43. The graph below is a combination of a line chart and a pie chart. The line chart depicts the total vehicle sales from 1993 to 2003. The pie charts for each year show the percentage light-duty truck sales are of total vehicle sales. Write a brief report summarizing the results. Be sure to include whether there has been a change in truck sales over the period. Also, has the percent that light-duty trucks are of the total vehicle sales changed over time? How?

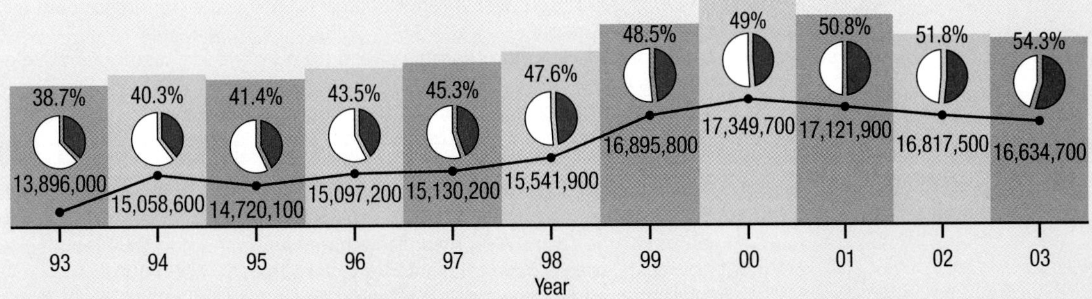

44. A pie chart shows the market shares of cola products. The "slice" for Pepsi-Cola has a central angle of 90 degrees. What is their market share?
45. The following graph shows the total wages paid by software and aircraft companies in the state of Washington from 1994 until 2002. Write a brief report summarizing this information.

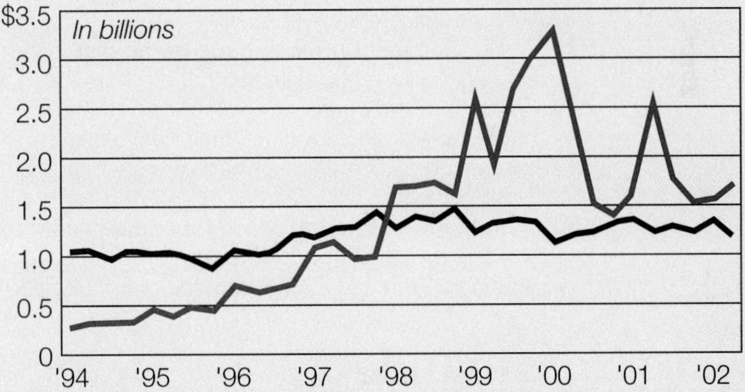

Source: Washington State Office of the Forecast Council

exercises.com

46. Monthly and year-to-date truck sales are available at the website: http://www.pickuptruck.com. Go to this site and search under **News** to obtain the most recent information. Make a pie chart or a bar chart showing the most recent information. What is the best selling truck? What are the four or five best selling trucks? What is their market share? You may wish to group some of the trucks into a category called "Other" to get a better picture of market share. Comment on your findings.

Dataset Exercises

47. Refer to the Real Estate data, which reports information on homes sold in the Denver, Colorado, area during the last year.
    a. Select an appropriate class interval and organize the selling prices into a frequency distribution.
        1. Around what values do the data tend to cluster?
        2. What is the largest selling price? What is the smallest selling price?
    b. Draw a cumulative frequency distribution based on the frequency distribution developed in part (a).
        1. How many homes sold for less than $200,000?
        2. Estimate the percent of the homes that sold for more than $220,000.
        3. What percent of the homes sold for less than $125,000?
    c. Write a report summarizing the selling prices of the homes.

48. Refer to the Baseball 2003 data, which reports information on the 30 Major League Baseball teams for the 2003 season.
   a. Organize the information on the team salaries into a frequency distribution. Select an appropriate class interval.
      1. What is a typical team salary? What is the range of salaries?
      2. Comment on the shape of the distribution. Does it appear that any of the team salaries are out of line with the others?
   b. Draw a cumulative frequency distribution based on the frequency distribution developed in part (a).
      1. Forty percent of the teams are paying less than what amount in total team salary?
      2. About how many teams have total salaries of less than $80,000,000?
      3. Below what amount do the lowest five teams pay in total salary?
   c. Organize the information on the size of the various stadiums into a frequency distribution.
      1. What is a typical stadium size? Where do the stadium sizes tend to cluster?
      2. Comment on the shape of the distribution. Does it appear that any of the stadium sizes are out of line with the others?
   d. Organize the information on the year in which the 30 major league stadiums were built into a frequency distribution. (You could also create a new variable called AGE by subtracting the year in which the stadium was built from the current year.)
      1. What is the year in which the typical stadium was built? Where do these years tend to cluster?
      2. Comment on the shape of the distribution. Does it appear that any of the stadium ages are out of line with the others? If so, which ones?
49. Refer to the Wage data, which reports information on annual wages for a sample of 100 workers. Also included are variables relating to industry, years of education, and gender for each worker. Draw a bar chart of the variable occupation. Write a brief report summarizing your findings.
50. Refer to the CIA data, which reports demographic and economic information on 46 countries. Develop a frequency distribution for the variable GNP per capita. Summarize your findings. What is the shape of the distribution?

Software Commands

1. The MegaStat commands for the frequency distribution on page 30 are:
   a. Open Excel and from the CD provided, select **Go to the Data Sets,** and select the Excel format; go to Chapter 2, and select **Table 2–1.** Click on **MegaStat, Frequency Distribution,** and select **Quantitative.**
   b. In the dialog box, input the range from *A1:A81,* select **Equal width intervals,** use 3,000 as the interval width, 15,000 as the lower boundary of the first interval, select **Histogram,** and then click **OK.**

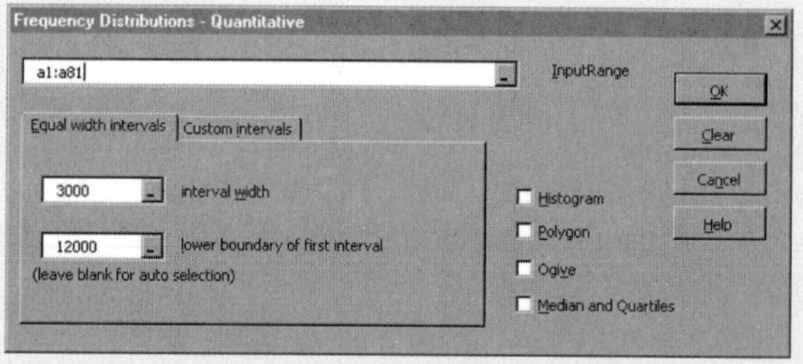

2. The Excel commands for the histogram on page 34 are:
   a. In cell *A1* indicate that the column of data is the selling price and in *B1* that it is the frequency. In columns *A2* to *A8* insert the midpoints of the selling prices in $000. In *B2* to *B8* record the class frequencies.
   b. With your mouse arrow on *A1,* click and drag to highlight the cells *A1:B8.*
   c. From the **Tool bar** select **Chart Wizard,** under **Chart type** select **Column,** under **Chart subtype** select the vertical bars in the upper left corner, and finally click on **Next** in the lower right corner.
   d. At the top select the **Series** tab. Under the Series list box, **Price** is highlighted. Select **Remove.** (We do not want Price to be a part of the values.) At the bottom, in the **Category (X)** axis labels text box, click the icon at the far right. Put your cursor on cell *A2,* click and drag to cell *A8.* There will be a running box around cells *A2* to *A8.* Touch the **Enter** key. This identifies the column of **Prices** as the *X*-axis labels. Click on **Next.**
   e. At the top of the dialog box click on **Titles.** Click on the **Chart title** box and key in *Selling Price of 80 Vehicles Sold at Whitner Autoplex.* Tab to the **Category (X)** axis box and key in the label *Selling Price in ($000).* Tab to the **Category (Y)** axis box and key in *Frequency.* At the top select **Legend** and remove the check from the **Show legend** box. Click **Finish.**
   f. To make the chart larger, click on the middle handle of the top line and drag the line to row 1.

Make sure the handles show on the chart box. With your right mouse button, click on one of the columns. Select **Format Data Series.** At the top select the **Options** tab. In the **Gap width** text box, click the down arrow until the gap width reads 0, and click **OK.**

3. The Excel commands for the pie chart on page 45 are:
   a. Set cell *A1* as the active cell and type the words *Use of Sales.* In cells *A2* through *A5* type *Prizes, Education, Bonuses,* and *Expense.*
   b. Set *B1* as the active cell and type *Amount ($ Millions)* and in cells *B2* through *B5* enter the data.
   c. From the **Tool Bar** select **Chart Wizard.** Select **Pie** as the type of chart, select the chart type in the upper left corner, and then click on **Next.**
   d. For the **Data Range** type *A1:B5,* indicate that the data are in **Columns,** and then click on **Next.**
   e. Click on the chart title area and type *Ohio Lottery Expenses 2002.* Then click **Finish.**

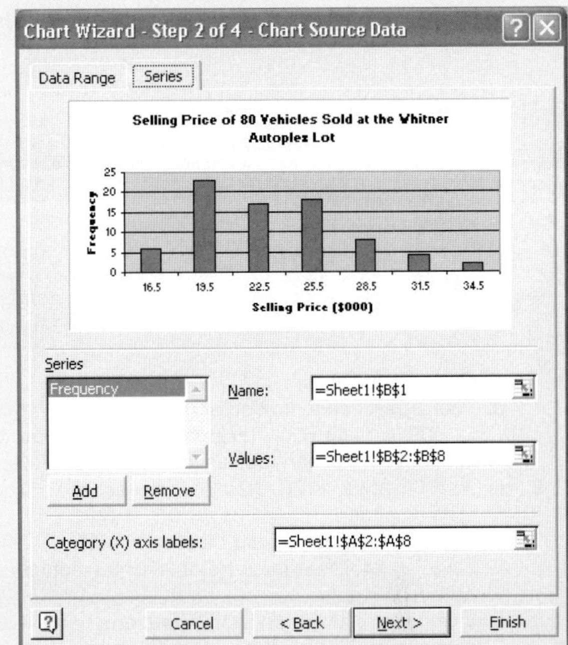

Chapter 2 Answers to Self-Review

2–1 **a.** The raw data or ungrouped data.

b.

Commission	Number of Salespeople
\$1,400 up to \$1,500	2
1,500 up to 1,600	5
1,600 up to 1,700	3
1,700 up to 1,800	1
Total	11

c. Class frequencies.

d. The largest concentration of commissions is \$1,500 up to \$1,600. The smallest commission is about \$1,400 and the largest is about \$1,800.

2–2 **a.** $2^6 = 64 < 73 < 128 = 2^7$. So 7 classes are recommended.

b. The interval width should be at least $(488 - 320)/7 = 24$. Class intervals of 25 or 30 feet are both reasonable.

c. If we use a class interval of 25 feet and begin with a lower limit of 300 feet, eight classes would be necessary. A class interval of 30 feet beginning with 300 feet is also reasonable. This alternative requires only seven classes.

2–3 **a.** 23

b. 28.75%, found by $(23/80) \times 100$

c. 7.5%, found by $(6/80) \times 100$

2–4 **a.**

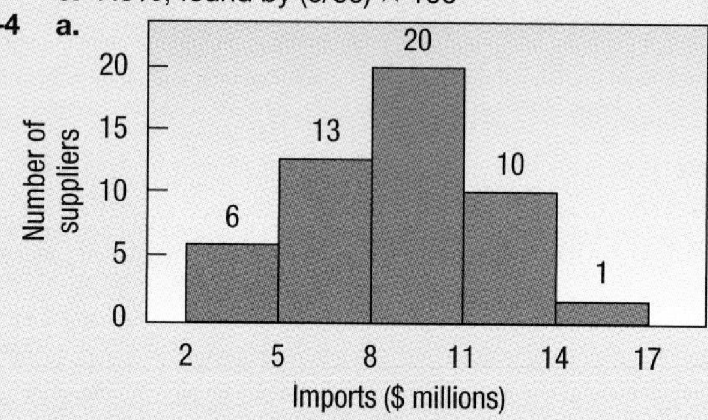

b.

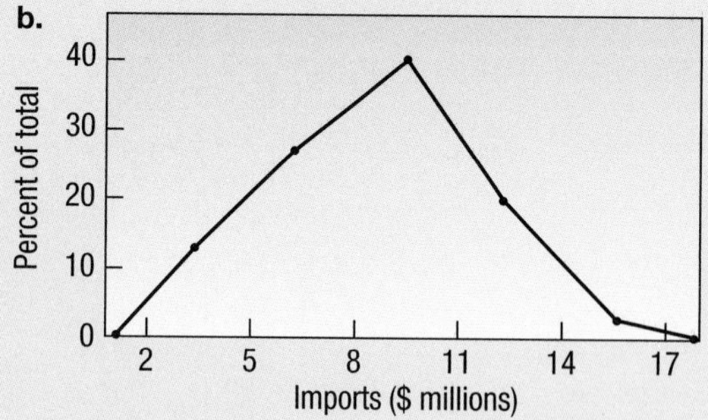

The plots are: (3.5, 12), (6.5, 26), (9.5, 40), (12.5, 20), and (15.5, 2).

c. The smallest annual sales volume of imports by a supplier is about \$2 million, the largest about \$17 million. The highest frequency is between \$8 million and \$11 million.

2–5 **a.** A frequency distribution.

b.

Hourly Wages	Cumulative Number
Less than \$8	0
Less than \$10	3
Less than \$12	10
Less than \$14	14
Less than \$16	15

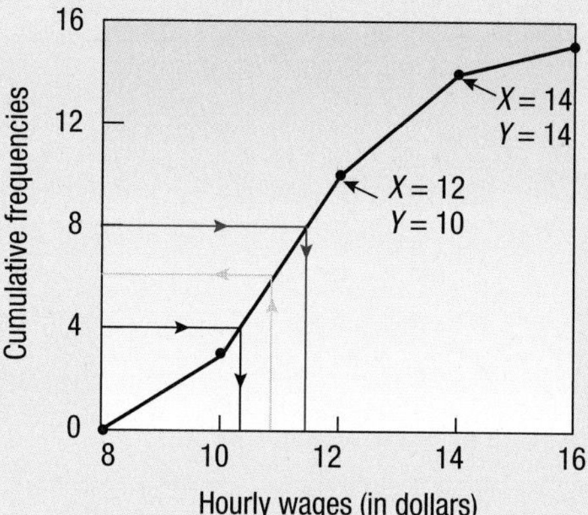

c. About seven employees earn \$11.00 or less. About half the employees earn \$11.25 or more. About four employees earn \$10.25 or less.

2–6

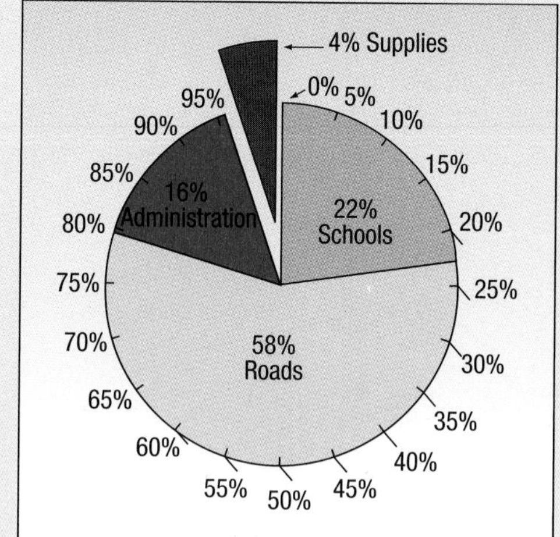

Describing Data:
Numerical Measures

3

The weights (in pounds) of a sample of five boxes being shipped to Texas using UPS are: 12, 6, 7, 3 and 10. Compute the standard deviation. (See Goal 4 and Exercise 66.)

GOALS

When you have completed this chapter you will be able to:

1 Calculate the *arithmetic mean, weighted mean, median, mode,* and *geometric mean.*

2 Explain the characteristics, uses, advantages, and disadvantages of each *measure of location.*

3 Identify the position of the mean, median, and mode for both *symmetric* and *skewed distributions.*

4 Compute and interpret the *range, mean deviation, variance,* and *standard deviation.*

5 Understand the characteristics, uses, advantages, and disadvantages of each *measure of dispersion.*

6 Understand *Chebyshev's theorem* and the *Empirical Rule* as they relate to a set of observations.

Introduction

Chapter 2 began our study of descriptive statistics. To transform a mass of raw data into a meaningful form, we organized it into a frequency distribution and portrayed it graphically in a histogram or a frequency polygon. We also looked at other graphical techniques such as line charts and pie charts.

This chapter is concerned with two numerical ways of describing data, namely, **measures of location** and **measures of dispersion.** Measures of location are often referred to as averages. The purpose of a measure of location is to pinpoint the center of a set of values.

Statistics in Action

Did you ever meet the "average" American? Well, his name is Robert (that is the nominal level of measurement), he is 31 years old (that is the ratio level), he is 69.5 inches tall (again the ratio level of measurement), weighs 172 pounds, wears a size 9½ shoe, has a 34-inch waist, and wears a size 40 suit. In addition, the average man eats 4 pounds of potato chips, watches 2,567 hours of TV, eats 26 pounds of bananas each year, and also, he sleeps 7.7 hours per night.

The average American woman is 5′4″ tall and weighs 140 pounds, while the average American model is 5′11″ tall and weighs 117 pounds. Most fashion models are thinner than 98% of American women. Four out of five American women say they're dissatisfied with the way they look. On any given day, almost half of the women in the United States are on a diet. Idolized in the 1950s, Marilyn Monroe would be considered overweight by today's standards. She fluctuated between a size 14 and 18 dress, and was a healthy and attractive woman.

You are familiar with the concept of an average. An average is a measure of location that shows the central value of the data. Averages appear daily on TV, in the newspaper, and in news magazines. Here are some examples:

- The average U.S. home changes ownership every 11.8 years.
- The average price of a gallon of gasoline last week in South Carolina was $1.94, according to a study by the American Automobile Association.
- The average cost to drive a private automobile is 55.8 cents per mile in Los Angeles, 49.8 cents per mile in Boston, 49.0 cents per mile in Philadelphia.
- An American receives an average of 568 pieces of mail per year.
- The average starting salary for a business school graduate last year was $36,357. For a graduate with a Liberal Arts major it was $31,599.
- There are 26.4 million golfers over the age of 12 in the United States. Approximately 6.1 million are avid golfers; that is, they play an average of 25 rounds a year. Some additional information on golfers and golfing: the median cost of a round of golf on an 18-hole course at a municipal course in the United States is $30. Today's typical golfer is male, 40 years old, has a household income of $68,209, and plays 21.3 rounds per year.
- In Chicago the mean high temperature is 84 degrees in July and 31 degrees in January. The mean amount of precipitation is 3.80 inches in July and 1.90 inches in January.

If we consider only the measures of location in a set of data, or if we compare several sets of data using central values, we may draw an erroneous conclusion. In addition to the measures of location, we should consider the **dispersion**—often called the *variation* or the *spread*—in the data. As an illustration, suppose the average annual income of executives for Internet-related companies is $80,000, and the average income for executives in pharmaceutical firms is also $80,000. If we looked only at the average incomes, we might wrongly conclude that the two salary distributions are identical or nearly identical. A look at the salary ranges indicates that this conclusion is not correct. The salaries for the executives in the Internet firms range from $70,000 to $90,000, but salaries for the marketing executives in pharmaceuticals range from $40,000 to $120,000. Thus, we conclude that although the average salaries are the same for the two industries, there is much more spread or dispersion in salaries for the pharmaceutical executives. To evaluate the dispersion we will consider the range, the mean deviation, the variance, and the standard deviation.

We begin by discussing measures of location. There is not just one measure of location; in fact, there are many. We will consider five: the arithmetic mean, the weighted mean, the median, the mode, and the geometric mean. The arithmetic mean is the most widely used and widely reported measure of location. We study the mean as both a population parameter and a sample statistic.

The Population Mean

Many studies involve all the values in a population. For example, there are 39 exits on I-75 through the state of Kentucky. The mean distance between these exits is 4.76 miles. This is an example of a population parameter because we have studied the distance between *all* the exits. There are 12 sales associates employed at the Reynolds Road outlet of Carpets by Otto. The mean amount of commission they earned last month was $1,345. This is a population value because we considered the commission of *all* the sales associates. Other examples of a population mean would be: the mean closing price for Johnson and Johnson stock for the last 5 days is $55.25; the mean annual rate of return for the last 10 years for Berger Funds is 5.21 percent; and the mean number of hours of overtime worked last week by the six welders in the welding department of Butts Welding, Inc., is 6.45 hours.

For raw data, that is, data that has not been grouped in a frequency distribution, the population mean is the sum of all the values in the population divided by the number of values in the population. To find the population mean, we use the following formula.

$$\text{Population mean} = \frac{\text{Sum of all the values in the population}}{\text{Number of values in the population}}$$

Instead of writing out in words the full directions for computing the population mean (or any other measure), it is more convenient to use the shorthand symbols of mathematics. The mean of a population using mathematical symbols is:

POPULATION MEAN $$\mu = \frac{\Sigma X}{N}$$ **[3–1]**

where:

μ represents the population mean. It is the Greek lowercase letter "mu."
N is the number of values in the population.
X represents any particular value.
Σ is the Greek capital letter "sigma" and indicates the operation of adding.
ΣX is the sum of the X values in the population.

Any measurable characteristic of a population is called a **parameter.** The mean of a population is a parameter.

PARAMETER A characteristic of a population.

EXAMPLE

There are 12 automobile manufacturing companies in the United States. Listed below is the number of patents granted by the United States government to each company in a recent year.

Company	Number of Patents Granted	Company	Number of Patents Granted
General Motors	511	Mazda	210
Nissan	385	Chrysler	97
DaimlerChrysler	275	Porsche	50
Toyota	257	Mitsubishi	36
Honda	249	Volvo	23
Ford	234	BMW	13

Is this information a sample or a population? What is the arithmetic mean number of patents granted?

SOLUTION

This is a population because we are considering all the automobile manufacturing companies obtaining patents. We add the number of patents for each of the 12 companies. The total number of patents for the 12 companies is 2,340. To find the arithmetic mean, we divide this total by 12. So the arithmetic mean is 195, found by 2340/12. From formula (3–1):

$$\mu = \frac{511 + 385 + \cdots + 13}{12} = \frac{2340}{12} = 195$$

How do we interpret the value of 195? The typical number of patents received by an automobile manufacturing company is 195. Because we considered all the companies receiving patents, this value is a population parameter.

The Sample Mean

As explained in Chapter 1, we often select a sample from the population to find something about a specific characteristic of the population. The quality assurance department, for example, needs to be assured that the ball bearings being produced have an acceptable outside diameter. It would be very expensive and time consuming to check the outside diameter of all the bearings produced. Therefore, a sample of five bearings is selected and the mean outside diameter of the five bearings is calculated to estimate the mean diameter of all the bearings.

For raw data, that is, ungrouped data, *the mean is the sum of all the sampled values divided by the total number of sampled values.* To find the mean for a sample:

Mean of ungrouped sample data

$$\text{Sample mean} = \frac{\text{Sum of all the values in the sample}}{\text{Number of values in the sample}}$$

The mean of a sample and the mean of a population are computed in the same way, but the shorthand notation used is different. The formula for the mean of a *sample* is:

SAMPLE MEAN $$\bar{X} = \frac{\Sigma X}{n}$$ **[3–2]**

where:

$\bar{X}$ *is* the sample mean. It is read "X bar."
n is the number of values in the sample.

The mean of a sample, or any other measure based on sample data, is called a **statistic.** If the mean outside diameter of a sample of five ball bearings is 0.625 inches, this is an example of a statistic.

STATISTIC A characteristic of a sample.

EXAMPLE

SunCom is studying the number of minutes used monthly by customers in their "Friends and Family" cell phone plan. A random sample of 12 clients enrolled in this plan showed the following number of minutes used last month.

90	77	94	89	119	112
91	110	92	100	113	83

SOLUTION

What is the arithmetic mean number of minutes used?

Using formula (3–2), the sample mean is:

$$\text{Sample mean} = \frac{\text{Sum of all the values in the sample}}{\text{Number of values in the sample}}$$

$$\bar{X} = \frac{\Sigma X}{n} = \frac{90 + 77 + \cdots + 83}{12} = \frac{1170}{12} = 97.5$$

The arithmetic mean number of minutes used last month by the sample of Friends and Family cell phone users is 97.5 minutes. To put it another way, the typical customer enrolled in the Friends and Family plan used 97.5 minutes of air time last month.

Properties of the Arithmetic Mean

The arithmetic mean is a widely used measure of location. It has several important properties:

1. Every set of interval- or ratio-level data has a mean. Recall from Chapter 1 that ratio-level data include such data as ages, incomes, and weights, with the distance between numbers being constant.
2. All the values are included in computing the mean.
3. A set of data has only one mean. The mean is unique. Later in the chapter we will discover an average that might appear twice, or more than twice, in a set of data.
4. The *sum of the deviations of each value from the mean will always be zero.* Expressed symbolically:

$$\Sigma(X - \bar{X}) = 0$$

As an example, the mean of 3, 8, and 4 is 5. Then:

$$\begin{aligned}\Sigma(X - \bar{X}) &= (3 - 5) + (8 - 5) + (4 - 5) \\ &= -2 + 3 - 1 \\ &= 0\end{aligned}$$

Mean as a balance point

Thus, we can consider the mean as a balance point for a set of data. To illustrate, we have a long board with the numbers 1, 2, 3, . . . , *n* evenly spaced on it. Suppose three bars of equal weight were placed on the board at numbers 3, 4, and 8, and the balance point was set at 5, the mean of the three numbers. We would find that the board is balanced perfectly! The deviations below the mean (−3) are equal to the deviations above the mean (+3). Shown schematically:

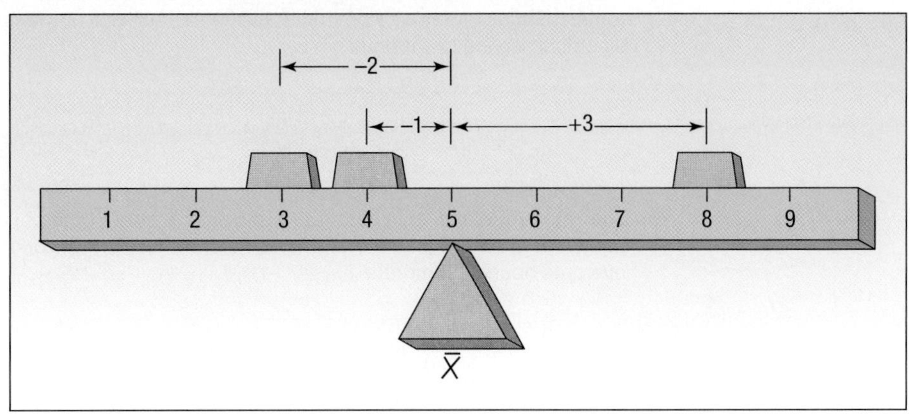

Mean unduly affected by unusually large or small values

The mean does have a weakness. Recall that the mean uses the value of every item in a sample, or population, in its computation. If one or two of these values are either extremely large or extremely small compared to the majority of data, the mean might not be an appropriate average to represent the data. For example, suppose the annual incomes of a small group of stockbrokers at Merrill Lynch are $62,900, $61,600, $62,500, $60,800, and $1,200,000. The mean income is $289,560. Obviously, it is not representative of this group, because all but one broker has an income in the $60,000 to $63,000 range. One income ($1.2 million) is unduly affecting the mean.

Self-Review 3–1

1. The annual incomes of a sample of middle-management employees at Westinghouse are: $62,900, $69,100, $58,300, and $76,800.
   (a) Give the formula for the sample mean.
   (b) Find the sample mean.
   (c) Is the mean you computed in (b) a statistic or a parameter? Why?
   (d) What is your best estimate of the population mean?
2. All the students in advanced Computer Science 411 are a population. Their course grades are 92, 96, 61, 86, 79, and 84.
   (a) Give the formula for the population mean.
   (b) Compute the mean course grade.
   (c) Is the mean you computed in (b) a statistic or a parameter? Why?

Exercises

The answers to the odd-numbered exercises are at the end of the book.

1. Compute the mean of the following population values: 6, 3, 5, 7, 6.
2. Compute the mean of the following population values: 7, 5, 7, 3, 7, 4.
3. **a.** Compute the mean of the following sample values: 5, 9, 4, 10.
   b. Show that $\Sigma(X - \bar{X}) = 0$.
4. **a.** Compute the mean of the following sample values: 1.3, 7.0, 3.6, 4.1, 5.0.
   b. Show that $\Sigma(X - \bar{X}) = 0$.
5. Compute the mean of the following sample values: 16.25, 12.91, 14.58.
6. Compute the mean hourly wage paid to carpenters who earned the following wages: $15.40, $20.10, $18.75, $22.76, $30.67, $18.00.

For Exercises 7–10, (a) compute the arithmetic mean and (b) indicate whether it is a statistic or a parameter.

7. There are 10 salespeople employed by Moody Insurance Agency in Venice, Florida. The numbers of new life insurance policies sold last month by the respective salespeople were: 15, 23, 4, 19, 18, 10, 10, 8, 28, 19.
8. The accounting department at a mail-order company counted the following numbers of incoming calls per day to the company's toll-free number during the first 7 days in May 2003: 14, 24, 19, 31, 36, 26, 17.
9. The Cambridge Power and Light Company selected a random sample of 20 residential customers. Following are the amounts, to the nearest dollar, the customers were charged for electrical service last month:

54	48	58	50	25	47	75	46	60	70
67	68	39	35	56	66	33	62	65	67

10. The Human Relations Director at Ford began a study of the overtime hours in the Inspection Department. A sample of 15 workers showed they worked the following number of overtime hours last month.

13	13	12	15	7	15	5	12
6	7	12	10	9	13	12	

The Weighted Mean

The weighted mean is a special case of the arithmetic mean. It occurs when there are several observations of the same value. To explain, suppose the nearby Wendy's Restaurant sold medium, large, and Biggie-sized soft drinks for \$.90, \$1.25, and \$1.50, respectively. Of the last 10 drinks sold, 3 were medium, 4 were large, and 3 were Biggie-sized. To find the mean price of the last 10 drinks sold, we could use formula (3–2).

$$\bar{X} = \frac{\$.90 + \$.90 + \$.90 + \$1.25 + \$1.25 + \$1.25 + \$1.25 + \$1.50 + \$1.50 + \$1.50}{10}$$

$$\bar{X} = \frac{\$12.20}{10} = \$1.22$$

The mean selling price of the last 10 drinks is \$1.22.

An easier way to find the mean selling price is to determine the weighted mean. That is, we multiply each observation by the number of times it happens. We will refer to the weighted mean as $\bar{X}_w$. This is read "X bar sub w."

$$\bar{X}_w = \frac{3(\$0.90) + 4(\$1.25) + 3(\$1.50)}{10} = \frac{\$12.20}{10} = \$1.22$$

In this case the weights are frequency counts. However, any measure of importance could be used as a weight. In general the weighted mean of a set of numbers designated $X_1, X_2, X_3, \ldots, X_n$ with the corresponding weights $w_1, w_2, w_3, \ldots, w_n$ is computed by:

WEIGHTED MEAN
$$\bar{X}_w = \frac{w_1X_1 + w_2X_2 + w_3X_3 + \cdots + w_nX_n}{w_1 + w_2 + w_3 + \cdots + w_n} \quad [3\text{–}3]$$

This may be shortened to:

$$\bar{X}_w = \frac{\Sigma(wX)}{\Sigma w}$$

EXAMPLE

The Carter Construction Company pays its hourly employees \$16.50, \$17.50, or \$18.50 per hour. There are 26 hourly employees, 14 are paid at the \$16.50 rate, 10 at the \$17.50 rate, and 2 at the \$18.50 rate. What is the mean hourly rate paid the 26 employees?

SOLUTION

To find the mean hourly rate, we weight or multiply each of the hourly rates by the number of employees earning that rate. From formula (3–3), the mean hourly rate is

$$\bar{X}_w = \frac{14(\$16.50) + 10(\$17.50) + 2(\$18.50)}{14 + 10 + 2} = \frac{\$443.00}{26} = \$17.038$$

The weighted mean hourly wage is rounded to \$17.04.

Self-Review 3–2

Springers sold 95 Antonelli men's suits for the regular price of \$400. For the spring sale the suits were reduced to \$200 and 126 were sold. At the final clearance, the price was reduced to \$100 and the remaining 79 suits were sold.

(a) What was the weighted mean price of an Antonelli suit?
(b) Springers paid \$200 a suit for the 300 suits. Comment on the store's profit per suit if a salesperson receives a \$25 commission for each one sold.

Exercises

11. In June an investor purchased 300 shares of Oracle (an information technology company) stock at $20 per share. In August she purchased an additional 400 shares at $25 per share. In November she purchased an additional 400 shares, but the stock declined to $23 per share. What is the weighted mean price per share?

12. The Bookstall, Inc., is a specialty bookstore concentrating on used books sold via the Internet. Paperbacks are $1.00 each, and hardcover books are $3.50. Of the 50 books sold last Tuesday morning, 40 were paperback and the rest were hardcover. What was the weighted mean price of a book?

13. Yesterday the Hess Mart at the junction of state highways 707 and 544 in Socastee, South Carolina sold 3,265 gallons of gasoline to motorists. They offered unleaded regular at $1.749 per gallon, unleaded plus at $1.849 per gallon, and unleaded supreme at $1.949 per gallon. Of the total gallons sold, 80.2 percent was unleaded regular, 15.2 percent unleaded plus, and the remaining 4.6 percent was unleaded supreme. Find the weighted mean selling price.

14. Andrews and Associates specialize in corporate law. They charge $100 an hour for researching a case, $75 an hour for consultations, and $200 an hour for writing a brief. Last week one of the associates spent 10 hours consulting with her client, 10 hours researching the case, and 20 hours writing the brief. What was the weighted mean hourly charge for her legal services?

The Median

We have stressed that for data containing one or two very large or very small values, the arithmetic mean may not be representative. The center for such data can be better described by a measure of location called the **median.**

To illustrate the need for a measure of location other than the arithmetic mean, suppose you are seeking to buy a condominium in Palm Aire. Your real estate agent says that the average price of the units currently available is $110,000. Would you still want to look? If you had budgeted your maximum purchase price at $75,000, you might think they are out of your price range. However, checking the individual prices of the units might change your mind. They are $60,000, $65,000, $70,000, $80,000, and a superdeluxe penthouse costs $275,000. The arithmetic mean price is $110,000, as the real estate agent reported, but one price ($275,000) is pulling the arithmetic mean upward, causing it to be an unrepresentative average. It does seem that a price around $70,000 is a more typical or representative average, and it is. In cases such as this, the median provides a more valid measure of location.

MEDIAN The midpoint of the values after they have been ordered from the smallest to the largest, or the largest to the smallest.

The data must be at least ordinal level of measurement. The median price of the units available is $70,000. To determine this, we ordered the prices from low ($60,000) to high ($275,000) and selected the middle value ($70,000).

Prices Ordered from Low to High		Prices Ordered from High to Low
$ 60,000		$275,000
65,000		80,000
70,000	← Median →	70,000
80,000		65,000
275,000		60,000

Median unaffected by extreme values

Note that there is the same number of prices below the median of $70,000 as above it. There are as many values below the median as above. The median is, therefore, unaffected by extremely low or high prices. Had the highest price been $90,000, or $300,000, or even $1 million, the median price would still be $70,000. Likewise, had the lowest price been $20,000 or $50,000, the median price would still be $70,000.

In the previous illustration there is an *odd* number of observations (five). How is the median determined for an *even* number of observations? As before, the observations are ordered. Then by convention to obtain a unique value we calculate the mean of the two middle observations. So for an even number of observations, the median may not be one of the given values.

EXAMPLE

The five-year annualized total returns of six mutual funds with emphasis on aggressive growth are listed below. What is the median annualized return?

SOLUTION

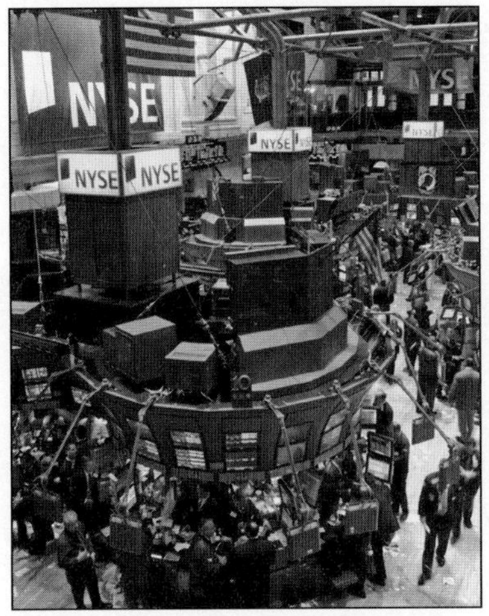

Name of Fund	Annualized Total Return
PBHG Growth	28.5%
Dean Witter Developing Growth	17.2
AIM Aggressive Growth	25.4
Twentieth Century Giftrust	28.6
Robertson Stevens Emerging Growth	22.6
Seligman Frontier A	21.0

Note that the number of returns is *even* (6). As before, the returns are first ordered from low to high. Then the two middle returns are identified. The arithmetic mean of the two middle observations gives us the median return. Arranging from low to high:

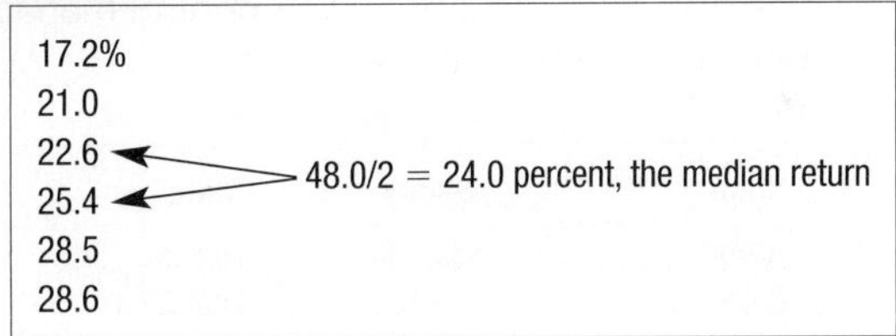

Notice that the median is not one of the values. Also, half of the returns are below the median and half are above it.

The major properties of the median are:

1. The median is unique; that is, like the mean, there is only one median for a set of data.
2. It is not affected by extremely large or small values and is therefore a valuable measure of location when such values do occur.
3. It can be computed for ratio-level, interval-level, and ordinal-level data. Recall from Chapter 1 that ordinal-level data can be ranked from low to high—such as the responses "excellent," "very good," "good," "fair," and "poor" to a question on a marketing survey. To use a simple illustration, suppose five people rated a new fudge bar. One person thought it was excellent, one rated it very good, one called it good, one rated it fair, and one considered it poor. The median response is "good." Half of the responses are above "good"; the other half are below it.

Median can be determined for all levels of data except nominal

The Mode

The **mode** is another measure of location.

MODE The value of the observation that appears most frequently.

The mode is especially useful in describing nominal and ordinal levels of measurement. As an example of its use for nominal-level data, a company has developed five bath oils. Chart 3–1 shows the results of a marketing survey designed to find which bath oil consumers prefer. The largest number of respondents favored Lamoure, as evidenced by the highest bar. Thus, Lamoure is the mode.

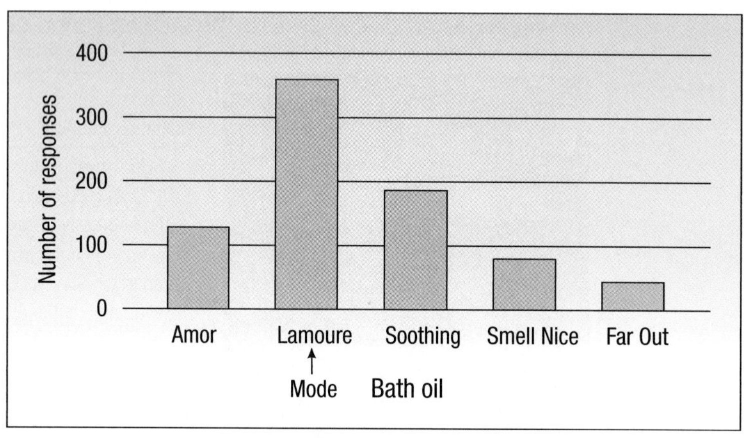

CHART 3–1 Number of Respondents Favoring Various Bath Oils

EXAMPLE

The annual salaries of quality-control managers in selected states are shown below. What is the modal annual salary?

State	Salary	State	Salary	State	Salary
Arizona	$35,000	Illinois	$58,000	Ohio	$50,000
California	49,100	Louisiana	60,000	Tennessee	60,000
Colorado	60,000	Maryland	60,000	Texas	71,400
Florida	60,000	Massachusetts	40,000	West Virginia	60,000
Idaho	40,000	New Jersey	65,000	Wyoming	55,000

SOLUTION

A perusal of the salaries reveals that the annual salary of $60,000 appears more often (six times) than any other salary. The mode is, therefore, $60,000.

In summary, we can determine the mode for all levels of data—nominal, ordinal, interval, and ratio. The mode also has the advantage of not being affected by extremely high or low values.

Disadvantages of the mode

The mode does have disadvantages, however, that cause it to be used less frequently than the mean or median. For many sets of data, there is no mode because no value appears more than once. For example, there is no mode for this set of price data: $19, $21, $23, $20, and $18. Since every value is different, however, it could be argued that every value is the mode. Conversely, for some data sets there is more than one mode. Suppose the ages of the individuals in a stock investment club are 22, 26, 27, 27, 31, 35, and 35. Both the ages 27 and 35 are modes. Thus, this grouping of ages is referred to as *bimodal* (having two modes). One would question the use of two modes to represent the location of this set of age data.

Self-Review 3–3

1. A sample of single persons in Towson, Texas, receiving Social Security payments revealed these monthly benefits: $426, $299, $290, $687, $480, $439, and $565.
   (a) What is the median monthly benefit?
   (b) How many observations are below the median? Above it?
2. The number of plant closings in the steel industry for selected months are 6, 0, 10, 14, 8, and 0.
   (a) What is the median number of closings?
   (b) How many observations are below the median? Above it?
   (c) What is the modal number of work closings?

Exercises

15. What would you report as the modal value for a set of observations if there were a total of:
a. 10 observations and no two values were the same?
b. 6 observations and they were all the same?
c. 6 observations and the values were 1, 2, 3, 3, 4, and 4?

For Exercises 16–19, (a) determine the median and (b) the mode.

16. The following is the number of oil changes for the last 7 days at the Jiffy Lube located at the corner of Elm Street and Pennsylvania Ave.

41	15	39	54	31	15	33

17. The following is the percent change in net income from 2003 to 2004 for a sample of 12 construction companies in Denver.

5	1	−10	−6	5	12	7	8	2	5	−1	11

18. The following are the ages of the 10 people in the video arcade at the Southwyck Shopping Mall at 10 A.M. this morning.

12	8	17	6	11	14	8	17	10	8

19. Listed below are several indicators of long-term economic growth in the United States. The projections are through the year 2008.

Economic Indicator	Percent Change	Economic Indicator	Percent Change
Inflation	4.5	Real GNP	2.9
Exports	4.7	Investment (residential)	3.6
Imports	2.3	Investment (nonresidential)	2.1
Real disposable income	2.9	Productivity (total)	1.4
Consumption	2.7	Productivity (manufacturing)	5.2

a. What is the median percent change?
b. What is the modal percent change?

20. Yesterday there were 22 arriving flights at the Appleton Outagamie County Regional Airport near Appleton, Wisconsin. The number of minutes each of the flights was earlier or later than the scheduled time is reported below. A negative value indicates the flight arrived *before* its scheduled time. A positive value reflects the number of minutes the flight arrived *after* its scheduled time.

−20	−15	−10	−4	−1	0	2	3	3	4	13	17
24	26	28	29	30	36	40	43	44	45		

Determine the median value. Interpret this value.

Software Solution

We can use a statistical software package to find many measures of location.

EXAMPLE

Table 2–1 on page 25 shows the prices of the 80 vehicles sold last month at Whitner Autoplex in Raytown, Missouri. Determine the mean and the median selling price.

SOLUTION

The mean and the median selling prices are reported in the following Excel output. (Remember: The instructions to create the output appear in the **Software Commands** section at the end of the chapter.) There are 80 vehicles in the study, so the calculations with a calculator would be tedious and prone to error.

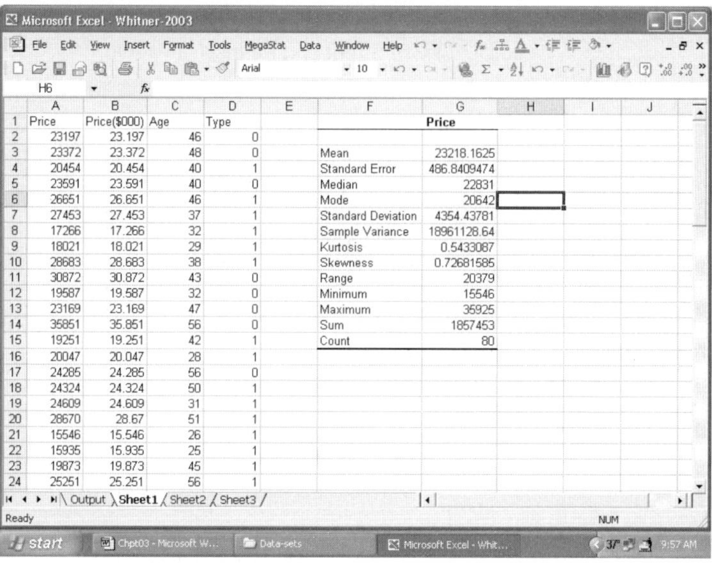

Microsoft Excel - Whitner-2003

	A	B	C	D	E	F	G
1	Price	Price($000)	Age	Type			Price
2	23197	23.197	46	0			
3	23372	23.372	48	0		Mean	23218.1625
4	20454	20.454	40	1		Standard Error	486.8409474
5	23591	23.591	40	0		Median	22831
6	26651	26.651	46	1		Mode	20642
7	27453	27.453	37	1		Standard Deviation	4354.43781
8	17266	17.266	32	1		Sample Variance	18961128.64
9	18021	18.021	29	1		Kurtosis	0.5433087
10	28683	28.683	38	1		Skewness	0.72681585
11	30872	30.872	43	0		Range	20379
12	19587	19.587	32	0		Minimum	15546
13	23169	23.169	47	0		Maximum	35925
14	35851	35.851	56	0		Sum	1857453
15	19251	19.251	42	1		Count	80
16	20047	20.047	28	1			
17	24285	24.285	56	0			
18	24324	24.324	50	1			
19	24609	24.609	31	1			
20	28670	28.67	51	1			
21	15546	15.546	26	1			
22	15935	15.935	25	1			
23	19873	19.873	45	1			
24	25251	25.251	56	1			

The mean selling price is $23,218 and the median is $22,831. These two values are less than $400 apart. So either value is reasonable. We can also see from the Excel output that there were 80 vehicles sold and their total price is $1,857,453. We will describe the meaning of standard error, standard deviation, and other measures later.

What can we conclude? The typical vehicle sold for about $23,000. Ms. Ball of Auto USA might use this value in her revenue projections. For example, if the dealership could increase the number sold in a month from 80 to 90, this would result in an additional estimated $230,000 of revenue, found by 10 × $23,000.

The Relative Positions of the Mean, Median, and Mode

Refer to the histogram in Chart 3–2. It is a symmetric distribution, which is also mound-shaped. This distribution *has the same shape on either side of the center.* If the

For a symmetric, mound-shaped distribution, mean, median, and mode are equal.

polygon were folded in half, the two halves would be identical. For this symmetric distribution, the mode, median, and mean are located at the center and are always equal. They are all equal to 20 years in Chart 3–2. We should point out that there are symmetric distributions that are not mound-shaped.

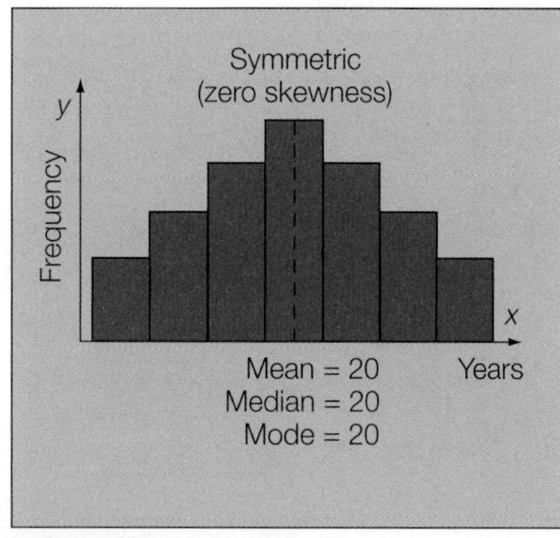

CHART 3–2 A Symmetric Distribution

The number of years corresponding to the highest point of the curve is the *mode* (20 years). Because the distribution is symmetrical, the *median* corresponds to the point where the distribution is cut in half (20 years). The total number of frequencies representing many years is offset by the total number representing few years, resulting in an *arithmetic mean* of 20 years. Logically, any of the three measures would be appropriate to represent the distribution's center.

A skewed distribution is not symmetrical.

If a distribution is nonsymmetrical, or **skewed,** the relationship among the three measures changes. In a **positively skewed distribution,** the arithmetic mean is the largest of the three measures. Why? Because the mean is influenced more than the median or mode by a few extremely high values. The median is generally the next largest measure in a positively skewed frequency distribution. The mode is the smallest of the three measures.

If the distribution is highly skewed, such as the weekly incomes in Chart 3–3, the mean would not be a good measure to use. The median and mode would be more representative.

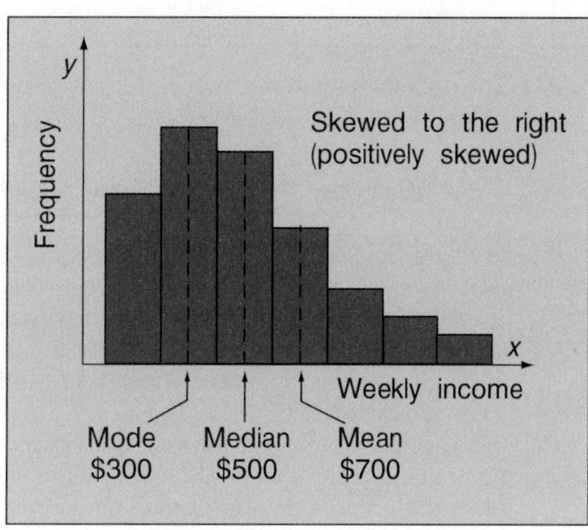

CHART 3–3 A Positively Skewed Distribution

Conversely, if a distribution is **negatively skewed,** the mean is the lowest of the three measures. The mean is, of course, influenced by a few extremely low observations. The median is greater than the arithmetic mean, and the modal value is the largest of the three measures. Again, if the distribution is highly skewed, such as the distribution of tensile strengths shown in Chart 3–4, the mean should not be used to represent the data.

Finally, note it is common practice to let the level of the data determine which measure is used to represent the center of the data. To put it another way, the mode is generally used for nominal data, median for ordinal, and mean for ratio-level data.

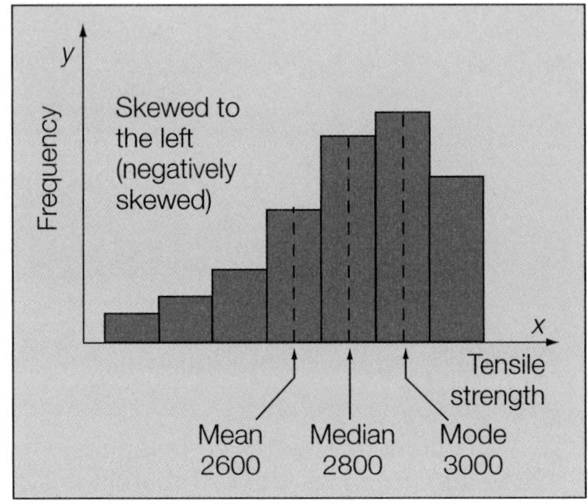

CHART 3–4 A Negatively Skewed Distribution

Self-Review 3–4

The weekly sales from a sample of Hi-Tec electronic supply stores were organized into a frequency distribution. The mean of weekly sales was computed to be $105,900, the median $105,000, and the mode $104,500.

(a) Sketch the sales in the form of a smoothed frequency polygon. Note the location of the mean, median, and mode on the *X*-axis.
(b) Is the distribution symmetrical, positively skewed, or negatively skewed? Explain.

Exercises

21. The unemployment rate in the state of Alaska for the 12 months of 2003 is given in the table below:

Jan	Feb	Mar	Apr	May	Jun	Jul	Aug	Sep	Oct	Nov	Dec
8.6	8.8	8.4	7.8	7.2	7.4	6.9	6.8	7.1	7.5	7.9	8.6

a. What is the arithmetic mean of the Alaskan unemployment rates?
b. Find the median and the mode for the unemployment rates.
c. Compute the arithmetic mean and median for just the winter (Dec–Mar) months. Is it much different?

22. Big Orange Trucking is designing an information system for use on "in-cab" communications. It must summarize data from eight sites throughout a region to describe typical conditions. Compute an appropriate measure of central location for each of the three variables shown in the table on the next page.

City	Wind Direction	Temperature	Pavement
Anniston, AL	West	89	Dry
Atlanta, GA	Northwest	86	Wet
Augusta, GA	Southwest	92	Wet
Birmingham, AL	South	91	Dry
Jackson, MS	Southwest	92	Dry
Meridian, MS	South	92	Trace
Monroe, LA	Southwest	93	Wet
Tuscaloosa, AL	Southwest	93	Trace

The Geometric Mean

The geometric mean is never greater than the arithmetic mean.

The geometric mean is useful in finding the average of percentages, ratios, indexes, or growth rates. It has a wide application in business and economics because we are often interested in finding the percentage changes in sales, salaries, or economic figures, such as the Gross Domestic Product, which compound or build on each other. The geometric mean of a set of n positive numbers is defined as the nth root of the product of n values. The formula for the geometric mean is written:

GEOMETRIC MEAN $$GM = \sqrt[n]{(X_1)(X_2)\cdots(X_n)}$$ **[3–4]**

The geometric mean will always be less than or equal to (never more than) the arithmetic mean. Also all the data values must be positive.

As an example of the geometric mean, suppose you receive a 5 percent increase in salary this year and a 15 percent increase next year. The average annual percent increase is 9.886, not 10.0. Why is this so? We begin by calculating the geometric mean. Recall, for example, that a 5 percent increase in salary is 105 percent. We will write it as 1.05.

$$GM = \sqrt{(1.05)(1.15)} = 1.09886$$

This can be verified by assuming that your monthly earning was $3,000 to start and you received two increases of 5 percent and 15 percent.

Raise 1 = $3,000 (.05) = $150.00

Raise 2 = $3,150 (.15) = 472.50

Total $622.50

Your total salary increase is $622.50. This is equivalent to:

$3,000.00 (.09886) = $296.58

$3,296.58 (.09886) = 325.90

$622.48 is about $622.50

The following example shows the geometric mean of several percentages.

EXAMPLE

The return on investment earned by Atkins Construction Company for four successive years was: 30 percent, 20 percent, −40 percent, and 200 percent. What is the geometric mean rate of return on investment?

SOLUTION

The number 1.3 represents the 30 percent return on investment, which is the "original" investment of 1.0 plus the "return" of 0.3. The number 0.6 represents the loss of 40 percent, which is the original investment of 1.0 less the loss of 0.4. This calculation assumes the total return each period is reinvested or becomes the base for the next period. In other words, the base for the second period is 1.3 and the base for the third period is (1.3)(1.2) and so forth.

Then the geometric mean rate of return is 29.4 percent, found by

$$GM = \sqrt[n]{(X_1)(X_2)\cdots(X_n)} = \sqrt[4]{(1.3)(1.2)(0.6)(3.0)} = \sqrt[4]{2.808} = 1.294$$

The geometric mean is the fourth root of 2.808. So, the average rate of return (compound annual growth rate) is 29.4 percent.

Notice also that if you compute the arithmetic mean [(30 + 20 − 40 + 200)/4 = 52.5], you would have a much larger number, which would overstate the true rate of return!

A second application of the geometric mean is to find an average percent increase over a period of time. For example, if you earned $30,000 in 1995 and $50,000 in 2005, what is your annual rate of increase over the period? The rate of increase is determined from the following formula.

AVERAGE PERCENT INCREASE OVER TIME

$$GM = \sqrt[n]{\frac{\text{Value at end of period}}{\text{Value at start of period}}} - 1 \qquad \textbf{[3–5]}$$

In the above box n is the number of periods. An example will show the details of finding the average annual percent increase.

EXAMPLE

During the decade of the 1990s, Las Vegas, Nevada, was the fastest-growing metropolitan area in the United States. The population increased from 852,737 in 1990 to 1,563,282 in 2000. This is an increase of 710,545 people or an 83 percent increase over the 10-year period. What is the average *annual* increase?

SOLUTION

There are 10 years between 1990 and 2000 so $n = 10$. Then formula (3–5) for the geometric mean as applied to this type of problem is:

$$GM = \sqrt[n]{\frac{\text{Value at end of period}}{\text{Value at start of period}}} - 1.0 = \sqrt[10]{\frac{1{,}563{,}282}{852{,}737}} - 1.0 = 1.0625 - 1.0 = .0625$$

The value of .0625 indicates that the average annual growth over the 10-year period was 6.25 percent. To put it another way, the population of Las Vegas increased at a rate of 6.25 percent per year from 1990 to 2000.

Self-Review 3–5

1. The percent increase in sales for the last 4 years at Combs Cosmetics were: 4.91, 5.75, 8.12, and 21.60.
   (a) Find the geometric mean percent increase.
   (b) Find the arithmetic mean percent increase.
   (c) Is the arithmetic mean equal to or greater than the geometric mean?
2. Production of Cablos trucks increased from 23,000 units in 1984 to 120,520 units in 2004. Find the geometric mean annual percent increase.

Exercises

23. Compute the geometric mean of the following percent increases: 8, 12, 14, 26, and 5.

24. Compute the geometric mean of the following percent increases: 2, 8, 6, 4, 10, 6, 8, and 4.

25. Listed below is the percent increase in sales for the MG Corporation over the last 5 years. Determine the geometric mean percent increase in sales over the period.

9.4	13.8	11.7	11.9	14.7

26. In 1996 a total of 14,968,000 taxpayers in the United States filed their individual tax returns electronically. By the year 2002 the number increased to 46,282,200. What is the geometric mean annual increase for the period?

27. The Consumer Price Index is reported monthly by the U.S. Bureau of Labor Statistics. It reports the change in prices for a market basket of goods from one period to another. The index for 1992 was 140.3, by 2003 it increased to 184.6. What was the geometric mean annual increase for the period?

28. In 1976 the nationwide average price of a gallon of unleaded gasoline at a self-serve pump was $0.605. By 2004 it increased to $1.941. What was the geometric mean annual increase for the period?

29. In 1999 there were 42.0 million pager subscribers. By 2004 the number of subscribers increased to 70.0 million. What is the geometric mean annual increase for the period?

30. The information below shows the cost for a year of college in public and private colleges in 1992 and 2003. What is the geometric mean annual increase for the period for the two types of colleges? Compare the rates of increase.

Type of College	1992	2003
Public	$ 4,975	$ 8,954
Private	12,284	22,608

Why Study Dispersion?

The average is not representative because of the large spread.

A measure of location, such as the mean or the median, only describes the center of the data. It is valuable from that standpoint, but it does not tell us anything about the spread of the data. For example, if your nature guide told you that the river ahead averaged 3 feet in depth, would you want to wade across on foot without additional information? Probably not. You would want to know something about the variation in the depth. Is the maximum depth of the river 3.25 feet and the minimum 2.75 feet? If that is the case, you would probably agree to cross. What if you learned the river depth ranged from 0.50 feet to 5.5 feet? Your decision would probably be not to cross. Before making a decision about crossing the river, you want information on both the typical depth and the dispersion in the depth of the river.

A small value for a measure of dispersion indicates that the data are clustered closely, say, around the arithmetic mean. The mean is therefore considered representative of the data. Conversely, a large measure of dispersion indicates that the mean is not reliable. Refer to Chart 3–5. The 100 employees of Hammond Iron Works, Inc., a steel fabricating company, are organized into a histogram based on the number of years of employment with the company. The mean is 4.9 years, but the spread of the data is from 6 months to 16.8 years. The mean of 4.9 years is not very representative of all the employees.

A second reason for studying the dispersion in a set of data is to compare the spread in two or more distributions. Suppose, for example, that the new PDM/3 computer is assembled in Baton Rouge and also in Tucson. The arithmetic mean hourly output in both the Baton Rouge plant and the Tucson plant is 50. Based on the two means, one might conclude that the distributions of the hourly outputs are identical. Production records for 9 hours at the two plants, however, reveal that this conclusion is not correct (see Chart 3–6). Baton Rouge production varies from 48 to 52 assemblies per hour. Production at the Tucson plant is more erratic, ranging from 40 to 60 per hour. Therefore, the hourly output for Baton Rouge is clustered near the mean of 50; the hourly output for Tucson is more dispersed.

Statistics in Action

The United States Postal Service has tried to become more "user friendly" in the last several years. A recent survey showed that customers were interested in more *consistency* in the time it takes to make a delivery. Under the old conditions, a local letter might take only one day to deliver, or it might take several. "Just tell me how many days ahead I need to mail the birthday card to Mom so it gets there on her birthday, not early, not late," was a common complaint. The level of consistency is measured by the standard deviation of the delivery times.

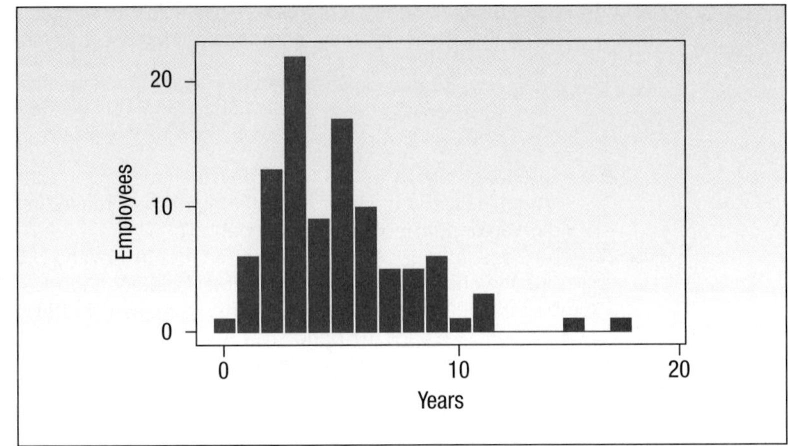

CHART 3–5 Histogram of Years of Employment at Hammond Iron Works, Inc.

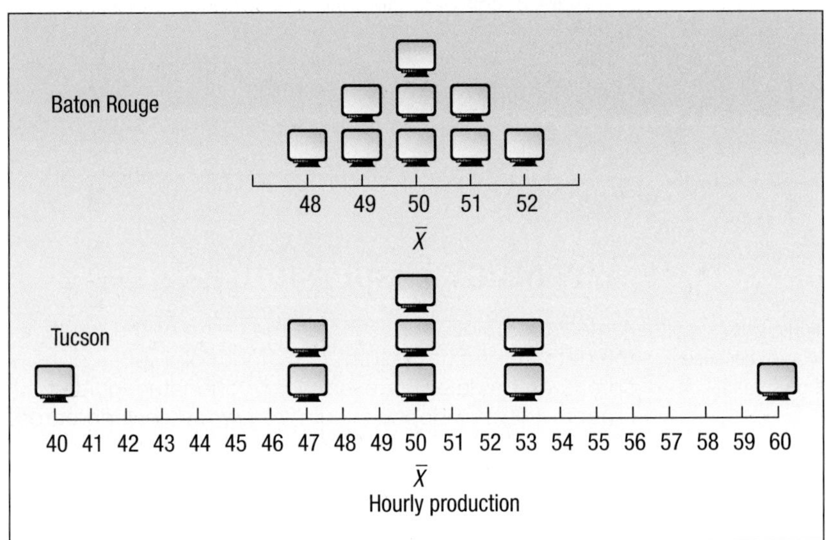

CHART 3–6 Hourly Production of Computers at the Baton Rouge and Tucson Plants

A measure of dispersion can be used to evaluate the reliability of two or more measures of location.

Measures of Dispersion

We will consider several measures of dispersion. The range is based on the largest and the smallest values in the data set. The mean deviation, the variance, and the standard deviation are all based on deviations from the arithmetic mean.

Range

The simplest measure of dispersion is the **range.** It is the difference between the largest and the smallest values in a data set. In the form of an equation:

RANGE	Range = Largest value − Smallest value	**[3–6]**

The range is widely used in statistical process control (SPC) applications because it is very easy to calculate and understand.

EXAMPLE

Refer to Chart 3–6. Find the range in the number of computers produced per hour for the Baton Rouge and the Tucson plants. Interpret the two ranges.

SOLUTION

The range of the hourly production of computers at the Baton Rouge plant is 4, found by the difference between the largest hourly production of 52 and the smallest of 48. The range in the hourly production for the Tucson plant is 20 computers, found by 60 − 40. We therefore conclude that (1) there is less dispersion in the hourly production in the Baton Rouge plant than in the Tucson plant because the range of 4 computers is less than a range of 20 computers, and (2) the production is clustered more closely around the mean of 50 at the Baton Rouge plant than at the Tucson plant (because a range of 4 is less than a range of 20). Thus, the mean production in the Baton Rouge plant (50 computers) is a more representative measure of location than the mean of 50 computers for the Tucson plant.

Mean Deviation

A defect of the range is that it is based on only two values, the highest and the lowest; it does not take into consideration all of the values. The mean deviation does. It measures the mean amount by which the values in a population, or sample, vary from their mean. In terms of a definition:

MEAN DEVIATION The arithmetic mean of the absolute values of the deviations from the arithmetic mean.

In terms of a formula, the mean deviation, designated *MD,* is computed for a sample by:

MEAN DEVIATION $$MD = \frac{\Sigma|X - \bar{X}|}{n}$$ **[3–7]**

where:

X is the value of each observation.
$\bar{X}$ is the arithmetic mean of the values.
n is the number of observations in the sample.
|| indicates the absolute value.

Why do we ignore the signs of the deviations from the mean? If we didn't, the positive and negative deviations from the mean would exactly offset each other, and the mean deviation would always be zero. Such a measure (zero) would be a useless statistic.

EXAMPLE

The number of cappuccinos sold at the Starbucks location in the Orange County Airport between 4 P.M. and 7 P.M. for a sample of 5 days last year were: 103, 97, 101, 106, and 103. Determine the mean deviation and interpret.

SOLUTION

The mean deviation is the mean of the amounts that individual observations differ from the arithmetic mean. To find the mean deviation of a set of data, we begin by finding the arithmetic mean. The mean number of cappuccinos sold is 102, found by (103 + 97 + 101 + 106 + 103)/5. Next we find the amount by which each observation differs from the mean. Then we sum these differences, ignoring the signs, and divide the sum by the number of observations. The result is the mean amount the observations differ from the mean. A small value for the mean deviation indicates that the data are clustered near the mean, whereas a large value for the mean deviation indicates greater dispersion in the data. Here are the details of the calculations using formula (3–7).

Number of Cappuccinos Sold	$(X - \bar{X})$	Absolute Deviation
103	(103 − 102) = 1	1
97	(97 − 102) = −5	5
101	(101 − 102) = −1	1
106	(106 − 102) = 4	4
103	(103 − 102) = 1	1
		Total 12

$$MD = \frac{\Sigma|X - \bar{X}|}{n} = \frac{12}{5} = 2.4$$

The mean deviation is 2.4 cappuccinos per day. The number of cappuccinos deviates, on average, by 2.4 cappuccinos from the mean of 102 cappuccinos per day.

Advantages of mean deviation

The mean deviation has two advantages. First, it uses all the values in the computation. Recall that the range uses only the highest and the lowest values. Second, it is easy to understand—it is the average amount by which values deviate from the mean. However, its drawback is the use of absolute values. Generally, absolute values are difficult to work with, so the mean deviation is not used as frequently as other measures of dispersion, such as the standard deviation.

Self-Review 3–6

The weights of containers being shipped to Ireland are (in thousands of pounds):

95	103	105	110	104	105	112	90

(a) What is the range of the weights?
(b) Compute the arithmetic mean weight.
(c) Compute the mean deviation of the weights.

Exercises

For Exercises 31–36, calculate the (a) range, (b) arithmetic mean, and (c) mean deviation, and (d) interpret the range and the mean deviation.

31. There were five customer service representatives on duty at the Electronic Super Store during last weekend's sale. The numbers of HDTVs these representatives sold are: 5, 8, 4, 10, and 3.

32. The Department of Statistics at Western State University offers eight sections of basic statistics. Following are the numbers of students enrolled in these sections: 34, 46, 52, 29, 41, 38, 36, and 28.

33. Dave's Automatic Door installs automatic garage door openers. The following list indicates the number of minutes needed to install a sample of 10 door openers: 28, 32, 24, 46, 44, 40, 54, 38, 32, and 42.

34. A sample of eight companies in the aerospace industry was surveyed as to their return on investment last year. The results are (in percent): 10.6, 12.6, 14.8, 18.2, 12.0, 14.8, 12.2, and 15.6.

35. Ten experts rated the taste of a newly developed sushi pizza topped with tuna, rice, and kelp on a scale of 1 to 50. The ratings were: 34, 35, 41, 28, 26, 29, 32, 36, 38, and 40.

36. A sample of the personnel files of eight employees at Acme Carpet Cleaners, Inc., revealed that, during a six-month period, they lost the following numbers of days due to illness: 2, 0, 6, 3, 10, 4, 1, and 2.

Variance and Standard Deviation

The **variance** and **standard deviation** are also based on the deviations from the mean. However, instead of using the absolute value of the deviations, the variance, and the standard deviation square the deviations.

Variance and standard deviation are based on squared deviations from the mean.

VARIANCE The arithmetic mean of the squared deviations from the mean.

The variance is nonnegative and is zero only if all observations are the same.

STANDARD DEVIATION The square root of the variance.

Population Variance The formulas for the population variance and the sample variance are slightly different. The population variance is considered first. (Recall that a population is the totality of all observations being studied.) The **population variance** is found by:

POPULATION VARIANCE
$$\sigma^2 = \frac{\Sigma(X - \mu)^2}{N} \quad \textbf{[3–8]}$$

where:

σ^2 is the symbol for the population variance (σ is the lowercase Greek letter sigma). It is usually referred to as "sigma squared."
X is the value of an observation in the population.
μ is the arithmetic mean of the population.
N is the number of observations in the population.

Note the process of computing the variance.

- We begin by finding the mean.
- Next we find the difference between each observation and the mean and square that difference.
- Then we sum all the squared differences.
- And finally we divide the sum of the squared differences by the number of items in the population.

So you might think of the population variance as the mean of the squared difference between each value and the mean. For populations whose values are near the mean, the variance will be small. For populations whose values are dispersed from the mean, the population variance will be large.

The variance overcomes the problem of the range by using all the values in the population, whereas the range uses only the largest and the smallest. We overcome the issue where $\Sigma(X - \mu) = 0$ by squaring the differences, instead of using the absolute values. Squaring the differences will always result in non-negative values. So, the variance will never be negative and it will be zero only when all the values in the data set are the same.

EXAMPLE

The number of traffic citations issued during the last five months in Beaufort County, South Carolina, is: 38, 26, 13, 41, and 22. What is the population variance?

SOLUTION

We consider these data a population because the last five months' citations are all the values possible over the period. The details of the calculations follow:

Number (X)	$X-\mu$	$(X-\mu)^2$	
38	+10	100	
26	−2	4	
13	−15	225	$\mu = \frac{\Sigma X}{N} = \frac{140}{5} = 28$
41	+13	169	
22	−6	36	
140	0*	534	$\sigma^2 = \frac{\Sigma(X-\mu)^2}{N} = \frac{534}{5} = 106.8$

*Sum of the deviations from mean must equal zero.

Like the range and the mean deviation, the variance can be used to compare the dispersion in two or more sets of observations. For example, the variance for the number of citations issued in Beaufort County was just computed to be 106.8. If the variance in the number of citations issued in Marlboro County, South Carolina, is 342.9, we conclude that (1) there is less dispersion in the distribution of the number of citations issued in Beaufort County than in Marlboro County (because 106.8 is less than 342.9); and (2) the number of citations in Beaufort County is more closely clustered around the mean of 28 than for the number of citations issued in Marlboro County. Thus the mean number of citations issued in Beaufort County is a more representative measure of location than the mean number of citations in Marlboro County.

Variance is difficult to interpret because the units are squared.

Standard deviation is in the same units as the data.

Population Standard Deviation Both the range and the mean deviation are easy to interpret. The range is the difference between the high and low values of a set of data, and the mean deviation is the mean of the deviations from the mean. However, the variance is difficult to interpret for a single set of observations. The variance of 106.8 for the number of citations is not in terms of citations, but rather "citations squared."

There is a way out of this dilemma. By taking the square root of the population variance, we can transform it to the same unit of measurement used for the original data. The square root of 106.8 citations squared is 10.3 citations. The square root of the population variance is called the **population standard deviation.**

POPULATION STANDARD DEVIATION $$\sigma = \sqrt{\frac{\Sigma(X-\mu)^2}{N}}$$ **[3–9]**

Self-Review 3–7

The Philadelphia office of Price Waterhouse Coopers LLP hired five accounting trainees this year. Their monthly starting salaries were: $3,536; $3,173; $3,448; $3,121; and $3,622.

(a) Compute the population mean.
(b) Compute the population variance.
(c) Compute the population standard deviation.
(d) The Pittsburgh office hired six trainees. Their mean monthly salary was $3,550, and the standard deviation was $250. Compare the two groups.

Exercises

37. Consider these five values a population: 8, 3, 7, 3, and 4.
  a. Determine the mean of the population.
  b. Determine the variance.

38. Consider these six values a population: 13, 3, 8, 10, 8, and 6.
  a. Determine the mean of the population.
  b. Determine the variance.

39. The annual report of Dennis Industries cited these primary earnings per common share for the past 5 years: \$2.68, \$1.03, \$2.26, \$4.30, and \$3.58. If we assume these are population values, what is:
  a. The arithmetic mean primary earnings per share of common stock?
  b. The variance?

40. Referring to Exercise 39, the annual report of Dennis Industries also gave these returns on stockholder equity for the same five-year period (in percent): 13.2, 5.0, 10.2, 17.5, and 12.9.
  a. What is the arithmetic mean return?
  b. What is the variance?

41. Plywood, Inc. reported these returns on stockholder equity for the past 5 years: 4.3, 4.9, 7.2, 6.7, and 11.6. Consider these as population values.
  a. Compute the range, the arithmetic mean, the variance, and the standard deviation.
  b. Compare the return on stockholder equity for Plywood, Inc. with that for Dennis Industries cited in Exercise 40.

42. The annual incomes of the five vice presidents of TMV Industries are: \$125,000; \$128,000; \$122,000; \$133,000; and \$140,000. Consider this a population.
  a. What is the range?
  b. What is the arithmetic mean income?
  c. What is the population variance? The standard deviation?
  d. The annual incomes of officers of another firm similar to TMV Industries were also studied. The mean was \$129,000 and the standard deviation \$8,612. Compare the means and dispersions in the two firms.

Sample Variance The formula for the population mean is $\mu = \Sigma X/N$. We just changed the symbols for the sample mean; that is $\bar{X} = \Sigma X/n$. Unfortunately, the conversion from the population variance to the sample variance is not as direct. It requires a change in the denominator. Instead of substituting n (number in the sample) for N (number in the population), the denominator is $n - 1$. Thus the formula for the **sample variance** is:

SAMPLE VARIANCE
$$s^2 = \frac{\Sigma(X - \bar{X})^2}{n - 1} \qquad \textbf{[3–10]}$$

where:

s^2 is the sample variance.
X is the value of each observation in the sample.
$\bar{X}$ is the mean of the sample.
n is the number of observations in the sample.

Why is this change made in the denominator? Although the use of n is logical, it tends to underestimate the population variance, σ^2. The use of $(n - 1)$ in the denominator provides the appropriate correction for this tendency. Because the primary use of sample statistics like s^2 is to estimate population parameters like σ^2, $(n - 1)$ is preferred to n in defining the sample variance. We will also use this convention when computing the sample standard deviation.

EXAMPLE

The hourly wages for a sample of part-time employees at Fruit Packers, Inc. are: \$12, \$20, \$16, \$18, and \$19. What is the sample variance?

Statistics in Action

Albert Pujols of the St. Louis Cardinals had the highest batting average at .359 during the 2003 season. Tony Gwynn hit .394 in the strike-shortened season of 1994, and Ted Williams hit .406 in 1941. No one has hit over .400 since 1941. The mean batting average has remained constant at about .260 for more than 100 years, but the standard deviation declined from .049 to .031. This indicates less dispersion in the batting averages today and helps explain the lack of any .400 hitters in recent times.

The sample variance is computed by using formula (3–10).

$$\bar{X} = \frac{\Sigma X}{n} = \frac{\$85}{5} = \$17$$

Hourly Wage (X)	$X - \bar{X}$	$(X - \bar{X})^2$
\$12	−\$5	25
20	3	9
16	−1	1
18	1	1
19	2	4
\$85	0	40

$$s^2 = \frac{\Sigma(X - \bar{X})^2}{n - 1} = \frac{40}{5 - 1}$$

$$= 10 \text{ in dollars squared}$$

Sample Standard Deviation The sample standard deviation is used as an estimator of the population standard deviation. As noted previously, the population standard deviation is the square root of the population variance. Likewise, the *sample standard deviation is the square root of the sample variance.* The sample standard deviation is most easily determined by:

STANDARD DEVIATION

$$s = \sqrt{\frac{\Sigma(X - \bar{X})^2}{n - 1}} \qquad \textbf{[3–11]}$$

EXAMPLE

The sample variance in the previous example involving hourly wages was computed to be 10. What is the sample standard deviation?

SOLUTION

The sample standard deviation is \$3.16, found by $\sqrt{10}$. Note again that the sample variance is in terms of dollars squared, but taking the square root of 10 gives us \$3.16, which is in the same units (dollars) as the original data.

Software Solution

On page 68 we used Excel to determine the mean and median of the Whitner Autoplex sales data. You will also note that it outputs the sample standard deviation. Excel, like most other statistical software, assumes the data are from a sample.

Another software package that we will use in this text is MINITAB. This package uses a spreadsheet format, much like Excel, but produces a wider variety of statistical output. The information for the Whitner Autoplex selling prices follows. Note that a histogram (although the default is to use a class interval of \$2,000 and 11 classes) is included as well as the mean and the sample standard deviation. The mean and standard deviation are reported in thousands of dollars.

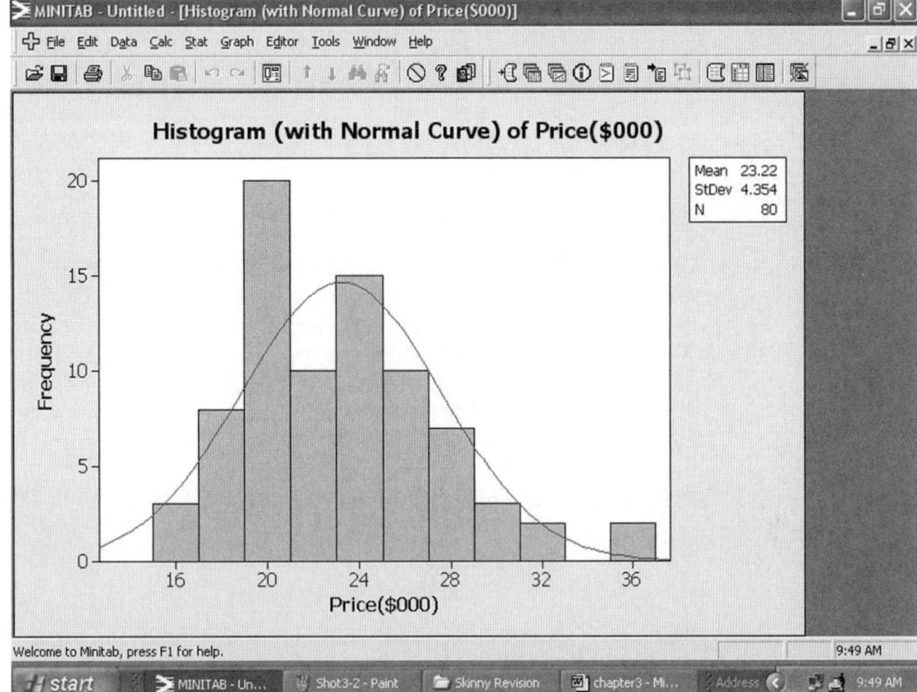

Self-Review 3–8 The weights of the contents of several small aspirin bottles are (in grams): 4, 2, 5, 4, 5, 2, and 6. What is the sample variance? Compute the sample standard deviation.

Exercises

For Exercises 43–48, do the following:

a. Compute the sample variance.
b. Determine the sample standard deviation.

43. Consider these values a sample: 7, 2, 6, 2, and 3.

44. The following five values are a sample: 11, 6, 10, 6, and 7.
a. Compute the sample variance.
b. Determine the sample standard deviation.

45. Dave's Automatic Door, referred to in Exercise 33, installs automatic garage door openers. Based on a sample, following are the times, in minutes, required to install 10 door openers: 28, 32, 24, 46, 44, 40, 54, 38, 32, and 42.

46. The sample of eight companies in the aerospace industry, referred to in Exercise 34, was surveyed as to their return on investment last year. The results are: 10.6, 12.6, 14.8, 18.2, 12.0, 14.8, 12.2, and 15.6.

47. The Houston, Texas, Motel Owner Association conducted a survey regarding weekday motel rates in the area. Listed below is the room rate for business class guests for a sample of 10 motels.

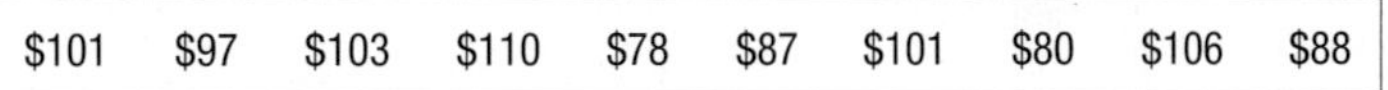

$101	$97	$103	$110	$78	$87	$101	$80	$106	$88

48. A consumer watchdog organization is concerned about credit card debt. A survey of 10 young adults with credit card debt of more than $2,000 showed they paid an average of just over $100 per month. Listed below is the amounts each young adult paid last month against their balances.

$110	$126	$103	$93	$99	$113	$87	$101	$109	$100

Statistics in Action

An average is a value used to represent all the data. However, often an average does not give the full picture of the data. Investors are often faced with this problem when considering two investments in mutual funds such as Vanguard's Index 500 and GNMA funds. In August 2003, the Index 500 fund's annualized return was −11.26 with a standard deviation of 16.9. The GNMA fund had an annualized return of 8.86% with a standard deviation of 2.68. These statistics reflect the well-known tradeoff between return and risk. The standard deviation shows that the Index 500 returns can vary widely. In fact, annual returns over the last 10 years ranged between −22.15 to 37.45%. The GNMA fund's standard deviation is much less. Its annual returns over the last 10 years ranged between −0.95 to 11.22% (www.vanguard.com)

Interpretation and Uses of the Standard Deviation

The standard deviation is commonly used as a measure to compare the spread in two or more sets of observations. For example, the standard deviation of the biweekly amounts invested in the Dupree Paint Company profit-sharing plan is computed to be $7.51. Suppose these employees are located in Georgia. If the standard deviation for a group of employees in Texas is $10.47, and the means are about the same, it indicates that the amounts invested by the Georgia employees are not dispersed as much as those in Texas (because $7.51 < $10.47). Since the amounts invested by the Georgia employees are clustered more closely about the mean, the mean for the Georgia employees is a more reliable measure than the mean for the Texas group.

Chebyshev's Theorem

We have stressed that a small standard deviation for a set of values indicates that these values are located close to the mean. Conversely, a large standard deviation reveals that the observations are widely scattered about the mean. The Russian mathematician P. L. Chebyshev (1821–1894) developed a theorem that allows us to determine the minimum proportion of the values that lie within a specified number of standard deviations of the mean. For example, according to Chebyshev's theorem, at least three of four values, or 75 percent, must lie between the mean plus two standard deviations and the mean minus two standard deviations. This relationship applies regardless of the shape of the distribution. Further, at least eight of nine values, or 88.9 percent, will lie between plus three standard deviations and minus three standard deviations of the mean. At least 24 of 25 values, or 96 percent, will lie between plus and minus five standard deviations of the mean.

Chebyshev's theorem states:

CHEBYSHEV'S THEOREM For any set of observations (sample or population), the proportion of the values that lie within k standard deviations of the mean is at least $1 - 1/k^2$, where k is any constant greater than 1.

EXAMPLE

The arithmetic mean biweekly amount contributed by the Dupree Paint employees to the company's profit-sharing plan is $51.54, and the standard deviation is $7.51. At least what percent of the contributions lie within plus 3.5 standard deviations and minus 3.5 standard deviations of the mean?

SOLUTION

About 92 percent, found by

$$1 - \frac{1}{k^2} = 1 - \frac{1}{(3.5)^2} = 1 - \frac{1}{12.25} = 0.92$$

The Empirical Rule

Empirical Rule applies only to symmetrical, bell-shaped distributions.

Chebyshev's theorem is concerned with any set of values; that is, the distribution of values can have any shape. However, for a symmetrical, bell-shaped distribution such as the one in Chart 3–7, we can be more precise in explaining the dispersion about the mean. These relationships involving the standard deviation and the mean are described by the **Empirical Rule,** sometimes called the **Normal Rule.**

> **EMPIRICAL RULE** For a symmetrical, bell-shaped frequency distribution, approximately 68 percent of the observations will lie within plus and minus one standard deviation of the mean; about 95 percent of the observations will lie within plus and minus two standard deviations of the mean; and practically all (99.7 percent) will lie within plus and minus three standard deviations of the mean.

These relationships are portrayed graphically in Chart 3–7 for a bell-shaped distribution with a mean of 100 and a standard deviation of 10.

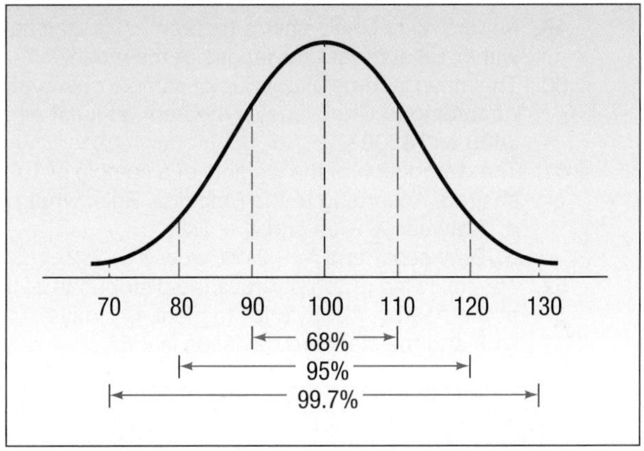

CHART 3–7 A Symmetrical, Bell-Shaped Curve Showing the Relationships between the Standard Deviation and the Observations

It has been noted that if a distribution is symmetrical and bell-shaped, practically all of the observations lie between the mean plus and minus three standard deviations. Thus, if $\overline{X} = 100$ and $s = 10$, practically all the observations lie between $100 + 3(10)$ and $100 - 3(10)$, or 70 and 130. The range is therefore 60, found by $130 - 70$. Conversely, if we know that the range is 60, we can approximate the standard deviation by dividing the range by 6. For this illustration: range $\div 6 = 60 \div 6 = 10$, the standard deviation.

EXAMPLE

A sample of the monthly rental rates at University Park Apartments approximates a symmetrical, bell-shaped distribution. The sample mean is \$500; the standard deviation is \$20. Using the Empirical Rule, answer these questions:

1. About 68 percent of the rental rates are between what two amounts?
2. About 95 percent of the rental rates are between what two amounts?
3. Almost all of the rental rates are between what two amounts?

SOLUTION

1. About 68 percent are between \$480 and \$520, found by $\bar{X} \pm 1s = \$500 \pm 1(\$20)$.
2. About 95 percent are between \$460 and \$540, found by $\bar{X} \pm 2s = \$500 \pm 2(\$20)$.
3. Almost all (99.7 percent) are between \$440 and \$560, found by $\bar{X} \pm 3s = \$500 \pm 3(\$20)$.

Self-Review 3–9

The Pitney Pipe Company is one of several domestic manufacturers of PVC pipe. The quality-control department sampled 600 10-foot lengths. At a point 1 foot from the end of the pipe they measured the outside diameter. The mean was 14.0 inches and the standard deviation 0.1 inches.

(a) If the shape of the distribution is not known, at least what percent of the observations will be between 13.85 inches and 14.15 inches?
(b) If we assume that the distribution of diameters is symmetrical and bell-shaped, about 95 percent of the observations will be between what two values?

Exercises

49. According to Chebyshev's theorem, at least what percent of any set of observations will be within 1.8 standard deviations of the mean?

50. The mean income of a group of sample observations is \$500; the standard deviation is \$40. According to Chebyshev's theorem, at least what percent of the incomes will lie between \$400 and \$600?

51. The distribution of the weights of a sample of 1,400 cargo containers is symmetric and bell-shaped. According to the Empirical Rule, what percent of the weights will lie:
a. Between $\bar{X} - 2s$ and $\bar{X} + 2s$?
b. Between $\bar{X}$ and $\bar{X} + 2s$? Below $\bar{X} - 2s$?

52. The following graph portrays the distribution of the number of Biggie-sized soft drinks sold at the nearby Wendy's for the last 141 days. The mean number of drinks sold per day is 91.9 and the standard deviation is 4.67.

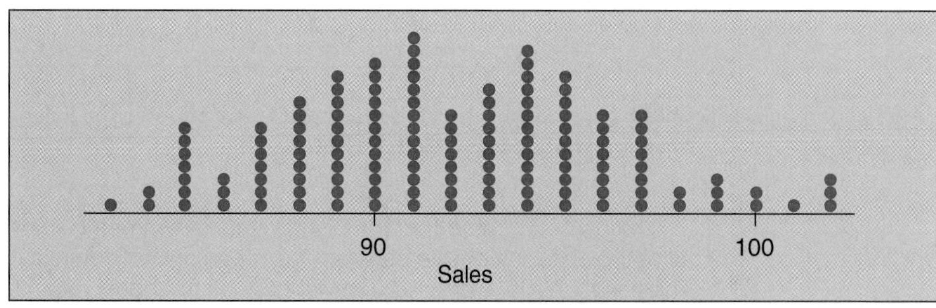

If we use the Empirical Rule, sales will be between what two values on 68 percent of the days? Sales will be between what two values on 95 percent of the days?

Chapter Outline

I. A measure of location is a value used to describe the center of a set of data.
A. The arithmetic mean is the most widely reported measure of location.
1. It is calculated by adding the values of the observations and dividing by the total number of observations.
a. The formula for a population mean of ungrouped or raw data is

Statistics in Action

Most colleges report the "average class size." This information can be misleading because average class size can be found several ways. If we find the number of students in each class at a particular university, the result is the mean number of students per class. If we compiled a list of the class sizes for each student and find the mean class size, we might find the mean to be quite different. One school found the mean number of students in each of their 747 classes to be 40. But when they found the mean from a list of the class sizes of each student it was 147. Why the disparity? Because there are few students in the small classes and a larger number of students in the larger classes, which has the effect of increasing the mean class size when it is calculated this way. A school could reduce this mean class size for each student by reducing the number of students in each class. That is, cut out the large freshman lecture classes.

$$\mu = \frac{\Sigma X}{N} \quad \textbf{[3–1]}$$

b. The formula for the mean of a sample is

$$\bar{X} = \frac{\Sigma X}{n} \quad \textbf{[3–2]}$$

2. The major characteristics of the arithmetic mean are:
  a. At least the interval scale of measurement is required.
  b. All the data values are used in the calculation.
  c. A set of data has only one mean. That is, it is unique.
  d. The sum of the deviations from the mean equals 0.

B. The weighted mean is found by multiplying each observation by its corresponding weight.
  1. The formula for determining the weighted mean is

$$\bar{X}_w = \frac{w_1X_1 + w_2X_2 + w_3X_3 + \cdots + w_nX_n}{w_1 + w_2 + w_3 + \cdots + w_n} \quad \textbf{[3–3]}$$

  2. It is a special case of the arithmetic mean.

C. The median is the value in the middle of a set of ordered data.
  1. To find the median, sort the observations from smallest to largest and identify the middle value.
  2. The major characteristics of the median are:
    a. At least the ordinal scale of measurement is required.
    b. It is not influenced by extreme values.
    c. Fifty percent of the observations are larger than the median.
    d. It is unique to a set of data.

D. The mode is the value that occurs most often in a set of data.
  1. The mode can be found for nominal-level data.
  2. A set of data can have more than one mode.

E. The geometric mean is the *n*th root of the product of *n* positive values.
  1. The formula for the geometric mean is

$$GM = \sqrt[n]{(X_1)(X_2)\cdots(X_n)} \quad \textbf{[3–4]}$$

  2. The geometric mean is also used to find the rate of change from one period to another.

$$GM = \sqrt[n]{\frac{\text{Value at end of period}}{\text{Value at beginning of period}}} - 1 \quad \textbf{[3–5]}$$

  3. The geometric mean is always equal to or less than the arithmetic mean.

II. The dispersion is the variation or spread in a set of data.

A. The range is the difference between the largest and the smallest value in a set of data.
  1. The formula for the range is

$$\text{Range} = \text{Largest value} - \text{Smallest value} \quad \textbf{[3–6]}$$

  2. The major characteristics of the range are:
    a. Only two values are used in its calculation.
    b. It is influenced by extreme values.
    c. It is easy to compute and to understand.

B. The mean absolute deviation is the sum of the absolute values of the deviations from the mean divided by the number of observations.
  1. The formula for computing the mean absolute deviation is

$$MD = \frac{\Sigma|X - \bar{X}|}{n} \quad \textbf{[3–7]}$$

  2. The major characteristics of the mean absolute deviation are:
    a. It is not unduly influenced by large or small values.
    b. All observations are used in the calculation.
    c. The absolute values are somewhat difficult to work with.

C. The variance is the mean of the squared deviations from the arithmetic mean.
  1. The formula for the population variance is

$$\sigma^2 = \frac{\Sigma(X - \mu)^2}{N} \quad \textbf{[3–8]}$$

2. The formula for the sample variance is

$$s^2 = \frac{\Sigma(X - \bar{X})^2}{n - 1} \quad \textbf{[3–10]}$$

3. The major characteristics of the variance are:
   a. All observations are used in the calculation.
   b. It is not unduly influenced by extreme observations.
   c. The units are somewhat difficult to work with; they are the original units squared.

D. The standard deviation is the square root of the variance.
   1. The major characteristics of the standard deviation are:
      a. It is in the same units as the original data.
      b. It is the square root of the average squared distance from the mean.
      c. It cannot be negative.
      d. It is the most widely reported measure of dispersion.
   2. The formula for the sample standard deviation is

$$s = \sqrt{\frac{\Sigma(X - \bar{X})^2}{n - 1}} \quad \textbf{[3–11]}$$

III. We interpret the standard deviation using two measures.
   A. Chebyshev's theorem states that regardless of the shape of the distribution, at least $1 - 1/k^2$ of the observations will be within k standard deviations of the mean, where k is greater than 1.
   B. The Empirical Rule states that for a bell-shaped distribution about 68 percent of the values will be within one standard deviation of the mean, 95 percent within two, and virtually all within three.

Pronunciation Key

SYMBOL	MEANING	PRONUNCIATION
μ	Population mean	*mu*
Σ	Operation of adding	*sigma*
ΣX	Adding a group of values	*sigma X*
$\bar{X}$	Sample mean	*X bar*
$\bar{X}_w$	Weighted mean	*X bar sub w*
GM	Geometric mean	*G M*
σ^2	Population variance	*sigma squared*
σ	Population standard deviation	*sigma*

Chapter Exercises

53. The accounting firm of Crawford and Associates has five senior partners. Yesterday the senior partners saw six, four, three, seven, and five clients, respectively.
   a. Compute the mean number and median number of clients seen by a partner.
   b. Is the mean a sample mean or a population mean?
   c. Verify that $\Sigma(X - \mu) = 0$.

54. Owens Orchards sells apples in a large bag by weight. A sample of seven bags contained the following numbers of apples: 23, 19, 26, 17, 21, 24, 22.
   a. Compute the mean number and median number of apples in a bag.
   b. Verify that $\Sigma(X - \bar{X}) = 0$.

55. A sample of young adults using the Alltel Local Freedom Plan revealed the following numbers of calls received last week. Determine the mean and the median number of calls received.

52	43	30	38	30	42	12	46	39	37
34	46	32	18	41	5				

56. The Citizens Banking Company is studying the number of times the ATM located in a Loblaws Supermarket at the foot of Market Street is used per day. Following are the numbers of times the machine was used over each of the last 30 days. Determine the mean number of times the machine was used per day. Assume the data to be a sample.

83	64	84	76	84	54	75	59	70	61
63	80	84	73	68	52	65	90	52	77
95	36	78	61	59	84	95	47	87	60

57. Listed below is the number of lampshades produced during the last 50 days at the American Lampshade Company in Rockville, GA. Compute the mean.

348	371	360	369	376	397	368	361	374
410	374	377	335	356	322	344	399	362
384	365	380	349	358	343	432	376	347
385	399	400	359	329	370	398	352	396
366	392	375	379	389	390	386	341	351
354	395	338	390	333				

58. Trudy Green works for the True-Green Lawn Company. Her job is to solicit lawn-care business via the telephone. Listed below are the numbers of appointments she made in each of the last 25 hours of calling. What is the arithmetic mean number of appointments she made per hour? What is the median number of appointments per hour? Write a brief report summarizing the findings.

9	5	2	6	5	6	4	4	7	2	3	6	3
4	4	7	8	4	4	5	5	4	8	3	3	

59. The Split-A-Rail Fence Company sells three types of fence to homeowners in suburban Seattle, Washington. Grade A costs $5.00 per running foot to install, Grade B costs $6.50 per running foot, and Grade C, the premium quality, costs $8.00 per running foot. Yesterday, Split-A-Rail installed 270 feet of Grade A, 300 feet of Grade B, and 100 feet of Grade C. What was the mean cost per foot of fence installed?

60. Rolland Poust is a sophomore in the College of Business at Scandia Tech. Last semester he took courses in statistics and accounting, 3 hours each, and earned an A in both. He earned a B in a five-hour history course and a B in a two-hour history of jazz course. In addition, he took a one-hour course dealing with the rules of basketball so he could get his license to officiate high school basketball games. He got an A in this course. What was his GPA for the semester? Assume that he receives 4 points for an A, 3 for a B, and so on. What measure of location did you just calculate?

61. The table below shows the percent of the labor force that is unemployed and the size of the labor force for three counties in Northwest Ohio. Jon Elsas is the Regional Director of Economic Development. He must present a report to several companies that are considering locating in Northwest Ohio. What would be an appropriate unemployment rate to show for the entire region?

County	Percent Unemployed	Size of Workforce
Wood	4.5	15,300
Ottawa	3.0	10,400
Lucas	10.2	150,600

62. The American Automobile Association checks the prices of gasoline before many holiday weekends. Listed below are the self-service prices ($) for a sample of 15 retail outlets during the May 2004 Memorial Day weekend in the Detroit, Michigan, area.

1.94	1.92	1.85	1.89	1.99	1.99	1.91	1.96
1.91	1.99	1.95	1.98	1.89	1.96	1.94	

a. What is the arithmetic mean selling price?
b. What is the median selling price?
c. What is the modal selling price?

63. The metropolitan area of Los Angeles–Long Beach, California, is the area expected to show the largest increase in the number of jobs between 1989 and 2010. The number of jobs is expected to increase from 5,164,900 to 6,286,800. What is the geometric mean expected yearly rate of increase?
64. A recent article suggested that if you earn $25,000 a year today and the inflation rate continues at 3 percent per year, you'll need to make $33,598 in 10 years to have the same buying power. You would need to make $44,771 if the inflation rate jumped to 6 percent. Confirm that these statements are accurate by finding the geometric mean rate of increase.
65. The ages of a sample of Canadian tourists flying from Toronto to Hong Kong were: 32, 21, 60, 47, 54, 17, 72, 55, 33, and 41.
    a. Compute the range.
    b. Compute the mean deviation.
    c. Compute the standard deviation.
66. The weights (in pounds) of a sample of five boxes being sent by UPS are: 12, 6, 7, 3, and 10.
    a. Compute the range.
    b. Compute the mean deviation.
    c. Compute the standard deviation.
67. The Apollo space program lasted from 1967 until 1972 and included 13 missions. The missions lasted from as little as 7 hours to as long as 301 hours. The duration of each flight is listed below.

9	195	241	301	216	260	7	244	192	147
10	295	142							

    a. Explain why the flight times are a population.
    b. Find the mean and median of the flight times.
    c. Find the range and the standard deviation of the flight times.
68. Creek Ratz is a very popular restaurant located along the coast of northern Florida. They serve a variety of steak and seafood dinners. During the summer beach season, they do not take reservations or accept "call ahead" seating. Management of the restaurant is concerned with the time a patron must wait before being seated for dinner. Listed below is the wait time, in minutes, for the 25 tables seated last Saturday night.

28	39	23	67	37	28	56	40	28	50
51	45	44	65	61	27	24	61	34	44
64	25	24	27	29					

    a. Explain why the times are a population.
    b. Find the mean and median of the times.
    c. Find the range and the standard deviation of the times.
69. The manager of the local Wal-Mart Super Store is studying the number of items purchased by customers in the evening hours. Listed below is the number of items for a sample of 30 customers.

15	8	6	9	9	4	18	10	10	12
12	4	7	8	12	10	10	11	9	13
5	6	11	14	5	6	6	5	13	5

    a. Find the mean and the median of the number of items.
    b. Find the range and the standard deviation of the number of items.

exercises.com

70. The State of Indiana and the Kelley School of Business of Indiana University offer links to many data sources. Go to www.stats.indiana.edu, under the heading **Data Tables**, select **Birth/Marriage/Death**, under the state comparison select **Birth and Death** rates. The information for live births by state should appear. You may access the site directly by using: www.stats.indiana.edu/web/state/birth_st02_final.html. Suppose you are interested in the typical number of births per state. Compute the mean, median, and the standard deviation of the *number of births per state* and the *number of births per 1000 population by state* for the latest year available. You should be able to download this information into a software package to perform the calculations. Which of the measures of location is the most representative? Which data set would you recommend using: *number of births per state* or the *number of births per 1000 population*? Why? Suppose you are interested in birth rates for the 50 states and Washington, D.C. Compute the mean, median, and standard deviation. Write a brief report summarizing the data.

71. There are many financial websites that provide information on stocks by industry. For example, go to http://biz.yahoo.com and select **Stock Research;** under **Analyst Research** select **Sector/Industry.** There are many choices available here such as **Energy, Financial,** and **Healthcare.** Select one of these sectors, such as **Healthcare.** Another list of choices is now available; select one such as **Major Drug.** A list of companies in that industry will appear. Select one of the variables available, such as the price to earnings ratio, listed as P/E. This variable is the ratio of the selling price of a share of the company's common stock to the earnings per share of common stock. Download this information into Excel and find the mean, median, and standard deviation. Go back to **Sector/Industry** and choose another **Sector** and **Industry.** You might want to select **Energy** and then **Coal.** A list of companies will appear. Select the same variable as before. Download the information to Excel and find the mean, median, and standard deviation for this industry. Compare the information on the two sectors. Write a brief report summarizing your findings. Are the means different? Is there more variability in one industry than another?

72. One of the most famous averages, the Dow Jones Industrial Average (DJIA), is not really an average. The following is a listing of the 30 companies whose stock prices make up the DJIA, their symbol, their current weight, and the closing value in May 2004. Use a software package to find the mean of the 30 stocks. The DJIA is 10,040.69. Is this the value you found for the average of the 30 stocks?

Company	Symbol	Price	Company	Symbol	Price
Alcoa Inc.	AA	$30.00	Johnson & Johnson	JNJ	55.07
Amer. Intl. Group	AIG	71.25	JP Morgan Chase	JPM	36.25
American Express	AXP	48.60	Coca-Cola Co.	KO	49.56
Boeing Co.	BA	43.43	McDonalds Corp.	MCD	26.00
Citigroup Inc.	C	46.50	3M Co.	MMM	84.59
Caterpillar Inc.	CAT	74.37	Altria Group Inc.	MO	48.84
Disney (Walt) Co.	DIS	23.15	Merck & Co.	MRK	46.72
DuPont (EI)	DD	41.65	Microsoft Corp.	MSFT	26.02
General Electric	GE	30.34	Pfizer Inc.	PFE	35.34
General Motors	GM	44.01	Procter & Gamble	PG	105.52
Home Depot Inc.	HD	33.63	SBC Communcation	SBC	24.60
Honeywell Intl.	HON	33.32	United Tech Corp.	UTX	83.23
Hewlett-Packard	HPQ	20.15	Verizon Communication	VZ	36.43
IBM	IBM	86.95	Wal-Mart Stores	WMT	55.20
Intel Corp.	INTC	27.36	Exxon Mobil Corp.	XOM	42.97

You may read about the history of the DJIA by going to *http://www.djindexes.com* and clicking on **About the Dow.** This will explain why it is not really an average. There are many sites you can visit to check the current value of the DJIA, *http://money.cnn.com, http://www.foxnews.com/news/features/dow,* and *http://www.usatoday.com* are three of the many sources. To find a list of the actual stocks that make up the average go to *http://www.bloomberg.com.* On the toolbar, click on **Market Data,** then down the left side of the screen select **Stocks,** and then select **Dow.** You should now have available a listing of the current selling price of 30 stocks that make up the DJIA.

Dataset Exercises

73. Refer to the Real Estate data, which reports information on homes sold in the Denver, Colorado, area last year.
  a. Select the variable selling price.
    1. Find the mean, median, and the standard deviation.
    2. Write a brief summary of the distribution of selling prices.
  b. Select the variable referring to the area of the home in square feet.
    1. Find the mean, median, and the standard deviation.
    2. Write a brief summary of the distribution of the area of homes.

74. Refer to the Baseball 2003 data, which reports information on the 30 major league teams for the 2003 baseball season.
  a. Select the variable team salary and find the mean, median, and the standard deviation.
  b. Select the variable that refers to the year in which the stadium was built. (Hint: Subtract the current year from the year in which the stadium was built to find the stadium age and work with that variable.) Find the mean, median, and the standard deviation.
  c. Select the variable that refers to the seating capacity of the stadium. Find the mean, median, and the standard deviation.

75. Refer to the CIA data, which reports demographic and economic information on 46 countries.
  a. Select the variable Life Expectancy.
    1. Find the mean, median, and the standard deviation.
    2. Write a brief summary of the distribution of life expectancy.
  b. Select the variable GDP/cap.
    1. Find the mean, median, and the standard deviation.
    2. Write a brief summary of the distribution GDP/cap.

Software Commands

1. The Excel Commands for the descriptive statistics on page 68 are:
  a. From the CD retrieve the Whitner data file, which is called **Table2–1.**
  b. From the menu bar select **Tools** and then **Data Analysis.** Select **Descriptive Statistics** and then click **OK.**
  c. For the **Input Range,** type *A1:A81,* indicate that the data are grouped by column and that the labels are in the first row. Click on **Output Range,** indicate that the output should go in D1 (or any place you wish), click on **Summary statistics,** then click **OK.**
  d. After you get your results, double-check the count in the output to be sure it contains the correct number of items.

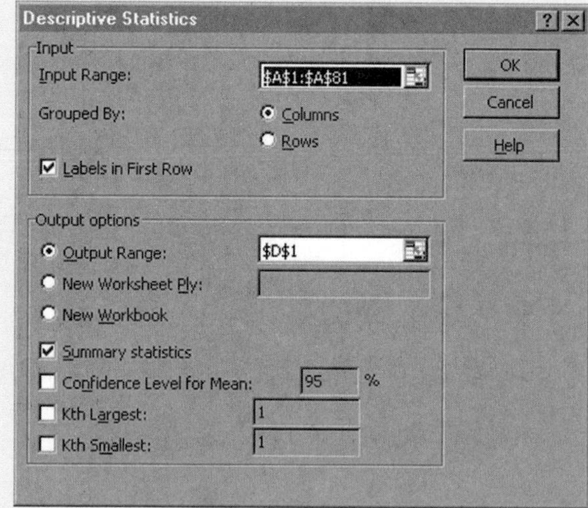

2. The MINITAB commands for the descriptive summary on page 81 are:
   a. From the CD retrieve the Whitner data, which is called **Whitner-Data.**
   b. Select **Stat, Basic Statistics,** and then **Display Descriptive Statistics.** In the dialog box select *Price* as the variable and then click on **Graphs** in the lower right-hand corner. Within the dialog box select **Histogram of data, with normal curve** and click **OK.** Click **OK** in the next dialog box.

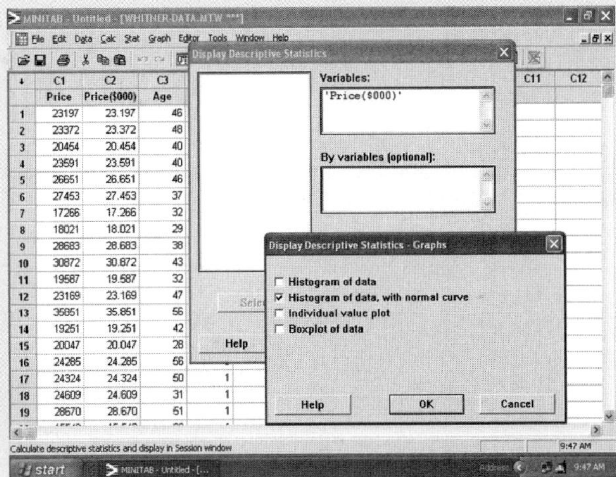

Chapter 3 Answers to Self-Review

3–1 **1. a.** 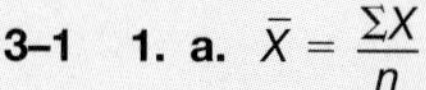 $\bar{X} = \frac{\Sigma X}{n}$

b. $\bar{X} = \frac{\$267{,}100}{4} = \$66{,}775$

c. Statistic, because it is a sample value.

d. $66,775. The sample mean is our best estimate of the population mean.

2. a. $\mu = \frac{\Sigma X}{N}$

b. $\mu = \frac{498}{6} = 83$

c. Parameter, because it was computed using all the population values.

3–2 **a.** $237, found by:

$$\frac{(95 \times \$400) + (126 \times \$200) + (79 \times \$100)}{95 + 126 + 79} = \$237.00$$

b. The profit per suit is $12, found by $237 − $200 cost − $25 commission. The total profit for the 300 suits is $3,600, found by 300 × $12.

3–3 **1. a.** $439

b. 3, 3

2. a. 7, found by (6 + 8)/2 = 7

b. 3, 3

c. 0

3–4 **a.**

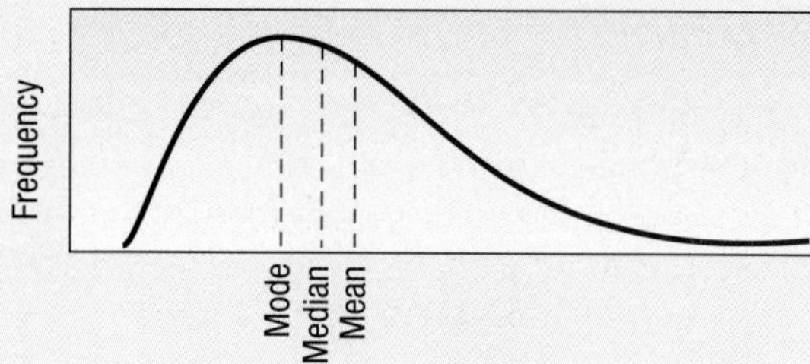

b. Positively skewed, because the mean is the largest average and the mode is the smallest.

3–5 **1. a.** About 9.9 percent, found by $\sqrt[4]{1.458602236}$, then 1.099 − 1.00 = .099

b. About 10.095 percent

c. Greater than, because 10.095 > 8.39

2. 8.63 percent, found by $\sqrt[20]{\frac{120{,}520}{23{,}000}} - 1 =$ 1.0863 − 1

3–6 **a.** 22 thousands of pounds, found by 112 − 90

b. $\bar{X} = \frac{824}{8} = 103$ thousands of pounds

c.

X	$\lvert X - \bar{X} \rvert$	Absolute Deviation
95	$\lvert -8 \rvert$	8
103	$\lvert 0 \rvert$	0
105	$\lvert +2 \rvert$	2
110	$\lvert +7 \rvert$	7
104	$\lvert +1 \rvert$	1
105	$\lvert +2 \rvert$	2
112	$\lvert +9 \rvert$	9
90	$\lvert -13 \rvert$	13
		Total 42

$MD = \frac{42}{8} = 5.25$ thousands of pounds

3–7 **a.** $\mu = \frac{\$16{,}900}{5} = \$3{,}380$

b. $\sigma^2 = \frac{(3{,}536 - 3{,}380)^2 + \cdots + (3{,}622 - 3{,}380)^2}{5}$

$= \frac{197{,}454}{5} = 39{,}490.8$

c. $\sigma = \sqrt{39{,}490.8} = 198.72$

d. There is more variation in the Pittsburgh office because the standard deviation is larger. The mean is also larger in the Pittsburgh office.

3–8 2.33, found by:

$$\bar{X} = \frac{\Sigma X}{n} = \frac{28}{7} = 4$$

X	$X - \bar{X}$	$(X - \bar{X})^2$
4	0	0
2	−2	4
5	1	1
4	0	0
5	1	1
2	−2	4
6	2	4
28	0	14

$s^2 = \frac{\Sigma(X - \bar{X})^2}{n - 1} = \frac{14}{7 - 1} = 2.33$

$s = \sqrt{2.33} = 1.53$

3–9 **a.** $k = \frac{14.15 - 14.00}{.10} = 1.5$

$1 - \frac{1}{(1.5)^2} = 1 - .44 = .56$

b. 13.8 and 14.2

4

Describing Data

Displaying and Exploring Data

A major airline wanted some information on those enrolled in their "frequent flyer" program. A sample of 48 members resulted in the data shown in exercise 27, for the number of miles flown last year, to the nearest 1,000 miles, by each participant. Does the distribution show any outliers? (See Goal 3, Exercise 27.)

GOALS

When you have completed this chapter you will be able to:

1. **Develop and interpret a *dot plot.***
2. **Develop and interpret *quartiles, deciles,* and *percentiles.***
3. **Construct and interpret *box plots.***
4. **Compute and understand the *coefficient of skewness.***
5. **Draw and interpret a *scatter diagram.***
6. **Set up and interpret a *contingency table.***

Introduction

Chapter 2 began our study of descriptive statistics. In order to transform raw or ungrouped data into a meaningful form, we organized the data into a frequency distribution. We presented the frequency distribution in graphic form as a histogram or a frequency polygon. This allowed us to visualize where the data tended to cluster, the largest and the smallest values, and the general shape of the data.

In Chapter 3 we first computed several measures of location, such as the mean and the median. These measures of location allow us to report a typical value in the set of observations. We also computed several measures of dispersion, such as the range and the standard deviation. These measures of dispersion allow us to describe the variation or the spread in a set of observations.

We continue our study of descriptive statistics in this chapter. We use several methods to display or describe distributions. We begin with graphical tools such as dot plots. These charts give us additional insight into the central location, dispersion, and general shape of a distribution. Next, we present some other numerical measures that let us see a distribution's dispersion, such as quartiles and percentiles. Finally, we consider techniques that show the relationship or association between two variables. When two variables are measured for each individual observation in a population or a sample the data are called *bivariate data.* Examples include: a student's age and class rank, whether a sampled product is acceptable or not and the shift on which it is manufactured, and the amount of electricity used in a month by a homeowner and the mean daily high temperature in the region for the month. A scatter diagram is a visual plot or graph of the bivariate data. On the other hand, a contingency table summarizes the data in a numerical cross tabulation.

Dot Plots

In Chapter 2, we described a distribution of data with a histogram. We grouped 80 observations from the Whitner Autoplex data in Table 2–1 into seven classes and used a histogram (Chart 2–2) to show the distribution. From this picture, we can visualize the approximate central location and dispersion of the distribution. However, when we arranged the data into classes we lost the exact values of the observations. A **dot plot,** on the other hand, groups the data less and we do not lose the identity of the individual observations. To develop a dot plot we display a dot for each observation along a horizontal number line indicating the possible values of the data. If there are identical observations or the observations are too close to be shown individually, the dots are "piled" on top of each other. This allows us to see the shape of the distribution, estimate the value of central location, and know the minimum and maximum values and calculate the range. Dot plots are most useful for smaller data sets, whereas histograms tend to be most useful for large data sets. An example will show how to construct and interpret dot plots.

EXAMPLE

Recall in Table 2–1 on page 25 we presented data on the price of 80 vehicles sold last month at Whitner Autoplex in Raytown, Missouri. Whitner is one of the many dealerships owned by AutoUSA. AutoUSA has many other dealerships located in small towns throughout the United States. Reported below are the number of vehicles sold in the last 24 months at Smith Ford Mercury Jeep, Inc., in Kane, Pennsylvania, and Brophy Honda Volkswagen in Greenville, Ohio. Construct dot plots for the two small town AutoUSA lots. Summarize your findings.

Smith Ford Mercury Jeep, Inc.									
23	27	30	27	32	31	32	32	35	33
28	39	32	29	35	36	33	25	35	37
26	28	36	30						

Brophy Honda Volkswagen									
31	44	30	36	37	34	43	38	37	35
36	34	31	32	40	36	31	44	26	30
37	43	42	33						

SOLUTION

The MINITAB system provides a dot plot and calculates the mean, median, maximum, and minimum values, and the standard deviation for the number of cars sold at each of the dealerships over the last 24 months.

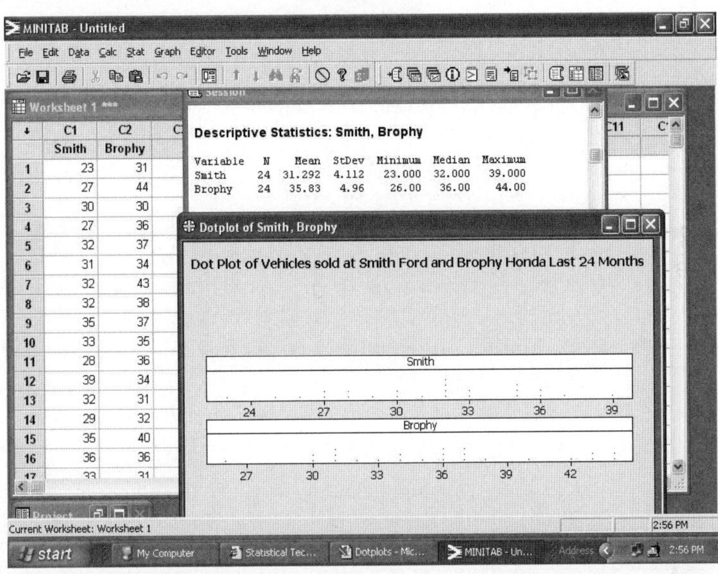

The dot plots in the lower right of the software output show the distributions for each dealership. The plots display the difference in location and dispersion of the individual observations. By examining the dot plots of the distributions, we observe the central location of Brophy's sales is greater than the central location of Smith's sales. In addition, the dot plots show that the distribution of Brophy's sales is more widely dispersed than Smith's sales. Several other features of the monthly sales are apparent:

- Smith sold the fewest cars in any month, 23.
- Brophy sold 26 cars in their lowest month which is 4 cars less than the next lowest month.
- Smith sold exactly 32 cars in four different months.
- The monthly sales cluster around 32 for Smith and 36 for Brophy.

The software output also shows the descriptive statistics, the mean and standard deviation. It reports that Brophy sold a mean of 35.83 vehicles per month and Smith a mean of 31.29 per month. So Brophy sells an average of 4.54 more vehicles per month. There is also more dispersion in Brophy's sales. How do we know this? The standard deviation at Brophy (4.96 cars per month) is larger than at Smith (4.11 cars per month). The descriptive statistics agree with the broad conclusions revealed in the dot plots.

Self-Review 4–1

The number of employees at each of the 142 Home Depot Stores in the Southeast region is shown in the following dot plot.

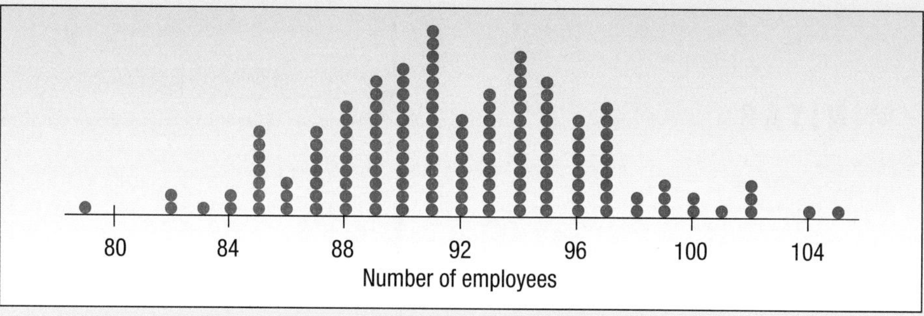

(a) What are the maximum and minimum numbers of employees per store?
(b) How many stores employ 91 people?
(c) Around what values does the number of employees per store tend to cluster?

Exercises

1. Consider the following chart.

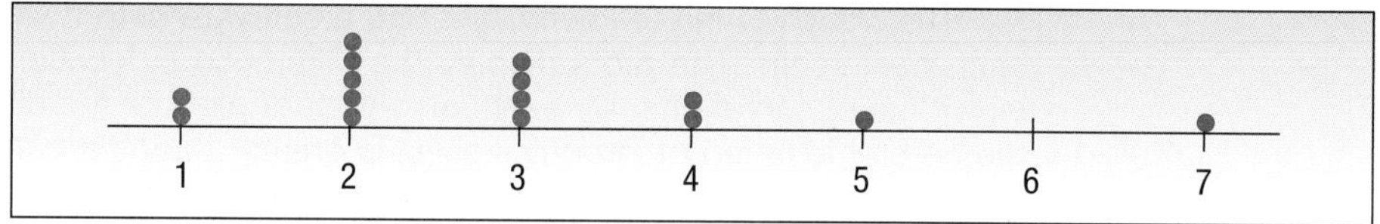

   a. What is this chart called?
   b. How many observations are in the study?
   c. What are the maximum and the minimum values? What is the range?
   d. Around what values do the observations tend to cluster?

2. The following chart reports the number of clocks sold each day at Shaver Clocks for the last 26 days.

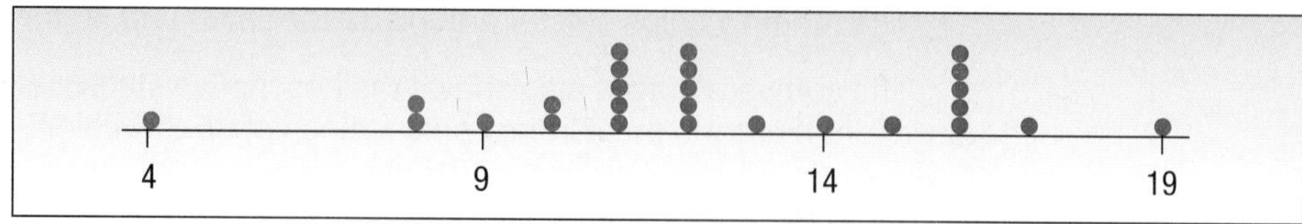

   a. What are the maximum and the minimum number of clocks sold in a day? What is the range?
   b. What is a typical number of clocks sold?

Quartiles, Deciles, and Percentiles

The standard deviation is the most widely used measure of dispersion. However, there are other ways of describing the variation or spread in a set of data. One method is to determine the *location* of values that divide a set of observations into equal parts. These measures include *quartiles, deciles,* and *percentiles.*

Quartiles divide a set of observations into four equal parts. To explain further, think of any set of values arranged from smallest to largest. In Chapter 3 we called the middle value of a set of data arranged from smallest to largest the median. That is, 50 percent of the observations are larger than the median and 50 percent are smaller. The median is a measure of location because it pinpoints the center of the data. In a similar fashion quartiles divide a set of observations into four equal parts. The first quartile, usually labeled Q_1, is the value below which 25 percent of the observations occur, and the third quartile, usually labeled Q_3, is the value below which 75 percent of the observations occur. Logically, Q_2 is the median. The values corresponding to Q_1, Q_2, and Q_3 divide a set of data into four equal parts. Q_1 can be thought of as the "median" of the lower half of the data and Q_3 the "median" of the upper half of the data.

In a similar fashion deciles divide a set of observations into 10 equal parts and percentiles into 100 equal parts. So if you found that your GPA was in the 8th decile at your university, you could conclude that 80 percent of the students had a GPA lower than yours and 20 percent had a higher GPA. A GPA in the 33rd percentile means that 33 percent of the students have a lower GPA and 67 percent have a higher GPA. Percentile scores are frequently used to report results on such national standardized tests as the SAT, ACT, GMAT (used to judge entry into many Master of Business Administration programs), and LSAT (used to judge entry into law school).

To formalize the computational procedure, let L_p refer to the location of a desired percentile. So if we wanted to find the 33rd percentile we would use L_{33} and if we wanted the median, the 50th percentile, then L_{50}. The number of observations is *n,* so if we want to locate the median, its position is at $(n + 1)/2$, or we could write this as $(n + 1)(P/100)$, where *P* is the desired percentile.

LOCATION OF A PERCENTILE $$L_p = (n + 1)\frac{P}{100} \qquad \textbf{[4–1]}$$

An example will help to explain further.

EXAMPLE

Listed below are the commissions earned last month by a sample of 15 brokers at Salomon Smith Barney's Oakland, California, office. Salomon Smith Barney is an investment company with offices located throughout the United States.

$2,038	$1,758	$1,721	$1,637	$2,097	$2,047	$2,205	$1,787	$2,287
1,940	2,311	2,054	2,406	1,471	1,460			

Locate the median, the first quartile, and the third quartile for the commissions earned.

SOLUTION

The first step is to organize the data from the smallest commission to the largest.

$1,460	$1,471	$1,637	$1,721	$1,758	$1,787	$1,940	$2,038
2,047	2,054	2,097	2,205	2,287	2,311	2,406	

The median value is the observation in the center. The center value or L_{50} is located at $(n + 1)(50/100)$, where n is the number of observations. In this case that is position number 8, found by $(15 + 1)(50/100)$. The eighth largest commission is \$2,038. So we conclude this is the median and that half the brokers earned commissions more than \$2,038 and half earned less than \$2,038.

Recall the definition of a quartile. Quartiles divide a set of observations into four equal parts. Hence 25 percent of the observations will be less than the first quartile. Seventy-five percent of the observations will be less than the third quartile. To locate the first quartile, we use formula (4–1), where $n = 15$ and $P = 25$:

$$L_{25} = (n + 1)\frac{P}{100} = (15 + 1)\frac{25}{100} = 4$$

and to locate the third quartile, $n = 15$ and $P = 75$:

$$L_{75} = (n + 1)\frac{P}{100} = (15 + 1)\frac{75}{100} = 12$$

Therefore, the first and third quartile values are located at positions 4 and 12. The fourth value in the ordered array is \$1,721 and the twelfth is \$2,205. These are the first and third quartiles, respectively. So, 25 percent of the brokers earn commissions of less than \$1,721 and 75 percent earn less than \$2,205. The quartiles provide information about the distribution of commissions earned by stock brokers.

In the above example the location formula yielded a whole number result. That is, we wanted to find the first quartile and there were 15 observations, so the location formula indicated we should find the fourth ordered value. What if there were 20 observations in the sample, that is $n = 20$, and we wanted to locate the first quartile? From the location formula (4–1):

$$L_{25} = (n + 1)\frac{P}{100} = (20 + 1)\frac{25}{100} = 5.25$$

We would locate the fifth value in the ordered array and then move .25 of the distance between the fifth and sixth values and report that as the first quartile. Like the median, the quartile does not need to be one of the actual values in the data set.

To explain further, suppose a data set contained the six values: 91, 75, 61, 101, 43, and 104. We want to locate the first quartile. We order the values from smallest to largest: 43, 61, 75, 91, 101, and 104. The first quartile is located at

$$L_{25} = (n + 1)\frac{P}{100} = (6 + 1)\frac{25}{100} = 1.75$$

The position formula tells us that the first quartile is located between the first and the second value and that it is .75 of the distance between the first and the second values. The first value is 43 and the second is 61. So the distance between these two values is 18. To locate the first quartile, we need to move .75 of the distance between the first and second values, so $.75(18) = 13.5$. To complete the procedure, we add 13.5 to the first value and report that the first quartile is 56.5. To put it another way, the first quartile is $43 + .75(61\text{-}43) = 56.5$.

We can extend the idea to include both deciles and percentiles. If we wanted to locate the 23rd percentile in a sample of 80 observations, we would look for the 18.63 position.

$$L_{23} = (n + 1)\frac{P}{100} = (80 + 1)\frac{23}{100} = 18.63$$

To find the value corresponding to the 23rd percentile, we would locate the 18th value and the 19th value and determine the distance between the two values. Next, we would multiply this difference by 0.63 and add the result to the smaller value. The result would be the 23rd percentile.

With a statistical software package, it is quite easy to sort the data from smallest to largest and to locate percentiles and deciles. Both MINITAB and Excel output summary statistics. The following Excel output includes the same information regarding the mean, median, and standard deviation. It will also output the quartiles, but the method of calculation is not as precise. To find the quartiles, we multiply the sample size by the desired percentile and report the integer of that value. To explain, in the Whitner Autoplex data there are 80 observations, and we wish to locate the 25th percentile. We multiply $n + 1 = 80 + 1 = 81$ by .25; the result is 20.25. Excel will not allow us to enter a fractional value, so we use 20 and request the location of the largest 20 values and the smallest 20 values. The result is a good approximation of the 25th and 75th percentiles.

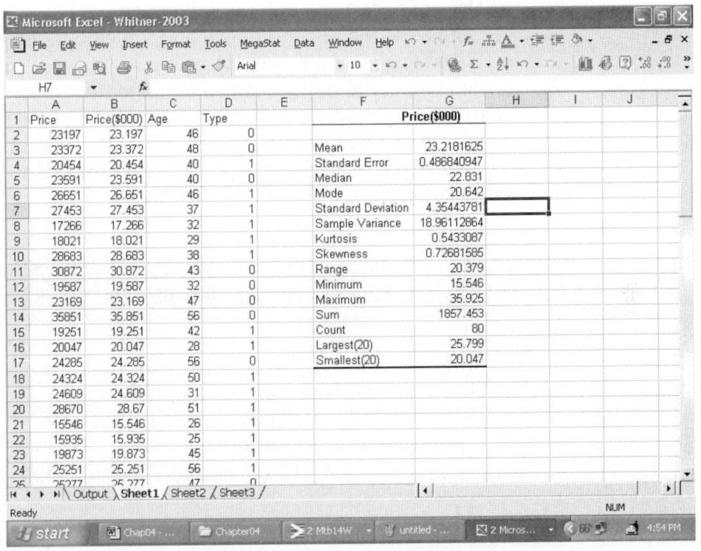

Self-Review 4–2

The quality control department of the Plainsville Peanut Company is checking the weight of the 8-ounce jar of peanut butter. The weights of a sample of nine jars produced last hour are:

7.69	7.72	7.80	7.86	7.90	7.94	7.97	8.06	8.09

(a) What is the median weight?
(b) Determine the weights corresponding to the first and third quartiles.

Exercises

3. Determine the median and the values corresponding to the first and third quartiles in the following data.

46	47	49	49	51	53	54	54	55	55	59

4. Determine the median and the values corresponding to the first and third quartiles in the following data.

5.24	6.02	6.67	7.30	7.59	7.99	8.03	8.35	8.81	9.45
9.61	10.37	10.39	11.86	12.22	12.71	13.07	13.59	13.89	15.42

5. The Thomas Supply Company, Inc. is a distributor of small electrical motors. As with any business, the length of time customers take to pay their invoices is important. Listed below, arranged from smallest to largest, is the time, in days, for a sample of The Thomas Supply Company, Inc. invoices.

13	13	13	20	26	27	31	34	34	34	35	35	36	37	38
41	41	41	45	47	47	47	50	51	53	54	56	62	67	82

a. Determine the first and third quartiles.
b. Determine the second decile and the eighth decile.
c. Determine the 67th percentile.

6. Kevin Horn is the national sales manager for National Textbooks, Inc. He has a sales staff of 40 who visit college professors all over the United States. Each Saturday morning he requires his sales staff to send him a report. This report includes, among other things, the number of professors visited during the previous week. Listed below, ordered from smallest to largest, are the number of visits last week.

38	40	41	45	48	48	50	50	51	51	52	52	53	54	55	55	55	56	56	57
59	59	59	62	62	62	63	64	65	66	66	67	67	69	69	71	77	78	79	79

a. Determine the median number of calls.
b. Determine the first and third quartiles.
c. Determine the first decile and the ninth decile.
d. Determine the 33rd percentile.

Box Plots

A **box plot** is a graphical display, based on quartiles, that helps us picture a set of data. To construct a box plot, we need only five statistics: the minimum value, Q_1 (the first quartile), the median, Q_3 (the third quartile), and the maximum value. An example will help to explain.

EXAMPLE

Alexander's Pizza offers free delivery of its pizza within 15 miles. Alex, the owner, wants some information on the time it takes for delivery. How long does a typical delivery take? Within what range of times will most deliveries be completed? For a sample of 20 deliveries, he determined the following information:

Minimum value = 13 minutes

Q_1 = 15 minutes

Median = 18 minutes

$$Q_3 = 22 \text{ minutes}$$
$$\text{Maximum value} = 30 \text{ minutes}$$

Develop a box plot for the delivery times. What conclusions can you make about the delivery times?

SOLUTION

The first step in drawing a box plot is to create an appropriate scale along the horizontal axis. Next, we draw a box that starts at Q_1 (15 minutes) and ends at Q_3 (22 minutes). Inside the box we place a vertical line to represent the median (18 minutes). Finally, we extend horizontal lines from the box out to the minimum value (13 minutes) and the maximum value (30 minutes). These horizontal lines outside of the box are sometimes called "whiskers" because they look a bit like a cat's whiskers.

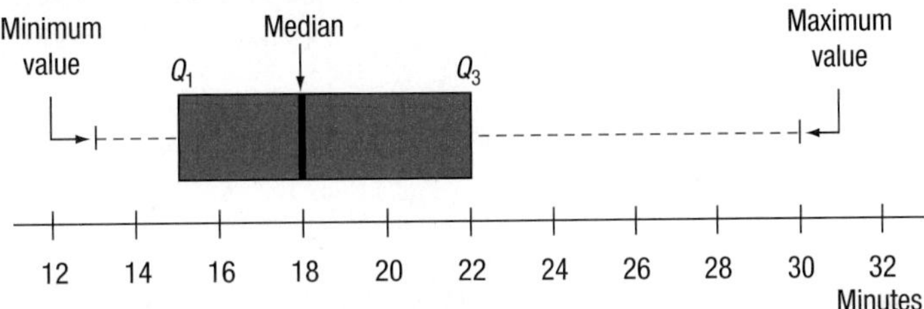

The box plot shows that the middle 50 percent of the deliveries take between 15 minutes and 22 minutes. The distance between the ends of the box, 7 minutes, is the **interquartile range.** The interquartile range is the distance between the first and the third quartile. It shows the spread or dispersion of the majority of deliveries.

The box plot also reveals that the distribution of delivery times is positively skewed. How do we know this? In this case there are actually two pieces of information that suggest that the distribution is positively skewed. Recall that skewness is the lack of symmetry in a set of values. First, the dashed line to the right of the box from 22 minutes (Q_3) to the maximum time of 30 minutes is longer than the dashed line from the left of 15 minutes (Q_1) to the minimum value of 13 minutes. To put it another way, the 25 percent of the data larger than the third quartile is more spread out than the 25 percent less than the first quartile. A second indication of positive skewness is that the median is not in the center of the box. The distance from the first quartile to the median is smaller than the distance from the median to the third quartile. We know that the number of delivery times between 15 minutes and 18 minutes is the same as the number of delivery times between 18 minutes and 22 minutes.

EXAMPLE

Refer to the Whitner Autoplex data in Table 2–1. Develop a box plot of the data. What can we conclude about the distribution of the vehicle selling prices?

SOLUTION

The MINITAB statistical software system was used to develop the chart on the next page.

We conclude that the median vehicle selling price is about $23,000, that about 25 percent of the vehicles sell for less than $20,000, and that about 25 percent sell for more than $26,000. About 50 percent of the vehicles sell for between $20,000 and $26,000. The distribution is somewhat positively skewed because the solid line above $26,000 is somewhat longer than the line below $20,000.

There is an asterisk (*) above the $35,000 selling price. An asterisk indicates an outlier. An **outlier** is a value that is inconsistent with the rest of the data. The standard definition of an outlier is a value that is more than 1.5 times the interquartile range smaller than Q_1 or larger than Q_3. In this example, an outlier would be a value larger than $35,000, found by

$$\text{Outlier} > Q_3 + 1.5(Q_3 - Q_1) = \$26{,}000 + 1.5(\$26{,}000 - \$20{,}000) = \$35{,}000$$

A value less than $11,000 is also an outlier.

$$\text{Outlier} < Q_1 - 1.5(Q_3 - Q_1) = \$20{,}000 - 1.5(\$26{,}000 - \$20{,}000) = \$11{,}000$$

The MINITAB box plot indicates that there is only one value larger than $35,000. However, if you look at the actual data in Table 2–1 on page 25 you will notice that there are actually two values ($35,851 and $35,925). The software was not able to graph two data points so close together, so it shows only one asterisk.

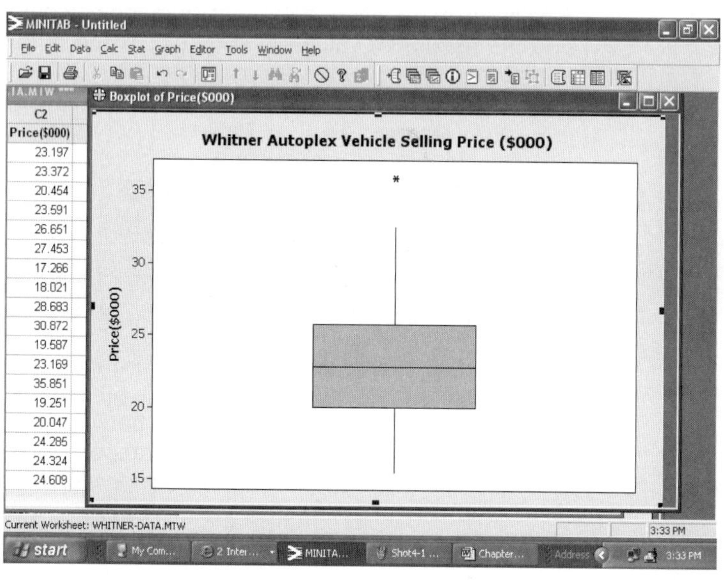

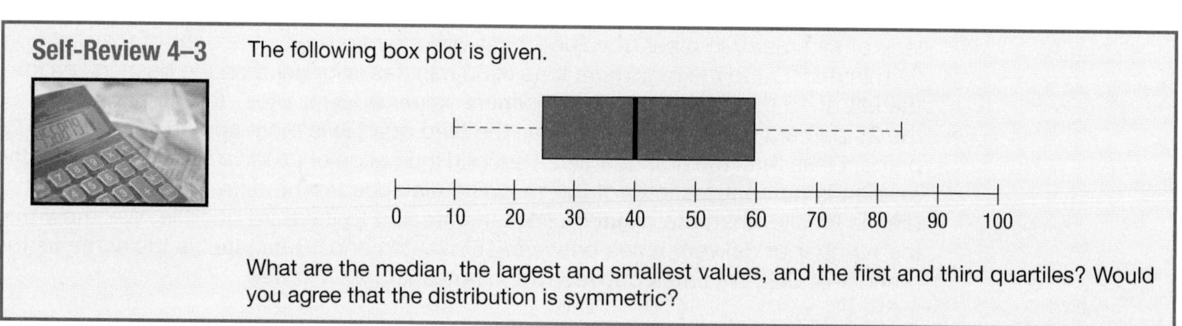

Self-Review 4–3 The following box plot is given.

What are the median, the largest and smallest values, and the first and third quartiles? Would you agree that the distribution is symmetric?

Exercises

7. Refer to the box plot below.

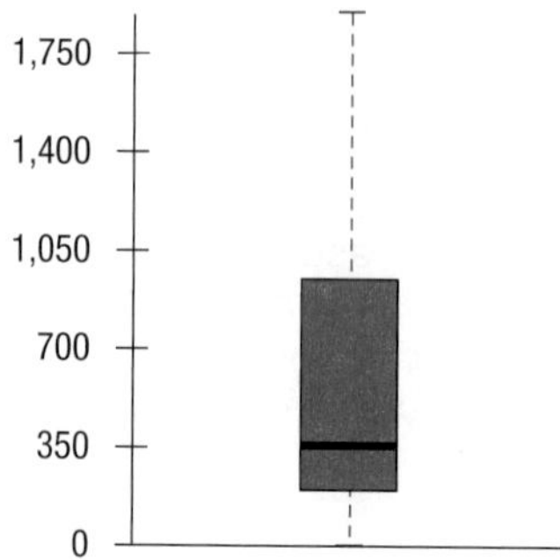

a. Estimate the median.
b. Estimate the first and third quartiles.
c. Determine the interquartile range.
d. Beyond what point is a value considered an outlier?
e. Identify any outliers and estimate their value.
f. Is the distribution symmetrical or positively or negatively skewed?

8. Refer to the following box plot.

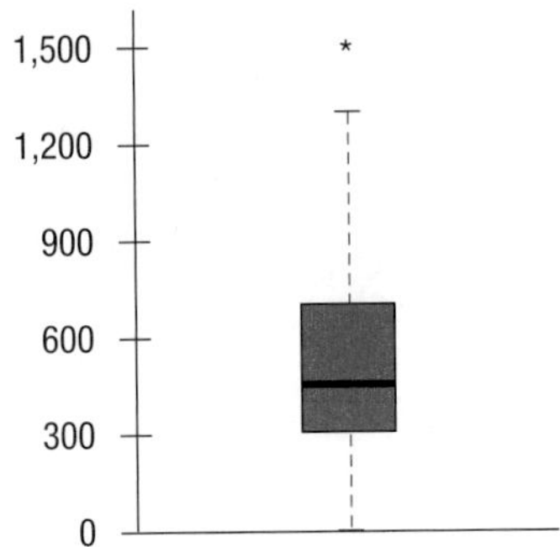

a. Estimate the median.
b. Estimate the first and third quartiles.
c. Determine the interquartile range.
d. Beyond what point is a value considered an outlier?
e. Identify any outliers and estimate their value.
f. Is the distribution symmetrical or positively or negatively skewed?

9. In a study of the gasoline mileage of model year 2004 automobiles, the mean miles per gallon was 27.5 and the median was 26.8. The smallest value in the study was 12.70 miles per gallon, and the largest was 50.20. The first and third quartiles were 17.95 and 35.45 miles per gallon, respectively. Develop a box plot and comment on the distribution. Is it a symmetric distribution?

10. A sample of 28 time shares in Florida revealed the following daily charges for a one-bedroom suite. For convenience the data are ordered from smallest to largest. Construct a box plot to represent the data. Comment on the distribution. Be sure to identify the first and third quartiles and the median.

$116	$121	$157	$192	$207	$209	$209
229	232	236	236	239	243	246
260	264	276	281	283	289	296
307	309	312	317	324	341	353

Skewness

In Chapter 3 we described measures of central location for a set of observations by reporting the mean, median, and mode. We also described measures that show the amount of spread or variation in a set of data, such as the range and the standard deviation.

Another characteristic of a set of data is the shape. There are four shapes commonly observed: symmetric, positively skewed, negatively skewed, and bimodal. In a **symmetric** set of observations the mean and median are equal and the data values are evenly spread around these values. The data values below the mean and median are a mirror image of those above. A set of values is **skewed to the right** or **positively skewed** if there is a single peak and the values extend much further to the right of the peak than to the left of the peak. In this case the mean is larger than the median. In a **negatively skewed** distribution there is a single peak but the observations extend further to the left, in the negative direction, than to the right. In a negatively skewed distribution the mean is smaller than the median. Positively skewed distributions are more common. Salaries often follow this pattern. Think of the salaries of those employed in a small company of about 100 people. The president and a few top executives would have very large salaries relative to the other workers and hence the distribution of salaries would exhibit positive skewness. A **bimodal distribution** will have two or more peaks. This is often the case when the values are from two populations. This information is summarized in Chart 4–1.

Statistics in Action

The late Stephen Jay Gould (1941–2002) was a professor of zoology and professor of geology at Harvard University. In 1982, he was diagnosed with cancer and had an expected survival time of eight months. However, never to be discouraged, his research showed that the distribution of survival time is dramatically skewed to the right and showed that not only do 50% of similar cancer patients survive more than 8 months, but that the survival time could be years rather than months! Based on his experience, he wrote a widely published essay titled, "The Median is not the Message."

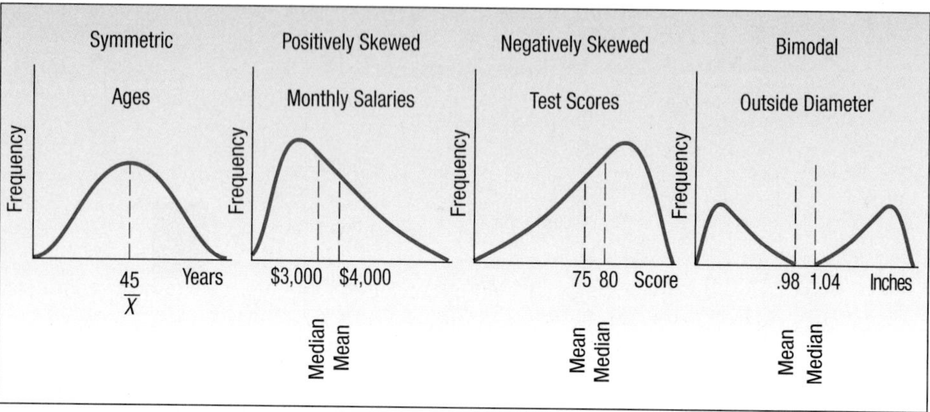

CHART 4–1 Shapes of Frequency Polygons

There are several formulas in the statistical literature used to calculate skewness. The simplest, developed by Professor Karl Pearson, is based on the difference between the mean and the median.

PEARSON'S COEFFICIENT OF SKEWNESS

$$sk = \frac{3(\bar{X} - \text{Median})}{s} \quad \textbf{[4–2]}$$

Using this relationship the coefficient of skewness can range from −3 up to 3. A value near −3, such as −2.57, indicates considerable negative skewness. A value such as 1.63 indicates moderate positive skewness. A value of 0, which will occur when the mean and median are equal, indicates the distribution is symmetrical and that there is no skewness present.

In this text we present output from the statistical software packages MINITAB and Excel. Both of these software packages compute a value for the coefficient of skewness that is based on the cubed deviations from the mean. The formula is:

SOFTWARE COEFFICIENT OF SKEWNESS

$$sk = \frac{n}{(n-1)(n-2)}\left[\sum\left(\frac{X - \bar{X}}{s}\right)^3\right] \quad \textbf{[4–3]}$$

Formula (4–3) offers an insight into skewness. The right-hand side of the formula is the difference between each value and the mean, divided by the standard deviation. That is the portion $(X - \bar{X})/s$ of the formula. This idea is called **standardizing.** We will discuss the idea of standardizing a value in more detail in Chapter 7 when we describe the normal probability distribution. At this point, observe that the result is to report the difference between each value and the mean in units of the standard deviation. If this difference is positive, the particular value is larger than the mean; if it is negative, it is smaller than the mean. When we cube these values, we retain the information on the direction of the difference. Recall that in the formula for the standard deviation [see formula (3–11)] we squared the difference between each value and the mean, so that the result was all non-negative values.

If the set of data values under consideration is symmetric, when we cube the standardized values and sum over all the values the result would be near zero. If there are several large values, clearly separate from the others, the sum of the cubed differences would be a large positive value. Several values much smaller will result in a negative cubed sum.

An example will illustrate the idea of skewness.

EXAMPLE

Following are the earnings per share for a sample of 15 software companies for the year 2005. The earnings per share are arranged from smallest to largest.

\$0.09	\$0.13	\$0.41	\$0.51	\$ 1.12	\$ 1.20	\$ 1.49	\$3.18
3.50	6.36	7.83	8.92	10.13	12.99	16.40	

Compute the mean, median, and standard deviation. Find the coefficient of skewness using Pearson's estimate and the software methods. What is your conclusion regarding the shape of the distribution?

SOLUTION

These are sample data, so we use formula (3–2) to determine the mean

$$\bar{X} = \frac{\Sigma X}{n} = \frac{\$74.26}{15} = \$4.95$$

The median is the middle value in a set of data, arranged from smallest to largest. In this case the middle value is \$3.18, so the median earnings per share is \$3.18.

We use formula (3–11) on page 80 to determine the sample standard deviation.

$$s = \sqrt{\frac{\Sigma(X - \bar{X})^2}{n - 1}} = \sqrt{\frac{(\$0.09 - \$4.95)^2 + \cdots + (\$16.40 - \$4.95)^2}{15 - 1}} = \$5.22$$

Pearson's coefficient of skewness is 1.017, found by

$$sk = \frac{3(\bar{X} - \text{Median})}{s} = \frac{3(\$4.95 - \$3.18)}{\$5.22} = 1.017$$

This indicates there is moderate positive skewness in the earnings per share data.

We obtain a similar, but not exactly the same, value from the software method. The details of the calculations are shown in Table 4–1. To begin we find the difference between each earnings per share value and the mean and divide this result by the standard deviation. Recall that we referred to this as standardizing. Next, we cube, that is, raise it to the third power, the result of the first step. Finally, we sum the cubed values. The details of the first row, that is, the company with an earnings per share of \$0.09, are:

$$\left(\frac{X - \bar{X}}{s}\right)^3 = \left(\frac{0.09 - 4.95}{5.22}\right)^3 = (-0.9310)^3 = -0.8070$$

When we sum the 15 cubed values, the result is 11.8274. That is, the term $\Sigma[(X - \bar{X})/s]^3 = 11.8274$. To find the coefficient of skewness, we use formula (4–3), with $n = 15$.

$$sk = \frac{n}{(n - 1)(n - 2)} \Sigma\left(\frac{X - \bar{X}}{s}\right)^3 = \frac{15}{(15 - 1)(15 - 2)}(11.8274) = 0.975$$

We conclude that the earnings per share values are somewhat positively skewed. The chart on the next page, from MINITAB, reports the descriptive measures, such as the mean, median, and standard deviation of the earnings per share data. Also included are the coefficient of skewness and a histogram with a bell-shaped curve superimposed.

TABLE 4–1 Calculation of the Coefficient of Skewness

Earnings per Share	$\frac{(X-\bar{X})}{s}$	$\left(\frac{(X-\bar{X})}{s}\right)^3$
0.09	−0.9310	−0.8070
0.13	−0.9234	−0.7873
0.41	−0.8697	−0.6579
0.51	−0.8506	−0.6154
1.12	−0.7337	−0.3950
1.20	−0.7184	−0.3708
1.49	−0.6628	−0.2912
3.18	−0.3391	−0.0390
3.50	−0.2778	−0.0214
6.36	0.2701	0.0197
7.83	0.5517	0.1679
8.92	0.7605	0.4399
10.13	0.9923	0.9772
12.99	1.5402	3.6539
16.40	2.1935	10.5537
		11.8274

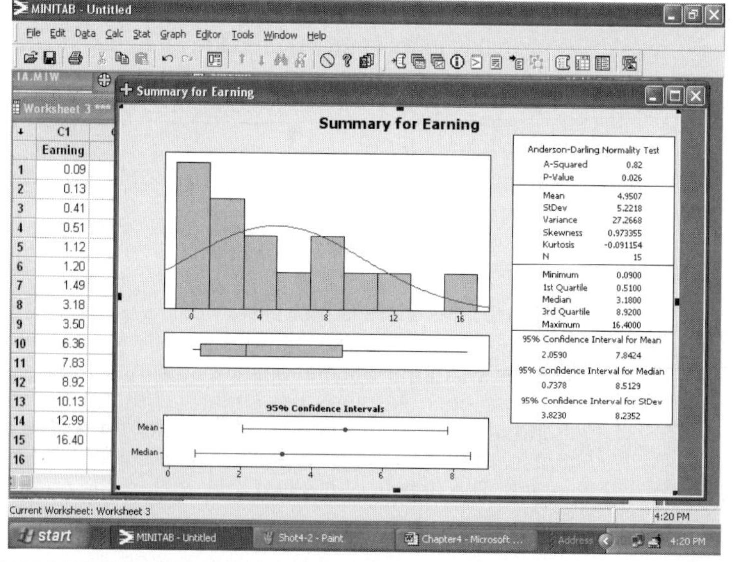

Self-Review 4–4

A sample of five data entry clerks employed in the Horry County Tax Office revised the following number of tax records last hour: 73, 98, 60, 92, and 84.

(a) Find the mean, median, and the standard deviation.
(b) Compute the coefficient of skewness using Pearson's method.
(c) Calculate the coefficient of skewness using the software method.
(d) What is your conclusion regarding the skewness of the data?

Exercises

For Exercises 11–14, do the following:

a. Determine the mean, median, and the standard deviation.
b. Determine the coefficient of skewness using Pearson's method.
c. Determine the coefficient of skewness using the software method.

11. The following values are the starting salaries, in $000, for a sample of five accounting graduates who accepted positions in public accounting last year.

36.0	26.0	33.0	28.0	31.0

12. Listed below are the salaries, in $000, for a sample of 15 chief financial officers in the electronics industry.

$516.0	$548.0	$566.0	$534.0	$586.0	$529.0
546.0	523.0	538.0	523.0	551.0	552.0
486.0	558.0	574.0			

13. Listed below are the commissions earned ($000) last year by the sales representatives at the Furniture Patch, Inc.

$ 3.9	$ 5.7	$ 7.3	$10.6	$13.0	$13.6	$15.1	$15.8	$17.1
17.4	17.6	22.3	38.6	43.2	87.7			

14. Listed below are the salaries for the New York Yankees for the year 2004. The salary information is reported in millions of dollars.

21.7	18.6	16.0	15.7	12.4	12.4	12.0	10.9	9.0	9.0
8.5	7.0	6.0	3.5	3.0	3.0	2.7	2.0	1.9	1.8
1.0	0.9	0.8	0.8	0.7	0.5	0.5	0.3	0.3	

Describing the Relationship Between Two Variables

In Chapter 2 and the first section of this chapter we presented graphical techniques to summarize the distribution of a single variable. We used a histogram in Chapter 2 to summarize the prices of vehicles sold at Whitner Autoplex. Earlier in this chapter we used dot plots to visually summarize a set of data. Because we are studying a single variable we refer to this as **univariate** data.

There are situations where we wish to study and visually portray the relationship between two variables. When two variables are measured for each individual or observation in the population or sample, the data are called **bivariate data.** Data analysts frequently wish to understand the relationship between two variables. Here are some examples:

- Tybo and Associates is a law firm that advertises extensively on local TV. The partners are considering increasing their advertising budget. Before doing so, they would like to know the relationship between the amount spent per month on advertising and the total amount of billings. To put it another way, will increasing the amount spent on advertising result in an increase in billings?

- Coastal Realty is studying the selling prices of homes. What variables seem to be related to the selling price of homes? For example, do larger homes sell for more than smaller ones? Probably. So Coastal might study the relationship between the area in square feet and the selling price.
- Dr. Stephen Givens is an expert in human development. He is studying the relationship between the height of fathers and the height of their sons. That is, do tall fathers tend to have tall children? Would you expect Shaquille O'Neal, the 7′1″, 335-pound professional basketball player, to have relatively tall sons?

One graphical technique we use to show the relationship between variables is called a **scatter diagram.**

To draw a scatter diagram we need two variables. We scale one variable along the horizontal axis (*X*-axis) of a graph and the other variable along the vertical axis (*Y*-axis). Usually one variable depends to some degree on the other. In the third example above, the height of the son *depends* on the height of the father. So we scale the height of the father on the horizontal axis and that of the son on the vertical axis.

We can use statistical software, such as Excel, to perform the plotting function for us. *Caution:* you should always be careful of the scale. Remember the example on page 17 (Chart 1–5). By changing the scale of either the vertical or the horizontal axis, you can affect the apparent visual strength of the relationship.

EXAMPLE

In the Introduction to Chapter 2 we presented data from AutoUSA. In this case the information concerned the prices of 80 vehicles sold last month at the Whitner Autoplex lot in Raytown, Missouri. The data shown below include the selling price of the vehicle as well as the age of the purchaser. Is there a relationship between the selling price of a vehicle and the age of the purchaser? Would it be reasonable to conclude that the more expensive vehicles are purchased by older buyers?

SOLUTION

We can investigate the relationship between vehicle selling price and the age of the buyer with a scatter diagram. We scale age on the horizontal, or *X*-axis, and the selling price on the vertical, or *Y*-axis. We use Microsoft Excel to develop the scatter diagram. The Excel commands necessary for the output are shown in the **Software Commands** section at the end of the chapter.

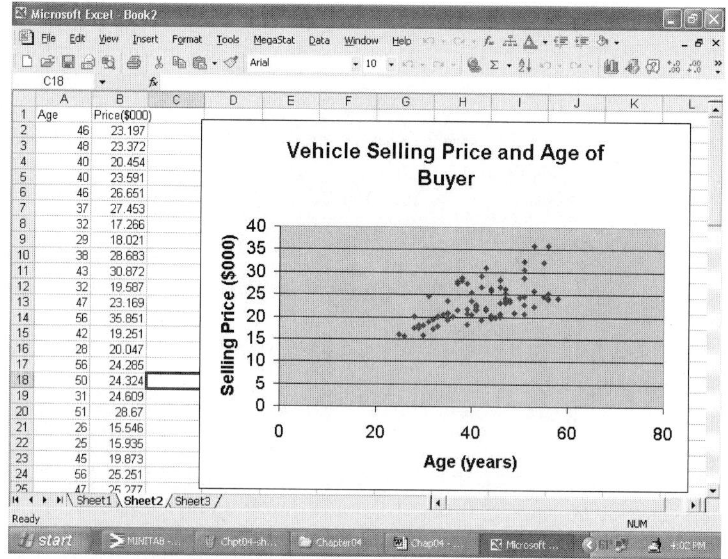

The scatter diagram shows a positive relationship between the variables. In fact, older buyers tend to buy more expensive cars. In Chapter 13 we will study the relationship between variables more extensively, even calculating several numerical measures to express the relationship.

In the Whitner Autoplex example there is a positive or direct relationship between the variables. That is, as age increased the vehicle selling price also increased. There are, however, many instances where there is a relationship between the variables, but that relationship is inverse or negative. For example:

- The value of a vehicle and the number of miles driven. As the number of miles increases, the value of the vehicle decreases.
- The premium for auto insurance and the age of the driver. Auto rates tend to be the highest for young adults and less for older people.
- For many law enforcement personnel as the number of years on the job increases the number of traffic citations decreases. This may be because personnel become more liberal in their interpretations or they may be in supervisor positions and not in a position to issue as many citations. But in any event as age increases the number of citations decreases.

A scatter diagram requires that both of the variables be at least interval scale. In the Whitner Autoplex example both age and selling price are ratio scale variables. Height is also ratio scale as used in the discussion of the relationship between the height of fathers and the height of their sons. What if we wish to study the relationship between two variables when one or both are nominal or ordinal scale? In this case we tally the results into a **contingency table.**

CONTINGENCY TABLE A table used to classify observations according to two identifiable characteristics.

A contingency table is a cross tabulation of two variables. It is a two dimensional frequency distribution in which the classes for one variable are presented on the rows and the classes for the other variable are presented on the columns. For example:

- Students at a university are classified by gender and class rank.
- A product is classified as acceptable or unacceptable and by the shift (day, afternoon, or night) on which it is manufactured.
- A voter in a school bond referendum is classified as to party affiliation (Democrat, Republican, other) and the number of children attending school in the district (0, 1, 2, etc.).

EXAMPLE

A manufacturer of preassembled windows produced 50 windows yesterday. This morning the quality assurance inspector reviewed each window for all quality aspects. Each was classified as acceptable or unacceptable and by the shift on which it was produced. Thus he reported two variables on a single item. The two variables are shift and quality. The results are reported in the following table.

	Shift			
	Day	**Afternoon**	**Night**	**Total**
Defective	3	2	1	6
Acceptable	17	13	14	44
Total	20	15	15	50

Compare the quality levels on each shift.

SOLUTION

The level of measurement for both variables is nominal. That is, the variables' shift and quality are such that a particular unit can only be classified or assigned into groups. By organizing the information into a contingency table we can compare the quality on the three shifts. For example, on the day shift, 3 out of 20 windows or 15 percent are defective. On the afternoon shift, 2 of 15 or 13 percent are defective and on the night shift 1 out of 15 or 7 percent are defective. Overall 12 percent of the windows are defective. Observe also that 40 percent of the windows are produced on the day shift, found by (20/50)(100). We will return to the study of contingency tables in Chapter 5 during the study of probability and in Chapter 15 during the study of nonparametric methods of analysis.

Self-Review 4–5

The following chart shows the relationship between concert seating capacity (00) and revenue in $000 for a sample of concerts.

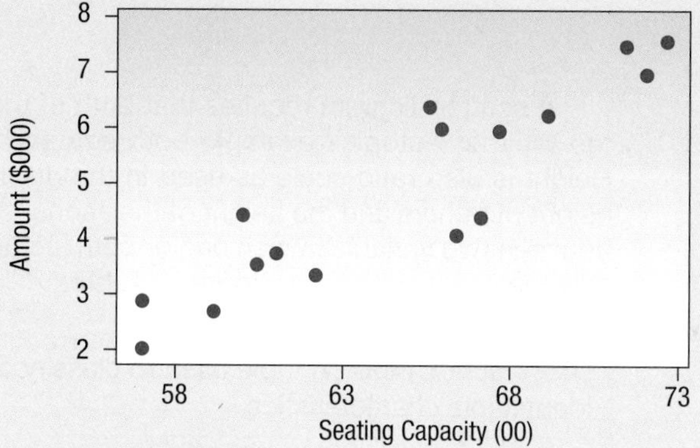

(a) What is the above diagram called?
(b) How many concerts were studied?
(c) Estimate the revenue for the concert with the largest seating capacity.
(d) How would you characterize the relationship between revenue and seating capacity? Is it strong or weak, direct or inverse?

Exercises

15. Develop a scatter diagram for the following sample data. How would you describe the relationship between the values?

X-Value	*Y*-Value
10	6
8	2
9	6
11	5
13	7
11	6
10	5
7	2
7	3
11	7

16. Silver Springs Moving and Storage, Inc. is studying the relationship between the number of rooms in a move and the number of labor hours required. As part of the analysis the CFO of Silver Springs developed the following scatter diagram.

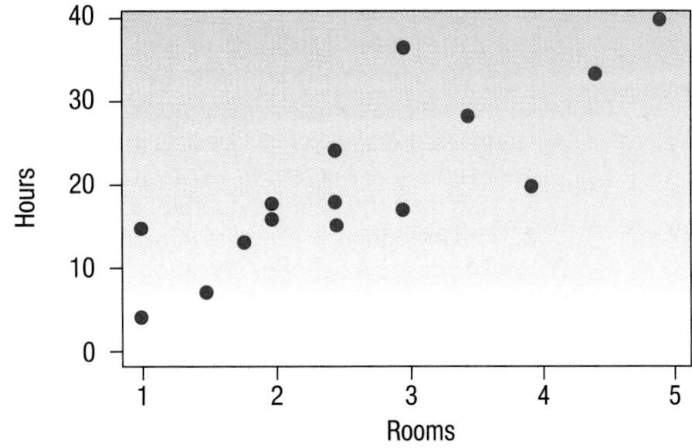

a. How many moves are in the sample?
b. Does it appear that more labor hours are required as the number of rooms increases, or does labor hours decrease as the number of rooms increases?

17. The manager of a restaurant wishes to study the relationship between the gender of a guest and whether the guest orders dessert. To investigate the relationship the manager collected the following information on 200 recent customers.

	Gender		
Dessert Ordered	**Male**	**Female**	**Total**
Yes	32	15	47
No	68	85	153
Total	100	100	200

a. What is the level of measurement of the two variables?
b. What is the above table called?
c. Does the evidence in the table suggest men are more likely to order dessert than women? Explain why.

18. A corporation is evaluating a proposed merger. The Board of Directors surveyed 50 stockholders concerning their position on the merger. The results are reported below.

	Opinion			
Number of Shares Held	**Favor**	**Opposed**	**Undecided**	**Total**
Under 200	8	6	2	16
200 to 1,000	6	8	1	15
1,000 or more	6	12	1	19
Total	20	26	4	50

a. What level of measurement is used in this table?
b. What is this table called?
c. What group seems most strongly opposed to the merger?

Chapter Outline

I. A dot plot shows the range of values on the horizontal axis and a dot is placed above each of the values.

A. Dot plots report the details of each observation.

B. They are useful for comparing two or more data sets.

II. Measures of location also describe the shape of a set of observations.

A. Quartiles divide a set of observations into four equal parts.

1. Twenty-five percent of the observations are less than the first quartile, 50 percent are less than the second quartile, and 75 percent are less than the third quartile.

2. The interquartile range is the difference between the third and the first quartile.

B. Deciles divide a set of observations in ten equal parts and percentiles into 100 equal parts.

C. A box plot is a graphic display of a set of data.

1. A box is drawn enclosing the regions between the first and third quartiles.

a. A line is drawn inside the box at the median value.

b. Dotted line segments are drawn from the third quartile to the largest value to show the highest 25 percent of the values and from the first quartile to the smallest value to show the lowest 25 percent of the values.

2. A box plot is based on five statistics: the maximum and minimum observations, the first and third quartiles, and the median.

III. The coefficient of skewness is a measure of the symmetry of a distribution.

A. There are two formulas for the coefficient of skewness.

1. The formula developed by Pearson is:

$$sk = \frac{3(\bar{X} - \text{Median})}{s} \qquad \textbf{[4–2]}$$

2. The coefficient of skewness computed by statistical software is:

$$sk = \frac{n}{(n-1)(n-2)}\left[\sum\left(\frac{X-\bar{X}}{s}\right)^3\right] \qquad \textbf{[4–3]}$$

IV. A scatter diagram is a graphic tool to portray the relationship between two variables.

A. Both variables are measured with interval or ratio scales.

B. If the scatter of points moves from the lower left to the upper right the variables under consideration are directly or positively related.

C. If the scatter of points moves from upper left to the lower right the variables are inversely or negatively related.

V. A contingency table is used to classify nominal scale observations according to two characteristics.

Pronunciation Key

SYMBOL	MEANING	PRONUNCIATION
L_p	Location of percentile	*L* sub *p*
Q_1	First quartile	*Q* sub 1
Q_3	Third quartile	*Q* sub 3

Chapter Exercises

19. A sample of students attending Southeast Florida University is asked the number of social activities in which they participated last week. The chart below was prepared from the sample data.

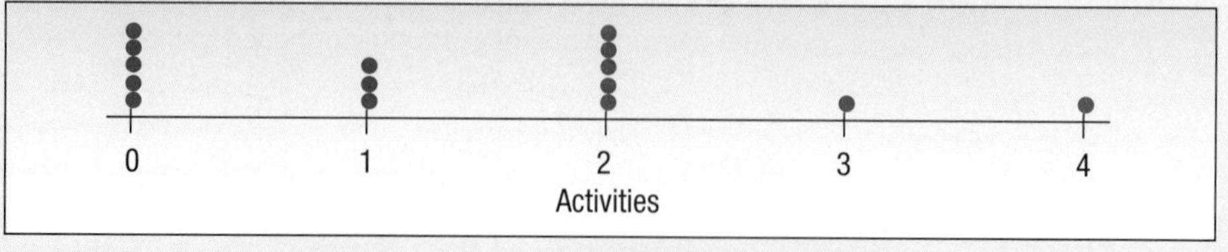

a. What is the name given to this chart?
b. How many students were in the study?
c. How many students reported attending no social activities?

20. Doctor's Care is a walk-in clinic, with locations in Georgetown, Monks Corners, and Aynor, at which patients may receive treatment for minor injuries, colds, and flu, as well as physical examinations. The following charts report the number of patients treated in each of the three locations last month.

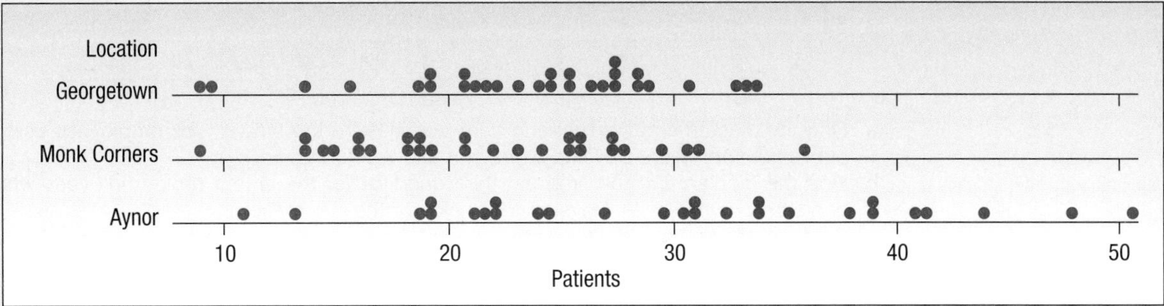

Describe the number of patients served at the three locations each day. What are the maximum and minimum numbers of patients served at each of the locations? What comparisons would you make among the three locations?

21. In the early 2000s interest rates were low so many homeowners refinanced their home mortgages. Linda Lahey is a mortgage officer at Down River Federal Savings and Loan. Below is the amount refinanced for twenty loans she processed last week. The data are reported in thousands of dollars and arranged from smallest to largest.

59.2	59.5	61.6	65.5	66.6	72.9	74.8	77.3	79.2
83.7	85.6	85.8	86.6	87.0	87.1	90.2	93.3	98.6
100.2	100.7							

a. Find the median, first quartile, and third quartile.
b. Find the 26th and 83rd percentiles.
c. Draw a box plot of the data.

22. A study is made by the recording industry in the United States of the number of music CDs owned by senior citizens and young adults. The information is reported below.

Seniors									
28	35	41	48	52	81	97	98	98	99
118	132	133	140	145	147	153	158	162	174
177	180	180	187	188					

Young Adults									
81	107	113	147	147	175	183	192	202	209
233	251	254	266	283	284	284	316	372	401
417	423	490	500	507	518	550	557	590	594

a. Find the median and the first and third quartiles for the number of CDs owned by senior citizens. Develop a box plot for the information.
b. Find the median and the first and third quartiles for the number of CDs owned by young adults. Develop a box plot for the information.
c. Compare the number of CDs owned by the two groups.

23. The corporate headquarters of *Bank.com*, a new Internet company that performs all banking transactions via the Internet, is located in downtown Philadelphia. The director of human resources is making a study of the time it takes employees to get to work. The city is planning to offer incentives to each downtown employer if they will encourage their

employees to use public transportation. Below is a listing of the time to get to work this morning according to whether the employee used public transportation or drove a car.

Public Transportation											
23	25	25	30	31	31	32	33	35	36	37	42

Private											
32	32	33	34	37	37	38	38	38	39	40	44

a. Find the median and the first and third quartiles for the time it took employees using public transportation. Develop a box plot for the information.
b. Find the median and the first and third quartiles for the time it took employees who drove their own vehicle. Develop a box plot for the information.
c. Compare the times of the two groups.

24. The following box plot shows the number of daily newspapers published in each state and the District of Columbia. Write a brief report summarizing the number published. Be sure to include information on the values of the first and third quartiles, the median, and whether there is any skewness. If there are any outliers, estimate their value.

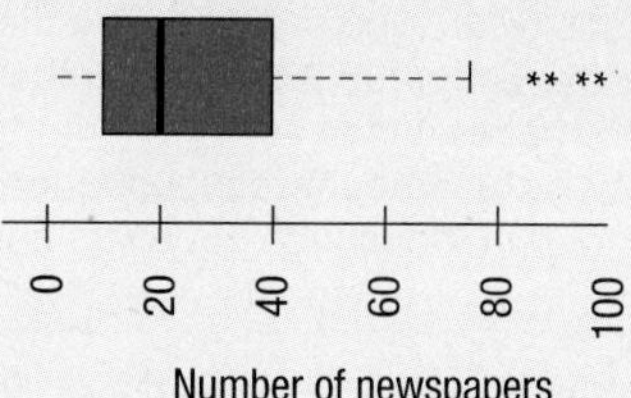

25. The Walter Gogel Company is an industrial supplier of fasteners, tools, and springs. The amounts of their invoices vary widely, from less than $20.00 to over $400.00. During the month of January they sent out 80 invoices. Here is a box plot of these invoices. Write a brief report summarizing the amounts of their invoices. Be sure to include information on the values of the first and third quartiles, the median, and whether there is any skewness. If there are any outliers, approximate the value of these invoices.

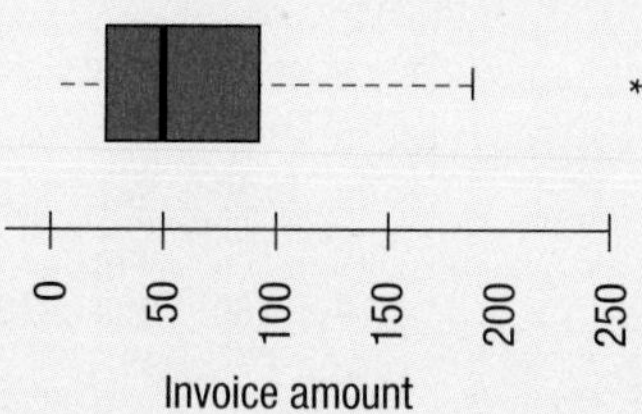

26. The National Muffler Company claims they will change your muffler in less than 30 minutes. An investigative reporter for WTOL Channel 11 monitored 30 consecutive muffler changes at the National outlet on Liberty Street. The number of minutes to perform changes is reported below.

44	12	22	31	26	22	30	26	18	28	12
40	17	13	14	17	25	29	15	30	10	28
16	33	24	20	29	34	23	13			

a. Develop a box plot for the time to change a muffler.
b. Does the distribution show any outliers?
c. Summarize your findings in a brief report.

27. A major airline wanted some information on those enrolled in their "frequent flyer" program. A sample of 48 members resulted in the following number of miles flown last year, to the nearest 1,000 miles, by each participant.

22	29	32	38	39	41	42	43	43	43	44	44
45	45	46	46	46	47	50	51	52	54	54	55
56	57	58	59	60	61	61	63	63	64	64	67
69	70	70	70	71	71	72	73	74	76	78	88

a. Develop a box plot for the information.
b. Does the distribution show any outliers?
c. Summarize your findings in a brief report.

28. Listed below is the amount of commissions earned last month for the eight members of the sales staff at Best Electronics. Calculate the coefficient of skewness using both methods. *Hint:* Use of a spreadsheet will expedite the calculations.

980.9	1036.5	1099.5	1153.9	1409.0	1456.4	1718.4	1721.2

29. Listed below is the number of car thefts per day in a large city over the last week. Calculate the coefficient of skewness using both methods. *Hint:* Use of a spreadsheet will expedite the calculations.

3	12	13	7	8	3	8

30. The manager of Information Services at Wilkin Investigations, a private investigation firm, is studying the relationship between the age (in months) of a combination printer, copy, and fax machine and its monthly maintenance cost. For a sample of 15 machines the manager developed the following chart. What can the manager conclude about the relationship between the variables?

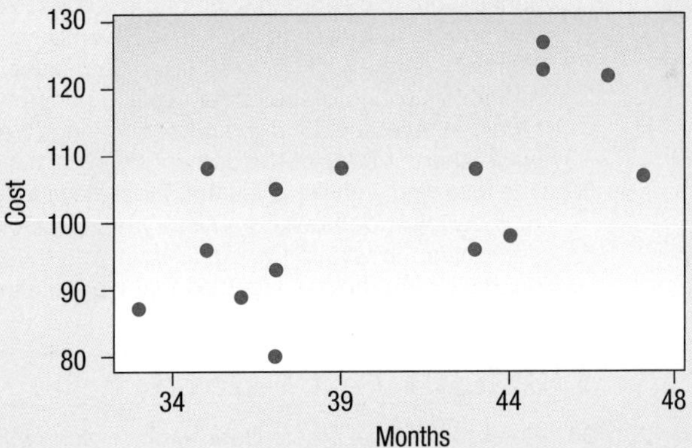

31. An auto insurance company reported the following information regarding the age of a driver and the number of accidents reported last year. Develop a scatter diagram for the data and write a brief summary.

Age	Accidents
16	4
24	2
18	5
17	4
23	0
27	1
32	1
22	3

32. Wendy's Old Fashion Hamburgers offers eight different condiments (mustard, catsup, onion, mayonnaise, pickle, lettuce, tomato, and relish) on hamburgers. A store manager collected the following information on the number of condiments ordered and the age group of the customer. What can you conclude regarding the information? Who tends to order the most or least number of condiments?

	Age			
Number of Condiments	**Under 18**	**18 up to 40**	**40 up to 60**	**60 or older**
0	12	18	24	52
1	21	76	50	30
2	39	52	40	12
3 or more	71	87	47	28

33. A nationwide poll of adults asked if they favor gun control, oppose it, or have no opinion, as well as their preferred political party. The results are reported in the following table.

	Opinion on Gun Control			
Party Affiliation	**Favor**	**Oppose**	**No Opinion**	**Total**
Democrat	88	96	36	220
Republican	64	96	20	180
Total	152	192	56	400

Analyze the information in the table. Who is more likely to favor gun control?

exercises.com

34. Refer to Exercise 72 on page 89, which suggests websites to find information on the Dow Jones Industrial Average. One of the websites suggested is Bloomberg, which is an excellent source of business data. The Bloomberg website is: http://bloomberg.com. Click on **Markets** on the tool bar select and then select **Stocks in the Dow.** You should now have available a listing of the current selling price of the 30 stocks that make up the Dow Jones Industrial Average. Find the percent change from yesterday for each of the 30 stocks. Develop charts to depict the percent change.

35. The following website gives the Super Bowl results since the game was first played in 1967: http://www.superbowl.com/history/recaps. Download the scores for each Super Bowl and determine the winning margin. What was the typical margin? What are the first and third quartiles? Are there any games that were outliers?

Dataset Exercises

36. Refer to the Real Estate Data, which reports information on homes sold in the Denver, Colorado, area last year. Select the variable selling price.

a. Develop a box plot. Estimate the first and the third quartiles. Are there any outliers?

b. Develop a scatter diagram with price on the vertical axis and the size of the home on the horizontal. Does there seem to be a relationship between these variables? Is the relationship direct or inverse?

c. Develop a scatter diagram with price on the vertical axis and distance from the center of the city on the horizontal axis. Does there seem to be a relationship between these variables? Is the relationship direct or inverse?

37. Refer to the Baseball 2003 data, which reports information on the 30 major league baseball teams for the 2003 season.

a. Select the variable that refers to the year in which the stadium was built. (*Hint:* Subtract the year in which the stadium was built from the current year to find the age of the stadium and work with this variable.) Develop a box plot. Are there any outliers?

b. Select the variable team salary and draw a box plot. Are there any outliers? What are the quartiles? Write a brief summary of your analysis. How do the salaries of the New York Yankees and the Montreal Expos compare with the other teams?
c. Draw a scatter diagram with the number of games won on the vertical axis and the team salary on the horizontal axis. What are your conclusions?
d. Select the variable wins. Draw a dot plot. What can you conclude from this plot?

38. Refer to the Wage data, which reports information on annual wages for a sample of 100 workers. Also included are variables relating to industry, years of education, and gender for each worker. Draw a bar chart of the variable occupation. Write a brief report summarizing your findings.
39. Refer to the CIA data, which reports demographic and economic information on 46 countries.
    a. Select the variable life expectancy. Develop a box plot. Find the first and third quartiles. Are there any outliers? Is the distribution skewed or symmetric? Write a paragraph summarizing your findings.
    b. Select the variable GDP/cap. Develop a box plot. Find the first and third quartiles. Are there any outliers? Is the distribution skewed or symmetric? Write a paragraph summarizing your findings.

Software Commands

1. The MINITAB commands for the dot plot on page 95 are:
   a. Enter the vehicles sold at Smith Ford Mercury Jeep in column C1 and Brophy Honda Volkswagen in C2. Name the variables accordingly.
   b. Select **Graph** and **Dot Plot**. In the first dialog box select **Simple** in the upper left corner and click **OK**. In the next dialog box select **Smith** and **Brophy** as the variables to **Graph**, click on **Labels** and write an appropriate title, click on **Multiple Graphs**, select **Options** and select the option **In separate panels on the same page** and click **OK** in the various dialog boxes.
   c. To calculate the descriptive statistics shown in the output select **Stat**, **Basic statistics**, and then **Display Descriptive statistics**. In the dialog box select Smith and Brophy as the **Variables**, click on **Statistics** and select the desired statistics to be output, and finally click **OK** twice.

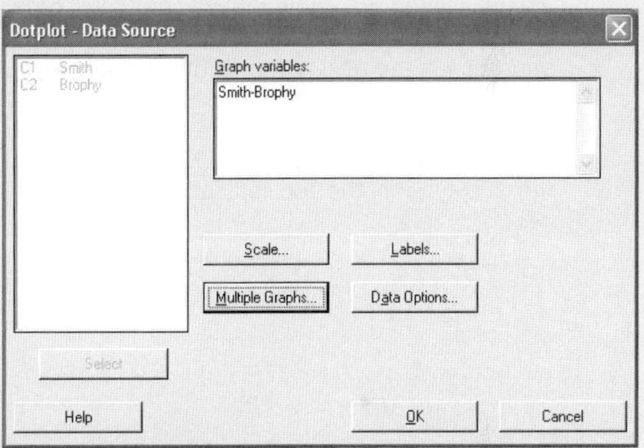

2. The Excel Commands for the descriptive statistics on page 99 are:
   a. From the CD retrieve the Whitner Autoplex data file, which is Whitner-Data.
   b. From the menu bar select **Tools**, and the **Data Analysis**. Select **Descriptive Statistics** and then click **OK.**
   c. For the **Input Range**, type *B1:B81*, indicate that the data are grouped by column and that the labels are in the first row. Click on **Output Range**, indicate that the output should go into *D1* (or any place you wish), click on **Summary Statistics**, then click **OK**.
   d. In the lower left click on **Kth Largest** and put *20* in the box and click on **Kth Smallest** and put *20* in that box.
   e. After you get your results, double-check the count in the output to be sure it contains the correct number of values.

Descriptive Statistics
Input
Input Range: $B$1:$B$81
Grouped By: Columns / Rows
Labels in first row
OK
Cancel
Help
Output options
Output Range:
New Worksheet Ply:
New Workbook
Summary statistics
Confidence Level for Mean: 95 %
Kth Largest: 20
Kth Smallest: 20

3. The MINITAB commands for the box plot on page 102 are:
   a. Import the data from the CD. The file name is **Table2–1.**
   b. Select **Graph** and then **Boxplot**. In the dialog box select **Simple** in the upper left corner and click **OK**. Select **Price** as the **Graph variable**, click on **Labels** and include an appropriate heading, and then click **OK**.
4. The MINITAB commands for the descriptive summary on page 106 are:
   a. Retrieve the data from **Table4–1** on the **CD**.
   b. Select **Stat**, **Basic Statistics**, and then click on **Graphical Summary**. Select **Earnings** as the variable, and then click **OK**.
5. The Excel commands for the scatter diagram on page 108 are:
   a. Retrieve the data from **Table2–1** on the **CD**.
   b. You will need to copy the variables to other columns on the spreadsheet with age in a column and price in the next column. This will allow you to place price on the vertical axis and age on the horizontal axis.
   c. Click on **Chart Wizard**, select **XY (Scatter)** and the sub-type in the top left, and then click on next.
   d. Select or highlight the variables age followed by price.
   e. Type in a title for the chart and a name for the two variables. In the final dialog box select a location for the charts.

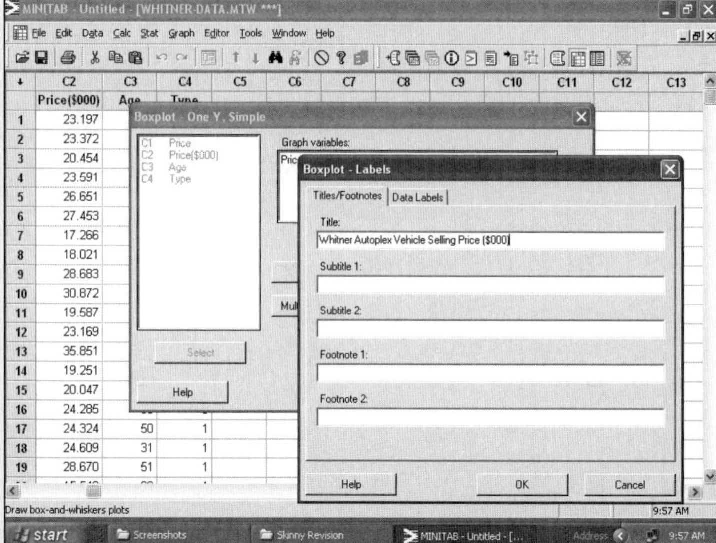

Chapter 4 Answers to Self-Review

4–1 **a.** 79, 105
b. 15
c. Between 89 and 91 accounts for 38 stores and 93 and 95 for 34 stores.

4–2 **a.** 7.9
b. $Q_1 = 7.76$, $Q_3 = 8.015$

4–3 The smallest value is 10 and the largest 85; the first quartile is 25 and the third 60. About 50 percent of the values are between 25 and 60. The median value is 40. The distribution is positively skewed.

4–4 **a.** $\bar{X} = \frac{407}{5} = 81.4$, Median = 84

$$s = \sqrt{\frac{923.2}{5-1}} = 15.19$$

b. $sk = \frac{3(81.4 - 84.0)}{15.19} = -0.51$

c.

X	$\frac{(X - \bar{X})}{s}$	$\left[\frac{(X - \bar{X})}{s}\right]^3$
73	−0.5530	−0.1691
98	1.0928	1.3051
60	−1.4088	−2.7962
92	0.6978	0.3398
84	0.1712	0.0050
		−1.3154

$$sk = \frac{5}{(4)(3)}[-1.3154]$$
$$= -0.5481$$

d. The distribution is somewhat negatively skewed.

4–5 **a.** Scatter diagram
b. 16
c. $7,500
d. Strong and direct

5

A Survey of Probability Concepts

GOALS

When you have completed this chapter you will be able to:

1 **Define *probability.***

2 **Describe the *classical, empirical,* and *subjective* approaches to probability.**

3 **Understand the terms *experiment, event, outcome, permutations,* and *combinations.***

4 **Define the terms *conditional probability* and *joint probability.***

5 **Calculate probabilities using the *rules of addition* and *rules of multiplication.***

6 **Use a tree diagram to organize and compute probabilities.**

Several years ago Wendy's Hamburgers advertised that there are 256 different ways to order your hamburger. You may choose to have, or omit, any combination of the following on your hamburger: mustard, ketchup, onion, pickle, tomato, relish, mayonnaise, and lettuce. Is the advertising correct? (See Goal 3 and Exercise 65.)

Introduction

The emphasis in Chapters 2, 3, and 4 is on descriptive statistics. In Chapter 2 we organize the prices of 80 vehicles sold last month at the Whitner Autoplex location of Auto USA into a frequency distribution. This frequency distribution shows the lowest and the highest selling prices and where the largest concentration of data occurs. In Chapter 3 we use measures of location and dispersion to locate a typical selling price and to examine the spread in the data. We describe the spread in the selling prices with measures of dispersion such as the range and the standard deviation. In Chapter 4 we develop charts and graphs, such as a scatter diagram, to further describe the data.

Descriptive statistics is concerned with summarizing data collected from past events. For example, we described the vehicle selling prices last month at Whitner Autoplex. We now turn to the second facet of statistics, namely, *computing the chance that something will occur in the future.* This facet of statistics is called **statistical inference** or **inferential statistics.**

Seldom does a decision maker have complete information from which to make a decision. For example:

- Toys and Things, a toy and puzzle manufacturer, recently developed a new game based on sports trivia. They want to know whether sports buffs will purchase the game. "Slam Dunk" and "Home Run" are two of the names under consideration. One way to minimize the risk of making a wrong decision is to hire a market research firm to take a sample of, say, 2,000 consumers from the population and ask each respondent for a reaction to the new game and its proposed titles. Using the sample results the company can estimate the proportion of the population that will purchase the game.
- The quality assurance department of a Bethlehem Steel mill must assure management that the quarter-inch wire being produced has an acceptable tensile strength. Obviously, not all the wire produced can be tested for tensile strength because testing requires the wire to be stretched until it breaks—thus destroying it. So a random sample of 10 pieces is selected and tested. Based on the test results, all the wire produced is deemed to be either satisfactory or unsatisfactory.

- Other questions involving uncertainty are: Should the daytime drama *Days of Our Lives* be discontinued immediately? Will a newly developed mint-flavored cereal be profitable if marketed? Will Charles Linden be elected to county auditor in Batavia County?

Statistical inference deals with conclusions about a population based on a sample taken from that population. (The populations for the preceding illustrations are: all consumers who like sports trivia games, all the quarter-inch steel wire produced, all television viewers who watch soaps, all who purchase breakfast cereal, and so on.)

Because there is uncertainty in decision making, it is important that all the known risks involved be scientifically evaluated. Helpful in this evaluation is *probability theory,* which has often been referred to as the science of uncertainty. The use of probability theory allows the decision maker with only limited information to analyze the risks and minimize the gamble inherent, for example, in marketing a new product or accepting an incoming shipment possibly containing defective parts.

Because probability concepts are so important in the field of statistical inference (to be discussed starting with Chapter 8), this chapter introduces the basic language of probability, including such terms as *experiment, event, subjective probability,* and *addition* and *multiplication rules.*

What Is a Probability?

No doubt you are familiar with terms such as *probability, chance,* and *likelihood.* They are often used interchangeably. The weather forecaster announces that there is a 70 percent chance of rain for Super Bowl Sunday. Based on a survey of consumers who tested a newly developed pickle with a banana taste, the probability is .03 that, if marketed, it will be a financial success. (This means that the chance of the banana-flavor pickle being accepted by the public is rather remote.) What is a probability? In general, it is a number that describes the chance that something will happen.

> **PROBABILITY** A value between zero and one, inclusive, describing the relative possibility (chance or likelihood) an event will occur.

A probability is frequently expressed as a decimal, such as .70, .27, or .50. However, it may be given as a fraction such as 7/10, 27/100, or 1/2. It can assume any number from 0 to 1, inclusive. If a company has only five sales regions, and each region's name or number is written on a slip of paper and the slips put in a hat, the probability of selecting one of the five regions is 1. The probability of selecting from the hat a slip of paper that reads "Pittsburgh Steelers" is 0. Thus, the probability of 1 represents something that is certain to happen, and the probability of 0 represents something that cannot happen.

The closer a probability is to 0, the more improbable it is the event will happen. The closer the probability is to 1, the more sure we are it will happen. The relationship is shown in the following diagram along with a few of our personal beliefs. You might, however, select a different probability for Slo Poke's chances to win the Kentucky Derby or for an increase in federal taxes.

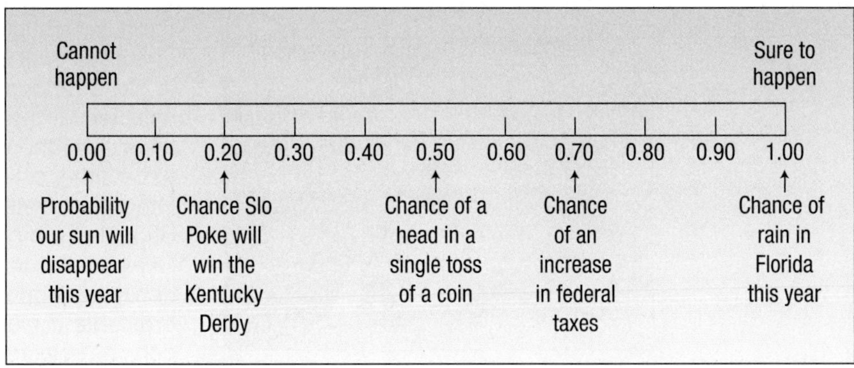

Three key words are used in the study of probability: **experiment, outcome,** and **event.** These terms are used in our everyday language, but in statistics they have specific meanings.

> **EXPERIMENT** A process that leads to the occurrence of one and only one of several possible observations.

This definition is more general than the one used in the physical sciences, where we picture someone manipulating test tubes or microscopes. In reference to probability, an experiment has two or more possible results, and it is uncertain which will occur.

> **OUTCOME** A particular result of an experiment.

For example, the tossing of a coin is an experiment. You may observe the toss of the coin, but you are unsure whether it will come up "heads" or "tails." Similarly, asking 500 college students whether they would purchase a new Dell computer system at a particular price is an experiment. If the coin is tossed, one particular outcome is a "head." The alternative outcome is a "tail." In the computer purchasing experiment, one possible outcome is that 273 students indicate they would purchase the computer. Another outcome is that 317 students would purchase the computer. Still another outcome is that 423 students indicate that they would purchase it. When one or more of the experiment's outcomes are observed, we call this an event.

EVENT A collection of one or more outcomes of an experiment.

Examples to clarify the definitions of the terms *experiment, outcome,* and *event* are presented in the following figure.

In the die-rolling experiment there are six possible outcomes, but there are many possible events. When counting the number of members of the board of directors for Fortune 500 companies over 60 years of age, the number of possible outcomes can be anywhere from zero to the total number of members. There are an even larger number of possible events in this experiment.

Experiment	Roll a die	Count the number of members of the board of directors for Fortune 500 companies who are over 60 years of age
All possible outcomes	Observe a 1 Observe a 2 Observe a 3 Observe a 4 Observe a 5 Observe a 6	None are over 60 One is over 60 Two are over 60 ... 29 are over 60 ... ... 48 are over 60 ...
Some possible events	Observe an even number Observe a number greater than 4 Observe a number 3 or less	More than 13 are over 60 Fewer than 20 are over 60

Self-Review 5–1

Video Games, Inc. recently developed a new video game. Its market potential is to be tested by 80 veteran game players.

(a) What is the experiment?
(b) What is one possible outcome?
(c) Suppose 65 players tried the new game and said they liked it. Is 65 a probability?
(d) The probability that the new game will be a success is computed to be −1.0. Comment.
(e) Specify one possible event.

Approaches to Assigning Probabilities

Two approaches to assigning probabilities will be discussed, namely, the *objective* and the *subjective* viewpoints. **Objective probability** is subdivided into (1) *classical probability* and (2) *empirical probability.*

Classical Probability

Classical probability is based on the assumption that the outcomes of an experiment are *equally likely.* Using the classical viewpoint, the probability of an event happening is computed by dividing the number of favorable outcomes by the number of possible outcomes:

DEFINITION OF CLASSICAL PROBABILITY

$$\text{Probability of an event} = \frac{\text{Number of favorable outcomes}}{\text{Total number of possible outcomes}} \qquad \textbf{[5–1]}$$

EXAMPLE

Consider an experiment of rolling a six-sided die. What is the probability of the event "an even number of spots appear face up"?

SOLUTION

The possible outcomes are:

a one-spot ⚀	a four-spot ⚃
a two-spot ⚁	a five-spot ⚄
a three-spot ⚂	a six-spot ⚅

There are three "favorable" outcomes (a two, a four, and a six) in the collection of six equally likely possible outcomes. Therefore:

$$\text{Probability of an even number} = \frac{3}{6} \begin{matrix} \leftarrow \\ \leftarrow \end{matrix} \boxed{\frac{\text{Number of favorable outcomes}}{\text{Total number of possible outcomes}}}$$

$$= .5$$

The mutually exclusive concept appeared earlier in our study of frequency distributions in Chapter 2. Recall that we create classes so that a particular event is included in only one of the classes and there is no overlap between classes. Thus, only one of several events can occur at a particular time.

MUTUALLY EXCLUSIVE The occurrence of one event means that none of the other events can occur at the same time.

The variable "gender" presents mutually exclusive outcomes, male and female. An employee selected at random is either male or female but cannot be both. A manufactured part is acceptable or unacceptable. The part cannot be both acceptable and unacceptable at the same time. In a sample of manufactured parts, the event of selecting an unacceptable part and the event of selecting an acceptable part are mutually exclusive.

If an experiment has a set of events that includes every possible outcome, such as the events "an even number" and "an odd number" in the die-tossing experiment, then the set of events is **collectively exhaustive.** For the die-tossing experiment, every outcome will be either even or odd. So the set is collectively exhaustive.

> **COLLECTIVELY EXHAUSTIVE** At least one of the events must occur when an experiment is conducted.

Sum of probabilities = 1

If the set of events is collectively exhaustive and the events are mutually exclusive, the sum of the probabilities is 1. Historically, the classical approach to probability was developed and applied in the 17th and 18th centuries to games of chance, such as cards and dice. It is unnecessary to do an experiment to determine the probability of an event occurring using the classical approach because the total number of outcomes is known before the experiment. The flip of a coin has two possible outcomes; the roll of a die has six possible outcomes. We can logically arrive at the probability of getting a tail on the toss of one coin or three heads on the toss of three coins.

The classical approach to probability can also be applied to lotteries. In South Carolina, one of the games of the Education Lottery is "Pick 3." A person buys a lottery ticket and selects three numbers between 0 and 9. Once per week, the three numbers are randomly selected from a machine that tumbles three containers each with balls numbered 0 through 9. One way to win is to match the numbers and the order of the numbers. Given that 1,000 possible outcomes exist (000 through 999), the probability of winning with any three-digit number is 0.001, or 1 in 1,000.

Empirical Probability

Another way to define probability is based on **relative frequencies.** The probability of an event happening is determined by observing what fraction of the time similar events happened in the past. In terms of a formula:

$$\text{Probability of event happening} = \frac{\text{Number of times event occurred in past}}{\text{Total number of observations}}$$

The empirical concept is illustrated with the following example.

EXAMPLE

On February 1, 2003, the space shuttle Columbia exploded. This was the second disaster in 113 space missions for NASA. On the basis of this information, what is the probability that a future mission is successfully completed?

SOLUTION

To simplify, letters or numbers may be used. *P* stands for probability, and in this case *P(A)* stands for the probability a future mission is successfully completed.

$$\text{Probability of a successful flight} = \frac{\text{Number of successful flights}}{\text{Total number of flights}}$$

$$P(A) = \frac{111}{113} = .98$$

We can use this as an estimate of probability. In other words, based on past experience, the probability is .98 that a future space shuttle mission will be successfully completed.

Subjective Probability

If there is little or no past experience or information on which to base a probability, it may be arrived at subjectively. Essentially, this means an individual evaluates the available opinions and other information and then estimates or assigns the probability. This probability is aptly called a **subjective probability.**

SUBJECTIVE CONCEPT OF PROBABILITY The likelihood (probability) of a particular event happening that is assigned by an individual based on whatever information is available.

Illustrations of subjective probability are:

1. Estimating the likelihood the New England Patriots will play in the Super Bowl next year.
2. Estimating the probability General Motors Corp. will lose its number 1 ranking in total units sold to Ford Motor Co. or DaimlerChrysler within 2 years.
3. Estimating the likelihood you will earn an *A* in this course.

The types of probability are summarized in Chart 5–1. A probability statement always assigns a likelihood of an event that has not yet occurred. There is, of course, a considerable latitude in the degree of uncertainty that surrounds this probability, based primarily on the knowledge possessed by the individual concerning the underlying process. The individual possesses a great deal of knowledge about the toss of a die and can state that the probability that a one-spot will appear face up on the toss of a true die is one-sixth. But we know very little concerning the acceptance in the marketplace of a new and untested product. For example, even though a market research director tests a newly developed product in 40 retail stores and states that there is a 70 percent chance that the product will have sales of more than 1 million units, she still has little knowledge of how consumers will react when it is marketed nationally. In both cases (the case of the person rolling a die and the testing of a new product) the individual is assigning a probability value to an event of interest, and a difference exists only in the predictor's confidence in the precision of the estimate. However, regardless of the viewpoint, the same laws of probability (presented in the following sections) will be applied.

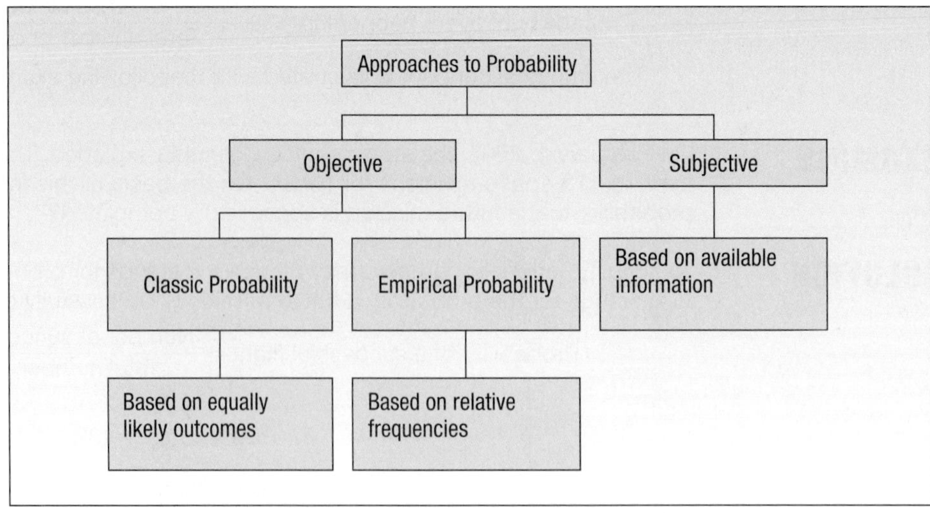

CHART 5–1 Summary of Approaches to Probability

Self-Review 5–2

1. One card will be randomly selected from a standard 52-card deck. What is the probability the card will be a queen? Which approach to probability did you use to answer this question?
2. The Center for Child Care reports on the parental status of 539 children. The parents of 333 children are married, 182 divorced, and 24 widowed. What is the probability a particular child chosen at random will have a parent who is divorced? Which approach did you use?
3. What is the probability that the Dow Jones Industrial Average will exceed 12,000 during the next 12 months? Which approach to probability did you use to answer this question?

Exercises

1. Some people are in favor of reducing federal taxes to increase consumer spending and others are against it. Two persons are selected and their opinions are recorded. List the possible outcomes.

2. A quality control inspector selects a part to be tested. The part is then declared acceptable, repairable, or scrapped. Then another part is tested. List the possible outcomes of this experiment regarding two parts.

3. A survey of 34 students at the Wall College of Business showed the following majors:

Accounting	10
Finance	5
Info. Systems	3
Management	6
Marketing	10

Suppose you select a student and observe his or her major.
   a. What is the probability he or she is a management major?
   b. Which concept of probability did you use to make this estimate?

4. A large company that must hire a new president prepares a final list of five candidates, all of whom are qualified. Two of these candidates are members of a minority group. To avoid bias in the selection of the candidate, the company decides to select the president by lottery.
   a. What is the probability one of the minority candidates is hired?
   b. Which concept of probability did you use to make this estimate?

5. In each of the following cases, indicate whether classical, empirical, or subjective probability is used.
   a. A basketball player makes 30 out of 50 foul shots. The probability is .6 that she makes the next foul shot attempted.
   b. A seven-member committee of students is formed to study environmental issues. What is the likelihood that any one of the seven is chosen as the spokesperson?
   c. You purchase one of 5 million tickets sold for Lotto Canada. What is the likelihood you win the $1 million jackpot?
   d. The probability of an earthquake in northern California in the next 10 years is .80.

6. A firm will promote two employees out of a group of six men and three women.
   a. List the outcomes of this experiment if there is particular concern about gender equity.
   b. Which concept of probability would you use to estimate these probabilities?

7. A sample of 40 oil industry executives was selected to test a questionnaire. One question about environmental issues required a yes or no answer.
   a. What is the experiment?
   b. List one possible event.
   c. Ten of the 40 executives responded "yes." Based on these sample responses, what is the probability that an oil industry executive will respond "yes"?
   d. What concept of probability does this illustrate?
   e. Are each of the possible outcomes equally likely and mutually exclusive?

8. A sample of 2,000 licensed drivers revealed the following number of speeding violations.

Number of Violations	Number of Drivers
0	1,910
1	46
2	18
3	12
4	9
5 or more	5
Total	2,000

a. What is the experiment?
b. List one possible event.
c. What is the probability that a particular driver had exactly two speeding violations?
d. What concept of probability does this illustrate?

9. Bank of America customers select their own three-digit personal identification number (PIN) for use at ATMs.
a. Think of this as an experiment and list four possible outcomes.
b. What is the probability Mr. Jones and Mrs. Smith select the same PIN?
c. Which concept of probability did you use to answer b?

10. An investor buys 100 shares of AT&T stock and records its price change daily.
a. List several possible events for this experiment.
b. Estimate the probability for each event you described in a.
c. Which concept of probability did you use in b?

Some Rules for Computing Probabilities

Now that we have defined probability and described the different approaches to probability, we turn our attention to computing the probability of two or more events by applying rules of addition and multiplication.

Rules of Addition

Mutually exclusive events cannot both happen.

Special Rule of Addition To apply the **special rule of addition,** the events must be mutually exclusive. Recall that *mutually exclusive* means that when one event occurs, none of the other events can occur at the same time. An illustration of mutually exclusive events in the die-tossing experiment is the events "a number 4 or larger" and "a number 2 or smaller." If the outcome is in the first group {4, 5, and 6}, then it cannot also be in the second group {1 and 2}. Another illustration is a product coming off the assembly line cannot be defective and satisfactory at the same time.

If two events *A* and *B* are mutually exclusive, the special rule of addition states that the probability of one *or* the other events occurring equals the sum of their probabilities. This rule is expressed in the following formula:

SPECIAL RULE OF ADDITION $P(A \text{ or } B) = P(A) + P(B)$ **[5–2]**

For three mutually exclusive events designated *A, B,* and *C,* the rule is written:

$$P(A \text{ or } B \text{ or } C) = P(A) + P(B) + P(C)$$

An example will help to show the details.

EXAMPLE

An automatic Shaw machine fills plastic bags with a mixture of beans, broccoli, and other vegetables. Most of the bags contain the correct weight, but because of the variation in the size of the beans and other vegetables, a package might be underweight or overweight. A check of 4,000 packages filled in the past month revealed:

Weight	Event	Number of Packages	Probability of Occurrence	
Underweight	*A*	100	.025	← $\frac{100}{4,000}$
Satisfactory	*B*	3,600	.900	
Overweight	*C*	300	.075	
		4,000	1.000	

What is the probability that a particular package will be either underweight or overweight?

SOLUTION

The outcome "underweight" is the event *A*. The outcome "overweight" is the event *C*. Applying the special rule of addition:

$$P(A \text{ or } C) = P(A) + P(C) = .025 + .075 = .10$$

Note that the events are mutually exclusive, meaning that a package of mixed vegetables cannot be underweight, satisfactory, and overweight at the same time. They are also collectively exhaustive; that is, a selected package must be either underweight, satisfactory, or overweight.

A Venn diagram is a useful tool to depict addition or multiplication rules.

English logician J. Venn (1835–1888) developed a diagram to portray graphically the outcome of an experiment. The *mutually exclusive* concept and various other rules for combining probabilities can be illustrated using this device. To construct a Venn diagram, a space is first enclosed representing the total of all possible outcomes. This space is usually in the form of a rectangle. An event is then represented by a circular area which is drawn inside the rectangle proportional to the probability of the event. The following Venn diagram represents the *mutually exclusive* concept. There is no overlapping of events, meaning that the events are mutually exclusive.

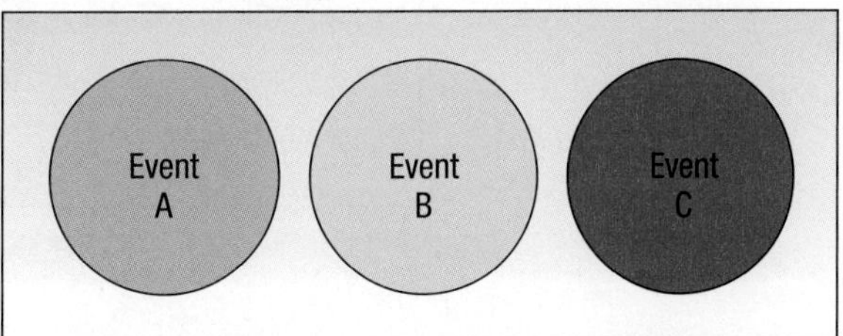

The **complement** of an event *A* is the event that *A* does **not** occur. To put it another way, the collection of outcomes when *A* does not happen is the complement of *A*. The probability that a bag of mixed vegetables selected is underweight, *P*(*A*), plus the probability that it is not an underweight bag, written *P*(~*A*) and read "not *A*," must logically equal 1. This is written:

$$P(A) + P(\sim A) = 1$$

This can be revised to read:

COMPLEMENT RULE	$P(A) = 1 - P(\sim A)$	[5–3]

This is the **complement rule.** It is used to determine the probability of an event occurring by subtracting the probability of the event not occurring from 1. This rule is useful because sometimes it is easier to calculate the probability of an event happening by determining the probability of it not happening and subtracting the result from 1. Notice that the events A and $\sim A$ are mutually exclusive and collectively exhaustive. Therefore, the probabilities of A and $\sim A$ sum to 1. A Venn diagram illustrating the complement rule is shown as:

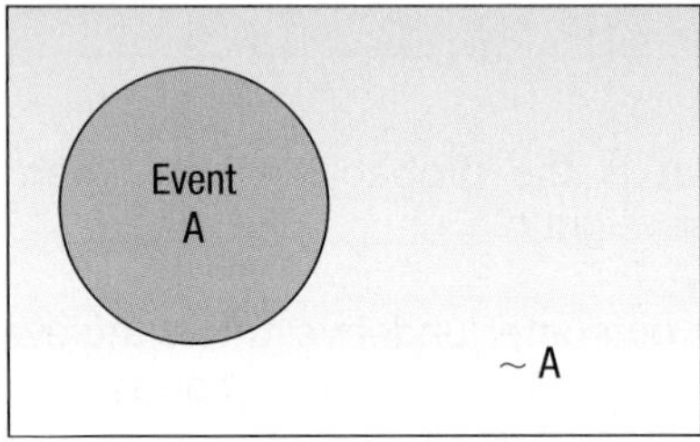

EXAMPLE

Recall the probability a bag of mixed vegetables is underweight is .025 and the probability of an overweight bag is .075. Use the complement rule to show the probability of a satisfactory bag is .900. Show the solution using a Venn diagram.

SOLUTION

The probability the bag is unsatisfactory equals the probability the bag is overweight plus the probability it is underweight. That is, $P(A \text{ or } C) = P(A) + P(C) = .025 + .075 = .100$. The bag is satisfactory if it is not underweight or overweight, so $P(B) = 1 - [P(A) + P(C)] = 1 - [.025 + .075] = 0.900$. The Venn diagram portraying this situation is:

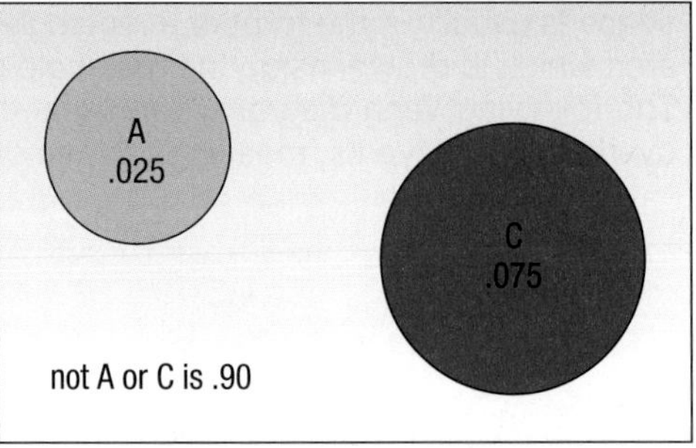

Self-Review 5–3

A sample of employees of Worldwide Enterprises is to be surveyed about a new pension plan. The employees are classified as follows:

Classification	Event	Number of Employees
Supervisors	A	120
Maintenance	B	50
Production	C	1,460
Management	D	302
Secretarial	E	68

(a) What is the probability that the first person selected is:
   (i) either in maintenance or a secretary?
   (ii) not in management?
(b) Draw a Venn diagram illustrating your answers to part (a).
(c) Are the events in part (a)(i) complementary or mutually exclusive or both?

Statistics in Action

If you wish to get some attention at the next gathering you attend, announce that you believe that at least two people present were born on the same date—that is, the same day of the year but not necessarily the same year. If there are 30 people in the room, the probability of a duplicate is .706. If there are 60 people in the room, the probability is .994 that at least two people share the same birthday. With as few as 23 people the chances are even, that is .50, that at least two people share the same birthday. Hint: To compute this, find the probability everyone was born on a different day and use the complement rule.

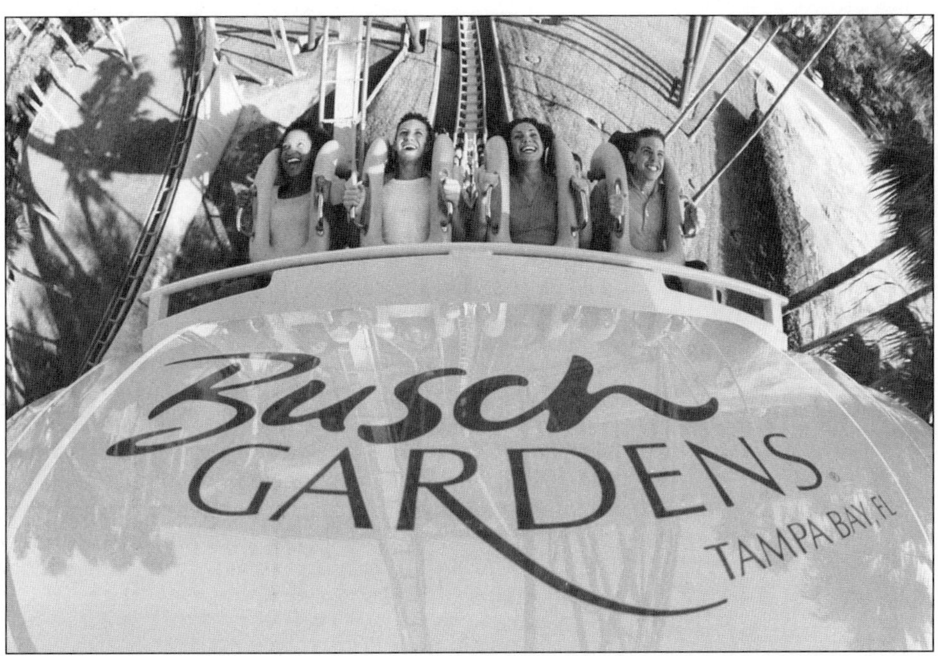

The General Rule of Addition The outcomes of an experiment may not be mutually exclusive. Suppose, for illustration, that the Florida Tourist Commission selected a sample of 200 tourists who visited the state during the year. The survey revealed that 120 tourists went to Disney World and 100 went to Busch Gardens near Tampa. What is the probability that a person selected visited either Disney World or Busch Gardens? If the special rule of addition is used, the probability of selecting a tourist who went to Disney World is .60, found by 120/200. Similarly, the probability of a tourist going to Busch Gardens is .50. The sum of these probabilities is 1.10. We know, however, that this probability cannot be greater than 1. The explanation is that many tourists visited both attractions and are being counted twice! A check of the survey responses revealed that 60 out of 200 sampled did, in fact, visit both attractions.

To answer our question, "What is the probability a selected person visited either Disney World or Busch Gardens?" (1) add the probability that a tourist visited Disney World and the probability he/she visited Busch Gardens, and (2) subtract the probability of visiting both. Thus:

$$P(\text{Disney or Busch}) = P(\text{Disney}) + P(\text{Busch}) - P(\text{both Disney and Busch})$$
$$= .60 + .50 - .30 = .80$$

When two events both occur, the probability is called a **joint probability.** The probability that a tourist visits both attractions (.30) is an example of a joint probability.

The following Venn diagram shows two events that are not mutually exclusive. The two events overlap to illustrate the joint event that some people have visited both attractions.

JOINT PROBABILITY A probability that measures the likelihood two or more events will happen concurrently.

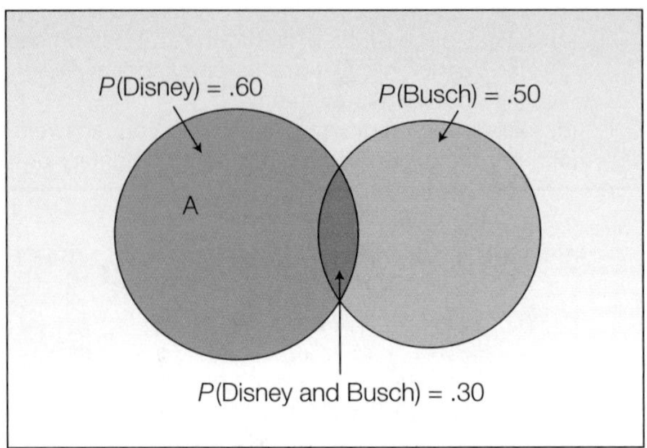

This rule for two events designated A and B is written:

GENERAL RULE OF ADDITION $P(A \text{ or } B) = P(A) + P(B) - P(A \text{ and } B)$ **[5–4]**

For the expression $P(A \text{ or } B)$, the word *or* suggests that A may occur or B may occur. This also includes the possibility that A and B may occur. This use of *or* is sometimes called an **inclusive.** You could also write $P(A \text{ or } B \text{ or both})$ to emphasize that the union of the events includes the intersection of A and B.

If we compare the general and special rules of addition, the important difference is determining if the events are mutually exclusive. If the events *are* mutually exclusive, then the joint probability $P(A \text{ and } B)$ is 0 and we could use the special rule of addition. Otherwise we must account for the joint probability and use the general rule of addition.

EXAMPLE

What is the probability that a card chosen at random from a standard deck of cards will be either a king or a heart?

SOLUTION

We may be inclined to add the probability of a king and the probability of a heart. But this creates a problem. If we do that, the king of hearts is counted with the kings and also with the hearts. So, if we simply add the probability of a king (there are 4 in a deck of 52 cards) to the probability of a heart (there are 13 in a deck of 52 cards) and report that 17 out of 52 cards meet the requirement, we have counted the king of hearts twice. We need to subtract 1 card from the 17 so the king of hearts is counted only once. Thus, there are 16 cards that are either hearts or kings. So the probability is 16/52 = .3077.

Card	Probability	Explanation
King	$P(A) = 4/52$	4 kings in a deck of 52 cards
Heart	$P(B) = 13/52$	13 hearts in a deck of 52 cards
King of hearts	$P(A \text{ and } B) = 1/52$	1 king of hearts in a deck of 52 cards

From formula (5–4):

$$\begin{aligned} P(A \text{ or } B) &= P(A) + P(B) - P(A \text{ and } B) \\ &= 4/52 + 13/52 - 1/52 \\ &= 16/52, \text{ or } .3077 \end{aligned}$$

A Venn diagram portrays these outcomes, which are not mutually exclusive.

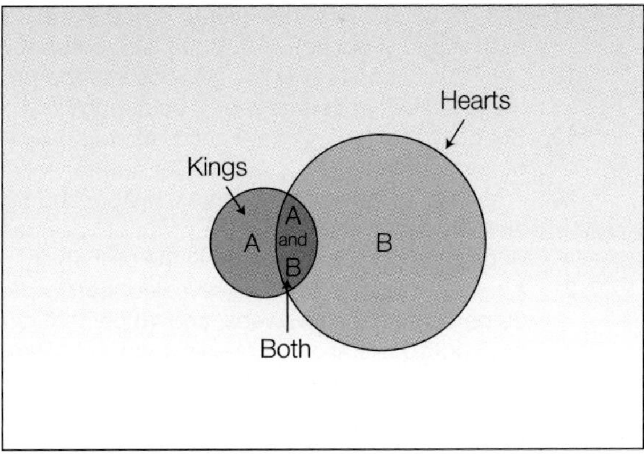

Self-Review 5–4

Routine physical examinations are conducted annually as part of a health service program for General Concrete, Inc., employees. It was discovered that 8 percent of the employees need corrective shoes, 15 percent need major dental work, and 3 percent need both corrective shoes and major dental work.

(a) What is the probability that an employee selected at random will need either corrective shoes or major dental work?
(b) Show this situation in the form of a Venn diagram.

Exercises

11. The events *A* and *B* are mutually exclusive. Suppose $P(A) = .30$ and $P(B) = .20$. What is the probability of either *A* or *B* occurring? What is the probability that neither *A* nor *B* will happen?

12. The events *X* and *Y* are mutually exclusive. Suppose $P(X) = .05$ and $P(Y) = .02$. What is the probability of either *X* or *Y* occurring? What is the probability that neither *X* nor *Y* will happen?

13. A study of 200 grocery chains revealed these incomes after taxes:

Income after Taxes	Number of Firms
Under $1 million	102
$1 million to $20 million	61
$20 million or more	37

a. What is the probability a particular chain has under $1 million in income after taxes?
b. What is the probability a grocery chain selected at random has either an income between $1 million and $20 million, or an income of $20 million or more? What rule of probability was applied?

14. The chair of the board of directors says, "There is a 50 percent chance this company will earn a profit, a 30 percent chance it will break even, and a 20 percent chance it will lose money next quarter."
a. Use an addition rule to find the probability they will not lose money next quarter.
b. Use the complement rule to find the probability they will not lose money next quarter.

15. Suppose the probability you will get a grade of A in this class is .25 and the probability you will get a B is .50. What is the probability your grade will be above a C?

16. Two coins are tossed. If *A* is the event "two heads" and *B* is the event "two tails," are *A* and *B* mutually exclusive? Are they complements?

17. The probabilities of the events *A* and *B* are .20 and .30, respectively. The probability that both *A* and *B* occur is .15. What is the probability of either *A* or *B* occurring?

18. Let $P(X) = .55$ and $P(Y) = .35$. Assume the probability that they both occur is .20. What is the probability of either *X* or *Y* occurring?

19. Suppose the two events *A* and *B* are mutually exclusive. What is the probability of their joint occurrence?

20. A student is taking two courses, history and math. The probability the student will pass the history course is .60, and the probability of passing the math course is .70. The probability of passing both is .50. What is the probability of passing at least one?

21. A survey of top executives revealed that 35 percent of them regularly read *Time* magazine, 20 percent read *Newsweek,* and 40 percent read *U.S. News and World Report.* Ten percent read both *Time* and *U.S. News and World Report.*
   a. What is the probability that a particular top executive reads either *Time* or *U.S. News and World Report* regularly?
   b. What is the probability .10 called?
   c. Are the events mutually exclusive? Explain.

22. A study by the National Park Service revealed that 50 percent of vacationers going to the Rocky Mountain region visit Yellowstone Park, 40 percent visit the Tetons, and 35 percent visit both.
   a. What is the probability a vacationer will visit at least one of these attractions?
   b. What is the probability .35 called?
   c. Are the events mutually exclusive? Explain.

Rules of Multiplication

When we use the rules of addition we find the likelihood of combining two events. Venn diagrams illustrate this as the "union" of two events. In this section we find the likelihood that two events both happen. For example, a marketing firm may want to estimate the likelihood that a person is 21 years old or older *and* buys a Hummer. Venn diagrams illustrate this as the intersection of two events. To find the likelihood of two events happening we use the rules of multiplication. There are two rules of multiplication, the Special Rule and the General Rule.

Special Rule of Multiplication

The special rule of multiplication requires that two events *A* and *B* are independent. Two events are independent if the occurrence of one event does not alter the probability of the occurrence of the other event.

INDEPENDENCE The occurrence of one event has no effect on the probability of the occurrence of another event.

One way to think about independence is to assume that events *A* and *B* occur at different times. For example, when event *B* occurs after event *A* occurs, does *A* have any effect on the likelihood that event *B* occurs? If the answer is no, then *A* and *B* are independent events. To illustrate independence, suppose two coins are tossed. The outcome of a coin toss (head or tail) is unaffected by the outcome of any other prior coin toss (head or tail).

For two independent events *A* and *B*, the probability that *A* and *B* will both occur is found by multiplying the two probabilities. This is the **special rule of multiplication** and is written symbolically as:

SPECIAL RULE OF MULTIPLICATION $P(A \text{ and } B) = P(A)P(B)$ **[5–5]**

For three independent events, *A*, *B*, and *C*, the special rule of multiplication used to determine the probability that all three events will occur is:

$$P(A \text{ and } B \text{ and } C) = P(A)P(B)P(C)$$

EXAMPLE

A survey by the American Automobile Association (AAA) revealed 60 percent of its members made airline reservations last year. Two members are selected at random. What is the probability both made airline reservations last year?

SOLUTION

The probability the first member made an airline reservation last year is .60, written $P(R_1) = .60$, where R_1 refers to the fact that the first member made a reservation. The probability that the second member selected made a reservation is also .60, so $P(R_2) = .60$. Since the number of AAA members is very large, you may assume that R_1 and R_2 are independent. Consequently, using formula (5–5), the probability they both make a reservation is .36, found by:

$$P(R_1 \text{ and } R_2) = P(R_1)P(R_2) = (.60)(.60) = .36$$

All possible outcomes can be shown as follows. *R* means a reservation is made, and *NR* means no reservation was made.

With the probabilities and the complement rule, we can compute the joint probability of each outcome. For example, the probability that neither member makes a reservation is .16. Further, the probability of the first or the second member (special addition rule) making a reservation is .48 (.24 + .24). You can also observe that the outcomes are mutually exclusive and collectively exhaustive. Therefore, the probabilities sum to 1.00.

Outcomes		Joint Probability	
R_1	R_2	(.60)(.60) =	.36
R_1	*NR*	(.60)(.40) =	.24
NR	R_2	(.40)(.60) =	.24
NR	*NR*	(.40)(.40) =	.16
Total			1.00

Self-Review 5–5

From experience, Teton Tire knows the probability is .80 that their XB-70 will last 60,000 miles before it becomes bald or fails. An adjustment is made on any tire that does not last 60,000 miles. You purchase four XB-70s. What is the probability all four tires will last at least 60,000 miles?

If two events are not independent, they are referred to as **dependent.** To illustrate dependency, suppose there are 10 rolls of film in a box, and it is known that 3 are defective. A roll of film is selected from the box. The probability of selecting a defective roll is 3/10, and the probability of selecting a good roll is 7/10. Then a second roll is selected from the box without the first one being returned to the box. The probability this second roll is defective *depends* on whether the first roll selected was defective or good. The probability that the second roll is defective is:

2/9, if the first roll was defective. (Only two defective rolls remain in the box containing nine rolls.)

3/9, if the first roll selected was good. (All three defective rolls are still in the box containing nine rolls.)

The fraction 2/9 (or 3/9) is aptly called a **conditional probability** because its value is conditional on (dependent on) whether a defective or a good roll of film is chosen in the first selection from the box.

CONDITIONAL PROBABILITY The probability of a particular event occurring, given that another event has occurred.

General Rule of Multiplication We use the general rule of multiplication to find the joint probability of two events when the events are not independent. For example, when event B occurs after event A occurs, and A has an effect on the likelihood that event B occurs, then A and B are not independent. To illustrate, suppose there are 10 rolls of film in a box, and it is known that 3 are defective. A roll of film is selected from the box. The probability of selecting a defective roll is 3/10, and the probability of selecting a good roll is 7/10. Then a second roll is selected from the box without returning the first one to the box. The probability that the second roll is defective is affected by the prior event that the first roll was defective or good. The probability that the second roll is defective is either:

P(second roll is defective | first roll was defective) is 2/9. (Only two defective rolls remain in the box that now contains nine rolls.)
P(second roll is defective | first roll was good) is 3/9. (All three defective rolls are still in the box that now contains nine rolls.)

The general rule of multiplication states that for two events, A and B, the joint probability that both events will happen is found by multiplying the probability event A will happen by the conditional probability of event B occurring given that A has occurred. Symbolically, the joint probability, $P(A \text{ and } B)$, is found by:

GENERAL RULE OF MULTIPLICATION $P(A \text{ and } B) = P(A)P(B/A)$ **[5–6]**

The symbols $P(B/A)$ stand for the conditional probability that B will occur after we have information that the related event A has occurred. The vertical line is usually read "given that." So $P(B/A)$ is the probability of B given A.

EXAMPLE

To illustrate the formula, let's use the problem with 10 rolls of film in a box, 3 of which are defective. Two rolls are to be selected, one after the other. What is the probability of selecting a defective roll followed by another defective roll?

SOLUTION

The first roll of film selected from the box being found defective is event D_1, $P(D_1) =$ 3/10 because 3 out of the 10 are defective. Selecting a second roll that is defective is event D_2. Therefore, $P(D_2|D_1) = 2/9$, because after the first selection was found to be defective, only 2 defective rolls of film remained in the box containing 9 rolls. Determining the probability of two defectives [see formula (5–6)]:

$$P(D_1 \text{ and } D_2) = P(D_1)P(D_2|D_1) = \left(\frac{3}{10}\right)\left(\frac{2}{9}\right) = \frac{6}{90}, \text{ or about .07}$$

Incidentally, it is assumed that this experiment was conducted without *replacement*—that is, the first defective roll of film was not thrown back in the box before the next roll was selected. It should also be noted that the general rule of multiplication can be extended to more than two events. For three events, A, B, and C, the formula would be:

$$P(A \text{ and } B \text{ and } C) = P(A)P(B|A)P(C|A \text{ and } B)$$

For illustration, the probability the first three rolls chosen from the box will all be defective is .00833, found by:

$$P(D_1 \text{ and } D_2 \text{ and } D_3) = P(D_1)P(D_2|D_1)P(D_3|D_1 \text{ and } D_2)$$

$$= \left(\frac{3}{10}\right)\left(\frac{2}{9}\right)\left(\frac{1}{8}\right) = \frac{6}{720} = .00833$$

Self-Review 5–6

The board of directors of Tarbell Industries consists of eight men and four women. A four-person search committee is to be chosen at random to conduct a nationwide search for a new company president.

(a) What is the probability all four members of the search committee will be women?
(b) What is the probability all four members will be men?
(c) Does the sum of the probabilities for the events described in parts (a) and (b) equal 1? Explain.

Statistics in Action

In 2000 George W. Bush won the Presidency by the slimmest of margins. Many election stories resulted, some involving voting irregularities, others raising interesting election questions. In a local Michigan election there was a tie between two candidates for an elected position. To break the tie the candidates drew a slip of paper from a box that contained two slips of paper, one marked "Winner" and the other unmarked. To determine which candidate drew first, election officials flipped a coin. The winner of the coin flip also drew the winning slip of paper. But was the coin flip really necessary? No, because the two events are independent. Winning the coin flip did not alter the probability of either candidate drawing the winning slip of paper.

Contingency Tables

Often we tally the results of a survey into a two-way table and use the results of the tally to determine various probabilities. We described this idea beginning on page 109 in Chapter 4. To review, we refer to a two-way table as a contingency table.

CONTINGENCY TABLE A table used to classify sample observations according to two or more identifiable characteristics.

A contingency table is a cross tabulation that simultaneously summarizes two variables of interest and their relationship. The level of measurement can be nominal. Below are several examples.

- A survey of 150 adults classified each as to gender and the number of movies attended last month. Each respondent is classified according to two criteria—the number of movies attended and gender.

	Gender		
Movies Attended	**Men**	**Women**	**Total**
0	20	40	60
1	40	30	70
2 or more	10	10	20
Total	70	80	150

- The American Coffee Producers Association reports the following information on age and the amount of coffee consumed in a month.

	Coffee Consumption			
Age (Years)	**Low**	**Moderate**	**High**	**Total**
Under 30	36	32	24	92
30 up to 40	18	30	27	75
40 up to 50	10	24	20	54
50 and over	26	24	29	79
Total	90	110	100	300

According to this table each of the 300 respondents is classified according to two criteria: (1) age and (2) the amount of coffee consumed.

The following example shows how the rules of addition and multiplication are used when we employ contingency tables.

EXAMPLE

A sample of executives was surveyed about their loyalty to the company. One of the questions was, "If you were given an offer by another company equal to or slightly better than your present position, would you remain with the company or take the other position?" The responses of the 200 executives in the survey were cross-classified with their length of service with the company. (See Table 5–1.)

TABLE 5–1 Loyalty of Executives and Length of Service with Company

	Length of Service				
Loyalty	**Less than 1 Year** B_1	**1–5 Years** B_2	**6–10 Years** B_3	**More than 10 Years** B_4	**Total**
Would remain, A_1	10	30	5	75	120
Would not remain, A_2	25	15	10	30	80
	35	45	15	105	200

What is the probability of randomly selecting an executive who is loyal to the company (would remain) and who has more than 10 years of service?

SOLUTION

Note that two events occur at the same time—the executive would remain with the company, and he or she has more than 10 years of service.

1. Event A_1 happens if a randomly selected executive will remain with the company despite an equal or slightly better offer from another company. To find the probability that event A_1 will happen, refer to Table 5–1. Note there are 120 executives out of the 200 in the survey who would remain with the company, so $P(A_1) = 120/200$, or .60.
2. Event B_4 happens if a randomly selected executive has more than 10 years of service with the company. Thus, $P(B_4|A_1)$ is the conditional probability that an executive with more than 10 years of service would remain with the company despite an equal or slightly better offer from another company. Referring to the contingency table, Table 5–1, 75 of the 120 executives who would remain have more than 10 years of service, so $P(B_4|A_1) = 75/120$.

Solving for the probability that an executive randomly selected will be one who would remain with the company and who has more than 10 years of service with the company, using the general rule of multiplication in formula (5–6), gives:

$$P(A_1 \text{ and } B_4) = P(A_1)P(B_4|A_1) = \left(\frac{120}{200}\right)\left(\frac{75}{120}\right) = \frac{9{,}000}{24{,}000} = .375$$

To find the probability of selecting an executive who would remain with the company *or* has less than 1 year of experience we use the general rule of addition, formula (5–4).

1. Event A_1 refers to executives that would remain with the company. So $P(A_1) = 120/200 = .60$.
2. Event B_1 refers to executives that have been with the company less than 1 year. The probability of B_1 is $P(B_1) = 35/200 = .175$.
3. The events A_1 and B_1 are not mutually exclusive. That is, an executive can both be willing to remain with the company and have less than 1 year of experience. We write this probability, which is called the joint probability, as $P(A_1 \text{ and } B_1)$. There are 10 executives who would both stay with the company and have less than 1 year of service, so $P(A_1 \text{ and } B_1) = 10/200 = .05$. These 10 people are in both

groups, those who would remain with the company and those with less than 1 year with the company. They are actually being counted twice, so we need to subtract out this value.

4. We insert these values in formula (5–4) and the result is as follows.

$$P(A_1 \text{ or } B_1) = P(A_1) + P(B_1) - P(A_1 \text{ and } B_1)$$
$$= .60 + .175 - .05 = .725$$

So the likelihood that a selected executive would either remain with the company or has been with the company less than 1 year is .725.

Self-Review 5–7

Refer to Table 5–1 to find the following probabilities.

(a) What is the probability of selecting an executive with more than 10 years of service?
(b) What is the probability of selecting an executive who would not remain with the company, given that he or she has more than 10 years of service?
(c) What is the probability of selecting an executive with more than 10 years of service or one who would not remain with the company?

Tree Diagrams

The **tree diagram** is a graph that is helpful in organizing calculations that involve several stages. Each segment in the tree is one stage of the problem. The branches of a tree diagram are weighted by probabilities. We will use the data in Table 5–1 to show the construction of a tree diagram.

Steps in constructing a tree diagram

1. To construct a tree diagram, we begin by drawing a heavy dot on the left to represent the root of the tree (see Chart 5–2).
2. For this problem, two main branches go out from the root, the upper one representing "would remain" and the lower one "would not remain." Their probabilities are written on the branches, namely, 120/200 and 80/200. These probabilities could also be denoted $P(A_1)$ and $P(A_2)$.
3. Four branches "grow" out of each of the two main branches. These branches represent the length of service—less than 1 year, 1–5 years, 6–10 years, and more than 10 years. The conditional probabilities for the upper branch of the tree, 10/120, 30/120, 5/120, and so on are written on the appropriate branches. These are $P(B_1|A_1)$, $P(B_2|A_1)$, $P(B_3|A_1)$, and $P(B_4|A_1)$, where B_1 refers to less than 1 year of service, B_2 1 to 5 years, B_3 6 to 10 years, and B_4 more than 10 years. Next, write the conditional probabilities for the lower branch.
4. Finally, joint probabilities, that the events A_1 and B_i or the events A_2 and B_i will occur together, are shown on the right side. For example, the joint probability of randomly selecting an executive who would remain with the company and who has less than 1 year of service, from formula (5–6), is:

$$P(A_1 \text{ and } B_1) = P(A_1)P(B_1|A_1) = \left(\frac{120}{200}\right)\left(\frac{10}{120}\right) = .05$$

Because the joint probabilities represent all possible outcomes (would remain, 6–10 years service; would not remain, more than 10 years of service; etc.), they must sum to 1.00 (see Chart 5–2).

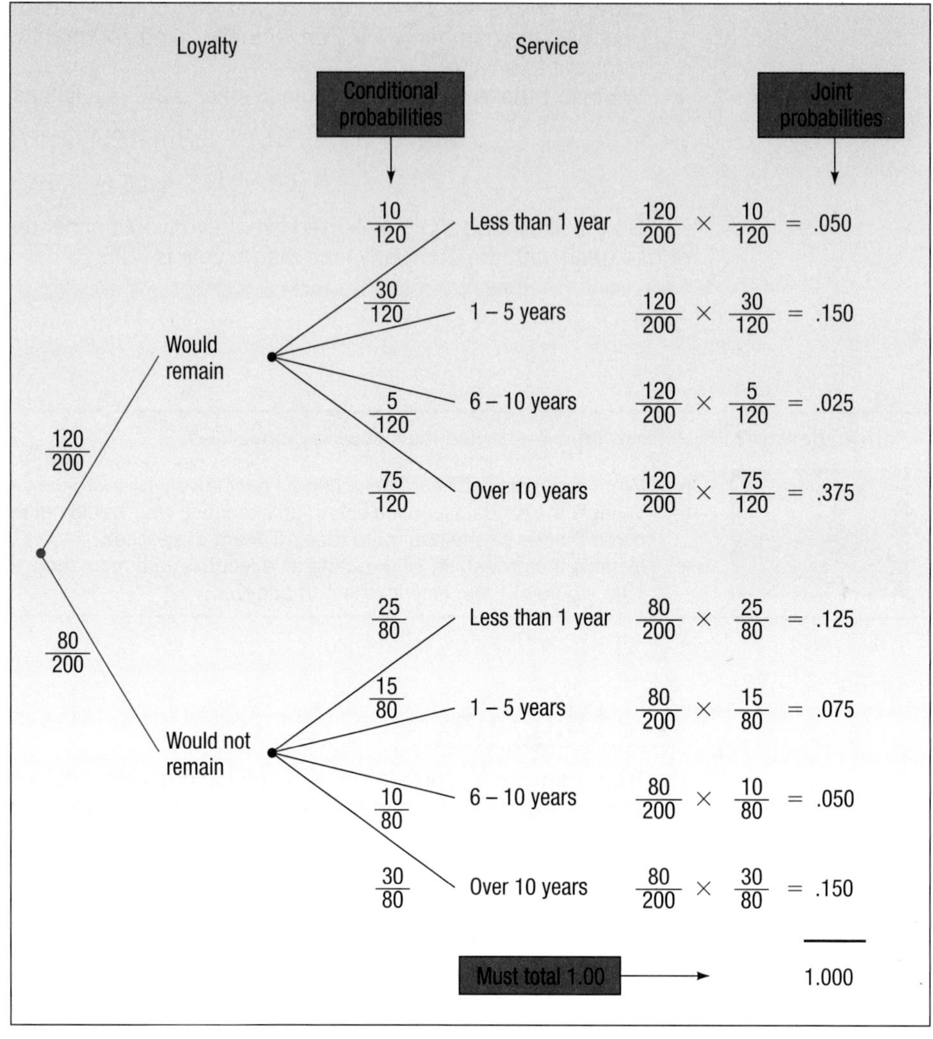

CHART 5–2 Tree Diagram Showing Loyalty and Length of Service

Self-Review 5–8

Consumers were surveyed on the relative number of visits to a Circuit City store (often, occasionally, and never) and if the store was conveniently located (yes and no).

	Convenient		
Visits	**Yes**	**No**	**Total**
Often	60	20	80
Occasional	25	35	60
Never	5	50	55
	90	105	195

(a) What is this table called?
(b) Are visits and convenience independent? Why? Interpret your conclusion.
(c) Draw a tree diagram and determine the joint probabilities

Exercises

23. Suppose $P(A) = .40$ and $P(B|A) = .30$. What is the joint probability of A and B?

24. Suppose $P(X_1) = .75$ and $P(Y_2|X_1) = .40$. What is the joint probability of X_1 and Y_2?

25. A local bank reports that 80 percent of its customers maintain a checking account, 60 percent have a savings account, and 50 percent have both. If a customer is chosen at random, what is the probability the customer has either a checking or a savings account? What is the probability the customer does not have either a checking or a savings account?

26. All Seasons Plumbing has two service trucks which frequently break down. If the probability the first truck is available is .75, the probability the second truck is available is .50, and the probability that both trucks are available is .30, what is the probability neither truck is available?

27. Refer to the following table.

	First Event			
Second Event	A_1	A_2	A_3	**Total**
B_1	2	1	3	6
B_2	1	2	1	4
Total	3	3	4	10

a. Determine $P(A_1)$.
b. Determine $P(B_1|A_2)$.
c. Determine $P(B_2$ and $A_3)$.

28. Three defective electric toothbrushes were accidentally shipped to a drugstore by Cleanbrush Products along with 17 nondefective ones.
a. What is the probability the first two electric toothbrushes sold will be returned to the drugstore because they are defective?
b. What is the probability the first two electric toothbrushes sold will not be defective?

29. Each salesperson at Stiles-Compton is rated either below average, average, or above average with respect to sales ability. Each salesperson is also rated with respect to his or her potential for advancement—either fair, good, or excellent. These traits for the 500 salespeople were cross-classified into the following table.

	Potential for Advancement		
Sales Ability	**Fair**	**Good**	**Excellent**
Below average	16	12	22
Average	45	60	45
Above average	93	72	135

a. What is this table called?
b. What is the probability a salesperson selected at random will have above average sales ability and excellent potential for advancement?
c. Construct a tree diagram showing all the probabilities, conditional probabilities, and joint probabilities.

30. An investor owns three common stocks. Each stock, independent of the others, has equally likely chances of (1) increasing in value, (2) decreasing in value, or (3) remaining the same value. List the possible outcomes of this experiment. Estimate the probability at least two of the stocks increase in value.

31. The board of directors of a small company consists of five people. Three of those are "strong leaders." If they buy an idea, the entire board will agree. The other "weak" members have no influence. Three sales reps are scheduled, one after the other, to make sales presentations to a board member of the sales rep's choice. The sales reps are convincing but do not know who the "strong leaders" are. However, they will know who the previous sales reps spoke to. The first sales rep to find a strong leader will win the account. Do the three sales reps have the same chance of winning the account? If not, find their respective probabilities of winning.

32. If you ask three strangers about their birthdays, what is the probability: (a) All were born on Wednesday? (b) All were born on different days of the week? (c) None were born on Saturday?

Principles of Counting

If the number of possible outcomes in an experiment is small, it is relatively easy to count them. There are six possible outcomes, for example, resulting from the roll of a die, namely:

If, however, there are a large number of possible outcomes, such as the number of heads and tails for an experiment with 10 tosses, it would be tedious to count all the possibilities. They could have all heads, one head and nine tails, two heads and eight tails, and so on. To facilitate counting, three counting formulas will be examined: the **multiplication formula** (not to be confused with the multiplication *rule* described earlier in the chapter), the **permutation formula,** and the **combination formula.**

The Multiplication Formula

MULTIPLICATION FORMULA If there are m ways of doing one thing and n ways of doing another thing, there are $m \times n$ ways of doing both.

In terms of a formula:

MULTIPLICATION FORMULA Total number of arrangements $= (m)(n)$ **[5–7]**

This can be extended to more than two events. For three events m, n, and o:

$$\text{Total number of arrangements} = (m)(n)(o)$$

EXAMPLE

An automobile dealer wants to advertise that for $29,999 you can buy a convertible, a two-door, or a four-door model with your choice of either wire wheel covers or solid wheel covers. How many different arrangements of models and wheel covers can the dealer offer?

SOLUTION

Of course the dealer could determine the total number of arrangements by picturing and counting them. There are six.

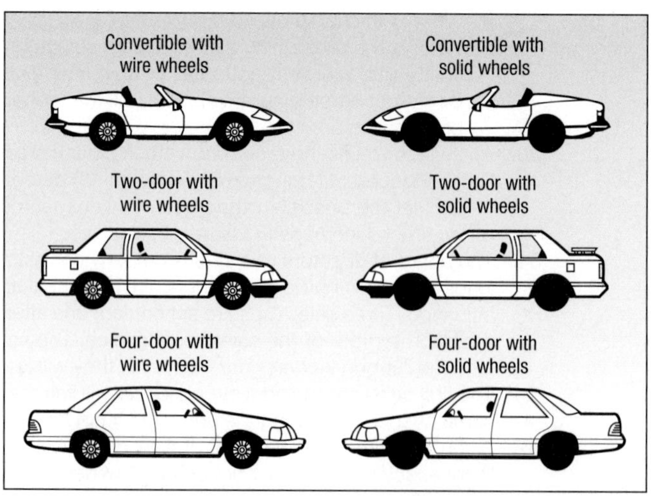

We can employ the multiplication formula as a check (where m is the number of models and n the wheel cover type). From formula (5–8):

$$\text{Total possible arrangements} = (m)(n) = (3)(2) = 6$$

It was not difficult to count all the possible model and wheel cover combinations in this example. Suppose, however, that the dealer decided to offer eight models and six types of wheel covers. It would be tedious to picture and count all the possible alternatives. Instead, the multiplication formula can be used. In this case, there are $(m)(n) = (8)(6) = 48$ possible arrangements.

Note in the preceding applications of the multiplication formula that there were *two or more groupings from which you made selections.* The automobile dealer, for example, offered a choice of models and a choice of wheel covers. If a home builder offered you four different exterior styles of a home to choose from and three interior floor plans, the multiplication formula would be used to find how many different arrangements were possible. The answer is there are 12 possibilities.

Self-Review 5–9

1. An Internet clothing retailer offers sweaters and slacks for women. The sweaters and slacks are offered in coordinating colors. If sweaters are available in five colors and the slacks are available in four colors, how many different outfits can be advertised?
2. Pioneer manufactures three models of stereo receivers, two cassette decks, four speakers, and three CD carousels. When the four types of components are sold together, they form a "system." How many different systems can the electronics firm offer?

The Permutation Formula

As noted, the multiplication formula is applied to find the number of possible arrangements for two or more groups. The **permutation formula** is applied to find the possible number of arrangements when there is only *one* group of objects. As illustrations of this type of problem:

- Three electronic parts are to be assembled into a plug-in unit for a television set. The parts can be assembled in any order. The question involving counting is: In how many different ways can the three parts be assembled?
- A machine operator must make four safety checks before starting his machine. It does not matter in which order the checks are made. In how many different ways can the operator make the checks?

One order for the first illustration might be: the transistor first, the LEDs second, and the synthesizer third. This arrangement is called a **permutation.**

PERMUTATION Any arrangement of r objects selected from a single group of n possible objects.

Note that the arrangements *a b c* and *b a c* are different permutations. The formula to count the total number of different permutations is:

PERMUTATION FORMULA $${}_nP_r = \frac{n!}{(n-r)!} \quad \textbf{[5–8]}$$

where:

n is the total number of objects.
r is the number of objects selected.

Before we solve the two problems illustrated, note that permutations and combinations (to be discussed shortly) use a notation called *n factorial.* It is written $n!$ and means the product of $n(n-1)(n-2)(n-3)\cdots(1)$. For instance, $5! = 5 \cdot 4 \cdot 3 \cdot 2 \cdot 1 = 120$.

As shown below, numbers can be canceled when the same numbers are included in the numerator and denominator.

$$\frac{6!3!}{4!} = \frac{6 \cdot 5 \cdot \not{4} \cdot \not{3} \cdot \not{2} \cdot \not{1}(3 \cdot 2 \cdot 1)}{\not{4} \cdot \not{3} \cdot \not{2} \cdot \not{1}} = 180$$

By definition, zero factorial, written 0!, is 1. That is, $0! = 1$.

EXAMPLE

Referring to the group of three electronic parts that are to be assembled in any order, in how many different ways can they be assembled?

SOLUTION

There are three electronic parts to be assembled, so $n = 3$. Because all three are to be inserted in the plug-in unit, $r = 3$. Solving using formula (5–8) gives:

$${}_nP_r = \frac{n!}{(n-r)!} = \frac{3!}{(3-3)!} = \frac{3!}{0!} = \frac{3!}{1} = \frac{3!}{1} = 6$$

We can check the number of permutations arrived at by using the permutation formula. We determine how many "spaces" have to be filled and the possibilities for each "space." In the problem involving three electronic parts, there are three locations in the plug-in unit for the three parts. There are three possibilities for the first place, two for the second (one has been used up), and one for the third, as follows:

$$(3)(2)(1) = 6 \text{ permutations}$$

The six ways in which the three electronic parts, lettered *A*, *B*, *C*, can be arranged are:

ABC	*BAC*	*CAB*	*ACB*	*BCA*	*CBA*

In the previous example we selected and arranged all the objects, that is $n = r$. In many cases, only some objects are selected and arranged from the *n* possible objects. We explain the details of this application in the following example.

EXAMPLE

The Betts Machine Shop, Inc., has eight screw machines but only three spaces available in the production area for the machines. In how many different ways can the eight machines be arranged in the three spaces available?

SOLUTION

There are eight possibilities for the first available space in the production area, seven for the second space (one has been used up), and six for the third space. Thus:

$$(8)(7)(6) = 336,$$

that is, there are a total of 336 different possible arrangements. This could also be found by using formula (5–8). If $n = 8$ machines, and $r = 3$ spaces available, the formula leads to

$${}_nP_r = \frac{n!}{(n-r)!} = \frac{8!}{(8-3)!} = \frac{8!}{5!} = \frac{(8)(7)(6)5!}{5!} = 336$$

The Combination Formula

If the order of the selected objects is *not* important, any selection is called a **combination.** The formula to count the number of r object combinations from a set of n objects is:

COMBINATION FORMULA $${}_nC_r = \frac{n!}{r!(n-r)!} \qquad [5\text{–}9]$$

For example, if executives Able, Baker, and Chauncy are to be chosen as a committee to negotiate a merger, there is only one possible combination of these three; the committee of Able, Baker, and Chauncy is the same as the committee of Baker, Chauncy, and Able. Using the combination formula:

$${}_nC_r = \frac{n!}{r!(n-r)!} = \frac{3 \cdot 2 \cdot 1}{3 \cdot 2 \cdot 1(1)} = 1$$

EXAMPLE

The marketing department has been given the assignment of designing color codes for the 42 different lines of compact discs sold by Goody Records. Three colors are to be used on each CD, but a combination of three colors used for one CD cannot be rearranged and used to identify a different CD. This means that if green, yellow, and violet were used to identify one line, then yellow, green, and violet (or any other combination of these three colors) cannot be used to identify another line. Would seven colors taken three at a time be adequate to color code the 42 lines?

SOLUTION

According to formula (5–9), there are 35 combinations, found by

$${}_7C_3 = \frac{n!}{r!(n-r)!} = \frac{7!}{3!(7-3)!} = \frac{7!}{3!4!} = 35$$

The seven colors taken three at a time (i.e., three colors to a line) would not be adequate to color-code the 42 different lines because they would provide only 35 combinations. Eight colors taken three at a time would give 56 different combinations. This would be more than adequate to color-code the 42 different lines.

When the number of permutations or combinations is large, the calculations are tedious. Computer software and handheld calculators have "functions" to compute these numbers. The Excel output for the location of the eight screw machines in the production area of Betts Machine Shop, Inc. is shown below. There are a total of 336 arrangements.

PERMUT

Number 8 = 8

Number_chosen 3 = 3

= 336

Returns the number of permutations for a given number of objects that can be selected from the total objects.

Number_chosen is the number of objects in each permutation.

Formula result =336 OK Cancel

Below is the output for the color codes at Goody Records, Inc. Three colors are chosen from among seven possible. The number of combinations possible is 35.

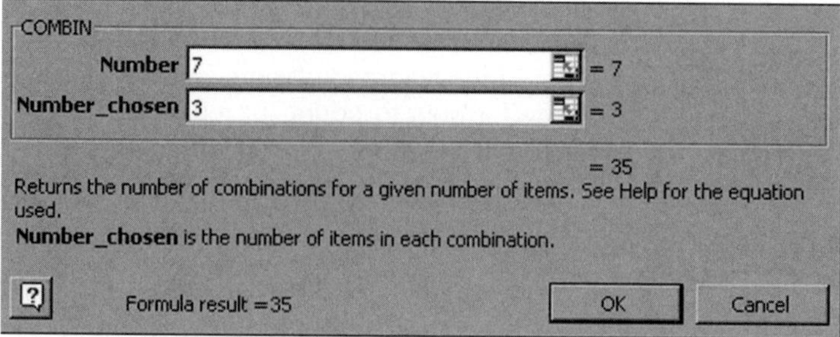

Self-Review 5–10

1. A musician wants to write a score based on only five chords: B-flat, C, D, E, and G. However, only three chords out of the five will be used in succession, such as C, B-flat, and E. Repetitions, such as B-flat, B-flat, and E, will not be permitted.
   (a) How many permutations of the five chords, taken three at a time, are possible?
   (b) Using formula (5–9), how many permutations are possible?
2. A machine operator must make four safety checks before starting to machine a part. It does not matter in which order the checks are made. In how many different ways can the operator make the checks?
3. The 10 numbers 0 through 9 are to be used in code groups of four to identify an item of clothing. Code 1083 might identify a blue blouse, size medium; the code group 2031 might identify a pair of pants, size 18; and so on. Repetitions of numbers are not permitted. That is, the same number cannot be used twice (or more) in a total sequence. For example, 2256, 2562, or 5559 would not be permitted. How many different code groups can be designed?
4. In the above example involving Goody Records, we said that eight colors taken three at a time would give 56 different combinations.
   (a) Use formula (5–9) to show this is true.
   (b) As an alternative plan for color coding the 42 different lines, it has been suggested that only two colors be placed on a disc. Would 10 colors be adequate to color code the 42 different lines? (Again, a combination of two colors could be used only once—that is, if pink and blue were coded for one line, blue and pink could not be used to identify a different line.)
5. In a lottery game, three numbers are randomly selected from a tumbler of balls numbered 1 through 50.
   (a) How many permutations are possible?
   (b) How many combinations are possible?

Exercises

33. Solve the following:
   a. 40!/35!
   b. ${}_7P_4$
   c. ${}_5C_2$

34. Solve the following:
   a. 20!/17!
   b. ${}_9P_3$
   c. ${}_7C_2$

35. Irwin Publishing, Inc., as part of its summer sales meeting, has arranged a golf outing at the Quail Creek Golf and Fish Club. Twenty people have signed up to play in the outing. The PGA Professional at Quail Creek is responsible for arranging the foursomes (four golfers playing together). How many different foursomes are possible?

36. A telephone number consists of seven digits, the first three representing the exchange. How many different telephone numbers are possible within the 537 exchange?

37. An overnight express company must include five cities on its route. How many different routes are possible, assuming that it does not matter in which order the cities are included in the routing?

38. A representative of the Environmental Protection Agency (EPA) wants to select samples from 10 landfills. The director has 15 landfills from which she can collect samples. How many different samples are possible?

39. A national pollster has developed 15 questions designed to rate the performance of the President of the United States. The pollster will select 10 of these questions. How many different arrangements are there for the order of the 10 selected questions?

40. A company is creating three new divisions and seven managers are eligible to be appointed head of a division. How many different ways could the three new heads be appointed?

Chapter Outline

I. A probability is a value between 0 and 1 inclusive that represents the likelihood a particular event will happen.
  A. An experiment is the observation of some activity or the act of taking some measurement.
  B. An outcome is a particular result of an experiment.
  C. An event is the collection of one or more outcomes of an experiment.

II. There are three definitions of probability.
  A. The classical definition applies when there are n equally likely outcomes to an experiment.
  B. The empirical definition occurs when the number of times an event happens is divided by the number of observations.
  C. A subjective probability is based on whatever information is available.

III. Two events are mutually exclusive if by virtue of one event happening the other cannot happen.

IV. Events are independent if the occurrence of one event does not affect the occurrence of another event.

V. The rules of addition refer to the union of events.
  A. The special rule of addition is used when events are mutually exclusive.

$$P(A \text{ or } B) = P(A) + P(B) \qquad \textbf{[5–2]}$$

  B. The general rule of addition is used when the events are not mutually exclusive.

$$P(A \text{ or } B) = P(A) + P(B) - P(A \text{ and } B) \qquad \textbf{[5–4]}$$

  C. The complement rule is used to determine the probability of an event happening by subtracting the probability of the event not happening from 1.

$$P(A) = 1 - P(\sim A) \qquad \textbf{[5–3]}$$

VI. The rules of multiplication refer to the product of events.
  A. The special rule of multiplication refers to events that are independent.

$$P(A \text{ and } B) = P(A)P(B) \qquad \textbf{[5–5]}$$

  B. The general rule of multiplication refers to events that are not independent.

$$P(A \text{ and } B) = P(A)P(B|A) \qquad \textbf{[5–6]}$$

  C. A joint probability is the likelihood that two or more events will happen at the same time.
  D. A conditional probability is the likelihood that an event will happen, given that another event has already happened.

VII. There are three counting rules that are useful in determining the number of outcomes in an experiment.
  A. The multiplication rule states that if there are m ways one event can happen and n ways another event can happen, then there are mn ways the two events can happen.

$$\text{Number of arrangements} = (m)(n) \qquad \textbf{[5–7]}$$

  B. A permutation is an arrangement in which the order of the objects selected from a specific pool of objects is important.

$${}_nP_r = \frac{n!}{(n-r)!} \qquad \textbf{[5–8]}$$

Statistics in Action

Government statistics show there are about 1.7 automobile caused fatalities for every 100,000,000 vehicle-miles. If you drive 1 mile to the store to buy your lottery ticket and then return home, you have driven 2 miles. Thus the probability that you will join this statistical group on your next 2 mile round trip is 2 × 1.7/100,000,000 = 0.000000034. This can also be stated as "One in 29,411,765." Thus if you drive to the store to buy your Powerball ticket, your chance of being killed (or killing someone else) is more than 4 times greater than the chance that you will win the Powerball Jackpot, one chance in 120,526,770. http://www.durangobill.com/PowerballOdds.html

C. A combination is an arrangement where the order of the objects selected from a specific pool of objects is not important.

$$_nC_r = \frac{n!}{r!(n-r)!} \quad \textbf{[5–9]}$$

Pronunciation Key

SYMBOL	MEANING	PRONUNCIATION
$P(A)$	Probability of *A*	*P* of *A*
$P(\sim A)$	Probability of not *A*	*P* of not *A*
$P(A \text{ and } B)$	Probability of *A* and *B*	*P* of *A* and *B*
$P(A \text{ or } B)$	Probability of *A* or *B*	*P* of *A* or *B*
$P(A\|B)$	Probability of *A* given *B* has happened	*P* of *A* given *B*
$_nP_r$	Permutation of *n* items selected *r* at a time	*Pnr*
$_nC_r$	Combination of *n* items selected *r* at a time	*Cnr*

Chapter Exercises

41. The marketing research department at Vernors plans to survey teenagers about a newly developed soft drink. Each will be asked to compare it with his or her favorite soft drink.
a. What is the experiment?
b. What is one possible event?

42. The number of times a particular event occurred in the past is divided by the number of occurrences. What is this approach to probability called?

43. The probability that the cause and the cure for all cancers will be discovered before the year 2010 is .20. What viewpoint of probability does this statement illustrate?

44. Berdine's Chicken Factory has several stores in the Hilton Head, South Carolina, area. When interviewing applicants for server positions, the owner would like to include information on the amount of tip a server can expect to earn per check (or bill). A study of 500 recent checks indicated the server earned the following tip.

Amount of Tip	Number
$ 0 up to $ 5	200
5 up to 10	100
10 up to 20	75
20 up to 50	75
50 or more	50
Total	500

a. What is the probability of a tip of $50 or more?
b. Are the categories "$0 up to $5," "$5 up to $10," and so on considered mutually exclusive?
c. If the probabilities associated with each outcome were totaled, what would that total be?
d. What is the probability of a tip of up to $10?
e. What is the probability of a tip of less than $50?

45. Define each of these items:
a. Conditional probability
b. Event
c. Joint probability

46. The first card selected from a standard 52-card deck was a king.
a. If it is returned to the deck, what is the probability that a king will be drawn on the second selection?
b. If the king is not replaced, what is the probability that a king will be drawn on the second selection?
c. What is the probability that a king will be selected on the first draw from the deck and another king on the second draw (assuming that the first king was not replaced)?

47. Armco, a manufacturer of traffic light systems, found that under accelerated-life tests, 95 percent of the newly developed systems lasted 3 years before failing to change signals properly.

a. If a city purchased four of these systems, what is the probability all four systems would operate properly for at least 3 years?

b. Which rule of probability does this illustrate?

c. Using letters to represent the four systems, write an equation to show how you arrived at the answer to part a.

48. Refer to the following picture.

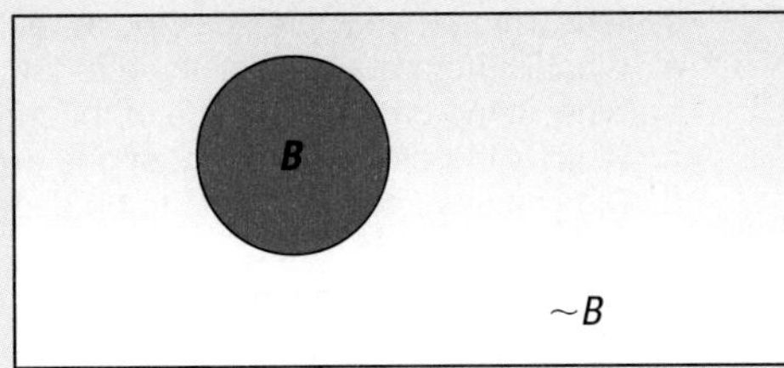

a. What is the picture called?

b. What rule of probability is illustrated?

c. B represents the event of choosing a family that receives welfare payments. What does $P(B) + P(\sim B)$ equal?

49. In a management trainee program at Claremont Enterprises, 80 percent of the trainees are female and 20 percent male. Ninety percent of the females attended college, and 78 percent of the males attended college.

a. A management trainee is selected at random. What is the probability that the person selected is a female who did not attend college?

b. Are gender and attending college independent? Why?

c. Construct a tree diagram showing all the probabilities, conditional probabilities, and joint probabilities.

d. Do the joint probabilities total 1.00? Why?

50. Assume the likelihood that any flight on Northwest Airlines arrives within 15 minutes of the scheduled time is .90. We select four flights from yesterday for study.

a. What is the likelihood all four of the selected flights arrived within 15 minutes of the scheduled time?

b. What is the likelihood that none of the selected flights arrived within 15 minutes of the scheduled time?

c. What is the likelihood at least one of the selected flights did not arrive within 15 minutes of the scheduled time?

51. There are 100 employees at Kiddie Carts International. Fifty-seven of the employees are production workers, 40 are supervisors, 2 are secretaries, and the remaining employee is the president. Suppose an employee is selected:

a. What is the probability the selected employee is a production worker?

b. What is the probability the selected employee is either a production worker or a supervisor?

c. Refer to part b. Are these events mutually exclusive?

d. What is the probability the selected employee is neither a production worker nor a supervisor?

52. Albert Pujols of the St. Louis Cardinals had the highest batting average in the 2003 Major League Baseball season. His average was .359. So assume the probability of getting a hit is .359 for each time he batted. In a particular game assume he batted three times.

a. This is an example of what type of probability?

b. What is the probability of getting three hits in a particular game?

c. What is the probability of not getting any hits in a game?

d. What is the probability of getting at least one hit?

53. The probability that a bomber hits its target on any particular mission is .80. Four bombers are sent after the same target. What is the probability:

a. They all hit the target?

b. None hit the target?

c. At least one hits the target?

54. Ninety students will graduate from Lima Shawnee High School this spring. Of the 90 students, 50 are planning to attend college. Two students are to be picked at random to carry flags at the graduation.
   a. What is the probability both of the selected students plan to attend college?
   b. What is the probability one of the two selected students plans to attend college?

55. Brooks Insurance, Inc. wishes to offer life insurance to men age 60 via the Internet. Mortality tables indicate the likelihood of a 60-year-old man surviving another year is .98. If the policy is offered to five men age 60:
   a. What is the probability all five men survive the year?
   b. What is the probability at least one does not survive?

56. Forty percent of the homes constructed in the Prince Creek development include a security system. Three homes are selected at random:
   a. What is the probability all three of the selected homes have a security system?
   b. What is the probability none of the three selected homes have a security system?
   c. What is the probability at least one of the selected homes has a security system?
   d. Did you assume the events to be dependent or independent?

57. Refer to Exercise 56, but assume there are 10 homes in the Prince Creek development and four of them have a security system. Three homes are selected at random:
   a. What is the probability all three of the selected homes have a security system?
   b. What is the probability none of the three selected homes have a security system?
   c. What is the probability at least one of the selected homes has a security system?
   d. Did you assume the events to be dependent or independent?

58. A juggler has a bag containing four blue balls, three green balls, two yellow balls, and one red ball. The juggler picks a ball at random. Then, without replacing it, he chooses a second ball. What is the probability the juggler first draws a yellow ball followed by a blue ball?

59. The board of directors of Saner Automatic Door Company consists of 12 members, 3 of whom are women. A new policy and procedures manual is to be written for the company. A committee of 3 is randomly selected from the board to do the writing.
   a. What is the probability that all members of the committee are men?
   b. What is the probability that at least 1 member of the committee is a woman?

60. A survey of undergraduate students in the School of Business at Northern University revealed the following regarding the gender and majors of the students:

	Major			
Gender	**Accounting**	**Management**	**Finance**	**Total**
Male	100	150	50	300
Female	100	50	50	200
Total	200	200	100	500

   a. What is the probability of selecting a female student?
   b. What is the probability of selecting a finance or accounting major?
   c. What is the probability of selecting a female or an accounting major? Which rule of addition did you apply?
   d. Are gender and major independent? Why?
   e. What is the probability of selecting an accounting major, given that the person selected is a male?
   f. Suppose two students are selected randomly to attend a lunch with the president of the university. What is the probability that both of those selected are accounting majors?

61. The Wood County sheriff classifies crimes by age (in years) of the criminal and whether the crime is violent or nonviolent. As shown below, a total of 150 crimes were reported by the sheriff last year.

	Age (in years)			
Type of Crime	**Under 20**	**20 to 40**	**Over 40**	**Total**
Violent	27	41	14	82
Nonviolent	12	34	22	68
Total	39	75	36	150

a. What is the probability of selecting a case to analyze and finding it involved a violent crime?
b. What is the probability of selecting a case to analyze and finding the crime was committed by someone less than 40 years old?
c. What is the probability of selecting a case that involved a violent crime or an offender less than 20 years old? Which rule of addition did you apply?
d. Given that a violent crime is selected for analysis, what is the probability the crime was committed by a person under 20 years old?
e. Two crimes are selected for review by Judge Tybo. What is the probability that both are violent crimes?

62. An investor purchased 100 shares of 5/3 Bank stock and 100 shares of Santee Cooper Electric stock. The probability the bank stock will appreciate over a year is .70. The probability the electric utility will increase over the same period is .60.
a. What is the probability both stocks appreciate during the period?
b. What is the probability the bank stock appreciates but the utility does not?
c. What is the probability at least one of the stocks appreciates?

63. With each purchase of a large pizza at Tony's Pizza, the customer receives a coupon that can be scratched to see if a prize will be awarded. The odds of winning a free soft drink are 1 in 10, and the odds of winning a free large pizza are 1 in 50. You plan to eat lunch tomorrow at Tony's. What is the probability:
a. That you will win either a large pizza or a soft drink?
b. That you will not win a prize?
c. That you will not win a prize on three consecutive visits to Tony's?
d. That you will win at least one prize on one of your next three visits to Tony's?

64. For the daily lottery game in Illinois, participants select three numbers between 0 and 9. A number cannot be selected more than once, so a winning ticket could be, say, 307. Purchasing one ticket allows you to select one set of numbers. The winning numbers are announced on TV each night.
a. How many different outcomes (three-digit numbers) are possible?
b. If you purchase a ticket for the game tonight, what is the likelihood you will win?
c. Suppose you purchase three tickets for tonight's drawing and select a different number for each ticket. What is the probability that you will not win with any of the tickets?

65. Several years ago Wendy's Hamburgers advertised that there are 256 different ways to order your hamburger. You may choose to have, or omit, any combination of the following on your hamburger: mustard, ketchup, onion, pickle, tomato, relish, mayonnaise, and lettuce. Is the advertisement correct? Show how you arrive at your answer.

66. It was found that 60 percent of the tourists to China visited the Forbidden City, the Temple of Heaven, the Great Wall, and other historical sites in or near Beijing. Forty percent visited Xi'an with its magnificent terracotta soldiers, horses, and chariots, which lay buried for over 2,000 years. Thirty percent of the tourists went to both Beijing and Xi'an. What is the probability that a tourist visited at least one of these places?

67. A new chewing gum has been developed that is helpful to those who want to stop smoking. If 60 percent of those people chewing the gum are successful in stopping smoking, what is the probability that in a group of four smokers using the gum at least one quits smoking?

68. Reynolds Construction Company has agreed not to erect all "look-alike" homes in a new subdivision. Five exterior designs are offered to potential home buyers. The builder has standardized three interior plans that can be incorporated in any of the five exteriors. How many different ways can the exterior and interior plans be offered to potential home buyers?

69. A new sports car model has defective brakes 15 percent of the time and a defective steering mechanism 5 percent of the time. Let's assume (and hope) that these problems occur independently. If one or the other of these problems is present, the car is called a "lemon." If both of these problems are present, the car is a "hazard." Your instructor purchased one of these cars yesterday. What is the probability it is:
a. A lemon?
b. A hazard?

70. The state of Maryland has license plates with three numbers followed by three letters. How many different license plates are possible?

71. There are four people being considered for the position of chief executive officer of Dalton Enterprises. Three of the applicants are over 60 years of age. Two are female, of which only one is over 60.
a. What is the probability that a candidate is over 60 and female?
b. Given that the candidate is male, what is the probability he is less than 60?
c. Given that the person is over 60, what is the probability the person is female?

72. Tim Bleckie is the owner of Bleckie Investment and Real Estate Company. The company recently purchased four tracts of land in Holly Farms Estates and six tracts in Newburg Woods. The tracts are all equally desirable and sell for about the same amount.
  a. What is the probability that the next two tracts sold will be in Newburg Woods?
  b. What is the probability that of the next four sold at least one will be in Holly Farms?
  c. Are these events independent or dependent?

73. A computer password consists of four characters. The characters can be one of the 26 letters of the alphabet. Each character may be used more than once. How many different passwords are possible?

74. A case of 24 cans contains 1 can that is contaminated. Three cans are to be chosen randomly for testing.
  a. How many different combinations of 3 cans could be selected?
  b. What is the probability that the contaminated can is selected for testing?

75. A puzzle in the newspaper presents a matching problem. The names of 10 U.S. presidents are listed in one column, and their vice presidents are listed in random order in the second column. The puzzle asks the reader to match each president with his vice president. If you make the matches randomly, how many matches are possible? What is the probability all 10 of your matches are correct?

76. The following diagram represents a system of two components, *A* and *B*, which are in series. (Being in series means that for the system to operate, both components *A* and *B* must work.) Assume the two components are independent. What is the probability the system works under these conditions? The probability *A* works is .90 and the probability *B* functions is also .90.

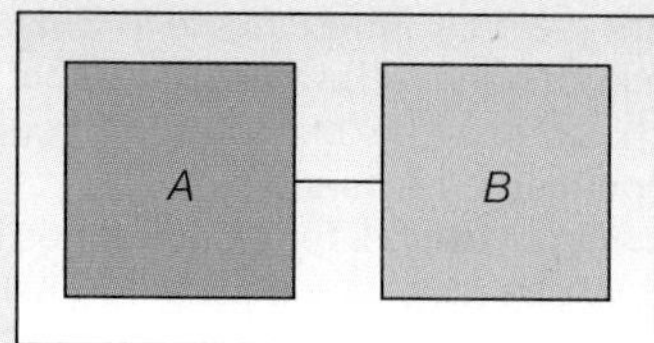

exercises.com

77. During the 1970s the game show *Let's Make a Deal* had a long run on TV. In the show a contestant was given a choice of three doors, behind one of which was a prize. The other two doors contained a gag gift of some type. After the contestant selected a door, the host of the show then revealed to them one of the doors from among the two not selected. The host asked the contestant if they wished to switch doors to one of those not chosen. Should the contestant switch? Are the odds of winning increased by switching doors?
Go to the following website, which is administered by the Department of Statistics at the University of South Carolina, and try your strategy: http://www.stat.sc.edu/~west/applets/LetsMakeaDeal.html; Go to the following website and read about the odds for the game: http://www.stat.sc.edu/~west/javahtml/LetsMakeaDeal.html. Was your strategy correct?

Dataset Exercises

78. Refer to the Real Estate data, which reports information on homes sold in the Denver, Colorado, area during the last year.
  a. Sort the data into a table that shows the number of homes that have a pool versus the number that don't have a pool in each of the five townships. If a home is selected at random, compute the following probabilities.
    (1) The home is in Township 1 or has a pool.
    (2) Given that it is in Township 3, that it has a pool.
    (3) Has a pool and is in Township 3.
  b. Sort the data into a table that shows the number of homes that have a garage versus those that don't have a garage in each of the five townships. If a home is selected at random, compute the following probabilities:
    (1) The home has a garage.
    (2) Given that it is in Township 5, that it does not have a garage.
    (3) The home has a garage and is in Township 3.
    (4) Does not have a garage or is in Township 2.

79. Refer to the Baseball 2003 data, which reports information on the 30 Major League Baseball teams for the 2003 season. Set up a variable that divides the teams into two groups, those that had a winning season and those that did not. That is, create a variable to count the teams that won 81 games or more, and those that won 80 or less. Next create a new variable for attendance, using three categories: attendance less than 2.0 million, attendance of 2.0 million up to 3.0 million, and attendance of 3.0 million or more.
   a. Create a table that shows the number of teams with a winning season versus those with a losing season by the three categories of attendance. If a team is selected at random, compute the following probabilities:
      (1) Having a winning season.
      (2) Having a winning season or attendance of more than 3.0 million.
      (3) Given attendance of more than 3.0 million, having a winning season.
      (4) Having a losing season and drawing less than 2.0 million.
   b. Create a table that shows the number of teams that play on artificial surfaces and natural surfaces by winning and losing records. If a team is selected at random, compute the following probabilities:
      (1) Selecting a team with a home field that has a natural surface.
      (2) Is the likelihood of selecting a team with a winning record larger for teams with natural or artificial surfaces?
      (3) Having a winning record or playing on an artificial surface.
80. Refer to the wage data set, which reports information on annual wages for a sample of 100 workers. Also included are variables relating to industry, years of education, and gender for each worker. Develop a table showing the industry of employment by gender. A worker is randomly selected; compute the probability the person selected is:
   a. Female.
   b. Female or in manufacturing.
   c. Female given that the selected person is in manufacturing.
   d. Female and in manufacturing.

Software Commands

1. The Excel commands to determine the number of permutations shown on page 145 are:
   a. Click on **Insert** on the toolbar, then select the f_x **function** and click **OK**.
   b. In the **Paste Function** box select **Statistical** and in the **Function name** column scroll down to **PERMUT** and click **OK**.
   c. In the **PERMUT** box after **Number** enter *8* and in the **Number_chosen** box enter *3*. The correct answer of 336 appears twice in the box.

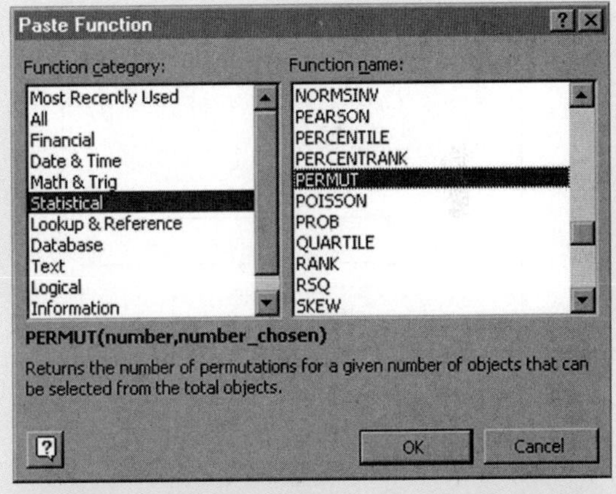

2. The Excel commands to determine the number of combinations shown on page 146 are:
   a. Click on **Insert** on the toolbar, then select the f_x **function** and click **OK**.
   b. In the **Paste Function** box select **Math & Trig** and in the Function name column scroll down to **COMBIN** and click **OK**.
   c. In the **COMBIN** box after **Number** enter *7* and in the **Number_chosen** box enter *3*. The correct answer 35 appears twice in the box.

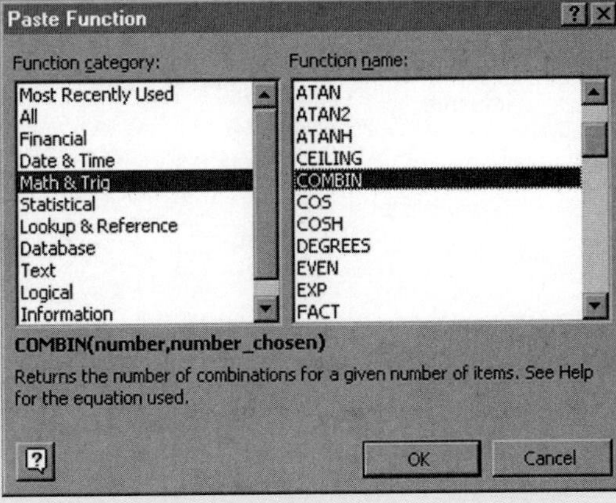

Chapter 5 Answers to Self-Review

5–1 **a.** Testing of the new computer game.
b. Seventy-three players liked the game.
c. No. Probability cannot be greater than 1. The probability that the game, if put on the market, will be successful is 65/80, or .8125.
d. Cannot be less than 0. Perhaps a mistake in arithmetic.
e. More than half of the persons testing the game liked it. (Of course, other answers are possible.)

5–2 **1.** $P(\text{Queen}) = \dfrac{4 \text{ queens in deck}}{52 \text{ cards total}}$

$= \dfrac{4}{52} = .0769$ Classical.

2. $P(\text{Divorced}) = \dfrac{182}{539} = .338$ Empirical.

3. The author's view when writing the text of the chance that the DJIA will climb to 12,000 is .25. You may be more optimistic or less optimistic. Subjective.

5–3 **a.** **i.** $P(B \text{ or } E) = \dfrac{(50 + 68)}{2{,}000} = .059$

ii. $P(\sim D) = 1 - P(D) = 1 - \dfrac{302}{2{,}000} = .849$

b.

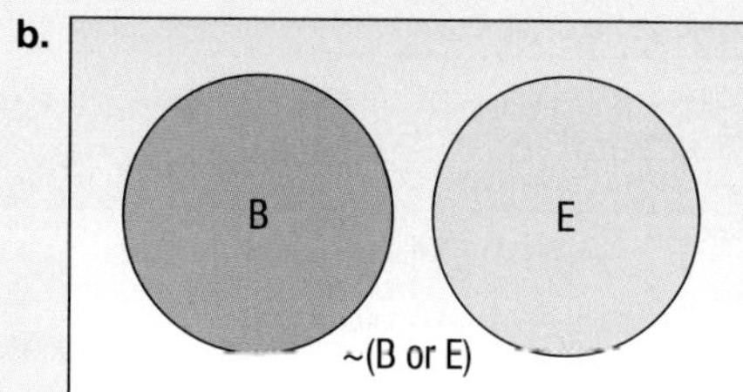

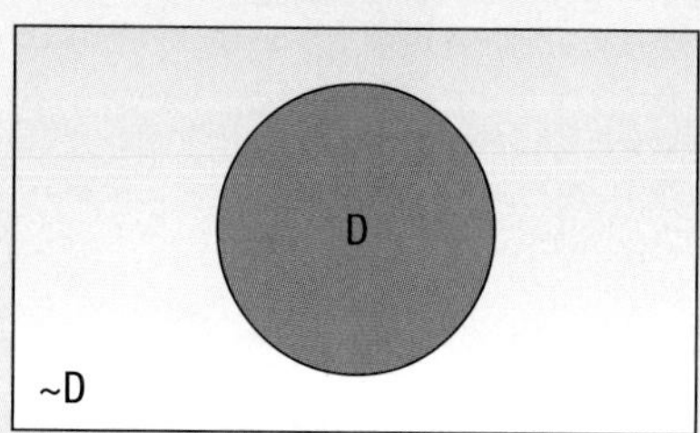

c. They are not complementary, but are mutually exclusive.

5–4 **a.** Need for corrective shoes is event A. Need for major dental work is event B.

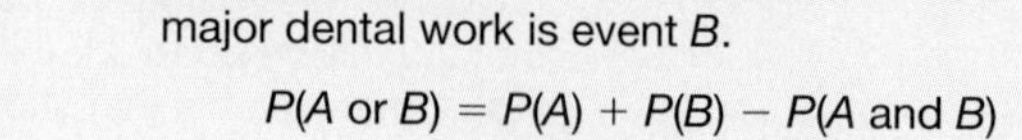

$$P(A \text{ or } B) = P(A) + P(B) - P(A \text{ and } B)$$
$$= .08 + .15 - .03$$
$$= .20$$

b. One possibility is:

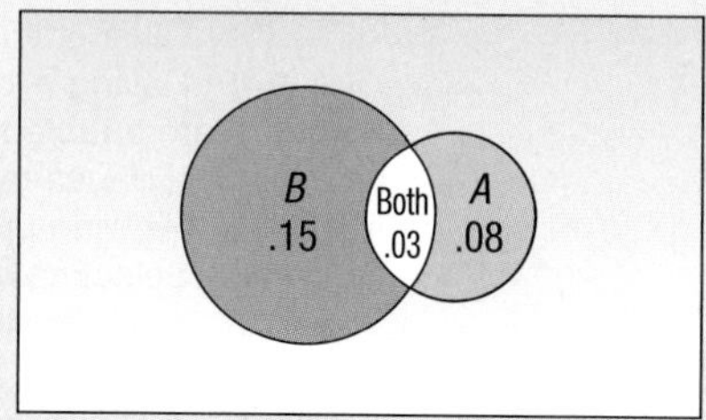

5–5 $(.80)(.80)(.80)(.80) = .4096$.

5–6 **a.** .002, found by:

$$\left(\frac{4}{12}\right)\left(\frac{3}{11}\right)\left(\frac{2}{10}\right)\left(\frac{1}{9}\right) = \frac{24}{11{,}880} = .002$$

b. .14, found by:

$$\left(\frac{8}{12}\right)\left(\frac{7}{11}\right)\left(\frac{6}{10}\right)\left(\frac{5}{9}\right) = \frac{1{,}680}{11{,}880} = .1414$$

c. No, because there are other possibilities, such as three women and one man.

5–7 **a.** $P(B_4) = \dfrac{105}{200} = .525$

b. $P(A_2 | B_4) = \dfrac{30}{105} = .286$

c. $P(A_2 \text{ or } B_4) = \dfrac{80}{200} + \dfrac{105}{200} - \dfrac{30}{200} = \dfrac{155}{200} = .775$

5–8 **a.** Contingency table
b. Independence requires that $P(A|B) = P(A)$. One possibility is:

$$P(\text{visit often} \mid \text{yes convenient location}) = P(\text{visit often})$$

Does $60/90 = 80/195$? No, the two variables are *not* independent.
Therefore, any joint probability in the table must be computed by using the general rule of multiplication.

c.

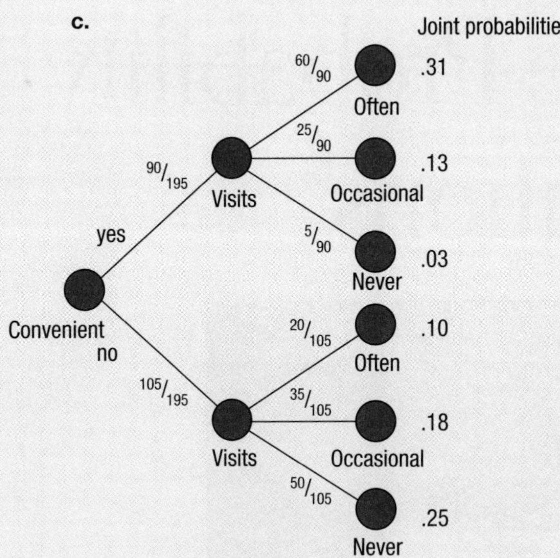

5–9 **1.** $(5)(4) = 20$

2. $(3)(2)(4)(3) = 72$

5–10 **1. a.** 60, found by $(5)(4)(3)$.

b. 60, found by:

$$\frac{5!}{(5-3)!} = \frac{5 \cdot 4 \cdot 3 \cdot \cancel{2 \cdot 1}}{\cancel{2 \cdot 1}}$$

2. 24, found by:

$$\frac{4!}{(4-4)!} = \frac{4!}{0!} = \frac{4!}{1} = \frac{4 \cdot 3 \cdot 2 \cdot 1}{1}$$

3. 5,040, found by:

$$\frac{10!}{(10-4)!} = \frac{10 \cdot 9 \cdot 8 \cdot 7 \cdot \cancel{6 \cdot 5 \cdot 4 \cdot 3 \cdot 2 \cdot 1}}{\cancel{6 \cdot 5 \cdot 4 \cdot 3 \cdot 2 \cdot 1}}$$

4. a. 56 is correct, found by:

$$_8C_3 = \frac{n!}{r!(n-r)!} = \frac{8!}{3!(8-3)!} = 56$$

b. Yes. There are 45 combinations, found by:

$$_{10}C_2 = \frac{n!}{r!(n-r)!} = \frac{10!}{2!(10-2)!} = 45$$

5. a. $_{50}P_3 = \dfrac{50!}{(50-3)!} = 117{,}600$

b. $_{50}C_3 = \dfrac{50!}{3!(50-3)!} = 19{,}600$

6 Discrete Probability Distributions

GOALS

When you have completed this chapter, you will be able to:

1 **Define the terms *probability distribution* and *random variable.***

2 **Distinguish between *discrete* and *continuous probability* distributions.**

3 **Calculate the *mean, variance,* and *standard deviation* of a discrete probability distribution.**

4 **Describe the characteristics of and compute probabilities using the *binomial probability* distribution.**

5 **Describe the characteristics of and compute probabilities using the *Poisson probability* distribution.**

Croissant Bakery, Inc. offers special decorated cakes for birthdays, weddings, and other occasions. They also have regular cakes available in their bakery. The table on page 179, exercise 38, gives the total number of cakes sold per day and the corresponding probability. Compute the mean, variance, and standard deviation of the number of cakes sold per day. (See Goal 3 and Exercise 38.)

Introduction

Chapters 2 through 4 are devoted to descriptive statistics. We describe raw data by organizing it into a frequency distribution and portraying the distribution in tables, graphs, and charts. Also, we compute a measure of location—such as the arithmetic mean, median, or mode—to locate a typical value near the center of the distribution. The range and the standard deviation are used to describe the spread in the data. These chapters focus on describing *something that has already happened.*

Starting with Chapter 5, the emphasis changes—we begin examining *something that would probably happen.* We note that this facet of statistics is called *statistical inference.* The objective is to make inferences (statements) about a population based on a number of observations, called a sample, selected from the population. In Chapter 5, we state that a probability is a value between 0 and 1 inclusive, and we examine how probabilities can be combined using rules of addition and multiplication.

This chapter will begin the study of **probability distributions.** A probability distribution gives the entire range of values that can occur based on an experiment. A probability distribution is similar to a relative frequency distribution. However, instead of describing the past, it describes the likelihood of some future event. For example, a drug manufacturer may claim a treatment will cause weight loss for 80 percent of the population. A consumer protection agency may test the treatment on a sample of six people. If the manufacturer's claim is true, it is *almost impossible* to have an outcome where no one in the sample loses weight and it is *most likely* that 5 out of the 6 do lose weight.

In this chapter we discuss the mean, variance, and standard deviation of a probability distribution. We also discuss frequently occurring probability distributions: the binomial and Poisson.

What Is a Probability Distribution?

A probability distribution shows the possible outcomes of an experiment and the probability of each of these outcomes.

PROBABILITY DISTRIBUTION A listing of all the outcomes of an experiment and the probability associated with each outcome.

How can we generate a probability distribution?

EXAMPLE

Suppose we are interested in the number of heads showing face up on three tosses of a coin. This is the experiment. The possible results are: zero heads, one head, two heads, and three heads. What is the probability distribution for the number of heads?

SOLUTION

There are eight possible outcomes. A tail might appear face up on the first toss, another tail on the second toss, and another tail on the third toss of the coin. Or we might get a tail, tail, and head, in that order. We use the multiplication formula for counting outcomes (5–7). There are (2)(2)(2) or 8 possible results. These results are listed below.

	Coin Toss			
Possible Result	**First**	**Second**	**Third**	**Number of Heads**
1	T	T	T	0
2	T	T	H	1
3	T	H	T	1
4	T	H	H	2
5	H	T	T	1
6	H	T	H	2
7	H	H	T	2
8	H	H	H	3

Note that the outcome "zero heads" occurred only once, "one head" occurred three times, "two heads" occurred three times, and the outcome "three heads" occurred only once. That is, "zero heads" happened one out of eight times or .125. Thus, the probability of zero heads is one eighth, the probability of one head is three eighths or .375, and so on. The probability distribution is shown in Table 6–1. Note that, since one of these outcomes must happen, the total of the probabilities of all possible events is 1.000. This is always true. The same information is shown in Chart 6–1.

TABLE 6–1 Probability Distribution for the Events of Zero, One, Two, and Three Heads Showing Face Up on Three Tosses of a Coin

Number of Heads, *x*	Probability of Outcome, *P*(*x*)
0	.125
1	.375
2	.375
3	.125
Total	1.000

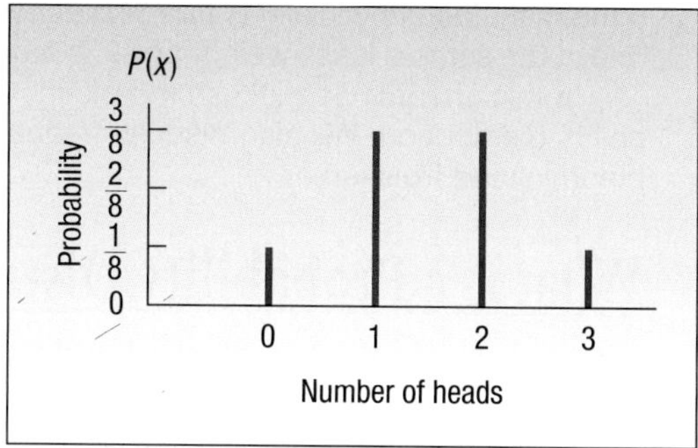

CHART 6–1 Graphical Presentation of the Number of Heads Resulting from Three Tosses of a Coin and the Corresponding Probability

Characteristics of a probability distribution

Before continuing, we should note two important characteristics of a probability distribution.

1. The probability of a particular outcome is between 0 and 1, inclusive. [The probabilities of *x*, written *P*(*x*) in the coin tossing example, were *P*(0 head) = 0.125, *P*(1 head) = 0.375, etc.]
2. The sum of the probabilities of all mutually exclusive events is 1.000. (Referring to Table 6–1, .125 + .375 + .375 + .125 = 1.000.)

Self-Review 6–1

The possible outcomes of an experiment involving the roll of a six-sided die are: a one-spot, a two-spot, a three-spot, a four-spot, a five-spot, and a six-spot.

(a) Develop a probability distribution for the number of possible spots.
(b) Portray the probability distribution graphically.
(c) What is the sum of the probabilities?

Random Variables

In any experiment of chance, the outcomes occur randomly. So it is often called a *random variable.* For example, rolling a single die is an experiment: any one of six possible outcomes can occur. Some experiments result in outcomes that are quantitative (such as dollars, weight, or number of children), and others result in qualitative outcomes (such as color or religious preference). A few examples will further illustrate what is meant by a **random variable.**

- If we count the number of employees absent from the day shift on Monday, the number might be 0, 1, 2, 3, ... The number absent is the random variable.
- If we weigh four steel ingots, the weights might be 2,492 pounds, 2,497 pounds, 2,506 pounds, and so on. The weight is the random variable.

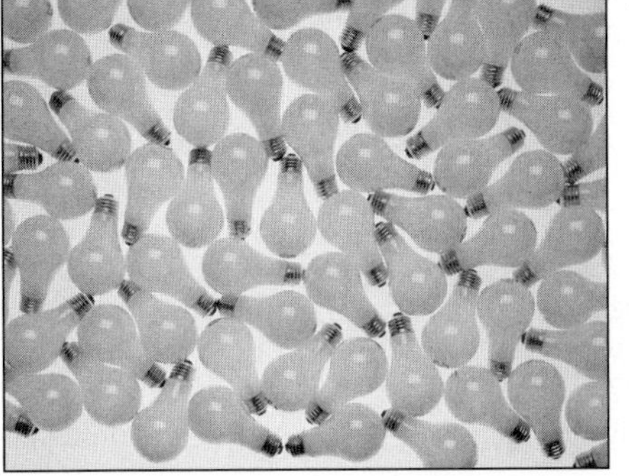

- If we toss two coins and count the number of heads, there could be zero, one, or two heads. Because the number of heads resulting from this experiment is due to chance, the number of heads appearing is the random variable.
- Other random variables might be: the number of defective light bulbs produced during each of the last 52 weeks at the Cleveland Bulb Company, Inc., the grade level (9, 10, 11, or 12) of the members of the St. James Girls' Varsity basketball team, the number of runners in the Boston Marathon for each of the last 20 years, and the number of drivers charged in each month for the last 36 months with driving under the influence of alcohol in Texas.

RANDOM VARIABLE A quantity resulting from an experiment that, by chance, can assume different values.

The following diagram illustrates the terms *experiment, outcome, event,* and *random variable.* First, for the experiment where a coin is tossed three times, there are eight possible outcomes. In this experiment, we are interested in the event that one head occurs in the three tosses. The random variable is the number of heads. In terms of probability, we want to know the probability of the event that the random variable equals 1. The result is $P(1 \text{ head in 3 tosses}) = 0.375$.

Possible *outcomes* for three coin tosses

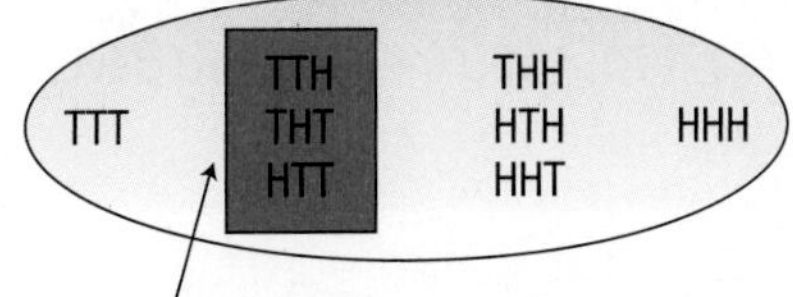

The *event* {one head} occurs and the *random variable* $x = 1$.

A random variable may be either *discrete* or *continuous.*

Discrete Random Variable

A discrete random variable can assume only a certain number of separated values. If there are 100 employees, then the count of the number absent on Monday can only be 0, 1, 2, 3, . . . , 100. A discrete random variable is usually the result of counting something. By way of definition:

DISCRETE RANDOM VARIABLE A random variable that can assume only certain clearly separated values.

A discrete random variable can, in some cases, assume fractional or decimal values. These values must be separated, that is, have distance between them. As an example, the scores awarded by judges for technical competence and artistic form in figure skating are decimal values, such as 7.2, 8.9, and 9.7. Such values are discrete because there is distance between scores of, say, 8.3 and 8.4. A score cannot be 8.34 or 8.347, for example.

Continuous Random Variable

On the other hand, if the random variable is continuous, then the distribution is a continuous probability distribution. If we measure something such as the width of a room, the height of a person, or the pressure in an automobile tire, the variable is a *continuous random variable.* It can assume one of an infinitely large number of values, within certain limitations. As examples:

- The times of commercial flights between Atlanta and Los Angeles are 4.67 hours, 5.13 hours, and so on. The random variable is the number of hours.
- Tire pressure, measured in pounds per square inch (psi), for a new Chevy Trailblazer might be 32.78 psi, 31.62 psi, 33.07 psi, and so on. In other words, any values between 28 and 35 could reasonably occur. The random variable is the tire pressure.

Logically, if we organize a set of possible values of a discrete random variable in a probability distribution, the distribution is a **discrete probability distribution.**

The tools used, as well as the probability interpretations, are different for discrete and continuous random variables. This chapter is limited to discrete probability distributions. The next chapter will address two continuous probability distributions.

The Mean, Variance, and Standard Deviation of a Probability Distribution

The mean reports the central location of the data and the variance describes the spread in the data. In a similar fashion, a probability distribution is summarized by its mean and variance. We identify the mean of a probability distribution by the lowercase Greek letter mu (μ) and the standard deviation by the lower case Greek letter sigma (σ).

Mean

The mean is a typical value used to represent the central location of a probability distribution. It also is the long-run average value of the random variable. The mean of a probability distribution is also referred to as its **expected value.** It is a weighted average where the possible values of a random variable are weighted by their corresponding probabilities of occurrence.

The mean of a discrete probability distribution is computed by the formula:

MEAN OF A PROBABILITY DISTRIBUTION $\mu = \Sigma[xP(x)]$ **[6–1]**

where $P(x)$ is the probability of a particular value x. In other words, multiply each x value by its probability of occurrence, and then add these products.

Variance and Standard Deviation

The mean is a typical value used to summarize a discrete probability distribution. However, it does not describe the amount of spread (variation) in a distribution. The variance does this. The formula for the variance of a probability distribution is:

VARIANCE OF A PROBABILITY DISTRIBUTION	$\sigma^2 = \Sigma[(x - \mu)^2 P(x)]$	[6–2]

The computational steps are:

1. Subtract the mean from each value, and square this difference.
2. Multiply each squared difference by its probability.
3. Sum the resulting products to arrive at the variance.

The standard deviation, σ, is found by taking the positive square root of σ^2; that is, $\sigma = \sqrt{\sigma^2}$.

EXAMPLE

John Ragsdale sells new cars for Pelican Ford. John usually sells the largest number of cars on Saturday. He has the following probability distribution for the number of cars he expects to sell on a particular Saturday.

Number of Cars Sold, x	Probability $P(x)$
0	.1
1	.2
2	.3
3	.3
4	.1
Total	1.0

1. What type of distribution is this?
2. On a typical Saturday, how many cars does John expect to sell?
3. What is the variance of the distribution?

SOLUTION

We begin by describing the type of probability distribution.

1. This is a discrete probability distribution for the random variable called "number of cars sold." Note that John expects to sell only within a certain range of cars; he does not expect to sell 5 cars or 50 cars. Further, he cannot sell half a car. He can sell only 0, 1, 2, 3, or 4 cars. Also, the outcomes are mutually exclusive—he cannot sell a total of both 3 and 4 cars on the same Saturday.
2. The mean number of cars sold is computed by multiplying the number of cars sold by the corresponding probability of selling that number of cars, and then summing the products. These steps are summarized in formula (6–1):

$$\begin{aligned}\mu &= \Sigma[xP(x)] \\ &= 0(.10) + 1(.20) + 2(.30) + 3(.30) + 4(.10) \\ &= 2.1\end{aligned}$$

These calculations are shown in the following table.

Number of Cars Sold, x	Probability $P(x)$	$x P(x)$
0	.10	0.00
1	.20	0.20
2	.30	0.60
3	.30	0.90
4	.10	0.40
Total	1.00	$\mu = 2.10$

How do we interpret a mean of 2.1? This value indicates that, over a large number of Saturdays, John Ragsdale expects to sell a mean of 2.1 cars a day. Of course, it is not possible for him to sell *exactly* 2.1 cars on any particular Saturday. However, the expected value can be used to predict the arithmetic mean number of cars sold on Saturdays in the long run. For example, if John works 50 Saturdays during a year, he can expect to sell (50)(2.1) or 105 cars just on Saturdays. Thus, the mean is sometimes called the expected value.

3. To find the variance we start by finding the difference between the value of the random variable and the mean. Next, we square these differences, and finally find the sum of the squared differences. A table is useful for systemizing the computations for the variance, which is 1.290.

Number of Cars Sold, x	Probability $P(x)$	$(x - \mu)$	$(x - \mu)^2$	$(x - \mu)^2 P(x)$
0	.10	0 − 2.1	4.41	0.441
1	.20	1 − 2.1	1.21	0.242
2	.30	2 − 2.1	0.01	0.003
3	.30	3 − 2.1	0.81	0.243
4	.10	4 − 2.1	3.61	0.361
				$\sigma^2 = 1.290$

Recall that the standard deviation, σ, is the positive square root of the variance. In this example, $\sqrt{\sigma^2} = \sqrt{1.290} = 1.136$ cars. How do we interpret a standard deviation of 1.136 cars? If salesperson Rita Kirsch also sold a mean of 2.1 cars on Saturdays, and the standard deviation in her sales was 1.91 cars, we would conclude that there is more variability in the Saturday sales of Ms. Kirsch than in those of Mr. Ragsdale (because $1.91 > 1.136$).

Self-Review 6–2

The Pizza Palace offers three sizes of cola—small, medium, and large—to go with its pizza. The colas are sold for \$0.80, \$0.90, and \$1.20, respectively. Thirty percent of the orders are for small, 50 percent are for medium, and 20 percent are for the large sizes. Organize the price of the colas and the probability of a sale into a probability distribution.

(a) Is this a discrete probability distribution? Indicate why or why not.
(b) Compute the mean amount charged for a cola.
(c) What is the variance in the amount charged for a cola? The standard deviation?

Exercises

1. Compute the mean and variance of the following discrete probability distribution.

x	*P*(*x*)
0	.2
1	.4
2	.3
3	.1

2. Compute the mean and variance of the following discrete probability distribution.

x	*P*(*x*)
2	.5
8	.3
10	.2

3. Three tables listed below show "random variables" and their "probabilities." However, only one of these is actually a probability distribution.

a. Which is it?

x	*P*(*x*)
5	.3
10	.3
15	.2
20	.4

x	*P*(*x*)
5	.1
10	.3
15	.2
20	.4

x	*P*(*x*)
5	.5
10	.3
15	−.2
20	.4

b. Using the correct probability distribution, find the probability that *x* is:

(1) Exactly 15.
(2) No more than 10.
(3) More than 5.

c. Compute the mean, variance, and standard deviation of this distribution.

4. Which of these variables are discrete and which are continuous random variables?

a. The number of new accounts established by a salesperson in a year.
b. The time between customer arrivals to a bank ATM.
c. The number of customers in Big Nick's barber shop.
d. The amount of fuel in your car's gas tank last week.
e. The number of minorities on a jury.
f. The outside temperature today.

5. Dan Woodward is the owner and manager of Dan's Truck Stop. Dan offers free refills on all coffee orders. He gathered the following information on coffee refills. Compute the mean, variance, and standard deviation for the distribution of number of refills.

Refills	Percent
0	30
1	40
2	20
3	10

6. The director of admissions at Kinzua University in Nova Scotia estimated the distribution of student admissions for the fall semester on the basis of past experience. What is the expected number of admissions for the fall semester? Compute the variance and the standard deviation of the number of admissions.

Admissions	Probability
1,000	.6
1,200	.3
1,500	.1

7. The following table lists the probability distribution for cash prizes in a lottery conducted at Lawson's Department Store.

Prize ($)	Probability
0	.45
10	.30
100	.20
500	.05

If you buy a single ticket, what is the probability that you win:

a. Exactly $100?
b. At least $10?
c. No more than $100?
d. Compute the mean, variance, and standard deviation of this distribution.

8. You are asked to match three songs with the performers who made those songs famous. If you guess, the probability distribution for the number of correct matches is:

Probability	.333	.500	0	.167
Number correct	0	1	2	3

What is the probability you get:

a. Exactly one correct?
b. At least one correct?
c. Exactly two correct?
d. Compute the mean, variance, and standard deviation of this distribution.

Binomial Probability Distribution

The **binomial probability distribution** is a widely occurring discrete probability distribution. One characteristic of a binomial distribution is that there are only two possible outcomes on a particular trial of an experiment. For example, the statement in a true/false question is either true or false. The outcomes are mutually exclusive, meaning that the answer to a true/false question cannot be both true and false at the same time. As other examples, a product is classified as either acceptable or not acceptable by the quality control department, a worker is classified as employed or unemployed, and a sales call results in the customer either purchasing the product or not purchasing the product. Frequently, we classify the two possible outcomes as "success" and "failure." However, this classification does *not* imply that one outcome is good and the other is bad.

Another characteristic of the binomial distribution is that the random variable is the result of counts. That is, we count the number of successes in the total number of trials. We flip a fair coin five times and count the number of times a head appears; we select 10 workers and count the number who are over 50 years of age, or we select 20 boxes of Kellogg's Raisin Bran and count the number that weigh more than the amount indicated on the package.

A third characteristic of a binomial distribution is that the probability of a success remains the same from one trial to another. Two examples are:

- The probability you will guess the first question of a true/false test correctly (a success) is one half. This is the first "trial." The probability that you will guess correctly on the second question (the second trial) is also one half, the probability of success on the third trial is one half, and so on.
- If past experience revealed the swing bridge over the Intracoastal Waterway in Socastee was raised one out of every 20 times you approach it, then the probability is one-twentieth that it will be raised (a "success") the next time you approach it, one-twentieth the following time, and so on.

The final characteristic of a binomial probability distribution is that each trial is *independent* of any other trial. Independent means that there is no pattern to the trials. The outcome of a particular trial does not affect the outcome of any other trial.

Characteristics of a binomial distribution

BINOMIAL PROBABILITY DISTRIBUTION

1. An outcome on each trial of an experiment is classified into one of two mutually exclusive categories—a success or a failure.
2. The random variable counts the number of successes in a fixed number of trials.
3. The probability of success and failure stay the same for each trial.
4. The trials are independent, meaning that the outcome of one trial does not affect the outcome of any other trial.

How Is a Binomial Probability Distribution Computed?

To construct a particular binomial probability distribution, we use (1) the number of trials and (2) the probability of success on each trial. For example, if an examination at the conclusion of a management seminar consists of 25 multiple-choice questions, the number of trials is 25. If each question has five choices and only one choice is correct, the probability of success on each trial is .20. Thus, the probability is .20 that a person with no knowledge of the subject matter will guess the answer to a question correctly. So the conditions of the binomial distribution just noted are met.

The binomial probability distribution is computed by the formula:

BINOMIAL PROBABILITY DISTRIBUTION $$P(x) = {}_nC_x \pi^x (1 - \pi)^{n-x} \quad \textbf{[6–3]}$$

where:

C denotes a combination.
n is the number of trials.
x is the random variable defined as the number of successes.
π is the probability of a success on each trial.

We use the Greek letter π (pi) to denote a binomial population parameter. Do not confuse it with the mathematical constant 3.1416.

EXAMPLE

There are five flights daily from Pittsburgh via US Airways into the Bradford, Pennsylvania Regional Airport. Suppose the probability that any flight arrives late is .20. What is the probability that none of the flights are late today? What is the probability that exactly one of the flights is late today?

SOLUTION

We can use Formula (6–3). The probability that a particular flight is late is .20, so let $\pi = .20$. There are five flights, so $n = 5$, and x, the random variable, refers to the number of successes. In this case a "success" is a plane that arrives late. Because there are no late arrivals $x = 0$.

$$P(0) = {}_nC_x(\pi)^x(1 - \pi)^{n-x}$$
$$= {}_5C_0(.20)^0(1 - .20)^{5-0} = (1)(1)(.3277) = .3277$$

The probability that exactly one of the five flights will arrive late today is .4096, found by

$$P(1) = {}_nC_x(\pi)^x(1 - \pi)^{n-x}$$
$$= {}_5C_1(.20)^1(1 - .20)^{5-1} = (5)(.20)(.4096) = .4096$$

The entire probability distribution is shown in Table 6–2.

TABLE 6–2 Binomial Probability Distribution for $n = 5, \pi = .20$

Number of Late Flights	Probability
0	.3277
1	.4096
2	.2048
3	.0512
4	.0064
5	.0003
Total	1.0000

The random variable in Table 6–2 is plotted in Chart 6–2. Note that the distribution of the number of late arriving flights is positively skewed.

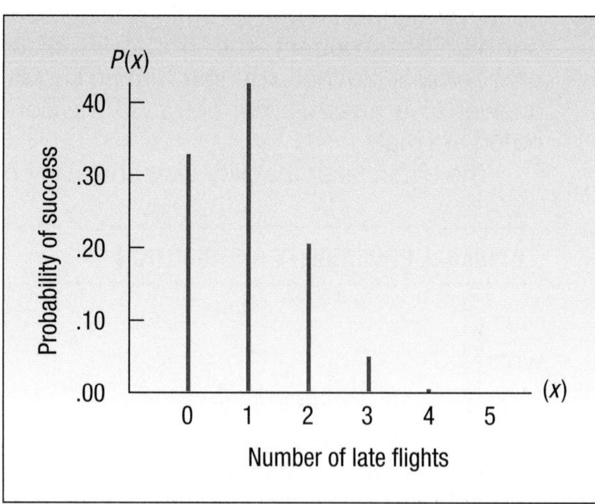

CHART 6–2 Binomial Probability Distribution for $n = 5, \pi = .20$

The mean (μ) and the variance (σ^2) of a binomial distribution can be computed in a "shortcut" fashion by:

MEAN OF A BINOMIAL DISTRIBUTION	$\mu = n\pi$	**[6–4]**

VARIANCE OF A BINOMIAL DISTRIBUTION	$\sigma^2 = n\pi(1 - \pi)$	**[6–5]**

For the example regarding the number of late flights, recall that $\pi = .20$ and $n = 5$. Hence:

$$\mu = n\pi = (5)(.20) = 1.0$$

$$\sigma^2 = n\pi(1 - \pi) = 5(.20)(1 - .20) = .80$$

The mean of 1.0 and the variance of .80 can be verified from formulas (6–1) and (6–2). The probability distribution from Table 6–2 and detailed calculations are shown below.

Number of Late Flights, x	$P(x)$	$xP(x)$	$x - \mu$	$(x - \mu)^2$	$(x - \mu)^2P(x)$
0	0.3277	0.0000	−1	1	0.3277
1	0.4096	0.4096	0	0	0
2	0.2048	0.4096	1	1	0.2048
3	0.0512	0.1536	2	4	0.2048
4	0.0064	0.0256	3	9	0.0576
5	0.0003	0.0015	4	16	0.0048
		$\mu = 1.0000$			$\sigma^2 = 0.7997$

Binomial Probability Tables

Formula (6–3) can be used to build a binomial probability distribution for any value of n and π. However, for larger n, the calculations take more time. For convenience, the tables in Appendix A show the result of using the formula for various values of n and π. Table 6–3 shows part of Appendix A for $n = 6$ and various values of π.

TABLE 6–3 Binomial Probabilities for $n = 6$ and Selected Values of π

	$n = 6$ Probability										
$x\backslash\pi$	.05	.1	.2	.3	.4	.5	.6	.7	.8	.9	.95
0	.735	.531	.262	.118	.047	.016	.004	.001	.000	.000	.000
1	.232	.354	.393	.303	.187	.094	.037	.010	.002	.000	.000
2	.031	.098	.246	.324	.311	.234	.138	.060	.015	.001	.000
3	.002	.015	.082	.185	.276	.313	.276	.185	.082	.015	.002
4	.000	.001	.015	.060	.138	.234	.311	.324	.246	.098	.031
5	.000	.000	.002	.010	.037	.094	.187	.303	.393	.354	.232
6	.000	.000	.000	.001	.004	.016	.047	.118	.262	.531	.735

EXAMPLE

Five percent of the worm gears produced by an automatic, high-speed Carter-Bell milling machine are defective. What is the probability that out of six gears selected at random none will be defective? Exactly one? Exactly two? Exactly three? Exactly four? Exactly five? Exactly six out of six?

SOLUTION

The binomial conditions are met: (a) there are only two possible outcomes (a particular gear is either defective or acceptable), (b) there is a fixed number of trials (6), (c) There is a constant probability of success (.05), and (d) the trials are independent.

Refer to Table 6–3 for the probability of exactly zero defective gears. Go down the left margin to an x of 0. Now move horizontally to the column headed by a π of .05 to find the probability. It is .735.

The probability of exactly one defective in a sample of six worm gears is .232. The complete binomial probability distribution for $n = 6$ and $\pi = .05$ is:

Number of Defective Gears, x	Probability of Occurrence, $P(x)$	Number of Defective Gears, x	Probability of Occurrence, $P(x)$
0	.735	4	.000
1	.232	5	.000
2	.031	6	.000
3	.002		

Of course, there is a slight chance of getting exactly five defective gears out of six random selections. It is .00000178, found by inserting the appropriate values in the binomial formula:

$$P(5) = {}_6C_5(.05)^5(.95)^1 = (6)(.05)^5(.95) = .00000178$$

For six out of the six, the exact probability is .000000016. Thus, the probability is very small that five or six defective gears will be selected in a sample of six.

We can compute the mean or expected value of the distribution of the number defective:

$$\mu = n\pi = (6)(.05) = 0.30$$

$$\sigma^2 = n\pi(1 - \pi) = 6(.05)(.95) = 0.285$$

The MegaStat software will also compute the probabilities for a binomial distribution. At the top of page 169 is the output for the previous example. In MegaStat p is used to represent the probability of success rather than π. The cumulative probability, expected value, variance, and standard deviation are also reported.

Self-Review 6–3

Eighty percent of the employees at the General Mills plant on Laskey Rd. have their bimonthly wages sent directly to their financial institution by electronic funds transfer. This is also called direct deposit. Suppose we select a random sample of seven recipients and count the number using direct deposit.

(a) Does this situation fit the assumptions of the binomial distribution?
(b) What is the probability that all seven employees use direct deposit?
(c) Use formula (6–3) to determine the exact probability that four of the seven sampled employees use direct deposit.
(d) Use Appendix A to verify your answers to parts (b) and (c).

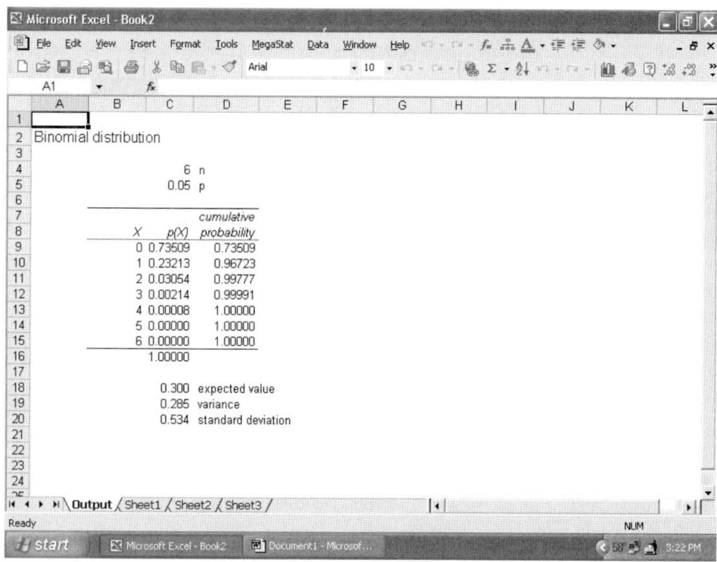

Binomial distribution

6 n
0.05 p

X	p(X)	cumulative probability
0	0.73509	0.73509
1	0.23213	0.96723
2	0.03054	0.99777
3	0.00214	0.99991
4	0.00008	1.00000
5	0.00000	1.00000
6	0.00000	1.00000
	1.00000	

0.300 expected value
0.285 variance
0.534 standard deviation

Appendix A is limited. It gives probabilities for n values from 1 to 15 and π values of .05, .10, . . ., .90, and .95. A software program can generate the probabilities for any specified number of successes, given n and π. The Excel output below shows the probability when $n = 40$ and $\pi = .09$. Note that the number of successes stops at 15 because the probability for each value between 16 and 40 is very close to 0.

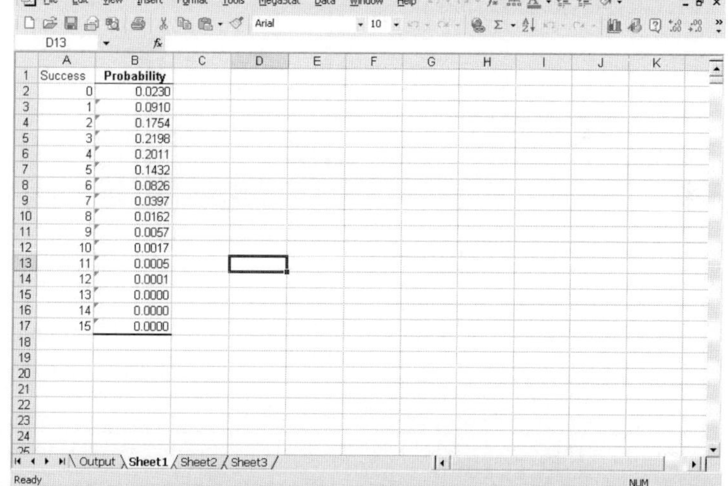

Success	Probability
0	0.0230
1	0.0910
2	0.1754
3	0.2198
4	0.2011
5	0.1432
6	0.0826
7	0.0397
8	0.0162
9	0.0057
10	0.0017
11	0.0005
12	0.0001
13	0.0000
14	0.0000
15	0.0000

Several additional points should be made regarding the binomial probability distribution.

1. If n remains the same but π increases from .05 to .95, the shape of the distribution changes. Look at Table 6–4 and Chart 6–3. The probabilities for a π of .05 are positively skewed. As π approaches .50, the distribution becomes symmetrical. As π goes beyond .50 and moves toward .95, the probability distribution becomes negatively skewed. Table 6–4 highlights probabilities for $n = 10$ and π of .05, .10, .20, .50, and .70. The graphs of these probability distributions are shown in Chart 6–3.

2. If π, the probability of success, remains the same but n becomes larger, the shape of the binomial distribution becomes more symmetrical. Chart 6–4 shows a situation where π remains constant at .10 but n increases from 7 to 40.

TABLE 6–4 Probability of 0, 1, 2, . . . Successes for a π of .05, .10, .20, .50, and .70 and an n of 10

$x \backslash \pi$	.05	.1	.2	.3	.4	.5	.6	.7	.8	.9	.95
0	.599	.349	.107	.028	.006	.001	.000	.000	.000	.000	.000
1	.315	.387	.268	.121	.040	.010	.002	.000	.000	.000	.000
2	.075	.194	.302	.233	.121	.044	.011	.001	.000	.000	.000
3	.010	.057	.201	.267	.215	.117	.042	.009	.001	.000	.000
4	.001	.011	.088	.200	.251	.205	.111	.037	.006	.000	.000
5	.000	.001	.026	.103	.201	.246	.201	.103	.026	.001	.000
6	.000	.000	.006	.037	.111	.205	.251	.200	.088	.011	.001
7	.000	.000	.001	.009	.042	.117	.215	.267	.201	.057	.010
8	.000	.000	.000	.001	.011	.044	.121	.233	.302	.194	.075
9	.000	.000	.000	.000	.002	.010	.040	.121	.268	.387	.315
10	.000	.000	.000	.000	.000	.001	.006	.028	.107	.349	.599

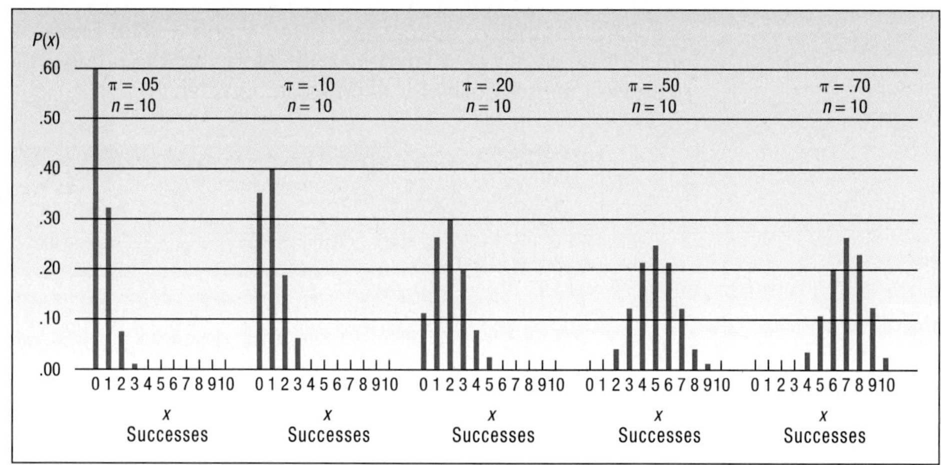

CHART 6–3 Graphing the Binomial Probability Distribution for a π of .05, .10, .20, .50, and .70 and an n of 10

Exercises

9. In a binomial situation $n = 4$ and $\pi = .25$. Determine the probabilities of the following events using the binomial formula.
   a. $x = 2$
   b. $x = 3$

10. In a binomial situation $n = 5$ and $\pi = .40$. Determine the probabilities of the following events using the binomial formula.
   a. $x = 1$
   b. $x = 2$

11. Assume a binomial distribution where $n = 3$ and $\pi = .60$.
   a. Refer to Appendix A, and list the probabilities for values of x from 0 to 3.
   b. Determine the mean and standard deviation of the distribution from the general definitions given in formulas (6–1) and (6–2).

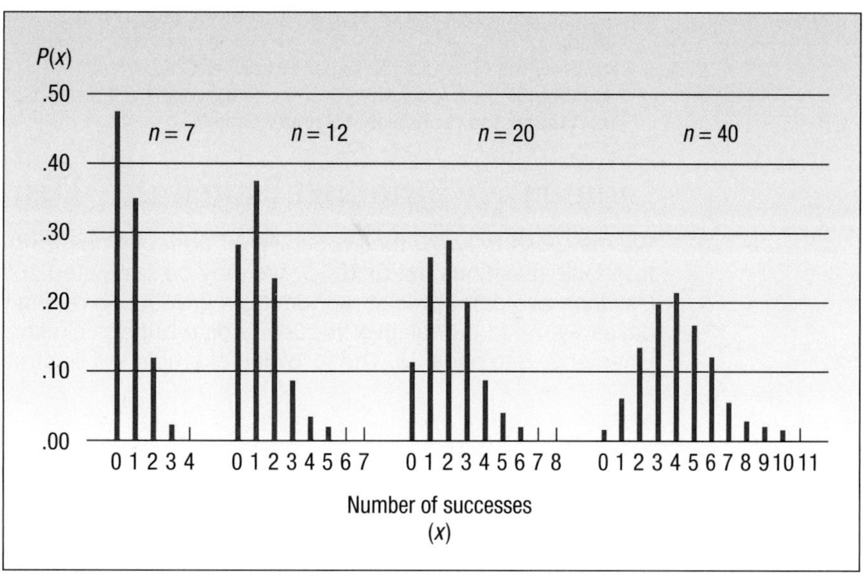

CHART 6–4 Chart Representing the Binomial Probability Distribution for a π of .10 and an n of 7, 12, 20, and 40

12. Assume a binomial distribution where $n = 5$ and $\pi = .30$.
    a. Refer to Appendix A, and list the probabilities for values of x from 0 to 5.
    b. Determine the mean and standard deviation of the distribution from the general definitions given in formulas (6–1) and (6–2).
13. An American Society of Investors survey found 30 percent of individual investors have used a discount broker. In a random sample of nine individuals, what is the probability:
    a. Exactly two of the sampled individuals have used a discount broker?
    b. Exactly four of them have used a discount broker?
    c. None of them have used a discount broker?
14. The United States Postal Service reports 95 percent of first class mail within the same city is delivered within two days of the time of mailing. Six letters are randomly sent to different locations.
    a. What is the probability that all six arrive within two days?
    b. What is the probability that exactly five arrive within two days?
    c. Find the mean number of letters that will arrive within two days.
    d. Compute the variance and standard deviation of the number that will arrive within two days.
15. The industry standards suggest that 10 percent of new vehicles require warranty service within the first year. Jones Nissan in Sumter, South Carolina, sold 12 Nissans yesterday.
    a. What is the probability that none of these vehicles requires warranty service?
    b. What is the probability exactly one of these vehicles requires warranty service?
    c. Determine the probability that exactly two of these vehicles require warranty service.
    d. Compute the mean and standard deviation of this probability distribution.
16. A telemarketer makes six phone calls per hour and is able to make a sale on 30 percent of these contacts. During the next two hours, find:
    a. The probability of making exactly four sales.
    b. The probability of making no sales.
    c. The probability of making exactly two sales.
    d. The mean number of sales in the two-hour period.
17. A recent survey by the American Accounting Association revealed 23 percent of students graduating with a major in accounting select public accounting. Suppose we select a sample of 15 recent graduates.
    a. What is the probability two select public accounting?
    b. What is the probability five select public accounting?
    c. How many graduates would you expect to select public accounting?

18. Suppose 60 percent of all people prefer Coke to Pepsi. We select 18 people for further study.
   a. How many would you expect to prefer Coke?
   b. What is the probability 10 of those surveyed will prefer Coke?
   c. What is the probability 15 prefer Coke?

Cumulative Binomial Probability Distributions

We may wish to know the probability of correctly guessing the answers to 6 *or more* true/false questions out of 10. Or we may be interested in the probability of *selecting less than two* defectives at random from production during the previous hour. In these cases we need cumulative frequency distributions similar to the ones developed in Chapter 2. See page 38. The following example will illustrate.

EXAMPLE

A recent study by the American Highway Patrolman's Association revealed that 60 percent of American drivers use their seat belts. A sample of 10 drivers on the Florida Turnpike is selected.

1. What is the probability that exactly 7 are wearing seat belts?
2. What is the probability that 7 or fewer of the drivers are wearing seat belts?

SOLUTION

This situation meets the binomial requirements, namely:

- A particular driver either is wearing a seat belt or is not. There are only two possible outcomes.
- There is a fixed number of trials—10 in this case, because 10 drivers are checked.
- The probability of "success" (wearing a seat belt) is the same from driver to driver: 60 percent.
- The trials are independent. If the fourth driver selected in the sample is wearing a seat belt, for example, it has no effect on whether the fifth driver selected is wearing a seat belt.

1. To find the likelihood of *exactly* 7 drivers, we use Appendix A. Locate the page for $n = 10$. Next find the column for $\pi = .60$ and the row for $x = 7$. The value is .215. Thus, the probability of finding 7 out of 10 drivers in the sample wearing their seat belts is .215. This is often written as follows:

$$P(x = 7|n = 10 \text{ and } \pi = .60) = .215$$

   where x refers to the number of successes, n the number of trials, and π the probability of a success. The bar "|" means "given that."
2. To find the probability that 7 or fewer of the drivers will be wearing seat belts, we apply the special rule of addition, formula (5–2), from Chapter 5. Because the events are mutually exclusive, we determine the probability that of the 10 drivers stopped, none was wearing a seat belt, 1 was wearing a seat belt, 2 were wearing a seat belt, and so on up to 7 drivers. The probabilities of the eight possible outcomes are then totaled. From Appendix A, $n = 10$, and $\pi = .60$.

$$\begin{aligned} P(x \leq 7|n = 10 \text{ and } \pi = .60) &= P(x = 0) + P(x = 1) + P(x = 2) + P(x = 3) \\ &\quad + P(x = 4) + P(x = 5) + P(x = 6) + P(x = 7) \\ &= .000 + .002 + .011 + .042 + .111 + .201 \\ &\quad + .251 + .215 \\ &= .833 \end{aligned}$$

So the probability of stopping 10 cars at random and finding 7 or fewer of the drivers wearing their seat belts is .833.

This value may also be determined, with less computation, using the complement rule. First, find $P(x > 7)$ given that $n = 10$ and $\pi = .60$. This probability is .167, found by $P(x = 8) + P(x = 9) + P(x = 10) = .121 + .040 + .006$. The probability that $x \leq 7$ is equal to $1 - P(x > 7)$, so $P(x \leq 7) = 1 - .167 = .833$, the same as computed above.

Self-Review 6–4

For a case where $n = 4$ and $\pi = .60$, determine the probability that:

(a) $x = 2$.
(b) $x \leq 2$.
(c) $x > 2$.

Exercises

19. In a binomial distribution $n = 8$ and $\pi = .30$. Find the probabilities of the following events.
- **a.** $x = 2$.
- **b.** $x \leq 2$ (the probability that x is equal to or less than 2).
- **c.** $x \geq 3$ (the probability that x is equal to or greater than 3).

20. In a binomial distribution $n = 12$ and $\pi = .60$. Find the following probabilities.
- **a.** $x = 5$.
- **b.** $x \leq 5$.
- **c.** $x \geq 6$.

21. In a recent study 90 percent of the homes in the United States were found to have large-screen TVs. In a sample of nine homes, what is the probability that:
- **a.** All nine have large-screen TVs?
- **b.** Less than five have large-screen TVs?
- **c.** More than five have large-screen TVs?
- **d.** At least seven homes have large-screen TVs?

22. A manufacturer of window frames knows from long experience that 5 percent of the production will have some type of minor defect that will require an adjustment. What is the probability that in a sample of 20 window frames:
- **a.** None will need adjustment?
- **b.** At least one will need adjustment?
- **c.** More than two will need adjustment?

23. The speed with which utility companies can resolve problems is very important. GTC, the Georgetown Telephone Company, reports they can resolve customer problems the same day they are reported in 70 percent of the cases. Suppose the 15 cases reported today are representative of all complaints.
- **a.** How many of the problems would you expect to be resolved today? What is the standard deviation?
- **b.** What is the probability 10 of the problems can be resolved today?
- **c.** What is the probability 10 or 11 of the problems can be resolved today?
- **d.** What is the probability more than 10 of the problems can be resolved today?

24. Steele Electronics, Inc. sells expensive brands of stereo equipment in several shopping malls throughout the northwest section of the United States. The Marketing Research Department of Steele reports that 30 percent of the customers entering the store that indicate they are browsing will, in the end, make a purchase. Let the last 20 customers who enter the store be a sample.
- **a.** How many of these customers would you expect to make a purchase?
- **b.** What is the probability that exactly five of these customers make a purchase?
- **c.** What is the probability ten or more make a purchase?
- **d.** Does it seem likely at least one will make a purchase?

Poisson Probability Distribution

Statistics in Action

Near the end of World War II, the Germans developed rocket bombs, which were fired at the city of London. The Allied military command didn't know whether these bombs were fired at random or whether they had an aiming device. To investigate, the city of London was divided into 576 square regions. The distribution of hits in each square was recorded as follows:

Hits					
0	1	2	3	4	5
Regions					
229	221	93	35	7	1

To interpret, the above chart indicates that 229 regions were not hit with one of the bombs. Seven regions were hit four times. Using the Poisson distribution, with a mean of 0.93 hits per region, the expected number of hits is as follows:

Hits					
0	1	2	3	4	5 or more
Regions					
227.3	211.3	98.3	30.5	7.1	1.6

Because the actual number of hits was close to the expected number of hits, the military command concluded that the bombs were falling at random. The Germans had not developed a bomb with an aiming device.

The **Poisson probability distribution** describes the number of times some event occurs during a specified interval. The interval may be time, distance, area, or volume.

The distribution is based on two assumptions. The first assumption is that the probability is proportional to the length of the interval. The second assumption is that the intervals are independent. To put it another way, the longer the interval the larger the probability, and the number of occurrences in one interval does not affect the other intervals. This distribution is also a limiting form of the binomial distribution when the probability of a success is very small and n is large. It is often referred to as the "law of improbable events," meaning that the probability, π, of a particular event's happening is quite small. The Poisson distribution is a discrete probability distribution because it is formed by counting.

In summary, a Poisson probability distribution has these characteristics:

POISSON PROBABILITY DISTRIBUTION

1. The random variable is the number of times some event occurs during a defined interval.
2. The probability of the event is proportional to the size of the interval.
3. The intervals which do not overlap are independent.

This distribution has many applications. It is used as a model to describe the distribution of errors in data entry, the number of scratches and other imperfections in newly painted car panels, the number of defective parts in outgoing shipments, the number of customers waiting to be served at a restaurant or waiting to get into an attraction at Disney World, and the number of accidents on I–75 during a three-month period.

The Poisson distribution can be described mathematically by the formula:

POISSON DISTRIBUTION $$P(x) = \frac{\mu^x e^{-\mu}}{x!} \quad \textbf{[6–6]}$$

where:

μ (mu) is the mean number of occurrences (successes) in a particular interval.
e is the constant 2.71828 (base of the Naperian logarithmic system).
x is the number of occurrences (successes).
$P(x)$ is the probability for a specified value of x.

The variance of the Poisson is also equal to its mean. If, for example, the probability that a check cashed by a bank will bounce is .0003, and 10,000 checks are cashed, the mean and the variance for the number of bad checks is 3.0, found by $\mu = n\pi = 10{,}000(.0003) = 3.0$.

Recall that for a binomial distribution there is a fixed number of trials. For example, for a four-question multiple-choice test there can only be zero, one, two, three, or four successes (correct answers). The random variable, x, for a Poisson distribution, however, can assume an *infinite number of values*—that is, 0, 1, 2, 3, 4, 5, ... However, *the probabilities become very small after the first few occurrences* (successes).

To illustrate the Poisson probability computation, assume baggage is rarely lost by Northwest Airlines. Most flights do not experience any mishandled bags; some have one bag lost; a few have two bags lost; rarely a flight will have three lost bags; and so on. Suppose a random sample of 1,000 flights shows a total of 300 bags were lost. Thus, the arithmetic mean number of lost bags per flight is 0.3, found by 300/1,000. If the number of lost bags per flight follows a Poisson distribution with μ = 0.3, we can compute the various probabilities using formula (6–6):

$$P(x) = \frac{\mu^x e^{-\mu}}{x!}$$

For example, the probability of not losing any bags is:

$$P(0) = \frac{(0.3)^0(e^{-0.3})}{0!} = 0.7408$$

In other words, 74 percent of the flights will have no lost baggage. The probability of exactly one lost bag is:

$$P(1) = \frac{(0.3)^1(e^{-0.3})}{1!} = 0.2222$$

Thus, we would expect to find exactly one lost bag on 22 percent of the flights.

Poisson probabilities can also be found in the table in Appendix C.

EXAMPLE

Recall from the previous illustration that the number of lost bags follows a Poisson distribution with a mean of 0.3. Use Appendix C to find the probability that no bags will be lost on a particular flight. What is the probability exactly one bag will be lost on a particular flight? When should the supervisor become suspicious that a flight is having too many lost bags?

SOLUTION

Part of Appendix C is repeated as Table 6–5. To find the probability of no lost bags, locate the column headed "0.3" and read down that column to the row labeled "0." The probability is .7408. That is the probability of no lost bags. The probability of one lost bag is .2222, which is in the next row of the table, in the same column. The probability of two lost bags is .0333, in the row below; for three lost bags it is .0033; and for four lost bags it is .0003. Thus, a supervisor should not be surprised to find one lost bag but should expect to see more than one lost bag infrequently.

TABLE 6–5 Poisson Table for Various Values of μ (from Appendix C)

	μ								
x	0.1	0.2	0.3	0.4	0.5	0.6	0.7	0.8	0.9
0	0.9048	0.8187	0.7408	0.6703	0.6065	0.5488	0.4966	0.4493	0.4066
1	0.0905	0.1637	0.2222	0.2681	0.3033	0.3293	0.3476	0.3595	0.3659
2	0.0045	0.0164	0.0333	0.0536	0.0758	0.0988	0.1217	0.1438	0.1647
3	0.0002	0.0011	0.0033	0.0072	0.0126	0.0198	0.0284	0.0383	0.0494
4	0.0000	0.0001	0.0003	0.0007	0.0016	0.0030	0.0050	0.0077	0.0111
5	0.0000	0.0000	0.0000	0.0001	0.0002	0.0004	0.0007	0.0012	0.0020
6	0.0000	0.0000	0.0000	0.0000	0.0000	0.0000	0.0001	0.0002	0.0003
7	0.0000	0.0000	0.0000	0.0000	0.0000	0.0000	0.0000	0.0000	0.0000

These probabilities can also be found using the MINITAB system. The commands necessary are reported at the end of the chapter.

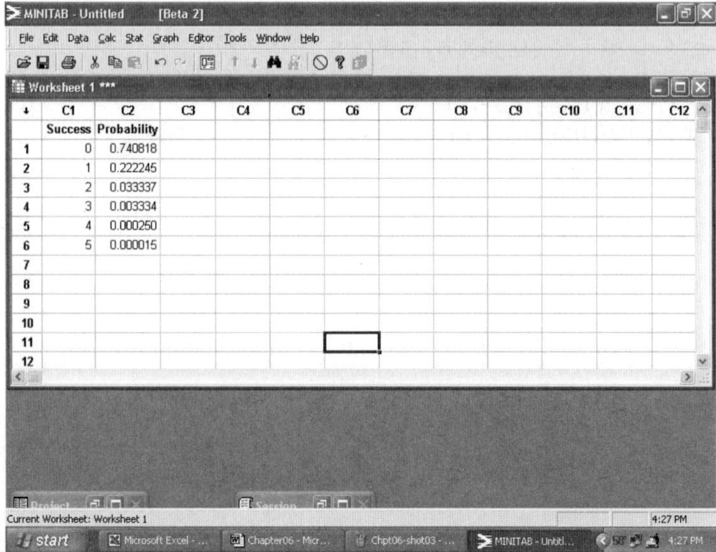

The Poisson probability distribution is always positively skewed. Also, the Poisson random variable has no specific upper limit. The Poisson distribution for the lost bags illustration, where $\mu = 0.3$, is highly skewed. As μ becomes larger, the Poisson distribution becomes more symmetrical. For example, Chart 6–5 shows the distributions of the number of transmission services, muffler replacements, and oil changes per day at Avellino's Auto Shop. They follow Poisson distributions with means of 0.7, 2.0, and 6.0, respectively.

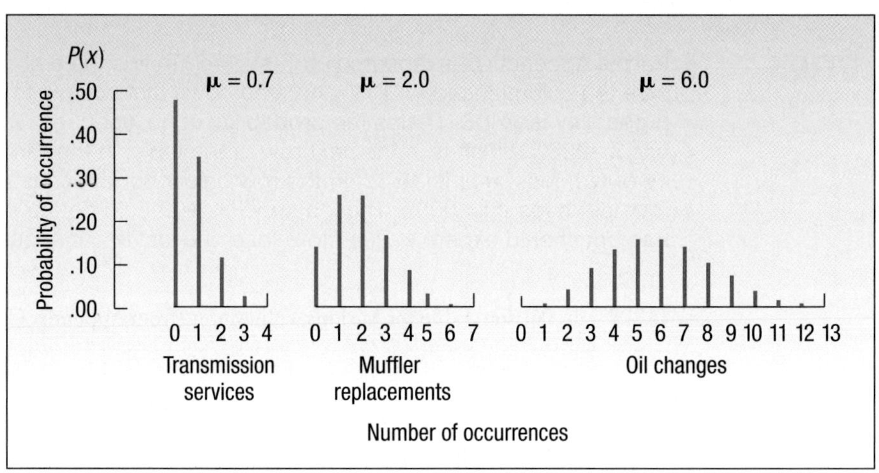

CHART 6–5 Poisson Probability Distributions for Means of 0.7, 2.0, and 6.0

Only μ needed to construct Poisson

In summary, the Poisson distribution is actually a family of discrete distributions. All that is needed to construct a Poisson probability distribution is the mean number of defects, errors, and so on—designated as μ.

Self-Review 6–5

From actuary tables the Washington Insurance Company determined the likelihood that a man age 25 will die within the next year is .0002. If Washington Insurance sells 4,000 policies to 25-year-old men this year, what is the probability they will pay on exactly one policy?

Exercises

25. In a Poisson distribution $\mu = 0.4$.
   a. What is the probability that $x = 0$?
   b. What is the probability that $x > 0$?

26. In a Poisson distribution $\mu = 4$.
   a. What is the probability that $x = 2$?
   b. What is the probability that $x \leq 2$?
   c. What is the probability that $x > 2$?

27. Ms. Bergen is a loan officer at Coast Bank and Trust. From her years of experience, she estimates that the probability is .025 that an applicant will not be able to repay his or her installment loan. Last month she made 40 loans.
   a. What is the probability that 3 loans will be defaulted?
   b. What is the probability that at least 3 loans will be defaulted?

28. Automobiles arrive at the Elkhart exit of the Indiana Toll Road at the rate of two per minute. The distribution of arrivals approximates a Poisson distribution.
   a. What is the probability that no automobiles arrive in a particular minute?
   b. What is the probability that at least one automobile arrives during a particular minute?

29. It is estimated that 0.5 percent of the callers to the Customer Service department of Dell, Inc. will receive a busy signal. What is the probability that of today's 1,200 callers at least 5 received a busy signal?

30. Textbook authors and publishers work very hard to minimize the number of errors in a text. However, some errors are unavoidable. Mr. J. A. Carmen, statistics editor, reports that the mean number of errors per chapter is 0.8. What is the probability that there are less than 2 errors in a particular chapter?

Chapter Outline

I. A random variable is a numerical value determined by the outcome of an experiment.

II. A probability distribution is a listing of all possible outcomes of an experiment and the probability associated with each outcome.
   A. A discrete probability distribution can assume only certain values. The main features are:
      1. The sum of the probabilities is 1.00.
      2. The probability of a particular outcome is between 0.00 and 1.00.
      3. The outcomes are mutually exclusive.
   B. A continuous distribution can assume an infinite number of values within a specific range.

III. The mean and variance of a probability distribution are computed as follows.
   A. The mean is equal to:

$$\mu = \Sigma[xP(x)] \qquad \textbf{[6–1]}$$

   B. The variance is equal to:

$$\sigma^2 = \Sigma[(x - \mu)^2P(x)] \qquad \textbf{[6–2]}$$

IV. The binomial distribution has the following characteristics.
   A. Each outcome is classified into one of two mutually exclusive categories.
   B. The distribution results from a count of the number of successes in a fixed number of trials.
   C. The probability of a success remains the same from trial to trial.
   D. Each trial is independent.
   E. A binomial probability is determined as follows:

$$P(x) = {}_nC_x\pi^x(1 - \pi)^{n-x} \qquad \textbf{[6–3]}$$

   F. The mean is computed as:

$$\mu = n\pi \qquad \textbf{[6–4]}$$

   G. The variance is

$$\sigma^2 = n\pi(1 - \pi) \qquad \textbf{[6–5]}$$

V. The Poisson distribution has the following characteristics.

A. It describes the number of times some event occurs during a specified interval.
B. The probability of a "success" is proportional to the length of the interval.
C. Nonoverlapping intervals are independent.
D. It is a limiting form of the binomial distribution when n is large and π is small.
E. A Poisson probability is determined from the following equation:

$$P(x) = \frac{\mu^x e^{-\mu}}{x!} \qquad \textbf{[6–6]}$$

F. The mean and the variance are equal.

Chapter Exercises

31. What is the difference between a random variable and a probability distribution?

32. For each of the following indicate whether the random variable is discrete or continuous.
- **a.** The length of time to get a haircut.
- **b.** The number of cars a jogger passes each morning while running.
- **c.** The number of hits for a team in a high school girls' softball game.
- **d.** The number of patients treated at the South Strand Medical Center between 6 and 10 P.M. each night.
- **e.** The number of miles your car traveled on the last fill-up.
- **f.** The number of customers at the Oak Street Wendy's who used the drive-through facility.
- **g.** The distance between Gainesville, Florida, and all Florida cities with a population of at least 50,000.

33. What are the requirements for the binomial distribution?

34. Under what conditions will the binomial and the Poisson distributions give roughly the same results?

35. Seaside Villas, Inc. has a large number of villas available to rent each month. A concern of management is the number of vacant villas each month. A recent study revealed the percent of the time that a given number of villas are vacant. Compute the mean and standard deviation of the number of vacant villas.

Number of Vacant Units	Probability
0	.1
1	.2
2	.3
3	.4

36. An investment will be worth $1,000, $2,000, or $5,000 at the end of the year. The probabilities of these values are .25, .60, and .15, respectively. Determine the mean and variance of the worth of the investment.

37. The vice president of human resources at Lowes is studying the number of on-the-job accidents over a period of one month. He developed the following probability distribution. Compute the mean, variance, and standard deviation of the number of accidents in a month.

Number of Accidents	Probability
0	.40
1	.20
2	.20
3	.10
4	.10

38. Croissant Bakery, Inc. offers special decorated cakes for birthdays, weddings, and other occasions. They also have regular cakes available in their bakery. The following table gives the total number of cakes sold per day and the corresponding probability. Compute the mean, variance, and standard deviation of the number of cakes sold per day.

Number of Cakes Sold in a Day	Probability
12	.25
13	.40
14	.25
15	.10

39. A recent survey reported that the average American adult eats ice cream 28 times per year. The same survey indicated 33 percent of the respondents said vanilla was their favorite flavor of ice cream. Nineteen percent said chocolate was their favorite flavor. There are 10 customers waiting for ice cream at the Highway 544 Ben and Jerry's ice cream and frozen yogurt store.

a. How many would you expect to purchase vanilla ice cream?
b. What is the probability exactly three will select vanilla ice cream?
c. What is the probability exactly three will select chocolate ice cream?
d. What is the probability at least one will select chocolate ice cream?

40. Thirty percent of the population in a southwestern community are Spanish-speaking Americans. A Spanish-speaking person is accused of killing a non-Spanish-speaking American. Of the first 12 potential jurors, only 2 are Spanish-speaking Americans, and 10 are not. The defendant's lawyer challenges the jury selection, claiming bias against her client. The government lawyer disagrees, saying that the probability of this particular jury composition is common. What do you think?

41. An auditor for Health Maintenance Services of Georgia reports 40 percent of the policyholders 55 years or older submit a claim during the year. Fifteen policyholders are randomly selected for company records.

a. How many of the policyholders would you expect to have filed a claim within the last year?
b. What is the probability that ten of the selected policyholders submitted a claim last year?
c. What is the probability that ten or more of the selected policyholders submitted a claim last year?
d. What is the probability that more than ten of the selected policyholders submitted a claim last year?

42. Tire and Auto Supply is considering a 2-for-1 stock split. Before the transaction is finalized, at least two-thirds of the 1,200 company stockholders must approve the proposal. To evaluate the likelihood the proposal will be approved, the director of finance selected a sample of 18 stockholders. He contacted each and found 14 approved of the proposed split. What is the likelihood of this event, assuming two-thirds of the stockholders approve?

43. A federal study reported that 7.5 percent of the U.S. workforce has a drug problem. A drug enforcement official for the State of Indiana wished to investigate this statement. In his sample of 20 employed workers:

a. How many would you expect to have a drug problem? What is the standard deviation?
b. What is the likelihood that *none* of the workers sampled has a drug problem?
c. What is the likelihood *at least one* has a drug problem?

44. The Bank of Hawaii reports that 7 percent of its credit card holders will default at some time in their life. The Hilo branch just mailed out 12 new cards today.

a. How many of these new cardholders would you expect to default? What is the standard deviation?
b. What is the likelihood that *none* of the cardholders will default?
c. What is the likelihood *at least one* will default?

45. Recent statistics suggest that 15 percent of those who visit a retail site on the World Wide Web make a purchase. A retailer wished to verify this claim. To do so, she selected a sample of 16 "hits" to her site and found that 4 had actually made a purchase.

a. What is the likelihood of exactly four purchases?
b. How many purchases should she expect?
c. What is the likelihood that four or more "hits" result in a purchase?

46. Dr. Richmond, a psychologist, is studying the daytime television viewing habits of college students. She believes 45 percent of college students watch soap operas during the afternoon. To further investigate, she selects a sample of 10.

a. Develop a probability distribution for the number of students in the sample who watch soap operas.
b. Find the mean and the standard deviation of this distribution.
c. What is the probability of finding exactly four watch soap operas?
d. What is the probability less than half of the students selected watch soap operas?

47. A recent study conducted by Penn, Shone, and Borland, on behalf of LastMinute.com, revealed that 52 percent of business travelers plan their trips less than two weeks before departure. The study is to be replicated in the tri-state area with a sample of 12 frequent business travelers.
a. Develop a probability distribution for the number of travelers who plan their trips within two weeks of departure.
b. Find the mean and the standard deviation of this distribution.
c. What is the probability exactly 5 of the 12 selected business travelers plan their trips within two weeks of departure?
d. What is the probability 5 or fewer of the 12 selected business travelers plan their trips within two weeks of departure?

48. A manufacturer of computer chips claims that the probability of a defective chip is .002. The manufacturer sells chips in batches of 1000 to major computer companies such as Dell and Gateway.
a. How many defective chips would you expect in a batch?
b. What is the probability that none of the chips are defective in a batch?
c. What is the probability at least one chip is defective in a batch?

49. The sales of Lexus automobiles in the Detroit area follow a Poisson distribution with a mean of 3 per day.
a. What is the probability that no Lexus is sold on a particular day?
b. What is the probability that for five consecutive days at least one Lexus is sold?

50. Suppose 1.5 percent of the antennas on new Nokia cell phones are defective. For a random sample of 200 antennas, find the probability that:
a. None of the antennas is defective.
b. Three or more of the antennas are defective.

51. A study of the checkout lines at the Safeway Supermarket in the South Strand area revealed that between 4 and 7 P.M. on weekdays there is an average of four customers waiting in line. What is the probability that you visit Safeway today during this period and find:
a. No customers are waiting?
b. Four customers are waiting?
c. Four or fewer are waiting?
d. Four or more are waiting?

52. An internal study at Lahey Electronics, a large software development company, revealed the mean time for an internal e-mail message to arrive at its destination was 2 seconds. Further, the distribution of the arrival times followed the Poisson distribution.
a. What is the probability a message takes exactly 1 second to arrive at its destination?
b. What is the probability it takes more than 4 seconds to arrive at its destination?
c. What is the probability it takes virtually no time, i.e., "zero" seconds?

53. Recent crime reports indicate that 3.1 motor vehicle thefts occur each minute in the United States. Assume that the distribution of thefts per minute can be approximated by the Poisson probability distribution.
a. Calculate the probability exactly four thefts occur in a minute.
b. What is the probability there are no thefts in a minute?
c. What is the probability there is *at least one* theft in a minute?

54. New Process, Inc., a large mail-order supplier of women's fashions, advertises same-day service on every order. Recently the movement of orders has not gone as planned, and there were a large number of complaints. Bud Owens, director of customer service, has completely redone the method of order handling. The goal is to have fewer than five unfilled orders on hand at the end of 95 percent of the working days. Frequent checks of the unfilled orders at the end of the day revealed that the distribution of the unfilled orders follows a Poisson distribution with a mean of two orders.
a. Has New Process, Inc. lived up to its internal goal? Cite evidence.
b. Draw a histogram representing the Poisson probability distribution of unfilled orders.

55. The National Aeronautics and Space Administration (NASA) has experienced two disasters. The *Challenger* exploded over the Atlantic Ocean in 1986 and the *Columbia* exploded over East Texas in 2003. There have been a total of 113 space missions. Use the Poisson distribution to estimate the probability of exactly two failures. What is the probability of no failures?

56. According to the "January theory," if the stock market is up for the month of January, it will be up for the year. If it is down in January, it will be down for the year. According to an article in *The Wall Street Journal,* this theory held for 29 out of the last 34 years. Suppose there is no truth to this theory. What is the probability this could occur by chance? (You will probably need a software package such as Excel or MINITAB.)

57. During the second round of the 1989 U.S. Open golf tournament, four golfers scored a hole in one on the sixth hole. The odds of a professional golfer making a hole in one are estimated to be 3,708 to 1, so the probability is 1/3,709. There were 155 golfers participating in the second round that day. Estimate the probability that four golfers would score a hole in one on the sixth hole.

58. On September 18, 2003, hurricane Isabel struck the North Carolina Coast causing extensive damage. For several days prior to reaching land the National Hurricane Center had been predicting the hurricane would come on shore between Cape Fear, North Carolina, and the North Carolina-Virginia border. It was estimated that the probability the hurricane would actually strike in this area was .95. In fact, the hurricane did come on shore almost exactly as forecast and was almost in the center of the strike area.

Suppose the National Hurricane Center forecasts that hurricanes will hit the strike area with a .95 probability. Answer the following questions:

a. What probability distribution does this follow?

b. What is the probability that 10 hurricanes reach landfall in the strike area?

c. What is the probability at least one of 10 hurricanes reaches land outside the strike area?

59. A recent CBS News survey reported that 67 percent of adults felt the U.S. Treasury should continue making pennies.

Suppose we select a sample of fifteen adults.

a. How many of the fifteen would we expect to indicate that the Treasury should continue making pennies? What is the standard deviation?

b. What is the likelihood that exactly 8 adults would indicate the Treasury should continue making pennies?

c. What is the likelihood at least 8 adults would indicate the Treasury should continue making pennies?

Dataset Exercises

60. Refer to the Real Estate data, which reports information on homes sold in the Denver, Colorado, area last year.

a. Create a probability distribution for the number of bedrooms. Compute the mean and the standard deviation of this distribution.

b. Create a probability distribution for the number of bathrooms. Compute the mean and the standard deviation of this distribution.

Software Commands

1. The MegaStat commands to create the binomial probability distribution on page 169 are:

a. Select the **MegaStat** option on the toolbar, click on **Probability**, and **Discrete Probability Distributions.**

b. In the dialog box select **Binomial**, the number of trials is *6*, the probability of a success is *.05*. If you wish to see a graph, click on **display graph**.

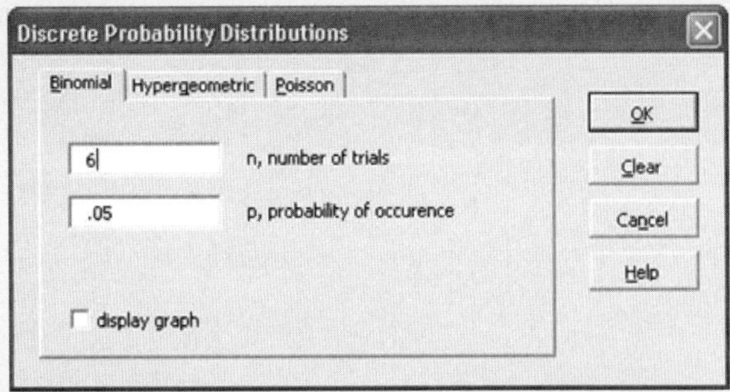

2. The Excel commands necessary to determine the binomial probability distribution on page 169 are:

a. On a blank Excel worksheet write the word *Success* in cell *A1* and the word *Probability* in *B1*. In cells A2 through *A14* write the integers *0* to *12*. Enter *B2* as the active cell.

b. From the toolbar select **Insert** and **Function Wizard.**

c. In the first dialog box select **Statistical** in the function category and **BINOMDIST** in the function name category, then click **OK.**

d. In the second dialog box enter the four items necessary to compute a binomial probability.

1. Enter *0* for the number of successes.
2. Enter *40* for the number of trials.
3. Enter *.09* for the probability of a success.
4. Enter the word *false* or the number *0* for the individual probabilities and click on **OK.**
5. Excel will compute the probability of 0 successes in 40 trials, with a .09 probability of success. The result, .02299618, is stored in cell B2.

e. To find the complete probability distribution, go to the formula bar and replace the *0* to the right of the open parentheses with *A2:A14.*

f. Move the mouse to the lower right corner of cell *B2* and highlight the B column to cell *B14.* The probability of a success for the various values of the random variable will appear.

BINOMDIST
Number_s 0 = 0
Trials 40 = 40
Probability_s .09 = 0.09
Cumulative 0 = FALSE
= 0.02299618
Returns the individual term binomial distribution probability.
Cumulative is a logical value: for the cumulative distribution function, use TRUE; for the probability mass function, use FALSE.
Formula result =0.02299618
OK Cancel

3. The MINITAB commands to generate the Poisson distribution on page 176 are:
   a. Label column *C1* as *Successes* and *C2* as *Probability.* Enter the integers *0* though *5* in the first column.
   b. Select **Calc**, then **Probability Distributions,** and **Poisson.**
   c. In the dialog box click on **Probability,** set the mean equal to *.3,* and select *C1* as the Input column. Designate *C2* as Optional storage, and then click **OK.**

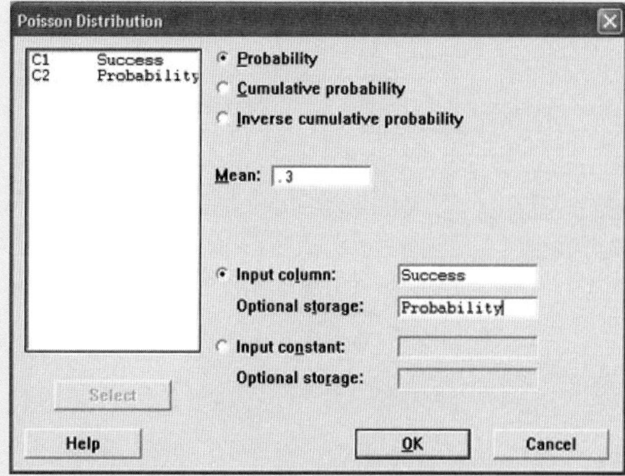

Chapter 6 Answers to Self-Review

6–1 a.

Number of Spots	Probability
1	$\frac{1}{6}$
2	$\frac{1}{6}$
3	$\frac{1}{6}$
4	$\frac{1}{6}$
5	$\frac{1}{6}$
6	$\frac{1}{6}$
Total	$\frac{6}{6} = 1.00$

b.

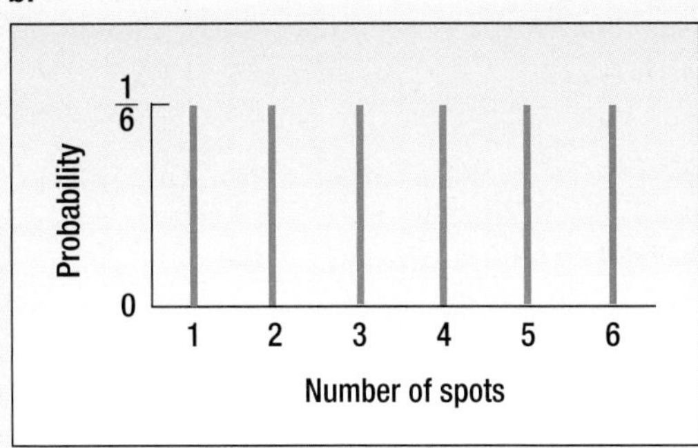

c. $\frac{6}{6}$, or 1.

6–2 a. It is discrete, because the values .80, .90, and 1.20 are clearly separated from each other. Also the sum of the probabilities is 1.00, and the outcomes are mutually exclusive.

b.

x	$P(x)$	$xP(x)$
\$ .80	.30	0.24
.90	.50	0.45
1.20	.20	0.24
		0.93

The mean is 93 cents.

c.

x	$P(x)$	$(x - \mu)$	$(x - \mu)^2 P(x)$
\$0.80	.30	−0.13	.00507
0.90	.50	−0.03	.00045
1.20	.20	0.27	.01458
			.02010

The variance is .02010, and the standard deviation is \$0.14.

6–3 a. It is reasonable because: each employee either uses direct deposit or does not; employees are independent; the probability of using direct deposit is .80 for all; and we count the number using the service out of 7.

b. $P(7) = {}_7C_7\,(.80)^7\,(.20)^0 = .2097$

c. $P(4) = {}_7C_4\,(.80)^4\,(.20)^3 = .1147$

d. Answers are in agreement.

6–4 $n = 4,\ \pi = .60$

a. $P(x = 2) = .346$

b. $P(x \leq 2) = .526$

c. $P(x > 2) = 1 - .526 = .474$

6–5 $\mu = 4{,}000(.0002) = 0.8$

$$P(1) = \frac{0.8^1 e^{-0.8}}{1!} = .3595$$

7

Continuous Probability Distributions

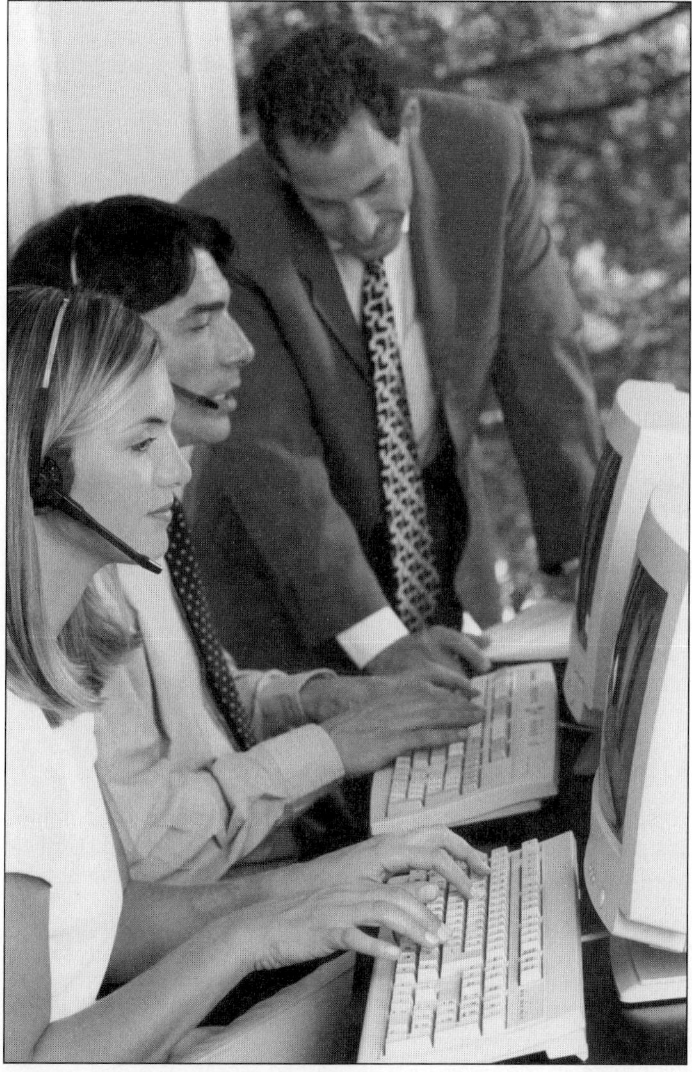

A telemarketing company DeKorte has telecommunications equipment including software for selecting numbers for calls. Some systems may be more effective than others and so DeKorte is testing claims by one of their system suppliers. (See Goal 7 and Exercise 53.)

GOALS

When you have completed this chapter you will be able to:

1 Understand the difference between *discrete* and *continuous* distributions.

2 Compute the mean and the standard deviation for a *uniform probability distribution.*

3 Compute probabilities by using the *uniform distribution.*

4 List the characteristics of the *normal probability distribution.*

5 Define and calculate *z values.*

6 Determine the probability an observation is between two points on a normal distribution by using the standard normal distribution.

7 Determine the probability an observation is above (or below) a point on a normal distribution by using the standard normal distribution.

Introduction

Chapter 6 began our study of probability distributions. We considered two *discrete* probability distributions: binomial and Poisson. These distributions are based on discrete random variables, which can assume only clearly separated values. For example, we select for study 10 small businesses which began operations during the year 2000. The number still operating in 2005 can be 0, 1, 2, . . . , 10. There cannot be 3.7, 12, or −7 still operating in 2005. In this example, only certain outcomes are possible and these outcomes are represented by clearly separated values. In addition, the result is usually found by counting the number of successes. We count the number of the businesses in the study that are still in operation in 2005.

In this chapter, we continue our study of probability distributions by examining *continuous* probability distributions. A continuous probability distribution usually results from measuring something, such as the distance from the dormitory to the classroom, the weight of an individual, or the amount of bonus earned by CEOs. Suppose we select five students and find the distance, in miles, they travel to attend class as 12.2, 8.9, 6.7, 3.6, and 14.6. When examining a continuous distribution we are usually interested in information such as the percent of students who travel less than 10 miles or the percent who travel more than 8 miles. In other words, for a continuous distribution we may wish to know the percent of observations that occur within a certain range. It is important to realize that a continuous random variable has an infinite number of values within a particular range. So you think of the probability a variable will have a value within a specified range, rather than the probability for a specific value.

We consider two families of continuous probability distributions, the **uniform probability distribution** and the **normal probability distribution.** These distributions describe the likelihood that a continuous random variable with an infinite number of possible values will fall within a specified range. For example, suppose the time to access the McGraw-Hill web page (www.mhhe.com) is uniformly distributed with a minimum time of 20 milliseconds and a maximum time of 60 milliseconds. Then we can determine the probability the page can be accessed in 30 milliseconds or less. The access time is measured on a continuous scale.

The second continuous distribution discussed in this chapter is the normal probability distribution. The normal distribution is described by its mean and standard deviation. For example, assume the life of an Energizer C-size battery follows a normal distribution with a mean of 45 hours and a standard deviation of 10 hours when used in a particular toy. We can determine the likelihood the battery will last more than 50 hours, between 35 and 62 hours, or less than 39 hours. The life of the battery is measured on a continuous scale.

The Family of Uniform Distributions

The uniform probability distribution is perhaps the simplest distribution for a continuous random variable. This distribution is rectangular in shape and is defined by minimum and maximum values. Here are some examples that follow a uniform distribution.

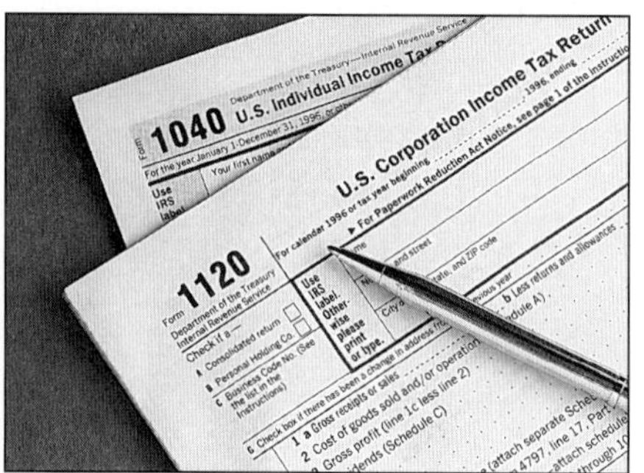

- The time to fly via a commercial airliner from Orlando, Florida to Atlanta, Georgia ranges from 60 minutes to 120 minutes. The random variable is the flight time within this interval. Note the variable of interest, flight time in minutes, is continuous in the interval from 60 minutes to 120 minutes.
- Volunteers at the Grand Strand Public Library prepare federal income tax forms. The time to prepare form 1040-EZ follows a uniform distribution over the interval between 10 minutes and 30 minutes. The random variable is the number of minutes to complete the form, and it can assume any value between 10 and 30.

A uniform distribution is shown in Chart 7–1. The distribution's shape is rectangular and has a minimum value of *a* and a maximum of *b*. Also notice in Chart 7–1 the height of the distribution is constant or uniform for all values between *a* and *b*. This implies that all the values in the range are equally likely.

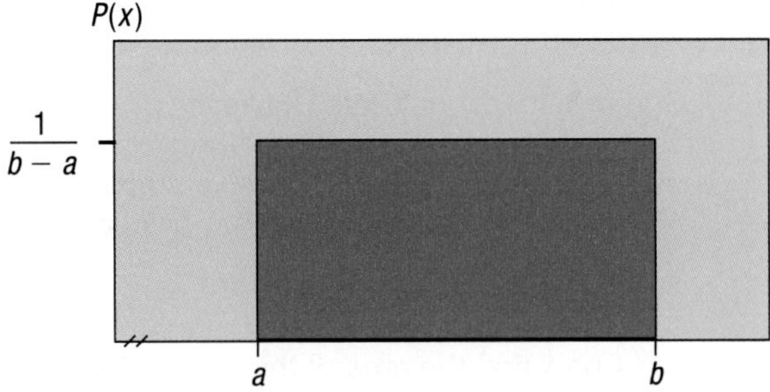

CHART 7–1 A Continuous Uniform Distribution

The mean of a uniform distribution is located in the middle of the interval between the minimum and maximum values. It is computed as:

MEAN OF THE UNIFORM DISTRIBUTION	$\mu = \frac{a + b}{2}$	**[7–1]**

The standard deviation describes the dispersion of a distribution. In the uniform distribution, the standard deviation is also related to the interval between the maximum and minimum values.

STANDARD DEVIATION OF THE UNIFORM DISTRIBUTION	$\sigma = \sqrt{\frac{(b - a)^2}{12}}$	**[7–2]**

The height of the distribution, $P(x)$, is equal for all values of the random variable, x. The height of the uniform probability distribution can be computed as:

UNIFORM DISTRIBUTION	$P(x) = \frac{1}{b - a}$ if $a \leq x \leq b$ and 0 elsewhere	**[7–3]**

As described in Chapter 6, probability distributions are useful for making probability statements concerning the values of a random variable. For distributions describing a continuous random variable, areas within the distribution represent probabilities. In the uniform distribution, its rectangular shape allows us to apply the area formula for a rectangle. Recall we find the area of a rectangle by multiplying its length by its height. For the uniform distribution the height of the rectangle is $P(x)$, which is $1/(b - a)$. The length or base of the distribution is $b - a$. Notice that if we multiply the height of the distribution by its entire range to find the area, the result is always 1.00. To put it another way, the total area within a continuous probability distribution is always equal to 1.00. In general

$$\text{Area} = (\text{height})(\text{base}) = \left(\frac{1}{b - a}\right)(b - a) = 1.00$$

So if a uniform distribution ranges from 10 to 15 the height is 0.20, found by 1/(15 − 10). The base is 5, found by 15 − 10. The total area is:

$$\text{Area} = (\text{height})(\text{base}) = \frac{1}{(15 - 10)}(15 - 10) = 1.00$$

An example will illustrate the features of a uniform distribution and how we calculate probabilities using it.

EXAMPLE

Southwest Arizona State University provides bus service to students while they are on campus. A bus arrives at the North Main Street and College Drive stop every 30 minutes between 6 A.M. and 11 P.M. during weekdays. Students arrive at the bus stop at random times. The time that a student waits is uniformly distributed from 0 to 30 minutes.

1. Draw a graph of this distribution.
2. Show that the area of this uniform distribution is 1.00.
3. How long will a student "typically" have to wait for a bus? In other words what is the mean waiting time? What is the standard deviation of the waiting times?
4. What is the probability a student will wait more than 25 minutes?
5. What is the probability a student will wait between 10 and 20 minutes?

SOLUTION

In this case the random variable is the length of time a student must wait. Time is measured on a continuous scale, and the wait times may range from 0 minutes up to 30 minutes.

1. The graph of the uniform distribution is shown in Chart 7–2. The horizontal line is drawn at a height of .0333, found by 1/(30 − 0). The range of this distribution is 30 minutes.

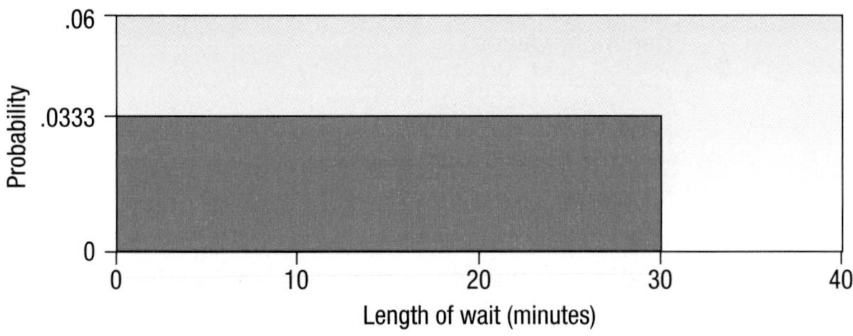

CHART 7–2 Uniform Probability Distribution of Student Waiting Times

2. The times students must wait for the bus is uniform over the interval from 0 minutes to 30 minutes, so in this case a is 0 and b is 30.

$$\text{Area} = (\text{height})(\text{base}) = \frac{1}{(30 - 0)}(30 - 0) = 1.00$$

3. To find the mean, we use formula (7–1).

$$\mu = \frac{a + b}{2} = \frac{0 + 30}{2} = 15$$

The mean of the distribution is 15 minutes, so the typical wait time for bus service is 15 minutes.

To find the standard deviation of the wait times, we use formula (7–2).

$$\sigma = \sqrt{\frac{(b-a)^2}{12}} = \sqrt{\frac{(30-0)^2}{12}} = 8.66$$

The standard deviation of the distribution is 8.66 minutes. This measures the variation in the student wait times.

4. The area within the distribution for the interval, 25 to 30, represents this particular probability. From the area formula:

$$P(25 < \text{wait time} < 30) = (\text{height})(\text{base}) = \frac{1}{(30-0)}(5) = .1667$$

So the probability a student waits between 25 and 30 minutes is .1667. This conclusion is illustrated by the following graph.

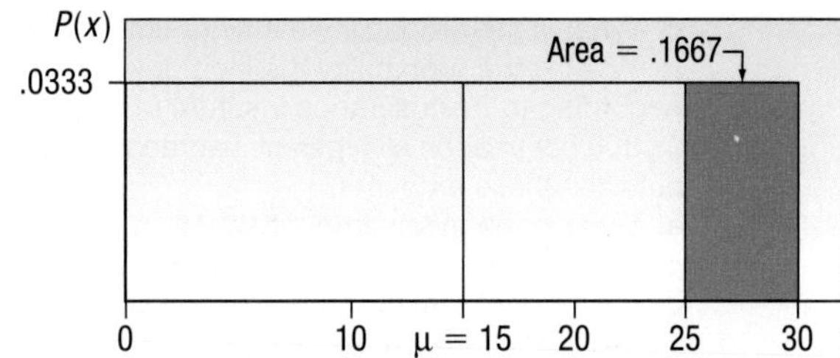

5. The area within the distribution for the interval, 10 to 20, represents the probability.

$$P(10 < \text{wait time} < 20) = (\text{height})(\text{base}) = \frac{1}{(30-0)}(10) = .3333$$

We can illustrate this probability as follows.

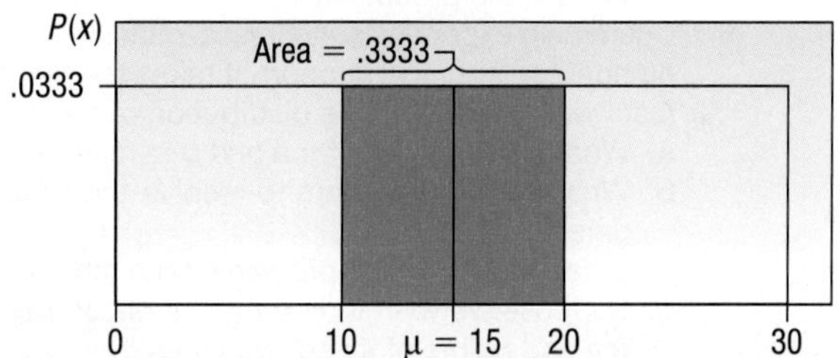

Self Review 7–1

Australian sheep dogs have a relatively short life. The length of their life follows a uniform distribution between 8 and 14 years.

(a) Draw this uniform distribution. What are the height and base values?
(b) Show the total area under the curve is 1.00.
(c) Calculate the mean and the standard deviation of this distribution.
(d) What is the probability a particular dog lives between 10 and 14 years?
(e) What is the probability a dog will live less than 9 years?

Exercises

1. A uniform distribution is defined over the interval from 6 to 10.
  a. What are the values for *a* and *b*?
  b. What is the mean of this uniform distribution?

c. What is the standard deviation?
d. Show that the total area is 1.00.
e. Find the probability of a value more than 7.
f. Find the probability of a value between 7 and 9.

2. A uniform distribution is defined over the interval from 2 to 5.
a. What are the values for *a* and *b*?
b. What is the mean of this uniform distribution?
c. What is the standard deviation?
d. Show that the total area is 1.00.
e. Find the probability of a value more than 2.6.
f. Find the probability of a value between 2.9 and 3.7.

3. America West Airlines reports the flight time from Los Angeles International Airport to Las Vegas is 1 hour and 5 minutes, or 65 minutes. Suppose the actual flying time is uniformly distributed between 60 and 70 minutes.
a. Show a graph of the continuous probability distribution.
b. What is the mean flight time? What is the variance of the flight times?
c. What is the probability the flight time is less than 68 minutes?
d. What is the probability the flight takes more than 64 minutes?

4. According to the Insurance Institute of America, a family of four spends between $400 and $3,800 per year on all types of insurance. Suppose the money spent is uniformly distributed between these amounts.
a. What is the mean amount spent on insurance?
b. What is the standard deviation of the amount spent?
c. If we select a family at random, what is the probability they spend less than $2,000 per year on insurance per year?
d. What is the probability a family spends more than $3,000 per year?

5. The April rainfall in Flagstaff, Arizona, follows a uniform distribution between 0.5 and 3.00 inches.
a. What are the values for *a* and *b*?
b. What is the mean amount of rainfall for the month? What is the standard deviation?
c. What is the probability of less than an inch of rain for the month?
d. What is the probability of "exactly" 1.00 inch of rain?
e. What is the probability of more than 1.50 inches of rain for the month?

6. Customers experiencing technical difficulty with their Internet cable hookup may call an 800 number for technical support. It takes the technician between 30 seconds to 10 minutes to resolve the problem. The distribution of this support time follows the uniform distribution.
a. What are the values for *a* and *b* in minutes?
b. What is the mean time to resolve the problem? What is the standard deviation of the time?
c. What percent of the problems take more than 5 minutes to resolve.
d. Suppose we wish to find the middle 50 percent of the problem-solving times. What are the end points of these two times?

The Family of Normal Probability Distributions

Next we consider the normal probability distribution. Unlike the uniform distribution [see formula (7–3)] the normal probability distribution has a very complex formula.

NORMAL PROBABILITY DISTRIBUTION

$$P(x) = \frac{1}{\sigma\sqrt{2\pi}} e^{-\left[\frac{(X-\mu)^2}{2\sigma^2}\right]} \qquad \textbf{[7–4]}$$

However, do not be bothered by how complex this formula looks. You are already familiar with many of the values. The symbols μ and σ refer to the mean and the standard deviation, as usual. The value of π is the mathematical constant of 22/7, or 3.1416, from your high school algebra. The letter *e* is also a mathematical constant. It is the base of the natural log system and is equal to 2.718. *X* is the value of a continuous random variable. So a normal distribution is based on—that is, it is defined by—its mean and standard deviation.

You will not need to make any calculations from formula (7–4). Instead you will be using a table, which is given as Appendix D or statistical software, to look up the various probabilities.

The normal probability distribution has the following major characteristics.

1. It is **bell-shaped** and has a single peak at the center of the distribution. The arithmetic mean, median, and mode are equal and located in the center of the distribution. Thus half the area under the normal curve is to the right of this center point and the other half to the left of it.
2. It is **symmetrical** about the mean. If we cut the normal curve vertically at the center value, the two halves will be mirror images.
3. It falls off smoothly in either direction from the central value. That is, the distribution is **asymptotic:** The curve gets closer and closer to the *X*-axis but never actually touches it. To put it another way, the tails of the curve extend indefinitely in both directions.
4. The location of a normal distribution is determined by the mean, μ. The dispersion or spread of the distribution is determined by the standard deviation, σ.

These characteristics are shown graphically in Chart 7–3.

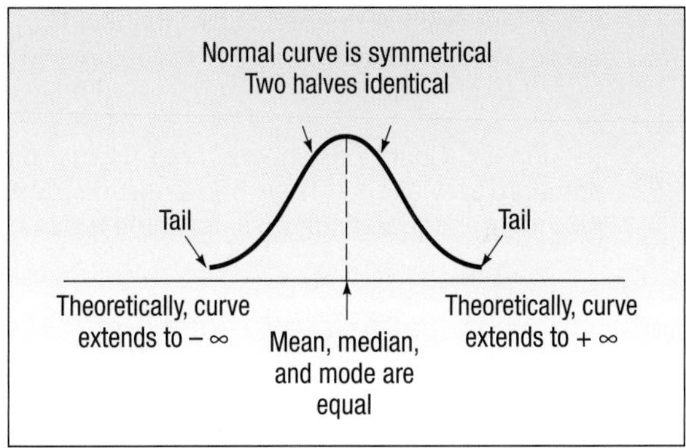

CHART 7–3 Characteristics of a Normal Distribution

There is not just one normal probability distribution, but rather a "family" of them. For example, in Chart 7–4 the probability distributions of length of employee service in three different plants can be compared. In the Camden plant, the mean is 20 years and the standard deviation is 3.1 years. There is another normal probability distribution for the length of service in the Dunkirk plant, where $\mu = 20$ years and $\sigma = 3.9$ years. In the Elmira plant, $\mu = 20$ years and $\sigma = 5.0$. Note that the means are the same but the standard deviations are different.

Equal means, unequal standard deviations

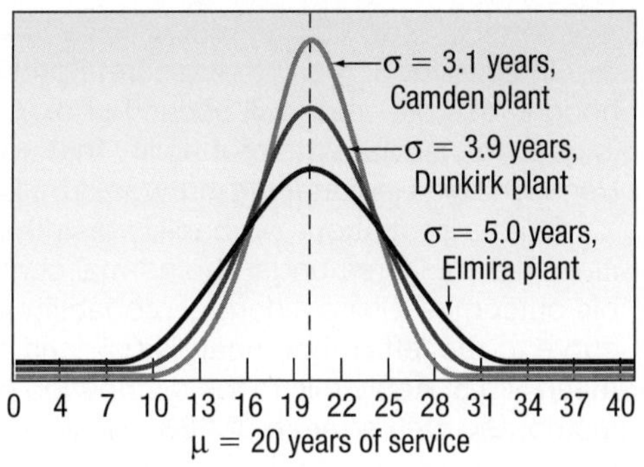

CHART 7–4 Normal Probability Distributions with Equal Means but Different Standard Deviations

Chart 7–5 shows the distribution of box weights of three different cereals. The weights follow a normal distribution with different means but identical standard deviations.

Unequal means, equal standard deviations

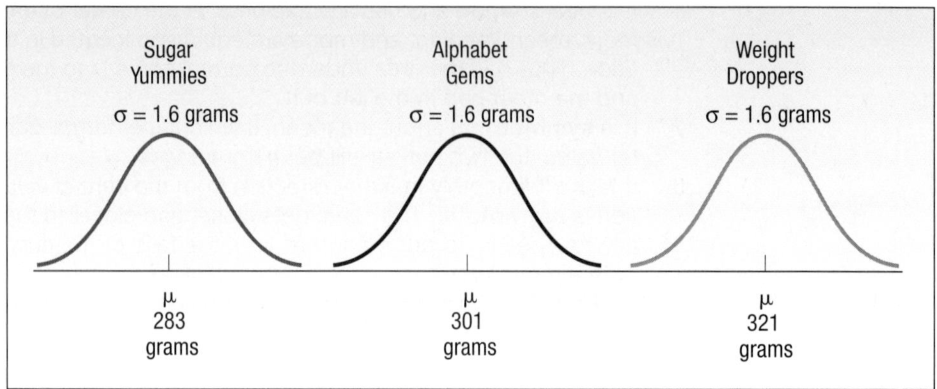

CHART 7–5 Normal Probability Distributions Having Different Means but Equal Standard Deviations

Finally, Chart 7–6 shows three normal distributions having different means and standard deviations. They show the distribution of tensile strengths, measured in pounds per square inch (psi), for three types of cables.

Unequal means, unequal standard deviations

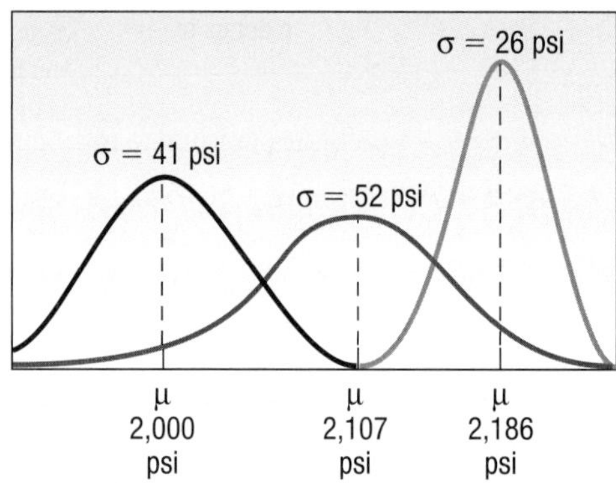

CHART 7–6 Normal Probability Distributions with Different Means and Standard Deviations

In Chapter 6, recall that discrete probability distributions show the specific likelihood a discrete value will occur. For example, on page 166, the binomial distribution is used to calculate the probability that none of the five flights arriving at the Bradford Pennsylvania Regional Airport would be late.

With a continuous probability distribution, areas below the curve define probabilities. The total area under the normal curve is always 1.0. This accounts for all possible outcomes. Since a normal probability distribution is symmetric, the area under the curve to the left of the mean is 0.5, and the area under the curve to the right of the mean is 0.5. Apply this to the distribution of Sugar Yummies in Chart 7–5. It is normally distributed with a mean of 283 grams. Therefore, the probability of filling a box with more than 283 grams is 0.5 and the probability of filling a box with less than 283 grams is 0.5. We can also determine the probability that a box weighs between 280 and 286 grams. However, to determine this probability we need to know about the standard normal probability distribution.

The Standard Normal Distribution

The number of normal distributions is unlimited, each having a different mean (μ), standard deviation (σ), or both. While it is possible to provide probability tables for discrete distributions such as the binomial and the Poisson, providing tables for the infinite number of normal distributions is impossible. Fortunately, one member of the family can be used to determine the probabilities for all normal distributions. It is called the **standard normal distribution,** and it is unique because it has a mean of 0 and a standard deviation of 1.

Any *normal distribution* can be converted into a *standard normal distribution* by subtracting the mean from each observation and dividing this difference by the standard deviation. The results are called ***z* values.** They are also referred to as ***z* scores,** the ***z* statistics,** the **standard normal deviates,** the **standard normal values,** or just the **normal deviate.**

***z* VALUE** The signed distance between a selected value, designated *X,* and the mean, μ, divided by the standard deviation, σ.

So, a *z* value is the distance from the mean, measured in units of the standard deviation.

In terms of a formula:

STANDARD NORMAL VALUE $$z = \frac{X - \mu}{\sigma}$$ **[7–5]**

where:

X is the value of any particular observation or measurement.
μ is the mean of the distribution.
σ is the standard deviation of the distribution.

As noted in the above definition, a *z* value expresses the distance or difference between a particular value of *X* and the arithmetic mean in units of the standard deviation. Once the normally distributed observations are standardized, the *z* values are normally distributed with a mean of 0 and a standard deviation of 1. The table in Appendix D (also on the inside back cover) lists the probabilities for the standard normal probability distribution.

To explain, suppose we wish to compute the probability that boxes of Sugar Yummies weigh between 283 and 285.4 grams. From Chart 7–5, we know that the box weight of Sugar Yummies follows the normal distribution with a mean of 283 grams and a standard deviation of 1.6 grams. We want to know the probability or area under the curve between the mean, 283 grams, and 285.4 grams. We can also express this problem using probability notation, similar to the style used in the previous chapter: $P(283 < \text{weight} < 285.4)$. To find the probability, it is necessary to convert both 283 grams and 285.4 grams to *z* values using formula (7–5). The *z* value corresponding to 283 is 0, found by (283 − 283)/1.6. The *z* value corresponding to 285.4 is 1.50 found by (285.4 − 283)/1.6. Next we go to the table in Appendix D. A portion of the table is repeated as Table 7–1. Go down the column of the table headed by the letter *z* to 1.5. Then move horizontally to the right and read the probability under the column headed 0.00. It is 0.4332. This means the area under the curve between 0.00 and 1.50 is 0.4332. This is the probability that a randomly selected box of Sugar Yummies will weigh between 283 and 285.4 grams. This is illustrated in the following graph.

TABLE 7–1 Areas under the Normal Curve

z	0.00	0.01	0.02	0.03	0.04	0.05	...
1.3	0.4032	0.4049	0.4066	0.4082	0.4099	0.4115	
1.4	0.4192	0.4207	0.4222	0.4236	0.4251	0.4265	
1.5	0.4332	0.4345	0.4357	0.4370	0.4382	0.4394	
1.6	0.4452	0.4463	0.4474	0.4484	0.4495	0.4505	
1.7	0.4554	0.4564	0.4573	0.4582	0.4591	0.4599	
1.8	0.4641	0.4649	0.4656	0.4664	0.4671	0.4678	
1.9	0.4713	0.4719	0.4726	0.4732	0.4738	0.4744	
.							
.							
.							

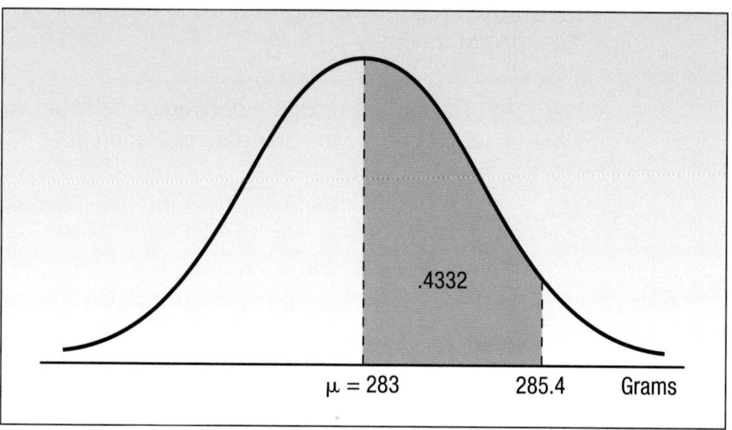

Now we will compute the z value given the population mean, μ, the population standard deviation, σ, and a selected X.

EXAMPLE

The weekly incomes of shift foremen in the glass industry are normally distributed with a mean of $1,000 and a standard deviation of $100. What is the z value for the income X of a foreman who earns $1,100 per week? For a foreman who earns $900 per week?

SOLUTION

Using formula (7–5), the z values for the two X values ($1,100 and $900) are:

For X = $1,100:

$$z = \frac{X - \mu}{\sigma} = \frac{\$1{,}100 - \$1{,}000}{\$100} = 1.00$$

For X = $900:

$$z = \frac{X - \mu}{\sigma} = \frac{\$900 - \$1{,}000}{\$100} = -1.00$$

The z of 1.00 indicates that a weekly income of $1,100 is one standard deviation above the mean, and a z of -1.00 shows that a $900 income is one standard deviation below the mean. Note that both incomes ($1,100 and $900) are the same distance ($100) from the mean.

Self-Review 7–2

Using the information in the preceding example ($\mu = \$1,000$, $\sigma = \$100$), convert:

(a) The weekly income of $1,225 to a *z* value.
(b) The weekly income of $775 to a *z* value.

The Empirical Rule

Statistics in Action

An individual's skills depend on a combination of many hereditary and environmental factors, each having about the same amount of weight or influence on the skills. Thus, much like a binomial distribution with a large number of trials, many skills and attributes follow the normal distribution. For example, scores on the Scholastic Aptitude Test (SAT) are normally distributed with a mean of 1000 and a standard deviation of 140.

Before examining further applications of the standard normal probability distribution, we will consider three areas under the normal curve that will be used extensively in the following chapters. These facts were called the Empirical Rule in Chapter 3, see page 83.

1. About 68 percent of the area under the normal curve is within one standard deviation of the mean. This can be written as $\mu \pm 1\sigma$.
2. About 95 percent of the area under the normal curve is within two standard deviations of the mean, written $\mu \pm 2\sigma$.
3. Practically all of the area under the normal curve is within three standard deviations of the mean, written $\mu \pm 3\sigma$.

This information is summarized in the following graph.

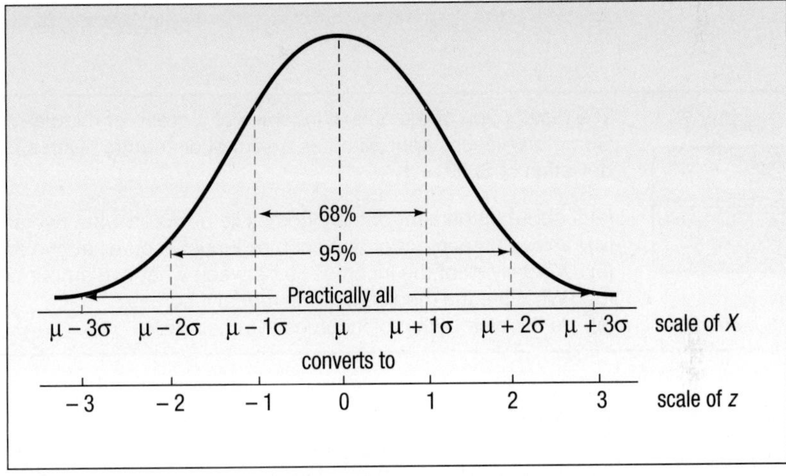

Transforming measurements to standard normal deviates changes the scale. The conversions are also shown in the graph. For example, $\mu + 1\sigma$ is converted to a *z* value of 1.00. Likewise, $\mu - 2\sigma$ is transformed to a *z* value of −2.00. Note that the center of the *z* distribution is zero, indicating no deviation from the mean, μ.

EXAMPLE

As part of their quality assurance program, the Autolite Battery Company conducts tests on battery life. For a particular D cell alkaline battery, the mean life is 19 hours. The useful life of the battery follows a normal distribution with a standard deviation of 1.2 hours. Answer the following questions.

1. About 68 percent of the batteries failed between what two values?
2. About 95 percent of the batteries failed between what two values?
3. Virtually all of the batteries failed between what two values?

SOLUTION

We can use the results of the Empirical Rule to answer these questions.

1. About 68 percent of the batteries will fail between 17.8 and 20.2 hours, found by 19.0 ± 1(1.2) hours.
2. About 95 percent of the batteries will fail between 16.6 and 21.4 hours, found by 19.0 ± 2(1.2) hours.
3. Virtually all failed between 15.4 and 22.6 hours, found by 19.0 ± 3(1.2) hours.

This information is summarized on the following chart.

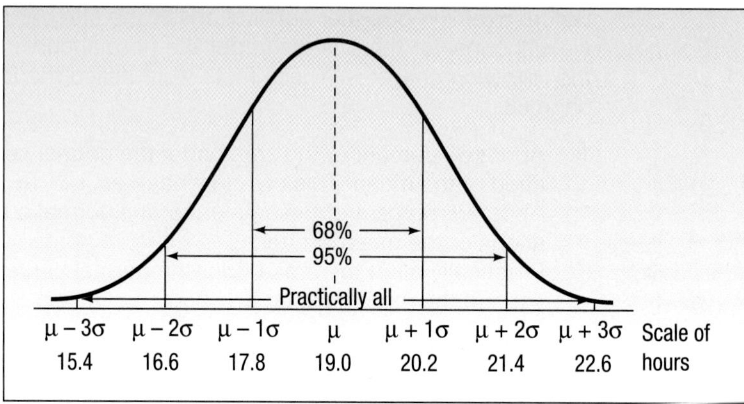

Self-Review 7–3

The distribution of the annual incomes of a group of middle-management employees at Compton Plastics approximates a normal distribution with a mean of $47,200 and a standard deviation of $800.

(a) About 68 percent of the incomes lie between what two amounts?
(b) About 95 percent of the incomes lie between what two amounts?
(c) Virtually all of the incomes lie between what two amounts?
(d) What are the median and the modal incomes?
(e) Is the distribution of incomes symmetrical?

Exercises

7. Explain what is meant by this statement: "There is not just one normal probability distribution but a 'family' of them."

8. List the major characteristics of a normal probability distribution.

9. The mean of a normal probability distribution is 500; the standard deviation is 10.
  a. About 68 percent of the observations lie between what two values?
  b. About 95 percent of the observations lie between what two values?
  c. Practically all of the observations lie between what two values?

10. The mean of a normal probability distribution is 60; the standard deviation is 5.
  a. About what percent of the observations lie between 55 and 65?
  b. About what percent of the observations lie between 50 and 70?
  c. About what percent of the observations lie between 45 and 75?

11. The Kamp family has twins, Rob and Rachel. Both Rob and Rachel graduated from college 2 years ago, and each is now earning $50,000 per year. Rachel works in the retail industry, where the mean salary for executives with less than 5 years' experience is $35,000 with a standard deviation of $8,000. Rob is an engineer. The mean salary for engineers with less than 5 years' experience is $60,000 with a standard deviation of $5,000. Compute the z values for both Rob and Rachel and comment on your findings.

12. A recent article in the *Cincinnati Enquirer* reported that the mean labor cost to repair a heat pump is $90 with a standard deviation of $22. Monte's Plumbing and Heating Service completed repairs on two heat pumps this morning. The labor cost for the first was $75 and it was $100 for the second. Compute z values for each and comment on your findings.

Finding Areas under the Normal Curve

The next application of the standard normal distribution involves finding the area in a normal distribution between the mean and a selected value, which we identify as *X*. The following example will illustrate the details.

EXAMPLE

Recall in an earlier example (see page 194) we reported that the mean weekly income of a shift foreman in the glass industry is normally distributed with a mean of $1,000 and a standard deviation of $100. That is, μ = $1,000 and σ = $100. What is the likelihood of selecting a foreman whose weekly income is between $1,000 and $1,100? We write this question in probability notation as: *P*($1,000 < weekly income < $1,100).

SOLUTION

We have already converted $1,100 to a *z* value of 1.00 using formula (7–5). To repeat:

$$z = \frac{X - \mu}{\sigma} = \frac{\$1{,}100 - \$1{,}000}{\$100} = 1.00$$

The probability associated with a *z* of 1.00 is available in Appendix D. A portion of Appendix D follows. To locate the probability, go down the left column to 1.0, and then move horizontally to the column headed .00. The value is .3413.

z	.00	.01	.02
.	.	.	.
.	.	.	.
.	.	.	.
0.7	.2580	.2611	.2642
0.8	.2881	.2910	.2939
0.9	.3159	.3186	.3212
1.0	.3413	.3438	.3461
1.1	.3643	.3665	.3686
.	.	.	.
.	.	.	.
.	.	.	.

Statistics in Action

Many processes, such as filling soda bottles and canning fruit, are normally distributed. Manufacturers must guard against both over- and underfilling. If they put too much in the can or bottle, they are giving away their product. If they put too little in, the customer may feel cheated and the government may question the label description. "Control charts," with limits drawn three standard deviations above and below the mean, are routinely used to monitor this type of production process.

The area under the normal curve between $1,000 and $1,100 is .3413. We could also say 34.13 percent of the shift foremen in the glass industry earn between $1,000 and $1,100 weekly, or the likelihood of selecting a foreman and finding his or her income is between $1,000 and $1,100 is .3413.

This information is summarized in the following diagram.

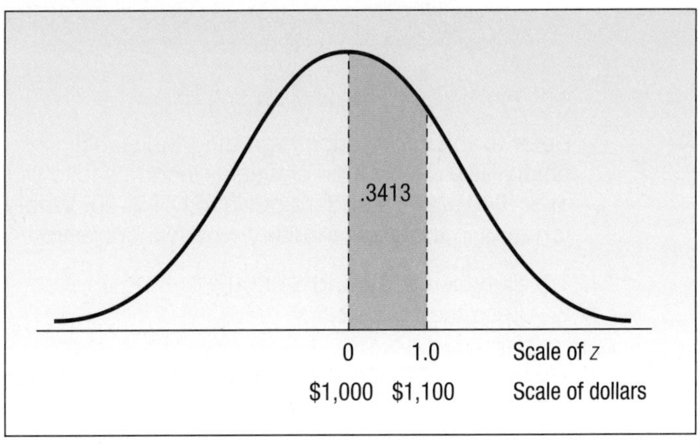

In the example just completed, we are interested in the probability between the mean and a given value. Let's change the question. Instead of wanting to know the probability of selecting at random a foreman who earned between $1,000 and $1,100, suppose we wanted the probability of selecting a foreman who earned less than $1,100. In probability notation we write this statement as *P*(weekly income < $1,100). The method of solution is the same. We find the probability of selecting a foreman who earns between $1,000, the mean, and $1,100. This probability is .3413. Next, recall that half the area, or probability, is above the mean and half is below. So the probability of selecting a foreman earning less than $1,000 is .5000. Finally, we add the two probabilities, so .3413 + .5000 = .8413. About 84 percent of the foremen in the glass industry earn less than $1,100 per month. See the following diagram.

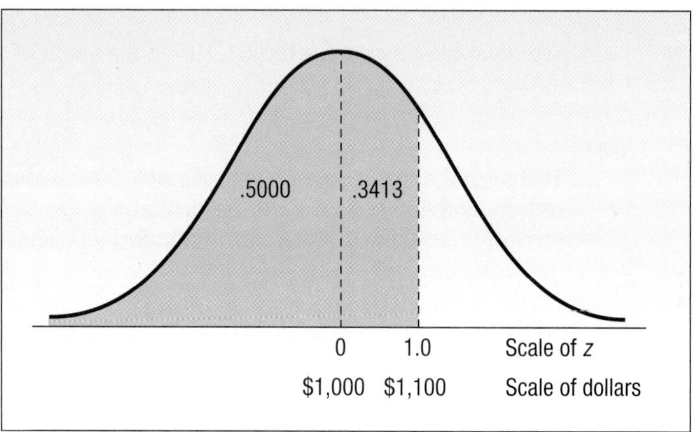

Excel will calculate this probability. The necessary commands are in the **Software Commands** section at the end of the chapter. The answer is .8413, the same as we calculated.

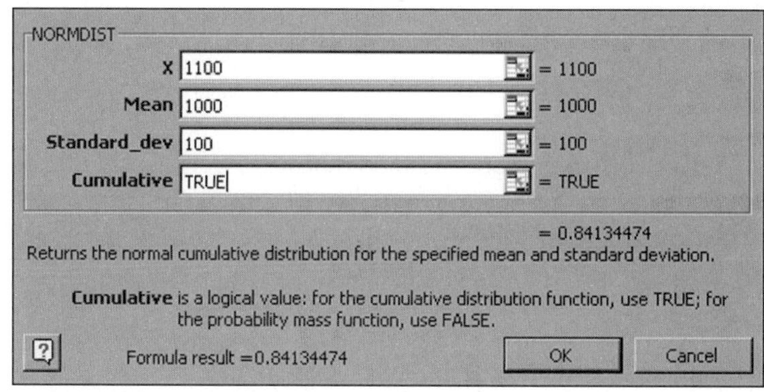

EXAMPLE

Refer to the information regarding the weekly income of shift foremen in the glass industry. The distribution of weekly incomes follows the normal distribution, with a mean of $1,000 and a standard deviation of $100. What is the probability of selecting a shift foreman in the glass industry whose income is:

1. Between $790 and $1,000?
2. Less than $790?

SOLUTION

We begin by finding the *z* value corresponding to a weekly income of $790. From formula (7–5):

$$z = \frac{X - \mu}{\sigma} = \frac{\$790 - \$1,000}{\$100} = -2.10$$

See Appendix D. Move down the left margin to the row 2.1 and across that row to the column headed 0.00. The value is .4821. So the area under the standard normal curve corresponding to a z value of 2.10 is .4821. However, because the normal distribution is symmetric, the area between 0 and a negative z value is the same as that between 0 and the corresponding positive z value. The likelihood of finding a foreman earning between \$790 and \$1,000 is .4821. In probability notation we write $P(\$790 < \text{weekly income} < \$1000) = .4821$.

z	0.00	0.01	0.02
.	.	.	.
.	.	.	.
.	.	.	.
2.0	.4772	.4778	.4783
2.1	.4821	.4826	.4830
2.2	.4861	.4864	.4868
2.3	.4893	.4896	.4898
.	.	.	.
.	.	.	.
.	.	.	.

The mean divides the normal curve into two identical halves. The area under the half to the left of the mean is .5000, and the area to the right is also .5000. Because the area under the curve between \$790 and \$1,000 is .4821, the area below \$790 is .0179, found by .5000 − .4821. In probability notation we write $P(\text{weekly income} < \$790) = .0179$.

This means that 48.21 percent of the foremen have weekly incomes between \$790 and \$1,000. Further, we can anticipate that 1.79 percent earn less than \$790 per week. This information is summarized in the following diagram.

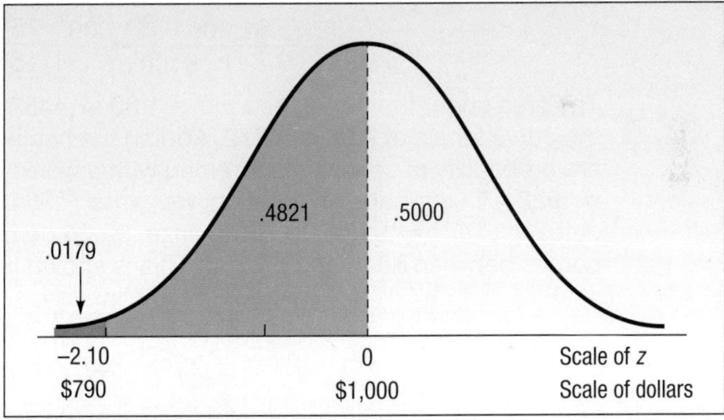

Self-Review 7–4

The employees of Cartwright Manufacturing are awarded efficiency ratings. The distribution of the ratings follows a normal distribution. The mean is 400, the standard deviation 50.

(a) What is the area under the normal curve between 400 and 482? Write this area in probability notation.
(b) What is the area under the normal curve for ratings greater than 482? Write this area in probability notation.
(c) Show the facets of this problem in a chart.

Exercises

13. A normal population has a mean of 20.0 and a standard deviation of 4.0.
a. Compute the z value associated with 25.0.

b. What proportion of the population is between 20.0 and 25.0?
c. What proportion of the population is less than 18.0?

14. A normal population has a mean of 12.2 and a standard deviation of 2.5.
a. Compute the z value associated with 14.3.
b. What proportion of the population is between 12.2 and 14.3?
c. What proportion of the population is less than 10.0?

15. A recent study of the hourly wages of maintenance crew members for major airlines showed that the mean hourly salary was \$20.50, with a standard deviation of \$3.50. If we select a crew member at random, what is the probability the crew member earns:
a. Between \$20.50 and \$24.00 per hour?
b. More than \$24.00 per hour?
c. Less than \$19.00 per hour?

16. The mean of a normal distribution is 400 pounds. The standard deviation is 10 pounds.
a. What is the area between 415 pounds and the mean of 400 pounds?
b. What is the area between the mean and 395 pounds?
c. What is the probability of selecting a value at random and discovering that it has a value of less than 395 pounds?

Another application of the normal distribution involves combining two areas, or probabilities. One of the areas is to the right of the mean and the other to the left.

EXAMPLE

Recall the distribution of weekly incomes of shift foremen in the glass industry. The weekly incomes follow the normal distribution, with a mean of \$1,000 and a standard deviation of \$100. What is the area under this normal curve between \$840 and \$1,200?

SOLUTION

The problem can be divided into two parts. For the area between \$840 and the mean of \$1,000:

$$z = \frac{\$840 - \$1{,}000}{\$100} = \frac{-\$160}{\$100} = -1.60$$

For the area between the mean of \$1,000 and \$1,200:

$$z = \frac{\$1{,}200 - \$1{,}000}{\$100} = \frac{\$200}{\$100} = 2.00$$

The area under the curve for a z of -1.60 is .4452 (from Appendix D). The area under the curve for a z of 2.00 is .4772. Adding the two areas: $.4452 + .4772 = .9224$. Thus, the probability of selecting a foreman with a weekly income between \$840 and \$1,200 is .9224. In probability notation we write $P(\$840 < \text{weekly income} < \$1{,}200) = .4452 + .4772 = .9224$. To summarize, 92.24 percent of the foremen have weekly incomes between \$840 and \$1,200. This is shown in a diagram:

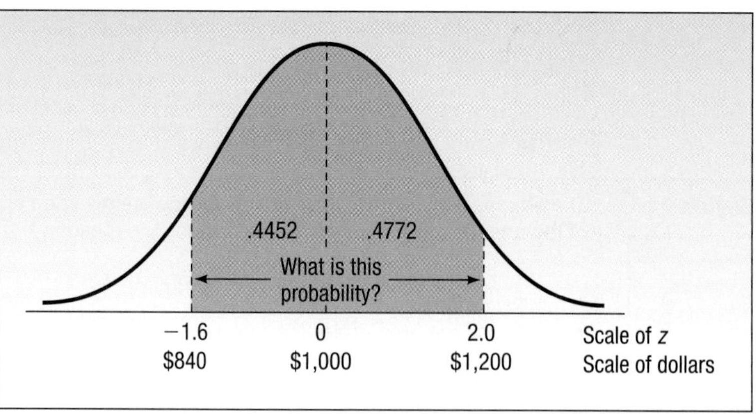

Another application of the normal distribution involves determining the area between values on the *same* side of the mean.

EXAMPLE

Returning to the weekly income distribution of shift foremen in the glass industry (μ = \$1,000, σ = \$100), what is the area under the normal curve between \$1,150 and \$1,250?

SOLUTION

The situation is again separated into two parts, and formula (7–5) is used. First, we find the z value associated with a weekly salary of \$1,250:

$$z = \frac{\$1{,}250 - \$1{,}000}{\$100} = 2.50$$

Next we find the z value for a weekly salary of \$1,150:

$$z = \frac{\$1{,}150 - \$1{,}000}{\$100} = 1.50$$

From Appendix D the area associated with a z value of 2.50 is .4938. So the probability of a weekly salary between \$1,000 and \$1,250 is .4938. Similarly, the area associated with a z value of 1.50 is .4332, so the probability of a weekly salary between \$1,000 and \$1,150 is .4332. The probability of a weekly salary between \$1,150 and \$1,250 is found by subtracting the area associated with a z value of 1.50 (.4332) from that associated with a z of 2.50 (.4938). Thus, the probability of a weekly salary between \$1,150 and \$1,250 is .0606. In probability notation we write $P(\$1{,}150 < \text{weekly income} < \$1{,}250) = .4938 - .4332 = .0606$.

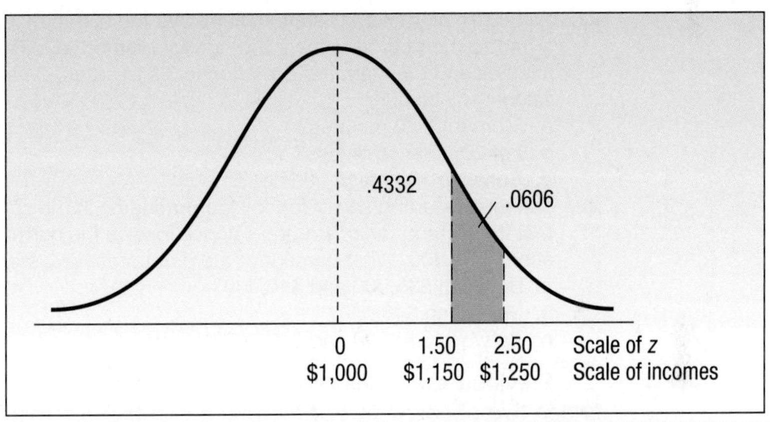

In brief, there are four situations for finding the area under the standard normal distribution.

1. To find the area between 0 and z (or $-z$), look up the probability directly in the table.
2. To find the area beyond z or ($-z$), locate the probability of z in the table and subtract that probability from .5000.
3. To find the area between two points on different sides of the mean, determine the z values and add the corresponding probabilities.
4. To find the area between two points on the same side of the mean, determine the z values and subtract the smaller probability from the larger.

Self-Review 7–5

Refer to the previous example, where the distribution of weekly incomes follows the normal distribution with a mean of \$1,000 and the standard deviation is \$100.

(a) What percent of shift foremen earn a weekly income between \$750 and \$1,225? Draw a normal curve and shade the desired area on your diagram.
(b) What percent of shift foremen earn a weekly income between \$1,100 and \$1,225? Draw a normal curve and shade the desired area on your diagram.

Exercises

17. A normal distribution has a mean of 50 and a standard deviation of 4.
a. Compute the probability of a value between 44.0 and 55.0.
b. Compute the probability of a value greater than 55.0.
c. Compute the probability of a value between 52.0 and 55.0.

18. A normal population has a mean of 80.0 and a standard deviation of 14.0.
a. Compute the probability of a value between 75.0 and 90.0.
b. Compute the probability of a value 75.0 or less.
c. Compute the probability of a value between 55.0 and 70.0.

19. A cola-dispensing machine is set to dispense on average 7.00 ounces of cola per cup. The standard deviation is 0.10 ounces. The distribution amounts dispensed follows a normal distribution.
a. What is the probability that the machine will dispense between 7.10 and 7.25 ounces of cola?
b. What is the probability that the machine will dispense 7.25 ounces of cola or more?
c. What is the probability that the machine will dispense between 6.80 and 7.25 ounces of cola?

20. The amounts of money requested on home loan applications at Down River Federal Savings follow the normal distribution, with a mean of $70,000 and a standard deviation of $20,000. A loan application is received this morning. What is the probability:
a. The amount requested is $80,000 or more?
b. The amount requested is between $65,000 and $80,000?
c. The amount requested is $65,000 or more?

21. WNAE, an all-news AM station, finds that the distribution of the lengths of time listeners are tuned to the station follows the normal distribution. The mean of the distribution is 15.0 minutes and the standard deviation is 3.5 minutes. What is the probability that a particular listener will tune in:
a. More than 20 minutes?
b. For 20 minutes or less?
c. Between 10 and 12 minutes?

22. The mean starting salary for college graduates in the spring of 2005 was $36,280. Assume that the distribution of starting salaries follows the normal distribution with a standard deviation of $3,300. What percent of the graduates have starting salaries:
a. Between $35,000 and $40,000?
b. More than $45,000?
c. Between $40,000 and $45,000?

Previous examples require finding the percent of the observations located between two observations or the percent of the observations above, or below, a particular observation *X*. A further application of the normal distribution involves finding the value of the observation *X* when the percent above or below the observation is given.

EXAMPLE

The Layton Tire and Rubber Company wishes to set a minimum mileage guarantee on its new MX100 tire. Tests reveal the mean mileage is 67,900 with a standard deviation of 2,050 miles and that the distribution of miles follows the normal distribution. They want to set the minimum guaranteed mileage so that no more than 4 percent of the tires will have to be replaced. What minimum guaranteed mileage should Layton announce?

SOLUTION

The facets of this case are shown in the following diagram, where *X* represents the minimum guaranteed mileage.

Statistics in Action

Many variables are approximately, normally distributed, such as IQ scores, life expectancies, and adult height. This implies that nearly all observations occur within 3 standard deviations of the mean. On the other hand, observations that occur beyond 3 standard deviations from the mean are extremely rare. For example, the mean adult male height is 68.2 inches (about 5 feet 8 inches) with a standard deviation of 2.74. This means that almost all males are between 60.0 inches (5 feet) and 76.4 inches (6 feet 4 inches). Shaquille O'Neal, a professional basketball player with the Los Angeles Lakers, is 86 inches or 7 feet 2 inches, which is clearly beyond 3 standard deviations from the mean. The height of a standard doorway is 6 feet 8 inches, and should be high enough for almost all adult males, except for a rare person like Shaquille O'Neal.

As another example, the driver's seat in most vehicles is set to comfortably fit a person who is at least 159 cm (62.5 inches) tall. The distribution of heights of adult women is approximately a normal distribution with a mean of 161.5 cm and a standard deviation of 6.3 cm. Thus about 35 percent of adult women will not fit comfortably in the driver's seat.

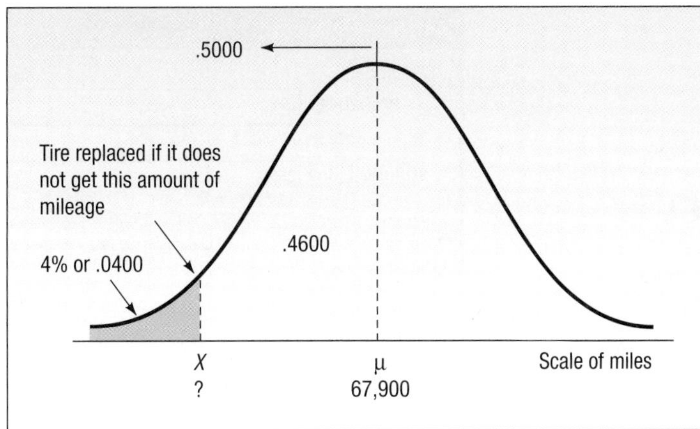

Inserting these values in formula (7–5) for z gives:

$$z = \frac{X - \mu}{\sigma} = \frac{X - 67{,}900}{2{,}050}$$

Notice that there are two unknowns, z and X. To find X, we first find z, and then solve for X. Notice the area under the normal curve to the left of μ is .5000. The area between μ and X is .4600, found by .5000 − .0400. Now refer to Appendix D. Search the body of the table for the area closest to .4600. The closest area is .4599. Move to the margins from this value and read the z value of 1.75. Because the value is to the left of the mean, it is actually −1.75. These steps are illustrated in Table 7–2.

TABLE 7–2 Selected Areas under the Normal Curve

z	.03	.04	.05	.06
.	.	.	.	.
.	.	.	.	.
.	.	.	.	.
1.5	.4370	.4382	.4394	.4406
1.6	.4484	.4495	.4505	.4515
1.7	.4582	.4591	.4599	.4608
1.8	.4664	.4671	.4678	.4686

Knowing that the distance between μ and X is -1.75σ or $z = -1.75$, we can now solve for X (the minimum guaranteed mileage):

$$z = \frac{X - 67{,}900}{2{,}050}$$

$$-1.75 = \frac{X - 67{,}900}{2{,}050}$$

$$-1.75(2{,}050) = X - 67{,}900$$

$$X = 67{,}900 - 1.75(2{,}050) = 64{,}312$$

So Layton can advertise that it will replace for free any tire that wears out before it reaches 64,312 miles, and the company will know that only 4 percent of the tires will be replaced under this plan.

Excel will also find the mileage value. See the following output. The necessary commands are given in the **Software Commands** section at the end of the chapter.

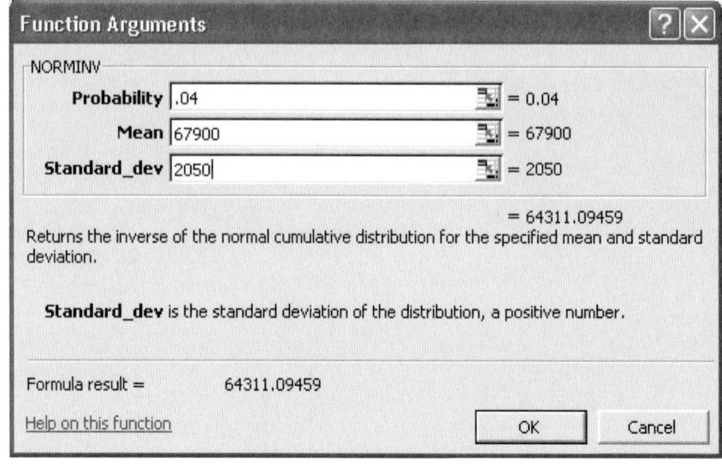

Self-Review 7–6

An analysis of the final test scores for Introduction to Business reveals the scores follow the normal distribution. The mean of the distribution is 75 and the standard deviation is 8. The professor wants to award an A to students whose score is in the highest 10 percent. What is the dividing point for those students who earn an A and those earning a B?

Exercises

23. A normal distribution has a mean of 50 and a standard deviation of 4. Determine the value below which 95 percent of the observations will occur.

24. A normal distribution has a mean of 80 and a standard deviation of 14. Determine the value above which 80 percent of the values will occur.

25. The amounts dispensed by a cola machine follow the normal distribution with a mean of 7 ounces and a standard deviation of 0.10 ounces per cup. How much cola is dispensed in the largest 1 percent of the cups?

26. Refer to Exercise 20, where the amount requested for home loans followed the normal distribution with a mean of $70,000 and a standard deviation of $20,000.

a. How much is requested on the largest 3 percent of the loans?

b. How much is requested on the smallest 10 percent of the loans?

27. Assume that the mean hourly cost to operate a commercial airplane follows the normal distribution with a mean $2,100 per hour and a standard deviation of $250. What is the operating cost for the lowest 3 percent of the airplanes?

28. The monthly sales of mufflers in the Richmond, Virginia, area follow the normal distribution with a mean of 1,200 and a standard deviation of 225. The manufacturer would like to establish inventory levels such that there is only a 5 percent chance of running out of stock. Where should the manufacturer set the inventory levels?

Chapter Outline

I. The uniform distribution is a continuous probability distribution with the following characteristics.

A. It is rectangular in shape.

B. The mean and the median are equal.

C. It is completely described by its minimum value *a* and its maximum value *b*.

D. It is also described by the following equation for the region from *a* to *b*:

$$P(x) = \frac{1}{b - a} \qquad \textbf{[7–3]}$$

E. The mean and standard deviation of a uniform distribution are computed as follows:

$$\mu = \frac{(a + b)}{2} \qquad \textbf{[7–1]}$$

$$\sigma = \sqrt{\frac{(b - a)^2}{12}} \qquad \textbf{[7–2]}$$

II. The normal distribution is a continuous distribution with the following characteristics.
- **A.** It is bell-shaped and has a single peak at the center of the distribution.
- **B.** The distribution is symmetric.
- **C.** It is asymptotic, meaning the curve approaches but never touches the *X*-axis.
- **D.** It is completely described by its mean and standard deviation.
- **E.** There is a family of normal distributions.
  1. Another normal distribution is created when either the mean or the standard deviation changes.
  2. A normal distribution is described by the following formula:

$$P(x) = \frac{1}{\sigma\sqrt{2\pi}} e^{-\left[\frac{(X-\mu)^2}{2\sigma^2}\right]} \qquad \textbf{[7–4]}$$

III. The standard normal distribution is a particular normal distribution.
- **A.** It has a mean of 0 and a standard deviation of 1.
- **B.** Any normal distribution can be converted to the standard normal distribution by the following formula.

$$z = \frac{X - \mu}{\sigma} \qquad \textbf{[7–5]}$$

- **C.** By standardizing a normal distribution, we can report the distance of a value from the mean in units of the standard deviation.

Chapter Exercises

29. The amount of cola in a 12-ounce can is uniformly distributed between 11.96 ounces and 12.05 ounces.
- **a.** What is the mean amount per can?
- **b.** What is the standard deviation amount per can?
- **c.** What is the probability of selecting a can of cola and finding it has less than 12 ounces?
- **d.** What is the probability of selecting a can of cola and finding it has more than 11.98 ounces?
- **e.** What is the probability of selecting a can of cola and finding it has more than 11.00 ounces?

30. A tube of Listerine Tartar Control toothpaste contains 4.2 ounces. As people use the toothpaste, the amount remaining in any tube is random. Assume the amount of toothpaste left in the tube follows a uniform distribution. From this information, we can determine the following information about the amount remaining in a toothpaste tube without invading anyone's privacy.
- **a.** How much toothpaste would you expect to be remaining in the tube?
- **b.** What is the standard deviation of the amount remaining in the tube?
- **c.** What is the likelihood there is less than 3.0 ounces remaining in the tube?
- **d.** What is the probability there is more than 1.5 ounces remaining in the tube?

31. Many retail stores offer their own credit cards. At the time of the credit application the customer is given a 10 percent discount on the purchase. The time required for the credit application process follows a uniform distribution with the times ranging from 4 minutes to 10 minutes.
- **a.** What is the mean time for the application process?
- **b.** What is the standard deviation of the process time?
- **c.** What is the likelihood a particular application will take less than 6 minutes?
- **d.** What is the likelihood an application will take more than 5 minutes?

32. The times patrons at the Grande Dunes Hotel in the Bahamas spend waiting for an elevator follows a uniform distribution between 0 and 3.5 minutes.
- **a.** Show that the area under the curve is 1.00.
- **b.** How long does the typical patron wait for elevator service?
- **c.** What is the standard deviation of the waiting time?

d. What percent of the patrons wait for less than a minute?
e. What percent of the patrons wait more than 2 minutes?

33. A recent report in *USA Today* indicated a typical family of four spends $490 per month on food. Assume the distribution of food expenditures for a family of four follows the normal distribution, with a mean of $490 and a standard deviation of $90.
a. What percent of the families spend more than $30 but less than $490 per month on food?
b. What percent of the families spend less than $430 per month on food?
c. What percent spend between $430 and $600 per month on food?
d. What percent spend between $500 and $600 per month on food?

34. A study of long distance phone calls made from the corporate offices of the Pepsi Bottling Group, Inc., in Somers, New York, showed the calls follow the normal distribution. The mean length of time per call was 4.2 minutes and the standard deviation was 0.60 minutes.
a. What fraction of the calls last between 4.2 and 5 minutes?
b. What fraction of the calls last more than 5 minutes?
c. What fraction of the calls last between 5 and 6 minutes?
d. What fraction of the calls last between 4 and 6 minutes?
e. As part of her report to the president, the Director of Communications would like to report the length of the longest (in duration) 4 percent of the calls. What is this time?

35. Shaver Manufacturing, Inc. offers dental insurance to its employees. A recent study by the Human Resource Director shows the annual cost per employee per year followed the normal distribution, with a mean of $1,280 and a standard deviation of $420 per year.
a. What fraction of the employees cost more than $1,500 per year for dental expenses?
b. What fraction of the employees cost between $1,500 and $2,000 per year?
c. Estimate the percent that did not have any dental expense.
d. What was the cost for the 10 percent of employees who incurred the highest dental expense?

36. The annual commissions earned by sales representatives of Machine Products, Inc. a manufacturer of light machinery, follow the normal distribution. The mean yearly amount earned is $40,000 and the standard deviation is $5,000.
a. What percent of the sales representatives earn more than $42,000 per year?
b. What percent of the sales representatives earn between $32,000 and $42,000?
c. What percent of the sales representatives earn between $32,000 and $35,000?
d. The sales manager wants to award the sales representatives who earn the largest commissions a bonus of $1,000. He can award a bonus to 20 percent of the representatives. What is the cutoff point between those who earn a bonus and those who do not?

37. According to the South Dakota Department of Health, the mean number of hours of TV viewing per week is higher among adult women than men. A recent study showed women spent an average of 34 hours per week watching TV and men 29 hours per week (www.state.sd.us/DOH/Nutrition/TV.pdf). Assume that the distribution of hours watched follows the normal distribution for both groups, and that the standard deviation among the women is 4.5 hours and it is 5.1 hours for the men.
a. What percent of the women watch TV less than 40 hours per week?
b. What percent of the men watch TV more than 25 hours per week?
c. How many hours of TV do the one percent of women who watch the most TV per week watch? Find the comparable value for the men.

38. According to a government study among adults in the 25- to 34-year age group, the mean amount spent per year on reading and entertainment is $1,994 (www.infoplease.com/ipa/A0908759.html). Assume that the distribution of the amounts spent follows the normal distribution with a standard deviation of $450.
a. What percent of the adults spend more than $2,500 per year on reading and entertainment?
b. What percent spend between $2,500 and $3,000 per year on reading and entertainment?
c. What percent spend less than $1,000 per year on reading and entertainment?

39. The weights of cans of Monarch pears follow the normal distribution with a mean of 1,000 grams and a standard deviation of 50 grams. Calculate the percentage of the cans that weigh:
a. Less than 860 grams.
b. Between 1,055 and 1,100 grams.
c. Between 860 and 1,055 grams.

40. The number of passengers on the *Carnival Sensation* during one-week cruises in the Caribbean follows the normal distribution. The mean number of passengers per cruise is 1,820 and the standard deviation is 120.
a. What percent of the cruises will have between 1,820 and 1,970 passengers?

b. What percent of the cruises will have 1,970 passengers or more?
c. What percent of the cruises will have 1,600 or fewer passengers?
d. How many passengers are on the cruises with the fewest 25 percent of passengers?

41. Management at Gordon Electronics is considering adopting a bonus system to increase production. One suggestion is to pay a bonus on the highest 5 percent of production based on past experience. Past records indicate weekly production follows the normal distribution. The mean of this distribution is 4,000 units per week and the standard deviation is 60 units per week. If the bonus is paid on the upper 5 percent of production, the bonus will be paid on how many units or more?

42. Fast Service Truck Lines uses the Ford Super Duty F-750 exclusively. Management made a study of the maintenance costs and determined the number of miles traveled during the year followed the normal distribution. The mean of the distribution was 60,000 miles and the standard deviation 2,000 miles.
a. What percent of the Ford Super Duty F-750s logged 65,200 miles or more?
b. What percent of the trucks logged more than 57,060 but less than 58,280 miles?
c. What percent of the Fords traveled 62,000 miles or less during the year?
d. Is it reasonable to conclude that any of the trucks were driven more than 70,000 miles? Explain.

43. Best Electronics, Inc. offers a "no hassle" returns policy. The number of items returned per day follows the normal distribution. The mean number of customer returns is 10.3 per day and the standard deviation is 2.25 per day.
a. In what percent of the days are there 8 or fewer customers returning items?
b. In what percent of the days are between 12 and 14 customers returning items?
c. Is there any chance of a day with no returns?

44. The current model Boeing 737 has a capacity of 189 passengers. Suppose Delta Airlines uses this equipment for its Atlanta to Houston flights. The distribution of the number of seats sold for the Atlanta to Houston flights follows the normal distribution with a mean of 155 seats and a standard deviation of 15 seats.
a. What is the likelihood of selling more than 134 seats?
b. What is the likelihood of selling less than 173 seats?
c. What is the likelihood of selling more than 134 seats but less than 173 seats?
d. What percent of the time would Delta be able to sell more seats than there are seats actually available?

45. The goal at U.S. airports handling international flights is to clear these flights within 45 minutes. Let's interpret this to mean that 95 percent of the flights are cleared in 45 minutes, so 5 percent of the flights take longer to clear. Let's also assume that the distribution is approximately normal.
a. If the standard deviation of the time to clear an international flight is 5 minutes, what is the mean time to clear a flight?
b. Suppose the standard deviation is 10 minutes, not the 5 minutes suggested in part a. What is the new mean?
c. A customer has 30 minutes from the time her flight landed to catch her limousine. Assuming a standard deviation of 10 minutes, what is the likelihood that she will be cleared in time?

46. The funds dispensed at the ATM machine located near the checkout line at the Kroger's in Union, Kentucky, follows a normal distribution with a mean of $4,200 per day and a standard deviation of $720 per day. The machine is programmed to notify the nearby bank if the amount dispensed is very low (less than $2,500) or very high (more than $6,000).
a. What percent of the days will the bank be notified because the amount dispensed is very low?
b. What percent of the time will the bank be notified because the amount dispensed is high?
c. What percent of the time will the bank not be notified regarding the amount of funds dispersed?

47. The weights of canned hams processed at the Henline Ham Company follow the normal distribution, with a mean of 9.20 pounds and a standard deviation of 0.25 pounds. The label weight is given as 9.00 pounds.
a. What proportion of the hams actually weigh less than the amount claimed on the label?
b. The owner, Glen Henline, is considering two proposals to reduce the proportion of hams below label weight. He can increase the mean weight to 9.25 and leave the standard deviation the same, or he can leave the mean weight at 9.20 and reduce the standard deviation from 0.25 pounds to 0.15. Which change would you recommend?

48. The *Cincinnati Enquirer,* as part of the Sunday business supplement, reported that the mean number of hours worked per week by those employed full time is 43.9. The article

further indicated that about one-third of those employed full time work less than 40 hours per week.

a. Given this information and assuming that number of hours worked follows the normal distribution, what is the standard deviation of the number of hours worked?

b. The article also indicated that 20 percent of those working full time work more than 49 hours per week. Determine the standard deviation with this information. Are the two estimates of the standard deviation similar? What would you conclude?

49. Most four-year automobile leases allow up to 60,000 miles. If the lessee goes beyond this amount, a penalty of 20 cents per mile is added to the lease cost. Suppose the distribution of miles driven on four-year leases follows the normal distribution. The mean is 52,000 miles and the standard deviation is 5,000 miles.

a. What percent of the leases will yield a penalty because of excess mileage?

b. If the automobile company wanted to change the terms of the lease so that 25 percent of the leases went over the limit, where should the new upper limit be set?

c. One definition of a low-mileage car is one that is 4 years old and has been driven less than 45,000 miles. What percent of the cars returned are considered low-mileage?

50. The price of shares of Bank of Florida at the end of trading each day for the last year followed the normal distribution. Assume there were 240 trading days in the year. The mean price was $42.00 per share and the standard deviation was $2.25 per share.

a. What percent of the days was the price over $45.00? How many days would you estimate?

b. What percent of the days was the price between $38.00 and $40.00?

c. What was the stock's price on the *highest* 15 percent of days?

51. The annual sales of romance novels follow the normal distribution. However, the mean and the standard deviation are unknown. Forty percent of the time sales are more than 470,000, and 10 percent of the time sales are more than 500,000. What are the mean and the standard deviation?

52. In establishing warranties on HDTV sets, the manufacturer wants to set the limits so that few will need repair at manufacturer expense. On the other hand, the warranty period must be long enough to make the purchase attractive to the buyer. For a new HDTV the mean number of months until repairs are needed is 36.84 with a standard deviation of 3.34 months. Where should the warranty limits be set so that only 10 percent of the HDTVs need repairs at the manufacturer's expense?

53. DeKorte Tele-Marketing, Inc., is considering purchasing a machine that randomly selects and automatically dials telephone numbers. DeKorte Tele-Marketing makes most of its calls during the evening, so calls to business phones are wasted. The manufacturer of the machine claims that their programming reduces the calling to business phones to 15 percent of all calls. To test this claim the Director of Purchasing at DeKorte programmed the machine to select a sample of 150 phone numbers. What is the likelihood that more than 30 of the phone numbers selected are those of businesses, assuming the manufacturer's claim is correct?

Dataset Exercises

54. Refer to the Real Estate dataset, which reports information on homes sold in the Denver, Colorado, area during the last year.

a. The mean selling price (in $ thousands) of the homes was computed earlier to be $221.10, with a standard deviation of $47.11. Use the normal distribution to estimate the percent of homes selling for more than $280.00. Compare this to the actual results. Does the normal distribution yield a good approximation of the actual results?

b. The mean distance from the center of the city is 14.629 miles with a standard deviation of 4.874 miles. Use the normal distribution to estimate the number of homes 18 or more miles but less than 22 miles from the center of the city. Compare this to the actual results. Does the normal distribution yield a good approximation of the actual results?

55. Refer to the Baseball 2003 dataset, which reports information on the 30 Major League Baseball teams for the 2003 season.

a. The mean attendance per team for the season was 2,254 (in 000s) with a standard deviation of 665 (in 000s). Use the normal distribution to estimate the number of teams with attendance of more than 3.5 million. Compare that estimate with the actual number. Comment on the accuracy of your estimate.

b. The mean team salary was $70.94 million with a standard deviation of $28.06 million. Use the normal distribution to estimate the number of teams with a team salary of more than \$50 million. Compare that estimate with the actual number. Comment on the accuracy of the estimate.

56. Refer to the CIA data, which report demographic and economic information on 46 countries.
   a. The mean of the GDP/capita variable is 16.58 with a standard deviation of 9.27. Use the normal distribution to estimate the percentage of countries with exports above 24. Compare this estimate with the actual proportion. Does the normal distribution appear accurate in this case? Explain.
   b. The mean of the Exports is 116.3 with a standard deviation of 157.4. Use the normal distribution to estimate the percentage of countries with Exports above 170. Compare this estimate with the actual proportion. Does the normal distribution appear accurate in this case? Explain.

Software Commands

1. The Excel commands necessary to produce the output on page 198 are:
   a. Select **Insert** and **Function,** then from the box select **Statistical** and **NORMDIST** and click **OK.**
   b. In the dialog box put *1100* in the box for *X, 1000* for the **Mean,** *100* for the **Standard_dev,** *True* in the **Cumulative** box, and click **OK.**
   c. The result will appear in the dialog box. If you click **OK,** the answer appears in your spreadsheet.
2. The Excel Commands necessary to produce the output on page 204 are:
   a. Select **Insert** and **Function,** then from the box select **Statistical** and **NORMINV** and click **OK.**
   b. In the dialog box, set the **Probability** to 0.04, the **Mean** to 67900, and the **Standard_dev** to 2050.
   c. The results will appear in the dialog box. Note that the answer is slightly different from page 203 because of rounding error. If you click **OK,** the answer also appears in your spreadsheet.
   d. Try entering a **Probability** of 0.04, a **Mean** of zero, and a **Standard_dev** of one. The *z* value will be computed.

Chapter 7 Answers to Self-Review

7–1 a.

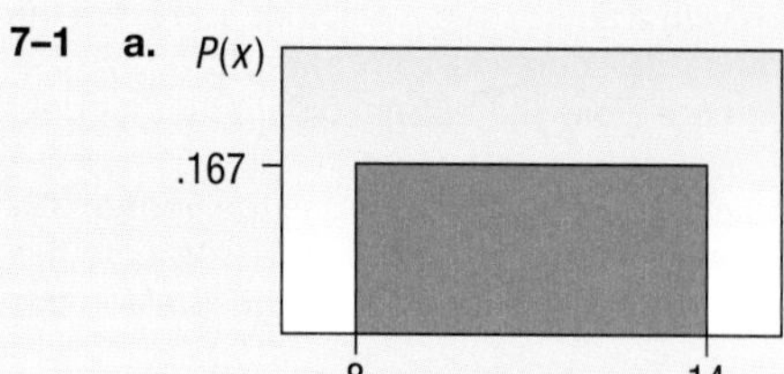

b. $P(x) = \text{(height)(base)}$

$$= \left(\frac{1}{14 - 8}\right)(14 - 8)$$

$$= \left(\frac{1}{6}\right)(6) = 1.00$$

c. $\mu = \frac{a + b}{2} = \frac{14 + 8}{2} = \frac{22}{2} = 11$

$$\sigma = \sqrt{\frac{(b - a)^2}{12}} = \sqrt{\frac{(14 - 8)^2}{12}} = \sqrt{\frac{36}{12}} = \sqrt{3}$$

$$= 1.73$$

d. $P(10 \leq x \leq 14) = \text{(height)(base)}$

$$= \left(\frac{1}{14 - 8}\right)(14 - 10)$$

$$= \frac{1}{6}(4)$$

$$= .667$$

e. $P(x \leq 9) = \text{(height)(base)}$

$$= \left(\frac{1}{14 - 8}\right)(9 - 8)$$

$$= 0.167$$

7–2 a. 2.25, found by:

$$z = \frac{\$1{,}225 - \$1{,}000}{\$100} = \frac{\$225}{\$100} = 2.25$$

b. −2.25, found by:

$$z = \frac{\$775 - \$1{,}000}{\$100} = \frac{-\$225}{\$100} = -2.25$$

7–3 a. \$46,400 and \$48,000, found by \$47,200 ± 1(\$800).

b. \$45,600 and \$48,800, found by \$47,200 ± 2(\$800).

c. \$44,800 and \$49,600, found by \$47,200 ± 3(\$800).

d. \$47,200. The mean, median, and mode are equal for a normal distribution.

e. Yes, a normal distribution is symmetrical.

7–4 a. Computing z:

$$z = \frac{482 - 400}{50} = +1.64$$

Referring to Appendix D, the area is .4495.

$P(400 < \text{rating} < 482) = .4495$

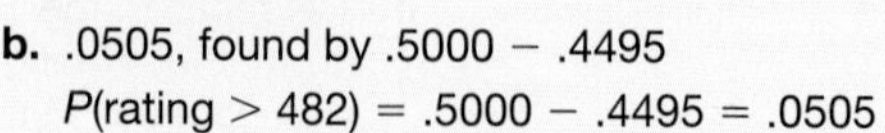

b. .0505, found by .5000 − .4495

$P(\text{rating} > 482) = .5000 - .4495 = .0505$

c.

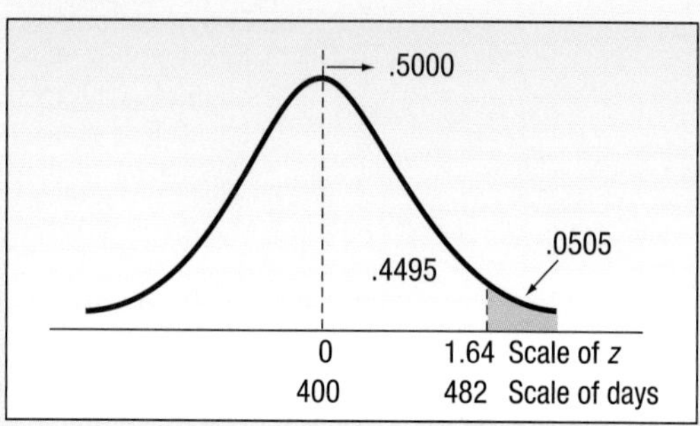

7–5 a. .9816, found by 0.4938 + 0.4878.

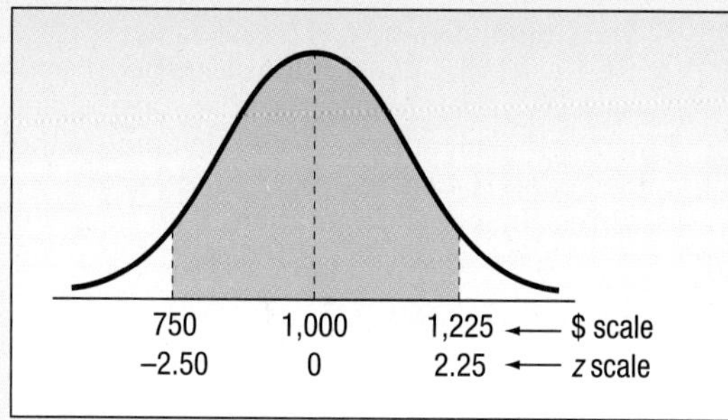

b. .1465, found by 0.4878 − 0.3413.

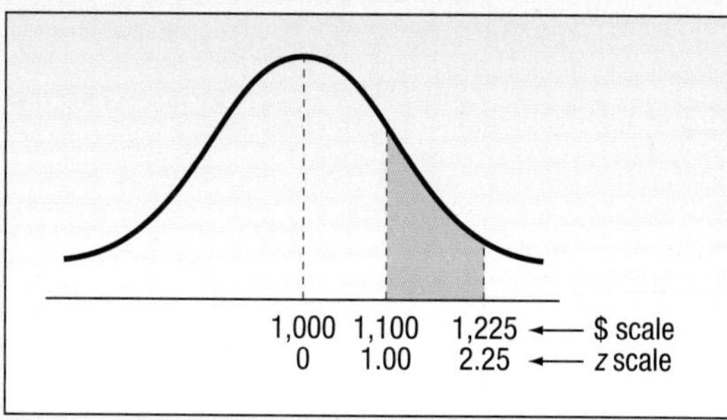

7–6 85.24 (instructor would no doubt make it 85). The closest area to .4000 is .3997; z is 1.28. Then:

$$1.28 = \frac{X - 75}{8}$$

$$10.24 = X - 75$$

$$X = 85.24$$

8

Sampling Methods and the Central Limit Theorem

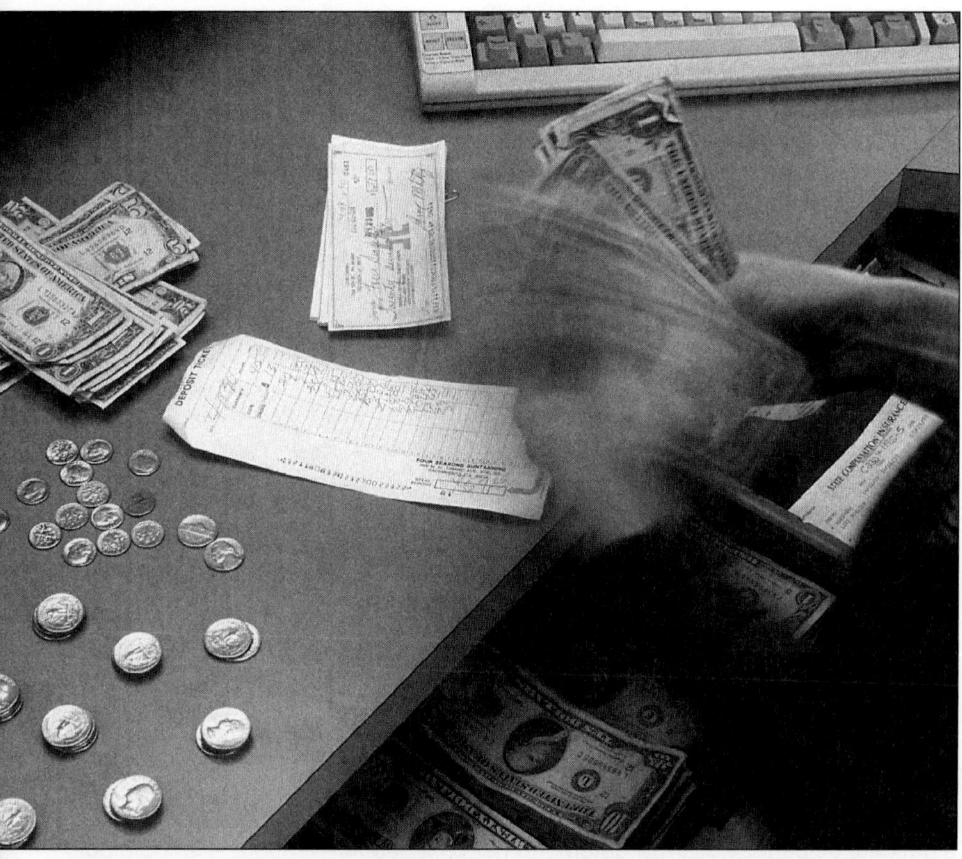

At the downtown office of First National Bank there are five tellers. How many different samples of two tellers are possible? (See Goal 3 and Exercise 28.)

GOALS

When you have completed this chapter you will be able to:

1 **Explain why a sample is often the only feasible way to learn something about a population.**

2 **Describe methods to select a sample.**

3 **Define and construct a sampling distribution of the sample mean.**

4 **Explain the *central limit theorem.***

5 **Use the central limit theorem to find probabilities of selecting possible sample means from a specified population.**

Statistics in Action

With the significant role played by inferential statistics in all branches of science, the availability of large sources of random numbers has become a necessity. The first book of random numbers, containing 41,600 random digits generated by L. Tippett, was published in 1927. In 1938, R. A. Fisher and F. Yates published 15,000 random digits generated using two decks of cards. In 1955, RAND Corporation published a million random digits, generated by the random frequency pulses of an electronic roulette wheel. By 1970, applications of sampling required billions of random numbers. Methods have since been developed for generating digits, using a computer, that are "almost" random and hence are called *pseudo-random*. The question of whether a computer program can be used to generate numbers that are truly random remains a debatable issue.

Introduction

Chapters 1 through 4 emphasize techniques to describe data. To illustrate these techniques, we organize the prices for the 80 vehicles sold last month at Whitner Autoplex into a frequency distribution and compute various measures of location and dispersion. Such measures as the mean and the standard deviation describe the typical selling price and the spread in the selling prices. In these chapters the emphasis is on describing the condition of the data. That is, we describe something that has already happened.

Chapter 5 starts to lay the foundation for statistical inference with the study of probability. Recall that in statistical inference our goal is to determine something about a *population* based only on the *sample.* The population is the entire group of individuals or objects under consideration, and the sample is a part or subset of that population. Chapter 6 extends the probability concepts by describing two discrete probability distributions: the binomial and the Poisson. Chapter 7 describes the uniform probability distribution and the normal probability distribution. Both of these are continuous distributions. Probability distributions encompass all possible outcomes of an experiment and the probability associated with each outcome. We use probability distributions to evaluate the likelihood something occurs in the future.

This chapter begins our study of sampling. A sample is a tool to infer something about a population. We begin this chapter by discussing methods of selecting a sample from a population. Next, we construct a distribution of the sample mean to understand how the sample means tend to cluster around the population mean. Finally, we show that for any population the shape of this sampling distribution tends to follow the normal probability distribution.

Sampling Methods

In Chapter 1, we said the purpose of inferential statistics is to find something about a population based on a sample. A sample is a portion or part of the population of interest. In many cases, sampling is more feasible than studying the entire population. In this section, we show major reasons for sampling, and then several methods for selecting a sample.

Reasons to Sample

When studying characteristics of a population, there are many practical reasons why we prefer to select portions or samples of a population to observe and measure. Some of the reasons for sampling are:

1. **The time to contact the whole population may be prohibitive.** A candidate for a national office may wish to determine her chances for election. A sample poll using the regular staff and field interviews of a professional polling firm would take only 1 or 2 days. By using the same staff and interviewers and working 7 days a week, it would take nearly 200 years to contact all the voting population! Even if a large staff of interviewers could be assembled, the benefit of contacting all of the voters would probably not be worth the time.
2. **The cost of studying all the items in a population may be prohibitive.** Public opinion polls and consumer testing organizations, such as Gallup Polls and Roper ASW, usually contact fewer than 2,000 of the nearly 60 million families in the United States. One consumer research organization charges about $40,000 to mail samples and tabulate responses in order to test a product (such as breakfast cereal, cat food, or perfume). The same product test using all 60 million families would cost about $1 billion.

3. **The physical impossibility of checking all items in the population.** The populations of fish, birds, snakes, mosquitoes, and the like are large and are constantly moving, being born, and dying. Instead of even attempting to count all the ducks in Canada or all the fish in Lake Erie, we make estimates using various techniques—such as counting all the ducks on a pond picked at random, making creel checks, or setting nets at predetermined places in the lake.
4. **The destructive nature of some tests.** If the wine tasters at the Sutter Home Winery in California drank all the wine to evaluate the vintage, they would consume the entire crop, and none would be available for sale. In the area of industrial production, steel plates, wires, and similar products must have a certain minimum tensile strength. To ensure that the product meets the minimum standard, the Quality Assurance Department selects a sample from the current production. Each piece is stretched until it breaks, and the breaking point (usually measured in pounds per square inch) recorded. Obviously, if all the wire or all the plates were tested for tensile strength, none would be available for sale or use. For the same reason, only a sample of photographic film is selected and tested by Kodak to determine the quality of all the film produced, and only a few seeds are tested for germination by Burpee prior to the planting season.
5. **The sample results are adequate.** Even if funds are available, it is doubtful the additional accuracy of a 100 percent sample—that is, studying the entire population—is essential in most problems. For example, the federal government uses a sample of grocery stores scattered throughout the United States to determine the monthly index of food prices. The prices of bread, beans, milk, and other major food items are included in the index. It is unlikely that the inclusion of all grocery stores in the United States would significantly affect the index, since the prices of milk, bread, and other major foods usually do not vary by more than a few cents from one chain store to another.

When selecting a sample, researchers or analysts must be very careful that the sample is a fair representation of the population. In other words, the sample must be unbiased. In Chapter 1, an example of abusing statistics was the intentional selection of dentists to report that "2 out of 3 dentists surveyed indicated they would recommend Brand X toothpaste to their patients." Clearly, people can select a sample that supports their own biases. The ethical side of statistics always requires unbiased sampling and objective reporting of results. Next, several sampling methods show how to select a fair and unbiased sample from a population.

Simple Random Sampling

The most widely used type of sampling is a **simple random sample.**

> **SIMPLE RANDOM SAMPLE** A sample selected so that each item or person in the population has the same chance of being included.

A table of random numbers is an efficient way to select members of the sample

To illustrate simple random sampling and selection, suppose a population consists of 845 employees of Nitra Industries. A sample of 52 employees is to be selected from that population. One way of ensuring that every employee in the population has the same chance of being chosen is to first write the name of each employee on a small slip of paper and deposit all of the slips in a box. After they have been thoroughly mixed, the first selection is made by drawing a slip out of the box without looking at it. This process is repeated until the sample size of 52 is chosen.

A more convenient method of selecting a random sample is to use the identification number of each employee and a **table of random numbers** such as the one in

Statistics in Action

Is discrimination taking a bite out of your paycheck? A recent article in Personnel Journal indicates that attractive men and women earn about 5 percent more than average lookers, who in turn earn about 5 percent more than their plain counterparts. This is true for both men and women. It is also true for a wide range of occupations, from construction to auto repair to telemarketing, occupations for which it seems looks should not matter.

Appendix E. As the name implies, these numbers have been generated by a random process (in this case, by a computer). For each digit of a number, the probability of 0, 1, 2, . . . , 9 is the same. Thus, the probability that employee number 011 will be selected is the same as for employee 722 or employee 382. By using random numbers to select employees, bias is eliminated from the selection process.

A portion of a table of random numbers is shown in the following illustration. To select a sample of employees, you first choose a starting point in the table. Any starting point will do. Suppose the time is 3:04. You might look at the third column and then move down to the fourth set of numbers. The number is 03759. Since there are only 845 employees, we will use the first three digits of a five-digit random number. Thus, 037 is the number of the first employee to be a member of the sample. Another way of selecting the starting point is to close your eyes and point at a number in the table. To continue selecting employees, you could move in any direction. Suppose you move right. The first three digits of the number to the right of 03759 are 447—the number of the employee selected to be the second member of the sample. The next three-digit number to the right is 961. You skip 961 because there are only 845 employees. You continue to the right and select employee 784, then 189, and so on.

50525	57454	28455	68226	34656	38884	39018
72507	53380	53827	42486	54465	71819	91199
34986	74297	00144	38676	89967	98869	39744
68851	27305	03759	44723	96108	78489	18910
06738	62879	03910	17350	49169	03850	18910
11448	10734	05837	24397	10420	16712	94496
		Starting point	Second employee		Third employee	Fourth employee

Most statistical software packages have available a routine that will select a simple random sample. The following Example uses the Excel system to select a random sample.

EXAMPLE

Jane and Joe Miley operate the Foxtrot Inn, a bed and breakfast in Tryon, North Carolina. There are eight rooms available for rent at this B&B. Listed below is the number of these eight rooms that was rented each day during June 2004. Use Excel to select a sample of five nights during the month of June.

June	Rentals	June	Rentals	June	Rentals
1	0	11	3	21	3
2	2	12	4	22	2
3	3	13	4	23	3
4	2	14	4	24	6
5	3	15	7	25	0
6	4	16	0	26	4
7	2	17	5	27	1
8	3	18	3	28	1
9	4	19	6	29	3
10	7	20	2	30	3

SOLUTION

Excel will select the random sample and report the results. On the first sampled date there were 4 of the eight rooms rented. On the second sampled date in June, 7 of the 8 rooms were rented. The information is reported in column D of the Excel spreadsheet. The Excel steps are listed in the **Software Commands** section at the end of the chapter. The Excel system performs the sampling *with* replacement. This means it is possible for the same day to appear more than once in a sample.

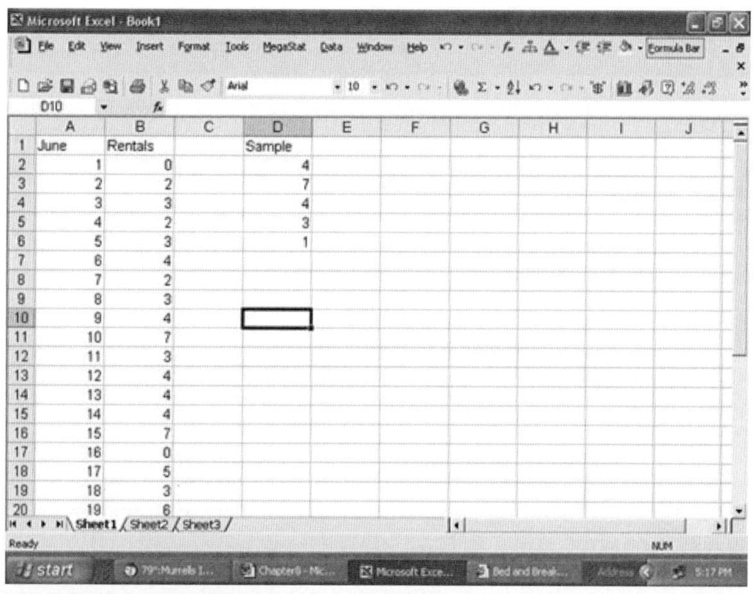

	A	B	C	D
1	June	Rentals		Sample
2	1	0		4
3	2	2		7
4	3	3		4
5	4	2		3
6	5	3		1
7	6	4		
8	7	2		
9	8	3		
10	9	4		
11	10	7		
12	11	3		
13	12	4		
14	13	4		
15	14	4		
16	15	7		
17	16	0		
18	17	5		
19	18	3		
20	19	6		

Self-Review 8–1

The following class roster lists the students enrolling in an introductory course in business statistics. Three students are to be randomly selected and asked various questions regarding course content and method of instruction.

(a) The numbers 00 through 45 are handwritten on slips of paper and placed in a bowl. The three numbers selected are 31, 7, and 25. Which students would be included in the sample?
(b) Now use the table of random digits, Appendix E, to select your own sample.
(c) What would you do if you encountered the number 59 in the table of random digits?

CSPM 264 01 BUSINESS & ECONOMIC STAT
8:00 AM 9:40 AM MW ST 118 LIND D

RANDOM NUMBER	NAME	CLASS RANK	RANDOM NUMBER	NAME	CLASS RANK
00	ANDERSON, RAYMOND	SO	23	MEDLEY, CHERYL ANN	SO
01	ANGER, CHERYL RENEE	SO	24	MITCHELL, GREG R	FR
02	BALL, CLAIRE JEANETTE	FR	25	MOLTER, KRISTI MARIE	SO
03	BERRY, CHRISTOPHER G	FR	26	MULCAHY, STEPHEN ROBERT	SO
04	BOBAK, JAMES PATRICK	SO	27	NICHOLAS, ROBERT CHARLES	JR
05	BRIGHT, M. STARR	JR	28	NICKENS, VIRGINIA	SO
06	CHONTOS, PAUL JOSEPH	SO	29	PENNYWITT, SEAN PATRICK	SO
07	DETLEY, BRIAN HANS	JR	30	POTEAU, KRIS E	JR
08	DUDAS, VIOLA	SO	31	PRICE, MARY LYNETTE	SO
09	DULBS, RICHARD ZALFA	JR	32	RISTAS, JAMES	SR
10	EDINGER, SUSAN KEE	SR	33	SAGER, ANNE MARIE	SO
11	FINK, FRANK JAMES	SR	34	SMILLIE, HEATHER MICHELLE	SO
12	FRANCIS, JAMES P	JR	35	SNYDER, LEISHA KAY	SR
13	GAGHEN, PAMELA LYNN	JR	36	STAHL, MARIA TASHERY	SO
14	GOULD, ROBYN KAY	SO	37	ST. JOHN, AMY J	SO
15	GROSENBACHER, SCOTT ALAN	SO	38	STURDEVANT, RICHARD K	SO
16	HEETFIELD, DIANE MARIE	SO	39	SWETYE, LYNN MICHELE	SO
17	KABAT, JAMES DAVID	JR	40	WALASINSKI, MICHAEL	SO
18	KEMP, LISA ADRIANE	FR	41	WALKER, DIANE ELAINE	SO
19	KILLION, MICHELLE A	SO	42	WARNOCK, JENNIFER MARY	SO
20	KOPERSKI, MARY ELLEN	SO	43	WILLIAMS, WENDY A	SO
21	KOPP, BRIDGETTE ANN	SO	44	YAP, HOCK BAN	SO
22	LEHMANN, KRISTINA MARIE	JR	45	YODER, ARLAN JAY	JR

Systematic Random Sampling

A table of random numbers is an efficient way to select members of the samples

The simple random sampling procedure may be awkward in some research situations. For example, suppose the sales division of Computer Printers Unlimited needs to quickly estimate the mean dollar revenue per sale during the past month. They find that 2,000 sales invoices were recorded and stored in file drawers, and decide to select 100 invoices to estimate the mean dollar revenue. Simple random sampling requires the numbering of each invoice before using the random number table to select the 100 invoices. The numbering process would be a very time consuming task. Instead, **systematic random sampling** can be used.

SYSTEMATIC RANDOM SAMPLE A random starting point is selected, and then every *k*th member of the population is selected.

Statistics in Action

Random and unbiased sampling methods are extremely important to making valid statistical inferences. In 1936, a straw vote to predict the outcome of the presidential race between Franklin Roosevelt and Alfred Landon was done. Ten million ballots in the form of returnable postcards were sent to addresses taken from telephone directories and automobile registrations. A high proportion of the ballots were returned, with 59 percent in favor of Landon and 41 percent favoring Roosevelt. On Election Day, Roosevelt won with 61 percent of the vote. Landon had 39 percent. In the mid-1930s people who had telephones and drove automobiles clearly did not represent American voters!

First, *k* is calculated as the population size divided by the sample size. For Computer Printers Unlimited, we would select every 20th (2,000/100) invoice from the file drawers; in so doing the numbering process is avoided. If *k* is not a whole number, then round down.

Random sampling is used in the selection of the first invoice. For example, a number from a random number table between 1 and *k*, or 20, would be selected. Say, the random number was 18. Then, starting with the 18th invoice, every 20th invoice (18, 38, 58, etc.) would be selected as the sample.

Before using systematic random sampling, we should carefully observe the physical order of the population. When the physical order is related to the population characteristic, then systematic random sampling should not be used. For example, if the invoices in the example were filed in order of increasing sales, systematic random sampling would not guarantee a random sample. Other sampling methods should be used.

Stratified Random Sampling

When a population can be clearly divided into groups based on some characteristic, then **stratified random sampling** can be used to guarantee that each group is represented in the sample. The groups are also called **strata.** For example, college students can be grouped as full time or part time, male or female, or traditional or nontraditional. Once the strata are defined, we can apply simple random sampling within each group or strata to collect the sample.

STRATIFIED RANDOM SAMPLE A population is divided into subgroups, called strata, and a sample is randomly selected from each stratum.

For instance, we might study the advertising expenditures for the 352 largest companies in the United States. Suppose the objective of the study is to determine whether firms with high returns on equity (a measure of profitability) spent more of each sales dollar on advertising than firms with a low return or deficit. To make sure that the sample is a fair representation of the 352 companies, the companies are grouped on percent return on equity. Table 8–1 shows the strata and the relative frequencies. If simple random sampling was used, observe that firms in the 3rd and 4th strata have a high chance of selection (probability of 0.87) while firms in the other strata have a low chance of selection (probability of 0.13). We might not select any firms in stratum 1 or 5 *simply by chance.* However, stratified random sampling will guarantee that at least one firm in strata 1 and 5 are represented in the sample. Let's say that 50 firms are selected for intensive study. Then 1 (0.02×50) firm from stratum 1 would be randomly selected, 5 (0.10×50) firms from stratum 2 would be randomly selected, and so on. In this case, the number of firms sampled from each stratum is proportional to the stratum's relative frequency in the population. Stratified sampling has the advantage, in some cases, of more accurately reflecting the characteristics of the population than does simple random or systematic random sampling.

TABLE 8–1 Number Selected for a Proportional Stratified Random Sample

Stratum	Profitability (return on equity)	Number of Firms	Relative Frequency	Number Sampled
1	30 percent and over	8	0.02	1*
2	20 up to 30 percent	35	0.10	5*
3	10 up to 20 percent	189	0.54	27
4	0 up to 10 percent	115	0.33	16
5	Deficit	5	0.01	1
Total		352	1.00	50

*0.02 of 50 = 1, 0.10 of 50 = 5, etc.

Cluster Sampling

Another common type of sampling is **cluster sampling.** It is often employed to reduce the cost of sampling a population scattered over a large geographic area.

CLUSTER SAMPLING A population is divided into clusters using naturally occurring geographic or other boundaries. Then, clusters are randomly selected and a sample is collected by randomly selecting from each cluster.

Suppose you want to determine the views of residents in a particular state about state and federal environmental protection policies. Selecting a random sample of residents in the state and personally contacting each one would be time consuming and very expensive. Instead, you could employ cluster sampling by subdividing the state into small units—either counties or regions. These are often called *primary units.*

Suppose you divided the state into 12 primary units, then selected at random four regions—2, 7, 4, and 12—and concentrated your efforts in these primary units. You could take a random sample of the residents in each of these regions and interview them. (Note that this is a combination of cluster sampling and simple random sampling.)

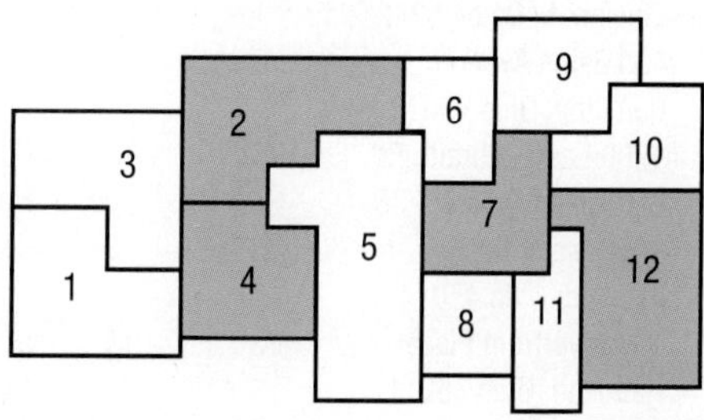

Many other sampling methods

The discussion of sampling methods in the preceding sections did not include all the sampling methods available to a researcher. Should you become involved in a major research project in marketing, finance, accounting, or other areas, you would need to consult books devoted solely to sample theory and sample design.

Self-Review 8–2

Refer to Self-Review 8–1 and the class roster on page 215. Suppose a systematic random sample will select every ninth student enrolled in the class. Initially, the fourth student on the list was selected at random. That student is numbered 03. Remembering that the random numbers start with 00, which students will be chosen to be members of the sample?

Exercises

1. The following is a list of Marco's Pizza stores in Lucas County. Also noted is whether the store is corporate-owned (C) or manager-owned (M). A sample of four locations is to be selected and inspected for customer convenience, safety, cleanliness, and other features.

ID No.	Address	Type	ID No.	Address	Type
00	2607 Starr Av	C	12	2040 Ottawa River Rd	C
01	309 W Alexis Rd	C	13	2116 N Reynolds Rd	C
02	2652 W Central Av	C	14	3678 Rugby Dr	C
03	630 Dixie Hwy	M	15	1419 South Av	C
04	3510 Dorr St	C	16	1234 W Sylvania Av	C
05	5055 Glendale Av	C	17	4624 Woodville Rd	M
06	3382 Lagrange St	M	18	5155 S Main	M
07	2525 W Laskey Rd	C	19	106 E Airport Hwy	C
08	303 Louisiana Av	C	20	6725 W Central	M
09	149 Main St	C	21	4252 Monroe	C
10	835 S McCord Rd	M	22	2036 Woodville Rd	C
11	3501 Monroe St	M	23	1316 Michigan Av	M

   a. The random numbers selected are 08, 18, 11, 54, 02, 41, and 54. Which stores are selected?
   b. Use the table of random numbers to select your own sample of locations.
   c. A sample is to consist of every seventh location. The number 03 is the starting point. Which locations will be included in the sample?
   d. Suppose a sample is to consist of three locations, of which two are corporate-owned and one is manager-owned. Select a sample accordingly.

2. The following is a list of hospitals in the Cincinnati (Ohio) and Northern Kentucky Region. Also included is whether the hospital is a general medical/surgical hospital (M/S) or a specialty hospital (S). We are interested in estimating the average number of full- and part-time nurses employed in the area hospitals.

ID Number	Name	Address	Type	ID Number	Name	Address	Type
00	Bethesda North	10500 Montgomery Cincinnati, Ohio 45242	M/S	10	Christ Hospital	2139 Auburn Avenue Cincinnati, Ohio 45219	M/S
01	Ft. Hamilton-Hughes	630 Eaton Avenue Hamilton, Ohio 45013	M/S	11	Deaconess Hospital	311 Straight Street Cincinnati, Ohio 45219	M/S
02	Jewish Hospital-Kenwood	4700 East Galbraith Rd. Cincinnati, Ohio 45236	M/S	12	Good Samaritan Hospital	375 Dixmyth Avenue Cincinnati, Ohio 45220	M/S
03	Mercy Hospital-Fairfield	3000 Mack Road Fairfield, Ohio 45014	M/S	13	Jewish Hospital	3200 Burnet Avenue Cincinnati, Ohio 45229	M/S
04	Mercy Hospital-Hamilton	100 Riverfront Plaza Hamilton, Ohio 45011	M/S	14	University Hospital	234 Goodman Street Cincinnati, Ohio 45267	M/S
05	Middletown Regional	105 McKnight Drive Middletown, Ohio 45044	M/S	15	Providence Hospital	2446 Kipling Avenue Cincinnati, Ohio 45239	M/S
06	Clermont Mercy Hospital	3000 Hospital Dr. Batavia, Ohio 45103	M/S	16	St. Francis-St. GeorgeHospital	3131 Queen City Avenue Cincinnati, Ohio 45238	M/S
07	Mercy Hospital-Anderson	7500 State Road Cincinnati, Ohio 45255	M/S	17	St. Elizabeth Medical Center, North Unit	401 E. 20th Street Covington, Kentucky 41014	M/S
08	Bethesda Oak Hospital	619 Oak Street Cincinnati, Ohio 45206	M/S	18	St. Elizabeth Medical Center, South Unit	One Medical Village Edgewood, Kentucky 41017	M/S
09	Children's Hospital Medical Center	3333 Burnet Avenue Cincinnati, Ohio 45229	M/S	19	St. Luke's Hospital West	7380 Turfway Dr. Florence, Kentucky 41075	M/S

(Continued)

ID Number	Name	Address	Type	ID Number	Name	Address	Type
20	St. Luke's Hospital East	85 North Grand Avenue Ft. Thomas, Kentucky 41042	M/S	25	Drake Center Rehab—Long Term	151 W. Galbraith Road Cincinnati, Ohio 45216	S
21	Care Unit Hospital Cinti.	3156 Glenmore Avenue Cincinnati, Ohio 45211	S	26	No. Kentucky Rehab Hospital—Short Term	201 Medical Village Edgewood, Kentucky	S
22	Emerson Behavioral Science	2446 Kipling Avenue Cincinnati, Ohio 45239	S	27	Shriners Burns Institute	3229 Burnet Avenue Cincinnati, Ohio 45229	S
23	Pauline Warfield Lewis Center for Psychiatric Treat.	1101 Summit Rd. Cincinnati, Ohio 45237	S	28	VA Medical Center	3200 Vine Cincinnati, Ohio 45220	S
24	Children's Psychiatric No. Kentucky	502 Farrell Drive Covington, Kentucky 41011	S				

a. A sample of five hospitals is to be randomly selected. The random numbers are 09, 16, 00, 49, 54, 12, and 04. Which hospitals are included in the sample?
b. Use a table of random numbers to develop your own sample of five hospitals.
c. A sample is to consist of every fifth location. We select 02 as the starting point. Which hospitals will be included in the sample?
d. A sample is to consist of four medical and surgical hospitals and one specialty hospital. Select an appropriate sample.

3. Listed below are the 35 members of the Metro Toledo Automobile Dealers Association. We would like to estimate the mean revenue from dealer service departments.

ID Number	Dealer	ID Number	Dealer	ID Number	Dealer
00	Dave White Acura	12	Spurgeon Chevrolet Motor Sales, Inc.	24	Lexus of Toledo
01	Autofair Nissan	13	Dunn Chevrolet	25	Mathews Ford Oregon, Inc.
02	Autofair Toyota-Suzuki	14	Don Scott Chevrolet-Pontiac-Geo, Inc.	26	Northtowne Chevrolet-GEO
03	George Ball's Buick GMC Truck	15	Dave White Chevrolet Co.	27	Quality Ford Sales, Inc.
04	Yark Automotive Group	16	Dick Wilson Pontiac	28	Rouen Chrysler Jeep Eagle
05	Bob Schmidt Chevrolet	17	Doyle Pontiac Buick	29	Saturn of Toledo
06	Bowling Green Lincoln Mercury Jeep Eagle	18	Franklin Park Lincoln Mercury	30	Ed Schmidt Pontiac Jeep Eagle
07	Brondes Ford	19	Genoa Motors	31	Southside Lincoln Mercury
08	Brown Honda	20	Great Lakes Ford Nissan	32	Valiton Chrysler
09	Brown Mazda	21	Grogan Towne Chrysler	33	Vin Divers
10	Charlie's Dodge	22	Hatfield Motor Sales	34	Whitman Ford
11	Thayer Chevrolet Geo Toyota	23	Kistler Ford, Inc.		

a. We want to select a random sample of five dealers. The random numbers are: 05, 20, 59, 21, 31, 28, 49, 38, 66, 08, 29, and 02. Which dealers would be included in the sample?
b. Use the table of random numbers to select your own sample of five dealers.
c. Use statistical software to select a simple random sample of five dealers. You must enter the ID numbers (00 through 34). See page 243 for instructions.
d. A sample is to consist of every seventh dealer. The number 04 is selected as the starting point. Which dealers are included in the sample?

4. Listed on the next page are the 27 Nationwide Insurance agents in the Toledo, Ohio, metropolitan area. We would like to estimate the mean number of years agents are employed with Nationwide.
a. We want to select a random sample of four agents. The random numbers are: 02, 59, 51, 25, 14, 29, 77, 69, and 18. Which dealers would be included in the sample?
b. Use the table of random numbers to select your own sample of four agents.
c. Use EXCEL to select a simple random sample of 10 dealers. You must enter the ID numbers (00 through 26). See page 243 for instructions.
d. A sample is to consist of every seventh dealer. The number 04 is selected as the starting point. Which agents will be included in the sample?

ID Number	Agent	ID Number	Agent	ID Number	Agent
00	**Bly Scott** 3332 W Laskey Rd	09	**Harris Ev** 2026 Albon Rd	18	**Priest Harvey** 5113 N Summit St
01	**Coyle Mike** 5432 W Central Av	10	**Heini Bernie** 7110 W Central	19	**Riker Craig** 2621 N Reynolds Rd
02	**Denker Brett** 7445 Airport Hwy	11	**Hinckley Dave** 14 N Holland Sylvania Rd	20	**Schwab Dave** 572 W Dussel Dr
03	**Denker Rollie** 7445 Airport Hwy	12	**Joehlin Bob** 3358 Navarre Av	21	**Seibert John** H 201 S Main
04	**Farley Ron** 1837 W Alexis Rd	13	**Keisser David** 3030 W Sylvania Av	22	**Smithers Bob** 229 Superior St
05	**George Mark** 7247 W Central Av	14	**Keisser Keith** 5902 Sylvania Av	23	**Smithers Jerry** 229 Superior St
06	**Gibellato Carlo** 6616 Monroe St 3521 Navarre Av	15	**Lawrence Grant** 342 W Dussel Dr	24	**Wright Steve** 105 S Third St
07	**Glemser Cathy** 5602 Woodville Rd	16	**Miller Ken** 2427 Woodville Rd	25	**Wood Tom** 112 Louisiana Av
08	**Green Mike** 4149 Holland Sylvania Rd	17	**O'Donnell Jim** 7247 W Central Av	26	**Yoder Scott** 6 Willoughby Av

Sampling "Error"

The previous section discussed sampling methods that can be used to select a sample that is a fair or unbiased representation of the population. In each method, it is important to note that the selection of every possible sample of a specified size from a population has a known chance or probability. This is another way to describe an unbiased sampling method.

Samples are used to estimate population characteristics. For example, the mean of a sample is used to estimate the population mean. However, since the sample is a part or portion of the population, it is unlikely that the sample mean would be *exactly equal* to the population mean. Similarly, it is unlikely that the sample standard deviation would be *exactly equal* to the population standard deviation. We can therefore expect a difference between a *sample statistic* and its corresponding *population parameter.* This difference is called **sampling error.**

SAMPLING ERROR The difference between a sample statistic and its corresponding population parameter.

The following example clarifies the idea of sampling error.

EXAMPLE

Refer to the previous example on page 214 where we studied the number of rooms rented at the Foxtrot Inn Bed and Breakfast in Tryon, North Carolina. The population is the number of rooms rented each of the 30 days in June of 2004. Find the mean of the population. Use Excel or other statistical software to select three random samples of five days. Calculate the mean of each sample and compare it to the population mean. What is the sampling error in each case?

SOLUTION

During the month there were a total of 94 rentals. So the mean number of units rented per night is 3.13. This is the population mean. Hence we designate this value with the Greek letter μ.

$$\mu = \frac{\Sigma X}{N} = \frac{0 + 2 + 3 + \cdots + 3}{30} = \frac{94}{30} = 3.13$$

The first random sample of five nights resulted in the following number of rooms rented: 4, 7, 4, 3, and 1. The mean of this sample of five nights is 3.8 rooms, which we designate as $\bar{X}_1$. The bar over the X reminds us that it is a sample mean and the subscript 1 indicates it is the mean of the first sample.

$$\bar{X}_1 = \frac{\Sigma X}{n} = \frac{4 + 7 + 4 + 3 + 1}{5} = \frac{19}{5} = 3.80$$

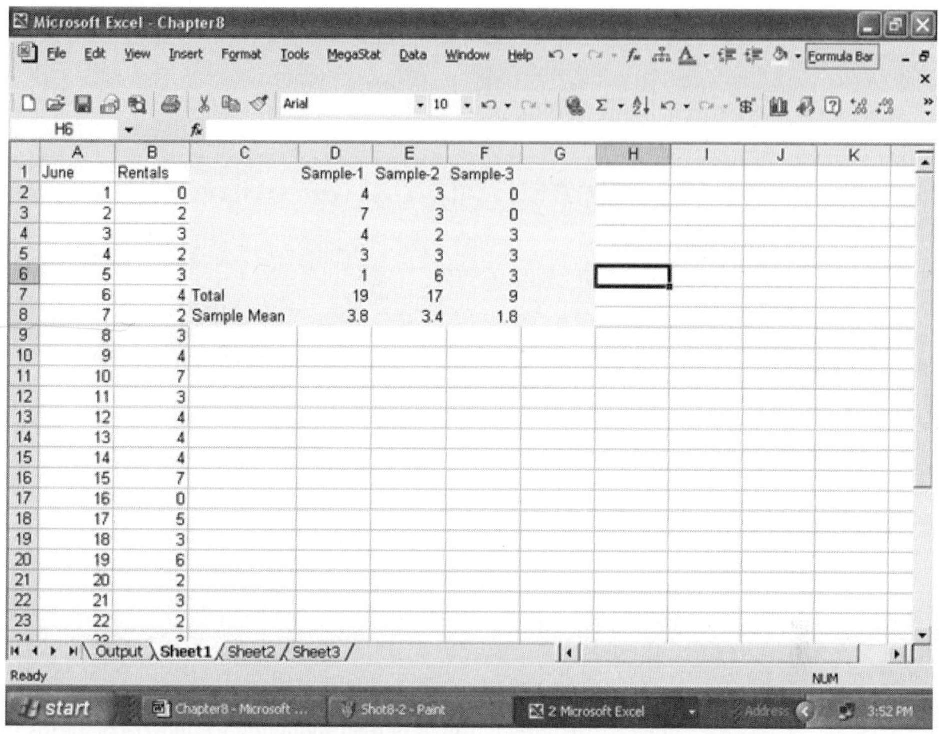

Microsoft Excel - Chapter8

	A	B	C	D	E	F
1	June	Rentals		Sample-1	Sample-2	Sample-3
2	1	0		4	3	0
3	2	2		7	3	0
4	3	3		4	2	3
5	4	2		3	3	3
6	5	3		1	6	3
7	6	4	Total	19	17	9
8	7	2	Sample Mean	3.8	3.4	1.8
9	8	3				
10	9	4				
11	10	7				
12	11	3				
13	12	4				
14	13	4				
15	14	4				
16	15	7				
17	16	0				
18	17	5				
19	18	3				
20	19	6				
21	20	2				
22	21	3				
23	22	2				

The sampling error for the first sample is the difference between the population mean (3.13) and the first sample mean (3.80). Hence, the sampling error is ($\bar{X}_1 - \mu = 3.80 - 3.13 = 0.67$). The second random sample of five days from the population of all 30 days in June revealed the following number of rooms rented: 3, 3, 2, 3, and 6. The mean of these five values is 3.4, found by

$$\bar{X}_2 = \frac{\Sigma X}{n} = \frac{3 + 3 + 2 + 3 + 6}{5} = 3.4$$

The sampling error is ($\bar{X}_2 - \mu = 3.4 - 3.13 = 0.27$).

In the third random sample the mean was 1.8 and the sampling error was -1.33.

Each of these differences, 0.67, 0.27, and -1.33, is the sampling error made in estimating the population mean. Sometimes these errors are positive values, indicating that the sample mean overestimated the population mean; other times they are negative values, indicating the sample mean was less than the population mean.

In this case where we have a population of 30 values and samples of 5 values there is a very large number of possible samples—142,506 to be exact! To find this value use the combination formula 5–9 on page 145. Each of the 142,506 different samples has the same chance of being selected. Each sample may have a different sample mean and therefore a different sampling error. The value of the sampling error is based on the particular one of the 142,506 different possible samples selected. Therefore, the sampling errors are random and occur by chance. If one were to determine the sum of these sampling errors over a large number of samples the result would be very close to zero.

Now that we have discovered the possibility of a sampling error when a sample statistic is used to estimate a population parameter, how can we make an accurate prediction about the possible success of a newly developed toothpaste or other product, based only on sample results? How can the quality-assurance department in a mass production firm release a shipment of microchips based only on a sample of 10 chips? How can the CNN/*USA Today* or ABC News/*Washington Post* polling organizations make an accurate prediction about a presidential race based on a sample of 2,000 registered voters out of a voting population of nearly 90 million? To answer these questions, we develop a *sampling distribution of the sample mean.*

Sampling Distribution of the Sample Mean

Sample means vary from sample to sample.

The sample means in the previous example showed the means for samples of a specified size vary from sample to sample. The mean of the first sample of 5 days was 3.80 days, and the second sample mean was 3.4 days. The population mean was 3.13 days. If we organized the means of all possible samples of 5 days into a probability distribution, we would obtain the **sampling distribution of the sample mean.**

SAMPLING DISTRIBUTION OF THE SAMPLE MEAN A probability distribution of all possible sample means of a given sample size.

The following example illustrates the construction of a sampling distribution of the sample mean.

EXAMPLE

Tartus Industries has seven production employees (considered the population). The hourly earnings of each employee are given in Table 8–2.

TABLE 8–2 Hourly Earnings of the Production Employees of Tartus Industries

Employee	Hourly Earnings
Joe	$7
Sam	7
Sue	8
Bob	8
Jan	7
Art	8
Ted	9

Answer the following questions.

1. What is the population mean?
2. What is the sampling distribution of the sample mean for samples of size 2?
3. What is the mean of the sampling distribution?
4. What observations can be made about the population and the sampling distribution?

SOLUTION

Here are the solutions to the questions proposed.

1. The population mean is $7.71, found by:

$$\mu = \frac{\$7 + \$7 + \$8 + \$8 + \$7 + \$8 + \$9}{7}$$

   We identify the population mean with the Greek letter μ. Our policy is to identify population parameters with Greek letters.
2. To arrive at the sampling distribution of the sample mean, all possible samples of 2 were selected without replacement from the population, and their means were computed. There are 21 possible samples, found by using formula (5–9) on page 145.

$$_NC_n = \frac{N!}{n!(N-n)!} = \frac{7!}{2!(7-2)!} = 21$$

where $N = 7$ is the number of items in the population and $n = 2$ is the number of items in the sample.

The 21 sample means from all possible samples of 2 that can be drawn from the population are shown in Table 8–3. These 21 sample means are used to construct a probability distribution which is the sampling distribution of the sample mean and is summarized in Table 8–4.

TABLE 8–3 Sample Means for All Possible Samples of 2 Employees

Sample	Employees	Hourly Earnings	Sum	Mean	Sample	Employees	Hourly Earnings	Sum	Mean
1	Joe, Sam	\$7, \$7	\$14	\$7.00	12	Sue, Bob	\$8, \$8	\$16	\$8.00
2	Joe, Sue	7, 8	15	7.50	13	Sue, Jan	8, 7	15	7.50
3	Joe, Bob	7, 8	15	7.50	14	Sue, Art	8, 8	16	8.00
4	Joe, Jan	7, 7	14	7.00	15	Sue, Ted	8, 9	17	8.50
5	Joe, Art	7, 8	15	7.50	16	Bob, Jan	8, 7	15	7.50
6	Joe, Ted	7, 9	16	8.00	17	Bob, Art	8, 8	16	8.00
7	Sam, Sue	7, 8	15	7.50	18	Bob, Ted	8, 9	17	8.50
8	Sam, Bob	7, 8	15	7.50	19	Jan, Art	7, 8	15	7.50
9	Sam, Jan	7, 7	14	7.00	20	Jan, Ted	7, 9	16	8.00
10	Sam, Art	7, 8	15	7.50	21	Art, Ted	8, 9	17	8.50
11	Sam, Ted	7, 9	16	8.00					

TABLE 8–4 Sampling Distribution of the Sample Mean for $n = 2$

Sample Mean	Number of Means	Probability
\$7.00	3	.1429
7.50	9	.4285
8.00	6	.2857
8.50	3	.1429
	21	1.0000

3. The mean of the sampling distribution of the sample mean is obtained by summing the various sample means and dividing the sum by the number of samples. The mean of all the sample means is usually written $\mu_{\bar{X}}$. The μ reminds us that it is a population value because we have considered all possible samples. The subscript $\bar{X}$ indicates that it is the population mean for the sampling distribution of the sample mean.

Population mean is equal to the mean of the sample means

$$\mu_{\bar{X}} = \frac{\text{Sum of all sample means}}{\text{Total number of samples}} = \frac{\$7.00 + \$7.50 + \cdots + \$8.50}{21}$$

$$= \frac{\$162}{21} = \$7.71$$

4. Refer to Chart 8–1 on the next page, which shows both the population distribution and the distribution of the sample mean. These observations can be made:
   a. The mean of the distribution of the sample mean (\$7.71) is equal to the mean of the population: $\mu = \mu_{\bar{X}}$.
   b. The spread in the distribution of the sample means is less than the spread in the population values. The sample means range from \$7.00 to \$8.50, while the population values vary from \$7.00 up to \$9.00. In fact, the standard deviation

of the distribution of the sample mean is equal to the population standard deviation divided by the square root of the sample size. So the formula for the standard deviation of the distribution of the sample mean is $\sigma/\sqrt{n}$. Notice, as we increase the size of the sample, the spread of the distribution of the sample mean becomes smaller.

c. The shape of the sampling distribution of the sample mean and the shape of the distribution of the population values are different. The distribution of the sample mean tends to be more bell-shaped and to approximate the normal probability distribution.

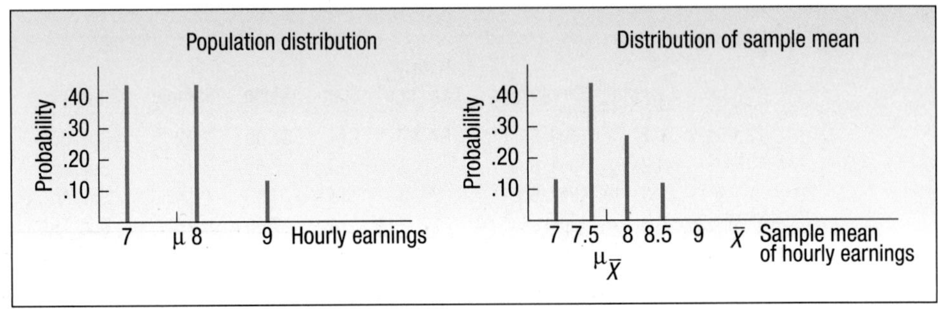

CHART 8–1 Distributions of Population Values and Sample Mean

In summary, we took all possible random samples from a population and for each sample calculated a sample statistic (the mean amount earned). This example illustrates important relationships between the population distribution and the sampling distribution of the sample mean:

1. The mean of the sample means is exactly equal to the population mean.
2. The dispersion of the sampling distribution of the sample means is narrower than the population distribution.
3. The sampling distribution of the sample means tends to become bell-shaped and to approximate the normal probability distribution.

Given a bell-shaped or normal probability distribution, we will be able to apply concepts from Chapter 7 to determine the probability of selecting a sample with a specified sample mean. In the next section, we will show the importance of sample size as it relates to the sampling distribution of sample means.

Self-Review 8–3

The lengths of service of all the executives employed by Standard Chemicals are:

Name	Years
Mr. Snow	20
Ms. Tolson	22
Mr. Kraft	26
Ms. Irwin	24
Mr. Jones	28

(a) Using the combination formula, how many samples of size 2 are possible?
(b) List all possible samples of 2 executives from the population and compute their means.
(c) Organize the means into a sampling distribution.
(d) Compare the population mean and the mean of the sample means.

(e) Compare the dispersion in the population with that in the distribution of the sample mean.
(f) A chart portraying the population values follows. Is the distribution of population values normally distributed (bell-shaped)?

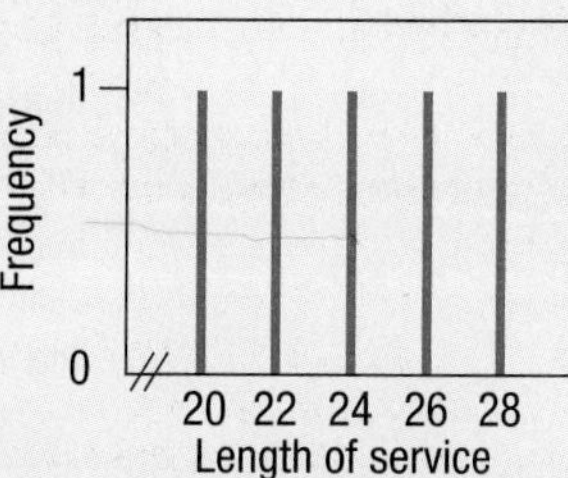

(g) Is the distribution of the sample mean computed in part (c) starting to show some tendency toward being bell-shaped?

Exercises

5. A population consists of the following four values: 12, 12, 14, and 16.
  a. List all samples of size 2, and compute the mean of each sample.
  b. Compute the mean of the distribution of the sample mean and the population mean. Compare the two values.
  c. Compare the dispersion in the population with that of the sample mean.

6. A population consists of the following five values: 2, 2, 4, 4, and 8.
  a. List all samples of size 2, and compute the mean of each sample.
  b. Compute the mean of the distribution of sample means and the population mean. Compare the two values.
  c. Compare the dispersion in the population with that of the sample means.

7. A population consists of the following five values: 12, 12, 14, 15, and 20.
  a. List all samples of size 3, and compute the mean of each sample.
  b. Compute the mean of the distribution of sample means and the population mean. Compare the two values.
  c. Compare the dispersion in the population with that of the sample means.

8. A population consists of the following five values: 0, 0, 1, 3, 6.
  a. List all samples of size 3, and compute the mean of each sample.
  b. Compute the mean of the distribution of sample means and the population mean. Compare the two values.
  c. Compare the dispersion in the population with that of the sample means.

9. In the law firm Tybo and Associates, there are six partners. Listed below is the number of cases each associate actually tried in court last month.

Associate	Number of Cases
Ruud	3
Wu	6
Sass	3
Flores	3
Wilhelms	0
Schueller	1

  a. How many different samples of 3 are possible?
  b. List all possible samples of size 3, and compute the mean number of cases in each sample.
  c. Compare the mean of the distribution of sample means to the population mean.
  d. On a chart similar to Chart 8–1, compare the dispersion in the population with that of the sample means.

10. There are five sales associates at Mid-Motors Ford. The five representatives and the number of cars they sold last week are:

Sales Representative	Cars Sold
Peter Hankish	8
Connie Stallter	6
Juan Lopez	4
Ted Barnes	10
Peggy Chu	6

a. How many different samples of size 2 are possible?
b. List all possible samples of size 2, and compute the mean of each sample.
c. Compare the mean of the sampling distribution of sample means with that of the population.
d. On a chart similar to Chart 8–1, compare the dispersion in sample means with that of the population.

The Central Limit Theorem

In this section, we examine the **central limit theorem.** Its application to the sampling distribution of the sample mean, introduced in the previous section, allows us to use the normal probability distribution to create confidence intervals for the population mean (described in Chapter 9) and perform tests of hypothesis (described in Chapter 10). The central limit theorem states that, for large random samples, the shape of the sampling distribution of the sample mean is close to a normal probability distribution. The approximation is more accurate for large samples than for small samples. This is one of the most useful conclusions in statistics. We can reason about the distribution of the sample mean with absolutely no information about the shape of the population distribution from which the sample is taken. In other words, the central limit theorem is true for all distributions.

A formal statement of the central limit theorem follows.

> **CENTRAL LIMIT THEOREM** If all samples of a particular size are selected from any population, the sampling distribution of the sample mean is approximately a normal distribution. This approximation improves with larger samples.

If the population follows a normal probability distribution, then for any sample size the sampling distribution of the sample mean will also be normal. If the population distribution is symmetrical (but not normal), you will see the normal shape of the distribution of the sample mean emerge with samples as small as 10. On the other hand, if you start with a distribution that is skewed or has thick tails, it may require samples of 30 or more to observe the normality feature. This concept is summarized in Chart 8–2. Observe the convergence to a normal distribution as the sample size increases regardless of the shape of the population distribution.

The idea that the distribution of the sample means from a population that is not normal will converge to normality is illustrated in Charts 8–3, 8–4, and 8–5. We will discuss this example in more detail shortly, but Chart 8–3 is a graph of a discrete probability distribution that is positively skewed. There are many possible samples of 5 that might be selected from this population. Suppose we randomly select 25 samples of size 5 each and compute the mean of each sample. These results are shown in Chart 8–4. Notice that the shape of the distribution of sample means has changed from the shape of the original population even though we selected only 25 of the many

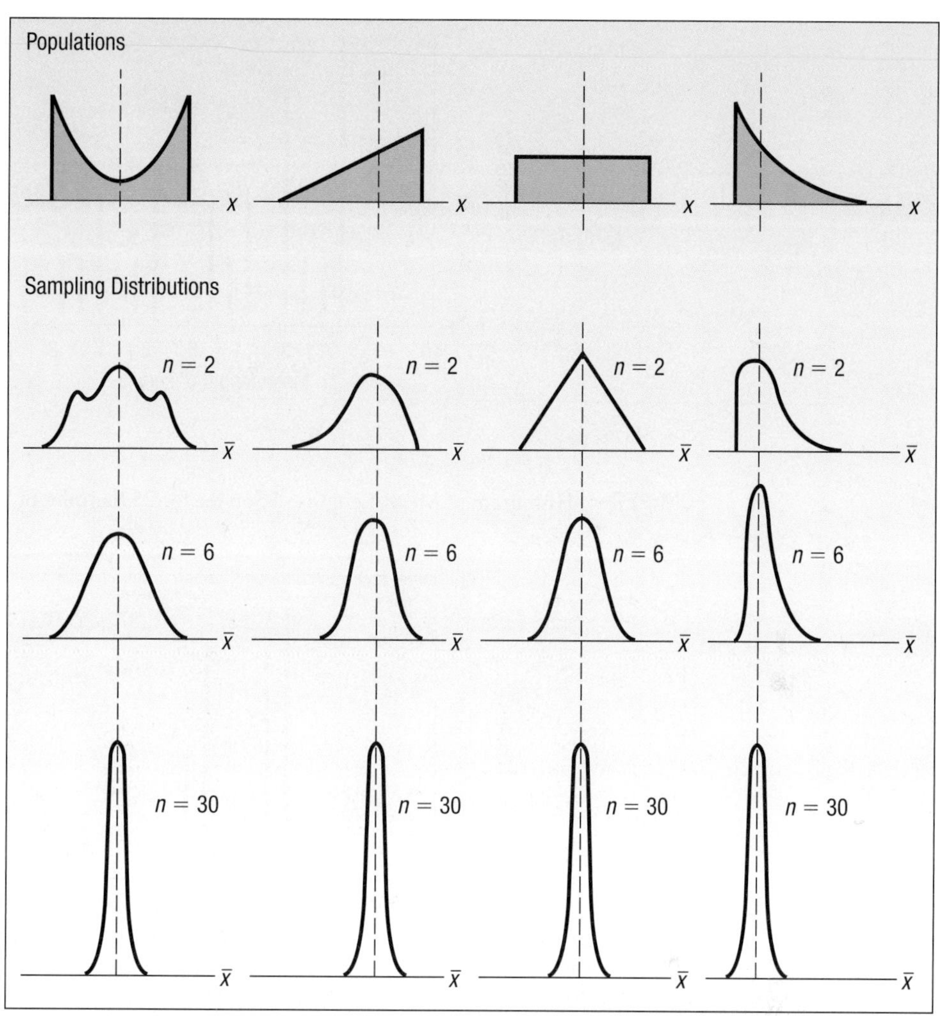

CHART 8–2 Results of the Central Limit Theorem for Several Populations

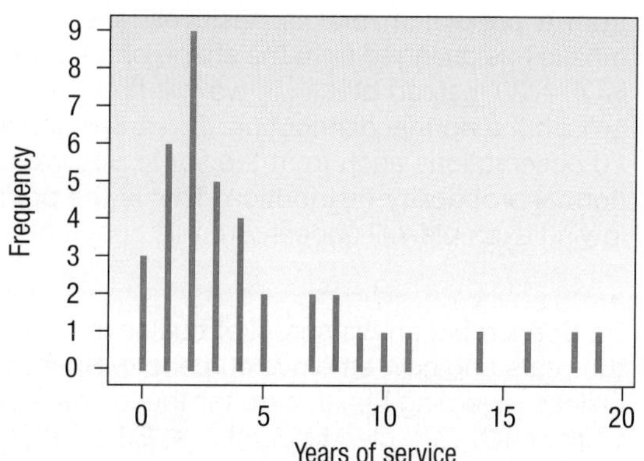

CHART 8–3 Length of Service for Spence Sprockets, Inc. Employees

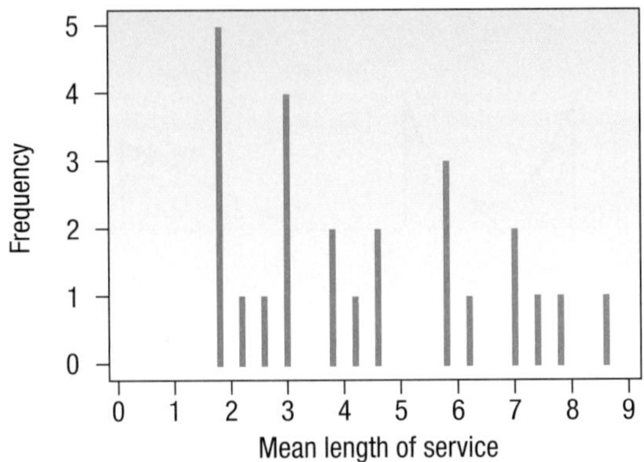

CHART 8–4 Histogram of Mean Lengths of Service for 25 Samples of Five Employees

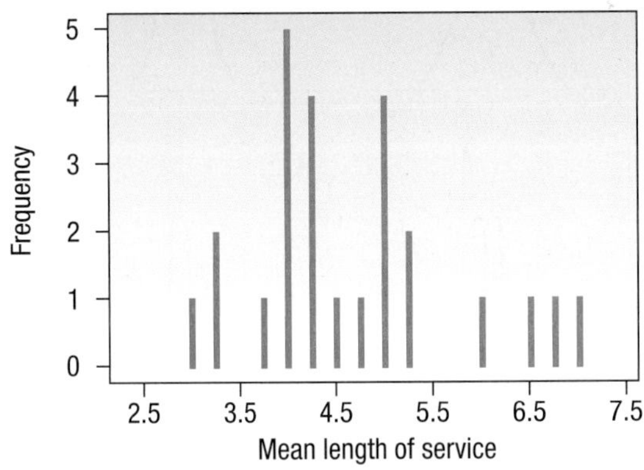

CHART 8–5 Histogram of Mean Lengths of Service for 25 Samples of 20 Employees

possible samples. To put it another way, we selected 25 random samples of 5 each from a population that is positively skewed and found the distribution of sample means has changed from the shape of the population. As we take larger samples, that is, $n = 20$ instead of $n = 5$, we will find the distribution of the sample mean will approach the normal distribution. Chart 8–5 shows the results of 25 random samples of 20 observations each from the same population. Observe the clear trend toward the normal probability distribution. This is the point of the central limit theorem. The following example will underscore this condition.

EXAMPLE

Ed Spence began his sprocket business 20 years ago. The business has grown over the years and now employs 40 people. Spence Sprockets, Inc. faces some major decisions regarding health care for these employees. Before making a final decision on what health care plan to purchase, Ed decides to form a committee of five representative employees. The committee will be asked to study the health care issue carefully and make a recommendation as to what plan best fits the employees' needs. Ed feels the views of newer employees toward health care may differ from those of more experienced employees. If Ed randomly selects this committee, what can he expect in terms of the mean years with Spence Sprockets for those on the committee? How does the shape of the distribution of years of experience of all employees (the population) compare with the shape of the sampling distribution of the mean? The lengths of service (rounded to the nearest year) of the 40 employees currently on the Spence Sprockets, Inc. payroll are as follows.

11	4	18	2	1	2	0	2	2	4
3	4	1	2	2	3	3	19	8	3
7	1	0	2	7	0	4	5	1	14
16	8	9	1	1	2	5	10	2	3

SOLUTION

Chart 8–3 shows the distribution of the years of experience for the population of 40 current employees. This distribution of lengths of service is positively skewed because there are a few employees who have worked at Spence Sprockets for a longer period of time. Specifically, six employees have been with the company 10 years or more. However, because the business has grown, the number of employees has increased in the last few years. Of the 40 employees, 18 have been with the company two years or less.

Let's consider the first of Ed Spence's problems. He would like to form a committee of five employees to look into the health care question and suggest what type of health care coverage would be most appropriate for the majority of workers. How should he select the committee? If he selects the committee randomly, what might he expect in terms of mean length of service for those on the committee?

To begin, Ed writes the length of service for each of the 40 employees on pieces of paper and puts them into an old baseball hat. Next, he shuffles the pieces of paper around and randomly selects five slips of paper. The lengths of service for these five employees are 1, 9, 0, 19, and 14 years. Thus, the mean length of service for these five sampled employees is 8.60 years. How does that compare with the population mean? At this point Ed does not know the population mean, but the number of employees in the population is only 40, so he decides to calculate the mean length of service for *all* his employees. It is 4.8 years, found by adding the lengths of service for *all* the employees and dividing the total by 40.

$$\mu = \frac{11 + 4 + 18 + \cdots + 2 + 3}{40} = 4.80$$

The difference between the sample mean ($\bar{X}$) and the population mean (μ) is called **sampling error.** In other words, the difference of 3.80 years between the population mean of 4.80 and the sample mean of 8.60 is the sampling error. It is due to chance. Thus, if Ed selected these five employees to constitute the committee, their mean length of service would be larger than the population mean.

What would happen if Ed put the five pieces of paper back into the baseball hat and selected another sample? Would you expect the mean of this second sample to be exactly the same as the previous one? Suppose he selects another sample of five employees and finds the lengths of service in this sample to be 7, 4, 4, 1, and 3. This sample mean is 3.80 years. The result of selecting 25 samples of five employees each is shown in Table 8–5 and Chart 8–4. There are actually 658,008 possible samples of 5 from the population of 40 employees, found by the combination formula (5–9) for 40 things taken 5 at a time. Notice the difference in the shape of the population and the distribution of these sample means. The population of the lengths of service for employees (Chart 8–3) is positively skewed, but the distribution of these 25 sample means does not reflect the same positive skew. There is also a difference in the range of the sample means versus the range of the population. The population ranged from 0 to 19 years, whereas the sample means range from 1.6 to 8.6 years.

TABLE 8–5 Twenty-Five Random Samples of Five Employees

Sample I.D.			Sample Data			Sample Mean
A	1	9	0	19	14	8.6
B	7	4	4	1	3	3.8
C	8	19	8	2	1	7.6
D	4	18	2	0	11	7.0
E	4	2	4	7	18	7.0
F	1	2	0	3	2	1.6
G	2	3	2	0	2	1.8
H	11	2	9	2	4	5.6
I	9	0	4	2	7	4.4
J	1	1	1	11	1	3.0
K	2	0	0	10	2	2.8
L	0	2	3	2	16	4.6
M	2	3	1	1	1	1.6
N	3	7	3	4	3	4.0
O	1	2	3	1	4	2.2
P	19	0	1	3	8	6.2
Q	5	1	7	14	9	7.2
R	5	4	2	3	4	3.6
S	14	5	2	2	5	5.6
T	2	1	1	4	7	3.0
U	3	7	1	2	1	2.8
V	0	1	5	1	2	1.8
W	0	3	19	4	2	5.6
X	4	2	3	4	0	2.6
Y	1	1	2	3	2	1.8

Table 8–6 reports the result of selecting 25 samples of 20 employees each and computing their sample means. These sample means are shown graphically in Chart 8–5. Compare the shape of this distribution to the population (Chart 8–3) and to the distribution of sample means where the sample is $n = 5$ (Chart 8–4). You should observe two important features:

1. The shape of the distribution of the sample mean is different from that of the population. In Chart 8–3 the distribution of all employees is positively skewed. However, as we select random samples from this population, the shape of the distribution of the sample mean changes. As we increase the size of the sample, the distribution of the sample mean approaches the normal probability distribution. This illustrates the central limit theorem.
2. There is less dispersion in the sampling distribution of sample means than in the population distribution. In the population the lengths of service ranged from 0 to 19 years. When we selected samples of 5, the sample means ranged from 1.6 to 8.6 years, and when we selected samples of 20, the means ranged from 3.05 to 7.10 years.

We can also compare the mean of the sample means to the population mean. The mean of the 25 samples reported in Table 8–6 is 4.676 years.

$$\mu_{\bar{X}} = \frac{3.95 + 3.25 + \cdots + 4.30 + 5.05}{25} = 4.676$$

We use the symbol $\mu_{\bar{X}}$ to identify the mean of the distribution of the sample mean. The subscript reminds us that the distribution is of the sample mean. It is read "mu sub X bar." We observe that the mean of the sample means, 4.676 years, is very close to the population mean of 4.80.

TABLE 8–6 Random Samples and Sample Means of 25 Samples of 20 Spence Sprocket, Inc. Employees

Sample Number										Sample Data (Length of Service)											Sample Mean
A	3	8	3	0	2	1	2	3	11	5	1	3	4	2	7	1	1	2	4	16	3.95
B	2	3	8	2	1	5	2	0	3	1	0	7	1	4	3	11	4	4	3	1	3.25
C	14	5	0	3	2	14	11	9	2	2	1	2	19	1	0	1	4	2	19	8	5.95
D	9	2	1	1	4	10	0	8	4	3	2	1	0	8	1	14	5	10	1	3	4.35
E	18	1	2	2	4	3	2	8	2	1	0	19	4	19	0	1	4	0	3	14	5.35
F	10	4	4	18	3	3	1	0	0	2	2	4	7	10	2	0	3	4	2	1	4.00
G	5	7	11	8	11	18	1	1	16	2	2	16	2	3	2	16	2	2	2	4	6.55
H	3	0	2	0	5	4	5	3	8	3	2	5	1	1	2	9	8	3	16	5	4.25
I	0	0	18	2	1	7	4	1	3	0	3	2	11	7	2	8	5	1	2	3	4.00
J	2	7	2	4	1	3	3	2	5	10	0	1	1	2	9	3	2	19	3	2	4.05
K	7	4	5	3	3	0	18	2	0	4	2	7	2	7	4	2	10	1	1	2	4.20
L	0	3	10	5	9	2	1	4	1	2	1	8	18	1	4	3	3	2	0	4	4.05
M	4	1	2	1	7	3	9	14	8	19	4	4	1	2	0	3	1	2	1	2	4.40
N	3	16	1	2	4	4	4	2	1	5	2	3	5	3	4	7	16	1	11	1	4.75
O	2	19	2	0	2	2	16	2	3	11	9	2	8	0	8	2	7	3	2	2	5.10
P	2	18	16	5	2	2	19	0	1	2	11	4	2	2	1	4	2	0	4	3	5.00
Q	3	2	3	11	10	1	1	5	19	16	7	10	3	1	1	1	2	2	3	1	5.10
R	2	3	1	2	7	4	3	19	9	2	2	1	1	2	2	2	1	8	0	2	3.65
S	2	14	19	1	19	2	8	4	2	2	14	2	8	16	4	7	2	9	0	7	7.10
T	0	1	3	3	2	2	3	1	1	0	3	2	3	5	2	10	14	4	2	0	3.05
U	1	0	1	2	16	1	1	2	5	1	4	1	2	2	2	2	2	8	9	3	3.25
V	1	9	4	4	2	8	7	1	14	18	1	5	10	11	19	0	3	7	2	11	6.85
W	8	1	9	19	3	19	0	5	2	1	5	3	3	4	1	5	3	1	8	7	5.35
X	4	2	0	3	1	16	1	11	3	3	2	18	2	0	1	5	0	7	2	5	4.30
Y	1	2	1	2	0	2	7	2	4	8	19	2	5	3	3	0	19	2	1	18	5.05

What should we conclude from this example? The central limit theorem indicates that, regardless of the shape of the population distribution, the sampling distribution of the sample mean will move toward the normal probability distribution. The larger the number of observations in each sample, the stronger the convergence. The Spence Sprockets, Inc., example shows how the central limit theorem works. We began with a positively skewed population (Chart 8–3). Next, we selected 25 random samples of 5 observations, computed the mean of each sample, and finally organized these 25 sample means into a graph (Chart 8–4). We observe a change in the shape of the sampling distribution of sample mean from that of the population. The movement is from a positively skewed distribution to a distribution that has the shape of the normal probability distribution.

To further illustrate the effects of the central limit theorem, we increased the number of observations in each sample from 5 to 20. We selected 25 samples of 20 observations each and calculated the mean of each sample. Finally, we organized these sample means into a graph (Chart 8–5). The shape of the histogram in Chart 8–5 is clearly moving toward the normal probability distribution.

If you go back to Chapter 6 where several binomial distributions with a "success" proportion of .10 are shown in Chart 6–4, you can see yet another demonstration of the central limit theorem. Observe as n increases from 7 through 12 and 20 up to 40 that the profile of the probability distributions moves closer and closer to a normal probability distribution. Chart 8–2 on page 227 also shows the convergence to normality as n increases. This again reinforces the fact that as more observations are sampled from any population distribution, the shape of the sampling distribution of the sample mean will get closer and closer to a normal distribution.

The central limit theorem itself (reread the definition on page 226) does not say anything about the dispersion of the sampling distribution of sample mean or about the comparison of the mean of the sampling distribution of sample mean to the mean of the population. However, in our example we did observe that there was less dispersion in the distribution of the sample mean than in the population distribution by noting the difference in the range in the population values and the range of the sample means. We observe that the mean of the sample means is close to the mean of the population. It can be demonstrated that the mean of the sampling distribution is the population mean, i.e., $\mu_{\bar{X}} = \mu$, and if the standard deviation in the population is σ, the standard deviation of the sample means is $\sigma/\sqrt{n}$, where n is the number of observations in each sample. We refer to $\sigma/\sqrt{n}$ as the **standard error of the mean.** Its longer name is actually the *standard deviation of the sampling distribution of the sample mean.*

STANDARD ERROR OF THE MEAN $$\sigma_{\bar{X}} = \frac{\sigma}{\sqrt{n}}$$ **[8–1]**

In this section we also came to other important conclusions.

1. The mean of the distribution of sample means will be *exactly* equal to the population mean if we are able to select all possible samples of the same size from a given population. That is:

$$\mu = \mu_{\bar{X}}$$

Even if we do not select all samples, we can expect the mean of the distribution of sample means to be close to the population mean.
2. There will be less dispersion in the sampling distribution of the sample mean than in the population. If the standard deviation of the population is σ, the standard deviation of the distribution of sample means is $\sigma/\sqrt{n}$. Note that when we increase the size of the sample the standard error of the mean decreases.

Self-Review 8–4

Refer to the Spence Sprockets, Inc. data on page 229. Select 10 random samples of 5 employees each. Use the methods described earlier in the chapter and the Table of Random Numbers (Appendix E) to find the employees to include in the sample. Compute the mean of each sample and plot the sample means on a chart similar to Chart 8–3. What is the mean of your 10 sample means?

Exercises

11. Appendix E is a table of random numbers. Hence, each digit from 0 to 9 has the same likelihood of occurrence.

a. Draw a graph showing the population distribution. What is the population mean? Is this an example of the uniform distribution? Why?

b. Following are the first 10 rows of five digits from Appendix E. Assume that these are 10 random samples of five values each. Determine the mean of each sample and plot the means on a chart similar to Chart 8–3. Compare the mean of the sampling distribution of the sample means with the population mean.

0	2	7	1	1
9	4	8	7	3
5	4	9	2	1
7	7	6	4	0
6	1	5	4	5
1	7	1	4	7
1	3	7	4	8
8	7	4	5	5
0	8	9	9	9
7	8	8	0	4

12. The Scrapper Elevator Company has 20 sales representatives who sell their product throughout the United States and Canada. The number of units sold by each representative is listed below. Assume these sales figures to be the population values.

2	3	2	3	3	4	2	4	3	2	2	7	3	4	5	3	3	3	3	5

a. Draw a graph showing the population distribution.
b. Compute the mean of the population.
c. Select five random samples of 5 each. Compute the mean of each sample. Use the methods described in this chapter and Appendix E to determine the items to be included in the sample.
d. Compare the mean of the sampling distribution of the sample means to the population mean. Would you expect the two values to be about the same?
e. Draw a histogram of the sample means. Do you notice a difference in the shape of the distribution of sample means compared to the shape of the population distribution?

13. Consider all of the coins (pennies, nickels, quarters, etc.) in your pocket or purse as a population. Make a frequency table beginning with the current year and counting backward to record the ages (in years) of the coins. For example, if the current year is 2005, then a coin with 2003 stamped on it is 2 years old.
a. Draw a histogram or other graph showing the population distribution.
b. Randomly select five coins and record the mean age of the sampled coins. Repeat this sampling process 20 times. Now draw a histogram or other graph showing the distribution of the sample means.
c. Compare the shapes of the two histograms.

14. Consider the digits in the phone numbers on a randomly selected page of your local phone book a population. Make a frequency table of the final digit of 30 randomly selected phone numbers. For example, if a phone number is 555-9704, record a 4.
a. Draw a histogram or other graph of this population distribution. Using the uniform distribution, compute the population mean and the population standard deviation.
b. Also record the sample mean of the final four digits (9704 would lead to a mean of 5). Now draw a histogram or other graph showing the distribution of the sample means.
c. Compare the shapes of the two histograms.

Using the Sampling Distribution of the Sample Mean

The previous discussion is important because most business decisions are made on the basis of sampling results. Here are some examples.

1. The Arm and Hammer Company wants to ensure that their laundry detergent actually contains 100 fluid ounces, as indicated on the label. Historical summaries from the filling process indicate the mean amount per container is 100 fluid ounces and the standard deviation is 2 fluid ounces. The quality technician in her 10 A.M. check of 40 containers finds the mean amount per container is 99.8 fluid ounces. Should the technician shut down the filling operation or is the sampling error reasonable?

2. The A. C. Nielsen Company provides information to companies advertising on television. Prior research indicates that adult Americans watch an average of 6.0 hours per day of television. The standard deviation is 1.5 hours. For a sample of 50 adults in the Greater Boston area, would it be reasonable that we could randomly select a sample and find that they watch an average of 6.5 hours of television per day?
3. The Haughton Elevator Company wishes to develop specifications for the number of people who can ride in a new oversized elevator. Suppose the mean weight for an adult is 160 pounds and the standard deviation is 15 pounds. However, the distribution of weights does not follow the normal probability distribution. It is positively skewed. What is the likelihood that for a sample of 50 adults their mean weight is 170 pounds or more?

In each of these situations we have a population about which we have some information. We take a sample from that population and wish to conclude whether the sampling error, that is, the difference between the population parameter and the sample statistic, is due to chance.

Using ideas discussed in the previous section, we can compute the probability that a sample mean will fall within a certain range. We know that the sampling distribution of the sample mean will follow the normal probability distribution under two conditions:

1. When the samples are taken from populations known to follow the normal distribution. In this case the size of the sample is not a factor.
2. When the shape of the population distribution is not known or the shape is known to be nonnormal, but our sample contains at least 30 observations.

We can use formula (7–5), from the previous chapter, to convert any normal distribution to the standard normal distribution. We also refer to this as a z value. Then we can use the standard normal table, Appendix D, to find the probability of selecting an observation that would fall within a specific range. The formula for finding a z value is:

$$z = \frac{X - \mu}{\sigma}$$

In this formula X is a value of the random variable, μ is the population mean, and σ the population standard deviation.

However, most business decisions refer to a sample mean—not just one observation. So we are interested in the distribution of $\bar{X}$, the sample mean, instead of X, the value of one observation. That is the first change we make in formula (7–5). The second is that we use the standard error of the mean of n observations instead of the population standard deviation. That is, we use $\sigma/\sqrt{n}$ in the denominator rather than σ. Therefore, to find the likelihood of a sample mean with a specified range, we first use the following formula to find the corresponding z value. Then we use Appendix D to locate the probability.

FINDING THE z VALUE OF $\bar{X}$ WHEN THE POPULATION STANDARD DEVIATION IS KNOWN

$$z = \frac{\bar{X} - \mu}{\sigma/\sqrt{n}} \quad \textbf{[8–2]}$$

The following example will show the application.

EXAMPLE

The Quality Assurance Department for Cola, Inc., maintains records regarding the amount of cola in their "Jumbo" bottle. The actual amount of cola in each bottle is critical, but varies a small amount from one bottle to the next. Cola, Inc., does not wish to underfill the bottles, because they will have a problem with truth in labeling. On the other hand, they cannot overfill each bottle, because they would be giving cola away, hence reducing their profits. Their records indicate that the amount of cola follows the normal probability distribution. The mean amount per bottle is 31.2 ounces. The population standard deviation of 0.4 ounces is based on hundreds of samples over the last several years. At 8 A.M. today the quality technician randomly selected 16 bottles from the filling line. The mean amount of cola contained in the bottles is 31.38 ounces. Is this an unlikely result? Is it likely the process is putting too much soda in the bottles? To put it another way, is the sampling error of 0.18 ounces unusual?

SOLUTION

We can use the results of the previous section to find the likelihood that we could select a sample of 16 (n) bottles from a normal population with a mean of 31.2 (μ) ounces and a population standard deviation of 0.4 (σ) ounces and find the sample mean to be 31.38 ($\bar{X}$). We use formula (8–2) to find the value of z.

$$z = \frac{\bar{X} - \mu}{\sigma/\sqrt{n}} = \frac{31.38 - 31.20}{0.4/\sqrt{16}} = 1.80$$

The numerator of this equation, $\bar{X} - \mu = 31.38 - 31.20 = .18$, is the sampling error. The denominator, $\sigma/\sqrt{n} = 0.40/\sqrt{16} = 0.1$, is the standard error of the sampling distribution of the sample mean. So the z values express the sampling error in standard units, in other words, the standard error.

Next, we compute the likelihood of a z value greater than 1.80. In Appendix D locate the probability corresponding to a z value of 1.80. It is .4641. The likelihood of a z value greater than 1.80 is .0359, found by .5000 − .4641.

What do we conclude? It is unlikely, less than a 4 percent chance, we could select a sample of 16 observations from a normal population with a mean of 31.2 ounces and a population standard deviation of 0.4 ounces and find the sample mean equal to or greater than 31.38 ounces. We conclude the process is putting too much cola in the bottles. The quality technician should see the production supervisor about reducing the amount of soda in each bottle. This information is summarized in Chart 8–6.

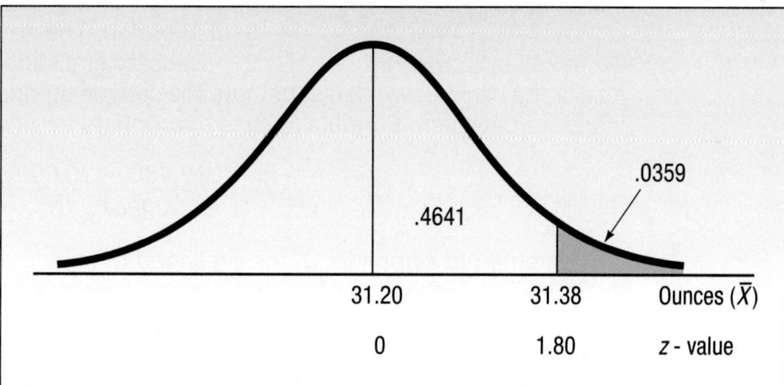

CHART 8–6 Sampling Distribution of the Mean Amount of Cola in a Jumbo Bottle

Self-Review 8–5 Refer to the Cola, Inc., information. Suppose the quality technician selected a sample of 16 Jumbo bottles that averaged 31.08 ounces. What can you conclude about the filling process?

There are many sampling situations in business when we wish to make an inference about the population mean, but we do not have much knowledge about the population. Here the power of the central limit theorem helps. We know that, for any shape of the population distribution, if we select a sample sufficiently large, the sampling distribution of the sample mean will follow the normal distribution. Statistical theory has shown that samples of at least 30 are sufficiently large to allow us to assume that the sampling distribution follows the normal distribution.

Often we do not know the value of the population standard deviation, σ. Because the sample is at least 30, we estimate the population standard deviation with the sample standard deviation. The actual distribution of the statistic is Student's t distribution which will be discussed in the next chapter. When we use s to replace σ, the new formula for finding the value of z is:

FINDING THE z VALUE OF $\bar{X}$ WHEN THE POPULATION STANDARD DEVIATION IS UNKNOWN

$$z = \frac{\bar{X} - \mu}{s/\sqrt{n}} \quad \textbf{[8–3]}$$

EXAMPLE

The Metropolitan New York Gas Station Dealers' Association estimates that the mean number of gallons of gasoline sold per day at a gas station is 20,000. The shape of this distribution is unknown. A sample of 70 dealers yesterday revealed the mean number of gallons sold was 19,480. The standard deviation of the sample of 70 dealers was 4,250 gallons. Is the assertion that the population mean is 20,000 gallons reasonable? What is the likelihood of finding a sample with the given statistics from the proposed population? What assumptions do you need to make?

SOLUTION

We are unsure of the shape of the population of gallons sold. However, the sample is sufficiently large to allow us to assume that the sampling distribution of the sample mean follows the normal distribution. The central limit theorem provides the necessary statistical theory. Again, because of the size of the sample, we can substitute the sample standard deviation for the population standard deviation. Formula (8–3) is appropriate for finding the z value.

$$z = \frac{\bar{X} - \mu}{s/\sqrt{n}} = \frac{19{,}480 - 20{,}000}{4{,}250/\sqrt{70}} = -1.02$$

Referring to Appendix D, the likelihood of finding a z value between 0 and -1.02 is .3461. The probability of finding a sample mean of 19,480 gallons or less from the specified population is .1539, found by .5000 − .3461. To put it another way, there is about a 15 percent chance we could select a sample of 70 gas stations and find the mean of this sample is 19,480 gallons or less, when the population mean is 20,000. It is reasonable to conclude that the population mean is 20,000 gallons. This information is summarized in Chart 8–7.

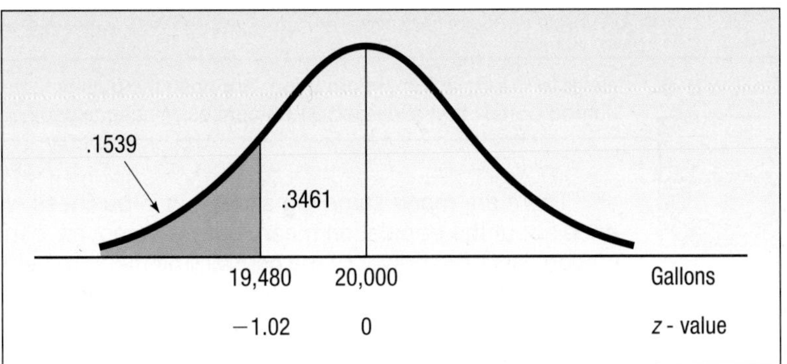

CHART 8–7 Sampling Distribution for the Sample Mean of the Number of Gallons Sold per Day

Self-Review 8–6

The mean hourly wage for plumbers in the Atlanta, Georgia, region is $28.00. What is the likelihood that we could select a sample of 50 plumbers with a mean wage of $28.50 or more? The standard deviation of the sample is $2.00 per hour.

Exercises

15. A normal population has a mean of 60 and a standard deviation of 12. You select a random sample of 9. Compute the probability the sample mean is:
a. Greater than 63.
b. Less than 56.
c. Between 56 and 63.

16. A population of unknown shape has a mean of 75. You select a sample of 40. The standard deviation of the sample is 5. Compute the probability the sample mean is:
a. Less than 74.
b. Between 74 and 76.
c. Between 76 and 77.
d. Greater than 77.

17. The mean rent for a one-bedroom apartment in Southern California is $2,200 per month. The distribution of the monthly costs does not follow the normal distribution. In fact, it is positively skewed. What is the probability of selecting a sample of 50 one-bedroom apartments and finding the mean to be at least $1,950 per month? The standard deviation of the sample is $250.

18. According to an IRS study, it takes an average of 330 minutes for taxpayers to prepare, copy, and electronically file a 1040 tax form. A consumer watchdog agency selects a random sample of 40 taxpayers and finds the standard deviation of the time to prepare, copy, and electronically file form 1040 is 80 minutes.
a. What assumption or assumptions do you need to make about the shape of the population?
b. What is the standard error of the mean in this example?
c. What is the likelihood the sample mean is greater than 320 minutes?
d. What is the likelihood the sample mean is between 320 and 350 minutes?
e. What is the likelihood the sample mean is greater than 350 minutes?

Chapter Outline

I. There are many reasons for sampling a population.
- **A.** The results of a sample may adequately estimate the value of the population parameter, thus saving time and money.
- **B.** It may be too time consuming to contact all members of the population.
- **C.** It may be impossible to check or locate all the members of the population.
- **D.** The cost of studying all the items in the population may be prohibitive.
- **E.** Often testing destroys the sampled item and it cannot be returned to the population.

II. In an unbiased sample all members of the population have a chance of being selected for the sample. There are several probability sampling methods.
- **A.** In a simple random sample all members of the population have the same chance of being selected for the sample.
- **B.** In a systematic sample a random starting point is selected, and then every *k*th item thereafter is selected for the sample.
- **C.** In a stratified sample the population is divided into several groups, called strata, and then a random sample is selected from each stratum.
- **D.** In cluster sampling the population is divided into primary units, then samples are drawn from the primary units.

III. The sampling error is the difference between a population parameter and a sample statistic.

IV. The sampling distribution of the sample mean is a probability distribution of all possible sample means of the same sample size.
- **A.** For a given sample size, the mean of all possible sample means selected from a population is equal to the population mean.
- **B.** There is less variation in the distribution of the sample mean than in the population distribution.
  - **1.** The standard error of the mean measures the variation in the sampling distribution of the sample mean.
    - **a.** If we know the population standard deviation, the standard error is

$$\sigma_{\bar{X}} = \frac{\sigma}{\sqrt{n}} \quad [8\text{–}1]$$

b. If we do not know the population standard deviation, the standard error is estimated by

$$s_{\bar{X}} = \frac{s}{\sqrt{n}}$$

C. If the population follows a normal distribution, the sampling distribution of the sample mean will also follow the normal distribution for samples of any size. Assume the population standard deviation is known. To determine the probability that a sample mean falls in a particular region, use the following formula.

$$z = \frac{\bar{X} - \mu}{\sigma/\sqrt{n}} \quad [8\text{–}2]$$

D. If the population is not normally distributed but the sample is of at least 30 observations, the sampling distribution of the sample mean is approximately normal. Assume the population standard deviation is not known. To determine the probability that a sample mean falls in a particular region, use the normal distribution and the following standardizing formula:

$$z = \frac{\bar{X} - \mu}{s/\sqrt{n}} \quad [8\text{–}3]$$

Pronunciation Key

SYMBOL	MEANING	PRONUNCIATION
$\mu_{\bar{X}}$	Mean of the sampling distribution of the sample mean	*mu sub X bar*
$\sigma_{\bar{X}}$	Population standard error of the sample mean	*sigma sub X bar*
$s_{\bar{X}}$	Estimate of the standard error of the sample mean	*s sub X bar*

Chapter Exercises

19. The retail stores located in the North Towne Square Mall are:

00	Elder-Beerman	09	Lion Store	18	County Seat
01	Montgomery Ward	10	Bootleggers	19	Kid Mart
02	Deb Shop	11	Formal Man	20	Lerner
03	Frederick's of Hollywood	12	Leather Ltd.	21	Coach House Gifts
04	Petries	13	B Dalton Bookseller	22	Spencer Gifts
05	Easy Dreams	14	Pat's Hallmark	23	CPI Photo Finish
06	Summit Stationers	15	Things Remembered	24	Regis Hairstylists
07	E. B. Brown Opticians	16	Pearle Vision Express		
08	Kay-Bee Toy & Hobby	17	Dollar Tree		

a. If the following random numbers are selected, which retail stores should be contacted for a survey? 11, 65, 86, 62, 06, 10, 12, 77, and 04

b. Select a random sample of four retail stores. Use Appendix E.

c. A systematic sampling procedure is to be used. The first store is to be contacted and then every third store. Which stores will be contacted?

20. Medical Mutual Insurance is investigating the cost of a routine office visit to family-practice physicians in the Rochester, New York, area. The following is a list of family-practice physicians in the region. Physicians are to be randomly selected and contacted regarding their charges. The 39 physicians have been coded from 00 to 38. Also noted is whether they are in practice by themselves (S), have a partner (P), or are in a group practice (G).

Number	Type of Physician	Practice	Number	Type of Physician	Practice
00	R. E. Scherbarth, M.D.	S	20	Gregory Yost, M.D.	P
01	Crystal R. Goveia, M.D.	P	21	J. Christian Zona, M.D.	P
02	Mark D. Hillard, M.D.	P	22	Larry Johnson, M.D.	P
03	Jeanine S. Huttner, M.D.	P	23	Sanford Kimmel, M.D.	P
04	Francis Aona, M.D.	P	24	Harry Mayhew, M.D.	S
05	Janet Arrowsmith, M.D.	P	25	Leroy Rodgers, M.D.	S
06	David DeFrance, M.D.	S	26	Thomas Tafelski, M.D.	S
07	Judith Furlong, M.D.	S	27	Mark Zilkoski, M.D.	G
08	Leslie Jackson, M.D.	G	28	Ken Bertka, M.D.	G
09	Paul Langenkamp, M.D.	S	29	Mark DeMichiei, M.D.	G
10	Philip Lepkowski, M.D.	S	30	John Eggert, M.D.	P
11	Wendy Martin, M.D.	S	31	Jeanne Fiorito, M.D.	P
12	Denny Mauricio, M.D.	P	32	Michael Fitzpatrick, M.D.	P
13	Hasmukh Parmar, M.D.	P	33	Charles Holt, D.O.	P
14	Ricardo Pena, M.D.	P	34	Richard Koby, M.D.	P
15	David Reames, M.D.	P	35	John Meier, M.D.	P
16	Ronald Reynolds, M.D.	G	36	Douglas Smucker, M.D.	S
17	Mark Steinmetz, M.D.	G	37	David Weldy, M.D.	P
18	Geza Torok, M.D.	S	38	Cheryl Zaborowski, M.D.	P
19	Mark Young, M.D.	P			

a. The random numbers obtained from Appendix E are: 31, 94, 43, 36, 03, 24, 17, and 09. Which physicians should be contacted?
b. Select a random sample of four physicians using the random numbers of Appendix E.
c. A sample is to consist of every fifth physician. The number 04 is selected as the starting point. Which physicians will be contacted?
d. A sample is to consist of two physicians in solo practice (S), two in partnership (P), and one in group practice (G). Select a sample accordingly. Explain your procedure.

21. What is sampling error? Could the value of the sampling error be zero? If it were zero, what would this mean?

22. List the reasons for sampling. Give an example of each reason for sampling.

23. The manufacturer of eMachines, an economy-priced computer, recently completed the design for a new laptop model. eMachine's top management would like some assistance in pricing the new laptop. Two market research firms were contacted and asked to prepare pricing strategy. Marketing-Gets-Results tested the new laptop E Machine with 50 randomly selected consumers, who indicated they plan to purchase a laptop within the next year. The second marketing research firm, called Marketing-Reaps-Profits, market-tested the new E Machine laptop with 200 current laptop owners. Which of the marketing research companies test results will be more useful? Discuss why.

24. Answer the following questions in one or two well-constructed sentences.
a. What happens to the standard error of the mean if the sample size is increased?
b. What happens to the distribution of the sample means if the sample size is increased?
c. When using the distribution of sample means to estimate the population mean, what is the benefit of using larger sample sizes?

25. A study of motel facilities in Rock Hill, South Carolina, showed there were 25 facilities. The city's convention and visitors bureau is studying the number of rooms at each location. The results are as follows:

90	72	75	60	75	72	84	72	88	74	105	115	68	74	80	64	104	82	48	58	60	80	48	58	100

a. Using a table of random numbers (Appendix E), select a random sample of five motels from this population.
b. Obtain a systematic sample by selecting a random starting point among the first five motels and then select every fifth motel.
c. Suppose the last five motels are "cut-rate" motels. Describe how you would select a random sample of three regular motels and two cut-rate motels.

26. As a part of their customer-service program, United Airlines randomly selected 10 passengers from today's 9 A.M. Chicago–Tampa flight. Each sampled passenger is to be interviewed in depth regarding airport facilities, service, food, and so on. To identify the sample, each passenger was given a number on boarding the aircraft. The numbers started with 001 and ended with 250.
a. Select 10 usable numbers at random using Appendix E.
b. The sample of 10 could have been chosen using a systematic sample. Choose the first number using Appendix E, and then list the numbers to be interviewed.
c. Evaluate the two methods by giving the advantages and possible disadvantages.
d. In what other way could a random sample be selected from the 250 passengers?

27. Suppose your statistics instructor gave six examinations during the semester. You received the following grades (percent correct): 79, 64, 84, 82, 92, and 77. Instead of averaging the six scores, the instructor indicated he would randomly select two grades and report that grade to the student records office.
a. How many different samples of two test grades are possible?
b. List all possible samples of size two and compute the mean of each.
c. Compute the mean of the sample means and compare it to the population mean.
d. If you were a student, would you like this arrangement? Would the result be different from dropping the lowest score? Write a brief report.

28. At the downtown office of First National Bank there are five tellers. Last week the tellers made the following number of errors each: 2, 3, 5, 3, and 5.
a. How many different samples of 2 tellers are possible?
b. List all possible samples of size 2 and compute the mean of each.
c. Compute the mean of the sample means and compare it to the population mean.

29. The quality control department employs five technicians during the day shift. Listed below is the number of times each technician instructed the production foreman to shut down the manufacturing process last week.

Technician	Shutdowns
Taylor	4
Hurley	3
Gupta	5
Rousche	3
Huang	2

a. How many different samples of two technicians are possible from this population?
b. List all possible samples of two observations each and compute the mean of each sample.
c. Compare the mean of the sample means with the population mean.
d. Compare the shape of the population distribution with the shape of the distribution of the sample means.

30. The Appliance Center has six sales representatives at their North Jacksonville outlet. Listed below is the number of refrigerators sold by each last month.

Sales Representative	Number Sold
Zina Craft	54
Woon Junge	50
Ernie DeBrul	52
Jan Niles	48
Molly Camp	50
Rachel Myak	52

a. How many samples of size two are possible?
b. Select all possible samples of size two and compute the mean number sold.
c. Organize the sample means into a frequency distribution.
d. What is the mean of the population? What is the mean of the sample means?

e. What is the shape of the population distribution?
f. What is the shape of the distribution of the sample mean?

31. The Sony Corporation produces a Walkman that requires two AA batteries. The mean life of these batteries in this product is 35.0 hours. The distribution of the battery lives closely follows the normal probability distribution with a standard deviation of 5.5 hours. As a part of their testing program Sony tests samples of 25 batteries.
a. What can you say about the shape of the distribution of the sample mean?
b. What is the standard error of the distribution of the sample mean?
c. What proportion of the samples will have a mean useful life of more than 36 hours?
d. What proportion of the samples will have a mean useful life greater than 34.5 hours?
e. What proportion of the samples will have a mean useful life between 34.5 and 36.0 hours?

32. CRA CDs, Inc. wants the mean lengths of the "cuts" on a CD to be 135 seconds (2 minutes and 15 seconds). This will allow the disk jockeys to have plenty of time for commercials within each 10-minute segment. Assume the distribution of the length of the cuts follows the normal distribution with a standard deviation of 8 seconds. Suppose we select a sample of 16 cuts from various CDs sold by CRA CDs, Inc.
a. What can we say about the shape of the distribution of the sample mean?
b. What is the standard error of the mean?
c. What percent of the sample means will be greater than 140 seconds?
d. What percent of the sample means will be greater than 128 seconds?
e. What percent of the sample means will be greater than 128 but less than 140 seconds?

33. Recent studies indicate that the typical 50-year-old woman spends $350 per year for personal-care products. The distribution of the amounts spent is positively skewed. We select a random sample of 40 women. The mean amount spent for those sampled is $335, and the standard deviation of the sample is $45. What is the likelihood of finding a sample mean this large or larger from the specified population?

34. Information from the American Institute of Insurance indicates the mean amount of life insurance per household in the United States is $110,000. This distribution is positively skewed. The standard deviation of the population is not known.
a. A random sample of 50 households revealed a mean of $112,000 and a standard deviation of $40,000. What is the standard error of the mean?
b. Suppose that you selected 50 samples of households. What is the expected shape of the distribution of the sample mean?
c. What is the likelihood of selecting a sample with a mean of at least $112,000?
d. What is the likelihood of selecting a sample with a mean of more than $100,000?
e. Find the likelihood of selecting a sample with a mean of more than $100,000 but less than $112,000.

35. The mean age at which men in the United States marry for the first time is 24.8 years. The shape and the standard deviation of the population are both unknown. For a random sample of 60 men, what is the likelihood that the age at which they were married for the first time is less than 25.1 years? Assume that the standard deviation of the sample is 2.5 years.

36. A recent study by the Greater Los Angeles Taxi Drivers Association showed that the mean fare charged for service from Hermosa Beach to the Los Angeles International Airport is $18.00 and the standard deviation is $3.50. We select a sample of 15 fares.
a. What is the likelihood that the sample mean is between $17.00 and $20.00?
b. What must you assume to make the above calculation?

37. The Crossett Trucking Company claims that the mean weight of their delivery trucks when they are fully loaded is 6,000 pounds and the standard deviation is 150 pounds. Assume that the population follows the normal distribution. Forty trucks are randomly selected and weighed. Within what limits will 95 percent of the sample means occur?

38. The mean amount purchased by each customer at Churchill's Grocery Store is $23.50. The population is positively skewed and the standard deviation is not known. For a sample of 50 customers, answer the following questions.
a. If the standard deviation of the sample is $5.00, what is the likelihood the sample mean is at least $25.00?
b. Again, assume the sample standard deviation is $5.00. What is the likelihood the sample mean is greater than $22.50 but less than $25.00?
c. Again, assume the sample standard deviation is $5.00. Within what limits will 90 percent of the sample means occur?

39. The mean SAT score for Division I student-athletes is 947 with a standard deviation of 205. If you select a random sample of 60 of these students, what is the probability the mean is below 900?

40. Suppose we roll a fair die two times.
  a. How many different samples are there?
  b. List each of the possible samples and compute the mean.
  c. On a chart similar to Chart 8–1, compare the distribution of sample means with the distribution of the population.
  d. Compute the mean and the standard deviation of each distribution and compare them.

41. The following table lists the most recent data available on per capita personal income (in dollars) for each of the 50 states.

Number	State	Income	Number	State	Income	Number	State	Income
	New England			**Plains**			**Southwest**	
01	Connecticut	$43,173	17	Iowa	29,043	36	Arizona	26,838
02	Maine	28,831	18	Kansas	29,935	37	New Mexico	25,541
03	Massachusetts	39,815	19	Minnesota	34,443	38	Oklahoma	26,656
04	New Hampshire	34,702	20	Missouri	29,252	39	Texas	29,372
05	Rhode Island	31,916	21	Nebraska	30,758		**Rocky Mountain**	
06	Vermont	30,740	22	North Dakota	29,204	40	Colorado	34,283
	Mideast		23	South Dakota	29,234	41	Idaho	25,911
07	Delaware	32,810		**Southeast**		42	Montana	25,920
08	Maryland	37,331	24	Alabama	26,338	43	Utah	24,977
09	New Jersey	40,427	25	Arkansas	24,289	44	Wyoming	32,808
10	New York	36,574	26	Florida	30,446		**Far West**	
11	Pennsylvania	31,998	27	Georgia	29,442	45	Alaska	33,568
	Great Lakes		28	Kentucky	26,252	46	California	33,749
12	Illinois	33,960	29	Louisiana	26,100	47	Hawaii	30,913
13	Indiana	28,783	30	Mississippi	23,448	48	Nevada	31,266
14	Michigan	30,439	31	North Carolina	28,235	49	Oregon	29,340
15	Ohio	29,944	32	South Carolina	26,132	50	Washington	33,332
16	Wisconsin	30,898	33	Tennessee	28,455			
			34	Virginia	33,671			
			35	West Virginia	24,379			

  a. You wish to select a sample of eight from this list. The selected random numbers are 45, 15, 81, 09, 39, 43, 90, 26, 06, 45, 01, and 42. Which states are included in the sample?
  b. You wish to use a systematic sample of every sixth item and the digit 02 is chosen as the starting point. Which states are included?
  c. A sample of one state from each region is to be selected. Describe how you would perform the sampling process in detail. That is, show the random numbers you selected and the corresponding states that are included in your sample.

exercises.com

42. You need to find the "typical" or mean annual dividend per share for large banks. You decide to sample six banks listed on the New York Stock Exchange. These banks and their trading symbol follow.

Bank	Symbol	Bank	Symbol	Bank	Symbol
AmSouth Bancorporation	ASO	Golden West Financial	GDW	SouthTrust Corp.	SOTR
Bank of America Corp.	BAC	Huntington Bancshares	HBAN	SunTrust Banks	STI
Bank of New York	BK	KeyCorp	KEY	Synovus Financial	SNV
Bank One Corp.	ONE	M&T Bank Corp.	MTB	Union Planters	UPC
BB&T Corporation	BBT	Mellon Financial Corp.	MEL	U.S. Bancorp	USB
Charter One Financial	CF	National City Corp.	NCC	Wachovia Corp.	WB
Comerica, Inc.	CMA	Northern Trust Corp.	NTRS	Washington Mutual, Inc.	WM
Fifth Third Bancorp	FITB	PNC Financial Services Group	PNC	Wells Fargo & Co. (New)	WFC
FleetBoston Financial Corp.	FBF			Zions Bancorp	ZION

a. After numbering the banks from 01 to 26, which banks would be included in a sample if the random numbers were 14, 08, 24, 25, 05, 44, 02, and 22? Go to the following website: http://www.quicken.com. Enter the trading symbol for each of the sampled banks and record the Annual Dividend per share (Annual div/shr). Determine the mean annual dividend per share for the sample of banks.

b. Which banks are selected if you use a systematic sample of every fourth bank starting with the random number 03?

43. There are several websites that will report the 30 stocks that make up the Dow Jones Industrial Average (DJIA). One site is www.dbc.com/dbcfiles/dowt.html. Compute the mean of the 30 stocks.

a. Use a random number table, such as Appendix E, to select a random sample of five companies that make up the DJIA. Compute the sample mean. Compare the sample mean to the population mean. What did you find? What did you expect to find?

b. You should not expect to find that the mean of these 30 stocks is the same as the current DJIA. Go to the Dow Jones website at http://averages.dowjones.com/jsp/index.jsp and read the reasons.

Dataset Exercises

44. Refer to the Real Estate data, which reports information on the homes sold in the Denver, Colorado, area last year.

a. Compute the mean and the standard deviation of the distribution of the selling prices for the homes. Assume this to be the population. Develop a histogram of the data. Would it seem reasonable from this histogram to conclude that the population of selling prices follows the normal distribution?

b. Let's assume a normal population. Select a sample of 10 homes. Compute the mean and the standard deviation of the sample. Determine the likelihood of finding a sample mean this large or larger from the population.

45. Refer to the CIA data, which reports demographic and economic information on 46 countries. Select a random sample of 10 countries. For this sample calculate the mean GDP/capita. Repeat this sampling and calculation process five more times. Then find the mean and standard deviation of your six sample means.

a. How do this mean and standard deviation compare with the mean and standard deviation of the original "population" of 46 countries?

b. Make a histogram of the six means and discuss whether the distribution is normal.

c. Suppose the population distribution is normal. For the first sample mean you computed, determine the likelihood of finding a sample mean this large or larger from the population.

Software Commands

The Excel commands to select a simple random sample on page 215 are:

1. Select **Tools**, **Data Analysis**, and then **Sampling**.
2. For the **Input Range** insert *B1:B31*. Since the column is named. Click the **Labels** box, select **Random,** and enter the sample size for the **Number of Samples**. In this case the sample size is 5, so select 5. Click on the **Output Range** and indicate the place in the spreadsheet you want the sample information. Note that your sample results will differ from those in the text. Also recall that Excel samples with replacement, so it is possible for a population value to appear more than once in the sample.

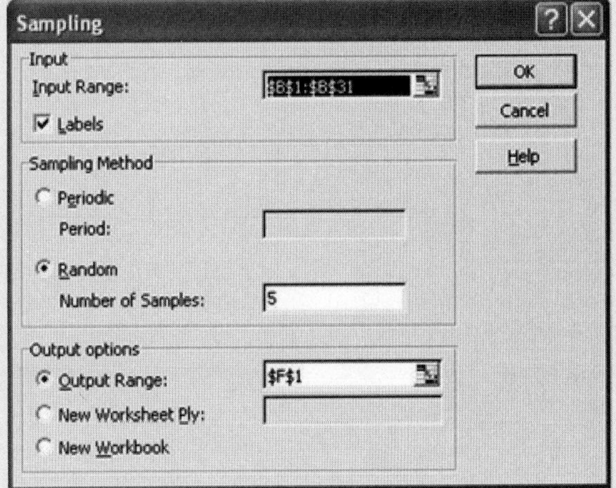

Chapter 8 Answers to Self-Review

8–1 **a.** Students selected are Price, Detley, and Molter.
b. Answers will vary.
c. Skip it and move to the next random number.

8–2 The students selected are Berry, Francis, Kopp, Poteau, and Swetye.

8–3 **a.** 10, found by:

$${}_5C_2 = \frac{5!}{2!(5-2)!}$$

b.

	Service	Sample Mean
Snow, Tolson	20, 22	21
Snow, Kraft	20, 26	23
Snow, Irwin	20, 24	22
Snow, Jones	20, 28	24
Tolson, Kraft	22, 26	24
Tolson, Irwin	22, 24	23
Tolson, Jones	22, 28	25
Kraft, Irwin	26, 24	25
Kraft, Jones	26, 28	27
Irwin, Jones	24, 28	26

c.

Mean	Number	Probability
21	1	.10
22	1	.10
23	2	.20
24	2	.20
25	2	.20
26	1	.10
27	1	.10
	10	1.00

d. Identical: population mean, μ, is 24, and mean of sample means, $\mu_{\bar{X}}$, is also 24.
e. Sample means range from 21 to 27. Population values go from 20 to 28.
f. Nonnormal.
g. Yes.

8–4 The answers will vary. Here is one solution.

	Sample Number									
	1	2	3	4	5	6	7	8	9	10
	8	2	2	19	3	4	0	4	1	2
	19	1	14	9	2	5	8	2	14	4
	8	3	4	2	4	4	1	14	4	1
	0	3	2	3	1	2	16	1	2	3
	2	1	7	2	19	18	18	16	3	7
Total	37	10	29	35	29	33	43	37	24	17
$\bar{X}$	7.4	2	5.8	7.0	5.8	6.6	8.6	7.4	4.8	3.4

Mean of the 10 sample means is 5.88.

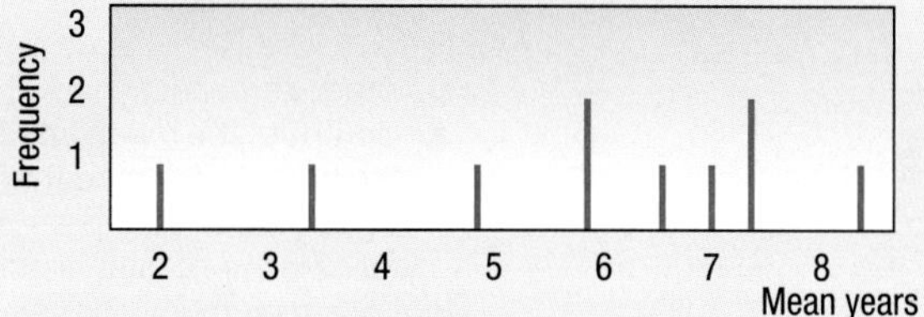

8–5 $z = \dfrac{31.08 - 31.20}{0.4/\sqrt{16}} = -1.20$

The probability that z is greater than -1.20 is $.5000 + .3849 = .8849$. There is less than a 12 percent chance of this event happening.

8–6 $z = \dfrac{\$28.50 - \$28.00}{\$2.00/\sqrt{50}} = 1.77$

The probability that z is greater than 1.77 is $.5000 - .4616 = .0384$.

9

Estimation and Confidence Intervals

The American Restaurant Association collected information on the number of meals eaten outside the home per week by young married couples. A survey of 60 couples showed the sample mean number of meals eaten outside the home was 2.76 meals per week. Construct a 97 percent confidence interval for the population mean. (See Goal 4 and Exercise 36.)

GOALS

When you have completed this chapter you will be able to:

1 **Define a *point estimate.***

2 **Define *level of confidence.***

3 **Construct a confidence interval for the population mean when the population standard deviation is known.**

4 **Construct a confidence interval for a population mean when the population standard deviation is unknown.**

5 **Construct a confidence interval for a population proportion.**

6 **Determine the sample size for attribute and variable sampling.**

Statistics in Action

On all new cars, a fuel economy estimate is prominently displayed on the window sticker as required by the Environmental Protection Agency (EPA). Often, fuel economy is a factor in a consumer's choice of a new car because of fuel costs or environmental concerns. For example, a 2004 Toyota Celica's (4 cylinder) fuel estimates are 36 miles per gallon on the highway and 29 mpg in the city. The EPA recognizes that actual fuel economy may differ from the estimates by noting, "No test can simulate all possible combinations of conditions and climate, driver behavior, and car care habits. Actual mileage depends on how, when, and where the vehicle is driven. EPA has found that the mpg obtained by most drivers will be within a few mpg of the estimates . . ." In fact, the window sticker also includes an interval estimate for fuel economy: 21 to 33 mpg in the city and 31 to 41 mpg on the highway. http://www.fueleconomy.gov/

Introduction

The previous chapter began our discussion of statistical inference. It introduced the reasons and methods of sampling. The reasons for sampling were:

- Contacting the entire population is too time consuming
- The cost of studying all the items in the population is often too expensive
- The sample results are usually adequate
- The destructive nature of certain tests
- The physical impossibility of checking all the items

There are several methods of sampling. Simple random sampling is the most widely used method. With this type of sampling, each member of the population has the same chance of being selected to be a part of the sample. Other methods of sampling include systematic sampling, stratified sampling, and cluster sampling.

Chapter 8 assumes information about the population, such as the mean, the standard deviation, or the shape of the population. In most business situations, such information is not available. In fact, the purpose of sampling may be to estimate some of these values. For example, you select a sample from a population and use the mean of the sample to estimate the mean of the population.

This chapter considers several important aspects of sampling. We begin by studying point estimates. A point estimate is a particular value used to estimate a population value. For example, suppose we select a sample of 50 junior executives and ask each the number of hours they worked last week. Compute the mean of this sample of 50 and use the value of the sample mean as a point estimate of the unknown population mean. However, a point estimate is a single value. A more informative approach is to present a range of values in which we expect the population parameter to occur. Such a range of values is called a confidence interval.

Frequently in business we need to determine the size of a sample. How many voters should a polling organization contact to forecast the election outcome? How many products do we need to examine to ensure our quality level? This chapter also develops a strategy for determining the appropriate size of the sample.

Point Estimates and Confidence Intervals

Known σ or a Large Sample

In the previous chapter, the data on the length of service of Spence Sprockets employees, presented in the example on page 229, is a population because we present the length of service for all 40 employees. In that case we can easily compute the population mean. We have all the data and the population is not too large. In most situations, however, the population is large or it is difficult to identify all members of the population, so we need to rely on sample information. In other words, we do not know the population parameter and we therefore want to estimate the value from a sample statistic. Consider the following business situations.

1. Tourism is a major source of income for many Caribbean countries, such as Barbados. Suppose the Bureau of Tourism for Barbados wants an estimate of the mean amount spent by tourists visiting the country. It would not be feasible to contact each tourist. Therefore, 500 tourists are randomly selected as they depart the country and asked in detail about their spending while visiting the island. The mean amount spent by the sample of 500 tourists is an estimate of the unknown population parameter. That is, we let $\bar{X}$, the sample mean, serve as an estimate of μ, the population mean.
2. Centex Home Builders, Inc., builds quality homes in the southeastern region of the United States. One of the major concerns of new buyers is the date on which the home will be completed. In recent times Centex has been telling customers, "Your home will be completed 45 working days from the date we begin installing

drywall." The customer relations department at Centex wishes to compare this pledge with recent experience. A sample of 50 homes completed this year revealed the mean number of working days from the start of drywall to the completion of the home was 46.7 days. Is it reasonable to conclude that the population mean is still 45 days and that the difference between the sample mean (46.7 days) and the proposed population mean is sampling error?

3. Recent medical studies indicate that exercise is an important part of a person's overall health. The director of human resources at OCF, a large glass manufacturer, wants an estimate of the number of hours per week employees spend exercising. A sample of 70 employees reveals the mean number of hours of exercise last week is 3.3. The sample mean of 3.3 hours estimates the unknown population mean, the mean hours of exercise for all employees.

A point estimate is a single statistic used to estimate a population parameter. Suppose Best Buy, Inc. wants to estimate the mean age of buyers of high-definition televisions. They select a random sample of 50 recent purchasers, determine the age of each purchaser, and compute the mean age of the buyers in the sample. The mean of this sample is a point estimate of the mean of the population.

POINT ESTIMATE The statistic, computed from sample information, which is used to estimate the population parameter.

The sample mean, $\bar{X}$, is a point estimate of the population mean, μ; *p,* a sample proportion, is a point estimate of π, the population proportion; and *s,* the sample standard deviation, is a point estimate of σ, the population standard deviation.

A point estimate, however, tells only part of the story. While we expect the point estimate to be close to the population parameter, we would like to measure how close it really is. A confidence interval serves this purpose.

CONFIDENCE INTERVAL A range of values constructed from sample data so that the population parameter is likely to occur within that range at a specified probability. The specified probability is called the *level of confidence.*

For example, we estimate the mean yearly income for construction workers in the New York–New Jersey area is \$65,000. The range of this estimate might be from \$61,000 to \$69,000. We can describe how confident we are that the population parameter is in the interval by making a probability statement. We might say, for instance, that we are 90 percent sure that the mean yearly income of construction workers in the New York–New Jersey area is between \$61,000 and \$69,000.

The information developed about the shape of a sampling distribution of the sample mean, that is, the sampling distribution of $\bar{X}$, allows us to locate an interval that has a specified probability of containing the population mean, μ. For reasonably large samples, the results of the central limit theorem allow us to state the following:

1. Ninety-five percent of the sample means selected from a population will be within 1.96 standard deviations of the population mean μ.
2. Ninety-nine percent of the sample means will lie within 2.58 standard deviations of the population mean.

The standard deviation discussed here is the standard deviation of the sampling distribution of the sample mean. It is usually called the "standard error." Intervals computed in this fashion are called the **95 percent confidence interval** and the **99 percent confidence interval.** How are the values of 1.96 and 2.58 obtained? The

95 percent and *99 percent* refer to the percent of similarly constructed intervals that would include the parameter being estimated. The *95 percent,* for example, refers to the middle 95 percent of the observations. Therefore, the remaining 5 percent are equally divided between the two tails.

See the following diagram.

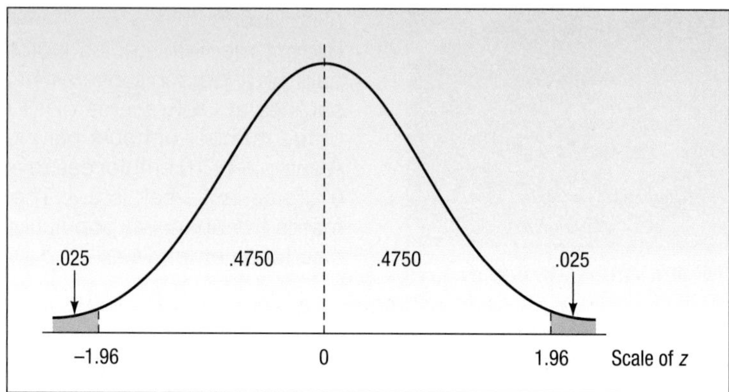

The central limit theorem, discussed in the previous chapter, states that the sampling distribution of the sample means is approximately normal when the sample contains at least 30 observations. Therefore, we can use Appendix D to find the appropriate z values. Locate .4750 in the body of the table. Read the corresponding row and column values. The value is 1.96. Thus, the probability of finding a z value between 0 and 1.96 is .4750. Likewise, the probability of being in the interval between −1.96 and 0 is also .4750. When we combine these two, the probability of being in the interval −1.96 to 1.96 is .9500. On the next page is a portion of Appendix D. The z value for the 90 percent level of confidence is determined in a similar manner. It is 1.65. For a 99 percent level of confidence the z value is 2.58.

How do you compute a 95 percent confidence interval? Assume your research involves the annual starting salary of accounting majors with a Bachelor's degree. You compute the sample mean to be $39,000 and the standard deviation (that is, the "standard error") of the sample mean to be $200. Assume your sample contains at least 30 observations. The 95 percent confidence interval is between $38,608 and $39,392, found by $39,000 ± 1.96($200). If 300 samples of the same size were selected from the population of interest and the corresponding 300 confidence intervals determined, you expect to find the population mean in about 285 of the 300 confidence intervals.

In the above example, the standard error of the sampling distribution of the sample mean was $200. This is, of course, the standard error of the sample means, discussed in the previous chapter. See formula (8–1) for the case when the population standard deviation is available. In most applied situations, the population standard deviation is not available, so we estimate it as follows:

$$s_{\bar{X}} = \frac{s}{\sqrt{n}}$$

The size of the standard error is affected by two values. The first is the standard deviation. If the standard deviation is large, then the standard error will also be large. However, the standard error is also affected by the sample size. As the sample size is increased, the standard error decreases, indicating that there is less variability in the sampling distribution of the sample mean. This conclusion is logical, because an estimate made with a large sample should be more precise than one made from a small sample.

z	0.00	0.01	0.02	0.03	0.04	0.05	0.06	0.07	0.08	0.09
.	.	.	.	.	.	.	.	.	.	.
.	.	.	.	.	.	.	.	.	.	.
.	.	.	.	.	.	.	.	.	.	.
1.5	0.4332	0.4345	0.4357	0.4370	0.4382	0.4394	0.4406	0.4418	0.4429	0.4441
1.6	0.4452	0.4463	0.4474	0.4484	0.4495	0.4505	0.4515	0.4525	0.4535	0.4545
1.7	0.4554	0.4564	0.4573	0.4582	0.4591	0.4599	0.4608	0.4616	0.4625	0.4633
1.8	0.4641	0.4649	0.4656	0.4664	0.4671	0.4678	0.4686	0.4693	0.4699	0.4706
1.9	0.4713	0.4719	0.4726	0.4732	0.4738	0.4744	0.4750	0.4756	0.4761	0.4767
2.0	0.4772	0.4778	0.4783	0.4788	0.4793	0.4798	0.4803	0.4808	0.4812	0.4817
2.1	0.4821	0.4826	0.4830	0.4834	0.4838	0.4842	0.4846	0.4850	0.4854	0.4857
2.2	0.4861	0.4864	0.4868	0.4871	0.4875	0.4878	0.4881	0.4884	0.4887	0.4890
2.3	0.4893	0.4896	0.4898	0.4901	0.4904	0.4906	0.4909	0.4911	0.4913	0.4916
2.4	0.4918	0.4920	0.4922	0.4925	0.4927	0.4929	0.4931	0.4932	0.4934	0.4936

As we state in Chapter 8, when the sample size, n, is at least 30, it is generally agreed that the central limit theorem will ensure that the sample mean follows the normal distribution. This is an important consideration. If the sample mean is normally distributed, we can use the standard normal distribution, that is, z, in our calculations.

The 95 percent confidence interval is computed as follows, when the number of observations in the sample is at least 30.

$$\bar{X} \pm 1.96 \frac{s}{\sqrt{n}}$$

Similarly, the 99 percent confidence interval is computed as follows. Again we assume that the sample size is at least 30.

$$\bar{X} \pm 2.58 \frac{s}{\sqrt{n}}$$

As we discussed earlier, the values 1.96 and 2.58 are the z values corresponding to the middle 95 percent and the middle 99 percent of the observations, respectively.

We can use other levels of confidence. For those cases the value of z changes accordingly. In general, a confidence interval for the population mean is computed by:

CONFIDENCE INTERVAL FOR THE POPULATION MEAN ($n \geq 30$) $$\bar{X} \pm z \frac{s}{\sqrt{n}} \quad \textbf{[9–1]}$$

where z depends on the level of confidence. Thus, for a 92 percent level of confidence, the value of z in formula (9–1) is 1.75. The value of z is from Appendix D. This table is based on half the normal distribution, so .9200/2 = .4600. The closest value in the body of the table is .4599 and the corresponding z value is 1.75.

Frequently, we also use the 90 percent level of confidence. In this case, we want the area between 0 and z to be .4500, found by .9000/2. To find the z value for this level of confidence, search the body of the table for an area close to .4500. The closest values in the table are .4495 and .4505. To be conservative we will use .4505. To find the corresponding z value, in the same row, refer to the left column and read 1.6. Then for the same column, refer to the top margin and find .05. Adding 1.6 and 0.05 the z value is 1.65. Try looking up the following levels of confidence and check your answers with the corresponding z values given on the right.

Confidence Level	Nearest Probability	*z* Value
80 percent	.3997	1.28
94 percent	.4699	1.88
96 percent	.4798	2.05

The following example shows the details for calculating a confidence interval and interpreting the result.

EXAMPLE

The American Management Association wishes to have information on the mean income of middle managers in the retail industry. A random sample of 256 managers reveals a sample mean of $45,420. The standard deviation of this sample is $2,050. The association would like answers to the following questions:

1. What is the population mean?
2. What is a reasonable range of values for the population mean?
3. What do these results mean?

SOLUTION

Generally, distributions of salary and income are positively skewed, because a few individuals earn considerably more than others, thus skewing the distribution in the positive direction. Fortunately, the central limit theorem stipulates that if we select a large sample, the distribution of the sample means will follow the normal distribution. In this instance, with a sample of 256 middle managers (remember, at least 30 is usually large enough), we can be assured that the sampling distribution will follow the normal distribution.

Another issue is that the population standard deviation is not known. Again, it is sound practice to use the sample standard deviation when we have a large sample. Now to answer the questions posed in the problem.

1. **What is the population mean?** In this case, we do not know. We do know the sample mean is $45,420. Hence, our best estimate of the unknown population value is the corresponding sample statistic. Thus the sample mean of $45,420 is a *point estimate* of the unknown population mean.
2. **What is a reasonable range of values for the population mean?** The Association decides to use the 95 percent level of confidence. To determine the corresponding confidence interval we use formula (9–1).

$$\bar{X} \pm z\frac{s}{\sqrt{n}} = \$45{,}420 \pm 1.96\frac{\$2{,}050}{\sqrt{256}} = \$45{,}420 \pm \$251$$

   These endpoints are $45,169 and $45,671. These endpoints are called the *confidence limits.* The degree of confidence or the *level of confidence* is 95 percent and the confidence interval is from $45,169 to $45,671.
3. **What do these results mean?** Suppose we select many samples of 256 managers, perhaps several hundred. For each sample, we compute the mean and the standard deviation and then construct a 95 percent confidence interval, such as we did in the previous section. We could expect about 95 percent of these confidence intervals to contain the *population* mean. About 5 percent of the intervals would not contain the population mean annual income, which is μ. However, a particular confidence interval either contains the population parameter or it does not. The following diagram shows the results of selecting samples from the population of middle managers in the retail industry, computing the mean and standard deviation of each, and then, using formula (9–1), determining a 95 percent confidence interval for the population mean. Note that not all intervals include the population mean. Both the endpoints of the fifth sample are less than the population mean. We attribute this to sampling error, and it is the risk we assume when we select the level of confidence.

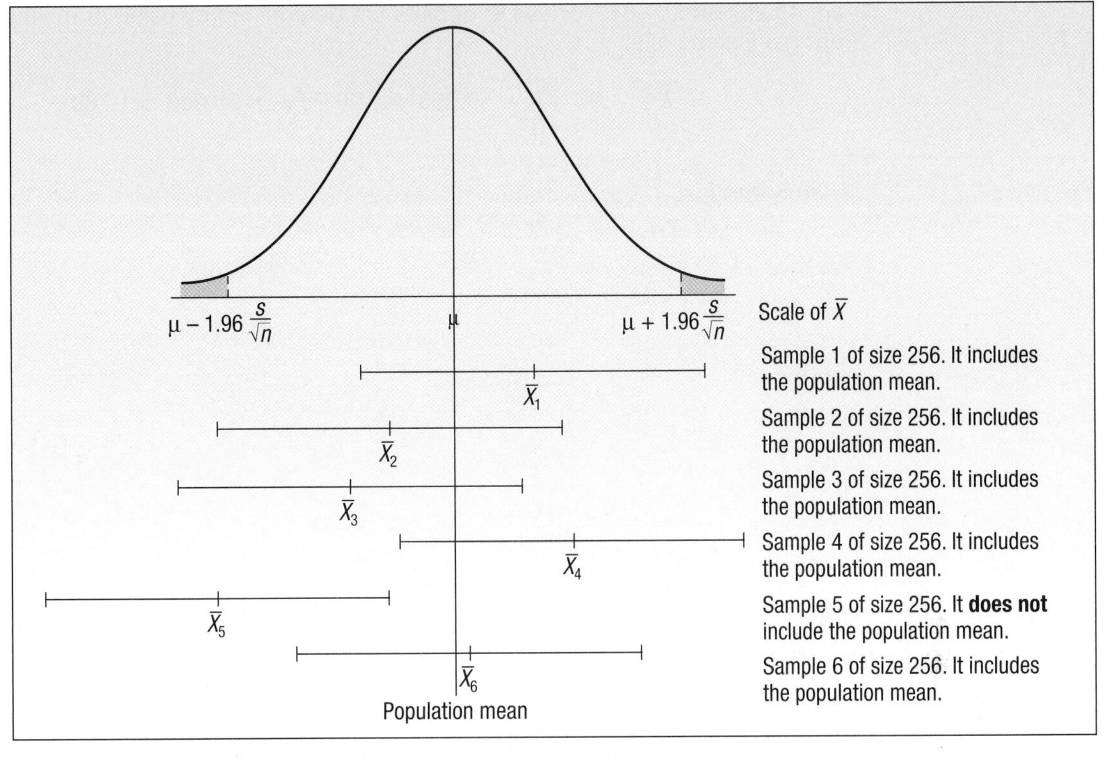

A Computer Simulation

With the aid of a computer, we can randomly select samples from a population, quickly compute the confidence interval, and show how confidence intervals usually, but not always, include the population parameter. The following example will help to explain.

EXAMPLE

From many years in the automobile leasing business, Town Bank knows the mean distance driven on a four-year lease is 50,000 miles and the standard deviation is 5,000. Suppose, using the MINITAB statistical software system, we want to find what proportion of the 95 percent confidence intervals will include the population mean of 50. To make the calculations easier to understand, we'll conduct the study in thousands of miles, instead of miles. We select 60 random samples of size 30 from a population with a mean of 50 and a standard deviation of 5.

SOLUTION

The results of 60 random samples of 30 automobiles each are summarized in the table on the next page. Of the 60 confidence intervals with a 95 percent confidence level, 2, or 3.33 percent, did not include the population mean of 50. The intervals (C3 and C59) that do *not* include the population mean are highlighted. A total of 3.33 percent is close to the estimate that 5 percent of the intervals will not include the population mean, and the 58 of 60, or 96.67 percent, is close to 95 percent.

To explain the first calculation in more detail: MINITAB began by selecting a random sample of 30 observations from a population with a mean of 50 and a standard deviation of 5. The mean of these 30 observations is 50.053. The sampling error is 0.053, found by $\bar{X} - \mu = 50.053 - 50.000$. The endpoints of the confidence interval are 48.264 and 51.842. These endpoints are determined by using formula (9–1), but using σ instead of s.

$$\bar{X} \pm 1.96\frac{\sigma}{\sqrt{n}} = 50.053 \pm 1.96\frac{5}{\sqrt{30}} = 50.053 \pm 1.789$$

One-Sample Z:

The assumed sigma = 5

Variable	N	Mean	StDev	SE Mean	95.0% CI
C1	30	50.053	5.002	0.913	(48.264, 51.842)
C2	30	49.025	4.450	0.913	(47.236, 50.815)
C3	30	52.023	5.918	0.913	(50.234, 53.812)
C4	30	50.056	3.364	0.913	(48.267, 51.845)
C5	30	49.737	4.784	0.913	(47.948, 51.526)
C6	30	51.074	5.495	0.913	(49.285, 52.863)
C7	30	50.040	5.930	0.913	(48.251, 51.829)
C8	30	48.910	3.645	0.913	(47.121, 50.699)
C9	30	51.033	4.918	0.913	(49.244, 52.822)
C10	30	50.692	4.571	0.913	(48.903, 52.482)
C11	30	49.853	4.525	0.913	(48.064, 51.642)
C12	30	50.286	3.422	0.913	(48.497, 52.076)
C13	30	50.257	4.317	0.913	(48.468, 52.046)
C14	30	49.605	4.994	0.913	(47.816, 51.394)
C15	30	51.474	5.497	0.913	(49.685, 53.264)
C16	30	48.930	5.317	0.913	(47.141, 50.719)
C17	30	49.870	4.847	0.913	(48.081, 51.659)
C18	30	50.739	6.224	0.913	(48.950, 52.528)
C19	30	50.979	5.520	0.913	(49.190, 52.768)
C20	30	48.848	4.130	0.913	(47.059, 50.638)
C21	30	49.481	4.056	0.913	(47.692, 51.270)
C22	30	49.183	5.409	0.913	(47.394, 50.973)
C23	30	50.084	4.522	0.913	(48.294, 51.873)
C24	30	50.866	5.142	0.913	(49.077, 52.655)
C25	30	48.768	5.582	0.913	(46.979, 50.557)
C26	30	50.904	6.052	0.913	(49.115, 52.694)
C27	30	49.481	5.535	0.913	(47.691, 51.270)
C28	30	50.949	5.916	0.913	(49.160, 52.739)
C29	30	49.106	4.641	0.913	(47.317, 50.895)
C30	30	49.994	5.853	0.913	(48.205, 51.784)
C31	30	49.601	5.064	0.913	(47.811, 51.390)
C32	30	51.494	5.597	0.913	(49.705, 53.284)
C33	30	50.460	4.393	0.913	(48.671, 52.249)
C34	30	50.378	4.075	0.913	(48.589, 52.167)
C35	30	49.808	4.155	0.913	(48.019, 51.597)
C36	30	49.934	5.012	0.913	(48.145, 51.723)
C37	30	50.017	4.082	0.913	(48.228, 51.806)
C38	30	50.074	3.631	0.913	(48.285, 51.863)
C39	30	48.656	4.833	0.913	(46.867, 50.445)
C40	30	50.568	3.855	0.913	(48.779, 52.357)
C41	30	50.916	3.775	0.913	(49.127, 52.705)
C42	30	49.104	4.321	0.913	(47.315, 50.893)
C43	30	50.308	5.467	0.913	(48.519, 52.097)
C44	30	49.034	4.405	0.913	(47.245, 50.823)
C45	30	50.399	4.729	0.913	(48.610, 52.188)
C46	30	49.634	3.996	0.913	(47.845, 51.424)
C47	30	50.479	4.881	0.913	(48.689, 52.268)
C48	30	50.529	5.173	0.913	(48.740, 52.318)
C49	30	51.577	5.822	0.913	(49.787, 53.366)
C50	30	50.403	4.893	0.913	(48.614, 52.192)
C51	30	49.717	5.218	0.913	(47.927, 51.506)
C52	30	49.796	5.327	0.913	(48.007, 51.585)
C53	30	50.549	4.680	0.913	(48.760, 52.338)
C54	30	50.200	5.840	0.913	(48.410, 51.989)
C55	30	49.138	5.074	0.913	(47.349, 50.928)

Variable	N	Mean	StDev	SE Mean	95.0% CI
C56	30	49.667	3.843	0.913	(47.878, 51.456)
C57	30	49.603	5.614	0.913	(47.814, 51.392)
C58	30	49.441	5.702	0.913	(47.652, 51.230)
C59	30	47.873	4.685	0.913	(46.084, 49.662)
C60	30	51.087	5.162	0.913	(49.297, 52.876)

Self-Review 9–1

The mean daily sales at the Bun-and-Run, a fast food outlet, is \$20,000 for a sample of 40 days. The standard deviation of the sample is \$3,000.

(a) What is the estimated mean daily sales of the population? What is this estimate called?
(b) What is the 99 percent confidence interval?
(c) Interpret your findings.

Exercises

1. A sample of 49 observations is taken from a normal population. The sample mean is 55, and the sample standard deviation is 10. Determine the 99 percent confidence interval for the population mean.
2. A sample of 81 observations is taken from a normal population. The sample mean is 40, and the sample standard deviation is 5. Determine the 95 percent confidence interval for the population mean.
3. A sample of 10 observations is selected from a normal population for which the population standard deviation is known to be 5. The sample mean is 20.
   a. Determine the standard error of the mean.
   b. Explain why we can use formula (9–1) to determine the 95 percent confidence interval even though the sample is less than 30.
   c. Determine the 95 percent confidence interval for the population mean.
4. Suppose you want an 85 percent confidence level. What value would you use to multiply the standard error of the mean?
5. A research firm conducted a survey to determine the mean amount steady smokers spend on cigarettes during a week. A sample of 49 steady smokers revealed that $\bar{X}$ = \$20 and s = \$5.
   a. What is the point estimate of the population mean? Explain what it indicates.
   b. Using the 95 percent level of confidence, determine the confidence interval for μ. Explain what it indicates.
6. Refer to the previous exercise. Suppose that 64 smokers (instead of 49) were sampled. Assume the sample mean and the sample standard deviation remained the same (\$20 and \$5, respectively).
   a. What is the 95 percent confidence interval estimate of μ?
   b. Explain why this confidence interval is narrower than the one determined in the previous exercise.
7. Bob Nale is the owner of Nale's Texaco GasTown. Bob would like to estimate the mean number of gallons of gasoline sold to his customers. From his records, he selects a random sample of 60 sales and finds the mean number of gallons sold is 8.60 and the standard deviation is 2.30 gallons.
   a. What is the point estimate of the population mean?
   b. Develop a 99 percent confidence interval for the population mean.
   c. Interpret the meaning of part b.
8. Dr. Patton is a Professor of English. Recently he counted the number of misspelled words in a group of student essays. For his class of 40 students, the mean number of misspelled words was 6.05 and the standard deviation 2.44 per essay. Construct a 95 percent confidence interval for the mean number of misspelled words in the population of student essays.

Unknown Population Standard Deviation and a Small Sample

In the previous section we used the standard normal distribution to express the level of confidence. We assumed either:

1. The population followed the normal distribution and the population standard deviation was known, or
2. The shape of the population was not known, but the number of observations in the sample was at least 30.

Statistics in Action

William Gosset was born in England in 1876 and died there in 1937. He worked for many years at Arthur Guinness & Sons Brewery. In fact, in his later years he was in charge of the Guinness Brewery in London. Guinness preferred their employees to use pen names when publishing papers, so in 1908, when Gosset wrote "The Probable Error of a Mean," he used the name "Student." In this paper he first described the properties of the t distribution.

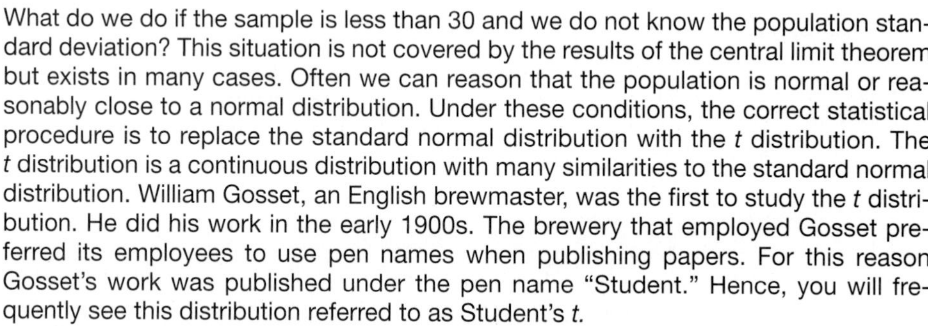

What do we do if the sample is less than 30 and we do not know the population standard deviation? This situation is not covered by the results of the central limit theorem but exists in many cases. Often we can reason that the population is normal or reasonably close to a normal distribution. Under these conditions, the correct statistical procedure is to replace the standard normal distribution with the t distribution. The t distribution is a continuous distribution with many similarities to the standard normal distribution. William Gosset, an English brewmaster, was the first to study the t distribution. He did his work in the early 1900s. The brewery that employed Gosset preferred its employees to use pen names when publishing papers. For this reason Gosset's work was published under the pen name "Student." Hence, you will frequently see this distribution referred to as Student's t.

Gosset was concerned with the behavior of the following term:

$$t = \frac{\bar{X} - \mu}{s/\sqrt{n}}$$

s is an estimate of σ. He was especially worried about the discrepancy between s and σ when s was calculated from a very small sample. The t distribution and the standard normal distribution are shown graphically in Chart 9–1. Note particularly that the t distribution is flatter, more spread out, than the standard normal distribution. This is because the standard deviation of the t distribution is larger than the standard normal distribution.

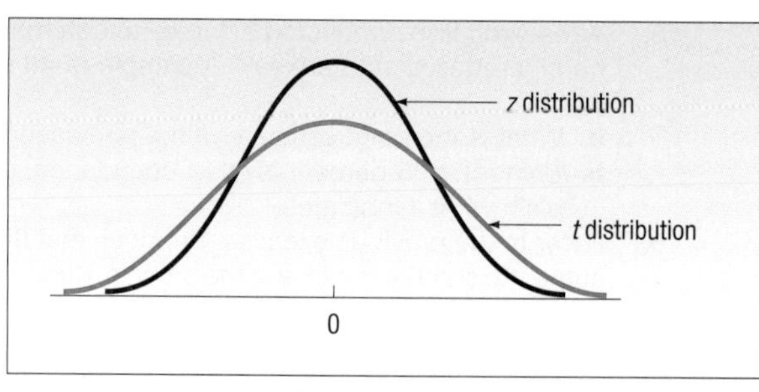

CHART 9–1 The Standard Normal Distribution and Student's t Distribution

The following characteristics of the t distribution are based on the assumption that the population of interest is normal, or nearly normal.

1. It is, like the z distribution, a continuous distribution.
2. It is, like the z distribution, bell-shaped and symmetrical.
3. There is not one t distribution, but rather a "family" of t distributions. All t distributions have a mean of 0, but their standard deviations differ according to the sample size, n. There is a t distribution for a sample size of 20, another for a sample size of 22, and so on. The standard deviation for a t distribution with 5 observations is larger than for a t distribution with 20 observations.

4. The t distribution is more spread out and flatter at the center than the standard normal distribution (see Chart 9–1). As the sample size increases, however, the t distribution approaches the standard normal distribution, because the errors in using s to estimate σ decrease with larger samples.

Because Student's t distribution has a greater spread than the z distribution, the value of t for a given level of confidence is larger in magnitude than the corresponding z values. Chart 9–2 shows the values of z for a 95 percent level of confidence and of t for the same level of confidence when the sample size is $n = 5$. How we obtained the actual value of t will be explained shortly. For now, observe that for the same level of confidence the t distribution is flatter and more spread out than the standard normal distribution.

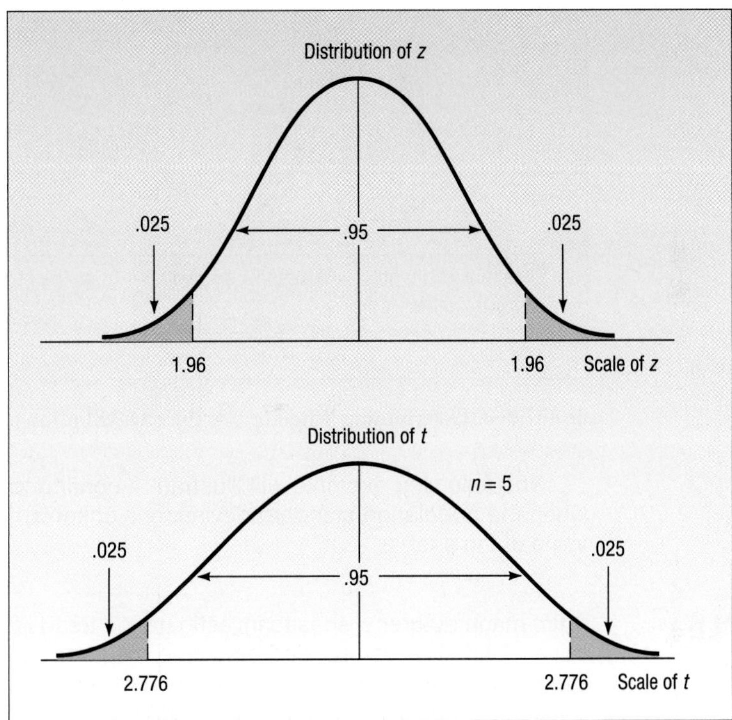

CHART 9–2 Values of z and t for the 95 Percent Level of Confidence

To develop a confidence interval for the population mean using the t distribution, we adjust formula (9–1) as follows.

CONFIDENCE INTERVAL FOR THE POPULATION MEAN, σ UNKNOWN $$\bar{X} \pm t\frac{s}{\sqrt{n}}$$ **[9–2]**

To put it another way, to develop a confidence interval for the population mean with an unknown population standard deviation we:

1. Assume the sample is from a normal population.
2. Estimate the population standard deviation (σ) with the sample standard deviation (s).
3. Use the t distribution rather than the z distribution.

We should be clear at this point. We usually employ the standard normal distribution when the sample size is at least 30. We should, strictly speaking, base the decision whether to use z or t on whether σ is known or not. When σ is known, we use z; when it is not, we use t. The rule of using z when the sample is 30 or more is based on the fact that the t distribution approaches the normal distribution as the sample size increases. When the sample reaches 30, there is little difference between the z and t values, so we may ignore the difference and use z. We will show this when we discuss the details of the t distribution and how to find values in a t distribution. Chart 9–3 summarizes the decision-making process.

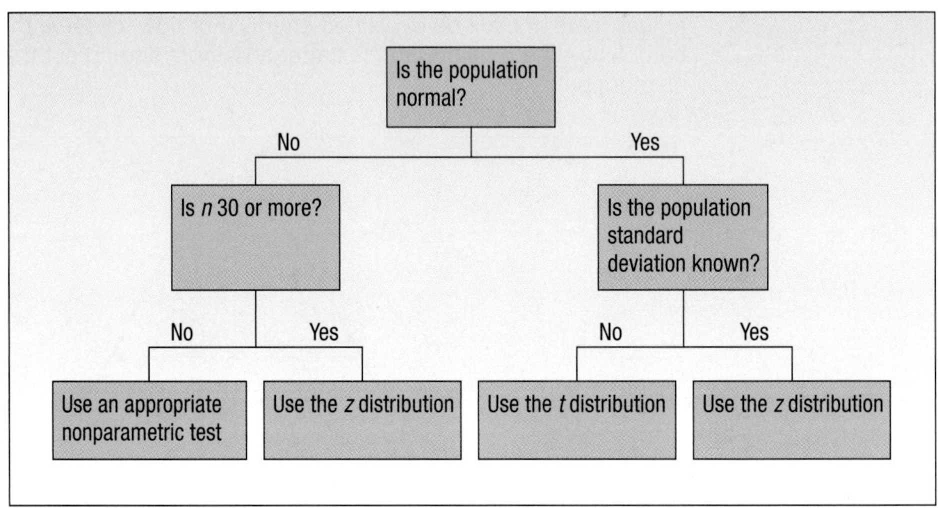

CHART 9–3 Determining When to Use the z Distribution or the t Distribution

The following example will illustrate a confidence interval for a population mean when the population standard deviation is unknown and how to find the appropriate value of t in a table.

EXAMPLE

A tire manufacturer wishes to investigate the tread life of its tires. A sample of 10 tires driven 50,000 miles revealed a sample mean of 0.32 inch of tread remaining with a standard deviation of 0.09 inch. Construct a 95 percent confidence interval for the population mean. Would it be reasonable for the manufacturer to conclude that after 50,000 miles the population mean amount of tread remaining is 0.30 inches?

SOLUTION

To begin, we assume the population distribution is normal. In this case, we don't have a lot of evidence, but the assumption is probably reasonable. We do not know the population standard deviation, but we know the sample standard deviation, which is .09 inches. To use the central limit theorem, we need a large sample, that is, a sample of 30 or more. In this instance there are only 10 observations in the sample. Hence, we cannot use the central limit theorem. That is, formula (9–1) is not applicable. We use formula (9–2):

$$\bar{X} \pm t\frac{s}{\sqrt{n}}$$

From the information given, $\bar{X} = 0.32$, $s = 0.09$, and $n = 10$. To find the value of t we use Appendix F, a portion of which is reproduced here as Chart 9–4. Appendix F is also reproduced on the back inside cover of the text. The first step for locating t is to move across the row identified for "Confidence Intervals" to the level of confidence requested. In this case we want the 95 percent level of confidence, so we move to the column headed "95%." The column on the left margin is identified as "*df.*" This refers to the number of degrees of freedom. The number of degrees of freedom is the number of observations in the sample minus the number of samples, written $n - 1$.[1] In this case it is $10 - 1 = 9$. For a 95 percent level of confidence and 9 degrees of freedom, we select the row with 9 degrees of freedom. The value of t is 2.262.

	Confidence Intervals				
	80%	90%	95%	98%	99%
	Level of Significance for One-Tailed Test, α				
df	0.100	0.050	0.025	0.010	0.005
	Level of Significance for Two-Tailed Test, α				
	0.20	0.10	0.05	0.02	0.01
1	3.078	6.314	12.706	31.821	63.657
2	1.886	2.920	4.303	6.965	9.925
3	1.638	2.353	3.182	4.541	5.841
4	1.533	2.132	2.776	3.747	4.604
5	1.476	2.015	2.571	3.365	4.032
6	1.440	1.943	2.447	3.143	3.707
7	1.415	1.895	2.365	2.998	3.499
8	1.397	1.860	2.306	2.896	3.355
9	1.383	1.833	2.262	2.821	3.250
10	1.372	1.812	2.228	2.764	3.169

CHART 9–4 A Portion of the t Distribution

To determine the confidence interval we substitute the values in formula (9–2).

$$\bar{X} \pm t\frac{s}{\sqrt{n}} = 0.32 \pm 2.262\frac{0.09}{\sqrt{10}} = 0.32 \pm .064$$

The endpoints of the confidence interval are 0.256 and 0.384. How do we interpret this result? It is reasonable to conclude that the population mean is in this interval. The manufacturer can be reasonably sure (95 percent confident) that the mean remaining tread depth is between 0.256 and 0.384 inches. Because the value of 0.30 is in this interval, it is possible that the mean of the population is 0.30.

[1]In brief summary, because sample statistics are being used, it is necessary to determine the number of values that are *free to vary.* To illustrate: assume that the mean of four numbers is known to be 5. The four numbers are 7, 4, 1, and 8. The deviations of these numbers from the mean must total 0. The deviations of +2, −1, −4, and +3 do total 0. If the deviations of +2, −1, and −4 are known, then the value of +3 is fixed (restricted) in order to satisfy the condition that the sum of the deviations must equal 0. Thus, 1 degree of freedom is lost in a sampling problem involving the standard deviation of the sample because one number (the arithmetic mean) is known.

Here is another example to clarify the use of confidence intervals. Suppose an article in your local newspaper reported that the mean time to sell a residential property in the area is 60 days. You select a random sample of 20 homes sold in the last year and find the mean selling time is 65 days. Based on the sample data, you develop a 95 percent confidence interval for the population mean. You find that the endpoints of the confidence interval are 62 days and 68 days. How do you interpret this result? You can be reasonably confident the population mean is within this range. The value proposed for the population mean, that is, 60 days, is not included in the interval. It is not likely that the population mean is 60 days. The evidence indicates the statement by the local newspaper may not be correct. To put it another way, it seems unreasonable to obtain the sample you did from a population that had a mean selling time of 60 days.

The following example will show additional details for determining and interpreting a confidence interval. We used MINITAB to perform the calculations.

EXAMPLE

The manager of the Inlet Square Mall, near Ft. Myers, Florida, wants to estimate the mean amount spent per shopping visit by customers. A sample of 20 customers reveals the following amounts spent.

\$48.16	\$42.22	\$46.82	\$51.45	\$23.78	\$41.86	\$54.86
37.92	52.64	48.59	50.82	46.94	61.83	61.69
49.17	61.46	51.35	52.68	58.84	43.88	

What is the best estimate of the population mean? Determine a 95 percent confidence interval. Interpret the result. Would it be reasonable to conclude that the population mean is \$50? What about \$60?

SOLUTION

The mall manager assumes that the population of the amounts spent follows the normal distribution. This is a reasonable assumption in this case. Additionally, the confidence interval technique is quite powerful and tends to commit any errors on the conservative side if the population is not normal. We should not make the normality assumption when the population is severely skewed or when the distribution has "thick tails." However, in this case, the normality assumption is reasonable.

The population standard deviation is not known and the size of the sample is less than 30. Hence, it is appropriate to use the t distribution and formula (9–2) to find the confidence interval. We use the MINITAB system to find the mean and standard deviation of this sample. The results are shown below.

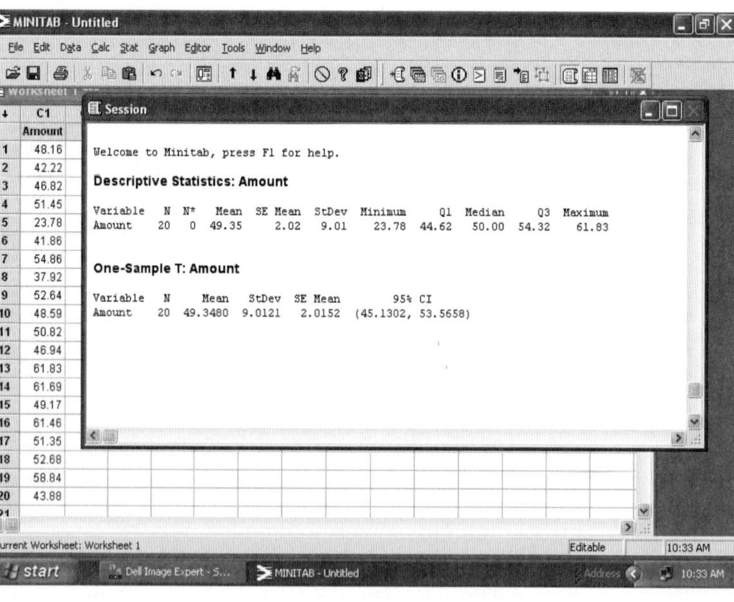

The mall manager does not know the population mean. The sample mean is the best estimate of that value. From the above MINITAB output, the mean is \$49.35, which is the best estimate, the *point estimate,* of the unknown population mean.

We use formula (9–2) to find the confidence interval. The value of t is available from Appendix F. There are $n - 1 = 20 - 1 = 19$ degrees of freedom. We move across the row with 19 degrees of freedom to the column for the 95% confidence level. The value at this intersection is 2.093. We substitute these values into formula (9–2) to find the confidence interval.

$$\bar{X} \pm t\frac{s}{\sqrt{n}} = \$49.35 \pm 2.093\frac{\$9.01}{\sqrt{20}} = \$49.35 \pm \$4.22$$

The endpoints of the confidence interval are \$45.13 and \$53.57. It is reasonable to conclude that the population mean is in that interval.

The manager of Inlet Square wondered whether the population mean could have been \$50 or \$60. The value of \$50 is within the confidence interval. It is reasonable that the population mean could be \$50. The value of \$60 is not in the confidence interval. Hence, we conclude that the population mean is unlikely to be \$60.

The calculations to construct a confidence interval are also available in Excel. The output is below. Note that the sample mean (\$49.35) and the sample standard deviation (\$9.01) are the same as those in the Minitab calculations. In the Excel information the last line of the output also includes the margin of error, which is the amount that is added and subtracted from the sample mean to form the endpoints of the confidence interval. This value is found from

$$t\frac{s}{\sqrt{n}} = 2.093\frac{\$9.01}{\sqrt{20}} = \$4.22.$$

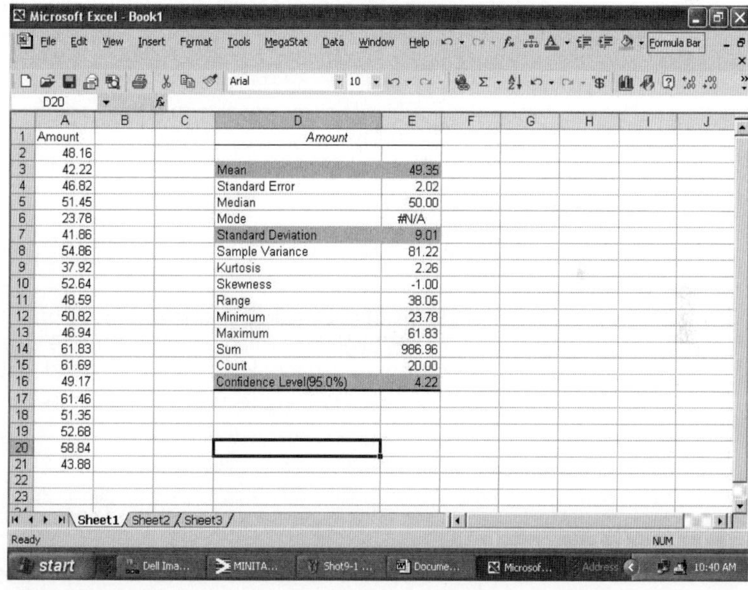

	A	D	E
1	Amount	Amount	
2	48.16		
3	42.22	Mean	49.35
4	46.82	Standard Error	2.02
5	51.45	Median	50.00
6	23.78	Mode	#N/A
7	41.86	Standard Deviation	9.01
8	54.86	Sample Variance	81.22
9	37.92	Kurtosis	2.26
10	52.64	Skewness	-1.00
11	48.59	Range	38.05
12	50.82	Minimum	23.78
13	46.94	Maximum	61.83
14	61.83	Sum	986.96
15	61.69	Count	20.00
16	49.17	Confidence Level(95.0%)	4.22
17	61.46		
18	51.35		
19	52.68		
20	58.84		
21	43.88		

Self-Review 9–2

Dottie Kleman is the "Cookie Lady." She bakes and sells cookies at 50 different locations in the Philadelphia area. Ms. Kleman is concerned about absenteeism among her workers. The information below reports the number of days absent for a sample of 10 workers during the last two-week pay period.

4	1	2	2	1	2	2	1	0	3

(a) Determine the mean and the standard deviation of the sample.
(b) What is the population mean? What is the best estimate of that value?
(c) Develop a 95 percent confidence interval for the population mean.
(d) Explain why the *t* distribution is used as a part of the confidence interval.
(e) Is it reasonable to conclude that the typical worker does not miss any days during a pay period?

Exercises

9. Use Appendix F to locate the value of t under the following conditions.
   a. The sample size is 12 and the level of confidence is 95 percent.
   b. The sample size is 20 and the level of confidence is 90 percent.
   c. The sample size is 8 and the level of confidence is 99 percent.
10. Use Appendix F to locate the value of t under the following conditions.
    a. The sample size is 15 and the level of confidence is 95 percent.
    b. The sample size is 24 and the level of confidence is 98 percent.
    c. The sample size is 12 and the level of confidence is 90 percent.
11. The owner of Britten's Egg Farm wants to estimate the mean number of eggs laid per chicken. A sample of 20 chickens shows they laid an average of 20 eggs per month with a standard deviation of 2 eggs per month.
    a. What is the value of the population mean? What is the best estimate of this value?
    b. Explain why we need to use the t distribution. What assumption do you need to make?
    c. For a 95 percent confidence interval, what is the value of t?
    d. Develop the 95 percent confidence interval for the population mean.
    e. Would it be reasonable to conclude that the population mean is 21 eggs? What about 25 eggs?
12. The American Sugar Producers Association wants to estimate the mean yearly sugar consumption. A sample of 16 people reveals the mean yearly consumption to be 60 pounds with a standard deviation of 20 pounds.
    a. What is the value of the population mean? What is the best estimate of this value?
    b. Explain why we need to use the t distribution. What assumption do you need to make?
    c. For a 90 percent confidence interval, what is the value of t?
    d. Develop the 90 percent confidence interval for the population mean.
    e. Would it be reasonable to conclude that the population mean is 63 pounds?
13. Merrill Lynch Securities and Health Care Retirement, Inc., are two large employers in downtown Toledo, Ohio. They are considering jointly offering child care for their employees. As a part of the feasibility study, they wish to estimate the mean weekly child-care cost of their employees. A sample of 10 employees who use child care reveals the following amounts spent last week.

$107	$92	$97	$95	$105	$101	$91	$99	$95	$104

    Develop a 90 percent confidence interval for the population mean. Interpret the result.
14. The Greater Pittsburgh Area Chamber of Commerce wants to estimate the mean time workers who are employed in the downtown area spend getting to work. A sample of 15 workers reveals the following number of minutes traveled.

29	38	38	33	38	21	45	34
40	37	37	42	30	29	35	

    Develop a 98 percent confidence interval for the population mean. Interpret the result.

A Confidence Interval for a Proportion

The material presented so far in this chapter uses the ratio scale of measurement. That is, we use such variables as incomes, weights, distances, and ages. We now want to consider situations such as the following:

- The career services director at Southern Technical Institute reports that 80 percent of its graduates enter the job market in a position related to their field of study.
- A company representative claims that 45 percent of Burger King sales are made at the drive-through window.

Statistics In Action

Many survey results reported in newspapers, in news magazines, and on TV use confidence intervals. For example, a recent survey of 800 TV viewers in Toledo, Ohio, found 44 percent watched the evening news on the local CBS affiliate. The article went on to indicate the margin of error was 3.4 percent. The margin of error is actually the amount that is added and subtracted from the point estimate to find the endpoints of a confidence interval. From formula (9–6) and the 95 percent level of confidence:

$$z\sqrt{\frac{p(1-p)}{n}}$$

$$= 1.96\sqrt{\frac{.44(1-.44)}{800}}$$

$$= 0.034$$

- A survey of homes in the Chicago area indicated that 85 percent of the new construction had central air conditioning.
- A recent survey of married men between the ages of 35 and 50 found that 63 percent felt that both partners should earn a living.

These examples illustrate the nominal scale of measurement. In the nominal scale an observation is classified into one of two or more mutually exclusive groups. For example, a graduate of Southern Tech either entered the job market in a position related to his or her field of study or not. A particular Burger King customer either made a purchase at the drive-through window or did not make a purchase at the drive-through window. There are only two possibilities, and the outcome must be classified into one of the two groups.

PROPORTION The fraction, ratio, or percent indicating the part of the sample or the population having a particular trait of interest.

As an example of a proportion, a recent survey indicated that 92 out of 100 surveyed favored the continued use of daylight savings time in the summer. The sample proportion is 92/100, or .92, or 92 percent. If we let p represent the sample proportion, X the number of "successes," and n the number of items sampled, we can determine a sample proportion as follows.

SAMPLE PROPORTION $$p = \frac{X}{n} \qquad \textbf{[9–3]}$$

The population proportion is identified by π. Therefore, π refers to the percent of successes in the population. Recall from Chapter 6 that π is the proportion of "successes" in a binomial distribution. This continues our practice of using Greek letters to identify population parameters and Roman letters to identify sample statistics.

To develop a confidence interval for a proportion, we need to meet the following assumptions.

1. The binomial conditions, discussed in Chapter 6, have been met. Briefly, these conditions are:
   a. The sample data is the result of counts.
   b. There are only two possible outcomes. (We usually label one of the outcomes a "success" and the other a "failure.")
   c. The probability of a success remains the same from one trial to the next.
   d. The trials are independent. This means the outcome on one trial does not affect the outcome on another.
2. The values $n\pi$ and $n(1 - \pi)$ should both be greater than or equal to 5. This condition allows us to employ the standard normal distribution, that is, z, to complete a confidence interval.

Developing a point estimate for a population proportion and a confidence interval for a population proportion is similar to doing so for a mean. To illustrate, John Gail is running for Congress from the third district of Nebraska. From a random sample of 100 voters in the district, 60 indicate they plan to vote for him in the upcoming election. The sample proportion is .60, but the population proportion is unknown. That is, we do not know what proportion of voters in the *population* will vote for Mr. Gail. The sample value, .60, is the best estimate we have of the unknown population parameter. So we let p, which is .60, be an estimate of π, which is not known.

To develop a confidence interval for a population proportion, we change formula (9–1) slightly:

CONFIDENCE INTERVAL FOR A POPULATION PROPORTION	$p \pm z\sigma_p$	[9–4]

The term σ_p is the "standard error" of the proportion. It measures the variability in the sampling distribution of the sample proportion.

STANDARD ERROR OF THE SAMPLE PROPORTION	$\sigma_p = \sqrt{\dfrac{p(1-p)}{n}}$	[9–5]

We can then construct a confidence interval for a population proportion from the following formula.

CONFIDENCE INTERVAL FOR A POPULATION PROPORTION	$p \pm z\sqrt{\dfrac{p(1-p)}{n}}$	[9–6]

EXAMPLE

The union representing the Bottle Blowers of America (BBA) is considering a proposal to merge with the Teamsters Union. According to BBA union bylaws, at least three-fourths of the union membership must approve any merger. A random sample of 2,000 current BBA members reveals 1,600 plan to vote for the merger proposal. What is the estimate of the population proportion? Develop a 95 percent confidence interval for the population proportion. Basing your decision on this sample information, can you conclude that the necessary proportion of BBA members favor the merger? Why?

SOLUTION

First, calculate the sample proportion from formula (9–3). It is .80, found by

$$p = \frac{X}{n} = \frac{1{,}600}{2{,}000} = .80$$

Thus, we estimate that 80 percent of the population favor the merger proposal. We determine the 95 percent confidence interval using formula (9–6). The z value corresponding to the 95 percent level of confidence is 1.96.

$$p \pm z\sqrt{\frac{p(1-p)}{n}} = .80 \pm 1.96\sqrt{\frac{.80(1-.80)}{2{,}000}} = .80 \pm .018$$

The endpoints of the confidence interval are .782 and .818. The lower endpoint is greater than .75. Hence, we conclude that the merger proposal will likely pass because the interval estimate includes values greater than 75 percent of the union membership.

Self-Review 9–3

A market survey was conducted to estimate the proportion of homemakers who would recognize the brand name of a cleanser based on the shape and the color of the container. Of the 1,400 homemakers sampled, 420 were able to identify the brand by name.

(a) Estimate the value of the population proportion.
(b) Compute the standard error of the proportion.
(c) Develop a 99 percent confidence interval for the population proportion.
(d) Interpret your findings.

Exercises

15. The owner of the West End Kwick Fill Gas Station wished to determine the proportion of customers who use a credit card or debit card to pay at the pump. He surveys 100 customers and finds that 80 paid at the pump.
a. Estimate the value of the population proportion.
b. Compute the standard error of the proportion.
c. Develop a 95 percent confidence interval for the population proportion.
d. Interpret your findings.

16. Ms. Maria Wilson is considering running for mayor of the town of Bear Gulch, Montana. Before completing the petitions, she decides to conduct a survey of voters in Bear Gulch. A sample of 400 voters reveals that 300 would support her in the November election.
a. Estimate the value of the population proportion.
b. Compute the standard error of the proportion.
c. Develop a 99 percent confidence interval for the population proportion.
d. Interpret your findings.

17. The Fox TV network is considering replacing one of its prime-time crime investigation shows with a new family-oriented comedy show. Before a final decision is made, network executives commission a sample of 400 viewers. After viewing the comedy, 250 indicated they would watch the new show and suggested it replace the crime investigation show.
a. Estimate the value of the population proportion.
b. Compute the standard error of the proportion.
c. Develop a 99 percent confidence interval for the population proportion.
d. Interpret your findings.

18. Schadek Silkscreen Printing, Inc. purchases plastic cups on which to print logos for sporting events, proms, birthdays, and other special occasions. Zack Schadek, the owner, received a large shipment this morning. To ensure the quality of the shipment, he selected a random sample of 300 cups. He found 15 to be defective.
a. What is the estimated proportion defective in the population?
b. Develop a 95 percent confidence interval for the proportion defective.
c. Zack has an agreement with his supplier that he is to return lots that are 10 percent or more defective. Should he return this lot? Explain your decision.

Finite-Population Correction Factor

The populations we have sampled so far have been very large or infinite. What if the sampled population is not very large? We need to make some adjustments in the way we compute the standard error of the sample means and the standard error of the sample proportions.

A population that has a fixed upper bound is *finite.* For example, there are 21,376 students enrolled at Eastern Illinois University, there are 40 employees at Spence Sprockets, DaimlerChrysler assembled 917 Jeep Wranglers at the Alexis Avenue plant yesterday, or there were 65 surgical patients at St. Rose Memorial Hospital in Sarasota yesterday. A finite population can be rather small; it could be all the students registered for this class. It can also be very large, such as all senior citizens living in Florida.

For a finite population, where the total number of objects is N and the size of the sample is n, the following adjustment is made to the standard errors of the sample means and proportions:

STANDARD ERROR OF THE SAMPLE MEAN, USING A FINITE POPULATION CORRECTION FACTOR

$$\sigma_{\bar{X}} = \frac{\sigma}{\sqrt{n}}\sqrt{\frac{N-n}{N-1}} \qquad [9\text{–}7]$$

STANDARD ERROR OF THE SAMPLE PROPORTION, USING A FINITE POPULATION CORRECTION FACTOR

$$\sigma_p = \sqrt{\frac{p(1-p)}{n}}\sqrt{\frac{N-n}{N-1}} \qquad [9\text{–}8]$$

This adjustment is called the **finite-population correction factor.** Why is it necessary to apply a factor, and what is its effect? Logically, if the sample is a substantial percentage of the population, the estimate is more precise. Note the effect of the term $(N - n)/(N - 1)$. Suppose the population is 1,000 and the sample is 100. Then this ratio is (1,000 − 100)/(1,000 − 1), or 900/999. Taking the square root gives the correction factor, .9492. Multiplying this correction factor by the standard error *reduces* the standard error by about 5 percent (1 − .9492 = .0508). This reduction in the size of the standard error yields a smaller range of values in estimating the population mean or the population proportion. If the sample is 200, the correction factor is .8949, meaning that the standard error has been reduced by more than 10 percent. Table 9–1 shows the effects of various sample sizes. Note that when the sample is less than about 5 percent of the population, the impact of the correction factor is quite small. The usual rule is if the ratio of n/N is less than .05, the correction factor is ignored.

TABLE 9–1 Finite-Population Correction Factor for Selected Samples When the Population Is 1,000

Sample Size	Fraction of Population	Correction Factor
10	.010	.9955
25	.025	.9879
50	.050	.9752
100	.100	.9492
200	.200	.8949
500	.500	.7075

EXAMPLE

There are 250 families in Scandia, Pennsylvania. A poll of 40 families reveals the mean annual church contribution is $450 with a standard deviation of $75. Construct a 90 percent confidence interval for the mean annual contribution.

SOLUTION

First, note that the population is finite. That is, there is a limit to the number of people in Scandia. Second, note that the sample constitutes more than 5 percent of the population; that is, $n/N = 40/250 = .16$. Hence, we use the finite-population correction factor. The 90 percent confidence interval is constructed as follows, using formula (9–7).

$$\overline{X} \pm z\frac{s}{\sqrt{n}}\left(\sqrt{\frac{N-n}{N-1}}\right) = \$450 \pm 1.65\frac{\$75}{\sqrt{40}}\left(\sqrt{\frac{250-40}{250-1}}\right) = \$450 \pm 19.57\left(\sqrt{.8434}\right)$$

$$= \$450 \pm \$17.97$$

The endpoints of the confidence interval are $432.03 and $467.97. It is likely that the population mean falls within this interval.

Self-Review 9–4

The same study of church contributions in Scandia revealed that 15 of the 40 families sampled attend church regularly. Construct the 95 percent confidence interval for the proportion of families attending church regularly. Should the finite-population correction factor be used? Why or why not?

Exercises

19. Thirty-six items are randomly selected from a population of 300 items. The sample mean is 35 and the sample standard deviation 5. Develop a 95 percent confidence interval for the population mean.

20. Forty-nine items are randomly selected from a population of 500 items. The sample mean is 40 and the sample standard deviation 9. Develop a 99 percent confidence interval for the population mean.

21. The attendance at the Savannah Colts minor league baseball game last night was 400. A random sample of 50 of those in attendance revealed that the mean number of soft drinks consumed per person was 1.86 with a standard deviation of 0.50. Develop a 99 percent confidence interval for the mean number of soft drinks consumed per person.

22. There are 300 welders employed at the Maine Shipyards Corporation. A sample of 30 welders revealed that 18 graduated from a registered welding course. Construct the 95 percent confidence interval for the proportion of all welders who graduated from a registered welding course.

Choosing an Appropriate Sample Size

A concern that usually arises when designing a statistical study is "How many items should be in the sample?" If a sample is too large, money is wasted collecting the data. Similarly, if the sample is too small, the resulting conclusions will be uncertain. The necessary sample size depends on three factors:

1. The level of confidence desired.
2. The margin of error the researcher will tolerate.
3. The variability in the population being studied.

The first factor is the *level of confidence.* Those conducting the study select the level of confidence. The 95 percent and the 99 percent levels of confidence are the most common, but any value between 0 and 100 percent is possible. The 95 percent level of confidence corresponds to a z value of 1.96, and a 99 percent level of confidence corresponds to a z value of 2.58. The higher the level of confidence selected, the larger the size of the corresponding sample.

The second factor is the *allowable error.* The maximum allowable error, designated as E, is the amount that is added and subtracted to the sample mean (or sample proportion) to determine the endpoints of the confidence interval. It is the amount of error those conducting the study are willing to tolerate. It is also one-half the width of the corresponding confidence interval. A small allowable error will require a large sample. A large allowable error will permit a smaller sample.

The third factor in determining the size of a sample is the *population standard deviation.* If the population is widely dispersed, a large sample is required. On the other hand, if the population is concentrated (homogeneous), the required sample size will be smaller. However, it may be necessary to use an estimate for the population standard deviation. Here are three suggestions for finding that estimate.

1. **Use a comparable study.** Use this approach when there is an estimate of the dispersion available from another study. Suppose we want to estimate the number of hours worked per week by refuse workers. Information from certain state or federal agencies who regularly sample the workforce might be useful to provide an estimate of the standard deviation. If a standard deviation observed in a previous study is thought to be reliable, it can be used in the current study to help provide an approximate sample size.
2. **Use a range-based approach.** To use this approach we need to know or have an estimate of the largest and smallest values in the population. Recall from Chapter 3, where we described the Empirical Rule, that virtually all the observations could be expected to be within plus or minus 3 standard deviations of the mean, assuming that the distribution was approximately normal. Thus, the distance between the largest and the smallest values is 6 standard deviations. We could estimate the standard deviation as one-sixth of the range. For example, the director of operations at University Bank wants an estimate of the number of checks written per month by college students. She believes that the distribution is approximately normal, the minimum number of checks written is 2 per month, and the most is 50 per month. The range of the number of checks written per

month is 48, found by 50 − 2. The estimate of the standard deviation then would be 8 checks per month, 48/6.

3. **Conduct a pilot study.** This is the most common method. Suppose we want an estimate of the number of hours per week worked by students enrolled in the College of Business at the University of Texas. To test the validity of our questionnaire, we use it on a small sample of students. From this small sample we compute the standard deviation of the number of hours worked and use this value to determine the appropriate sample size.

We can express the interaction among these three factors and the sample size in the following formula.

$$E = z\frac{s}{\sqrt{n}}$$

Solving this equation for n yields the following result.

SAMPLE SIZE FOR ESTIMATING THE POPULATION MEAN $$n = \left(\frac{zs}{E}\right)^2 \quad \textbf{[9–9]}$$

where:

n is the size of the sample.
z is the standard normal value corresponding to the desired level of confidence.
s is an estimate of the population standard deviation.
E is the maximum allowable error.

The result of this calculation is not always a whole number. When the outcome is not a whole number, the usual practice is to round up *any* fractional result. For example, 201.22 would be rounded up to 202.

EXAMPLE

A student in public administration wants to determine the mean amount members of city councils in large cities earn per month as remuneration for being a council member. The error in estimating the mean is to be less than \$100 with a 95 percent level of confidence. The student found a report by the Department of Labor that estimated the standard deviation to be \$1,000. What is the required sample size?

SOLUTION

The maximum allowable error, E, is \$100. The value of z for a 95 percent level of confidence is 1.96, and the estimate of the standard deviation is \$1,000. Substituting these values into formula (9–9) gives the required sample size as:

$$n = \left(\frac{zs}{E}\right)^2 = \left(\frac{(1.96)(\$1{,}000)}{\$100}\right)^2 = (19.6)^2 = 384.16$$

The computed value of 384.16 is rounded up to 385. A sample of 385 is required to meet the specifications. If the student wants to increase the level of confidence, for example to 99 percent, this will require a larger sample. The z value corresponding to the 99 percent level of confidence is 2.58.

$$n = \left(\frac{zs}{E}\right)^2 = \left(\frac{(2.58)(\$1{,}000)}{\$100}\right)^2 = (25.8)^2 = 665.64$$

We recommend a sample of 666. Observe how much the change in the confidence level changed the size of the sample. An increase from the 95 percent to the 99 percent level of confidence resulted in an increase of 281 observations. This could greatly increase the cost of the study, both in terms of time and money. Hence, the level of confidence should be considered carefully.

The procedure just described can be adapted to determine the sample size for a proportion. Again, three items need to be specified:

1. The desired level of confidence.
2. The margin of error in the population proportion.
3. An estimate of the population proportion.

The formula to determine the sample size of a proportion is:

SAMPLE SIZE FOR THE POPULATION PROPORTION $$n = p(1 - p)\left(\frac{z}{E}\right)^2$$ **[9–10]**

If an estimate of π is available from a pilot study or some other source, it can be used. Otherwise, .50 is used because the term $p(1 - p)$ can never be larger than when $p = .50$. For example, if $p = .30$, then $p(1 - p) = .3(1 - 3) = .21$, but when $p = .50$, $p(1 - p) = .5(1 - 5) = .25$

EXAMPLE

The study in the previous example also estimates the proportion of cities that have private refuse collectors. The student wants the estimate to be within .10 of the population proportion, the desired level of confidence is 90 percent, and no estimate is available for the population proportion. What is the required sample size?

SOLUTION

The estimate of the population proportion is to be within .10, so $E = .10$. The desired level of confidence is .90, which corresponds to a z value of 1.65. Because no estimate of the population proportion is available, we use .50. The suggested number of observations is

$$n = (.5)(1 - .5)\left(\frac{1.65}{.10}\right)^2 = 68.0625$$

The student needs a random sample of 69 cities.

Self-Review 9–5

Will you assist the college registrar in determining how many transcripts to study? The registrar wants to estimate the arithmetic mean grade point average (GPA) of all graduating seniors during the past 10 years. GPAs range between 2.0 and 4.0. The mean GPA is to be estimated within plus or minus .05 of the population mean. The standard deviation is estimated to be 0.279. Use the 99 percent level of confidence.

Exercises

23. A population is estimated to have a standard deviation of 10. We want to estimate the population mean within 2, with a 95 percent level of confidence. How large a sample is required?

24. We want to estimate the population mean within 5, with a 99 percent level of confidence. The population standard deviation is estimated to be 15. How large a sample is required?

25. The estimate of the population proportion is to be within plus or minus .05, with a 95 percent level of confidence. The best estimate of the population proportion is .15. How large a sample is required?

26. The estimate of the population proportion is to be within plus or minus .10, with a 99 percent level of confidence. The best estimate of the population proportion is .45. How large a sample is required?

27. A survey is being planned to determine the mean amount of time corporation executives watch television. A pilot survey indicated that the mean time per week is 12 hours, with a standard deviation of 3 hours. It is desired to estimate the mean viewing time within one-quarter hour. The 95 percent level of confidence is to be used. How many executives should be surveyed?

28. A processor of carrots cuts the green top off each carrot, washes the carrots, and inserts six to a package. Twenty packages are inserted in a box for shipment. To test the weight of the boxes, a few were checked. The mean weight was 20.4 pounds, the standard deviation 0.5 pounds. How many boxes must the processor sample to be 95 percent confident that the sample mean does not differ from the population mean by more than 0.2 pounds?

29. Suppose the President wants an estimate of the proportion of the population who support his current policy toward gun control. The President wants the estimate to be within .04 of the true proportion. Assume a 95 percent level of confidence. The President's political advisors estimated the proportion supporting the current policy to be .60.

a. How large of a sample is required?

b. How large of a sample would be necessary if no estimate were available for the proportion that support current policy?

30. Past surveys reveal that 30 percent of tourists going to Las Vegas to gamble during a weekend spend more than $1,000. The Las Vegas Area Chamber of Commerce wants to update this percentage.

a. The new study is to use the 90 percent confidence level. The estimate is to be within 1 percent of the population proportion. What is the necessary sample size?

b. Management said that the sample size determined above is too large. What can be done to reduce the sample? Based on your suggestion recalculate the sample size.

Chapter Outline

I. A point estimate is a single value (statistic) used to estimate a population value (parameter).

II. A confidence interval is a range of values within which the population parameter is expected to occur.

A. The factors that determine the width of a confidence interval for a mean are:

1. The number of observations in the sample, *n*.
2. The variability in the population, usually estimated by the sample standard deviation, *s*.
3. The level of confidence.

a. To determine the confidence limits when the population standard deviation is known or the sample is 30 or more, we use the *z* distribution. The formula is

$$\bar{X} \pm z\frac{s}{\sqrt{n}} \qquad \textbf{[9–1]}$$

b. To determine the confidence limits when the population standard deviation is unknown and the sample is less than 30, we use the *t* distribution. The formula is

$$\bar{X} \pm t\frac{s}{\sqrt{n}} \qquad \textbf{[9–2]}$$

III. The major characteristics of the *t* distribution are:

A. It is a continuous distribution.

B. It is mound-shaped and symmetrical.

C. It is flatter, or more spread out, than the standard normal distribution.

D. There is a family of *t* distributions, depending on the number of degrees of freedom.

IV. A proportion is a ratio, fraction, or percent that indicates the part of the sample or population that has a particular characteristic.

A. A sample proportion is found by *X*, the number of successes, divided by *n*, the number of observations.

B. The standard error of the sample proportion reports the variability in the distribution of sample proportions. It is found by

$$\sigma_p = \sqrt{\frac{p(1-p)}{n}} \qquad \textbf{[9–5]}$$

C. We construct a confidence interval for a sample proportion from the following formula.

$$p \pm z\sqrt{\frac{p(1-p)}{n}} \quad \textbf{[9–6]}$$

V. We can determine an appropriate sample size for estimating a variable and a proportion.

A. There are three factors that determine the sample size when we wish to estimate the mean.

1. The desired level of confidence, which is usually expressed by *z*.
2. The maximum allowable error, *E*.
3. The variation in the population, expressed by *s*.
4. The formula to determine the sample size for the mean is

$$n = \left(\frac{zs}{E}\right)^2 \quad \textbf{[9–9]}$$

B. There are three factors that determine the sample size when we wish to estimate a proportion.

1. The desired level of confidence, which is usually expressed by *z*.
2. The maximum allowable error, *E*.
3. An estimate of the population proportion. If no estimate is available, use .50.
4. The formula to determine the sample size for a proportion is

$$n = p(1-p)\left(\frac{z}{E}\right)^2 \quad \textbf{[9–10]}$$

VI. For a finite population, the standard error is adjusted by the factor $\sqrt{\frac{N-n}{N-1}}$

Pronunciation Key

SYMBOL	MEANING	PRONUNCIATION
$\sigma_{\bar{X}}$	The standard error of the sample means	*sigma sub X bar*
σ_p	Standard error of the sample proportion	*sigma sub p*

Chapter Exercises

31. A random sample of 85 group leaders, supervisors, and similar personnel at General Motors revealed that, on the average, they spent 6.5 years on the job before being promoted. The standard deviation of the sample was 1.7 years. Construct a 95 percent confidence interval.

32. A state meat inspector in Iowa has been given the assignment of estimating the mean net weight of packages of ground chuck labeled "3 pounds." Of course, he realizes that the weights cannot be precisely 3 pounds. A sample of 36 packages reveals the mean weight to be 3.01 pounds, with a standard deviation of 0.03 pounds.

a. What is the estimated population mean?

b. Determine a 95 percent confidence interval for the population mean.

33. A recent study of 50 self-service gasoline stations in the Greater Cincinnati–Northern Kentucky metropolitan area in the spring of 2004 revealed that the mean price of unleaded gas was \$2.029 per gallon. The sample standard deviation was \$0.03 per gallon.

a. Determine a 99 percent confidence interval for the population mean price.

b. Would it be reasonable to conclude that the population mean was \$1.50? Why or why not?

34. A recent survey of 50 executives who were laid off from their previous position revealed it took a mean of 26 weeks for them to find another position. The standard deviation of the sample was 6.2 weeks. Construct a 95 percent confidence interval for the population mean. Is it reasonable that the population mean is 28 weeks? Justify your answer.

35. Marty Rowatti recently assumed the position of director of the YMCA of South Jersey. He would like some current data on how long current members of the YMCA have been members. To investigate, suppose he selects a random sample of 40 current members. The mean length of membership of those included in the sample is 8.32 years and the standard deviation is 3.07 years.

a. What is the mean of the population?

b. Develop a 90 percent confidence interval for the population mean.

c. The previous director, in the summary report she prepared as she retired, indicated the mean length of membership was now "almost 10 years." Does the sample information substantiate this claim? Cite evidence.

36. The American Restaurant Association collected information on the number of meals eaten outside the home per week by young married couples. A survey of 60 couples showed the sample mean number of meals eaten outside the home was 2.76 meals per week, with a standard deviation of 0.75 meals per week. Construct a 97 percent confidence interval for the population mean.

37. The National Collegiate Athletic Association (NCAA) reported that the mean number of hours spent per week on coaching and recruiting by college football assistant coaches during the season is 70. A random sample of 50 assistant coaches showed the sample mean to be 68.6 hours, with a standard deviation of 8.2 hours.

a. Using the sample data, construct a 99 percent confidence interval for the population mean.

b. Does the 99 percent confidence interval include the value suggested by the NCAA? Interpret this result.

c. Suppose you decided to switch from a 99 to a 95 percent confidence interval. Without performing any calculations, will the interval increase, decrease, or stay the same? Which of the values in the formula will change?

38. The Human Relations Department of Electronics, Inc., would like to include a dental plan as part of the benefits package. The question is: How much does a typical employee and his or her family spend per year on dental expenses? A sample of 45 employees reveals the mean amount spent last year was $1,820, with a standard deviation of $660.

a. Construct a 95 percent confidence interval for the population mean.

b. The information from part (a) was given to the president of Electronics, Inc. He indicated he could afford $1,700 of dental expenses per employee. Is it possible that the population mean could be $1,700? Justify your answer.

39. A student conducted a study and reported that the 95 percent confidence interval for the mean ranged from 46 to 54. He was sure that the mean of the sample was 50, that the standard deviation of the sample was 16, and that the sample was at least 30, but could not remember the exact number. Can you help him out?

40. A recent study by the American Automobile Dealers Association revealed the mean amount of profit per car sold for a sample of 20 dealers was $290, with a standard deviation of $125. Develop a 95 percent confidence interval for the population mean.

41. A study of 25 graduates of four-year colleges by the American Banker's Association revealed the mean amount owed by a student in student loans was $14,381. The standard deviation of the sample was $1,892. Construct a 90 percent confidence interval for the population mean. Is it reasonable to conclude that the mean of the population is actually $15,000? Tell why or why not.

42. An important factor in selling a residential property is the number of people who look through the home. A sample of 15 homes recently sold in the Buffalo, New York, area revealed the mean number looking through each home was 24 and the standard deviation of the sample was 5 people. Develop a 98 percent confidence interval for the population mean.

43. The Warren County Telephone Company claims in its annual report that "the typical customer spends $60 per month on local and long distance service." A sample of 12 subscribers revealed the following amounts spent last month.

$64	$66	$64	$66	$59	$62	$67	$61	$64	$58	$54	$66

a. What is the point estimate of the population mean?

b. Develop a 90 percent confidence interval for the population mean.

c. Is the company's claim that the "typical customer" spends $60 per month reasonable? Justify your answer.

44. The manufacturer of a new line of ink jet printers would like to include as part of their advertising the number of pages a user can expect from a print cartridge. A sample of 10 cartridges revealed the following number of pages printed.

2,698	2,028	2,474	2,395	2,372	2,475	1,927	3,006	2,334	2,379

a. What is the point estimate of the population mean?
b. Develop a 95 percent confidence interval for the population mean.

45. Dr. Susan Benner is an industrial psychologist. She is currently studying stress among executives of Internet companies. She has developed a questionnaire that she believes measures stress. A score above 80 indicates stress at a dangerous level. A random sample of 15 executives revealed the following stress level scores.

94	78	83	90	78	99	97	90	97	90	93	94	100	75	84

a. Find the mean stress level for this sample. What is the point estimate of the population mean?
b. Construct a 95 percent confidence level for the population mean.
c. Is it reasonable to conclude that Internet executives have a mean stress level in the dangerous level, according to Dr. Benner's test?

46. As a condition of employment, Fashion Industries applicants must pass a drug test. Of the last 220 applicants 14 failed the test. Develop a 99 percent confidence interval for the proportion of applicants that fail the test. Would it be reasonable to conclude that more than 10 percent of the applicants are now failing the test? In addition to the testing of applicants, Fashion Industries randomly tests its employees throughout the year. Last year in the 400 random tests conducted, 14 employees failed the test. Would it be reasonable to conclude that less than 5 percent of the employees are not able to pass the random drug test?

47. There are 20,000 eligible voters in York County, South Carolina. A random sample of 500 York County voters revealed 350 plan to vote to return Louella Miller to the state senate. Construct a 99 percent confidence interval for the proportion of voters in the county who plan to vote for Ms. Miller. From this sample information, can you confirm she will be reelected?

48. In a poll to estimate presidential popularity, each person in a random sample of 1,000 voters was asked to agree with one of the following statements:
    1. The President is doing a good job.
    2. The President is doing a poor job.
    3. I have no opinion.

    A total of 560 respondents selected the first statement, indicating they thought the President was doing a good job.
    a. Construct a 95 percent confidence interval for the proportion of respondents who feel the President is doing a good job.
    b. Based on your interval in part (a), is it reasonable to conclude that a majority (more than half) of the population believes the President is doing a good job?

49. Police Chief Aaron Ard of River City reports 500 traffic citations were issued last month. A sample of 35 of these citations showed the mean amount of the fine was $54, with a standard deviation of $4.50. Construct a 95 percent confidence interval for the mean amount of a citation in River City.

50. The First National Bank of Wilson has 650 checking account customers. A recent sample of 50 of these customers showed 26 to have a Visa card with the bank. Construct the 99 percent confidence interval for the proportion of checking account customers who have a Visa card with the bank.

51. It is estimated that 60 percent of U.S. households subscribe to cable TV. You would like to verify this statement for your class in mass communications. If you want your estimate to be within 5 percentage points, with a 95 percent level of confidence, how large of a sample is required?

52. You need to estimate the mean number of travel days per year for outside salespeople. The mean of a small pilot study was 150 days, with a standard deviation of 14 days. If you must estimate the population mean within 2 days, how many outside salespeople should you sample? Use the 90 percent confidence level.

53. You are to conduct a sample survey to determine the mean family income in a rural area of central Florida. The question is, how many families should be sampled? In a pilot sample of 10 families, the standard deviation of the sample was $500. The sponsor of the survey wants you to use the 95 percent confidence level. The estimate is to be within $100. How many families should be interviewed?

54. You plan to conduct a survey to find what proportion of the workforce has two or more jobs. You decide on the 95 percent confidence level and state that the estimated proportion must be within 2 percent of the population proportion. A pilot survey reveals that 5 of the 50

sampled hold two or more jobs. How many in the workforce should be interviewed to meet your requirements?

55. The proportion of public accountants who have changed companies within the last three years is to be estimated within 3 percent. The 95 percent level of confidence is to be used. A study conducted several years ago revealed that the percent of public accountants changing companies within three years was 21.
   a. To update this study, the files of how many public accountants should be studied?
   b. How many public accountants should be contacted if no previous estimates of the population proportion are available?

56. The Huntington National Bank, like most other large banks, found that using automatic teller machines (ATMs) reduces the cost of routine bank transactions. Huntington installed an ATM in the corporate offices of the Fun Toy Company. The ATM is for the exclusive use of Fun's 605 employees. After several months of operation, a sample of 100 employees revealed the following use of the ATM machine by Fun employees in a month.

Number of Times ATM Used	Frequency
0	25
1	30
2	20
3	10
4	10
5	5

   a. What is the estimate of the proportion of employees who do not use the ATM in a month?
   b. Develop a 95 percent confidence interval for this estimate. Can Huntington be sure that at least 40 percent of the employees of Fun Toy Company will use the ATM?
   c. How many transactions does the average Fun employee make per month?
   d. Develop a 95 percent confidence interval for the mean number of transactions per month.
   e. Is it possible that the population mean is 0? Explain.

57. In a recent Zogby poll of 1,000 adults nationwide, 613 said they believe other forms of life exist elsewhere in the universe. Construct the 99 percent confidence interval for the population proportion of those believing life exists elsewhere in the universe. Does your result imply that a majority of Americans believe life exists outside of Earth?

58. As part of an annual review of its accounts, a discount brokerage selects a random sample of 36 customers. Their accounts are reviewed for total account valuation, which showed a mean of $32,000, with a sample standard deviation of $8,200. What is a 90 percent confidence interval for the mean account valuation of the population of customers?

59. A sample of 352 subscribers to *Wired* magazine shows the mean time spent using the Internet is 13.4 hours per week, with a sample standard deviation of 6.8 hours. Find the 95 percent confidence interval for the mean time *Wired* subscribers spend on the Internet.

60. The Tennessee Tourism Institute (TTI) plans to sample information center visitors entering the state to learn the fraction of visitors who plan to camp in the state. Current estimates are that 35 percent of visitors are campers. How large a sample would you take to estimate at a 95 percent confidence level the population proportion with an allowable error of 2 percent?

exercises.com

61. Hoover is an excellent source of business information. It includes daily summaries as well as information about various industries and specific companies. Go to the site at www.hoovers.com. Click on **Browse Industries,** select an industry sector, such as **Financial Services.** This should give you a list of companies. Use a table of random numbers, such as Appendix E, to randomly select 5 to 10 companies in the list. For each company, click on the **Financials** tab to get information about the selected companies. One suggestion is to find the earnings per share. Compute the mean of each sample, and then develop a confidence interval for the mean earnings per share. Because the sample is a large part of the population, you will want to include the correction factor. Interpret the result.

62. The online edition of the *Information Please Almanac* is a valuable source of business information. Go to the Website at www.infoplease.com. Click on **Business.** Then in the **Almanac Section,** click on **Taxes,** then click on **State Taxes on Individuals.** The result is a listing of the 50 states and the District of Columbia. Use a table of random numbers to randomly select 5 to 10 states. Compute the mean state tax rate on individuals. Develop a confidence interval for the mean amount. Because the sample is a large part of the population, you will want to include the finite population correction factor. Interpret your result. You might, as an additional exercise, download all the information and use Excel or MINITAB to compute the population mean. Compare that value with the results of your confidence interval.

Dataset Exercises

63. Refer to the Real Estate data, which reports information on the homes sold in Denver, Colorado, last year.
    a. Develop a 95 percent confidence interval for the mean selling price of the homes.
    b. Develop a 95 percent confidence interval for the mean distance the home is from the center of the city.
    c. Develop a 95 percent confidence interval for the proportion of homes with an attached garage.
64. Refer to the Baseball 2003 data, which reports information on the 30 Major League Baseball teams for the 2003 season. Use the *t* distribution.
    a. Develop a 95 percent confidence interval for the mean number of home runs per team.
    b. Develop a 95 percent confidence interval for the mean number of errors committed by each team.
    c. Develop a 95 percent confidence interval for the mean number of stolen bases for each team.
65. Refer to the Wage data, which reports information on annual wages for a sample of 100 workers. Also included are variables relating to industry, years of education, and gender for each worker.
    a. Develop a 95 percent confidence interval for the mean wage of the workers. Is it reasonable to conclude that the population mean is $35,000?
    b. Develop a 95 percent confidence interval for the mean years of education. Is it reasonable that the population mean is 13 years?
    c. Develop a 95 percent confidence interval for the mean age of the workers. Could the mean age be 40 years?
66. Refer to the CIA data, which reports demographic and economic information on 46 countries.
    a. Develop a 90 percent confidence interval for the mean percent of the population over 65 years.
    b. Develop a 90 percent confidence interval for the mean Gross Domestic Product (GDP) per capita.
    c. Develop a 90 percent confidence interval for the mean imports.

Software Commands

1. The MINITAB commands for the 60 columns of 30 random numbers used in the Example/Solution on page 252 are:
    a. Select **Calc, Random Data,** and then click on **Normal.**
    b. From the dialog box click on **Generate** and type *30* for the number of rows of data, **Store** in *C1-C60,* the **Mean** is *50,* the **Standard Deviation** is *5.0,* and finally click **OK.**

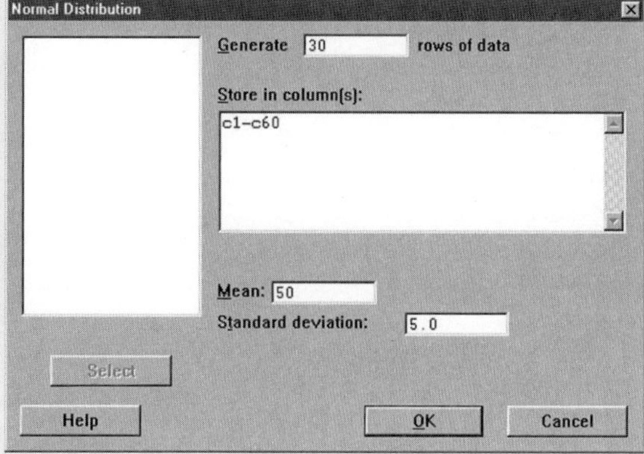

2. The MINITAB commands for the 60 confidence intervals on page 252 follow.
   a. Select **Stat, Basic Statistics,** and then click on **1-Sample-z.**
   b. In the dialog box indicate that the **Variables** are *C1-C60* and that **Sigma** is *5.0.* Next click on **Options** in the lower right corner, in the next dialog box indicate that the **Confidence level** is *95.0,* and then click **OK.** Click **OK** in the main dialog box.

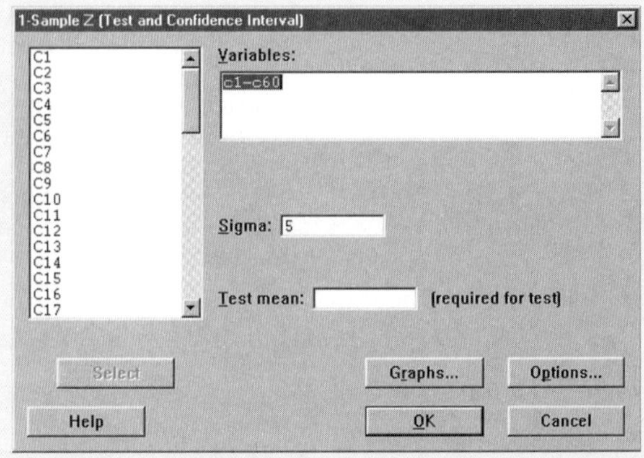

3. The MINITAB commands for the descriptive statistics on page 258 are the same as those used on page 81 in Chapter 3. Enter the data in the first column and label this column *Amount.* On the Toolbar select **Stat, Basic Statistics,** and **Display Basic Statistics.** In the dialog box select *Amount* as the **Variable** and click **OK.**
4. The MINITAB commands for the confidence interval for the amount spent at the Inlet Square Mall on page 258 are:
   a. Enter the 20 amounts spent in column c1 and name the variable *Amounts,* or locate the data on the student data disk.
   b. On the Toolbar select **Stat, Basic Statistics,** and click on **1-Sample t.**
   c. Select *Amount* as the **Variable** and click **OK.**

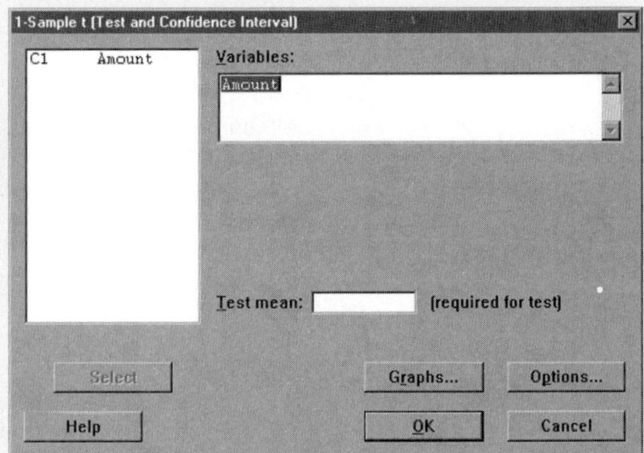

5. The Excel commands for the confidence interval for the amounts spent at the Inlet Square Mall on page 259 are:
   a. From the menu bar select **Tools, Data Analysis,** and **Descriptive Statistics,** and then click **OK.**
   b. For the **Input Range** type *A1:A21,* click on **Labels in first row,** *D1* as the **Output Range,** click on **Summary Statistics** and **Confidence Level for Mean,** and then click on **OK.**

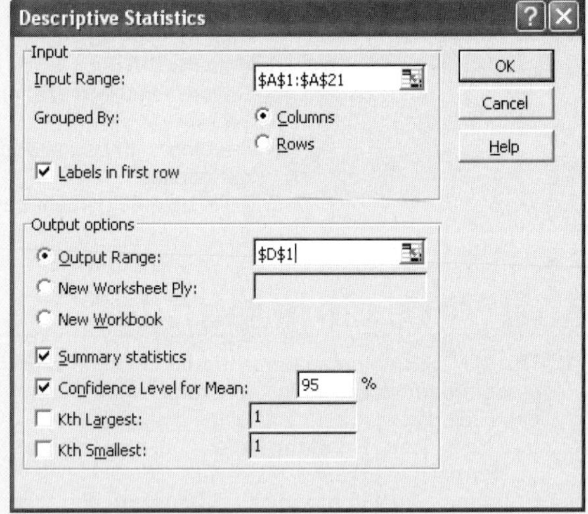

Chapter 9 Answers to Self-Review

9–1 a. \$20,000. This is called the point estimate.

b. $\$20{,}000 \pm 2.58 \dfrac{\$3{,}000}{\sqrt{40}} = \$20{,}000 \pm 1{,}224$

c. The endpoints of the confidence interval are \$18,776 and \$21,224. About 99 percent of the intervals similarly constructed would include the population mean.

9–2 a. $\bar{X} = \dfrac{18}{10} = 1.8 \quad s = \sqrt{\dfrac{11.6}{10 - 1}} = 1.1353$

b. The population mean is not known. The best estimate is the sample mean, 1.8 days.

c. $1.80 \pm 2.262 \dfrac{1.1353}{\sqrt{10}} = 1.80 \pm 0.81$

d. t is used because the population standard deviation is unknown and the sample contains less than 30 observations.

e. The value of 0 is not in the interval. It is unreasonable to conclude that the mean number of days of work missed is 0 per employee.

9–3 a. $p = \dfrac{420}{1400} = .30$

b. $\sigma_p = \sqrt{\dfrac{.30(1 - .30)}{1400}} = .0122$

c. $.30 \pm 2.58(.0122) = .30 \pm .03$

d. The interval is between .27 and .33. About 99 percent of the similarly constructed intervals would include the population mean.

9–4 $.375 \pm 1.96\sqrt{\dfrac{.375(1 - .375)}{40}}\sqrt{\dfrac{250 - 40}{250 - 1}} =$

$.375 \pm 1.96(.0765)(.9184) = .375 \pm .138$

The correction factor should be applied because $40/250 > .05$.

9–5 $n = \left(\dfrac{2.58(.279)}{.05}\right)^2 = 207.26$. The sample should be rounded to 208.

10

One-Sample Tests of Hypothesis

GOALS

When you have completed this chapter you will be able to:

1 **Define a *hypothesis* and *hypothesis testing.***

2 **Describe the five-step hypothesis-testing procedure.**

3 **Distinguish between a one-tailed and a two-tailed test of hypothesis.**

4 **Conduct a test of hypothesis about a population mean.**

5 **Conduct a test of hypothesis about a population proportion.**

6 **Define *Type I* and *Type II* errors.**

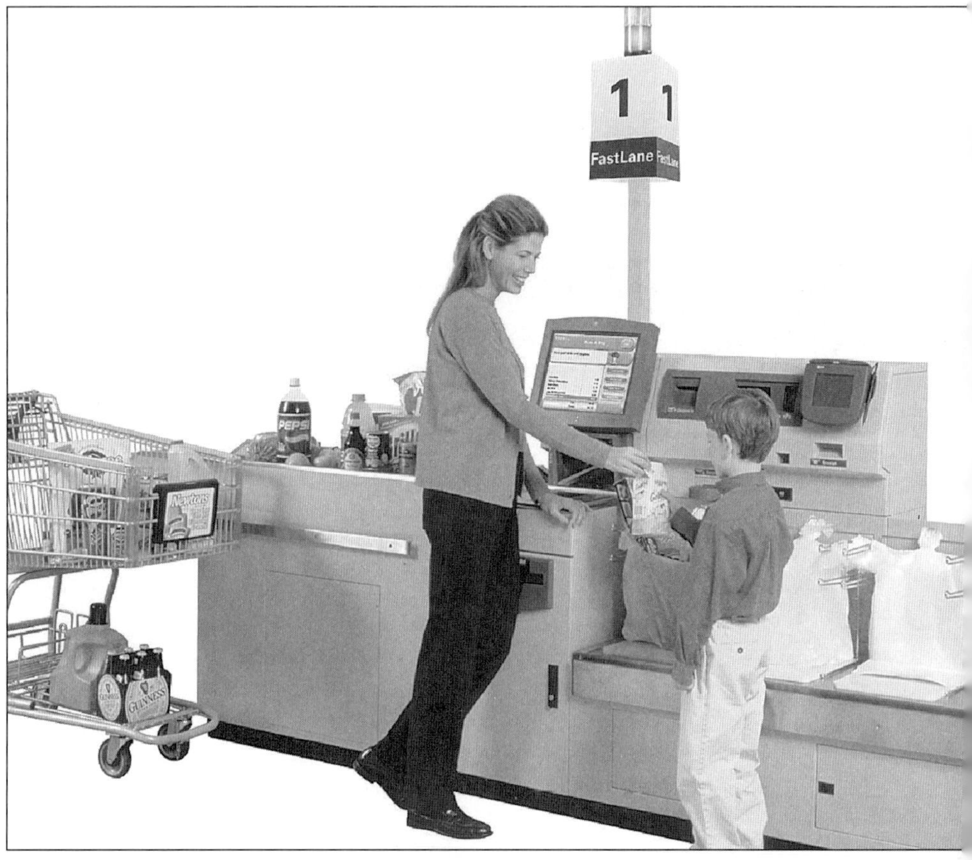

Many grocery stores and large retailers such as Wal-Mart and K-Mart have installed self-checkout systems so shoppers can scan their own items and cash out themselves. A sample of customers using the service was taken for 15 days at the Wal-Mart on Highway 544 in Surfside Beach, South Carolina, to see how often it is used. Using the .05 significance level, is it reasonable to conclude that the mean number of customers using the system is more than 100 per day? (See Goal 4 and Exercise 49.)

Introduction

Chapter 8 began our study of statistical inference. We described how we could select a random sample and from this sample estimate the value of a population parameter. For example, we selected a sample of 5 employees at Spence Sprockets, found the number of years of service for each sampled employee, computed the mean years of service, and used the sample mean to estimate the mean years of service for all employees. In other words, we estimated a population parameter from a sample statistic.

Chapter 9 continued the study of statistical inference by developing a confidence interval. A confidence interval is a range of values within which we expect the population parameter to occur. In this chapter, rather than develop a range of values within which we expect the population parameter to occur, we develop a procedure to test the validity of a statement about a population parameter. Some examples of statements we might want to test are:

- The mean speed of automobiles passing milepost 150 on the West Virginia Turnpike is 68 miles per hour.

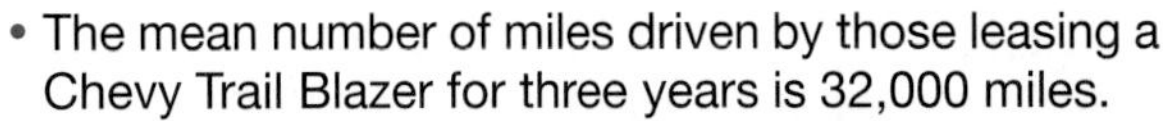

- The mean number of miles driven by those leasing a Chevy Trail Blazer for three years is 32,000 miles.
- The mean time an American family lives in a particular single-family dwelling is 11.8 years.
- The mean starting salary for graduates of four-year business schools is $3,200 per month.
- Thirty-five percent of retirees in the upper Midwest sell their home and move to a warm climate within 1 year of their retirement.
- Eighty percent of those who play the state lotteries regularly never win more than $100 in any one play.

This chapter and several of the following chapters are concerned with statistical hypothesis testing. We begin by defining what we mean by a statistical hypothesis and statistical hypothesis testing. Next, we outline the steps in statistical hypothesis testing. Then we conduct tests of hypothesis for means and proportions.

What Is a Hypothesis?

A hypothesis is a statement about a population parameter.

A hypothesis is a statement about a population. Data are then used to check the reasonableness of the statement. To begin we need to define the word *hypothesis.* In the United States legal system, a person is innocent until proven guilty. A jury hypothesizes that a person charged with a crime is innocent and subjects this hypothesis to verification by reviewing the evidence and hearing testimony before reaching a verdict. In a similar sense, a patient goes to a physician and reports various symptoms. On the basis of the symptoms, the physician will order certain diagnostic tests, then, according to the symptoms and the test results, determine the treatment to be followed.

In statistical analysis we make a claim, that is, state a hypothesis, collect data, then use the data to test the assertion. We define a statistical hypothesis as follows.

HYPOTHESIS A statement about a population developed for the purpose of testing.

In most cases the population is so large that it is not feasible to study all the items, objects, or persons in the population. For example, it would not be possible to contact every systems analyst in the United States to find his or her monthly income. Likewise, the quality assurance department at Cooper Tire cannot check each tire produced to determine whether it will last more than 60,000 miles.

As noted in Chapter 8, an alternative to measuring or interviewing the entire population is to take a sample from the population. We can, therefore, test a statement to determine whether the sample does or does not support the statement concerning the population.

Statistics in Action

LASIK is a 15-minute surgical procedure that uses a laser to reshape an eye's cornea with the goal of improving eyesight. Research shows that about 5% of all surgeries involve complications such as glare, corneal haze, overcorrection or undercorrection of vision, and loss of vision. In a statistical sense, the research tests a Null Hypothesis that the surgery will not improve eyesight with the Alternative Hypothesis that the surgery will improve eyesight. The sample data of LASIK surgery shows that 5% of all cases result in complications. The 5% represents a Type I error rate. When a person decides to have the surgery, he or she expects to reject the Null Hypothesis. In 5% of future cases, this expectation will not be met. (Source: American Academy of Ophthalmology, San Francisco, Vol. 16, no. 43.)

What Is Hypothesis Testing?

The terms *hypothesis testing* and *testing a hypothesis* are used interchangeably. Hypothesis testing starts with a statement, or assumption, about a population parameter—such as the population mean. As noted, this statement is referred to as a *hypothesis.* A hypothesis might be that the mean monthly commission of sales associates in retail electronics stores, such as Circuit City, is $2,000. We cannot contact all these sales associates to ascertain that the mean is in fact $2,000. The cost of locating and interviewing every electronics sales associate in the United States would be exorbitant. To test the validity of the assumption ($\mu = \$2{,}000$), we must select a sample from the population of all electronics sales associates, calculate sample statistics, and based on certain decision rules accept or reject the hypothesis. A sample mean of $1,000 for the electronics sales associates would certainly cause rejection of the hypothesis. However, suppose the sample mean is $1,995. Is that close enough to $2,000 for us to accept the assumption that the population mean is $2,000? Can we attribute the difference of $5 between the two means to sampling error, or is that difference statistically significant?

HYPOTHESIS TESTING A procedure based on sample evidence and probability theory to determine whether the hypothesis is a reasonable statement.

Five-Step Procedure for Testing a Hypothesis

There is a five-step procedure that systematizes hypothesis testing; when we get to step 5, we are ready to reject or not reject the hypothesis. However, hypothesis testing as used by statisticians does not provide proof that something is true, in the manner in which a mathematician "proves" a statement. It does provide a kind of "proof beyond a reasonable doubt," in the manner of the court system. Hence, there are specific rules of evidence, or procedures, that are followed. The steps are shown in the diagram at the bottom of this page. We will discuss in detail each of the steps.

Step 1: State the Null Hypothesis (H_0) and the Alternate Hypothesis (H_1)

The first step is to state the hypothesis being tested. It is called the **null hypothesis,** designated H_0, and read "*H sub zero.*" The capital letter *H* stands for hypothesis, and

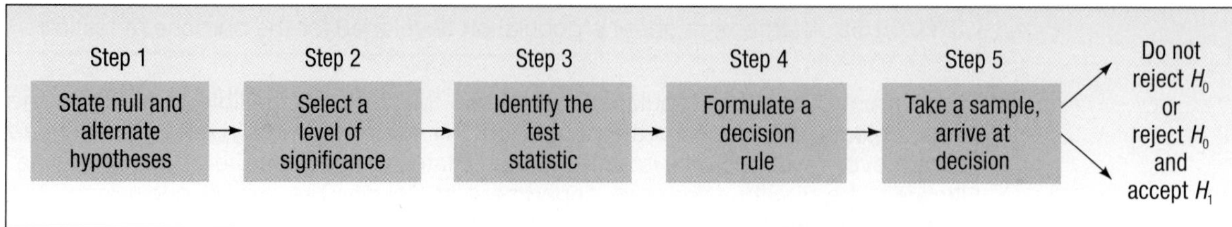

Five-step systematic procedure.

the subscript zero implies "no difference." There is usually a "not" or a "no" term in the null hypothesis, meaning that there is "no change." For example, the null hypothesis is that the mean number of miles driven on the steel-belted tire is not different from 60,000. The null hypothesis would be written H_0: $\mu = 60{,}000$. Generally speaking, the null hypothesis is developed for the purpose of testing. We either reject or fail to reject the null hypothesis. The null hypothesis is a statement that is not rejected unless our sample data provide convincing evidence that it is false.

We should emphasize that if the null hypothesis is not rejected on the basis of the sample data, we cannot say that the null hypothesis is true. To put it another way, failing to reject the null hypothesis does not prove that H_0 is true, it means we have *failed to disprove* H_0. To prove without any doubt the null hypothesis is true, the population parameter would have to be known. To actually determine it, we would have to test, survey, or count every item in the population. This is usually not feasible. The alternative is to take a sample from the population.

State the null hypothesis and the alternative hypothesis.

It should also be noted that we often begin the null hypothesis by stating, "There is no *significant* difference between . . . ," or "The mean impact strength of the glass is not *significantly* different from. . . . " When we select a sample from a population, the sample statistic is usually numerically different from the hypothesized population parameter. As an illustration, suppose the hypothesized impact strength of a glass plate is 70 psi, and the mean impact strength of a sample of 12 glass plates is 69.5 psi. We must make a decision about the difference of 0.5 psi. Is it a true difference, that is, a significant difference, or is the difference between the sample statistic (69.5) and the hypothesized population parameter (70.0) due to chance (sampling)? As noted, to answer this question we conduct a test of significance, commonly referred to as a test of hypothesis. To define what is meant by a null hypothesis:

NULL HYPOTHESIS A statement about the value of a population parameter.

The **alternate hypothesis** describes what you will conclude if you reject the null hypothesis. It is written H_1 and is read "*H sub one.*" It is often called the research hypothesis. The alternate hypothesis is accepted if the sample data provide us with enough statistical evidence that the null hypothesis is false.

ALTERNATE HYPOTHESIS A statement that is accepted if the sample data provide sufficient evidence that the null hypothesis is false.

The following example will help clarify what is meant by the null hypothesis and the alternate hypothesis. A recent article indicated the mean age of U.S. commercial aircraft is 15 years. To conduct a statistical test regarding this statement, the first step is to determine the null and the alternate hypotheses. The null hypothesis represents the current or reported condition. It is written H_0: $\mu = 15$. The alternate hypothesis is that the statement is not true, that is, H_1: $\mu \neq 15$. It is important to remember that no matter how the problem is stated, *the null hypothesis will always contain the equal sign.* The equal sign (=) will never appear in the alternate hypothesis. Why? Because the null hypothesis is the statement being tested, and we need a specific value to include in our calculations. We turn to the alternate hypothesis only if the data suggests the null hypothesis is untrue.

Step 2: Select a Level of Significance

Select a level of significance or risk.

After establishing the null hypothesis and alternate hypothesis, the next step is to select the level of significance.

LEVEL OF SIGNIFICANCE The probability of rejecting the null hypothesis when it is true.

The level of significance is designated α, the Greek letter alpha. It is also sometimes called the level of risk. This may be a more appropriate term because it is the risk you take of rejecting the null hypothesis when it is really true.

There is no one level of significance that is applied to all tests. A decision is made to use the .05 level (often stated as the 5 percent level), the .01 level, the .10 level, or any other level between 0 and 1. Traditionally, the .05 level is selected for consumer research projects, .01 for quality assurance, and .10 for political polling. You, the researcher, must decide on the level of significance *before* formulating a decision rule and collecting sample data.

To illustrate how it is possible to reject a true hypothesis, suppose a firm manufacturing personal computers uses a large number of printed circuit boards. Suppliers bid on the boards, and the one with the lowest bid is awarded a sizable contract. Suppose the contract specifies that the computer manufacturer's quality-assurance department will sample all incoming shipments of circuit boards. If more than 6 percent of the boards sampled are substandard, the shipment will be rejected. The null hypothesis is that the incoming shipment of boards contains 6 percent or less substandard boards. The alternate hypothesis is that more than 6 percent of the boards are defective.

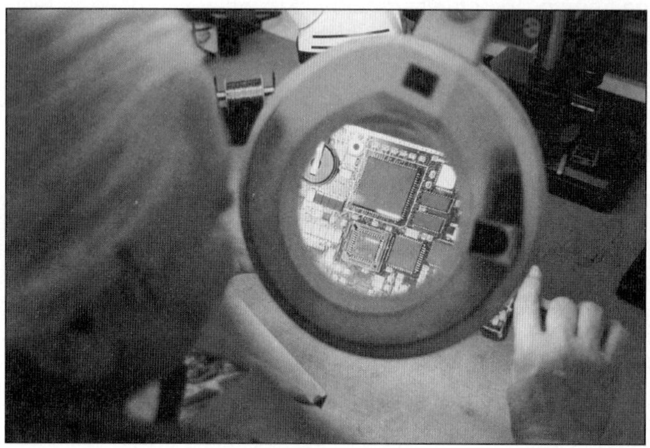

A sample of 50 circuit boards received July 21 from Allied Electronics revealed that 4 boards, or 8 percent, were substandard. The shipment was rejected because it exceeded the maximum of 6 percent substandard printed circuit boards. If the shipment was actually substandard, then the decision to return the boards to the supplier was correct. However, suppose the 4 substandard printed circuit boards selected in the sample of 50 were the only substandard boards in the shipment of 4,000 boards. Then only ⅒ of 1 percent were defective (4/4,000 = .001). In that case, less than 6 percent of the entire shipment was substandard and rejecting the shipment was an error. In terms of hypothesis testing, we rejected the null hypothesis that the shipment was not substandard when we should have accepted the null hypothesis. By rejecting a true null hypothesis, we committed a Type I error. The probability of committing a Type I error is α.

TYPE I ERROR Rejecting the null hypothesis, H_0, when it is true.

The probability of committing another type of error, called a Type II error, is designated by the Greek letter beta (β).

TYPE II ERROR Accepting the null hypothesis when it is false.

The firm manufacturing personal computers would commit a Type II error if, unknown to the manufacturer, an incoming shipment of printed circuit boards from Allied Electronics contained 15 percent substandard boards, yet the shipment was accepted. How could this happen? Suppose 2 of the 50 boards in the sample (4 percent) tested were substandard, and 48 of the 50 were good boards. According to the stated procedure, because the sample contained less than 6 percent substandard boards, the shipment was accepted. It could be that *by chance* the 48 good boards selected in the sample were the only acceptable ones in the entire shipment consisting of thousands of boards!

In retrospect, the researcher cannot study every item or individual in the population. Thus, there is a possibility of two types of error—a Type I error, wherein the null hypothesis is rejected when it should have been accepted, and a Type II error, wherein the null hypothesis is not rejected when it should have been rejected.

We often refer to the probability of these two possible errors as *alpha,* α, and *beta,* β. Alpha (α) is the probability of making a Type I error, and beta (β) is the probability of making a Type II error.

The following table summarizes the decisions the researcher could make and the possible consequences.

Null Hypotheses	Researcher Accepts H_0	Researcher Rejects H_0
H_0 is true	Correct decision	Type I error
H_0 is false	Type II error	Correct decision

Step 3: Select the Test Statistic

There are many test statistics. In this chapter we use both *z* and *t* as the test statistic. In other chapters we will use such test statistics as *F* and χ^2, called chi-square.

TEST STATISTIC A value, determined from sample information, used to determine whether to reject the null hypothesis.

In hypothesis testing for the mean (μ) when σ is known or the sample size is large, the test statistic *z* is computed by:

z DISTRIBUTION AS A TEST STATISTIC

$$z = \frac{\overline{X} - \mu}{\sigma/\sqrt{n}} \quad \textbf{[10–1]}$$

The *z* value is based on the sampling distribution of $\overline{X}$, which follows the normal distribution when the sample is reasonably large with a mean ($\mu_{\overline{X}}$) equal to μ, and a standard deviation $\sigma_{\overline{X}}$, which is equal to $\sigma/\sqrt{n}$. We can thus determine whether the difference between $\overline{X}$ and μ is statistically significant by finding the number of standard deviations $\overline{X}$ is from μ, using formula (10–1).

Step 4: Formulate the Decision Rule

The decision rule states the conditions when H_0 is rejected.

A decision rule is a statement of the specific conditions under which the null hypothesis is rejected and the conditions under which it is not rejected. The region or area of rejection defines the location of all those values that are so large or so small that the probability of their occurrence under a true null hypothesis is rather remote.

Chart 10–1 portrays the rejection region for a test of significance that will be conducted later in the chapter.

Statistics in Action

During World War II, allied military planners needed estimates of the number of German tanks. The information provided by traditional spying methods was not reliable, but statistical methods proved to be valuable. For example, espionage and reconnaissance led analysts to estimate that 1,550 tanks were produced during June of 1941. However, using the serial numbers of captured tanks and statistical analysis, military planners estimated 244. The actual number produced, as determined from German production records, was 271. The estimate using statistical analysis turned out to be much more accurate. A similar type of analysis was used to estimate the number of Iraqi tanks destroyed during Desert Storm.

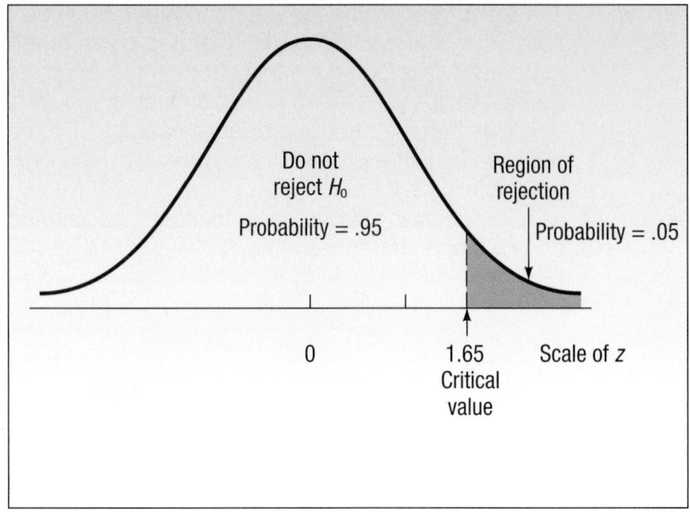

CHART 10–1 Sampling Distribution of the Statistic z, a Right-Tailed Test, .05 Level of Significance

Note in the chart that:

1. The area where the null hypothesis is not rejected is to the left of 1.65. We will explain how to get the 1.65 value shortly.
2. The area of rejection is to the right of 1.65.
3. A one-tailed test is being applied. (This will also be explained later.)
4. The .05 level of significance was chosen.
5. The sampling distribution of the statistic z is normally distributed.
6. The value 1.65 separates the regions where the null hypothesis is rejected and where it is not rejected.
7. The value 1.65 is the **critical value.**

CRITICAL VALUE The dividing point between the region where the null hypothesis is rejected and the region where it is not rejected.

Step 5: Make a Decision

The fifth and final step in hypothesis testing is computing the test statistic, comparing it to the critical value, and making a decision to reject or not to reject the null hypothesis. Referring to Chart 10–1, if, based on sample information, the test statistic z is computed to be 2.34, the null hypothesis is rejected at the .05 level of significance. The decision to reject H_0 was made because 2.34 lies in the region of rejection, that is, beyond 1.65. We would reject the null hypothesis, reasoning that it is highly improbable that a computed z value this large is due to sampling error (chance).

Had the computed test statistic been 1.65 or less, say 0.71, the null hypothesis would not be rejected. It would be reasoned that such a small computed value could be attributed to chance, that is, sampling error.

As noted, only one of two decisions is possible in hypothesis testing—either accept or reject the null hypothesis. Instead of "accepting" the null hypothesis, H_0, some researchers prefer to phrase the decision as: "Do not reject H_0," "We fail to reject H_0," or "The sample results do not allow us to reject H_0."

SUMMARY OF THE STEPS IN HYPOTHESIS TESTING

1. Establish the null hypothesis (H_0) and the alternate hypothesis (H_1).
2. Select the level of significance, that is α.
3. Select an appropriate test statistic.
4. Formulate a decision rule based on steps 1, 2, and 3 above.
5. Make a decision regarding the null hypothesis based on the sample information. Interpret the results of the test.

It should be reemphasized that there is always a possibility that the null hypothesis is rejected when it should not be rejected (a Type I error). Also, there is a definable chance that the null hypothesis is accepted when it should be rejected (a Type II error). Before actually conducting a test of hypothesis, we will differentiate between a one-tailed test of significance and a two-tailed test.

One-Tailed and Two-Tailed Tests of Significance

Refer to Chart 10–1 (previous page). It depicts a one-tailed test. The region of rejection is only in the right (upper) tail of the curve. To illustrate, suppose that the packaging department at General Foods Corporation is concerned that some boxes of Grape Nuts are significantly overweight. The cereal is packaged in 453-gram boxes, so the null hypothesis is H_0: $\mu \leq 453$. This is read, "the population mean (μ) is equal to or less than 453." The alternate hypothesis is, therefore, H_1: $\mu > 453$. This is read, "μ is greater than 453." Note that the inequality sign in the alternate hypothesis ($>$) points to the region of rejection in the upper tail. (See Chart 10–1.) Also note that the null hypothesis includes the equal sign. That is, H_0: $\mu \leq 453$. The equality condition *always* appears in H_0, *never* in H_1.

Chart 10–2 portrays a situation where the rejection region is in the left (lower) tail of the normal distribution. As an illustration, consider the problem of automobile manufacturers, large automobile leasing companies, and other organizations that purchase large quantities of tires. They want the tires to average, say, 60,000 miles of wear under normal usage. They will, therefore, reject a shipment of tires if tests reveal that the life of the tires is significantly below 60,000 miles on the average. They gladly

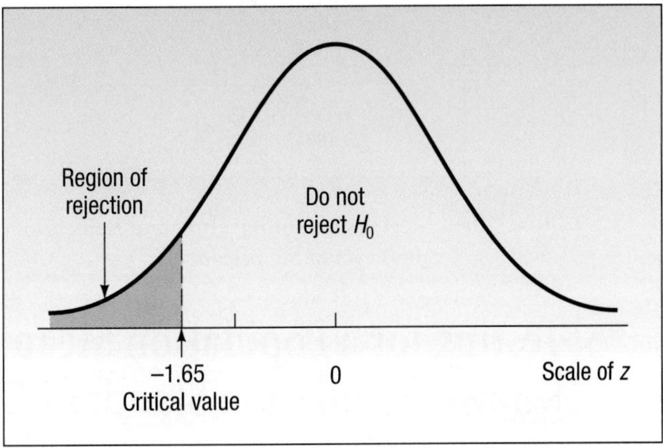

CHART 10–2 Sampling Distribution for the Statistic z, Left-Tailed Test, .05 Level of Significance

accept a shipment if the mean life is greater than 60,000 miles! They are not concerned with this possibility, however. They are concerned only if they have sample evidence to conclude that the tires will average less than 60,000 miles of useful life. Thus, the test is set up to satisfy the concern of the automobile manufacturers that *the mean life of the tires is less than 60,000 miles.* The null and alternate hypotheses in this case are written H_0: $\mu \geq 60{,}000$ and H_1: $\mu < 60{,}000$.

Test is one-tailed if H_1 states $\mu >$ or $\mu <$.

One way to determine the location of the rejection region is to look at the direction in which the inequality sign in the alternate hypothesis is pointing (either < or >). In this problem it is pointing to the left, and the rejection region is therefore in the left tail.

If H_1 states a direction, test is one-tailed.

In summary, a test is *one-tailed* when the alternate hypothesis, H_1, states a direction, such as:

H_0: The mean income of women financial planners is *less than or equal to* \$65,000 per year.
H_1: The mean income of women financial planners is *greater than* \$65,000 per year.

If no direction is specified in the alternate hypothesis, we use a *two-tailed* test. Changing the previous problem to illustrate, we can say:

H_0: The mean income of women financial planners is \$65,000 per year.
H_1: The mean income of women financial planners is *not equal to* \$65,000 per year.

If the null hypothesis is rejected and H_1 accepted in the two-tailed case, the mean income could be significantly greater than \$65,000 per year, or it could be significantly less than \$65,000 per year. To accommodate these two possibilities, the 5 percent area of rejection is divided equally into the two tails of the sampling distribution (2.5 percent each). Chart 10–3 shows the two areas and the critical values. Note that the total area in the normal distribution is 1.0000, found by .9500 + .0250 + .0250.

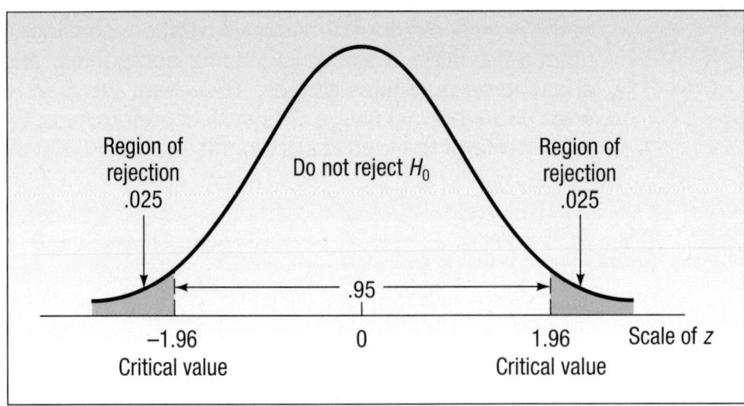

CHART 10–3 Regions of Nonrejection and Rejection for a Two-Tailed Test, .05 Level of Significance

Testing for a Population Mean with a Known Population Standard Deviation

A Two-Tailed Test

An example will show the details of the five-step hypothesis testing procedure. We also wish to use a two-tailed test. That is, we are *not* concerned whether the sample results are larger or smaller than the proposed population mean. Rather, we are interested in whether it is *different from* the proposed value for the population mean. We begin, as we did in the previous chapter, with a situation in which we have historical information about the population and in fact know its standard deviation.

EXAMPLE

The Jamestown Steel Company manufactures and assembles desks and other office equipment at several plants in western New York State. The weekly production of the Model A325 desk at the Fredonia Plant follows the normal distribution, with a mean of 200 and a standard deviation of 16. Recently, because of market expansion, new production methods have been introduced and new employees hired. The vice president of manufacturing would like to investigate whether there has been a change in the weekly production of the Model A325 desk. To put it another way, is the mean number of desks produced at the Fredonia Plant different from 200 at the .01 significance level?

SOLUTION

We use the statistical hypothesis testing procedure to investigate whether the production rate has changed from 200 per week.

Step 1: State the null hypothesis and the alternate hypothesis. The null hypothesis is "The population mean is 200." The alternate hypothesis is "The mean is different from 200" or "The mean is not 200." These two hypotheses are written:

$$H_0: \mu = 200$$
$$H_1: \mu \neq 200$$

This is a *two-tailed* test because the alternate hypothesis does not state a direction. In other words, it does not state whether the mean production is greater than 200 or less than 200. The vice president wants only to find out whether the production rate is different from 200.

Step 2: Select the level of significance. As noted, the .01 level of significance is used. This is α, the probability of committing a Type I error, and it is the probability of rejecting a true null hypothesis.

Step 3: Select the test statistic. In this case, because we know that the population follows the normal distribution and we know σ, the population standard deviation, we use z as the test statistic. It was discussed at length in Chapter 7. Transforming the production data to standard units (z values) permits their use not only in this problem but also in other hypothesis-testing problems. Formula (10–1) for z is repeated below with the various letters identified.

Formula for the test statistic

[10–1]

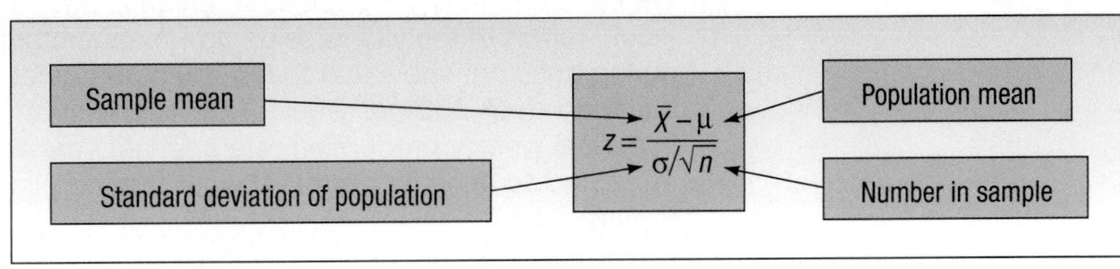

Step 4: Formulate the decision rule. The decision rule is formulated by finding the critical values of z from Appendix D. Since this is a two-tailed test, half of .01, or .005, is placed in each tail. The area where H_0 is not rejected, located between the two tails, is therefore .99. Appendix D is based on half of the area under the curve, or .5000. Then, .5000 − .0050 is .4950, so .4950 is the area between 0 and the critical value. Locate .4950 in the body of the table. The value nearest to .4950 is .4951. Then read the critical value in the row and column corresponding to .4951. It is 2.58. For your convenience, Appendix D, Areas under the Normal Curve, is repeated in the inside back cover.

All the facets of this problem are shown in the diagram in Chart 10–4.

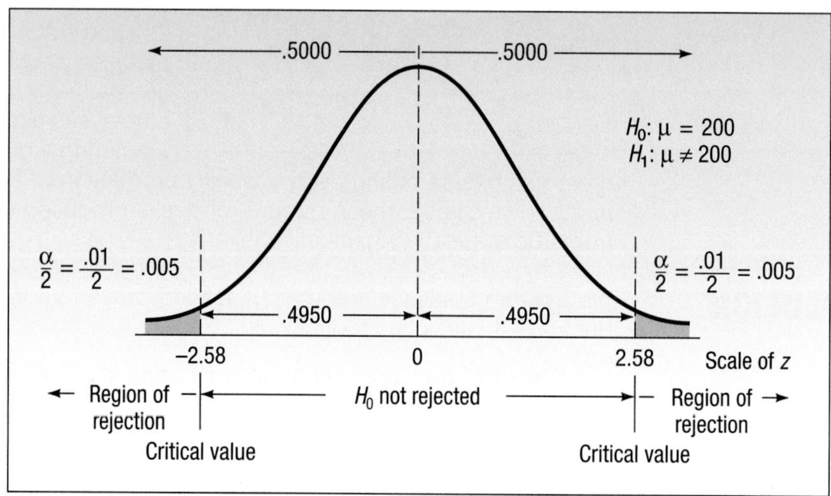

CHART 10–4 Decision Rule for the .01 Significance Level

The decision rule is, therefore: Reject the null hypothesis and accept the alternate hypothesis (which states that the population mean is not 200) if the computed value of z is not between −2.58 and +2.58. Do not reject the null hypothesis if z falls between −2.58 and +2.58.

Step 5: Make a decision and interpret the result. Take a sample from the population (weekly production), compute z, apply the decision rule, and arrive at a decision to reject H_0 or not to reject H_0. The mean number of desks produced last year (50 weeks, because the plant was shut down 2 weeks for vacation) is 203.5. The standard deviation of the population is 16 desks per week. Computing the z value from formula (10–1):

$$z = \frac{\bar{X} - \mu}{\sigma/\sqrt{n}} = \frac{203.5 - 200}{16/\sqrt{50}} = 1.55$$

Because 1.55 does not fall in the rejection region, H_0 is not rejected. We conclude that the population mean is *not* different from 200. So we would report to the vice president of manufacturing that the sample evidence does not show that the production rate at the Fredonia Plant has changed from 200 per week. The difference of 3.5 units between the historical weekly production rate and last year's rate can reasonably be attributed to sampling error. This information is summarized in the following chart.

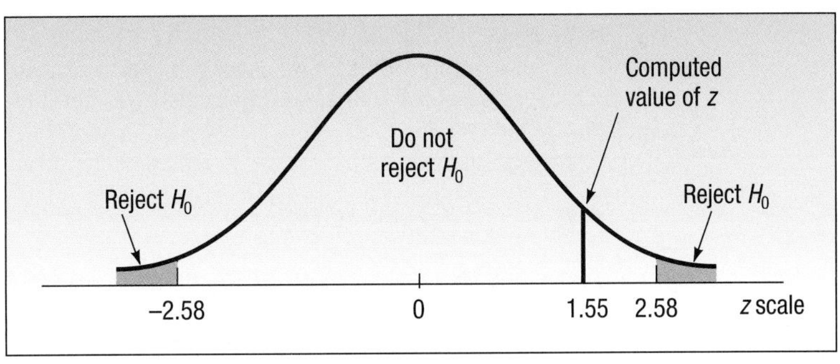

Did we prove that the assembly rate is still 200 per week? Not really. What we did, technically, was *fail to disprove the null hypothesis.* Failing to disprove the hypothesis that the population mean is 200 is not the same thing as proving it to be true. As we suggested in the chapter introduction, the conclusion is analogous to the American judicial system. To explain, suppose a person is accused of a crime but is acquitted by a jury. If a person is acquitted of a crime, the conclusion is that there was not enough evidence to prove the person guilty. The trial did not prove that the individual was innocent, only that there was not enough evidence to prove the defendant guilty. That is what we do in statistical hypothesis testing when we do not reject the null hypothesis. The correct interpretation is that we have failed to disprove the null hypothesis.

We selected the significance level, .01 in this case, before setting up the decision rule and sampling the population. This is the appropriate strategy. The significance level should be set by the investigator, but it should be determined *before* gathering the sample evidence and not changed based on the sample evidence.

How does the hypothesis testing procedure just described compare with that of confidence intervals discussed in the previous chapter? When we conducted the test of hypothesis regarding the production of desks we changed the units from desks per week to a z value. Then we compared the computed value of the test statistic (1.55) to that of the critical values (−2.58 and 2.58). Because the computed value was in the region where the null hypothesis was not rejected, we concluded that the population mean could be 200. To use the confidence interval approach, on the other hand, we would develop a confidence interval, based on formula (9–1). See page 249. The interval would be from 197.66 to 209.34, found by $203.5 \pm 2.58(16/\sqrt{50})$. Note that the proposed population value, 200, is within this interval. Hence, we would conclude that the population mean could reasonably be 200.

In general, H_0 is rejected if the confidence interval does not include the hypothesized value. If the confidence interval includes the hypothesized value, then H_0 is not rejected. So the "do not reject region" for a test of hypothesis is equivalent to the proposed population value occurring in the confidence interval. The primary difference between a confidence interval and the "do not reject" region for a hypothesis test is whether the interval is centered around the sample statistic, such as $\bar{X}$, as in the confidence interval, or around 0, as it is for a test of hypothesis.

SELF-REVIEW 10–1

The annual turnover rate of the 200-count bottle of Bayer Aspirin follows the normal distribution with a mean of 6.0 and a standard deviation of 0.50. (This indicates that the stock of Bayer turns over on the pharmacy shelves an average of 6 times per year.) It is suspected that the mean turnover has changed and is not 6.0. Use the .05 significance level.

(a) State the null hypothesis and the alternate hypothesis.
(b) What is the probability of a Type I error?
(c) Give the formula for the test statistic.

(d) State the decision rule.
(e) A random sample of 64 bottles of the 200-count size Bayer Aspirin showed a mean turnover rate of 5.84. Shall we reject the hypothesis that the population mean is 6.0? Interpret the result.

A One-Tailed Test

In the previous example, we emphasized that we were concerned only with reporting to the vice president whether there had been a change in the mean number of desks assembled at the Fredonia Plant. We were not concerned with whether the change was an increase or a decrease in the production.

To illustrate a one-tailed test, let's change the problem. Suppose the vice president wants to know whether there has been an *increase* in the number of units assembled. To put it another way, can we conclude, because of the improved production methods, that the mean number of desks assembled in the last 50 weeks was more than 200? Look at the difference in the way the problem is formulated. In the first case we wanted to know whether there was a *difference* in the mean number assembled, but now we want to know whether there has been an *increase.* Because we are investigating different questions, we will set our hypotheses differently. The biggest difference occurs in the alternate hypothesis. Before, we stated the alternate hypothesis as "different from"; now we want to state it as "greater than." In symbols:

A two-tailed test:	A one-tailed test:
H_0: $\mu = 200$	H_0: $\mu \leq 200$
H_1: $\mu \neq 200$	H_1: $\mu > 200$

The critical values for a one-tailed test are different from a two-tailed test at the same significance level. In the previous example, we split the significance level in half and put half in the lower tail and half in the upper tail. In a one-tailed test we put all the rejection region in one tail. See Chart 10–5.

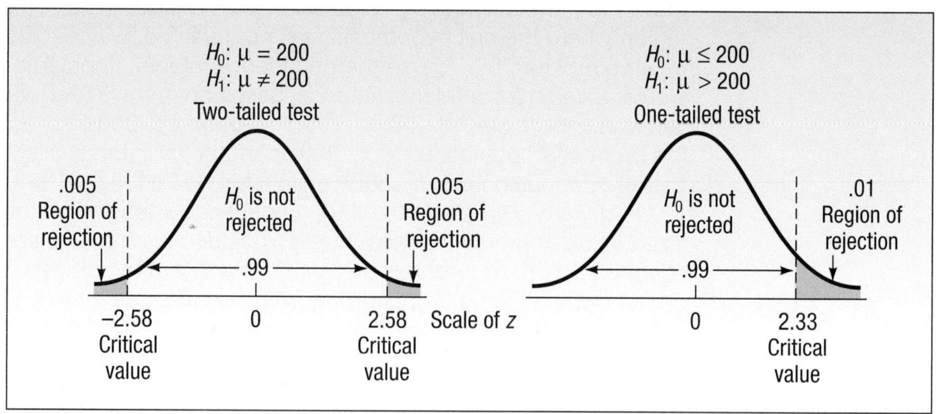

CHART 10-5 Rejection Regions for Two-Tailed and One-Tailed Tests, $\sigma = .01$

For the one-tailed test, the critical value is 2.33, found by: (1) subtracting .01 from .5000 and (2) finding the z value corresponding to .4900.

p-Value in Hypothesis Testing

In testing a hypothesis, we compare the test statistic to a critical value. A decision is made to either reject the null hypothesis or not to reject it. So, for example, if the critical value is 1.96 and the computed value of the test statistic is 2.19, the decision is to reject the null hypothesis.

In recent years, spurred by the availability of computer software, additional information is often reported on the strength of the rejection or acceptance. That is, how confident are we in rejecting the null hypothesis? This approach reports the probability (assuming that the null hypothesis is true) of getting a value of the test statistic at least as extreme as the value actually obtained. This process compares the probability, called the ***p*-value,** with the significance level. If the *p*-value is smaller than the significance level, H_0 is rejected. If it is larger than the significance level, H_0 is not rejected.

Statistics in Action

There is a difference between *statistically significant* and *practically significant.* To explain, suppose we develop a new diet pill and test it on 100,000 people. We conclude that the typical person taking the pill for two years lost one pound. Do you think many people would be interested in taking the pill to lose one pound? The results of using the new pill were statistically significant but not practically significant.

> ***p*-VALUE** The probability of observing a sample value as extreme as, or more extreme than, the value observed, given that the null hypothesis is true.

Determining the *p*-value not only results in a decision regarding H_0, but it gives us additional insight into the strength of the decision. A very small *p*-value, such as .0001, indicates that there is little likelihood the H_0 is true. On the other hand, a *p*-value of .2033 means that H_0 is not rejected, and there is little likelihood that it is false.

How do we compute the *p*-value? To illustrate we will use the example in which we tested the null hypothesis that the mean number of desks produced per week at Fredonia was 200. We did not reject the null hypothesis, because the *z* value of 1.55 fell in the region between −2.58 and 2.58. We agreed not to reject the null hypothesis if the computed value of *z* fell in this region. The probability of finding a *z* value of 1.55 or more is .0606, found by .5000 − .4394. To put it another way, the probability of obtaining an $\bar{X}$ greater than 203.5 if $\mu = 200$ is .0606. To compute the *p*-value, we need to be concerned with the region less than −1.55 as well as the values greater than 1.55 (because the rejection region is in both tails). The two-tailed *p*-value is .1212, found by 2(.0606). The *p*-value of .1212 is greater than the significance level of .01 decided upon initially, so H_0 is not rejected. The details are shown in the following graph. In general, the area is doubled in a two-sided test. Then the *p*-value can easily be compared with the significance level. The same decision rule is used as in the one-sided test.

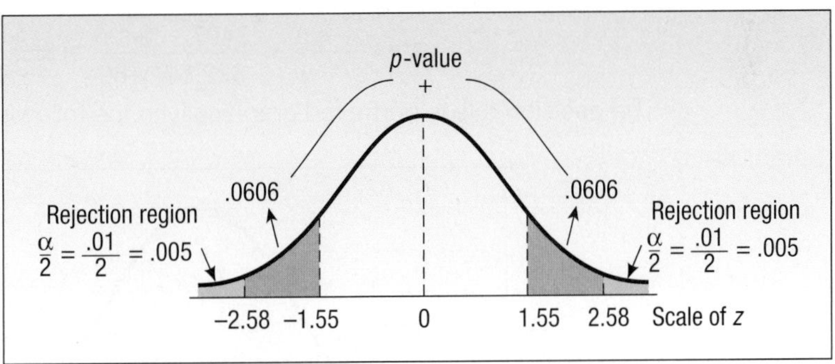

A *p*-value is a way to express the likelihood that H_0 is false. But how do we interpret a *p*-value? We have already said that if the *p*-value is less than the significance level, then we reject H_0; if it is greater than the significance level, then we do not reject H_0. Also, if the *p*-value is very large, then it is likely that H_0 is true. If the *p*-value is small, then it is likely that H_0 is not true. The following box will help to interpret *p*-values.

> **INTERPRETING THE WEIGHT OF EVIDENCE AGAINST H_0** If the *p*-value is less than
> (a) .10, we have *some evidence* that H_0 is not true.
> (b) .05, we have *strong evidence* that H_0 is not true.
> (c) .01, we have *very strong evidence* that H_0 is not true.
> (d) .001, we have *extremely strong evidence* that H_0 is not true.

Testing for a Population Mean: Large Sample, Population Standard Deviation Unknown

In the preceding example, we knew that the population followed the normal distribution and σ, the population standard deviation. In most cases, however, we may not know for certain that the population follows the normal distribution or the population standard deviation. Thus, σ must be based on prior studies or estimated by the sample standard deviation, *s*. The population standard deviation in the following example is not known, so the sample standard deviation is used to estimate σ. As long as the sample size, *n*, is at least 30, *s* can be substituted for σ, as illustrated in the following formula:

z STATISTIC, σ UNKNOWN $$z = \frac{\bar{X} - \mu}{s/\sqrt{n}}$$ **[10–2]**

EXAMPLE

The Thompson's Discount Appliance Store issues its own credit card. The credit manager wants to find whether the mean monthly unpaid balance is more than \$400. The level of significance is set at .05. A random check of 60 unpaid balances revealed the sample mean is \$407 and the standard deviation of the sample is \$22.50. Should the credit manager conclude the population mean is greater than \$400, or is it reasonable that the difference of \$7 (\$407 − \$400 = \$7) is due to chance?

SOLUTION

The null and alternate hypotheses are:

H_0: $\mu \leq \$400$
H_1: $\mu > \$400$

Because the alternate hypothesis states a direction, a one-tailed test is applied. The critical value of *z* is 1.65. The computed value of *z* is 2.41, found by using formula (10–2):

$$z = \frac{\bar{X} - \mu}{s/\sqrt{n}} = \frac{\$407 - \$400}{\$22.50/\sqrt{60}} = \frac{\$7}{2.9047} = 2.41$$

The decision rule is portrayed graphically in the following chart.

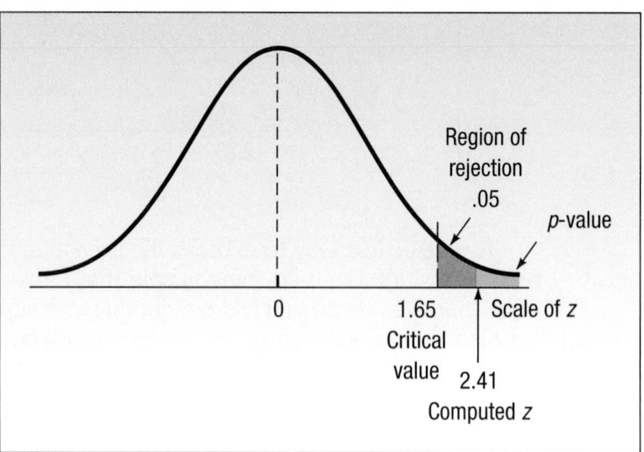

Because the computed value of the test statistic (2.41) is larger than the critical value (1.65), the null hypothesis is rejected. The credit manager can conclude the mean unpaid balance is greater than \$400.

The p-value provides additional insight into the decision. Recall the p-value is the probability of finding a test statistic as large as or larger than that obtained, when the null hypothesis is true. So we find the probability of a z value greater than 2.41. From Appendix D the probability of a z value between 0 and 2.41 is .4920. We want to determine the likelihood of a value *greater than* 2.41, so .5000 − .4920 = .0080. We conclude that the likelihood of finding a z value of 2.41 or larger when the null hypothesis is true is 0.80 percent. It is unlikely, therefore, that the null hypothesis is true.

SELF-REVIEW 10-2 According to recent information from the American Automobile Association, the mean age of passenger cars in the United States is 8.4 years. A sample of 40 cars in the student lots at the University of Tennessee showed the mean age to be 9.2 years. The standard deviation of this sample was 2.8 years. At the .01 significance level can we conclude the mean age is more than 8.4 years for the cars of Tennessee students?

(a) State the null hypothesis and the alternate hypothesis.
(b) Explain why z is the test statistic.
(c) What is the critical value of the test statistic?
(d) Compute the value of the test statistic.
(e) What is your decision regarding the null hypothesis?
(f) Interpret your decision from part e in a single sentence.
(g) What is the p-value?

Exercises

For Exercises 1–4 answer the questions: (a) Is this a one- or two-tailed test? (b) What is the decision rule? (c) What is the value of the test statistic? (d) What is your decision regarding H_0? (e) What is the p-value? Interpret it.

1. The following information is available.

H_0: $\mu = 50$
H_1: $\mu \neq 50$

The sample mean is 49, and the sample size is 36. The population follows the normal distribution and the standard deviation is 5. Use the .05 significance level.

2. The following information is available.

H_0: $\mu \leq 10$
H_1: $\mu > 10$

The sample mean is 12 for a sample of 36. The population follows the normal distribution and the standard deviation is 3. Use the .02 significance level.

3. A sample of 36 observations is selected from a normal population. The sample mean is 21, and the sample standard deviation is 5. Conduct the following test of hypothesis using the .05 significance level.

H_0: $\mu \leq 20$
H_1: $\mu > 20$

4. A sample of 64 observations is selected from a normal population. The sample mean is 215, and the sample standard deviation is 15. Conduct the following test of hypothesis using the .03 significance level.

H_0: $\mu \geq 220$
H_1: $\mu < 220$

For Exercises 5–8: (a) State the null hypothesis and the alternate hypothesis. (b) State the decision rule. (c) Compute the value of the test statistic. (d) What is your decision regarding H_0? (e) What is the p-value? Interpret it.

5. The manufacturer of the X-15 steel-belted radial truck tire claims that the mean mileage the tire can be driven before the tread wears out is 60,000 miles. The Crosset Truck Company bought 48 tires and found that the mean mileage for their trucks is 59,500 miles with a standard deviation of 5,000 miles. Is Crosset's experience different from that claimed by the manufacturer at the .05 significance level?

6. The MacBurger restaurant chain claims that the waiting time of customers for service is normally distributed, with a mean of 3 minutes and a standard deviation of 1 minute. The quality-assurance department found in a sample of 50 customers at the Warren Road MacBurger that the mean waiting time was 2.75 minutes. At the .05 significance level, can we conclude that the mean waiting time is less than 3 minutes?
7. A recent national survey found that high school students watched an average (mean) of 6.8 DVDs per month. A random sample of 36 college students revealed that the mean number of DVDs watched last month was 6.2, with a standard deviation of 0.5. At the .05 significance level, can we conclude that college students watch fewer DVDs a month than high school students?
8. At the time she was hired as a server at the Grumney Family Restaurant, Beth Brigden was told, "You can average more than $80 a day in tips." Over the first 35 days she was employed at the restaurant, the mean daily amount of her tips was $84.85, with a standard deviation of $11.38. At the .01 significance level, can Ms. Brigden conclude that she is earning an average of more than $80 in tips?

Tests Concerning Proportions

In the previous chapter we discussed confidence intervals for proportions. We can also conduct a test of hypothesis for a proportion. Recall that a proportion is the ratio of the number of successes to the number of observations. We let X refer to the number of successes and n the number of observations, so the proportion of successes in a fixed number of trials is X/n. Thus, the formula for computing a sample proportion, p, is $p = X/n$. Consider the following potential hypothesis-testing situations.

- Historically, General Motors reports that 70 percent of leased vehicles are returned with less than 36,000 miles. A recent sample of 200 vehicles returned at the end of their lease showed 158 had less than 36,000 miles. Has the proportion increased?
- The American Association of Retired Persons (AARP) reports that 60 percent of retired persons under the age of 65 would return to work on a full-time basis if a suitable job were available. A sample of 500 retirees under 65 revealed 315 would return to work. Can we conclude that more than 60 percent would return to work?
- Able Moving and Storage, Inc., advises its clients for long distance residential moves that their household goods will be delivered in 3 to 5 days from the time they are picked up. Able's records show that they are successful 90 percent of the time with this claim. A recent audit revealed they were successful 190 times out of 200. Can they conclude that their success rate has increased?

Some assumptions must be made and conditions met before testing a population proportion. To test a hypothesis about a population proportion, a random sample is chosen from the population. It is assumed that the binomial assumptions discussed in Chapter 6 are met: (1) the sample data collected are the result of counts; (2) the outcome of an experiment is classified into one of two mutually exclusive categories—a "success" or a "failure"; (3) the probability of a success is the same for each trial; and (4) the trials are independent, meaning the outcome of one trial does not affect the outcome of any other trial. The test we will conduct shortly is appropriate when both $n\pi$ and $n(1 - \pi)$ are at least 5. n is the sample size, and π is the population proportion. It takes advantage of the fact that a binomial distribution can be approximated by the normal distribution.

$n\pi$ and $n(1 - \pi)$ must be at least 5.

EXAMPLE

Prior elections in Indiana indicate it is necessary for a candidate for governor to receive at least 80 percent of the vote in the northern section of the state to be elected. The incumbent governor is interested in assessing his chances of returning to office and plans to conduct a survey of 2,000 registered voters in the northern section of Indiana.

Using the hypothesis-testing procedure, assess the governor's chances of reelection.

SOLUTION

The following test of hypothesis can be conducted because both $n\pi$ and $n(1 - \pi)$ exceed 5. In this case, $n = 2{,}000$ and $\pi = .80$ (π is the proportion of the vote in the northern part of Indiana, or 80 percent, needed to be elected). Thus, $n\pi = 2{,}000(.80) = 1{,}600$ and $n(1 - \pi) = 2{,}000(1 - .80) = 400$. Both 1,600 and 400 are greater than 5.

Step 1: State the null hypothesis and the alternate hypothesis. The null hypothesis, H_0, is that the population proportion π is .80 or larger. The alternate hypothesis, H_1, is that the proportion is less than .80. From a practical standpoint, the incumbent governor is concerned only when the proportion is less than .80. If it is equal to or greater than .80, he will have no problem; that is, the sample data would indicate he will probably be reelected. These hypotheses are written symbolically as:

$$H_0: \pi \geq .80$$
$$H_1: \pi < .80$$

H_1 states a direction. Thus, as noted previously, the test is one-tailed with the inequality sign pointing to the tail of the distribution containing the region of rejection.

Step 2: Select the level of significance. The level of significance is .05. This is the likelihood that a true hypothesis will be rejected.

Step 3: Select the test statistic. z is the appropriate statistic, found by:

TEST OF HYPOTHESIS, ONE PROPORTION $$z = \frac{p - \pi}{\sigma_p} \quad \textbf{[10–3]}$$

where:

π is the population proportion.
p is the sample proportion.
n is the sample size.
σ_p is the standard error of the proportion. It is computed by $\sqrt{\pi(1 - \pi)/n}$, so the formula for z becomes:

TEST OF HYPOTHESIS, ONE PROPORTION $$z = \frac{p - \pi}{\sqrt{\dfrac{\pi(1 - \pi)}{n}}} \quad \textbf{[10–4]}$$

Finding the critical value

Step 4: Formulate the decision rule. The critical value or values of z form the dividing point or points between the regions where H_0 is rejected and where it is not rejected. Since the alternate hypothesis states a direction, this is a one-tailed test. The sign of the inequality points to the left, so we use only the left side of the distribution. (See Chart 10–6.) The significance level was given as .05 in **Step 2.** This probability is in the left tail and determines the region of rejection. The area between zero and the critical value is .4500, found by $.5000 - .0500$. Referring to Appendix D and searching for .4500, we find the critical value of z is -1.65. The decision rule is, therefore: Reject the null hypothesis and accept the alternate hypothesis if the computed value of z falls to the left of -1.65; otherwise do not reject H_0.

Select a sample and make a decision regarding H_0.

Step 5: Make a decision and interpret the result. Select a sample and make a decision about H_0. A sample survey of 2,000 potential voters in the northern part of Indiana revealed that 1,550 planned to vote for the

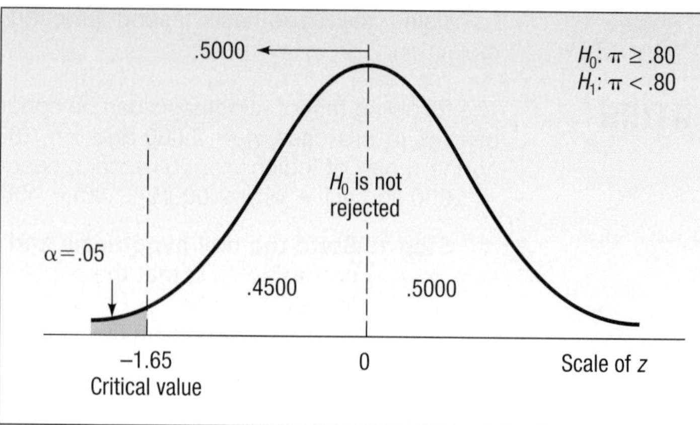

CHART 10–6 Rejection Region for the .05 Level of Significance, One-Tailed Test

incumbent governor. Is the sample proportion of .775 (found by 1,550/2,000) close enough to .80 to conclude that the difference is due to sampling error? In this case:

p is .775, the proportion in the sample who plan to vote for the governor.
n is 2,000, the number of voters surveyed.
π is .80, the hypothesized population proportion.
z is a normally distributed test statistic when the hypothesis is true and the other assumptions are true.

Using formula (10–4) and computing *z* gives

$$z = \frac{p - \pi}{\sqrt{\frac{\pi(1-\pi)}{n}}} = \frac{\frac{1{,}550}{2{,}000} - .80}{\sqrt{\frac{.80(1-.80)}{2{,}000}}} = \frac{.775 - .80}{\sqrt{.00008}} = -2.80$$

The computed value of *z* (−2.80) is in the rejection region, so the null hypothesis is rejected at the .05 level. The difference of 2.5 percentage points between the sample percent (77.5 percent) and the hypothesized population percent in the northern part of the state necessary to carry the state (80 percent) is statistically significant. It is likely not due to sampling error. To put it another way, the evidence at this point does not support the claim that the incumbent governor will return to the governor's mansion for another four years.

The *p*-value is the probability of finding a *z* value less than −2.80. From Appendix D, the probability of a *z* value between zero and −2.80 is .4974. So the *p*-value is .0026, found by .5000 − .4974. The governor cannot be confident of reelection because the *p*-value is less than the significance level.

SELF-REVIEW 10–3 A recent insurance industry report indicated that 40 percent of those persons involved in minor traffic accidents this year have been involved in at least one other traffic accident in the last five years. An advisory group decided to investigate this claim, believing it was too large. A sample of 200 traffic accidents this year showed 74 persons were also involved in another accident within the last five years. Use the .01 significance level.

(a) Can we use *z* as the test statistic? Tell why or why not.

(b) State the null hypothesis and the alternate hypothesis.
(c) Show the decision rule graphically.
(d) Compute the value of z and state your decision regarding the null hypothesis.
(e) Determine and interpret the p-value.

Exercises

9. The following hypotheses are given.

H_0: $\pi \leq .70$
H_1: $\pi > .70$

A sample of 100 observations revealed that $p = .75$. At the .05 significance level, can the null hypothesis be rejected?
a. State the decision rule.
b. Compute the value of the test statistic.
c. What is your decision regarding the null hypothesis?

10. The following hypotheses are given.

H_0: $\pi = .40$
H_1: $\pi \neq .40$

A sample of 120 observations revealed that $p = .30$. At the .05 significance level, can the null hypothesis be rejected?
a. State the decision rule.
b. Compute the value of the test statistic.
c. What is your decision regarding the null hypothesis?

Note: It is recommended that you use the five-step hypothesis-testing procedure in solving the following problems.

11. The National Safety Council reported that 52 percent of American turnpike drivers are men. A sample of 300 cars traveling southbound on the New Jersey Turnpike yesterday revealed that 170 were driven by men. At the .01 significance level, can we conclude that a larger proportion of men were driving on the New Jersey Turnpike than the national statistics indicate?

12. A recent article in *USA Today* reported that a job awaits only one in three new college graduates. The major reasons given were an overabundance of college graduates and a weak economy. A survey of 200 recent graduates from your school revealed that 80 students had jobs. At the .02 significance level, can we conclude that a larger proportion of students at your school have jobs?

13. Chicken Delight claims that 90 percent of its orders are delivered within 10 minutes of the time the order is placed. A sample of 100 orders revealed that 82 were delivered within the promised time. At the .10 significance level, can we conclude that less than 90 percent of the orders are delivered in less than 10 minutes?

14. Research at the University of Toledo indicates that 50 percent of the students change their major area of study after their first year in a program. A random sample of 100 students in the College of Business revealed that 48 had changed their major area of study after their first year of the program. Has there been a significant decrease in the proportion of students who change their major after the first year in this program? Test at the .05 level of significance.

Testing for a Population Mean: Small Sample, Population Standard Deviation Unknown

We are able to use the standard normal distribution, that is z, under two conditions:

1. The population is known to follow a normal distribution and the population standard deviation is known, or
2. The shape of the population is not known, but the number of observations in the sample is at least 30.

What do we do when the sample is less than 30 and the population standard deviation is not known? We encountered this same situation when constructing confidence intervals in the previous chapter. See pages 254–259 in Chapter 9. We summarized this problem in Chart 9–3 on page 256. Under these conditions the correct statistical procedure is to replace the standard normal distribution with the *t* distribution. To review, the major characteristics of the *t* distribution are:

1. It is a continuous distribution.
2. It is bell-shaped and symmetrical.
3. There is a family of *t* distributions. Each time the degrees of freedom change, a new distribution is created.
4. As the number of degrees of freedom increases, the shape of the *t* distribution approaches that of the standard normal distribution.
5. The *t* distribution is flatter, or more spread out, than the standard normal distribution.

To conduct a test of hypothesis using the *t* distribution, we adjust formula (10–2) as follows.

SMALL SAMPLE TEST FOR MEAN

$$t = \frac{\bar{X} - \mu}{s/\sqrt{n}} \qquad \textbf{[10–5]}$$

with $n - 1$ degrees of freedom, where:

$\bar{X}$ is the mean of the sample.
μ is the hypothesized population mean.
s is the standard deviation of the sample.
n is the number of observations in the sample.

The following example shows the details

EXAMPLE

The McFarland Insurance Company Claims Department reports the mean cost to process a claim is $60. An industry comparison showed this amount to be larger than most other insurance companies, so they instituted cost-cutting measures. To evaluate the effect of the cost-cutting measures, the Supervisor of the Claims Department selected a random sample of 26 claims processed last month and determined the cost to process these selected claims. The sample information is reported below.

$45	$49	$62	$40	$43	$61
48	53	67	63	78	64
48	54	51	56	63	69
58	51	58	59	56	57
38	76				

At the .01 significance level is it reasonable to conclude that mean cost to process a claim is now less than $60?

SOLUTION

We will use the five-step hypothesis testing procedure.

Step 1: State the null hypothesis and the alternate hypothesis. The null hypothesis is that the population mean is at least $60. The alternate hypothesis is that the population mean is less than $60. We can express the null and alternate hypotheses as follows:

H_0: $\mu \geq \$60$
H_1: $\mu < \$60$

The test is *one*-tailed because we want to determine whether there has been a *reduction* in the cost. The inequality in the alternate hypothesis points to the region of rejection in the left tail of the distribution.

Step 2: Select the level of significance. We decided on the .01 significance level.

Step 3: Select the test statistic. The test statistic in this situation is the t distribution. Why? First it is reasonable to conclude that the distribution of the cost per claim follows the normal distribution. We can confirm this from the histogram on the right-hand side of the following MINITAB output. Observe the normal distribution superimposed on the frequency distribution.

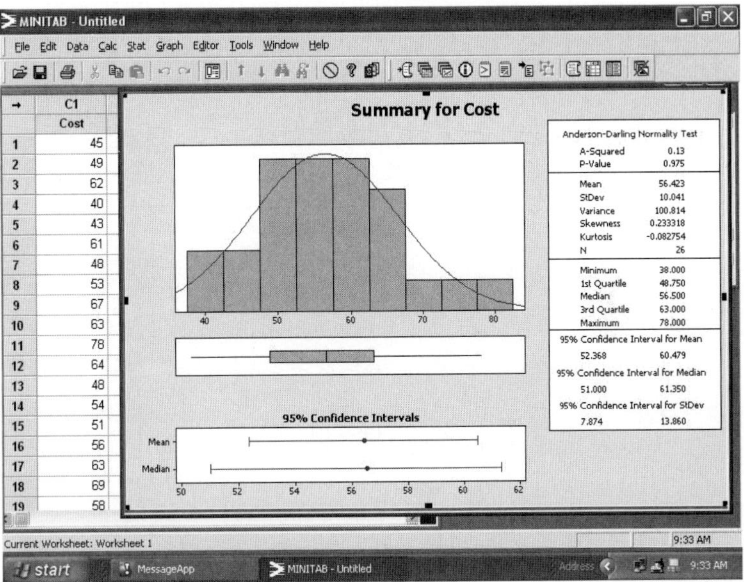

We do not know the standard deviation of the population. So we substitute the sample standard deviation. When the sample is large we can make the substitution and still use the standard normal distribution. We usually define large as 30 or more observations. In this case there are only 26 observations. Consequently we cannot use the standard normal distribution. Instead, we use t. The value of the test statistic is computed by formula (10–5):

$$t = \frac{\bar{X} - \mu}{s/\sqrt{n}}$$

Step 4: Formulate the decision rule. The critical values of t are given in Appendix F, a portion of which is shown in Table 10–1. Appendix F is also repeated in the back inside cover of the text. The far left column of the table is labeled "df" for degrees of freedom. The number of degrees of freedom is the total number of observations in the sample minus the number of samples, written $n - 1$. In this case the number of observations in the sample is 26, so there are $26 - 1 = 25$ degrees of freedom. To find the critical value, first locate the row with the appropriate degrees of freedom. This row is shaded in Table 10–1. Next, determine whether the test is one-tailed or two-tailed. In this case, we have a one-tailed test, so find the portion of the table that is labeled "one-tailed." Locate the column with the selected significance level. In this example, the significance level is .01. Move down the column labeled "0.010" until it intersects the row with 25 degrees of freedom. The value is 2.485. Because

TABLE 10–1 A Portion of the *t* Distribution Table

	Confidence Intervals					
	80%	90%	95%	98%	99%	99.9%
	Level of Significance for One-Tailed Test, α					
df	0.100	0.050	0.025	0.010	0.005	0.0005
	Level of Significance for Two-Tailed Test, α					
	0.20	0.10	0.05	0.02	0.01	0.001
⋮	⋮	⋮	⋮	⋮	⋮	⋮
21	1.323	1.721	2.080	2.518	2.831	3.819
22	1.321	1.717	2.074	2.508	2.819	3.792
23	1.319	1.714	2.069	2.500	2.807	3.768
24	1.318	1.711	2.064	2.492	2.797	3.745
25	1.316	1.708	2.060	2.485	2.787	3.725
26	1.315	1.706	2.056	2.479	2.779	3.707
27	1.314	1.703	2.052	2.473	2.771	3.690
28	1.313	1.701	2.048	2.467	2.763	3.674
29	1.311	1.699	2.045	2.462	2.756	3.659
30	1.310	1.697	2.042	2.457	2.750	3.646

this is a one-sided test and the rejection region is in the left tail, the critical value is negative. The decision rule is to reject H_0 if the value of t is less than −2.485.

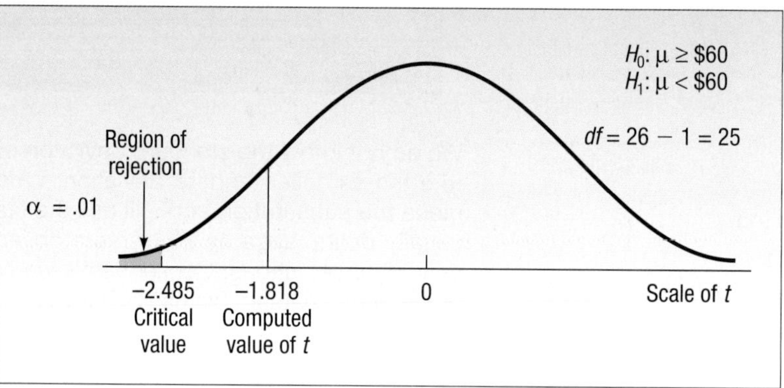

CHART 10-7 Rejection Region, *t* Distribution, .01 Significance Level

Step 5: Make a decision and interpret the result. From the MINITAB output on page 297, next to the histogram, the mean cost per claim for the sample of 26 observations is \$56.42. The standard deviation of this sample is \$10.04. We insert these values in formula (10–5) and compute the value of *t*:

$$t = \frac{\overline{X} - \mu}{s/\sqrt{n}} = \frac{\$56.42 - \$60}{\$10.04/\sqrt{26}} = -1.818$$

Because −1.818 lies in the region to the right of the critical value of −2.485, the null hypothesis is not rejected at the .01 significance level. We have not demonstrated that the cost-cutting measures reduced the mean cost per claim to less than \$60. To put it another way, the difference of \$3.58 (\$56.42 − \$60) between the sample mean and the population mean could be due to sampling error. The computed value of t is shown in Chart 10–7. It is in the region where the null hypothesis is *not* rejected.

In the previous example the mean and the standard deviation were calculated by MINITAB. The following example requires this information to be computed from the sample data.

EXAMPLE

The mean length of a small counterbalance bar is 43 millimeters. The production supervisor is concerned that the adjustments of the machine producing the bars have changed. He asks the Engineering Department to investigate. Engineering selects a random sample of 12 bars and measures each. The results are reported below in millimeters.

42	39	42	45	43	40	39	41	40	42	43	42

Is it reasonable to conclude that there has been a change in the mean length of the bars? Use the .02 significance level.

SOLUTION

We begin by stating the null hypothesis and the alternate hypothesis.

H_0: $\mu = 43$
H_1: $\mu \neq 43$

The alternate hypothesis does not state a direction, so this is a two-tailed test. There are 11 degrees of freedom, found by $n - 1 = 12 - 1 = 11$. The t value is 2.718, found by referring to Appendix F for a two-tailed test, using the .02 significance level, with 11 degrees of freedom. The decision rule is: Reject the null hypothesis if the computed test statistic, t, is to the left of −2.718 or to the right of 2.718. This information is summarized in Chart 10–8.

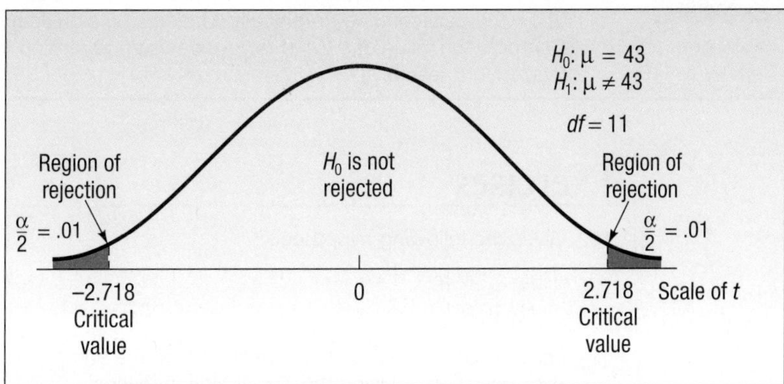

CHART 10–8 Regions of Rejection, Two-Tailed Test, Student's t Distribution, $\alpha = .02$

We calculate the standard deviation of the sample using formula (3–11). The mean, $\bar{X}$, is 41.5 millimeters, and the standard deviation, s, is 1.784 millimeters. The details are shown in Table 10–2.

TABLE 10–2 Calculations of the Sample Standard Deviation

X (mm)	$X - \bar{X}$	$(X - \bar{X})^2$
42	0.5	0.25
39	−2.5	6.25
42	0.5	0.25
45	3.5	12.25
43	1.5	2.25
40	−1.5	2.25
39	−2.5	6.25
41	−0.5	0.25
40	−1.5	2.25
42	0.5	0.25
43	1.5	2.25
42	0.5	0.25
498	0	35.00

$$\bar{X} = \frac{498}{12} = 41.5 \text{ mm}$$

$$s = \sqrt{\frac{\Sigma(X - \bar{X})^2}{n - 1}} = \sqrt{\frac{35}{12 - 1}} = 1.784$$

Now we are ready to compute the value of *t*, using formula (10–5).

$$t = \frac{\bar{X} - \mu}{s/\sqrt{n}} = \frac{41.5 - 43.0}{1.784/\sqrt{12}} = -2.913$$

The null hypothesis that the population mean is 43 millimeters is rejected because the computed *t* of −2.913 lies in the area to the left of −2.718. We accept the alternate hypothesis and conclude that the population mean is not 43 millimeters. The machine is out of control and needs adjustment.

SELF-REVIEW 10–4 The mean life of a battery used in a digital clock is 305 days. The lives of the batteries follow the normal distribution. The battery was recently modified with the objective of making it last longer. A sample of 20 of the modified batteries had a mean life of 311 days with a standard deviation of 12 days. Did the modification increase the mean life of the battery?

(a) State the null hypothesis and the alternate hypothesis.
(b) Show the decision rule graphically. Use the .05 significance level.
(c) Compute the value of *t*. What is your decision regarding the null hypothesis? Briefly summarize your results.

Exercises

15. Given the following hypothesis:

H_0: $\mu \leq 10$
H_1: $\mu > 10$

For a random sample of 10 observations, the sample mean was 12 and the sample standard deviation 3. Using the .05 significance level:

a. State the decision rule.
b. Compute the value of the test statistic.
c. What is your decision regarding the null hypothesis?

16. Given the following hypothesis:

H_0: $\mu = 400$
H_1: $\mu \neq 400$

For a random sample of 12 observations, the sample mean was 407 and the sample standard deviation 6. Using the .01 significance level:

a. State the decision rule.
b. Compute the value of the test statistic.
c. What is your decision regarding the null hypothesis?

17. The Rocky Mountain district sales manager of Rath Publishing, Inc., a college textbook publishing company, claims that the sales representatives make an average of 40 sales calls per week on professors. Several reps say that this estimate is too low. To investigate, a random sample of 28 sales representatives reveals that the mean number of calls made last week was 42. The standard deviation of the sample is 2.1 calls. Using the .05 significance level, can we conclude that the mean number of calls per salesperson per week is more than 40?

18. The management of White Industries is considering a new method of assembling its golf cart. The present method requires 42.3 minutes, on the average, to assemble a cart. The mean assembly time for a random sample of 24 carts, using the new method, was 40.6 minutes, and the standard deviation of the sample was 2.7 minutes. Using the .10 level of significance, can we conclude that the assembly time using the new method is faster?

19. A spark plug manufacturer claimed that its plugs have a mean life in excess of 22,100 miles. Assume the life of the spark plugs follows the normal distribution. A fleet owner purchased a large number of sets. A sample of 18 sets revealed that the mean life was 23,400 miles and the standard deviation was 1,500 miles. Is there enough evidence to substantiate the manufacturer's claim at the .05 significance level?

20. Most air travelers now use e-tickets. Electronic ticketing allows passengers to not worry about a paper ticket, and it costs the airline companies less to handle than a paper ticketing. However, in recent times the airlines have received complaints from passengers regarding their e-tickets, particularly when connecting flights and a change of airlines were involved. To investigate the problem an independent watchdog agency contacted a random sample of 20 airports and collected information on the number of complaints the airport had with e-tickets for the month of March. The information is reported below.

14	14	16	12	12	14	13	16	15	14
12	15	15	14	13	13	12	13	10	13

At the .05 significance level can the watchdog agency conclude the mean number of complaints per airport is less than 15 per month?

a. What assumption is necessary before conducting a test of hypothesis?
b. Plot the number of complaints per airport in a frequency distribution or a dot plot. Is it reasonable to conclude that the population follows a normal distribution?
c. Conduct a test of hypothesis and interpret the results.

A Software Solution

The MINITAB statistical software system, used in earlier chapters, provides an efficient way of conducting a one-sample test of hypothesis for a population mean. The steps to generate the following output are shown in the Software Commands section at the end of the chapter.

An additional feature of most statistical software packages is to report the *p*-value, which gives additional information on the null hypothesis. The *p*-value is the probability of a *t* value as extreme as that computed, given that the null hypothesis is true. In the case of the Example on page 299, the *p*-value of .014 is the likelihood of a *t* value of −2.91 or less plus the likelihood of a *t* value of 2.91 or larger, given a population mean of 43. Thus, comparing the *p*-value to the significance level tells us whether the null hypothesis was close to being rejected, barely rejected, and so on.

To explain further, refer to the diagram on the next page, in which the *p*-value of .014 is shown in color and the significance level is the color area plus the grey area. Because the *p*-value of .014 is less than the significance level of .02, the null

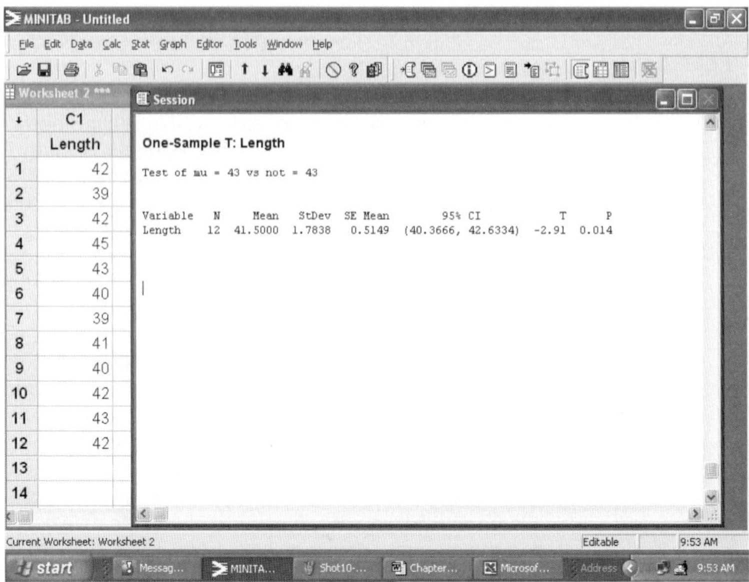

hypothesis is rejected. Had the *p*-value been larger than the significance level—say, .06, .19, or .57—the null hypothesis would not be rejected. If the significance level had initially been selected as .01, the null hypothesis would not be rejected.

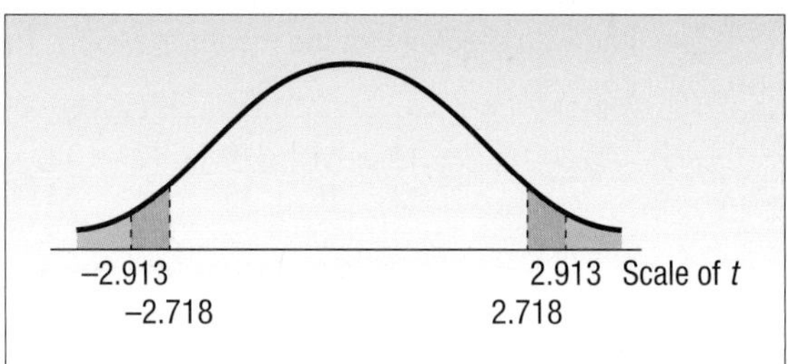

In the preceding example the alternate hypothesis was two-sided, so there were rejection areas in both the upper and the lower tails. To determine the *p*-value, it was necessary to determine the area to the left of -2.913 for a *t* distribution with 11 degrees of freedom and add to it the value of the area to the right of 2.913, also with 11 degrees of freedom.

What if we were conducting a one-sided test, so that the entire rejection region would be in either the upper or the lower tail? In that case, we would report the area from only the one tail. In the counterbalance example, if H_1 were stated as $\mu < 43$, the inequality would point to the left. Thus, we would have reported the *p*-value as the area to the left of -2.913. This value is .007, found by .014/2. Thus, the *p*-value for a one-tailed test would be .007.

How can we estimate a *p*-value without a computer? To illustrate, recall that, in the example regarding the length of a counterbalance, we rejected the null hypothesis that $\mu = 43$ and accepted the alternate hypothesis that $\mu \neq 43$. The significance level was .02, so logically the *p*-value is less than .02. To estimate the *p*-value more accurately, go to Appendix F and find the row with 11 degrees of freedom. The computed *t* value of 2.913 is between 2.718 and 3.106. (A portion of Appendix F is reproduced as Table 10–3.) The two-tailed significance level corresponding to 2.718 is .02, and for 3.106 it is .01. Therefore, the *p*-value is between .01 and .02. The usual practice is to report that the *p*-value is less than the larger of the two significance levels. So we would report, “the *p*-value is less than .02.”

TABLE 10–3 A Portion of Student's *t* Distribution

	Confidence Intervals					
	80%	90%	95%	98%	99%	99.9%
	Level of Significance for One-Tailed Test, α					
df	0.100	0.050	0.025	0.010	0.005	0.0005
	Level of Significance for Two-Tailed Test, α					
	0.20	0.10	0.05	0.02	0.01	0.001
⋮	⋮	⋮	⋮	⋮	⋮	⋮
9	1.383	1.833	2.262	2.821	3.250	4.781
10	1.372	1.812	2.228	2.764	3.169	4.587
11	1.363	1.796	2.201	2.718	3.106	4.437
12	1.356	1.782	2.179	2.681	3.055	4.318
13	1.350	1.771	2.160	2.650	3.012	4.221
14	1.345	1.761	2.145	2.624	2.977	4.140
15	1.341	1.753	2.131	2.602	2.947	4.073

SELF-REVIEW 10–5 A machine is set to fill a small bottle with 9.0 grams of medicine. A sample of eight bottles revealed the following amounts (grams) in each bottle.

9.2	8.7	8.9	8.6	8.8	8.5	8.7	9.0

At the .01 significance level, can we conclude that the mean weight is less than 9.0 grams?

(a) State the null hypothesis and the alternate hypothesis.
(b) How many degrees of freedom are there?
(c) Give the decision rule.
(d) Compute the value of *t*. What is your decision regarding the null hypothesis?
(e) Estimate the *p*-value.

Exercises

21. Given the following hypothesis:

H_0: $\mu \geq 20$
H_1: $\mu < 20$

A random sample of five resulted in the following values: 18, 15, 12, 19, and 21. Using the .01 significance level, can we conclude the population mean is less than 20?

a. State the decision rule.
b. Compute the value of the test statistic.
c. What is your decision regarding the null hypothesis?
d. Estimate the *p*-value.

22. Given the following hypothesis:

H_0: $\mu = 100$
H_1: $\mu \neq 100$

A random sample of six resulted in the following values: 118, 105, 112, 119, 105, and 111. Using the .05 significance level, can we conclude the mean is different from 100?

a. State the decision rule.
b. Compute the value of the test statistic.
c. What is your decision regarding the null hypothesis?
d. Estimate the *p*-value.

23. Experience raising New Jersey Red chickens revealed the mean weight of the chickens at five months is 4.35 pounds. The weights follow the normal distribution. In an effort to increase their weight, a special additive is added to the chicken feed. The subsequent weights of a sample of five-month-old chickens were (in pounds):

4.41	4.37	4.33	4.35	4.30	4.39	4.36	4.38	4.40	4.39

At the .01 level, has the special additive increased the mean weight of the chickens? Estimate the *p*-value.

24. The liquid chlorine added to swimming pools to combat algae has a relatively short shelf life before it loses its effectiveness. Records indicate that the mean shelf life of a 5-gallon jug of chlorine is 2,160 hours (90 days). As an experiment, Holdlonger was added to the chlorine to find whether it would increase the shelf life. A sample of nine jugs of chlorine had these shelf lives (in hours):

2,159	2,170	2,180	2,179	2,160	2,167	2,171	2,181	2,185

At the .025 level, has Holdlonger increased the shelf life of the chlorine? Estimate the *p*-value.

25. Wyoming fisheries contend that the mean number of cutthroat trout caught during a full day of fly-fishing on the Snake, Buffalo, and other rivers and streams in the Jackson Hole area is 4.0. To make their yearly update, the fishery personnel asked a sample of fly-fishermen to keep a count of the number caught during the day. The numbers were: 4, 4, 3, 2, 6, 8, 7, 1, 9, 3, 1, and 6. At the .05 level, can we conclude that the mean number caught is greater than 4.0? Estimate the *p*-value.

26. Hugger Polls contends that an agent conducts a mean of 53 in-depth home surveys every week. A streamlined survey form has been introduced, and Hugger wants to evaluate its effectiveness. The number of in-depth surveys conducted during a week by a random sample of agents are:

53	57	50	55	58	54	60	52	59	62	60	60	51	59	56

At the .05 level of significance, can we conclude that the mean number of interviews conducted by the agents is more than 53 per week? Estimate the *p*-value.

Chapter Outline

I. The objective of hypothesis testing is to check the validity of a statement about a population.

II. The steps in conducting a test of hypothesis are:

A. State the null hypothesis (H_0) and the alternate hypothesis (H_1).

B. Select the level of significance.

1. The level of significance is the likelihood of rejecting a true null hypothesis.
2. The most frequently used significance levels are .01, .05, and .10, but any value between 0 and 1.00 is possible.

C. Select the test statistic.

1. A test statistic is a value calculated from sample information used to determine whether to reject the null hypothesis.
2. Two test statistics were considered in this chapter.
   - **a.** The standard normal distribution is used when the population follows the normal distribution and the population standard deviation is known.
   - **b.** The standard normal distribution is used when the population standard deviation is unknown, but the sample contains at least 30 observations.
   - **c.** The *t* distribution is used when the population follows the normal distribution, the population standard deviation is unknown, and the sample contains fewer than 30 observations.

D. State the decision rule.

1. The decision rule indicates the condition or conditions when the null hypothesis is rejected.
2. In a two-tailed test, the rejection region is evenly split between the upper and lower tails.
3. In a one-sample test, all of the rejection region is in either the upper or the lower tail.

E. Select a sample, compute the value of the test statistic, make a decision regarding the null hypothesis, and interpret the results.

III. A *p*-value is the probability that the value of the test statistic is as extreme as the value computed, when the null hypothesis is true.

IV. Testing a hypothesis about a population mean.

A. If the population follows a normal distribution and the population standard deviation, σ, is known, the test statistic is the standard normal distribution and is determined from:

$$z = \frac{\bar{X} - \mu}{\sigma/\sqrt{n}} \quad \textbf{[10–1]}$$

B. If the population standard deviation is not known, but there are at least 30 observations in the sample, s is substituted for σ. The test statistic is the standard normal distribution, and its value is determined from:

$$z = \frac{\bar{X} - \mu}{s/\sqrt{n}} \quad \textbf{[10–2]}$$

C. If the population standard deviation is not known, but there are fewer than 30 observations in the sample, s is substituted for σ. The test statistic is the t distribution, and its value is determined from:

$$t = \frac{\bar{X} - \mu}{s/\sqrt{n}} \quad \textbf{[10–5]}$$

The major characteristics of the t distribution are:

1. It is a continuous distribution.
2. It is mound-shaped and symmetric.
3. It is flatter, or more spread out, than the standard normal distribution.
4. There is a family of t distributions, depending on the number of degrees of freedom.

V. Testing about a population proportion.

A. Both $n\pi$ and $n(1 - \pi)$ must be at least 5.

B. The test statistic is

$$z = \frac{p - \pi}{\sqrt{\frac{\pi(1 - \pi)}{n}}} \quad \textbf{[10-4]}$$

Pronunciation Key

SYMBOL	MEANING	PRONUNCIATION
H_0	Null hypothesis	*H sub zero*
H_1	Alternate hypothesis	*H sub one*
$\alpha/2$	Two-tailed significance level	*Alpha over 2*

Chapter Exercises

27. A new weight-watching company, Weight Reducers International, advertises that those who join will lose, on the average, 10 pounds the first two weeks. A random sample of 50 people who joined the new weight reduction program revealed the mean loss to be 9 pounds with a standard deviation of 2.8 pounds. At the .05 level of significance, can we conclude that those joining Weight Reducers on average will lose less than 10 pounds? Determine the *p*-value.

28. Dole Pineapple, Inc. is concerned that the 16-ounce can of sliced pineapple is being overfilled. The quality-control department took a random sample of 50 cans and found that the arithmetic mean weight was 16.05 ounces, with a sample standard deviation of 0.03

ounces. At the 5 percent level of significance, can we conclude that the mean weight is greater than 16 ounces? Determine the *p*-value.

29. According to a recent survey, Americans get a mean of 7 hours of sleep per night. A random sample of 50 students at West Virginia University revealed the mean number of hours slept last night was 6 hours and 48 minutes (6.8 hours). The standard deviation of the sample was 0.9 hours. Is it reasonable to conclude that students at West Virginia sleep less than the typical American? Compute the *p*-value.

30. A statewide real estate sales agency, Farm Associates, specializes in selling farm property in the state of Nebraska. Their records indicate that the mean selling time of farm property is 90 days. Because of recent drought conditions, they believe that the mean selling time is now greater than 90 days. A statewide survey of 100 farms sold recently revealed that the mean selling time was 94 days, with a standard deviation of 22 days. At the .10 significance level, has there been an increase in selling time?

31. According to the local union president, the mean income of plumbers in the Salt Lake City follows the normal distribution. This normal distribution has a mean of $45,000 and a standard deviation of $3,000. A recent investigative reporter for KYAK TV found, for a sample of 120 plumbers, the mean gross income was $45,500. At the .10 significance level, is it reasonable to conclude that the mean income is not equal to $45,000? Determine the *p*-value.

32. A recent article in *Vitality* magazine reported that the mean amount of leisure time per week for American men is 40.0 hours. You believe this figure is too large and decide to conduct your own test. In a random sample of 60 men, you find that the mean is 37.8 hours of leisure per week and that the standard deviation of the sample is 12.2 hours. Can you conclude that the information in the article is untrue? Use the .05 significance level. Determine the *p*-value and explain its meaning.

33. NBC TV news, in a segment on the price of gasoline, reported last evening that the mean price nationwide is $2.10 per gallon for self-serve regular unleaded. A random sample of 35 stations in the Milwaukee, Wisconsin, area revealed that the mean price was $2.12 per gallon and that the standard deviation was $0.05 per gallon. At the .05 significance level, can we conclude that the price of gasoline is higher in the Milwaukee area? Determine the *p*-value.

34. The Rutter Nursery Company packages their pine bark mulch in 50-pound bags. From a long history, the production department reports that the distribution of the bag weights follows the normal distribution and the standard deviation of this process is 3 pounds per bag. At the end of each day, Jeff Rutter, the production manager, weighs 10 bags and computes the mean weight of the sample. Below are the weights of 10 bags from today's production.

45.6	47.7	47.6	46.3	46.2	47.4	49.2	55.8	47.5	48.5

a. Can Mr. Rutter conclude that the mean weight of the bags is less than 50 pounds? Use the .01 significance level.
b. In a brief report, tell why Mr. Rutter can use the *z* distribution as the test statistic.
c. Compute the *p*-value.

35. Tina Dennis is the comptroller for Meek Industries. She believes that the current cash-flow problem at Meek is due to the slow collection of accounts receivable. She believes that more than 60 percent of the accounts are in arrears more than three months. A random sample of 200 accounts showed that 140 were more than three months old. At the .01 significance level, can she conclude that more than 60 percent of the accounts are in arrears for more than three months?

36. The policy of the Suburban Transit Authority is to add a bus route if more than 55 percent of the potential commuters indicate they would use the particular route. A sample of 70 commuters revealed that 42 would use a proposed route from Bowman Park to the downtown area. Does the Bowman-to-downtown route meet the STA criterion? Use the .05 significance level.

37. Past experience at the Crowder Travel Agency indicated that 44 percent of those persons who wanted the agency to plan a vacation for them wanted to go to Europe. During the most recent busy season, a sampling of 1,000 plans was selected at random from the files. It was found that 480 persons wanted to go to Europe on vacation. Has there been a significant shift upward in the percentage of persons who want to go to Europe? Test at the .05 significance level.

38. From past experience a television manufacturer found that 10 percent or less of its sets needed any type of repair in the first two years of operation. In a sample of 50 sets manufactured two years ago, 9 needed repair. At the .05 significance level, has the percent of sets needing repair increased? Determine the *p*-value.

39. An urban planner claims that, nationally, 20 percent of all families renting condominiums move during a given year. A random sample of 200 families renting condominiums in Dallas Metroplex revealed that 56 had moved during the past year. At the .01 significance level, does this evidence suggest that a larger proportion of condominium owners moved in the Dallas area? Determine the *p*-value.

40. The cost of weddings in the United States has skyrocketed in recent years. As a result many couples are opting to have their weddings in the Caribbean. A Caribbean vacation resort recently advertised in *Bride Magazine* that the cost of a Caribbean wedding was less than $10,000. Listed below is a total cost in $000 for a sample of 8 Caribbean weddings.

9.7	9.4	11.7	9.0	9.1	10.5	9.1	9.8

At the .05 significance level is it reasonable to conclude the mean wedding cost is less than $10,000 as advertised?

41. In recent years the interest rate on home mortgages has declined to less than 6.0 percent. However, according to a study by the Federal Reserve Board the rate charged on credit card debit is more than 14 percent. Listed below is the interest rate charged on a sample of 10 credit cards.

14.6	16.7	17.4	17.0	17.8	15.4	13.1	15.8	14.3	14.5

Is it reasonable to conclude the mean rate charged is greater than 14 percent? Use the .01 significance level.

42. A recent article in the *Wall Street Journal* reported that the 30-year mortgage rate is now less than 6 percent. A sample of eight small banks in the Midwest revealed the following 30-year rates (in percent):

4.8	5.3	6.5	4.8	6.1	5.8	6.2	5.6

At the .01 significance level, can we conclude that the 30-year mortgage rate for small banks is less than 6 percent? Estimate the *p*-value.

43. According to the Coffee Research Organization (http://www.coffeeresearch.org) the typical American coffee drinker consumes an average of 3.1 cups per day. A sample of 12 senior citizens revealed they consumed the following amounts, reported in cups, of coffee yesterday.

3.1	3.3	3.5	2.6	2.6	4.3	4.4	3.8	3.1	4.1	3.1	3.2

At the .05 significance level does this sample data suggest there is a difference between the national average and the sample mean from senior citizens?

44. The postanesthesia care area (recovery room) at St. Luke's Hospital in Maumee, Ohio, was recently enlarged. The hope was that with the enlargement the mean number of patients per day would be more than 25. A random sample of 15 days revealed the following numbers of patients.

25	27	25	26	25	28	28	27	24	26	25	29	25	27	24

At the .01 significance level, can we conclude that the mean number of patients per day is more than 25? Estimate the *p*-value and interpret it.

45. egolf.com receives an average of 6.5 returns per day from online shoppers. For a sample of 12 days, they received the following number of returns.

0	4	3	4	9	4	5	9	1	6	7	10

At the .01 significance level, can we conclude the mean number of returns is less than 6.5?

46. During recent seasons, Major League Baseball has been criticized for the length of the games. A report indicated that the average game lasts 3 hours and 30 minutes. A sample of 17 games revealed the following times to completion. (Note that the minutes have been changed to fractions of hours, so that a game that lasted 2 hours and 24 minutes is reported as 2.40 hours.)

2.98	2.40	2.70	2.25	3.23	3.17	2.93	3.18	2.80
2.38	3.75	3.20	3.27	2.52	2.58	4.45	2.45	

Can we conclude that the mean time for a game is less than 3.50 hours? Use the .05 significance level.

47. The Watch Corporation of Switzerland claims that their watches on average will neither gain nor lose time during a week. A sample of 18 watches provided the following gains (+) or losses (−) in seconds per week.

−0.38	−0.20	−0.38	−0.32	+0.32	−0.23	+0.30	+0.25	−0.10
−0.37	−0.61	−0.48	−0.47	−0.64	−0.04	−0.20	−0.68	+0.05

Is it reasonable to conclude that the mean gain or loss in time for the watches is 0? Use the .05 significance level. Estimate the *p*-value.

48. Listed below is the rate of return for one year (reported in percent) for a sample of 12 mutual funds that are classified as taxable money market funds.

4.63	4.15	4.76	4.70	4.65	4.52	4.70	5.06	4.42	4.51	4.24	4.52

Using the .05 significance level is it reasonable to conclude that the mean rate of return is more than 4.50 percent?

49. Many grocery stores and large retailers such as Wal-Mart and K-Mart have installed self-checkout systems so shoppers can scan their own items and cash out themselves. How do customers like this service and how often do they use it? Listed below is the number of customers using the service for a sample of 15 days at the Wal-Mart on Highway 544 in Surfside, South Carolina.

120	108	120	114	118	91	118	92	104	104
112	97	118	108	117					

Is it reasonable to conclude that the mean number of customers using the self-checkout system is more than 100 per day? Use the .05 significance level.

50. In the year 2003 the mean fare to fly from Charlotte, North Carolina, to Seattle, Washington, on a discount ticket was \$267. A random sample of round-trip discount fares on this route last month gives:

\$321	\$286	\$290	\$330	\$310	\$250	\$270	\$280	\$299	\$265	\$291	\$275	\$281

At the .01 significance level can we conclude that the mean fare has increased? What is the *p*-value?

51. The President's call for designing and building a missile defense system that ignores restrictions of the Anti-Ballistic Missile Defense System treaty (ABM) is supported by 483 of the respondents in a nationwide poll of 1,002 adults. Is it reasonable to conclude that the nation is evenly divided on the issue? Use the .05 significance level.

exercises.com

52. The *USA Today* (http://www.usatoday.com/sports/baseball/front.htm) and Major League Baseball (http://www.majorleaguebaseball.com) websites regularly report information on individual player salaries. Go to one of these sites and find the individual salaries for your favorite team. Compute the mean and the standard deviation. Is it reasonable to conclude that the mean salary on your favorite team is *different from* $90.0 million? If you are more of a football, basketball, or hockey enthusiast, information is also available on their teams' salaries.
53. The Gallup Organization in Princeton, New Jersey, is one of the best-known polling organizations in the United States. They often combine with *USA Today* or CNN to conduct polls of current interest. They also maintain a website at: http://www.gallup.com/. Consult this website to find the most recent polling results on Presidential approval ratings. You may need to click on Fast Facts. Test whether the majority (more than 50 percent) approve of the President's performance. If the article does not report the number of respondents included in the survey, assume that it is 1,000, a number that is typically used.

Dataset Exercises

54. Refer to the Real Estate data, which reports information on the homes sold in Denver, Colorado, last year.
    a. A recent article in the *Denver Post* indicated that the mean selling price of the homes in the area is more than $220,000. Can we conclude that the mean selling price in the Denver area is more than $220,000? Use the .01 significance level. What is the *p*-value?
    b. The same article reported the mean size was more than 2,100 square feet. Can we conclude that the mean size of homes sold in the Denver area is more than 2,100 square feet? Use the .01 significance level. What is the *p*-value?
    c. Determine the proportion of homes that have an attached garage. At the .05 significance level can we conclude that more than 60 percent of the homes sold in the Denver area had an attached garage? What is the *p*-value?
    d. Determine the proportion of homes that have a pool. At the .05 significance level, can we conclude that less than 40 percent of the homes sold in the Denver area had a pool? What is the *p*-value?
55. Refer to the Baseball 2003 data, which reports information on the 30 Major League Baseball teams for the 2003 season.
    a. Conduct a test of hypothesis to determine whether the mean salary of the teams was different from $80.0 million. Use the .05 significance level.
    b. Conduct a test of hypothesis to determine whether the mean attendance was more than 2,000,000 per team.
56. Refer to the Wage data, which reports information on the annual wages for a sample of 100 workers. Also included are variables relating to the industry, years of education, and gender for each worker.
    a. Conduct a test of hypothesis to determine if the mean annual wage is greater than $30,000. Use the .05 significance level. Determine the *p*-value and interpret the result.
    b. Conduct a test of hypothesis to determine if the mean years of experience is different from 20. Use the .05 significance level. Determine the *p*-value and interpret the result.
    c. Conduct a test of hypothesis to determine if the mean age is less than 40. Use the .05 significance level. Determine the *p*-value and interpret the result.
    d. Conduct a test of hypothesis to determine if the proportion of union workers is greater than 15 percent. Use the .05 significance level and report the *p*-value.
57. Refer to the CIA data, which reports demographic and economic information on 46 different countries.
    a. Conduct a test of hypothesis to determine if the mean number of cell phones is greater than 4.0. Use the .05 significance level. What is the *p*-value?
    b. Conduct a test of hypothesis to determine if the mean size of the labor force is less than 50. Use the .05 significance level. What is the *p*-value?

Software Commands

1. The MINITAB commands for the histogram and the descriptive statistics on page 297 are:
   a. Enter the 26 sample observations in column C1 and name the variable **Cost.**
   b. From the menu bar select **Stat, Basic Statistics,** and **Graphical Summary.** In the dialog box select **Cost** as the variable and click **OK.**

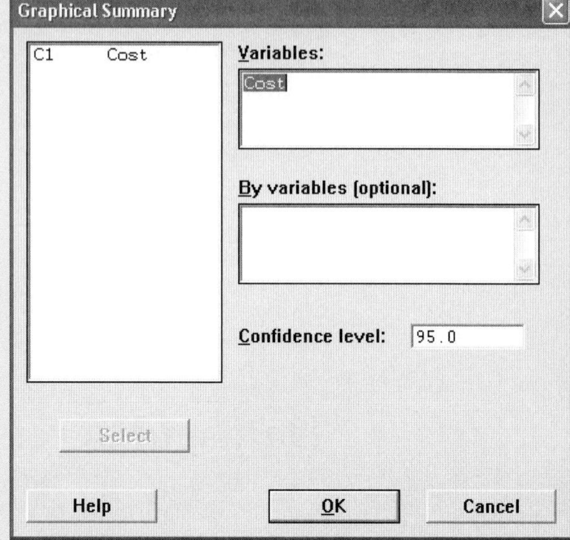

2. The MINITAB commands for the one-sample t test on page 302 are:
   a. Enter the sample data into column C1 and name the variable **Length.**
   b. From the menu bar select **Stat, Basic Statistics,** and **1-Sample t** and then hit **Enter.**
   c. Select **Length** as the variable, select **Test mean,** insert the number **43** and click **OK.**

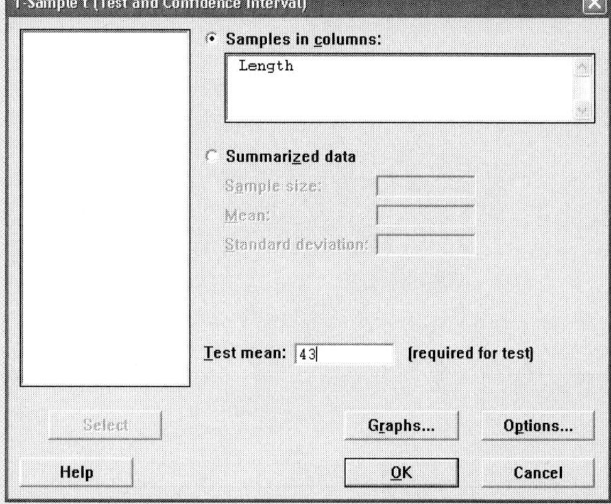

Chapter 10 Answers to Self-Review

10–1 **a.** H_0: $\mu = 6.0$; H_1: $\mu \neq 6.0$

b. .05.

c. $z = \dfrac{\bar{X} - \mu}{\sigma/\sqrt{n}}$

d. Do not reject the null hypothesis if the computed z value falls between -1.96 and $+1.96$.

e. Yes. Computed $z = -2.56$, found by:

$$z = \frac{5.84 - 6.0}{0.5/\sqrt{64}} = \frac{-0.16}{.0625} = -2.56$$

Reject H_0 at the .05 level. Accept H_1. The mean turnover rate is not equal to 6.0.

10–2 **a.** H_0: $\mu \leq 8.4$; H_1: $\mu > 8.4$

b. Large sample, $n > 30$.

c. Reject H_0 if $z > 2.33$.

d. $z = \dfrac{9.2 - 8.4}{2.8/\sqrt{40}} = 1.81$

e. Do not reject H_0.

f. We cannot conclude that the mean age is greater than 8.4 years.

g. p-value $= .5000 - .4649 = .0351$

10–3 **a.** Yes, because both $n\pi$ and $n(1 - \pi)$ exceed 5: $n\pi = 200(.40) = 80$, and $n(1 - \pi) = 200(.60) = 120$.

b. H_0: $\pi \geq .40$
H_1: $\pi < .40$

c.

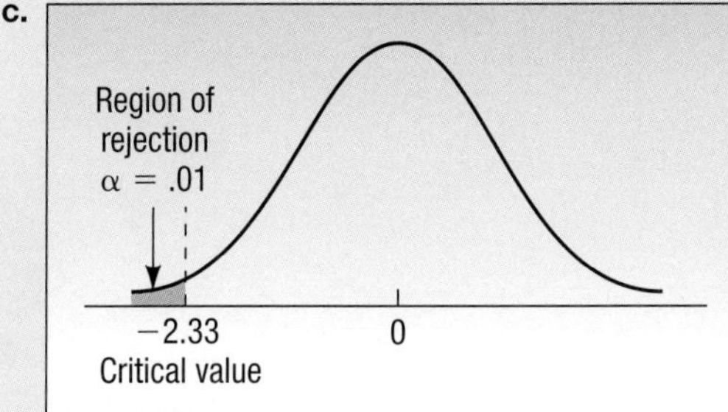

d. $z = -0.87$, found by:

$$z = \frac{.37 - .40}{\sqrt{\dfrac{.40(1 - .40)}{200}}} = \frac{-.03}{\sqrt{.0012}} = -0.87$$

Do not reject H_0.

e. The p-value is .1922, found by $.5000 - .3078$.

10–4 **a.** H_0: $\mu \leq 305$, H_1: $\mu > 305$.

b. $df = n - 1 = 20 - 1 = 19$

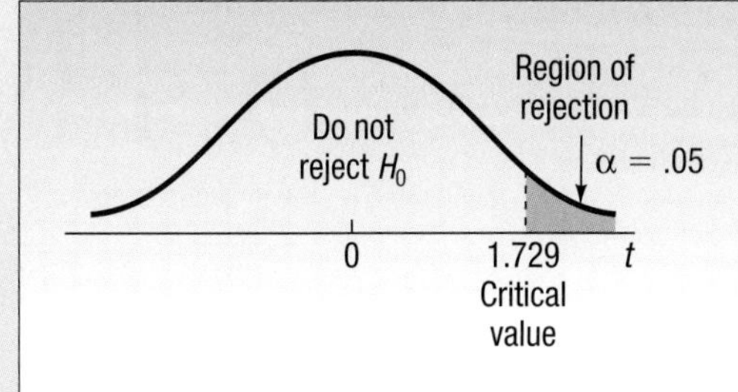

c. $t = \dfrac{\bar{X} - \mu}{s/\sqrt{n}} = \dfrac{311 - 305}{12/\sqrt{20}} = 2.236$

Reject H_0 because $2.236 > 1.729$. The modification increased the mean battery life to more than 305 days.

10–5 **a.** H_0: $\mu \geq 9.0$, H_1: $\mu < 9.0$.

b. 7, found by $n - 1 = 8 - 1 = 7$.

c. Reject H_0 if $t < -2.998$.

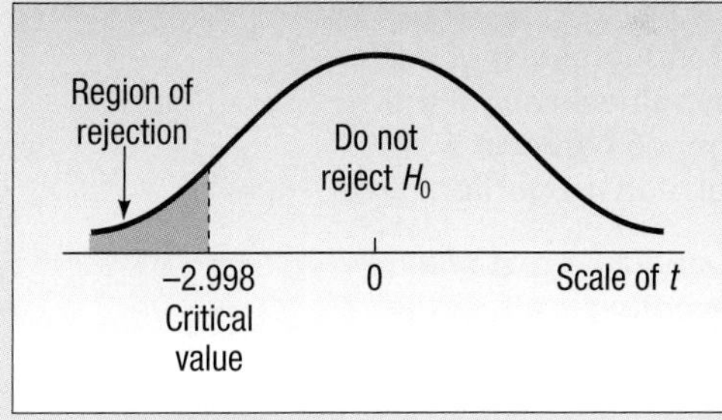

d. $t = -2.494$, found by:

$$s = \sqrt{\frac{0.36}{8 - 1}} = 0.2268$$

$$\bar{X} = \frac{70.4}{8} = 8.8$$

Then

$$t = \frac{8.8 - 9.0}{0.2268/\sqrt{8}} = -2.494$$

Since -2.494 lies to the right of -2.998, H_0 is not rejected. We have not shown that the mean is less than 9.0.

e. The p-value is between .025 and .010.

11 Two-Sample Tests of Hypothesis

GOALS

When you have completed this chapter, you will be able to:

1 Conduct a test of a hypothesis about the difference between two independent population means.

2 Conduct a test of a hypothesis about the difference between two population proportions.

3 Conduct a test of a hypothesis about the mean difference between paired or dependent observations.

4 Understand the difference between dependent and independent samples.

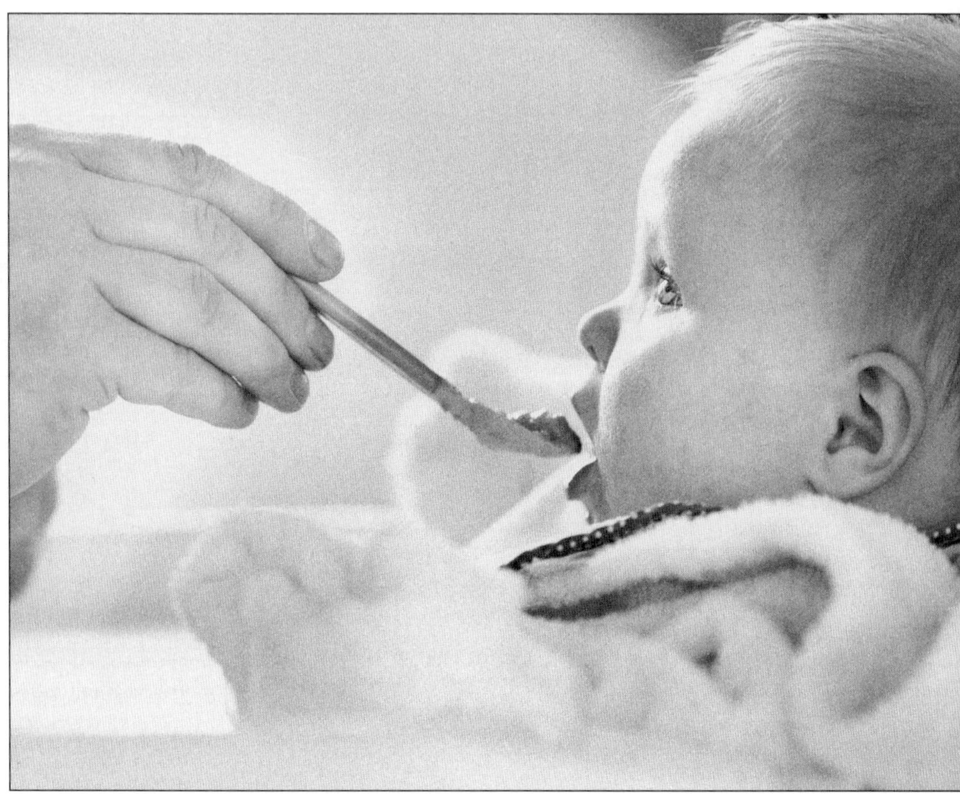

The Gibbs Baby Food Company wishes to compare the weight gain of infants using their brand versus their competitor's. A sample of 40 babies using the Gibbs products revealed a mean weight gain of 7.6 pounds in the first three months after birth. The standard deviation of the sample was 2.3 pounds. A sample of 55 babies using the competitor's brand revealed a mean increase in weight of 8.1 pounds, with a standard deviation of 2.9 pounds. At the .05 significance level, can we conclude that babies using the Gibbs brand gained less weight? Compute the *p*-value and interpret it. (See Goal 1 and Exercise 3.)

Introduction

Statistics in Action

The Election of 2000 turned out to be one of the closest in history. The news media were unable to project a winner, and the final decision, including recounts and court decisions, took more than five weeks. This was not the only election in which there was controversy. Shortly before the 1936 presidential election, the *New York Times* carried the headline: "*Digest* Poll Gives Landon 32 States: Landon Leads 4–3." However, Alfred Landon of Kansas was not elected President. In fact, Roosevelt won by more than 11 million votes and received 523 Electoral College votes. How could the headline have been so wrong?

The *Literary Digest* collected a sample of voters from lists of telephone numbers, automobile registrations, and *Digest* readers. In 1936 not many people could afford a telephone or an automobile. In addition those who read the *Digest* tended to be wealthier and vote

Chapter 10 began our study of hypothesis testing. We described the nature of hypothesis testing and conducted tests of a hypothesis in which we compared the results of a single sample to a population value. That is, we selected a single random sample from a population and conducted a test of whether the proposed population value was reasonable. Recall, in Chapter 10 we selected a sample of the number of desks assembled per week at the Jamestown Steel Company to determine whether there was a change in the production rate. Similarly, we sampled voters in one area of Indiana to determine whether the population proportion that would support the governor for reelection was less than .80. In both of these cases, we compared the results of a *single* sample statistic to a population parameter.

In this chapter we expand the idea of hypothesis testing to two samples. That is, we select random samples from two different populations to determine whether the population means or the population proportions are equal. Some questions we might want to test are:

1. Is there a difference in the mean value of residential real estate sold by male agents and female agents in south Florida?
2. Is there a difference in the mean number of defects produced on the day and the afternoon shifts at Kimble Products?
3. Is there a difference in the mean number of days absent between young workers (under 21 years of age) and older workers (more than 60 years of age) in the fast-food industry?
4. Is there is a difference in the proportion of Ohio State University graduates and University of Cincinnati graduates who pass the state Certified Public Accounting Examination on their first attempt?
5. Is there an increase in the production rate if music is piped into the production area?

We begin this chapter with the case in which we select random samples from two populations and wish to investigate whether these populations have the same mean.

Two-Sample Tests of Hypothesis: Independent Samples

A city planner in Florida wishes to know whether there is a difference in the mean hourly wage rate of plumbers and electricians in central Florida. A financial accountant wishes to know whether the mean rate of return for high yield mutual funds is different from the mean rate of return on global mutual funds. In each of these cases there are two independent populations. In the first case, the plumbers represent one population and the electricians the other. In the second case, high yield mutual funds are one population and global mutual funds the other.

In each of these cases, to investigate the question, we would select a random sample from each population and compute the mean of the two samples. If the two population means are the same, that is, the mean hourly rate is the same for the plumbers and the electricians, we would expect the *difference* between the two

Republican. Thus, the population that was sampled did not represent the population of voters. A second problem was with the nonresponses. More than 10 million people were sent surveys, and more than 2.3 million responded. However, no attempt was made to see whether those responding represented a cross-section of all the voters.

With modern computers and survey methods, samples are carefully selected and checked to ensure they are representative. What happened to the *Literary Digest?* It went out of business shortly after the 1936 election.

sample means to be zero. But what if our sample results yield a difference other than zero? Is that difference due to chance or is it because there is a real difference in the hourly earnings? A two-sample test of means will help to answer this question.

We do need to return to the results of Chapter 8. Recall that we showed that a distribution of sample means would tend to approximate the normal distribution when the sample size is at least 30. We need to again assume that a distribution of sample means will follow the normal distribution. It can be shown mathematically that the distribution of the differences between sample means for two normal distributions is also normal.

We can illustrate this theory in terms of the city planner in Tampa, Florida. To begin, let's assume some information that is not usually available. Suppose that the population of plumbers has a mean of \$30.00 per hour and a standard deviation of \$5.00 per hour. The population of electricians has a mean of \$29.00 and a standard deviation of \$4.50. Now, from this information it is clear that the two population means are not the same. The plumbers actually earn \$1.00 per hour more than the electricians. But we cannot expect to uncover this difference each time we sample the two populations.

Suppose we select a random sample of 40 plumbers and a random sample of 35 electricians and compute the mean of each sample. Then, we determine the difference between the sample means. It is this difference between the sample means that holds our interest. If the populations have the same mean, then we would expect the difference between the two sample means to be zero. If there is a difference between the population means, then we expect to find a difference between the sample means.

To understand the theory, we need to take several pairs of samples, compute the mean of each, determine the difference between the sample means, and study the distribution of the differences in the sample means. Because of our study of the distribution of sample means in Chapter 8, we know that the distribution of the sample means follows the normal distribution (assume n is at least 30). If the two distributions of sample means follow the normal distribution, then we can reason that the distribution of their differences will also follow the normal distribution. This is the first hurdle.

The second hurdle refers to the mean of this distribution of differences. If we find the mean of this distribution is zero, that implies that there is no difference in the two populations. On the other hand, if the mean of the distribution of differences is equal to some value other than zero, either positive or negative, then we conclude that the two populations do not have the same mean.

To report some concrete results, let's return to the city planner in Tampa, Florida. Table 11–1 shows the result of selecting 20 different samples of 40 plumbers and 35 electricians, computing the mean of each sample, and finding the difference between the two sample means. In the first case the sample of 40 plumbers has a mean of \$29.80, and for the 35 electricians the mean is \$28.76. The difference between the sample means is \$1.04. This process was repeated 19 more times. Observe that in 17 of the 20 cases the mean of the plumbers is larger than the mean of the electricians.

Our final hurdle is that we need to know something about the *variability* of the distribution of differences. To put it another way, what is the standard deviation of this distribution of differences? Statistical theory shows that when we have independent populations, such as the case here, the distribution of the differences has a variance (standard deviation squared) equal to the sum of the two individual variances. This means that we can add the variances of the two sampling distributions.

VARIANCE OF THE DISTRIBUTION OF DIFFERENCES IN MEANS

$$s^2_{\bar{X}_1-\bar{X}_2} = \frac{s_1^2}{n_1} + \frac{s_2^2}{n_2} \quad \textbf{[11–1]}$$

The term $s^2_{\bar{X}_1-\bar{X}_2}$ looks complex but need not be difficult to interpret. The s^2 portion reminds us that it is a sample variance, and the subscript $\bar{X}_1 - \bar{X}_2$ that it is a distribution of differences in the sample means.

TABLE 11–1 The Means of Random Samples of Plumbers and Electricians

Sample	Plumbers	Electricians	Difference
1	$29.80	$28.76	$1.04
2	30.32	29.40	0.92
3	30.57	29.94	0.63
4	30.04	28.93	1.11
5	30.09	29.78	0.31
6	30.02	28.66	1.36
7	29.60	29.13	0.47
8	29.63	29.42	0.21
9	30.17	29.29	0.88
10	30.81	29.75	1.06
11	30.09	28.05	2.04
12	29.35	29.07	0.28
13	29.42	28.79	0.63
14	29.78	29.54	0.24
15	29.60	29.60	0.00
16	30.60	30.19	0.41
17	30.79	28.65	2.14
18	29.14	29.95	−0.81
19	29.91	28.75	1.16
20	28.74	29.21	−0.47

We can put this equation in a more usable form by taking the square root, so that we have the standard deviation of the distribution of the differences. Finally, we standardize the distribution of the differences. The result is the following equation.

TEST STATISTIC FOR THE DIFFERENCE BETWEEN TWO MEANS

$$z = \frac{\bar{X}_1 - \bar{X}_2}{\sqrt{\frac{s_1^2}{n_1} + \frac{s_2^2}{n_2}}} \qquad [11\text{–}2]$$

Before we present an example, let's review the assumptions necessary for using formula (11–2).

Assumptions for large sample test

1. The two samples must be unrelated, that is, independent.
2. The samples must be large enough that the distribution of the sample means follows the normal distribution. The usual practice is to require that both samples have at least 30 observations.

The following example shows the details of the two-sample test of hypothesis for two population means.

EXAMPLE

Customers at FoodTown Super Markets have a choice when paying for their groceries. They may check out and pay using the standard cashier assisted checkout, or they may use the new U-Scan procedure. In the standard procedure a FoodTown employee scans each item, puts it on a short conveyor where another employee puts it in a bag and then into the grocery cart. In the U-Scan procedure the customer scans each item, bags it, and places the bags in the cart themselves. The U-Scan procedure is designed to reduce the time a customer spends in the checkout line.

The U-Scan facility was recently installed at the Byrne Road FoodTown location. The store manager would like to know if the mean checkout time using the standard checkout method is longer than using the U-Scan. She gathered the following sample information. The time is measured from when the customer enters the line until their bags are in the cart. Hence the time includes both waiting in line and checking out.

Customer Type	Sample Mean	Sample Standard Deviation	Sample Size
Standard	5.50 minutes	0.40 minutes	50
U-Scan	5.30 minutes	0.30 minutes	100

SOLUTION

We use the five-step hypothesis testing procedure to investigate the question.

Step 1: State the null hypothesis and the alternate hypothesis. The null hypothesis is that there is no difference in the mean checkout times for the two groups. In other words, the difference of 0.20 minutes between the mean checkout time for the standard method and the mean checkout time for U-Scan is due to chance. The alternate hypothesis is that the mean checkout time is longer for those using the standard method. We will let μ_s refer to the mean checkout time for the population of standard customers and μ_u the mean checkout time for the U-Scan customers. The null and alternative hypotheses are:

$$H_0: \mu_s \leq \mu_u$$
$$H_1: \mu_s > \mu_u$$

Statistics in Action

Do you live to work or work to live? A recent poll of 802 working Americans revealed that, among those who considered their work as a career, the mean number of hours worked per day was 8.7. Among those who considered their work a job, the mean number of hours worked per day was 7.6.

Step 2: Select the level of significance. The significance level is the probability that we reject the null hypothesis when it is actually true. This likelihood is determined prior to selecting the sample or performing any calculations. The .05 and .01 significance levels are the most common, but other values, such as .02 and .10, are also used. In theory, we may select any value between 0 and 1 for the significance level. In this case we selected the .01 significance level.

Step 3: Determine the test statistic. In Chapter 10 we used the standard normal distribution (that is z) and t as test statistics. In this case, because the samples are large, we use the z distribution as the test statistic.

Step 4: Formulate a decision rule. The decision rule is based on the null and the alternate hypotheses (i.e., one-tailed or two-tailed test), the level of significance, and the test statistic used. We selected the .01 significance level, the z distribution as the test statistic, and we wish to determine whether the mean checkout time is longer using the standard method. We set the alternate hypothesis to indicate that the mean checkout time is longer for those using the standard method than the U-Scan method. Hence, the rejection region is in the upper tail of the standard normal distribution. To find the critical value, place .01 of the total area in the upper tail. This means that .4900 (.5000 − .0100) of the area is located between the z value of 0 and the critical value. Next, we search the body of Appendix D for a value located near .4900. It is 2.33, so our decision rule is to reject H_0 if the value computed from the test statistic exceeds 2.33. Chart 11–1 depicts the decision rule.

Step 5: Make the decision regarding H_0 and interpret the result. We use formula (11–2) to compute the value of the test statistic.

$$z = \frac{\bar{X}_s - \bar{X}_u}{\sqrt{\frac{s_s^2}{n_s} + \frac{s_u^2}{n_u}}} = \frac{5.5 - 5.3}{\sqrt{\frac{0.40^2}{50} + \frac{0.30^2}{100}}} = \frac{0.2}{0.064} = 3.13$$

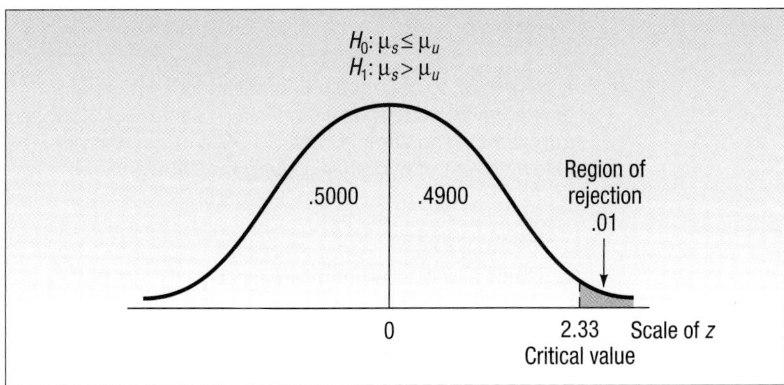

CHART 11–1 Decision Rule for One-Tailed Test at .01 Significance Level

The computed value of 3.13 is larger than the critical value of 2.33. Our decision is to reject the null hypothesis and accept the alternate hypothesis. The difference of .20 minutes between the mean checkout time using the standard method is too large to have occurred by chance. To put it another way, we conclude the U-Scan method is faster.

What is the *p*-value for the test statistic? Recall that the *p*-value is the probability of finding a value of the test statistic this extreme when the null hypothesis is true. To calculate the *p*-value we need the probability of a z value larger than 3.13. From Appendix D we cannot find the probability associated with 3.13. The largest value available is 3.09. The area corresponding to 3.09 is .4990. In this case we can report that the *p*-value is less than .0010, found by .5000 − .4990. We conclude that there is very little likelihood that the null hypothesis is true!

In summary, the criteria for using the large sample test of means are:

1. *The samples are from independent populations*. This means, for example, that the sample checkout time for the U-Scan customers is unrelated to the checkout time for the other customers. If Mr. Smith is a FoodTown customer and his response time is sampled, that does not affect the checkout time for any other customers.
2. *Both sample sizes are at least 30*. In the FoodTown example, one sample was 50 and the other 100. Because both samples are considered large, we can substitute the sample standard deviations for the population standard deviations and use formula (11–2) to find the value of the test statistic.

Self-Review 11–1

Tom Sevits is the owner of the Appliance Patch. Recently Tom observed a difference in the dollar value of sales between the men and women he employs as sales associates. A sample of 40 days revealed the men sold a mean of $1,400 worth of appliances per day with a standard deviation of $200. For a sample of 50 days, the women sold a mean of $1,500 worth of appliances per day with a standard deviation of $250. At the .05 significance level can Mr. Sevits conclude that the mean amount sold per day is larger for the women?

(a) State the null hypothesis and the alternate hypothesis.
(b) What is the decision rule?
(c) What is the value of the test statistic?
(d) What is your decision regarding the null hypothesis?
(e) What is the *p*-value?
(f) Interpret the result.

Exercises

1. A sample of 40 observations is selected from one population. The sample mean is 102 and the sample standard deviation is 5. A sample of 50 observations is selected from a second population. The sample mean is 99 and the sample standard deviation is 6. Conduct the following test of hypothesis using the .04 significance level.

   $H_0: \mu_1 = \mu_2$
   $H_1: \mu_1 \neq \mu_2$

   a. Is this a one-tailed or a two-tailed test?
   b. State the decision rule.
   c. Compute the value of the test statistic.
   d. What is your decision regarding H_0?
   e. What is the *p*-value? Compute and interpret the *p*-value.
2. A sample of 65 observations is selected from one population. The sample mean is 2.67 and the sample standard deviation is 0.75. A sample of 50 observations is selected from a second population. The sample mean is 2.59 and the sample standard deviation is 0.66. Conduct the following test of hypothesis using the .08 significance level.

   $H_0: \mu_1 \leq \mu_2$
   $H_1: \mu_1 > \mu_2$

   a. Is this a one-tailed or a two-tailed test?
   b. State the decision rule.
   c. Compute the value of the test statistic.
   d. What is your decision regarding H_0?
   e. What is the *p*-value? Compute and interpret the *p*-value.

Note: Use the five-step hypothesis testing procedure to solve the following exercises.

3. The Gibbs Baby Food Company wishes to compare the weight gain of infants using their brand versus their competitor's. A sample of 40 babies using the Gibbs products revealed a mean weight gain of 7.6 pounds in the first three months after birth. The standard deviation of the sample was 2.3 pounds. A sample of 55 babies using the competitor's brand revealed a mean increase in weight of 8.1 pounds, with a standard deviation of 2.9 pounds. At the .05 significance level, can we conclude that babies using the Gibbs brand gained less weight? Compute the *p*-value and interpret it.
4. As part of a study of corporate employees, the Director of Human Resources for PNC, Inc. wants to compare the distance traveled to work by employees at their office in downtown Cincinnati with the distance for those in downtown Pittsburgh. A sample of 35 Cincinnati employees showed they travel a mean of 370 miles per month, with a standard deviation of 30 miles per month. A sample of 40 Pittsburgh employees showed they travel a mean of 380 miles per month, with a standard deviation of 26 miles per month. At the .05 significance level, is there a difference in the mean number of miles traveled per month between Cincinnati and Pittsburgh employees? Use the five-step hypothesis-testing procedure.
5. A financial analyst wants to compare the turnover rates, in percent, for shares of oil-related stocks versus other stocks, such as GE and IBM. She selected 32 oil-related stocks and 49 other stocks. The mean turnover rate of oil-related stocks is 31.4 percent and the standard deviation 5.1 percent. For the other stocks, the mean rate was computed to be 34.9 percent and the standard deviation 6.7 percent. Is there a significant difference in the turnover rates of the two types of stock? Use the .01 significance level.
6. Mary Jo Fitzpatrick is the Vice President for Nursing Services at St. Luke's Memorial Hospital. Recently she noticed that unionized jobs for nurses seem to offer higher wages. She decided to investigate and gathered the following sample information.

Group	Mean Wage	Sample Standard Deviation	Sample Size
Union	\$20.75	\$2.25	40
Nonunion	\$19.80	\$1.90	45

Would it be reasonable for her to conclude that union nurses earn more? Use the .02 significance level. What is the *p*-value? Compute and interpret the *p*-value.

Two-Sample Tests about Proportions

In the previous section, we considered a test involving population means. However, we are often interested also in whether two sample proportions came from populations that are equal. Here are several examples.

- The Vice President of Human Resources wishes to know whether there is a difference in the proportion of hourly employees who miss more than 5 days of work per year at the Atlanta and the Houston plants.
- General Motors is considering a new design for the Pontiac Grand Am. The design is shown to a group of potential buyers under 30 years of age and another group over 60 years of age. Pontiac wishes to know whether there is a difference in the proportion of the two groups who like the new design.
- A consultant to the airline industry is investigating the fear of flying among adults. Specifically, they wish to know whether there is a difference in the proportion of men versus women who are fearful of flying.

In the above cases each sampled item or individual can be classified as a "success" or a "failure." That is, in the Pontiac Grand Am example each potential buyer is classified as "liking the new design" or "not liking the new design." We then compare the proportion in the under 30 group with the proportion in the over 60 group who indicated they liked the new design. Can we conclude that the differences are due to chance? In this study there is no measurement obtained, only classifying the individuals or objects. Then we assume the nominal scale of measurement.

To conduct the test, we assume each sample is large enough that the normal distribution will serve as a good approximation of the binomial distribution. The test statistic follows the standard normal distribution. We compute the value of z from the following formula:

TWO-SAMPLE TEST OF PROPORTIONS

$$z = \frac{p_1 - p_2}{\sqrt{\dfrac{p_c(1-p_c)}{n_1} + \dfrac{p_c(1-p_c)}{n_2}}} \quad \textbf{[11–3]}$$

Formula (11–3) is formula (11–2) with the respective sample proportions replacing the sample means and $p_c(1 - p_c)$ replacing the two sample standard deviations. In addition:

n_1 is the number of observations in the first sample.
n_2 is the number of observations in the second sample.
p_1 is the proportion in the first sample possessing the trait.
p_2 is the proportion in the second sample possessing the trait.
p_c is the pooled proportion possessing the trait in the combined samples. It is called the pooled estimate of the population proportion and is computed from the following formula.

POOLED PROPORTION

$$p_c = \frac{X_1 + X_2}{n_1 + n_2} \quad \textbf{[11–4]}$$

where:

X_1 is the number possessing the trait in the first sample.
X_2 is the number possessing the trait in the second sample.

The following example will illustrate the two-sample test of proportions.

EXAMPLE

The Manelli Perfume Company recently developed a new fragrance that they plan to market under the name "Heavenly." A number of market studies indicate that Heavenly has very good market potential. The Sales Department at Manelli is particularly interested in whether there is a difference in the proportions of younger and older women who would purchase Heavenly if it were marketed. There are two independent populations, a population consisting of the younger women and a population consisting of the older women. Each sampled woman will be asked to smell Heavenly and indicate whether she likes the fragrance well enough to purchase a bottle.

SOLUTION

We will use the usual five-step hypothesis-testing procedure.

Step 1: State H_0 and H_1. In this case the null hypothesis is: "There is no difference in the proportion of young women and older women who prefer Heavenly." We designate π_1 as the proportion of young women who would purchase Heavenly and π_2 as the proportion of older women who would purchase. The alternate hypothesis is that the two proportions are not equal.

$$H_0: \pi_1 = \pi_2$$
$$H_1: \pi_1 \neq \pi_2$$

Step 2: Select the level of significance. We selected the .05 significance level in this example.

Step 3: Determine the test statistic. If each sample is large enough, the test statistic follows the standard normal distribution. The value of the test statistic can be computed from formula (11–3).

Step 4: Formulate the decision rule. Recall that the alternate hypothesis from step 1 does not state a direction, so this is a two-tailed test. To determine the critical value, we divide the significance level in half and place this amount in each tail of the z distribution. Next, we subtract this amount from the total area to the right of zero. That is $.5000 - .0250 = .4750$. Finally, we search the body of the z table (Appendix D) for the closest value. It is 1.96. The critical values are -1.96 and $+1.96$. As before, if the computed z value falls in the region between $+1.96$ and -1.96, the null hypothesis is not rejected. If that does occur, it is assumed that any difference between the two sample proportions is due to chance variation. This information is summarized in Chart 11–2.

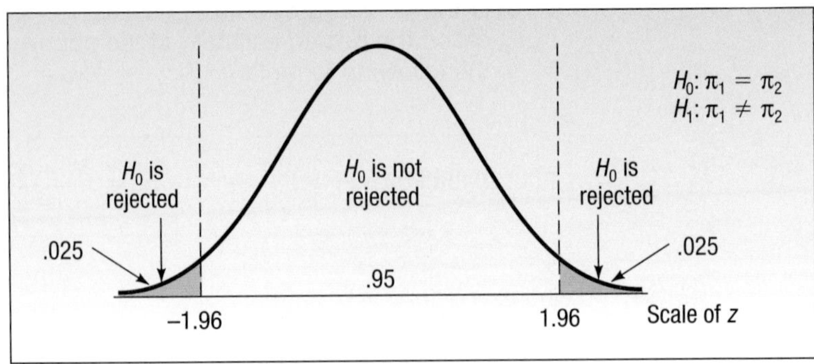

CHART 11–2 Decision Rules for Heavenly Fragrance Test, .05 Significance Level

Step 5: Select a sample and make a decision. A random sample of 100 young women revealed 20 liked the Heavenly fragrance well enough to purchase it. Similarly, a sample of 200 older women revealed 100 liked the fragrance well enough to make a purchase. We let p_1 refer to the young women and p_2 to the older women.

$$p_1 = \frac{X_1}{n_1} = \frac{20}{100} = .20 \qquad p_2 = \frac{X_2}{n_2} = \frac{100}{200} = .50$$

The research question is whether the difference of .30 in the two sample proportions is due to chance or whether there is a difference in the proportion of younger and older women who like the Heavenly fragrance.

Next, we combine or pool the sample proportions. We use formula (11–4).

$$p_c = \frac{X_1 + X_2}{n_1 + n_2} = \frac{20 + 100}{100 + 200} = .40$$

Note that the pooled proportion is closer to .50 than to .20 because more older women than younger women were sampled.

We use formula (11–3) to find the value of the test statistic.

$$z = \frac{p_1 - p_2}{\sqrt{\dfrac{p_c(1 - p_c)}{n_1} + \dfrac{p_c(1 - p_c)}{n_2}}} = \frac{.20 - .50}{\sqrt{\dfrac{.40(1 - .40)}{100} + \dfrac{.40(1 - .40)}{200}}} = -5.00$$

The computed value of -5.00 is in the area of rejection; that is, it is to the left of -1.96. Therefore, the null hypothesis is rejected at the .05 significance level. To put it another way, we reject the null hypothesis that the proportion of young women who would purchase Heavenly is equal to the proportion of older women who would purchase Heavenly. It is unlikely that the difference between the two sample proportions is due to chance. To find the p-value we go to Appendix D and look for the likelihood of finding a z value less than -5.00 or greater than 5.00. The largest value of z reported is 3.09, with a corresponding probability of .4990. So the probability of finding a z value greater than 5.00 or less than -5.00 is virtually zero. So we report zero as the p-value. There is very little likelihood the null hypothesis is true. We conclude that there is a difference in the proportion of younger and older women who would purchase Heavenly.

Self-Review 11–2

Of 150 adults who tried a new peach-flavored peppermint patty, 87 rated it excellent. Of 200 children sampled, 123 rated it excellent. Using the .10 level of significance, can we conclude that there is a significant difference in the proportion of adults and the proportion of children who rate the new flavor excellent?

(a) State the null hypothesis and the alternate hypothesis.
(b) What is the probability of a Type I error?
(c) Is this a one-tailed or a two-tailed test?
(d) What is the decision rule?
(e) What is the value of the test statistic?
(f) What is your decision regarding the null hypothesis?
(g) What is the p-value? Explain what it means in terms of this problem.

Exercises

7. The null and alternate hypotheses are:

H_0: $\pi_1 \leq \pi_2$
H_1: $\pi_1 > \pi_2$

A sample of 100 observations from the first population indicated that X_1 is 70. A sample of 150 observations from the second population revealed X_2 to be 90. Use the .05 significance level to test the hypothesis.

a. State the decision rule.
b. Compute the pooled proportion.
c. Compute the value of the test statistic.
d. What is your decision regarding the null hypothesis?

8. The null and alternate hypotheses are:

$$H_0: \pi_1 = \pi_2$$
$$H_1: \pi_1 \neq \pi_2$$

A sample of 200 observations from the first population indicated that X_1 is 170. A sample of 150 observations from the second population revealed X_2 to be 110. Use the .05 significance level to test the hypothesis.

a. State the decision rule.
b. Compute the pooled proportion.
c. Compute the value of the test statistic.
d. What is your decision regarding the null hypothesis?

Note: Use the five-step hypothesis-testing procedure in solving the following exercises.

9. The Damon family owns a large grape vineyard in western New York along Lake Erie. The grapevines must be sprayed at the beginning of the growing season to protect against various insects and diseases. Two new insecticides have just been marketed: Pernod 5 and Action. To test their effectiveness, three long rows were selected and sprayed with Pernod 5, and three others were sprayed with Action. When the grapes ripened, 400 of the vines treated with Pernod 5 were checked for infestation. Likewise, a sample of 400 vines sprayed with Action were checked. The results are:

Insecticide	Number of Vines Checked (sample size)	Number of Infested Vines
Pernod 5	400	24
Action	400	40

At the .05 significance level, can we conclude that there is a difference in the proportion of vines infested using Pernod 5 as opposed to Action?

10. The Roper Organization conducted identical surveys in 1995 and 2005. One question asked women was "Are most men basically kind, gentle, and thoughtful?" The 1995 survey revealed that, of the 3,000 women surveyed, 2,010 said that they were. In 2005, 1,530 of the 3,000 women surveyed thought that men were kind, gentle, and thoughtful. At the .05 level, can we conclude that women think men are less kind, gentle, and thoughtful in 2005 compared with 1995?

11. A nationwide sample of influential Republicans and Democrats was asked as a part of a comprehensive survey whether they favored lowering environmental standards so that high-sulfur coal could be burned in coal-fired power plants. The results were:

	Republicans	Democrats
Number sampled	1,000	800
Number in favor	200	168

At the .02 level of significance, can we conclude that there is a larger proportion of Democrats in favor of lowering the standards?

12. The research department at the home office of New Hampshire Insurance conducts ongoing research on the causes of automobile accidents, the characteristics of the drivers, and so on. A random sample of 400 policies written on single persons revealed 120 had at least one accident in the previous three-year period. Similarly, a sample of 600 policies written on married persons revealed that 150 had been in at least one accident. At the .05 significance level, is there a significant difference in the proportions of single and married persons having an accident during a three-year period?

Comparing Population Means with Small Samples

In an earlier section we assumed that the two population standard deviations were unknown but that we selected random samples containing 30 or more observations each. The large number of observations in our samples allowed us to use z as the test statistic. In this section we consider the case in which the population standard deviations are unknown and the number of observations in at least one of the samples is less than 30. We often refer to this as a "small sample test of means." The requirements for the small sample test are more stringent. The three required assumptions are:

Assumptions for small sample test of means

1. The sampled populations follow the normal distribution.
2. The two samples are from independent populations.
3. The standard deviations of the two populations are equal.

In this case, the t distribution is used to compare two population means. The formula for computing the test statistic t is similar to (11–2), but an additional calculation is necessary. The third assumption above indicates that the population standard deviations must be equal. The two sample standard deviations are pooled to form a single estimate of the unknown population standard deviation. In essence, we compute a weighted mean of the two sample standard deviations and use this as an estimate of the population standard deviation. The weights are the degrees of freedom that each sample provides. Why do we need to pool the standard deviations? In most cases when the samples each have fewer than 30 observations, the population standard deviations are not known. Thus, we calculate s, the sample standard deviation, and substitute it for σ, the population standard deviation. Because we assume that the two populations have equal standard deviations, the best estimate we can make of that value is to combine or pool all the information we have about the value of the population standard deviation.

The following formula is used to pool the sample standard deviations. Notice that two factors are involved: the number of observations in each sample and the sample standard deviations themselves.

POOLED VARIANCE

$$s_p^2 = \frac{(n_1 - 1)s_1^2 + (n_2 - 1)s_2^2}{n_1 + n_2 - 2} \qquad \textbf{[11–5]}$$

where:

s_1^2 is the variance (standard deviation squared) of the first sample.
s_2^2 is the variance of the second sample.

The value of t is computed from the following equation.

TWO-SAMPLE TEST OF MEANS—SMALL SAMPLES

$$t = \frac{\overline{X}_1 - \overline{X}_2}{\sqrt{s_p^2\left(\frac{1}{n_1} + \frac{1}{n_2}\right)}} \qquad \textbf{[11–6]}$$

where:

$\overline{X}_1$ is the mean of the first sample.
$\overline{X}_2$ is the mean of the second sample.
n_1 is the number of observations in the first sample.
n_2 is the number of observations in the second sample.
s_p^2 is the pooled estimate of the population variance.

The number of degrees of freedom in the test is the total number of items sampled minus the total number of samples. Because there are two samples, there are $n_1 + n_2 - 2$ degrees of freedom.

An example will help explain the details of the test.

EXAMPLE

Owens Lawn Care, Inc. manufactures and assembles lawnmowers that are shipped to dealers throughout the United States and Canada. Two different procedures have been proposed for mounting the engine on the frame of the lawnmower. The question is: Is there a difference in the mean time to mount the engines on the frames of the lawnmowers? The first procedure was developed by longtime Owens employee Herb Welles (designated as procedure 1), and the other procedure was developed by Owens Vice-President of Engineering William Atkins (designated as procedure 2). To evaluate the two methods, it was decided to conduct a time and motion study. A sample of five employees was timed using the Welles method and six using the Atkins method. The results, in minutes, are shown below. Is there a difference in the mean mounting times? Use the .10 significance level.

Welles (minutes)	Atkins (minutes)
2	3
4	7
9	5
3	8
2	4
	3

SOLUTION

Following the five steps to test a hypothesis, the null hypothesis states that there is no difference in mean mounting times between the two procedures. The alternate hypothesis indicates that there is a difference.

$$H_0: \mu_1 = \mu_2$$
$$H_1: \mu_1 \neq \mu_2$$

The required assumptions are:

1. The observations in the Welles sample are *independent* of the observations in the Atkins sample.
2. The two populations follow the normal distribution.
3. The two populations have equal standard deviations.

Is there a difference between the mean assembly times using the Welles and the Atkins methods? The degrees of freedom are equal to the total number of items sampled minus the number of samples. In this case that is $n_1 + n_2 - 2$. Five assemblers used the Welles method and six the Atkins method. Thus, there are 9 degrees of freedom, found by $5 + 6 - 2$. The critical values of t, from Appendix F for $df = 9$, a two-tailed test, and the .10 significance level, are -1.833 and 1.833. The decision rule is portrayed graphically in Chart 11–3. We do not reject the null hypothesis if the computed value of t falls between -1.833 and 1.833.

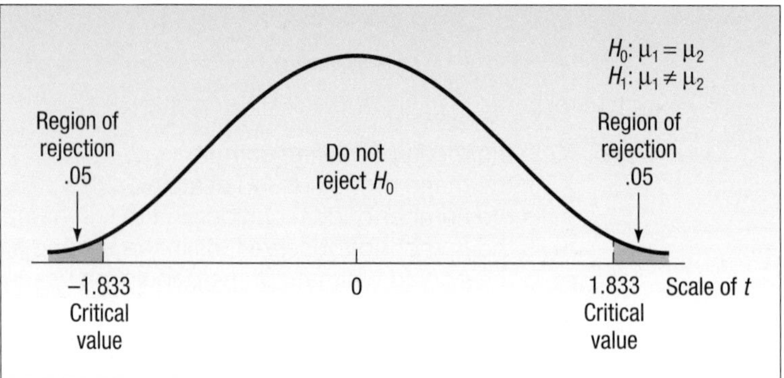

CHART 11–3 Regions of Rejection, Two-Tailed Test, $df = 9$, and .10 Significance Level

We use three steps to compute the value of t.

Step 1: Calculate the Sample Standard Deviations. See the details below.

Welles Method		Atkins Method	
X_1	$(X_1 - \bar{X}_1)^2$	X_2	$(X_2 - \bar{X}_2)^2$
2	$(2-4)^2 = 4$	3	$(3-5)^2 = 4$
4	$(4-4)^2 = 0$	7	$(7-5)^2 = 4$
9	$(9-4)^2 = 25$	5	$(5-5)^2 = 0$
3	$(3-4)^2 = 1$	8	$(8-5)^2 = 9$
2	$(2-4)^2 = 4$	4	$(4-5)^2 = 1$
20	34	3	$(3-5)^2 = 4$
		30	22

$$\bar{X}_1 = \frac{\Sigma X_1}{n_1} = \frac{20}{5} = 4 \qquad \bar{X}_2 = \frac{\Sigma X_2}{n_2} = \frac{30}{6} = 5$$

$$s_1 = \sqrt{\frac{\Sigma(X_1 - \bar{X}_1)^2}{n_1 - 1}} = \sqrt{\frac{34}{5-1}} = 2.9155 \qquad s_2 = \sqrt{\frac{\Sigma(X_2 - \bar{X}_2)^2}{n_2 - 1}} = \sqrt{\frac{22}{6-1}} = 2.0976$$

Step 2: Pool the Sample Variances. We use formula (11–5) to pool the sample variances (standard deviations squared).

$$s_p^2 = \frac{(n_1 - 1)s_1^2 + (n_2 - 1)s_2^2}{n_1 + n_2 - 2} = \frac{(5-1)(2.9155)^2 + (6-1)(2.0976)^2}{5+6-2} = 6.2222$$

Step 3: Determine the value of *t*. The mean mounting time for the Welles method is 4.00 minutes, found by $\bar{X}_1 = 20/5$. The mean mounting time for the Atkins method is 5.00 minutes, found by $\bar{X}_2 = 30/6$. We use formula (11–6) to calculate the value of t.

$$t = \frac{\bar{X}_1 - \bar{X}_2}{\sqrt{s_p^2\left(\frac{1}{n_1} + \frac{1}{n_2}\right)}} = \frac{4.00 - 5.00}{\sqrt{6.2222\left(\frac{1}{5} + \frac{1}{6}\right)}} = -0.662$$

The decision is not to reject the null hypothesis, because -0.662 falls in the region between -1.833 and 1.833. We conclude that there is no difference in the mean times to mount the engine on the frame using the two methods.

We can also estimate the p-value using Appendix F. Locate the row with 9 degrees of freedom, and use the two-tailed test column. Find the t value, without regard to the sign, which is closest to our computed value of 0.662. It is 1.383, corresponding to a significance level of .20. Thus, even had we used the 20 percent significance level, we would not have rejected the null hypothesis of equal means. We can report that the p-value is greater than .20.

Excel has a procedure called "t-Test: Two Sample Assuming Equal Variances" that will perform the calculations of formulas (11–5) and (11–6) as well as find the sample means and sample variances. The data are input in the first two columns of the Excel spreadsheet. They are labeled "Welles" and "Atkins." The output follows. The value of t, called the "t Stat," is -0.662, and the two-tailed p-value is .525. As we would expect, the p-value is larger than the significance level of .10. The conclusion is not to reject the null hypothesis.

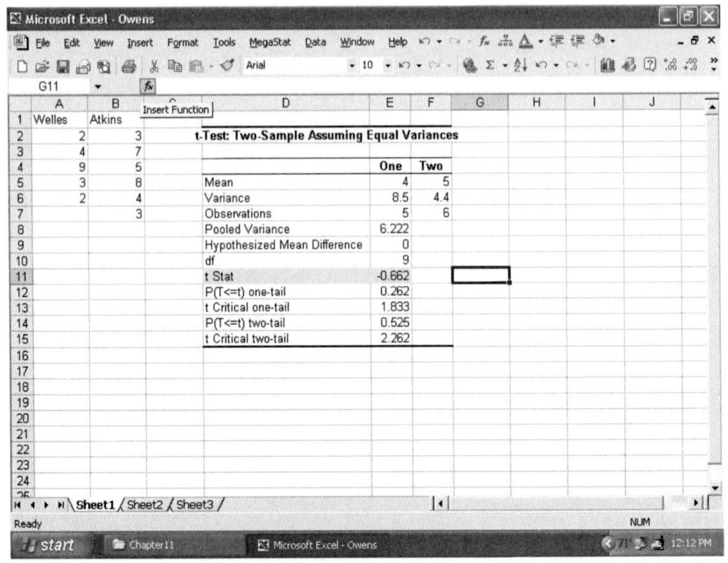

Welles	Atkins
2	3
4	7
9	5
3	8
2	4
	3

t-Test: Two-Sample Assuming Equal Variances

	One	Two
Mean	4	5
Variance	8.5	4.4
Observations	5	6
Pooled Variance	6.222	
Hypothesized Mean Difference	0	
df	9	
t Stat	-0.662	
P(T<=t) one-tail	0.262	
t Critical one-tail	1.833	
P(T<=t) two-tail	0.525	
t Critical two-tail	2.262	

Self-Review 11–3

The production manager at Bellevue Steel, a manufacturer of wheelchairs, wants to compare the number of defective wheelchairs produced on the day shift with the number on the afternoon shift. A sample of the production from 6 day shifts and 8 afternoon shifts revealed the following number of defects.

Day	5	8	7	6	9	7		
Afternoon	8	10	7	11	9	12	14	9

At the .05 significance level, is there a difference in the mean number of defects per shift?

(a) State the null hypothesis and the alternate hypothesis.
(b) What is the decision rule?
(c) What is the value of the test statistic?
(d) What is your decision regarding the null hypothesis?
(e) What is the *p*-value?
(f) Interpret the result.
(g) What are the assumptions necessary for this test?

Exercises

For Exercises 13 and 14: (a) state the decision rule, (b) compute the pooled estimate of the population variance, (c) compute the test statistic, (d) state your decision about the null hypothesis, and (e) estimate the *p*-value.

13. The null and alternate hypotheses are:

H_0: $\mu_1 = \mu_2$
H_1: $\mu_1 \neq \mu_2$

A random sample of 10 observations from one population revealed a sample mean of 23 and a sample deviation of 4. A random sample of 8 observations from another population revealed a sample mean of 26 and a sample standard deviation of 5. At the .05 significance level, is there a difference between the population means?

14. The null and alternate hypotheses are:

H_0: $\mu_1 = \mu_2$
H_1: $\mu_1 \neq \mu_2$

A random sample of 15 observations from the first population revealed a sample mean of 350 and a sample standard deviation of 12. A random sample of 17 observations from the second population revealed a sample mean of 342 and a sample standard deviation of 15. At the .10 significance level, is there a difference in the population means?

Note: Use the five-step hypothesis testing procedure for the following exercises.

15. A sample of scores on an examination given in Statistics 201 are:

Men	72	69	98	66	85	76	79	80	77
Women	81	67	90	78	81	80	76		

At the .01 significance level, is the mean grade of the women higher than that of the men?

16. A recent study compared the time spent together by single- and dual-earner couples. According to the records kept by the wives during the study, the mean amount of time spent together watching television among the single-earner couples was 61 minutes per day, with a standard deviation of 15.5 minutes. For the dual-earner couples, the mean number of minutes spent watching television was 48.4 minutes, with a standard deviation of 18.1 minutes. At the .01 significance level, can we conclude that the single-earner couples on average spend more time watching television together? There were 15 single-earner and 12 dual-earner couples studied.

17. Ms. Lisa Monnin is the budget director for Nexus Media, Inc. She would like to compare the daily travel expenses for the sales staff and the audit staff. She collected the following sample information.

Sales ($)	131	135	146	165	136	142	
Audit ($)	130	102	129	143	149	120	139

At the .10 significance level, can she conclude that the mean daily expenses are greater for the sales staff than the audit staff? What is the *p*-value?

18. The Tampa Bay (Florida) Area Chamber of Commerce wanted to know whether the mean weekly salary of nurses was larger than that of school teachers. To investigate, they collected the following information on the amounts earned last week by a sample of school teachers and nurses.

School teachers ($)	845	826	827	875	784	809	802	820	829	830	842	832
Nurses ($)	841	890	821	771	850	859	825	829				

Is it reasonable to conclude that the mean weekly salary of nurses is higher? Use the .01 significance level. What is the *p*-value?

Two-Sample Tests of Hypothesis: Dependent Samples

On page 324, we tested the difference between the means from two independent samples. We compared the mean time required to mount an engine using the Welles method to the time to mount the engine using the Atkins method. The samples were *independent,* meaning that the sample of assembly times using the Welles method was in no way related to the sample of assembly times using the Atkins method.

There are situations, however, in which the samples are not independent. To put it another way, the samples are **dependent** or related. As an example, Nickel Savings and Loan employs two firms, Schadek Appraisals and Bowyer Real Estate, to appraise the value of the real estate properties on which they make loans. It is important that these two firms be similar in their appraisal values. To review the consistency of

the two appraisal firms, Nickel Savings randomly selects 10 homes and has both Schadek Appraisals and Bowyer Real Estate appraise the value of the selected homes. For each home, there will be a pair of appraisal values. That is, for each home there will be an appraised value from both Schadek Appraisals and Bowyer Real Estate. The appraised values depend on, or are related to, the home selected. This is also referred to as a **paired sample.**

For hypothesis testing, we are interested in the distribution of the *differences* in the appraised value of each home. Hence, there is only one sample. To put it more formally, we are investigating whether the mean of the distribution of differences in the appraised values is 0. The sample is made up of the *differences* between the appraised values determined by Schadek Appraisals and the values from Bowyer Real Estate. If the two appraisal firms are reporting similar estimates, then sometimes Schadek Appraisals will be the higher value and sometimes Bowyer Real Estate will have the higher value. However, the mean of the distribution of differences will be 0. On the other hand, if one of the firms consistently reports the larger appraisal values, then the mean of the distribution of the differences will not be 0.

We will use the symbol μ_d to indicate the population mean of the distribution of differences. We assume the distribution of the population of differences follows the normal distribution. The test statistic follows the t distribution and we calculate its value from the following formula:

PAIRED *t* TEST

$$t = \frac{\bar{d}}{s_d/\sqrt{n}} \qquad \textbf{[11–7]}$$

There are $n - 1$ degrees of freedom and

$\bar{d}$ is the mean of the differences between the paired or related observations.
s_d is the standard deviation of the differences between the paired or related observations.
n is the number of paired observations.

The standard deviation of the differences is computed by the familiar formula for the standard deviation, except d is substituted for X. The formula is:

$$s_d = \sqrt{\frac{\Sigma(d - \bar{d})^2}{n - 1}}$$

The following example illustrates this test.

EXAMPLE

Recall that Nickel Savings and Loan wishes to compare the two companies they use to appraise the value of residential homes. Nickel Savings selected a sample of 10 residential properties and scheduled both firms for an appraisal. The results, reported in $000, are:

Home	Schadek	Bowyer
1	135	128
2	110	105
3	131	119
4	142	140
5	105	98
6	130	123
7	131	127
8	110	115
9	125	122
10	149	145

At the .05 significance level, can we conclude there is a difference in the mean appraised values of the homes?

SOLUTION

The first step is to state the null and the alternate hypotheses. In this case a two-tailed alternative is appropriate because we are interested in determining whether there is a *difference* in the appraised values. We are not interested in showing whether one particular firm appraises property at a higher value than the other. The question is whether the sample differences in the appraised values could have come from a population with a mean of 0. If the population mean of the differences is 0, then we conclude that there is no difference in the appraised values. The null and alternate hypotheses are:

H_0: $\mu_d = 0$
H_1: $\mu_d \neq 0$

There are 10 homes appraised by both firms, so $n = 10$, and $df = n - 1 = 10 - 1 = 9$. We have a two-tailed test, and the significance level is .05. To determine the critical value, go to Appendix F, move across the row with 9 degrees of freedom to the column for a two-tailed test and the .05 significance level. The value at the intersection is 2.262. This value appears in the box in Table 11–2 on page 330. The decision rule is to reject the null hypothesis if the computed value of t is less than −2.262 or greater than 2.262. Here are the computational details.

Home	Schadek	Bowyer	Difference, d	$(d - \bar{d})$	$(d - \bar{d})^2$
1	135	128	7	2.4	5.76
2	110	105	5	0.4	0.16
3	131	119	12	7.4	54.76
4	142	140	2	−2.6	6.76
5	105	98	7	2.4	5.76
6	130	123	7	2.4	5.76
7	131	127	4	−0.6	0.36
8	110	115	−5	−9.6	92.16
9	125	122	3	−1.6	2.56
10	149	145	4	−0.6	0.36
			46	0	174.40

$$\bar{d} = \frac{\Sigma d}{n} = \frac{46}{10} = 4.60$$

$$s_d = \sqrt{\frac{\Sigma(d - \bar{d})^2}{n - 1}} = \sqrt{\frac{174.4}{10 - 1}} = 4.402$$

Using formula (11–7), the value of the test statistic is 3.305, found by

$$t = \frac{\bar{d}}{s_d / \sqrt{n}} = \frac{4.6}{4.402 / \sqrt{10}} = \frac{4.6}{1.3920} = 3.305$$

Because the computed t falls in the rejection region, the null hypothesis is rejected. The population distribution of differences does not have a mean of 0. We conclude that there is a difference in the mean appraised values of the homes. The largest differences are for homes 3 and 8. Perhaps this would be an appropriate place to begin a more detailed review.

To find the p-value, we use Appendix F and the section for a two-tailed test. Move along the row with 9 degrees of freedom and find the values of t that are closest to our calculated value. For a .01 significance level, the value of t is 3.250. The computed value is larger than this value, but smaller than the value of 4.781 corresponding to the

.001 significance level. Hence, the *p*-value is less than .01. This information is highlighted in Table 11–2.

TABLE 11–2 A Portion of the *t* Distribution from Appendix F

	Confidence Intervals					
	80%	**90%**	**95%**	**98%**	**99%**	**99.9%**
	Level of Significance for One-Tailed Test, α					
df	**0.100**	**0.050**	**0.025**	**0.010**	**0.005**	**0.0005**
	Level of Significance for Two-Tailed Test, α					
	0.20	**0.10**	**0.05**	**0.02**	**0.01**	**0.001**
1	3.078	6.314	12.706	31.821	63.657	636.619
2	1.886	2.920	4.303	6.965	9.925	31.599
3	1.638	2.353	3.182	4.541	5.841	12.924
4	1.533	2.132	2.776	3.747	4.604	8.610
5	1.476	2.015	2.571	3.365	4.032	6.869
6	1.440	1.943	2.447	3.143	3.707	5.959
7	1.415	1.895	2.365	2.998	3.499	5.408
8	1.397	1.860	2.306	2.896	3.355	5.041
9	1.383	1.833	2.262	2.821	3.250	4.781
10	1.372	1.812	2.228	2.764	3.169	4.587

Excel has a procedure called "t-Test: Paired Two-Sample for Means" that will perform the calculations of formula (11–7). The output from this procedure is given below.

The computed value of *t* is 3.3045, and the two-tailed *p*-value is .00916. Because the *p*-value is less than .05, we reject the hypothesis that the mean of the distribution of the differences between the appraised values is zero. In fact, this *p*-value is less than 1.0 percent. There is a small likelihood that the null hypothesis is true.

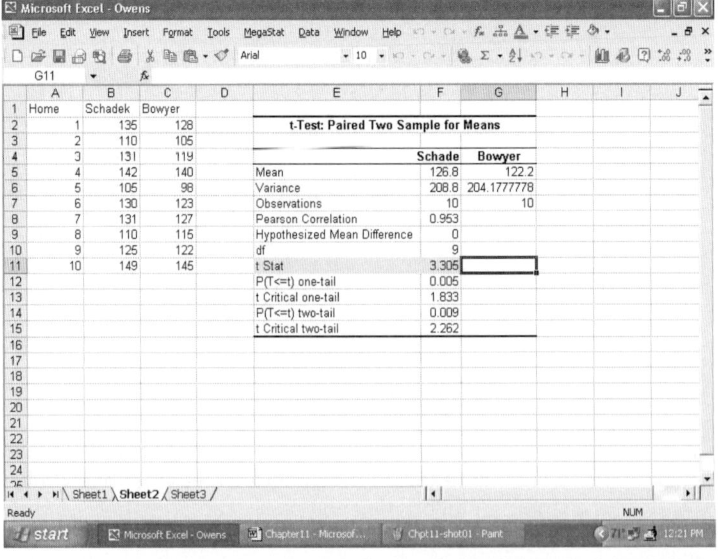

Home	Schadek	Bowyer
1	135	128
2	110	105
3	131	119
4	142	140
5	105	98
6	130	123
7	131	127
8	110	115
9	125	122
10	149	145

t-Test: Paired Two Sample for Means

	Schade	Bowyer
Mean	126.8	122.2
Variance	208.8	204.1777778
Observations	10	10
Pearson Correlation	0.953	
Hypothesized Mean Difference	0	
df	9	
t Stat	3.305	
P(T<=t) one-tail	0.005	
t Critical one-tail	1.833	
P(T<=t) two-tail	0.009	
t Critical two-tail	2.262	

Comparing Dependent and Independent Samples

Beginning students are often confused by the difference between tests for independent samples [formula (11–6)] and tests for dependent samples [formula (11–7)]. How do we tell the difference between dependent and independent samples? There are two types of dependent samples: (1) those characterized by a measurement, an intervention of some type, and then another measurement; and (2) a matching or pairing of the observations. To explain further:

1. The first type of dependent sample is characterized by a measurement followed by an intervention of some kind and then another measurement. This could be called a "before" and "after" study. Two examples will help to clarify. Suppose we want to show that, by placing speakers in the production area and playing soothing music, we are able to increase production. We begin by selecting a sample of workers and measuring their output under the current conditions. The speakers are then installed in the production area, and we again measure the output of the same workers. There are two measurements, before placing the speakers in the production area and after. The intervention is playing music in the production area.

   A second example involves an educational firm that offers courses designed to increase test scores and reading ability. Suppose the firm wants to offer a course that will help high school juniors increase their SAT scores. To begin, each student takes the SAT in the junior year in high school. During the summer between the junior and senior year, they participate in the course that gives them tips on taking tests. Finally, during the fall of their senior year in high school, they retake the SAT. Again, the procedure is characterized by a measurement (taking the SAT as a junior), an intervention (the summer workshops), and another measurement (taking the SAT during their senior year).
2. The second type of dependent sample is characterized by matching or pairing observations. Nickel Savings in the previous example is a dependent sample of this type. They selected a property for appraisal and then had two appraisals on the same property. As a second example, suppose an industrial psychologist wishes to study the intellectual similarities of newly married couples. She selects a sample of newlyweds. Next, she administers a standard intelligence test to both the man and woman to determine the difference in the scores. Notice the matching that occurred: compare the scores that are paired or matched by marriage.

Why do we prefer dependent samples to independent samples? By using dependent samples, we are able to reduce the variation in the sampling distribution. To illustrate, we will use the Nickel Savings and Loan example just completed. Suppose we assume that we have two independent samples of real estate property for appraisal and conduct the following test of hypothesis, using formula (11–6). The null and alternate hypotheses are:

H_0: $\mu_1 = \mu_2$
H_1: $\mu_1 \neq \mu_2$

There are now two independent samples of 10 each. So the number of degrees of freedom is $10 + 10 - 2 = 18$. From Appendix D, for the .05 significance level, H_0 is rejected if t is less than -2.101 or greater than 2.101.

We use the same Excel commands as on page 90 in Chapter 3 to find the mean and the standard deviation of the two independent samples. We use the Excel commands on page 341 of this chapter to find the pooled variance and the value of the "t-Stat." These values are highlighted with shading.

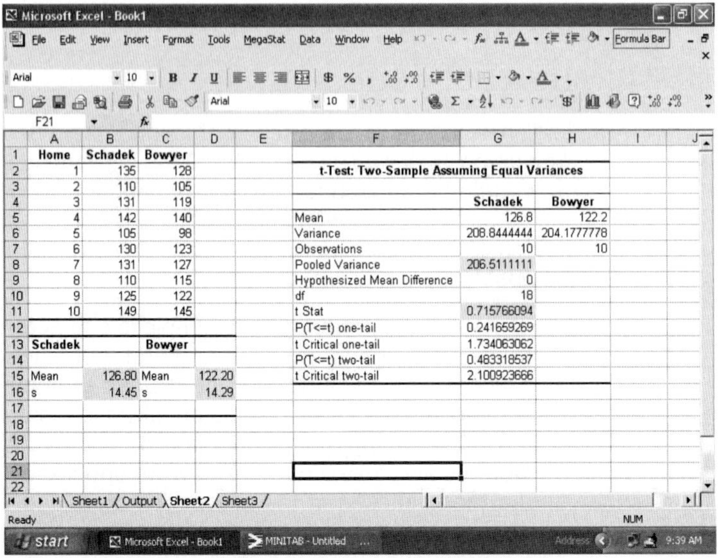

Home	Schadek	Bowyer
1	135	128
2	110	105
3	131	119
4	142	140
5	105	98
6	130	123
7	131	127
8	110	115
9	125	122
10	149	145

Schadek		Bowyer	
Mean	126.80	Mean	122.20
s	14.45	s	14.29

t-Test: Two-Sample Assuming Equal Variances

	Schadek	Bowyer
Mean	126.8	122.2
Variance	208.8444444	204.1777778
Observations	10	10
Pooled Variance	206.5111111	
Hypothesized Mean Difference	0	
df	18	
t Stat	0.715766094	
P(T<=t) one-tail	0.241659269	
t Critical one-tail	1.734063062	
P(T<=t) two-tail	0.483318537	
t Critical two-tail	2.100923666	

The mean of the appraised value of the 10 properties by Schadek is \$126,800, and the standard deviation is \$14,450. For Bowyer Real Estate the mean appraised value is \$122,200, and the standard deviation is \$14,290. To make the calculations easier, we use \$000 instead of \$. The value of the pooled estimate of the variance from formula (11–5) is

$$s_p^2 = \frac{(n_1 - 1)s_1^2 + (n_2 - 1)s_2^2}{n_1 + n_2 - 2} = \frac{(10 - 1)(14.45^2) + (10 - 1)(14.29)^2}{10 + 10 - 2} = 206.50$$

From formula (11–6), t is 0.716.

$$t = \frac{\overline{X}_1 - \overline{X}_2}{\sqrt{s_p^2\left(\frac{1}{n_1} + \frac{1}{n_2}\right)}} = \frac{126.8 - 122.2}{\sqrt{206.50\left(\frac{1}{10} + \frac{1}{10}\right)}} = \frac{4.6}{6.4265} = 0.716$$

The computed t (0.716) is less than 2.101, so the null hypothesis is not rejected. We cannot show that there is a difference in the mean appraisal value. That is not the same conclusion that we got before! Why does this happen? The numerator is the same in the paired observations test (4.6). However, the denominator is smaller. In the paired test the denominator is 1.3920 (see the calculations on page 329). In the case of the independent samples, the denominator is 6.4265. There is more variation or uncertainty. This accounts for the difference in the t values and the difference in the statistical decisions. The denominator measures the standard error of the statistic. When the samples are *not* paired, two kinds of variation are present: differences between the two appraisal firms and the difference in the value of the real estate. Properties numbered 4 and 10 have relatively high values, whereas number 5 is relatively low. These data show how different the values of the property are, but we are really interested in the difference between the two appraisal firms.

The trick is to pair the values to reduce the variation among the properties. The paired test uses only the difference between the two appraisal firms for the same property. Thus, the paired or dependent statistic focuses on the variation between Schadek Appraisals and Bowyer Real Estate. Thus, its standard error is always smaller. That, in turn, leads to a larger test statistic and a greater chance of rejecting the null hypothesis. So whenever possible you should pair the data.

There is a bit of bad news here. In the paired observations test, the degrees of freedom are half of what they are if the samples are not paired. For the real estate example, the degrees of freedom drop from 18 to 9 when the observations are paired. However, in most cases, this is a small price to pay for a better test.

Self-Review 11–4

Advertisements by Rivertown Fitness Center claim that completing their course will result in losing weight. A random sample of eight recent participants showed the following weights before and after completing the course. At the .01 significance level, can we conclude the students lost weight?

Name	Before	After
Hunter	155	154
Cashman	228	207
Mervine	141	147
Massa	162	157
Creola	211	196
Peterson	164	150
Redding	184	170
Poust	172	165

(a) State the null hypothesis and the alternate hypothesis.
(b) What is the critical value of t?
(c) What is the computed value of t?
(d) Interpret the result. What is the p-value?
(e) What assumption needs to be made about the distribution of the differences?

Exercises

19. The null and alternate hypotheses are:

H_0: $\mu_d \leq 0$
H_1: $\mu_d > 0$

The following sample information shows the number of defective units produced on the day shift and the afternoon shift for a sample of four days last month.

	Day			
	1	2	3	4
Day shift	10	12	15	19
Afternoon shift	8	9	12	15

At the .05 significance level, can we conclude there are more defects produced on the afternoon shift?

20. The null and alternate hypotheses are:

H_0: $\mu_d = 0$
H_1: $\mu_d \neq 0$

The following paired observations show the number of traffic citations given for speeding by Officer Dhondt and Officer Meredith of the South Carolina Highway Patrol for the last five months.

	Day				
	May	June	July	August	September
Officer Dhondt	30	22	25	19	26
Officer Meredith	26	19	20	15	19

At the .05 significance level, is there a difference in the mean number of citations given by the two officers?

Note: Use the five-step hypothesis testing procedure to solve the following exercises.

21. The management of Discount Furniture, a chain of discount furniture stores in the Northeast, designed an incentive plan for salespeople. To evaluate this innovative plan, 12 salespeople were selected at random, and their weekly incomes before and after the plan were recorded.

Salesperson	Before	After
Sid Mahone	$320	$340
Carol Quick	290	285
Tom Jackson	421	475
Andy Jones	510	510
Jean Sloan	210	210
Jack Walker	402	500
Peg Mancuso	625	631
Anita Loma	560	560
John Cuso	360	365
Carl Utz	431	431
A. S. Kushner	506	525
Fern Lawton	505	619

Was there a significant increase in the typical salesperson's weekly income due to the innovative incentive plan? Use the .05 significance level. Estimate the *p*-value, and interpret it.

22. The federal government recently granted funds for a special program designed to reduce crime in high-crime areas. A study of the results of the program in eight high-crime areas of Miami, Florida, yielded the following results.

	Number of Crimes by Area							
	A	B	C	D	E	F	G	H
Before	14	7	4	5	17	12	8	9
After	2	7	3	6	8	13	3	5

Has there been a decrease in the number of crimes since the inauguration of the program? Use the .01 significance level. Estimate the *p*-value.

Chapter Outline

I. In comparing two population means we wish to know whether they could be equal.

A. We are investigating whether the distribution of the difference between the means could have a mean of 0.

B. The test statistic is the standard normal *z* if the samples both contain at least 30 observations and the population standard deviations are unknown.

1. No assumption about the shape of either population is required.
2. The samples are from independent populations.
3. The formula to compute the value of *z* is

$$z = \frac{\bar{X}_1 - \bar{X}_2}{\sqrt{\frac{s_1^2}{n_1} + \frac{s_2^2}{n_2}}} \qquad \textbf{[11-2]}$$

II. We can also test whether two samples come from populations with an equal proportion of successes.

A. The two sample proportions are pooled using the following formula:

$$p_c = \frac{X_1 + X_2}{n_1 + n_2} \qquad \textbf{[11-4]}$$

B. We compute the value of the test statistic from the following formula:

$$z = \frac{p_1 - p_2}{\sqrt{\frac{p_c(1-p_c)}{n_1} + \frac{p_c(1-p_c)}{n_2}}} \quad \textbf{[11-3]}$$

III. The test statistic to compare two means is the t distribution if one or both of the samples contain fewer than 30 observations.

A. Both populations must follow the normal distribution.

B. The populations must have equal standard deviations.

C. The samples are independent.

D. Finding the value of t requires two steps.

1. The first step is to pool the standard deviations according to the following formula:

$$s_p^2 = \frac{(n_1 - 1)s_1^2 + (n_2 - 1)s_2^2}{n_1 + n_2 - 2} \quad \textbf{[11-5]}$$

2. The value of t is computed from the following formula:

$$t = \frac{\bar{X}_1 - \bar{X}_2}{\sqrt{s_p^2\left(\frac{1}{n_1} + \frac{1}{n_2}\right)}} \quad \textbf{[11-6]}$$

IV. For dependent samples, we assume the distribution of the paired differences between the populations has a mean of 0.

A. We first compute the mean and the standard deviation of the sample differences.

B. The value of the test statistic is computed from the following formula:

$$t = \frac{\bar{d}}{s_d/\sqrt{n}} \quad \textbf{[11-7]}$$

Pronunciation Key

SYMBOL	MEANING	PRONUNCIATION
p_c	Pooled proportion	*p sub c*
s_p^2	Pooled sample variance	*s sub p squared*
$\bar{X}_1$	Mean of the first sample	*X bar sub 1*
$\bar{X}_2$	Mean of the second sample	*X bar sub 2*
$\bar{d}$	Mean of the difference between dependent observations	*d bar*
s_d	Standard deviation of the difference between dependent observations	*s sub d*

Chapter Exercises

23. A recent study focused on the number of times men and women who live alone buy take-out dinners in a month. The information is summarized below.

Statistic	Men	Women
Mean	24.51	22.69
Standard deviation	4.48	3.86
Sample size	35	40

At the .01 significance level, is there a difference in the mean number of times men and women order takeout dinners in a month? What is the p-value?

24. Clark Heter is an industrial engineer at Lyons Products. He would like to determine whether there are more units produced on the afternoon shift than on the day shift. A sample of 54 day-shift workers showed that the mean number of units produced was 345, with a standard deviation of 21. A sample of 60 afternoon-shift workers showed that the mean number of units produced was 351, with a standard deviation of 28 units. At the .05 significance level, is the number of units produced on the afternoon shift larger?

25. Fry Brothers Heating and Air Conditioning, Inc. employs Larry Clark and George Murnen to make service calls to repair furnaces and air conditioning units in homes. Tom Fry, the owner, would like to know whether there is a difference in the mean number of service calls they make per day. A random sample of 40 days last year showed that Larry Clark made an average of 4.77 calls per day, with a standard deviation of 1.05 calls per day. For a sample of 50 days George Murnen made an average of 5.02 calls per day, with a standard deviation of 1.23 calls per day. At the .05 significance level, is there a difference in the mean number of calls per day between the two employees? What is the *p*-value?

26. A coffee manufacturer is interested in whether the mean daily consumption of regular coffee drinkers is less than that of decaffeinated-coffee drinkers. A random sample of 50 regular-coffee drinkers showed a mean of 4.35 cups per day, with a standard deviation of 1.20 cups per day. A sample of 40 decaffeinated-coffee drinkers showed a mean of 5.84 cups per day, with a standard deviation of 1.36 cups per day. Use the .01 significance level. Compute the *p*-value.

27. A cell phone company offers two plans to it subscribers. At the time new subscribers sign up, they are asked to provide some demographic information. The mean yearly income for a sample of 40 subscribers to Plan A is $57,000 with a standard deviation of $9,200. This distribution is positively skewed; the actual coefficient of skewness is 2.11. For a sample of 30 subscribers to Plan B the mean income is $61,000 with a standard deviation of $7,100. The distribution of Plan B subscribers is also positively skewed, but not as severely. The coefficient of skewness is 1.54. At the .05 significance level, is it reasonable to conclude the mean income of those selecting Plan B is larger? What is the *p*-value? Do the coefficients of skewness affect the results of the hypothesis test? Why?

28. A computer manufacturer offers a help line that purchasers can call for help 24 hours a day 7 days a week. Clearing these calls for help in a timely fashion is important to the company's image. After telling the caller that resolution of the problem is important the caller is asked whether the issue is "software" or "hardware" related. The mean time it takes a technician to resolve a software issue is 18 minutes with a standard deviation of 4.2 minutes. This information was obtained from a sample of 35 monitored calls. For a study of 45 hardware issues, the mean time for the technician to resolve the problem was 15.5 minutes with a standard deviation of 3.9 minutes. This information was also obtained from monitored calls. At the .05 significance level is it reasonable to conclude that it takes longer to resolve software issues? What is the *p*-value?

29. The manufacturer of Advil, a common headache remedy, recently developed a new formulation of the drug that is claimed to be more effective. To evaluate the new drug, a sample of 200 current users is asked to try it. After a one-month trial, 180 indicated the new drug was more effective in relieving a headache. At the same time a sample of 300 current Advil users is given the current drug but told it is the new formulation. From this group, 261 said it was an improvement. At the .05 significance level can we conclude that the new drug is more effective?

30. Each month the National Association of Purchasing Managers publishes the NAPM index. One of the questions asked on the survey to purchasing agents is: Do you think the economy is expanding? Last month, of the 300 responses 160 answered yes to the question. This month, 170 of the 290 responses indicated they felt the economy was expanding. At the .05 significance level, can we conclude that a larger proportion of the agents believe the economy is expanding this month?

31. As part of a recent survey among dual-wage-earner couples, an industrial psychologist found that 990 men out of the 1,500 surveyed believed the division of household duties was fair. A sample of 1,600 women found 970 believed the division of household duties was fair. At the .01 significance level, is it reasonable to conclude that the proportion of men who believe the division of household duties is fair is larger? What is the *p*-value?

32. There are two major Internet providers in the Colorado Springs, Colorado, area, one called HTC and the other Mountain Communications. We want to investigate whether there is a difference in the proportion of times a customer is able to access the Internet. During a one-week period, 500 calls were placed at random times throughout the day and night to HTC. A connection was made to the Internet on 450 occasions. A similar one-week study with Mountain Communications showed the Internet to be available on 352 of 400 trials. At the .01 significance level, is there a difference in the percent of time that access to the Internet is successful?

33. The owner of Bun 'N' Run Hamburger wishes to compare the sales per day at two locations. The mean number sold for 10 randomly selected days at the Northside site was

83.55, and the standard deviation was 10.50. For a random sample of 12 days at the Southside location, the mean number sold was 78.80 and the standard deviation was 14.25. At the .05 significance level, is there a difference in the mean number of hamburgers sold at the two locations? What is the *p*-value?

34. The Engineering Department at Sims Software, Inc., recently developed two chemical solutions designed to increase the usable life of computer disks. A sample of disks treated with the first solution lasted 86, 78, 66, 83, 84, 81, 84, 109, 65, and 102 hours. Those treated with the second solution lasted 91, 71, 75, 76, 87, 79, 73, 76, 79, 78, 87, 90, 76, and 72 hours. At the .10 significance level, can we conclude that there is a difference in the length of time the two types of treatment lasted?

35. The Willow Run Outlet Mall has two Gap Outlet Stores, one located on Peach Street and the other on Plum Street. The two stores are laid out differently, but both store managers claim their layout maximizes the amounts customers will purchase on impulse. A sample of 10 customers at the Peach Street store revealed they spent the following amounts more than planned: $17.58, $19.73, $12.61, $17.79, $16.22, $15.82, $15.40, $15.86, $11.82, and $15.85. A sample of 14 customers at the Plum Street store revealed they spent the following amounts more than they planned: $18.19, $20.22, $17.38, $17.96, $23.92, $15.87, $16.47, $15.96, $16.79, $16.74, $21.40, $20.57, $19.79, and $14.83. At the .01 significance level, is there a difference in the mean amounts purchased on impulse at the two stores?

36. The Grand Strand Family Medical Center is specifically set up to treat minor medical emergencies for visitors to the Myrtle Beach area. There are two facilities, one in the Little River Area and the other in Murrells Inlet. The Quality Assurance Department wishes to compare the mean waiting time for patients at the two locations. Samples of the waiting times, reported in minutes, follow:

Location	Waiting Time											
Little River	31.73	28.77	29.53	22.08	29.47	18.60	32.94	25.18	29.82	26.49		
Murrells Inlet	22.93	23.92	26.92	27.20	26.44	25.62	30.61	29.44	23.09	23.10	26.69	22.31

At the .05 significance level, is there a difference in the mean waiting time?

37. The Commercial Bank and Trust Company is studying the use of its automatic teller machines (ATMs). Of particular interest is whether young adults (under 25 years) use the machines more than senior citizens. To investigate further, samples of customers under 25 years of age and customers over 60 years of age were selected. The number of ATM transactions last month was determined for each selected individual, and the results are shown below. At the .01 significance level, can bank management conclude that younger customers use the ATMs more?

Under 25	10	10	11	15	7	11	10	9			
Over 60	4	8	7	7	4	5	1	7	4	10	5

38. Two boats, the *Prada* (Italy) and the *Oracle* (U.S.A.), are competing for a spot in the upcoming *America's Cup* race. They race over a part of the course several times. Below are the sample times in minutes. At the .05 significance level, can we conclude that there is a difference in their mean times?

Boat	Times (minutes)											
Prada (Italy)	12.9	12.5	11.0	13.3	11.2	11.4	11.6	12.3	14.2	11.3		
Oracle (U.S.A.)	14.1	14.1	14.2	17.4	15.8	16.7	16.1	13.3	13.4	13.6	10.8	19.0

39. The manufacturer of an MP3 player wanted to know whether a 10 percent reduction in price is enough to increase the sales of their product. To investigate, the owner randomly selected eight outlets and sold the MP3 player at the reduced price. At seven randomly selected outlets, the MP3 player was sold at the regular price. Reported below is the number of units sold last month at the sampled outlets. At the .01 significance level, can the manufacturer conclude that the price reduction resulted in an increase in sales?

Regular price	138	121	88	115	141	125	96	
Reduced price	128	134	152	135	114	106	112	120

40. A number of minor automobile accidents occur at various high-risk intersections in Teton County despite traffic lights. The Traffic Department claims that a modification in the type of light will reduce these accidents. The county commissioners have agreed to a proposed experiment. Eight intersections were chosen at random, and the lights at those intersections were modified. The numbers of minor accidents during a six-month period before and after the modifications were:

	Number of Accidents							
	A	B	C	D	E	F	G	H
Before modification	5	7	6	4	8	9	8	10
After modification	3	7	7	0	4	6	8	2

At the .01 significance level is it reasonable to conclude that the modification reduced the number of traffic accidents?

41. Lester Hollar is Vice President for Human Resources for a large manufacturing company. In recent years he has noticed an increase in absenteeism that he thinks is related to the general health of the employees. Four years ago, in an attempt to improve the situation, he began a fitness program in which employees exercise during their lunch hour. To evaluate the program, he selected a random sample of eight participants and found the number of days each was absent in the six months before the exercise program began and in the last six months. Below are the results. At the .05 significance level, can he conclude that the number of absences has declined? Estimate the *p*-value.

Employee	Before	After
1	6	5
2	6	2
3	7	1
4	7	3
5	4	3
6	3	6
7	5	3
8	6	7

42. The president of the American Insurance Institute wants to compare the yearly costs of auto insurance offered by two leading companies. He selects a sample of 15 families, some with only a single insured driver, others with several teenage drivers, and pays each family a stipend to contact the two companies and ask for a price quote. To make the data comparable, certain features, such as the amount deductible and limits of liability, are standardized. The sample information is reported below. At the .10 significance level, can we conclude that there is a difference in the amounts quoted?

Family	Progressive Car Insurance	GEICO Mutual Insurance
Becker	$2,090	$1,610
Berry	1,683	1,247
Wong	1,402	2,327
Debuck	1,830	1,367
DuBrul	930	1,461
Eckroate	697	1,789
German	1,741	1,621
Ruska	1,129	1,914
King	1,018	1,956
Kucic	1,881	1,772
Meredith	1,571	1,375
Obeid	874	1,527
Orlando	1,579	1,767
Phillips	1,577	1,636
Suzuki	860	1,188

43. Fairfield Homes is developing two parcels of land near Pigeon Fork, Tennessee. In order to test different advertising approaches, they use different media to reach potential buyers. The mean annual family income for 75 people making inquiries at the first development is \$150,000, with a standard deviation of \$40,000. A corresponding sample of 120 people at the second development had a mean of \$180,000, with a standard deviation of \$30,000. At the .05 significance level, can Fairfield conclude that the population means are different?

44. The following data resulted from a taste test of two different chocolate bars. The first number is a rating of the taste, which could range from 0 to 5, with a 5 indicating the person liked the taste. The second number indicates whether a "secret ingredient" was present. If the ingredient was present a code of "1" was used and a "0" otherwise. At the .05 significance level, does this data show a difference in the taste ratings?

Rating	"With/Without"	Rating	"With/Without"
3	1	1	1
1	1	4	0
0	0	4	0
2	1	2	1
3	1	3	0
1	1	4	0

45. An investigation of the effectiveness of an antibacterial soap in reducing operating room contamination resulted in the accompanying table. The new soap was tested in a sample of eight operating rooms in the greater Seattle area during the last year.

	Operating Room							
	A	B	C	D	E	F	G	H
Before	6.6	6.5	9.0	10.3	11.2	8.1	6.3	11.6
After	6.8	2.4	7.4	8.5	8.1	6.1	3.4	2.0

At the .05 significance level, can we conclude the contamination measurements are lower after use of the new soap?

46. The following data on annual rates of return were collected from five stocks listed on the New York Stock Exchange ("the big board") and five stocks listed on NASDAQ. At the .10 significance level, can we conclude that the annual rates of return are higher on the big board?

NYSE	NASDAQ
17.16	15.80
17.08	16.28
15.51	16.21
8.43	17.97
25.15	7.77

47. The city of Laguna Beach operates two public parking lots. The one on Ocean Drive can accommodate up to 125 cars and the one on Rio Rancho can accommodate up to 130 cars. City planners are considering both increasing the size of the lots and changing the fee structure. To begin, the Planning Office would like some information on the number of cars in the lots at various times of the day. A junior planner officer is assigned the task of visiting the two lots at random times of the day and evening and counting the number of cars in the lots. The study lasted over a period of one month. Below is the number of cars in the lots for 25 visits of the Ocean Drive lot and 28 visits of the Rio Rancho lot.

Ocean												
89	115	93	79	113	77	51	75	118	105	106	91	54
63	121	53	81	115	67	53	69	95	121	88	64	

Rio Rancho												
128	110	81	126	82	114	93	40	94	45	84	71	74
92	66	69	100	114	113	107	62	77	80	107	90	129
105	124											

Is it reasonable to conclude that there is a difference in the mean number of cars in the two lots? Use the .05 significance level.

48. The amount spent on housing is an important component of the cost of living. The total costs of housing for homeowners might include mortgage payments, property taxes, and utility costs (water, heat, electricity). An economist selected a sample of 20 homeowners in New England and then calculated these total housing costs as a percent of monthly income, five years ago and now. The information is reported below. Is it reasonable to conclude the percent is less now than five years ago?

Homeowner	Five Years Ago	Now	Homeowner	Five Years Ago	Now
1	17	10	11	35	32
2	20	39	12	16	32
3	29	37	13	23	21
4	43	27	14	33	12
5	36	12	15	44	40
6	43	41	16	44	42
7	45	24	17	28	22
8	19	26	18	29	19
9	49	28	19	39	35
10	49	26	20	22	12

exercises.com

49. Listed below are several prominent companies and their stock prices in June 2004. Go to the Web and look up today's price. There are many sources to find stock prices, such as Yahoo and CNNFI. The Yahoo address is http://www.finance.yahoo.com. Enter the symbol identification to find the current price. At the .05 significance level, can we conclude that the prices have changed?

Company	Symbol	Price
Coca-Cola	KO	$51.89
Walt Disney	DIS	24.06
Eastman Kodak	EK	25.31
Ford Motor Company	F	14.81
General Motors	GM	45.60
Goodyear Tire	GT	8.49
IBM	IBM	87.59
McDonald's	MCD	26.58
McGraw-Hill Publishing	MHP	77.18
Oracle	ORCL	11.01
Johnson and Johnson	JNJ	56.72
General Electric	GE	31.01
Home Depot	HD	35.60

50. The *USA Today* (http://www.usatoday.com/sports/baseball/front.htm) and Major League Baseball's (http://www.majorleaguebaseball.com) websites regularly report information on individual player salaries in the American League and the National League. Go to one of these sites and find the individual salaries for your favorite team in each league. Compute the mean and the standard deviation. Is it reasonable to conclude that there is a difference in the salaries of the two teams?

Dataset Exercises

51. Refer to the Real Estate data, which reports information on the homes sold in Denver, Colorado, last year.
    a. At the .05 significance level, can we conclude that there is a difference in the mean selling price of homes with a pool and homes without a pool?
    b. At the .05 significance level, can we conclude that there is a difference in the mean selling price of homes with an attached garage and homes without a garage?
    c. At the .05 significance level, can we conclude that there is a difference in the mean selling price of homes in Township 1 and Township 2?
    d. Find the median selling price of the homes. Divide the homes into two groups, those that sold for more than (or equal to) the median price and those that sold for less. Is there a difference in the proportion of homes with a pool for those that sold at or above the median price versus those that sold for less than the median price? Use the .05 significance level.
52. Refer to the Baseball 2003 data, which reports information on the 30 Major League Baseball teams for the 2003 season.
    a. At the .05 significance level, can we conclude that there is a difference in the mean salary of teams in the American League versus teams in the National League?
    b. At the .05 significance level, can we conclude that there is a difference in the mean home attendance of teams in the American League versus teams in the National League?
    c. At the .05 significance level, can we conclude that there is a difference in the mean number of wins for teams that have artificial turf home fields versus teams that have grass home fields?
    d. At the .05 significance level, can we conclude that there is a difference in the mean number of home runs for teams that have artificial turf home fields versus teams that have grass home fields?
53. Refer to the Wage data, which reports information on annual wages for a sample of 100 workers. Also included are variables relating to industry, years of education, and gender for each worker.
    a. Conduct a test of hypothesis to determine if there is a difference in the mean annual wages of southern residents versus nonsouthern residents.
    b. Conduct a test of hypothesis to determine if there is a difference in the mean annual wages of white and nonwhite wage earners.
    c. Conduct a test of hypothesis to determine if there is a difference in the mean annual wages of Hispanic and non-Hispanic wage earners.
    d. Conduct a test of hypothesis to determine if there is a difference in the mean annual wages of female and male wage earners.
    e. Conduct a test of hypothesis to determine if there is a difference in the mean annual wages of married and nonmarried wage earners.
54. Refer to the CIA data, which reports demographic and economic information on 46 countries. Conduct a test of hypothesis to determine whether the mean percent of the population over 65 years of age in G20 countries is different from those that are not G20 members.

Software Commands

1. The Excel commands for the two-sample *t*-test on page 326 are:
    a. Enter the data into columns A and B (or any other columns) in the spreadsheet. Use the first row of each column to enter the variable name.
    b. From the menu bar select **Tools** and **Data Analysis.** Select **t-Test: Two-Sample Assuming Equal Variances,** then click **OK.**
    c. In the dialog box indicate that the range of **Variable 1** is from *A1* to *A6* and **Variable 2** from *B1* to *B7*, the **Hypothesized Mean Difference** is 0, the **Labels** are in the first row, **Alpha** is *0.05*, and the **Output Range** is *D2*. Click **OK.**

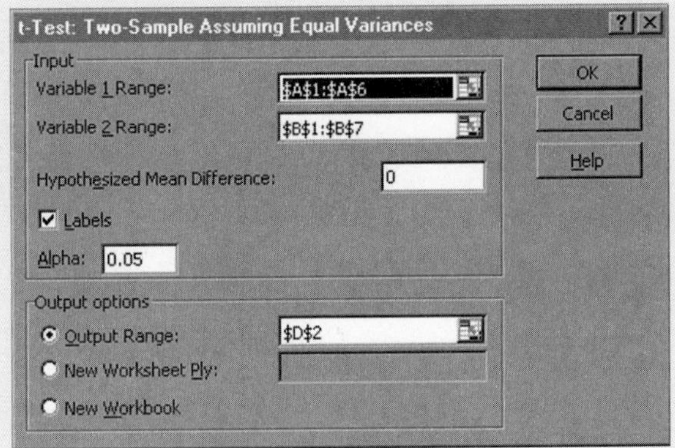

2. The Excel commands for the paired *t*-test on page 330 are:
   a. Enter the data into columns B and C (or any other two columns) in the spreadsheet, with the variable names in the first row.
   b. From the menu bar select **Tools** and **Data Analysis.** Select **t-Test: Paired Two Sample for Means,** then click **OK.**
   c. In the dialog box indicate that the range of **Variable 1** is from *B1* to *B11* and **Variable 2** from *C1* to *C11*, the **Hypothesized Mean Difference** is *0*, the **Labels** are in the first row, **Alpha** is *.05*, and the **Output Range** is *D2*. Click **OK.**

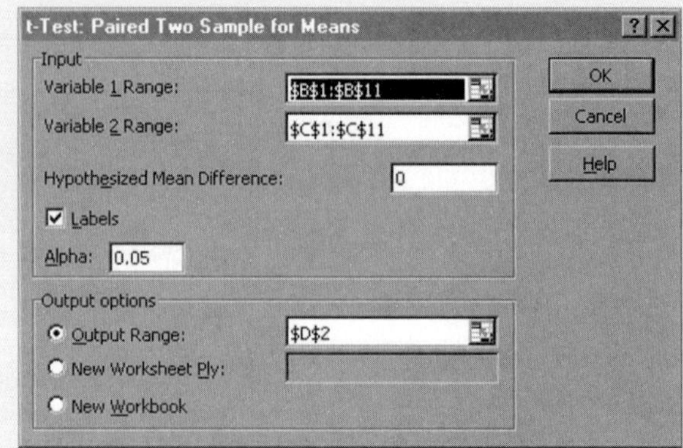

Chapter 11 Answers to Self-Review

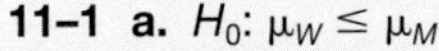

11–1 **a.** H_0: $\mu_W \le \mu_M$
H_1: $\mu_W > \mu_M$
The subscript W refers to the women and M to the men.

b. Reject H_0 if $z > 1.65$

c. $$z = \frac{\$1,500 - \$1,400}{\sqrt{\frac{(\$250)^2}{50} + \frac{(\$200)^2}{40}}} = 2.11$$

d. Reject the null hypothesis

e. p-value = .5000 − .4826 = .0174

f. The mean amount sold per day is larger for women.

11–2 **a.** H_0: $\pi_1 = \pi_2$
H_1: $\pi_1 \ne \pi_2$

b. .10

c. Two-tailed

d. Reject H_0 if z is less than −1.65 or greater than 1.65.

e. $$p_c = \frac{87 + 123}{150 + 200} = \frac{210}{350} = .60$$

$$p_1 = \frac{87}{150} = .58 \quad p_2 = \frac{123}{200} = .615$$

$$z = \frac{.58 - .615}{\sqrt{\frac{.60(.40)}{150} + \frac{.60(.40)}{200}}} = -0.66$$

f. Do not reject H_0.

g. p-value = 2(.5000 − .2454) = .5092
There is no difference in the proportion of adults and children that liked the proposed flavor.

11–3 **a.** H_0: $\mu_d = \mu_a$
H_1: $\mu_d \ne \mu_a$

b. $df = 6 + 8 - 2 = 12$
Reject H_0 if t is less than −2.179 or t is greater than 2.179.

c. $$\bar{X}_1 = \frac{42}{6} = 7.00 \quad s_1 = \sqrt{\frac{10}{6 - 1}} = 1.4142$$

$$\bar{X}_2 = \frac{80}{8} = 10.00 \quad s_2 = \sqrt{\frac{36}{8 - 1}} = 2.2678$$

$$s_p^2 = \frac{(6 - 1)(1.4142)^2 + (8 - 1)(2.2678)^2}{6 + 8 - 2}$$

$$= 3.8333$$

$$t = \frac{7.00 - 10.00}{\sqrt{3.8333\left(\frac{1}{6} + \frac{1}{8}\right)}} = -2.837$$

d. Reject H_0 because −2.837 is less than the critical value.

e. The p-value is less than .02.

f. The mean number of defects is not the same on the two shifts.

g. Independent populations, populations follow the normal distribution, populations have equal standard deviations.

11–4 **a.** H_0: $\mu_d \le 0$, H_1: $\mu_d > 0$.

b. Reject H_0 if $t > 2.998$.

c.

Name	Before	After	d	$(d - \bar{d})$	$(d - \bar{d})^2$
Hunter	155	154	1	−7.875	62.0156
Cashman	228	207	21	12.125	147.0156
Mervine	141	147	−6	−14.875	221.2656
Massa	162	157	5	−3.875	15.0156
Creola	211	196	15	6.125	37.5156
Peterson	164	150	14	5.125	26.2656
Redding	184	170	14	5.125	26.2656
Poust	172	165	7	−1.875	3.5156
			71		538.8750

$$\bar{d} = \frac{71}{8} = 8.875$$

$$s_d = \sqrt{\frac{538.875}{8 - 1}} = 8.774$$

$$t = \frac{8.875}{8.774 / \sqrt{8}} = 2.861$$

d. Do not reject H_0. We cannot conclude that the students lost weight. The p-value is less than .025 but larger than .01.

e. The distribution of the differences must follow a normal distribution.

12 Analysis of Variance

GOALS

When you have completed this chapter, you will be able to:

1 List the characteristics of the F distribution.

2 Conduct a test of hypothesis to determine whether the variances of two populations are equal.

3 Discuss the general idea of analysis of variance.

4 Organize data into a one-way ANOVA table.

5 Conduct a test of hypothesis among three or more treatment means.

6 Develop confidence intervals for the difference in treatment means.

A grocery store wants to monitor the amount of withdrawals that its customers make from automatic teller machines (ATMs) located within their stores. They sample 10 withdrawals from each location: Use a .01 level of significance to test if there is a difference in the mean amount of money withdrawn, based on the output on page 369. (See Goal 5 and Exercise 29.)

Introduction

In this chapter we continue our discussion of hypothesis testing. Recall that in Chapters 10 and 11 we examined the general theory of hypothesis testing. We described the case where a large sample was selected from the population. We used the *z* distribution (the standard normal distribution) to determine whether it was reasonable to conclude that the population mean was equal to a specified value. We tested whether two population means are the same. We also conducted both one- and two-sample tests for population proportions, again using the standard normal distribution as the distribution of the test statistic. We described methods for conducting tests of means where the populations were assumed normal but the samples were small (contained fewer than 30 observations). In that case the *t* distribution was used as the distribution of the test statistic. In this chapter we expand further our idea of hypothesis tests. We describe a test for variances and then a test that simultaneously compares several means to determine if they came from equal populations.

The *F* Distribution

The probability distribution used in this chapter is the *F* distribution. It was named to honor Sir Ronald Fisher, one of the founders of modern-day statistics. This probability distribution is used as the distribution of the test statistic for several situations. It is used to test whether two samples are from populations having equal variances, and it is also applied when we want to compare several population means simultaneously. The simultaneous comparison of several population means is called **analysis of variance (ANOVA).** In both of these situations, the populations must follow a normal distribution, and the data must be at least interval-scale.

What are the characteristics of the *F* distribution?

Characteristics of the *F* distribution

1. **There is a "family" of *F* distributions.** A particular member of the family is determined by two parameters: the degrees of freedom in the numerator and the degrees of freedom in the denominator. The shape of the distribution is illustrated by the following graph. There is one *F* distribution for the combination of 29 degrees of freedom in the numerator and 28 degrees of freedom in the denominator. There is another *F* distribution for 19 degrees in the numerator and 6 degrees of freedom in the denominator. Note that the shape of the curves changes as the degrees of freedom changes.

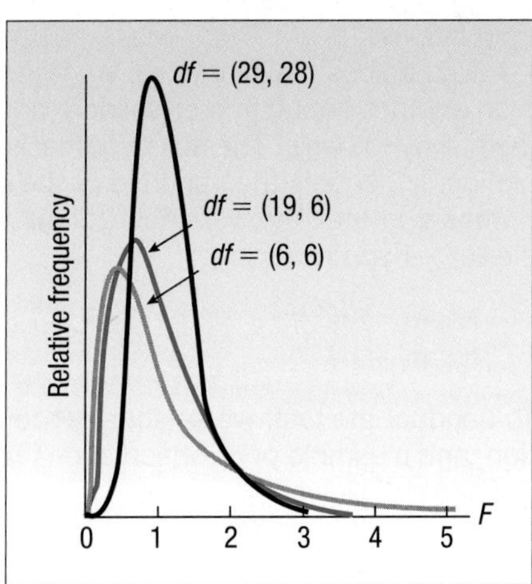

2. **The *F* distribution is continuous.** This means that it can assume an infinite number of values between zero and positive infinity.

3. **The *F* distribution cannot be negative.** The smallest value *F* can assume is 0.
4. **It is positively skewed.** The long tail of the distribution is to the right-hand side. As the number of degrees of freedom increases in both the numerator and denominator the distribution approaches a normal distribution.
5. **It is asymptotic.** As the values of *X* increase, the *F* curve approaches the *X*-axis but never touches it. This is similar to the behavior of the normal distribution, described in Chapter 7.

Comparing Two Population Variances

The *F* distribution is used to test the hypothesis that the variance of one normal population equals the variance of another normal population. The following examples will show the use of the test:

- Two Barth shearing machines are set to produce steel bars of the same length. The bars, therefore, should have the same mean length. We want to ensure that in addition to having the same mean length they also have similar variation.

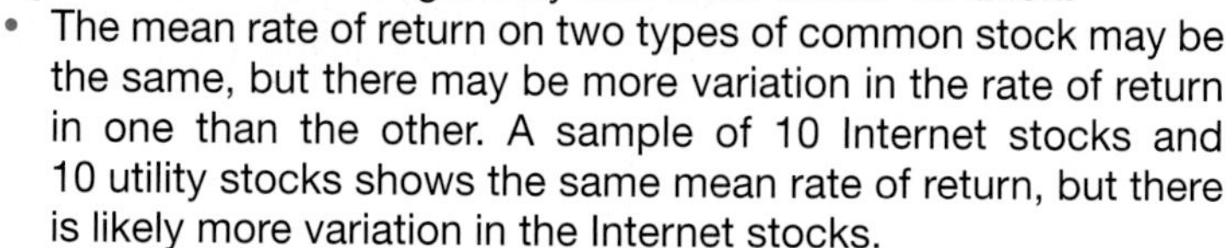

- The mean rate of return on two types of common stock may be the same, but there may be more variation in the rate of return in one than the other. A sample of 10 Internet stocks and 10 utility stocks shows the same mean rate of return, but there is likely more variation in the Internet stocks.
- A study by the marketing department for a large newspaper found that men and women spent about the same amount of time per day reading the paper. However, the same report indicated there was nearly twice as much variation in time spent per day among the men than the women.

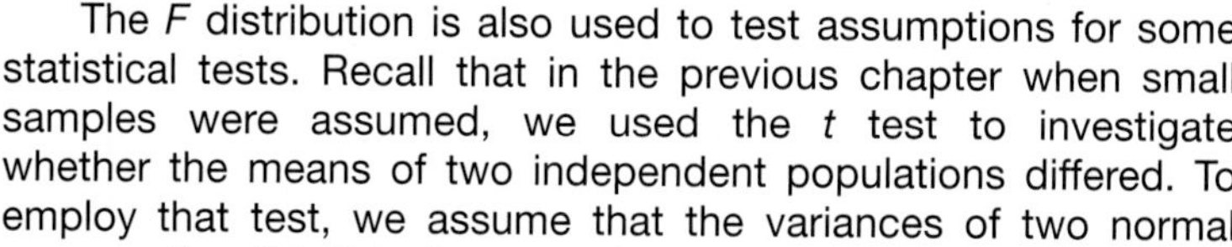

The *F* distribution is also used to test assumptions for some statistical tests. Recall that in the previous chapter when small samples were assumed, we used the *t* test to investigate whether the means of two independent populations differed. To employ that test, we assume that the variances of two normal populations are the same. See this list of assumptions on page 323. The *F* distribution provides a means for conducting a test regarding the variances of two normal populations.

Regardless of whether we want to determine if one population has more variation than another population or validate an assumption for a statistical test, we first state the null hypothesis. The null hypothesis could be that the variance of one normal population, σ_1^2, equals the variance of the other normal population, σ_2^2. The alternate hypothesis is that the variances differ. In this instance the null hypothesis and the alternate hypothesis are:

$$H_0: \sigma_1^2 = \sigma_2^2$$
$$H_1: \sigma_1^2 \neq \sigma_2^2$$

To conduct the test, we select a random sample of n_1 observations from one population, and a sample of n_2 observations from the second population. The test statistic is defined as follows.

TEST STATISTIC FOR COMPARING TWO VARIANCES $$F = \frac{s_1^2}{s_2^2} \quad [12\text{–}1]$$

The terms s_1^2 and s_2^2 are the respective sample variances. The test statistic follows the *F* distribution with $n_1 - 1$ and $n_2 - 1$ degrees of freedom. In order to reduce the size of the table of critical values, the *larger* sample variance is placed in the numerator; hence, the tabled *F* ratio is always larger than 1.00. Thus, the right-tail critical value is the only one required. The critical value of *F* for a two-tailed test is found by dividing the significance level in half ($\alpha/2$) and then referring to the appropriate degrees of freedom in Appendix G. An example will illustrate.

EXAMPLE

Lammers Limos offers limousine service from the city hall in Toledo, Ohio, to Metro Airport in Detroit. Sean Lammers, president of the company, is considering two routes. One is via U.S. 25 and the other via I-75. He wants to study the time it takes to drive to the airport using each route and then compare the results. He collected the following sample data, which is reported in minutes. Using the .10 significance level, is there a difference in the variation in the driving times for the two routes?

U.S. Route 25	Interstate 75
52	59
67	60
56	61
45	51
70	56
54	63
64	57
	65

SOLUTION

The mean driving times along the two routes are nearly the same. The mean time is 58.29 minutes for the U.S. 25 route and 59.0 minutes along the I-75 route. However, in evaluating travel times, Mr. Lammers is also concerned about the variation in the travel times. The first step is to compute the two sample variances. We'll use formula (3–11) to compute the sample standard deviations. To obtain the sample variances, we square the standard deviations.

U.S. Route 25

$$\bar{X} = \frac{\Sigma X}{n} = \frac{408}{7} = 58.29 \qquad s = \sqrt{\frac{\Sigma(X - \bar{X})^2}{n - 1}} = \sqrt{\frac{485.43}{7 - 1}} = 8.9947$$

Interstate 75

$$\bar{X} = \frac{\Sigma X}{n} = \frac{472}{8} = 59.00 \qquad s = \sqrt{\frac{\Sigma(X - \bar{X})^2}{n - 1}} = \sqrt{\frac{134}{8 - 1}} = 4.3753$$

There is more variation, as measured by the standard deviation, in the U.S. 25 route than in the I-75 route. This is somewhat consistent with his knowledge of the two routes; the U.S. 25 route contains more stoplights, whereas I-75 is a limited-access interstate highway. However, the I-75 route is several miles longer. It is important that the service offered be both timely and consistent, so he decides to conduct a statistical test to determine whether there really is a difference in the variation of the two routes.

The usual five-step hypothesis-testing procedure will be employed.

Step 1: We begin by stating the null hypothesis and the alternate hypothesis. The test is two-tailed because we are looking for a difference in the variation of the two routes. We are *not* trying to show that one route has more variation than the other.

$$H_0: \sigma_1^2 = \sigma_2^2$$
$$H_1: \sigma_1^2 \neq \sigma_2^2$$

Step 2: We selected the .10 significance level.

Step 3: The appropriate test statistic follows the F distribution.

Step 4: The critical value is obtained from Appendix G, a portion of which is reproduced as Table 12–1. Because we are conducting a two-tailed test, the tabled significance level is .05, found by $\alpha/2 = .10/2 = .05$. There are $n_1 - 1 = 7 - 1 = 6$ degrees of freedom in the numerator, and $n_2 - 1 = 8 - 1 = 7$ degrees of freedom in the denominator. To find the critical value, move horizontally across the top portion of the F table (Table 12–1 or Appendix G) for the .05 significance level to 6 degrees of freedom in the numerator. Then move down that column to the critical value opposite 7 degrees of freedom in the denominator. The critical value is 3.87. Thus, the decision rule is: Reject the null hypothesis if the ratio of the sample variances exceeds 3.87.

TABLE 12–1 Critical Values of the F Distribution, $\alpha = .05$

Degrees of Freedom for Denominator	Degrees of Freedom for Numerator			
	5	6	7	8
1	230	234	237	239
2	19.3	19.3	19.4	19.4
3	9.01	8.94	8.89	8.85
4	6.26	6.16	6.09	6.04
5	5.05	4.95	4.88	4.82
6	4.39	4.28	4.21	4.15
7	3.97	3.87	3.79	3.73
8	3.69	3.58	3.50	3.44
9	3.48	3.37	3.29	3.23
10	3.33	3.22	3.14	3.07

Step 5: The final step is to take the ratio of the two sample variances, determine the value of the test statistic, and make a decision regarding the null hypothesis. Note that formula (12–1) refers to the sample *variances* but we calculated the sample *standard deviations*. We need to square the standard deviations to determine the variances.

$$F = \frac{s_1^2}{s_2^2} = \frac{(8.9947)^2}{(4.3753)^2} = 4.23$$

The decision is to reject the null hypothesis, because the computed F value (4.23) is larger than the critical value (3.87). We conclude that there is a difference in the variation of the travel times along the two routes.

As noted, the usual practice is to determine the *F* ratio by putting the larger of the two sample variances in the numerator. This will force the *F* ratio to be at least 1.00. This allows us to always use the right tail of the *F* distribution, thus avoiding the need for more extensive *F* tables.

A logical question arises regarding one-tailed tests. For example, suppose in the previous example we suspected that the variance of the times using the U.S. 25 route is *larger* than the variance of the times along the I-75 route. We would state the null and the alternate hypothesis as

$$H_0: \sigma_1^2 \leq \sigma_2^2$$
$$H_1: \sigma_1^2 > \sigma_2^2$$

The test statistic is computed as s_1^2/s_2^2. Notice that we labeled the population with the suspected largest variance as population 1. So s_1^2 appears in the numerator. The *F* ratio will be larger than 1.00, so we can use the upper tail of the *F* distribution. Under these conditions, it is not necessary to divide the significance level in half. Because Appendix G gives us only the .05 and .01 significance levels, we are restricted to these levels for one-tailed tests and .10 and .02 for two-tailed tests unless we consult a more complete table or use statistical software to compute the *F* statistic.

The Excel software system has a procedure to perform a test of variances. Below is the output. The computed value of *F* is the same as determined by using formula (12–1). The computed value of *F* is highlighted by shading.

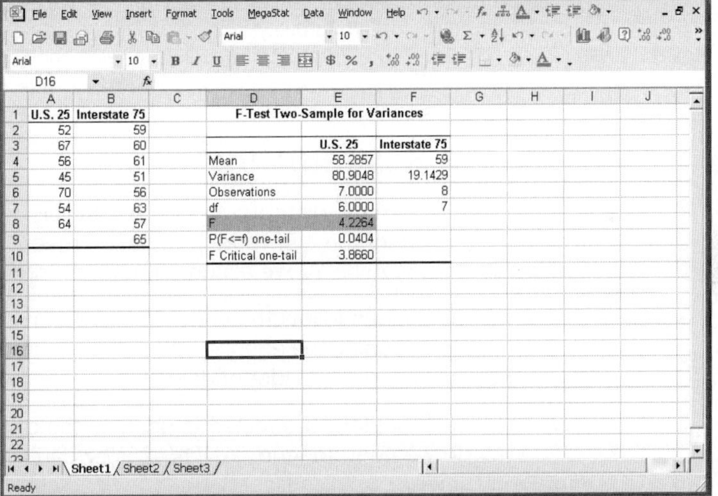

	A	B	C	D	E	F
1	U.S. 25	Interstate 75		F-Test Two-Sample for Variances		
2	52	59				
3	67	60			U.S. 25	Interstate 75
4	56	61		Mean	58.2857	59
5	45	51		Variance	80.9048	19.1429
6	70	56		Observations	7.0000	8
7	54	63		df	6.0000	7
8	64	57		F	4.2264	
9		65		P(F<=f) one-tail	0.0404	
10				F Critical one-tail	3.8660	

Self-Review 12–1 Steele Electric Products, Inc. assembles electrical components for cell phones. For the last 10 days Mark Nagy has averaged 9 rejects, with a standard deviation of 2 rejects per day. Debbie Richmond averaged 8.5 rejects, with a standard deviation of 1.5 rejects, over the same period. At the .05 significance level, can we conclude that there is more variation in the number of rejects per day attributed to Mark?

Exercises

1. What is the critical *F* value for a sample of six observations in the numerator and four in the denominator? Use a two-tailed test and the .10 significance level.

2. What is the critical F value for a sample of four observations in the numerator and seven in the denominator? Use a one-tailed test and the .01 significance level.
3. The following hypotheses are given.

$$H_0: \sigma_1^2 = \sigma_2^2$$
$$H_1: \sigma_1^2 \neq \sigma_2^2$$

A random sample of eight observations from the first population resulted in a standard deviation of 10. A random sample of six observations from the second population resulted in a standard deviation of 7. At the .02 significance level, is there a difference in the variation of the two populations?
4. The following hypotheses are given.

$$H_0: \sigma_1^2 \leq \sigma_2^2$$
$$H_1: \sigma_1^2 > \sigma_2^2$$

A random sample of five observations from the first population resulted in a standard deviation of 12. A random sample of seven observations from the second population showed a standard deviation of 7. At the .01 significance level, is there more variation in the first population?
5. Arbitron Media Research, Inc. conducted a study of the radio listening habits of men and women. One facet of the study involved the mean listening time. It was discovered that the mean listening time for men was 35 minutes per day. The standard deviation of the sample of the 10 men studied was 10 minutes per day. The mean listening time for the 12 women studied was also 35 minutes, but the standard deviation of the sample was 12 minutes. At the .10 significance level, can we conclude that there is a difference in the variation in the listening times for men and women?
6. A stockbroker at Critical Securities reported that the mean rate of return on a sample of 10 oil stocks was 12.6 percent with a standard deviation of 3.9 percent. The mean rate of return on a sample of 8 utility stocks was 10.9 percent with a standard deviation of 3.5 percent. At the .05 significance level, can we conclude that there is more variation in the oil stocks?

ANOVA Assumptions

Another use of the F distribution is the analysis of variance (ANOVA) technique in which we compare three or more population means to determine whether they could be equal. To use ANOVA, we assume the following:

1. The populations follow the normal distribution.
2. The populations have equal standard deviations (σ).
3. The populations are independent.

When these conditions are met, F is used as the distribution of the test statistic.

Why do we need to study ANOVA? Why can't we just use the test of differences in population means discussed in the previous chapter? We could compare the treatment means two at a time. The major reason is the unsatisfactory buildup of Type I error. To explain further, suppose we have four different methods (A, B, C, and D) of training new recruits to be firefighters. We randomly assign each of the 40 recruits in this year's class to one of the four methods. At the end of the training program, we administer to the four groups a common test to measure understanding of firefighting techniques. The question is: Is there a difference in the mean test scores among the four groups? An answer to this question will allow us to compare the four training methods.

Using the *t* distribution leads to a buildup of Type I error.

Using the t distribution to compare the four population means, we would have to conduct six different t tests. That is, we would need to compare the mean scores for the four methods as follows: A versus B, A versus C, A versus D, B versus C, B versus D, and C versus D. If we set the significance level at .05, the probability of a correct statistical decision is .95, found by $1 - .05$. Because we conduct six separate (independent) tests the probability that we do *not* make an incorrect decision due to sampling in any of the six independent tests is:

$$P(All\ correct) = (.95)(.95)(.95)(.95)(.95)(.95) = .735$$

To find the probability of at least one error due to sampling, we subtract this result from 1. Thus, the probability of at least one incorrect decision due to sampling is 1 − .735 = .265. To summarize, if we conduct six independent tests using the *t* distribution, the likelihood of rejecting a true null hypothesis because of sampling error is increased from .05 to an unsatisfactory level of .265. It is obvious that we need a better method than conducting six *t* tests. ANOVA will allow us to compare the treatment means simultaneously and avoid the buildup of the Type I error.

ANOVA was developed for applications in agriculture, and many of the terms related to that context remain. In particular the term *treatment* is used to identify the different populations being examined. The following illustration will clarify the term *treatment* and demonstrate an application of ANOVA.

EXAMPLE

Joyce Kuhlman manages a regional financial center. She wishes to compare the productivity, as measured by the number of customers served, among three employees. Four days are randomly selected and the number of customers served by each employee is recorded. The results are:

Wolfe	White	Korosa
55	66	47
54	76	51
59	67	46
56	71	48

SOLUTION

Is there a difference in the mean number of customers served? Chart 12–1 illustrates how the populations would appear if there was a difference in the treatment means. Note that the populations follow the normal distribution and the variation in each population is the same. However, the population means are *not* the same.

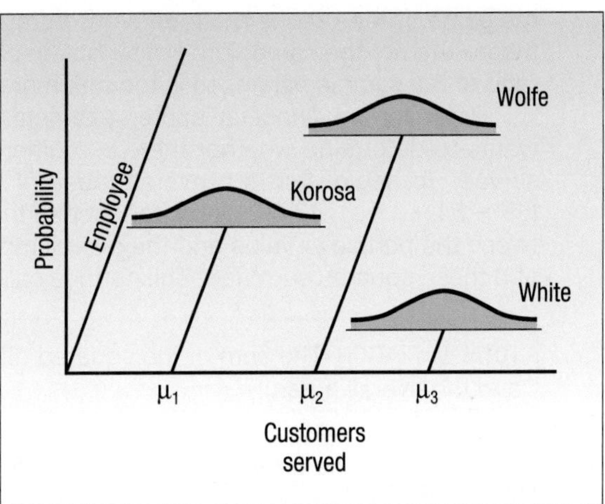

CHART 12–1 Case Where Treatment Means Are Different

Suppose the populations are the same. That is, there is no difference in the (treatment) means. This is shown in Chart 12–2. This would indicate that the population means are the same. Note again that the populations follow the normal distribution and the variation in each of the populations is the same.

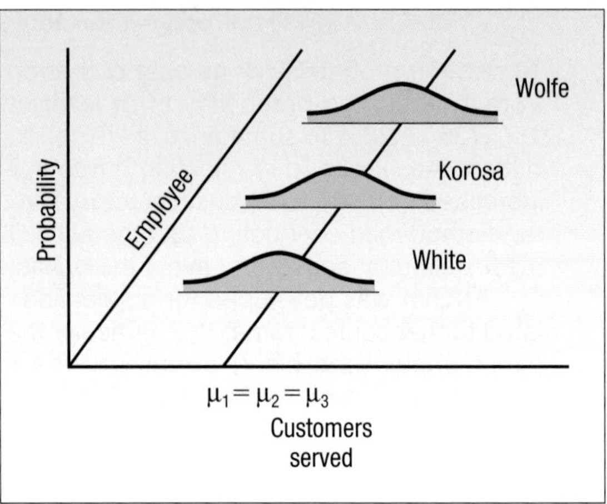

CHART 12–2 Case Where Treatment Means Are the Same

The ANOVA Test

How does the ANOVA test work? Recall that we want to determine whether the various sample means came from a single population or populations with different means. We actually compare these sample means through their variances. To explain, recall that on page 350 we listed the assumptions required for ANOVA. One of those assumptions was that the standard deviations of the various normal populations had to be the same. We take advantage of this requirement in the ANOVA test. The underlying strategy is to estimate the population variance (standard deviation squared) two ways and then find the ratio of these two estimates. If this ratio is about 1, then logically the two estimates are the same, and we conclude that the population means are the same. If the ratio is quite different from 1, then we conclude that the population means are not the same. The *F* distribution serves as a referee by indicating when the ratio of the sample variances is too much greater than 1 to have occurred by chance.

Refer to the financial center example in the previous section. The manager wants to determine whether there is a difference in the mean number of customers served. To begin, find the overall mean of the 12 observations. It is 58, found by $(55 + 54 + \cdots + 48)/12$. Next, for each of the 12 observations find the difference between the particular value and the overall mean. Each of these differences is squared and these squares summed. This term is called the **total variation.**

TOTAL VARIATION The sum of the squared differences between each observation and the overall mean.

In our example the total variation is 1,082, found by $(55 - 58)^2 + (54 - 58)^2 + \cdots + (48 - 58)^2$.

Next, break this total variation into two components: that which is due to the **treatments** and that which is **random.** To find these two components, determine the mean of each of the treatments. The first source of variation is due to the treatments.

TREATMENT VARIATION The sum of the squared differences between each treatment mean and the grand or overall mean.

In the example the variation due to the treatments is the sum of the squared differences between the mean of each employee and the overall mean. This term is 992. To calculate it we first find the mean of each of the three treatments. The mean for Wolfe is 56, found by $(55 + 54 + 59 + 56)/4$. The other means are 70 and 48, respectively. The sum of the squares due to the treatments is:

$$(56 - 58)^2 + (56 - 58)^2 + \cdots + (48 - 58)^2 = 4(56 - 58)^2 + 4(70 - 58)^2 + 4(48 - 58)^2$$
$$= 992$$

If there is considerable variation among the treatment means, it is logical that this term will be large. If the treatment means are similar, this term will be a small value. The smallest possible value would be zero. This would occur when all the treatment means are the same and equal to the overall mean.

The other source of variation is referred to as the **random** component, or the error component.

> **RANDOM VARIATION** The sum of the squared differences between each observation and its treatment mean.

In the example this term is the sum of the squared differences between each value and the mean for that particular employee. The error variation is 90.

$$(55 - 56)^2 + (54 - 56)^2 + \cdots + (48 - 48)^2 = 90$$

We determine the test statistic, which is the ratio of the two estimates of the population variance, from the following equation.

$$F = \frac{\text{Estimate of the population variance based on the differences among the sample means}}{\text{Estimate of the population variance based on the variation within the samples}}$$

Our first estimate of the population variance is based on the treatments, that is, the difference *between* the means. It is 992/2. Why did we divide by 2? Recall from Chapter 3, to find a sample variance [see formula (3–11)], we divide by the number of observations minus one. In this case there are three treatments, so we divide by 2. Our first estimate of the population variance is 992/2.

The variance estimate *within* the treatments is the random variation divided by the total number of observations less the number of treatments. That is $90/(12 - 3)$. Hence, our second estimate of the population variance is 90/9. This is actually a generalization of formula (11–5), where we pooled the sample variances from two populations.

The last step is to take the ratio of these two estimates.

$$F = \frac{992/2}{90/9} = 49.6$$

Because this ratio is quite different from 1, we can conclude that the population means are not the same. There is a difference in the mean number of customers served by the three employees.

Here's another example of the ANOVA technique which deals with samples of different sizes. It will provide additional insight into the technique.

EXAMPLE

Professor James Brunner had the 22 students in his 10 A.M. Introduction to Marketing rate his performance as Excellent, Good, Fair, or Poor. A graduate student collected the ratings and assured the students that Professor Brunner would not receive them until after course grades had been sent to the Registrar's office. The rating (i.e., the treatment) a student gave the professor was matched with his or her course grade, which could range from 0 to 100. The sample information is reported below. Is there a difference in the mean score of the students in each of the four rating categories? Use the .01 significance level.

Course Grades			
Excellent	**Good**	**Fair**	**Poor**
94	75	70	68
90	68	73	70
85	77	76	72
80	83	78	65
	88	80	74
		68	65
		65	

SOLUTION

We will follow the usual five-step hypothesis-testing procedure.

Step 1: State the null hypothesis and the alternate hypothesis. The null hypothesis is that the mean scores are the same for the four ratings.

$$H_0: \mu_1 = \mu_2 = \mu_3 = \mu_4$$

The alternate hypothesis is that the mean scores are not all the same for the four ratings.

H_1: The mean scores are not all equal.

We can also think of the alternate hypothesis as "at least two mean scores are not equal."

If the null hypothesis is not rejected, we conclude that there is no difference in the mean course grades based on the instructor ratings. If H_0 is rejected, we conclude that there is a difference in at least one pair of mean ratings, but at this point we do not know which pair or how many pairs differ.

Step 2: Select the level of significance. We selected the .01 significance level.

Step 3: Determine the test statistic. The test statistic follows the F distribution.

Step 4: Formulate the decision rule. To determine the decision rule, we need the critical value. The critical value for the F statistic is found in Appendix G. The critical values for the .05 significance level are found on the first page and the .01 significance level on the second page. To use this table we need to know the degrees of freedom in the numerator and the denominator. The degrees of freedom in the numerator equals the number of treatments, designated as k, minus 1. The degrees of freedom in the denominator is the total number of observations, n, minus the number of treatments. For this problem there are four treatments and a total of 22 observations.

Degrees of freedom in the numerator $= k - 1 = 4 - 1 = 3$
Degrees of freedom in the denominator $= n - k = 22 - 4 = 18$

Refer to Appendix G and the .01 significance level. Move horizontally across the top of the page to 3 degrees of freedom in the numerator. Then move down that column to the row with 18 degrees of freedom. The value at this intersection is 5.09. So the decision rule is to reject H_0 if the computed value of F exceeds 5.09.

Step 5: Select the sample, perform the calculations, and make a decision. It is convenient to summarize the calculations of the F statistic in an

ANOVA table. The format for an ANOVA table is as follows. Statistical software packages also use this format.

ANOVA Table

Source of Variation	Sum of Squares	Degrees of Freedom	Mean Square	F
Treatments	SST	$k - 1$	SST/(k − 1) = MST	MST/MSE
Error	SSE	$n - k$	SSE/(n − k) = MSE	
Total	SS total	$n - 1$		

There are three values, or sum of squares, used to compute the test statistic F. You can determine these values by obtaining SS total and SSE, then finding SST by subtraction. The SS total term is the total variation, SST is the variation due to the treatments, and SSE is the variation within the treatments.

We usually start the process by finding SS total. This is the sum of the squared differences between each observation and the overall mean. The formula for finding SS total is:

$$\text{SS total} = \Sigma(X - \bar{X}_G)^2 \quad \textbf{[12–2]}$$

where:

X is each sample observation.
$\bar{X}_G$ is the overall or grand mean. The subscript G refers to the "grand" mean.

Next determine SSE or the sum of the squared errors. This is the sum of the squared differences between each observation and its respective treatment mean. The formula for finding SSE is:

$$\text{SSE} = \Sigma(X - \bar{X}_c)^2 \quad \textbf{[12–3]}$$

where:

$\bar{X}_c$ is the sample mean for treatment c. The subscript c refers to the particular column.

The detailed calculations of SS total and SSE for this example follow. To determine the values of SS total and SSE we start by calculating the overall or grand mean. There are 22 observations and the total is 1,664, so the grand mean is 75.64.

$$\bar{X}_G = \frac{1{,}664}{22} = 75.64$$

	Excellent	Good	Fair	Poor	Total
	94	75	70	68	
	90	68	73	70	
	85	77	76	72	
	80	83	78	65	
		88	80	74	
			68	65	
			65		
Column total	349	391	510	414	1664
n	4	5	7	6	22
Mean	87.25	78.20	72.86	69.00	75.64

Next we find the deviation of each observation from the grand mean, square those deviations, and sum this result for all 22 observations. For example, the first student who rated Dr. Brunner Excellent had a score of 94 and the overall or grand mean is 75.64. So $(X - \bar{X}_G) = 94 - 75.64 = 18.36$. To find the value for the first student who rated Dr. Brunner Good: $75 - 75.64 = -0.64$. The calculations for all students follow.

Excellent	Good	Fair	Poor
18.36	−0.64	−5.64	−7.64
14.36	−7.64	−2.64	−5.64
9.36	1.36	0.36	−3.64
4.36	7.36	2.36	−10.64
	12.36	4.36	−1.64
		−7.64	−10.64
		−10.64	

Then square each of these differences and sum all the values. Thus for the first student:

$$(X - \bar{X}_G)^2 = (94 - 75.64)^2 = (18.36)^2 = 337.09.$$

Finally sum all the squared differences as formula (12–2) directs. Our SS total value is 1,485.09.

	Excellent	Good	Fair	Poor	Total
	337.09	0.41	31.81	58.37	
	206.21	58.37	6.97	31.81	
	87.61	1.85	0.13	13.25	
	19.0	54.17	5.57	113.21	
		152.77	19.01	2.69	
			58.37	113.21	
			113.21		
Total	649.91	267.57	235.07	332.54	1,485.09

To compute the term SSE find the deviation between each observation and its treatment mean. In the example the mean of the first treatment (that is the students who rated Professor Brunner "Excellent") is 87.25. The first student earned a score of 94, so $(X - \bar{X}_c) = (94 - 87.25) = 6.75$. For the first student in the "Good" group $(X - \bar{X}_c) = (75 - 78.20) = -3.20$. The details of each of these calculations follow.

Excellent	Good	Fair	Poor
6.75	−3.2	−2.86	−1
2.75	−10.2	0.14	1
−2.25	−1.2	3.14	3
−7.25	4.8	5.14	−4
	9.8	7.14	5
		−4.86	−4
		−7.86	

Each of these values is squared and then summed for all 22 observations. The values are shown in the following table.

Statistics in Action

Have you ever waited in line for a telephone and it seemed like the person using the phone talked on and on? There is evidence that people actually talk longer on public telephones when someone is waiting. In a recent survey, researchers measured the length of time that 56 shoppers in a mall spent on the phone (1) when they were alone, (2) when a person was using the adjacent phone, and (3) when a person was using an adjacent phone and someone was waiting to use the phone. The study, using the one-way ANOVA technique, showed that the mean time using the telephone was significantly less when the person was alone.

	Excellent	Good	Fair	Poor	Total
	45.5625	10.24	8.18	1	
	7.5625	104.04	0.02	1	
	5.0625	1.44	9.86	9	
	52.5625	23.04	26.42	16	
		96.04	50.98	25	
			23.62	16	
			61.78		
Total	110.7500	234.80	180.86	68	594.41

So the SSE value is 594.41. That is $\Sigma(X - \bar{X}_c)^2 = 594.41$.

Finally we determine SST, the sum of the squares due to the treatments, by subtraction.

$$SST = SS\ total - SSE \qquad [12\text{–}4]$$

For this example:

$$SST = SS\ total - SSE = 1{,}485.09 - 594.41 = 890.68.$$

To find the computed value of F, work your way across the ANOVA table. The degrees of freedom for the numerator and the denominator are the same as in **step 4** above when we were finding the critical value of F. The term **mean square** is another expression for an estimate of the variance. The mean square for treatments is SST divided by its degrees of freedom. The result is the **mean square for treatments** and is written MST. Compute the **mean square error** in a similar fashion. To be precise, divide SSE by its degrees of freedom. To complete the process and find F, divide MST by MSE.

Insert the particular values of F into an ANOVA table and compute the value of F as follows.

Source of Variation	Sum of Squares	Degrees of Freedom	Mean Square	F
Treatments	890.68	3	296.89	8.99
Error	594.41	18	33.02	
Total	1,485.09	21		

The computed value of F is 8.99, which is greater than the critical value of 5.09, so the null hypothesis is rejected. We conclude the population means are not all equal. The mean scores are not the same in each of the four ratings groups. It is likely that the grades students earned in the course are related to the opinion they have of the overall competency and classroom performance of Dr. Brunner the instructor. At this point we can only conclude there is a difference in the treatment means. We cannot determine which treatment groups differ or how many treatment groups differ.

As noted in the previous example, the calculations are tedious if the number of observations in each treatment is large. There are many software packages that will output the results. Following is the Excel output in the form of an ANOVA table for the previous example involving student ratings in Dr. Brunner's Introduction to Marketing. There are some slight differences between the software output and the previous calculations. These differences are due to rounding.

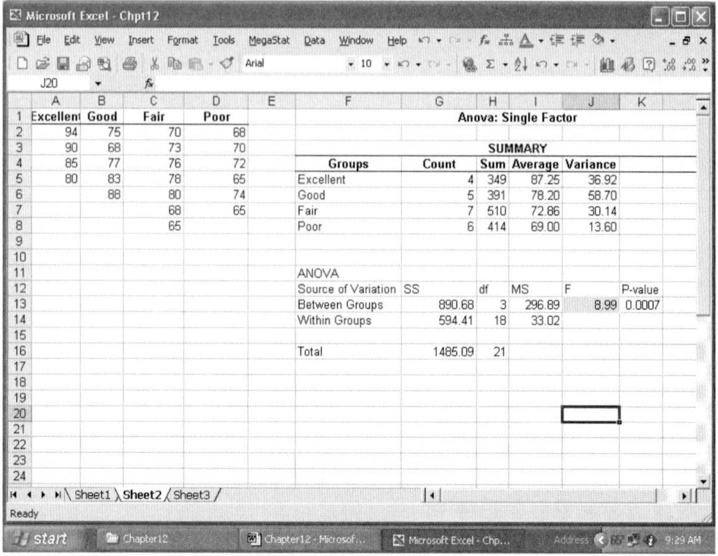

	A	B	C	D	E	F	G	H	I	J	K
1	Excellent	Good	Fair	Poor		Anova: Single Factor					
2	94	75	70	68							
3	90	68	73	70		SUMMARY					
4	85	77	76	72		Groups	Count	Sum	Average	Variance	
5	80	83	78	65		Excellent	4	349	87.25	36.92	
6		88	80	74		Good	5	391	78.20	58.70	
7			68	65		Fair	7	510	72.86	30.14	
8			65			Poor	6	414	69.00	13.60	
11						ANOVA					
12						Source of Variation	SS	df	MS	F	P-value
13						Between Groups	890.68	3	296.89	8.99	0.0007
14						Within Groups	594.41	18	33.02		
16						Total	1485.09	21			

Notice Excel uses the term "Between Groups" for "Treatments" and "Within Groups" for "Error." However, they have the same meanings. The *p*-value is .0007. This is the probability of finding a value of the test statistic this large or larger when the null hypothesis is true. To put it another way, it is the likelihood of calculating an *F* value larger than 8.99 with 3 degrees of freedom in the numerator and 18 degrees of freedom in the denominator. So when we reject the null hypothesis in this instance there is a very small likelihood of committing a Type I error!

Following is the MINITAB output from the student ratings example, which is similar to the Excel output. The output is also in the form of an ANOVA table. In addition, MINITAB provides information about the differences between means. This is discussed in the next section.

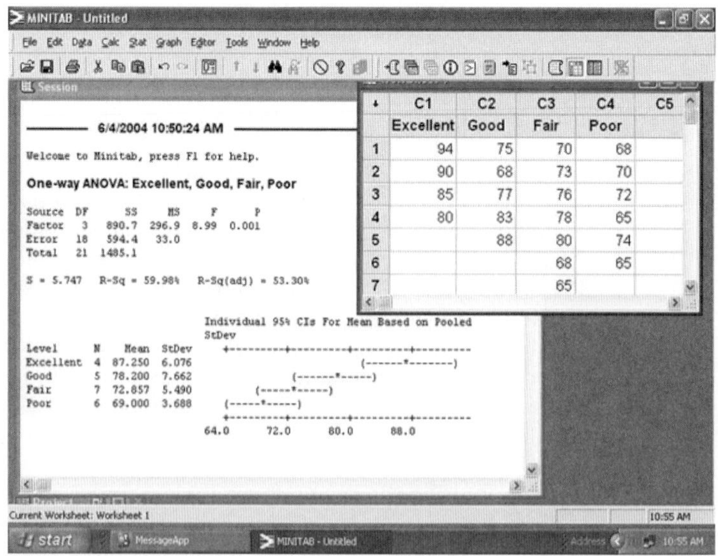

6/4/2004 10:50:24 AM

Welcome to Minitab, press F1 for help.

One-way ANOVA: Excellent, Good, Fair, Poor

Source	DF	SS	MS	F	P
Factor	3	890.7	296.9	8.99	0.001
Error	18	594.4	33.0		
Total	21	1485.1			

S = 5.747 R-Sq = 59.98% R-Sq(adj) = 53.30%

Individual 95% CIs For Mean Based on Pooled StDev

Level	N	Mean	StDev
Excellent	4	87.250	6.076
Good	5	78.200	7.662
Fair	7	72.857	5.490
Poor	6	69.000	3.688

64.0 72.0 80.0 88.0

	C1 Excellent	C2 Good	C3 Fair	C4 Poor
1	94	75	70	68
2	90	68	73	70
3	85	77	76	72
4	80	83	78	65
5		88	80	74
6			68	65
7			65	

The MINITAB system uses the term *factor* instead of *treatment,* with the same intended meaning.

Self-Review 12–2

Citrus Clean is a new all-purpose cleaner being test marketed by placing displays in three different locations within various supermarkets. The number of 12-ounce bottles sold from each location within the supermarket is reported below.

Near bread	18	14	19	17
Near beer	12	18	10	16
Other cleaners	26	28	30	32

At the .05 significance level, is there a difference in the mean number of bottles sold at the three locations?

(a) State the null hypothesis and the alternate hypothesis.
(b) What is the decision rule?
(c) Compute the values of SS total, SST, and SSE.
(d) Develop an ANOVA table.
(e) What is your decision regarding the null hypothesis?

Exercises

7. The following is sample information. Test the hypothesis that the treatment means are equal. Use the .05 significance level.

Treatment 1	Treatment 2	Treatment 3
8	3	3
6	2	4
10	4	5
9	3	4

a. State the null hypothesis and the alternate hypothesis.
b. What is the decision rule?
c. Compute SST, SSE, and SS total.
d. Complete an ANOVA table.
e. State your decision regarding the null hypothesis.

8. The following is sample information. Test the hypothesis at the .05 significance level that the treatment means are equal.

Treatment 1	Treatment 2	Treatment 3
9	13	10
7	20	9
11	14	15
9	13	14
12		15
10		

a. State the null hypothesis and the alternate hypothesis.
b. What is the decision rule?
c. Compute SST, SSE, and SS total.
d. Complete an ANOVA table.
e. State your decision regarding the null hypothesis.

9. A real estate developer is considering investing in a shopping mall on the outskirts of Atlanta, Georgia. Three parcels of land are being evaluated. Of particular importance is the income in the area surrounding the proposed mall. A random sample of four families is selected near each proposed mall. Following are the sample results. At the .05 significance level, can the developer conclude there is a difference in the mean income? Use the usual five-step hypothesis testing procedure.

Southwyck Area ($000)	Franklin Park ($000)	Old Orchard ($000)
64	74	75
68	71	80
70	69	76
60	70	78

10. The manager of a computer software company wishes to study the number of hours senior executives spend at their desktop computers by type of industry. The manager selected a sample of five executives from each of three industries. At the .05 significance level, can she conclude there is a difference in the mean number of hours spent per week by industry?

Banking	Retail	Insurance
12	8	10
10	8	8
10	6	6
12	8	8
10	10	10

Inferences about Pairs of Treatment Means

Suppose we carry out the ANOVA procedure and make the decision to reject the null hypothesis. This allows us to conclude that all the treatment means are not the same. Sometimes we may be satisfied with this conclusion, but in other instances we may want to know which treatment means differ. This section provides the details for such a test.

Recall the example regarding student opinions and final scores in Dr. Brunner's Introduction to Marketing. We concluded that there was a difference in the treatment means. That is, the null hypothesis was rejected and the alternate hypothesis accepted. If the student opinions do differ, the question is: Between which groups do the treatment means differ?

Several procedures are available to answer this question. The simplest is through the use of confidence intervals, that is, formula (9–2). From the MINITAB output of the previous example (see page 358), note that the sample mean score for those students rating the instruction Excellent is 87.250, and for those rating the instruction Poor it is 69.000. Thus, those students who rated the instruction Excellent seemingly earned higher grades than those who rated the instruction Poor. Is there enough disparity to justify the conclusion that there is a significant difference in the mean scores of the two groups?

The t distribution, described in Chapters 10 and 11, is used as the basis for this test. Recall that one of the assumptions of ANOVA is that the population variances are the same for all treatments. This common population value is the **mean square error,** or MSE, and is determined by SSE/$(n - k)$. A confidence interval for the difference between two population means is found by:

CONFIDENCE INTERVAL FOR THE DIFFERENCE IN TREATMENT MEANS

$$\left(\bar{X}_1 - \bar{X}_2\right) \pm t\sqrt{\text{MSE}\left(\frac{1}{n_1} + \frac{1}{n_2}\right)} \qquad \textbf{[12–5]}$$

where:

$\bar{X}_1$ is the mean of the first sample.
$\bar{X}_2$ is the mean of the second sample.
t is obtained from Appendix F. The degrees of freedom is equal to $n - k$.
MSE is the mean square error term obtained from the ANOVA table [SSE/$(n - k)$].
n_1 is the number of observations in the first sample.
n_2 is the number of observations in the second sample.

How do we decide whether there is a difference in the treatment means? If the confidence interval includes zero, there is *not* a difference between the treatment means. For example, if the left endpoint of the confidence interval has a negative sign and the right endpoint has a positive sign, the interval includes zero and the two means do not differ. So if we develop a confidence interval from formula (12–5) and find the difference in the sample means was 5.00, that is, if $\bar{X}_1 - \bar{X}_2 = 5$ and $t\sqrt{\text{MSE}\left(\frac{1}{n_1} + \frac{1}{n_2}\right)} = 12$, the confidence interval would range from -7.00 up to 17.00. To put it in symbols:

$$(\bar{X}_1 - \bar{X}_2) \pm t\sqrt{\text{MSE}\left(\frac{1}{n_1} + \frac{1}{n_2}\right)} = 5.00 \pm 12.00 = -7.00 \text{ up to } 17.00$$

Note that zero is included in this interval. Therefore, we conclude that there is no significant difference in the selected treatment means.

On the other hand, if the endpoints of the confidence interval have the same sign, this indicates that the treatment means differ. For example, if $\bar{X}_1 - \bar{X}_2 = -0.35$ and $t\sqrt{\text{MSE}\left(\frac{1}{n_1} + \frac{1}{n_2}\right)} = 0.25$, the confidence interval would range from -0.60 up to -0.10. Because -0.60 and -0.10 have the same sign, both negative, zero is not in the interval and we conclude that these treatment means differ.

Using the previous student opinion example let us compute the confidence interval for the difference between the mean scores of all students who provide "Excellent" and "Poor" ratings. Assume the populations are labeled 1 and 4. With a 95 percent level of confidence, the endpoints of the confidence interval are 10.46 and 26.04.

$$(\bar{X}_1 - \bar{X}_4) \pm t\sqrt{\text{MSE}\left(\frac{1}{n_1} + \frac{1}{n_4}\right)} = (87.25 - 69.00) \pm 2.101\sqrt{33.0\left(\frac{1}{4} + \frac{1}{6}\right)}$$
$$= 18.25 \pm 7.79$$

where:

$\bar{X}_1$ is 87.25.
$\bar{X}_4$ is 69.00.
t is 2.101: from Appendix F with $(n - k) = 22 - 4 = 18$ degrees of freedom.
MSE is 33.0: from the ANOVA table with SSE/$(n - k) = 594.4/18$.
n_1 is 4.
n_4 is 6.

The 95 percent confidence interval ranges from 10.46 up to 26.04. Both endpoints are positive; hence, we can conclude these treatment means differ significantly. That is, students who rated the instructor Excellent have significantly higher scores than those who rated the instructor as Poor.

Approximate results can also be obtained directly from the MINITAB output. On the next page is the lower portion of the output from page 358. On the left side is the number of observations, the mean, and the standard deviation for each treatment. Seven students, for example, rated the instructor as Fair. The mean score they earned is 72.857. The standard deviation of their scores is 5.490.

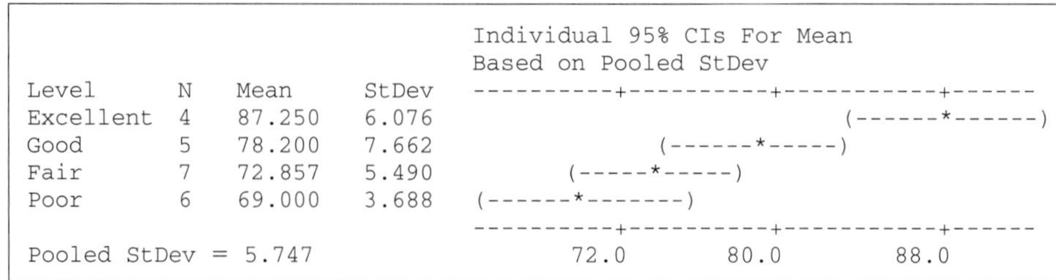

```
                                   Individual 95% CIs For Mean
                                   Based on Pooled StDev
Level      N   Mean     StDev    ----------+----------+----------+------
Excellent  4   87.250   6.076                             (------*------)
Good       5   78.200   7.662                 (------*-----)
Fair       7   72.857   5.490          (-----*-----)
Poor       6   69.000   3.688    (------*-------)
                                 ----------+----------+----------+------
Pooled StDev = 5.747                      72.0       80.0       88.0
```

On the right side of the printout is a confidence interval for each treatment mean. The asterisk (*) indicates the location of the treatment mean and the open parenthesis and close parenthesis, the endpoints of the confidence interval. In those instances where the intervals overlap, the treatment means may not differ. If there is no common area in the confidence intervals, that pair of means differ.

The endpoints of a 95 percent confidence interval for the scores of students rating the instructor Fair are about 69 and 77. For students rating the instructor Poor, the endpoints of the confidence interval are about 64 and 74. There is common area in this confidence interval, so we conclude that this pair of means does not differ. In other words, there is no significant difference between the scores of students rating the instructor Fair and those rating him Poor.

There are two pairs of means that differ. The scores of students who rated the instructor Excellent differ from the scores of the students who rated the instructor Fair and those who rated the instructor Poor. There is no common area between the two pairs of confidence intervals.

We should emphasize that this investigation is a step-by-step process. The initial step is to conduct the ANOVA test. Only if the null hypothesis that the treatment means are equal is rejected should any analysis of the individual treatment means be attempted.

Self-Review 12–3

The following data are the semester tuition charges ($000) for a sample of private colleges in various regions of the United States. At the .05 significance level, can we conclude there is a difference in the mean tuition rates for the various regions?

Northeast ($000)	Southeast ($000)	West ($000)
10	8	7
11	9	8
12	10	6
10	8	7
12		6

(a) State the null and the alternate hypotheses.
(b) What is the decision rule?
(c) Develop an ANOVA table. What is the value of the test statistic?
(d) What is your decision regarding the null hypothesis?
(e) Could there be a significant difference between the mean tuition in the Northeast and that of the West? If so, develop a 95 percent confidence interval for that difference.

Exercises

11. Given the following sample information, test the hypothesis that the treatment means are equal at the .05 significance level.

Treatment 1	Treatment 2	Treatment 3
8	3	3
11	2	4
10	1	5
	3	4
	2	

a. State the null hypothesis and the alternate hypothesis.
b. What is the decision rule?
c. Compute SST, SSE, and SS total.
d. Complete an ANOVA table.
e. State your decision regarding the null hypothesis.
f. If H_0 is rejected, can we conclude that treatment 1 and treatment 2 differ? Use the 95 percent level of confidence.

12. Given the following sample information, test the hypothesis that the treatment means are equal at the .05 significance level.

Treatment 1	Treatment 2	Treatment 3
3	9	6
2	6	3
5	5	5
1	6	5
3	8	5
1	5	4
	4	1
	7	5
	6	
	4	

a. State the null hypothesis and the alternate hypothesis.
b. What is the decision rule?
c. Compute SST, SSE, and SS total.
d. Complete an ANOVA table.
e. State your decision regarding the null hypothesis.
f. If H_0 is rejected, can we conclude that treatment 2 and treatment 3 differ? Use the 95 percent level of confidence.

13. A senior accounting major at Midsouth State University has job offers from four CPA firms. To explore the offers further, she asked a sample of recent trainees how many months each worked for the firm before receiving a raise in salary. The sample information is submitted to MINITAB with the following results:

```
Analysis of Variance
Source        DF        SS        MS         F         P
Factor         3     32.33     10.78      2.36     0.133
Error         10     45.67      4.57
Total         13     78.00
```

At the .05 level of significance, is there a difference in the mean number of months before a raise was granted among the four CPA firms?

14. A stock analyst wants to determine whether there is a difference in the mean rate of return for three types of stock: utility, retail, and banking stocks. The following output is obtained:

```
Analysis of Variance
Source    DF       SS       MS        F        P
Factor     2    86.49    43.25    13.09    0.001
Error     13    42.95     3.30
Total     15   129.44
                                 Individual 95% CIs For Mean
                                 Based on Pooled StDev
Level       N     Mean    StDev  ----------+----------+-----------+------
Utility     5   17.400    1.916                      (------*------)
Retail      5   11.620    0.356  (------*-----)
Banking     6   15.400    2.356             (-----*-----)
                                 ----------+----------+-----------+------
Pooled StDev = 1.818                    12.0       15.0        18.0
```

a. Using the .05 level of significance, is there a difference in the mean rate of return among the three types of stock?

b. Suppose the null hypothesis is rejected. Can the analyst conclude there is a difference between the mean rates of return for the utility and the retail stocks? Explain.

Chapter Outline

I. The characteristics of the *F* distribution are:
- **A.** There is a family of *F* distributions. Each time the degrees of freedom in either the numerator or the denominator changes, a new distribution is created.
- **B.** It is continuous.
- **C.** Its values cannot be negative.
- **D.** It is positively skewed.
- **E.** It is asymptotic.

II. The *F* distribution is used to test whether two population variances are the same.
- **A.** The sampled populations must follow the normal distribution.
- **B.** The larger of the two sample variances is placed in the numerator, forcing the ratio to be at least 1.00.
- **C.** The value of *F* is computed using the following equation:

$$F = \frac{s_1^2}{s_2^2} \quad \textbf{[12–1]}$$

III. A one-way ANOVA is used to compare several treatment means.
- **A.** A treatment is a source of variation.
- **B.** The assumptions underlying ANOVA are:
  1. The samples are from populations which follow the normal distribution.
  2. The populations have equal standard deviations.
  3. The samples are independent.
- **C.** The information for finding the value of *F* is summarized in an ANOVA table.
  1. The formula for SS total, the sum of squares total, is:

$$\text{SS total} = \Sigma(X - \bar{X}_G)^2 \quad \textbf{[12–2]}$$

  2. The SSE, the sum of squares error, is:

$$\text{SSE} = \Sigma(X - \bar{X}_c)^2 \quad \textbf{[12–3]}$$

  3. The formula for the SST, the sum of squares treatment, is:

$$\text{SST} = \text{SS total} - \text{SSE} \quad \textbf{[12–4]}$$

  4. This information is summarized in the following table and the value of *F* determined.

ANOVA Table				
Source of Variation	**Sum of Squares**	**Degrees of Freedom**	**Mean Square**	***F***
Treatments	SST	$k-1$	$\text{SST}/(k-1) = \text{MST}$	MST/MSE
Error	SSE	$n-k$	$\text{SSE}/(n-k) = \text{MSE}$	
Total	SS total	$n-1$		

IV. If a null hypothesis of equal treatment means is rejected, we can identify the pairs of means that differ from the following confidence interval.

$$(\bar{X}_1 - \bar{X}_2) \pm t\sqrt{\text{MSE}\left(\frac{1}{n_1} + \frac{1}{n_2}\right)} \quad \textbf{[12–5]}$$

Pronunciation Key

SYMBOL	MEANING	PRONUNCIATION
SS total	Sum of squares total	*S S total*
SST	Sum of squares treatment	*S S T*
SSE	Sum of squares error	*S S E*
MSE	Mean square error	*M S E*

Chapter Exercises

15. A real estate agent in the coastal area of Georgia wants to compare the variation in the selling price of homes on the oceanfront with those one to three blocks from the ocean. A sample of 21 oceanfront homes sold within the last year revealed the standard deviation of the selling prices was $45,600. A sample of 18 homes, also sold within the last year, that were one to three blocks from the ocean revealed that the standard deviation was $21,330. At the .01 significance level, can we conclude that there is more variation in the selling prices of the oceanfront homes?

16. A computer manufacturer is about to unveil a new, faster personal computer. The new machine clearly is faster, but initial tests indicate there is more variation in the processing time. The processing time depends on the particular program being run, the amount of input data, and the amount of output. A sample of 16 computer runs, covering a range of production jobs, showed that the standard deviation of the processing time was 22 (hundredths of a second) for the new machine and 12 (hundredths of a second) for the current machine. At the .05 significance level can we conclude that there is more variation in the processing time of the new machine?

17. There are two Chevrolet dealers in Jamestown, New York. The mean monthly sales at Sharkey Chevy and Dave White Chevrolet are about the same. However, Tom Sharkey, the owner of Sharkey Chevy, believes his sales are more consistent. Below is the number of new cars sold at Sharkey in the last seven months and for the last eight months at Dave White. Do you agree with Mr. Sharkey? Use the .01 significance level.

Sharkey	98	78	54	57	68	64	70	
Dave White	75	81	81	30	82	46	58	101

18. Random samples of five were selected from each of three populations. The sum of squares total was 100. The sum of squares due to the treatments was 40.

a. Set up the null hypothesis and the alternate hypothesis.
b. What is the decision rule? Use the .05 significance level.
c. Complete the ANOVA table. What is the value of *F*?
d. What is your decision regarding the null hypothesis?

19. In an ANOVA table MSE was equal to 10. Random samples of six were selected from each of four populations, where the sum of squares total was 250.

a. Set up the null hypothesis and the alternate hypothesis.
b. What is the decision rule? Use the .05 significance level.
c. Complete the ANOVA table. What is the value of *F*?
d. What is your decision regarding the null hypothesis?

20. The following is a partial ANOVA table.

Source	Sum of Squares	*df*	Mean Square	*F*
Treatment		2		
Error			20	
Total	500	11		

Complete the table and answer the following questions. Use the .05 significance level.

a. How many treatments are there?
b. What is the total sample size?
c. What is the critical value of *F*?
d. Write out the null and alternate hypotheses.
e. What is your conclusion regarding the null hypothesis?

21. A consumer organization wants to know whether there is a difference in the price of a particular toy at three different types of stores. The price of the toy was checked in a sample of five discount stores, five variety stores, and five department stores. The results are shown below. Use the .05 significance level.

Discount	Variety	Department
$12	$15	$19
13	17	17
14	14	16
12	18	20
15	17	19

22. A physician who specializes in weight control has three different diets she recommends. As an experiment, she randomly selected 15 patients and then assigned 5 to each diet. After three weeks the following weight losses, in pounds, were noted. At the .05 significance level, can she conclude that there is a difference in the mean amount of weight loss among the three diets?

Plan A	Plan B	Plan C
5	6	7
7	7	8
4	7	9
5	5	8
4	6	9

23. The City of Maumee comprises four districts. Chief of police Andy North wants to determine whether there is a difference in the mean number of crimes committed among the four districts. He recorded the number of crimes reported in each district for a sample of six days. At the .05 significance level, can the chief of police conclude there is a difference in the mean number of crimes?

Number of Crimes			
Rec Center	**Key Street**	**Monclova**	**Whitehouse**
13	21	12	16
15	13	14	17
14	18	15	18
15	19	13	15
14	18	12	20
15	19	15	18

24. The personnel director of Cander Machine Products is investigating "perfectionism" on the job. A test designed to measure perfectionism was administered to a random sample of 18 employees. The scores ranged from 20 to about 40. One of the facets of the study involved the early background of each employee. Did the employee come from a rural background, a small city, or a large city? The scores are:

Rural Area	Small Urban Area	Large Urban Area
35	28	24
30	24	28
36	25	26
38	30	30
29	32	34
34	28	
31		

a. At the .05 level, can it be concluded that there is a difference in the three mean scores?
b. If the null hypothesis is rejected, can you state that the mean score of those with a rural background is different from the score of those with a large-city background?

25. When only two treatments are involved, ANOVA and the Student *t* test (Chapter 10) result in the same conclusions. Also, $t^2 = F$. As an example, suppose that 14 randomly selected students were divided into two groups, one consisting of 6 students and the other of 8. One group was taught using a combination of lecture and programmed instruction, the other using a combination of lecture and television. At the end of the course, each group was given a 50-item test. The following is a list of the number correct for each of the two groups.

Lecture and Programmed Instruction	Lecture and Television
19	32
17	28
23	31
22	26
17	23
16	24
	27
	25

a. Using analysis of variance techniques, test H_0 that the two mean test scores are equal; $\alpha = .05$.
b. Using the *t* test from Chapter 10, compute *t*.
c. Interpret the results.

26. There are four auto body shops in a community and all claim to promptly serve customers. To check if there is any difference in service, customers are randomly selected from each repair shop and their waiting times in days are recorded. The output from a statistical software package is:

Summary				
Groups	Count	Sum	Average	Variance
Body Shop A	3	15.4	5.133333	0.323333
Body Shop B	4	32	8	1.433333
Body Shop C	5	25.2	5.04	0.748
Body Shop D	4	25.9	6.475	0.595833

ANOVA					
Source of Variation	SS	*df*	MS	*F*	*p*-value
Between Groups	23.37321	3	7.791069	9.612506	0.001632
Within Groups	9.726167	12	0.810514		
Total	33.09938	15			

Is there evidence to suggest a difference in the mean waiting times at the four body shops? Use the .05 significance level.

27. The fuel efficiencies for a sample of 27 compact, midsize, and large cars are entered into a statistical software package. Analysis of variance is used to investigate if there is a difference in the mean mileage of the three cars. What do you conclude? Use the .01 significance level.

Summary				
Groups	Count	Sum	Average	Variance
Compact	12	268.3	22.35833	9.388106
Midsize	9	172.4	19.15556	7.315278
Large	6	100.5	16.75	7.303

Additional results are shown below.

ANOVA					
Source of Variation	SS	*df*	MS	*F*	*p*-value
Between Groups	136.4803	2	68.24014	8.258752	0.001866
Within Groups	198.3064	24	8.262766		
Total	334.7867	26			

28. Three assembly lines are used to produce a certain component for an airliner. To examine the production rate, a random sample of six hourly periods is chosen for each assembly line and the number of components produced during these periods for each line is recorded. The output from a statistical software package is:

Summary				
Groups	Count	Sum	Average	Variance
Line A	6	250	41.66667	0.266667
Line B	6	260	43.33333	0.666667
Line C	6	249	41.5	0.7

ANOVA					
Source of Variation	**SS**	***df***	**MS**	***F***	***p*-value**
Between Groups	12.33333	2	6.166667	11.32653	0.001005
Within Groups	8.166667	15	0.544444		
Total	20.5	17			

a. Use a .01 level of significance to test if there is a difference in the mean production of the three assembly lines.

b. Develop a 99 percent confidence interval for the difference in the means between Line B and Line C.

29. A grocery store wants to monitor the amount of withdrawals that its customers make from automatic teller machines (ATMs) located within their stores. They sample 10 withdrawals from each location and the output from a statistical software package is:

Summary				
Groups	**Count**	**Sum**	**Average**	**Variance**
Location X	10	825	82.5	1,808.056
Location Y	10	540	54	921.1111
Location Z	10	382	38.2	1,703.733

ANOVA					
Source of Variation	**SS**	***df***	**MS**	***F***	***p*-value**
Between Groups	1,0081.27	2	5,040.633	3.411288	0.047766
Within Groups	3,9896.1	27	1,477.633		
Total	4,9977.37	29			

a. Use a .01 level of significance to test if there is a difference in the mean amount of money withdrawn.

b. Develop a 90 percent confidence interval for the difference in the means between Location X and Location Z.

30. One reads that a business school graduate with an undergraduate degree earns more than a high school graduate with no additional education, and a person with a master's degree or a doctorate earns even more. To investigate we select a sample of 25 mid-level managers of companies with less than 200 employees. Their incomes, classified by highest level of education, follow.

Income ($thousands)		
High School or Less	**Undergraduate Degree**	**Master's Degree or More**
45	49	51
47	57	73
53	85	82
62	73	59
39	81	94
43	84	89
54	89	89
	92	95
	62	73

Test at the .05 level of significance that there is no difference in the arithmetic mean salaries of the three groups. If the null hypothesis is rejected, conduct further tests to determine which groups differ.

31. Listed below are the weights (in grams) of a sample of M&M's Plain candies, classified according to color. Use a statistical software system to determine whether there is a difference in the mean weights of candies of different colors. Use the .05 significance level.

Red	Orange	Yellow	Brown	Tan	Green
0.946	0.902	0.929	0.896	0.845	0.935
1.107	0.943	0.960	0.888	0.909	0.903
0.913	0.916	0.938	0.906	0.873	0.865
0.904	0.910	0.933	0.941	0.902	0.822
0.926	0.903	0.932	0.838	0.956	0.871
0.926	0.901	0.899	0.892	0.959	0.905
1.006	0.919	0.907	0.905	0.916	0.905
0.914	0.901	0.906	0.824	0.822	0.852
0.922	0.930	0.930	0.908		0.965
1.052	0.883	0.952	0.833		0.898
0.903		0.939			
0.895		0.940			
		0.882			
		0.906			

32. There are four radio stations in Midland. The stations have different formats (hard rock, classical, country/western, and easy listening), but each is concerned with the number of minutes of music played per hour. From a sample of 10 hours from each station, the following sample means were offered.

$$\bar{X}_1 = 51.32 \qquad \bar{X}_2 = 44.64 \qquad \bar{X}_3 = 47.2 \qquad \bar{X}_4 = 50.85$$

$$\text{SS total} = 650.75$$

a. Determine SST.
b. Determine SSE.
c. Complete an ANOVA table.
d. At the .05 significance level, is there a difference in the treatment means?
e. Is there a difference in the mean amount of music time between station 1 and station 4? Use the .05 significance level.

exercises.com

33. Many real estate companies and rental agencies now publish their listings on the Web. One example is the Dunes Realty Company, located in Garden City Beach, South Carolina. Go to their website, http://www.dunes.com, select **Vacation Rentals, Beach House Search,** then indicate 5 bedroom, accommodations for 14 people, second row (this means it is across the street from the beach), no pool or floating dock, select a period in July and August, indicate that you are willing to spend $8,000 per week, and then click on **Search the Beach Houses.** The output should include details on the beach houses that met your criteria. At the .05 significance level, is there a difference in the mean rental prices for the different number of bedrooms? (You may want to combine some of the larger homes, such as 8 or more bedrooms.) Which pairs of means differ?
34. The percentages of quarterly changes in the gross domestic product for 20 countries are available at the following site: http://www.oecd.org, select **Statistics, National Accounts,** and select **Quarterly Growth Rates in GDP.** Copy the data for Germany, Japan, and the United States into three columns in MINITAB or Excel. Perform an ANOVA to see whether there is a difference in the means. What can you conclude?

Dataset Exercises

35. Refer to the Real Estate data, which reports information on the homes sold in the Denver, Colorado, area last year.

a. At the .02 significance level, is there a difference in the variability of the selling prices of the homes that have a pool versus those that do not have a pool?
b. At the .02 significance level, is there a difference in the variability of the selling prices of the homes with an attached garage versus those that do not have an attached garage?
c. At the .05 significance level, is there a difference in the mean selling price of the homes among the five townships?

36. Refer to the Baseball 2003 data, which reports information on the 30 Major League Baseball teams for the 2003 season.
a. At the .10 significance level, is there a difference in the variation of the number of stolen bases among the teams that play their home games on natural grass versus on artificial turf?
b. Create a variable that classifies a team's total attendance into three groups: less than 2.0 (million), 2.0 up to 3.0, and 3.0 or more. At the .05 significance level, is there a difference in the mean number of games won among the three groups? Use the .01 significance level.
c. Using the same attendance variable developed in part (b), is there a difference in the mean team batting average? Use the .01 significance level.
d. Using the same attendance variable developed in part (b), is there a difference in the mean salary of the three groups? Use the .01 significance level.

37. Refer to the Wage data, which reports information on annual wages for a sample of 100 workers. Also included are variables relating to industry, years of education, and gender for each worker.
a. Conduct a test of hypothesis to determine if there is a difference in the mean annual wages for workers in the three industries. If there is a difference in the means, which pair or pairs of means differ? Use the .05 significance level.
b. Conduct a test of hypothesis to determine if there is a difference in the mean annual wages for workers in the six different occupations. If there is a difference in the means, which pair or pairs of means differ? Use the .05 significance level.

Software Commands

1. The Excel commands for the test of variances on page 349 are:
   a. Enter the data for U.S. 25 in column A and for I-75 in column B. Label the two columns.
   b. Click on **Tools**, **Data Analysis**, select **F-Test: Two-Sample for Variances,** and click **OK**.
   c. The range of the first variable is *A1:A8* and *B1:B9* for the second, click on **Labels,** select *D1* for the output range, and click **OK.**

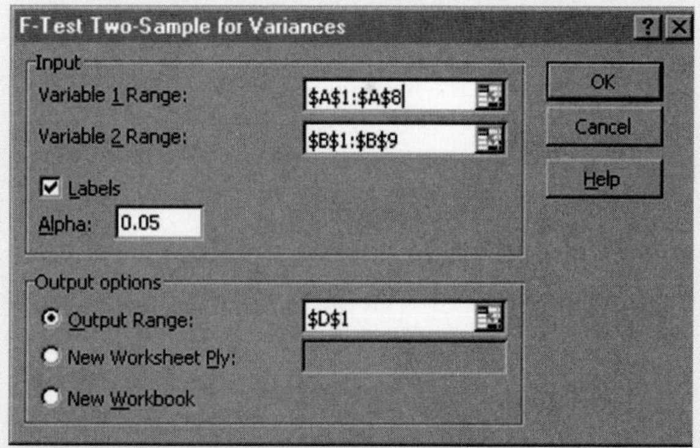

2. The Excel commands for the one-way ANOVA on page 358 are:
   a. Key in data into four columns labeled: Excellent, Good, Fair, and Poor.
   b. Click on **Tools** on the Excel Toolbar and select **Data Analysis.** In the dialog box select **ANOVA, Single Factor ANOVA,** and click **OK.**
   c. In the subsequent dialog box make the input range *A1:D8,* click on **Grouped by Columns,** click on **Labels in First Row,** the **Alpha** text box is .05, and finally select **Output range** as *G1* and click **OK.**

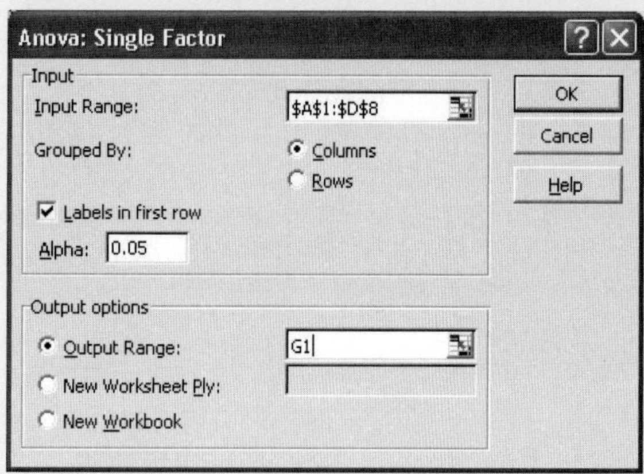

3. The MINITAB commands for the one-way ANOVA on page 358 are:
   a. Input the data into four columns and identify the columns as *Excellent, Good, Fair,* and *Poor.*
   b. Select **Stat**, **ANOVA**, and **Oneway (Unstacked)** and click **OK.**
   c. Select column C1 to C4 and click **OK.**

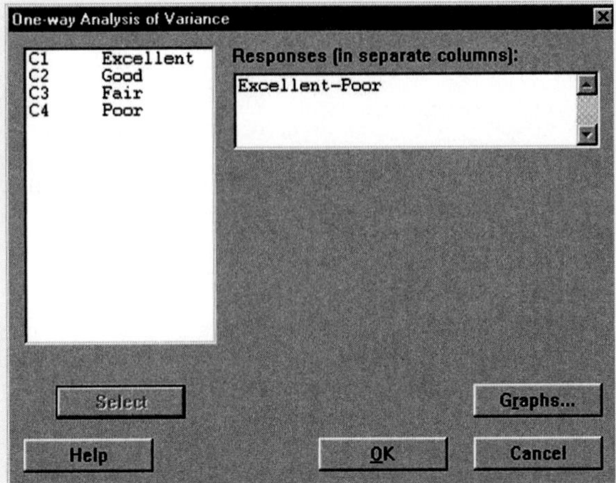

Chapter 12 Answers to Self-Review

12–1 Let Mark's assemblies be population 1, then H_0: $\sigma_1^2 \le \sigma_2^2$; H_1: $\sigma_1^2 > \sigma_2^2$; $df_1 = 10 - 1 = 9$; and df_2 also equals 9. H_0 is rejected if $F > 3.18$.

$$F = \frac{(2.0)^2}{(1.5)^2} = 1.78$$

H_0 is not rejected. The variation is the same for both employees.

12–2 **a.** H_0: $\mu_1 = \mu_2 = \mu_3$
H_1: At least one treatment mean is different.

b. Reject H_0 if $F > 4.26$

c. $$\bar{X} = \frac{240}{12} = 20$$

$$\text{SS total} = (18 - 20)^2 + \cdots + (32 - 20)^2 = 578$$

$$\text{SSE} = (18 - 17)^2 + (14 - 17)^2 + \cdots + (32 - 29)^2 = 74$$

$$\text{SST} = 578 - 74 = 504$$

d.

Source	Sum of Squares	Degrees of Freedom	Mean Square	F
Treatment	504	2	252	30.65
Error	74	9	8.22	

e. H_0 is rejected. There is a difference in the mean number of bottles sold at the various locations.

12–3 **a.** H_0: $\mu_1 = \mu_2 = \mu_3$
H_1: Not all means are equal.

b. H_0 is rejected if $F > 3.98$.

c. $\bar{X}_G = 8.86$, $\bar{X}_1 = 11$, $\bar{X}_2 = 8.75$, $\bar{X}_3 = 6.8$
SS total = 53.71
SST = 44.16
SSE = 9.55

Source	Sum of Squares	df	Mean Square	F
Treatment	44.16	2	22.08	25.43
Error	9.55	11	0.8682	
Total	53.71	13		

d. H_0 is rejected. The treatment means differ.

e. $(11.0 - 6.8) \pm 2.201\sqrt{0.8682(1/5 + 1/5)} = 4.2 \pm 1.30 = 2.90$ and 5.50
These treatment means differ because both endpoints of the confidence interval are of the same sign—positive in this problem.

13

Linear Regression and Correlation

GOALS

When you have completed this chapter, you will be able to:

1 **Understand and interpret the terms *dependent* and *independent variable.***

2 **Calculate and interpret the *coefficient of correlation, the coefficient of determination,* and the *standard error of estimate.***

3 **Conduct a test of hypothesis to determine whether the coefficient of correlation in the population is zero.**

4 **Calculate the *least squares regression line.***

5 **Construct and interpret *confidence* and *prediction intervals* for the dependent variable.**

6 **Set up and interpret an ANOVA table.**

Use the data given in Exercise 55 showing the retail price for 12 randomly selected laptop computers with their corresponding processor speeds to develop a linear equation that can be used to describe how the price depends on the processor speed. (See Goal 4 and Exercise 55.)

Introduction

Chapters 2 through 4 dealt with *descriptive statistics.* We organized raw data into a frequency distribution, and computed several measures of location and measures of dispersion to describe the major characteristics of the data. Chapter 5 started the study of *statistical inference.* The main emphasis was on inferring something about a population parameter, such as the population mean, on the basis of a sample. We tested for the reasonableness of a population mean or a population proportion, the difference between two population means, or whether several population means were equal. All of these tests involved just *one* interval- or ratio-level variable, such as the weight of a plastic soft drink bottle, the income of bank presidents, or the number of patients admitted to a particular hospital.

We shift the emphasis in this chapter to the study of two variables. Recall in Chapter 4 we introduced the idea of showing the relationship between two variables with a scatter diagram. We plotted the price of vehicles sold at Whitner Autoplex on the vertical axis and the age of the buyer on the horizontal axis. See the statistical software output on page 108. In that case we observed that as the age of the buyer increased, the amount spent for the vehicle also increased. In this chapter we carry this idea further. That is, we develop numerical measures to express the relationship between two variables. Is the relationship strong or weak, is it direct or inverse? In addition we develop an equation to express the relationship between variables. This will allow us to estimate one variable on the basis of another. Here are some examples.

- Is there a relationship between the amount Healthtex spends per month on advertising and the sales in the month?
- Can we base an estimate of the cost to heat a home in January on the number of square feet in the home?
- Is there a relationship between the miles per gallon achieved by large pickup trucks and the size of the engine?
- Is there a relationship between the number of hours that students studied for an exam and the score earned?

Note in each of these cases there are two variables observed for each sampled observation. For the last example, we find, for each student selected for the sample, the hours studied and the score earned.

We begin this chapter by examining the meaning and purpose of **correlation analysis.** We continue our study by developing a mathematical equation that will allow us to estimate the value of one variable based on the value of another. This is called **regression analysis.** We will (1) determine the equation of the line that best fits the data, (2) use the equation to estimate the value of one variable based on another, (3) measure the error in our estimate, and (4) establish confidence and prediction intervals for our estimate.

What Is Correlation Analysis?

Correlation analysis is the study of the relationship between variables. To explain, suppose the sales manager of Copier Sales of America, which has a large sales force throughout the United States and Canada, wants to determine whether there is a

Statistics in Action

The space shuttle Challenger exploded on January 28, 1986. An investigation of the cause examined four contractors: Rockwell International for the shuttle and engines, Lockheed for ground support, Martin Marietta for the external fuel tanks, and Morton Thiokol for the solid fuel booster rockets. After several months, the investigation blamed the explosion on defective O-rings produced by Morton Thiokol. A study of the contractor's stock prices showed an interesting happenstance. On the day of the crash, Morton Thiokol stock was down 11.86% and the stock of the other three lost only 2 to 3%. Can we conclude that financial markets predicted the outcome of the investigation?

relationship between the number of sales calls made in a month and the number of copiers sold that month. The manager selects a random sample of 10 representatives and determines the number of sales calls each representative made last month and the number of copiers sold. The sample information is shown in Table 13–1.

TABLE 13–1 Sales Calls and Copiers Sold for 10 Salespeople

Sales Representative	Number of Sales Calls	Number of Copiers Sold
Tom Keller	20	30
Jeff Hall	40	60
Brian Virost	20	40
Greg Fish	30	60
Susan Welch	10	30
Carlos Ramirez	10	40
Rich Niles	20	40
Mike Kiel	20	50
Mark Reynolds	20	30
Soni Jones	30	70

By reviewing the data we observe that there does seem to be some relationship between the number of sales calls and the number of units sold. That is, the salespeople who made the most sales calls sold the most units. However, the relationship is not "perfect" or exact. For example, Soni Jones made fewer sales calls than Jeff Hall, but she sold more units.

Instead of talking in generalities as we did in Chapter 4 and have so far in this chapter, we will develop some statistical measures to portray more precisely the relationship between the two variables, sales calls and copiers sold. This group of statistical techniques is called **correlation analysis.**

CORRELATION ANALYSIS A group of techniques to measure the association between two variables.

The basic idea of correlation analysis is to report the association between two variables. The usual first step is to plot the data in a **scatter diagram** as we described in Chapter 4. An example will show how a scatter diagram is used.

EXAMPLE

Copier Sales of America sells copiers to businesses of all sizes throughout the United States and Canada. Ms. Marcy Bancer was recently promoted to the position of national sales manager. At the upcoming sales meeting, the sales representatives from all over the country will be in attendance. She would like to impress upon them the importance of making that extra sales call each day. She decides to gather some information on the relationship between the number of sales calls and the number of copiers sold. She selected a random sample of 10 sales representatives and determined the number of sales calls they made last month and the number of copiers they sold. The sample information is reported in Table 13–1. What observations can you make about the relationship between the number of sales calls and the number of copiers sold? Develop a scatter diagram to display the information.

SOLUTION

Based on the information in Table 13–1, Ms. Bancer suspects there is a relationship between the number of sales calls made in a month and the number of copiers sold. Soni Jones sold the most copiers last month, and she was one of three representatives making 30 or more sales calls. On the other hand, Susan Welch and Carlos

Ramirez made only 10 sales calls last month. Ms. Welch had the lowest number of copiers sold among the sampled representatives.

The implication is that the number of copiers sold is related to the number of sales calls made. As the number of sales calls increases, it appears the number of copiers sold also increases. We refer to number of sales calls as the **independent variable** and number of copiers sold as the **dependent variable.**

DEPENDENT VARIABLE The variable that is being predicted or estimated.

INDEPENDENT VARIABLE A variable that provides the basis for estimation. It is the predictor variable.

It is common practice to scale the dependent variable (copiers sold) on the vertical or *Y*-axis and the independent variable (number of sales calls) on the horizontal or *X*-axis. To develop the scatter diagram of the Copier Sales of America sales information, we begin with the first sales representative, Tom Keller. Tom made 20 sales calls last month and sold 30 copiers, so $X = 20$ and $Y = 30$. To plot this point, move along the horizontal axis to $X = 20$, then go vertically to $Y = 30$ and place a dot at the intersection. This process is continued until all the paired data are plotted, as shown in Chart 13–1.

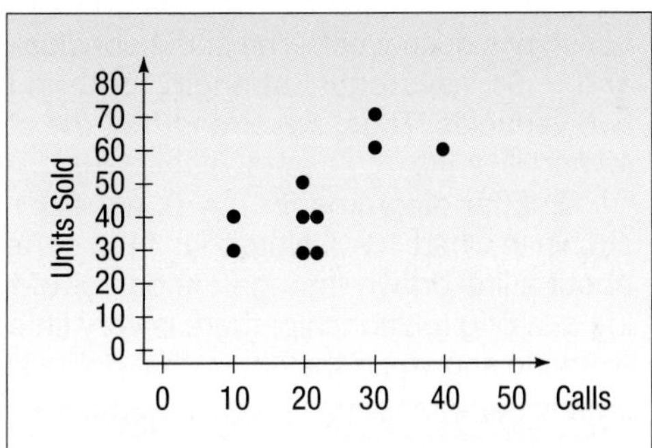

CHART 13–1 Scatter Diagram Showing Sales Calls and Copiers Sold

The scatter diagram shows graphically that the sales representatives who make more calls tend to sell more copiers. It is reasonable for Ms. Bancer, the national sales manager at Copier Sales of America, to tell her salespeople that the more sales calls they make the more copiers they can expect to sell. Note that while there appears to be a positive relationship between the two variables, all the points do not fall on a line. In the following section you will measure the strength and direction of this relationship between two variables by determining the coefficient of correlation.

The Coefficient of Correlation

Interval- or ratio-level data are required

Originated by Karl Pearson about 1900, the **coefficient of correlation** describes the strength of the relationship between two sets of interval-scaled or ratio-scaled variables. Designated *r,* it is often referred to as *Pearson's r* and as the *Pearson product-moment correlation coefficient.* It can assume any value from -1.00 to $+1.00$ inclusive. A correlation coefficient of -1.00 or $+1.00$ indicates *perfect correlation.* For example, a correlation coefficient for the preceding example computed to be $+1.00$

Characteristics of r

would indicate that the number of sales calls and the number of copiers sold are perfectly related in a positive linear sense. A computed value of -1.00 reveals that sales calls and the number of copiers sold are perfectly related in an inverse linear sense. How the scatter diagram would appear if the relationship between the two sets of data were linear and perfect is shown in Chart 13–2.

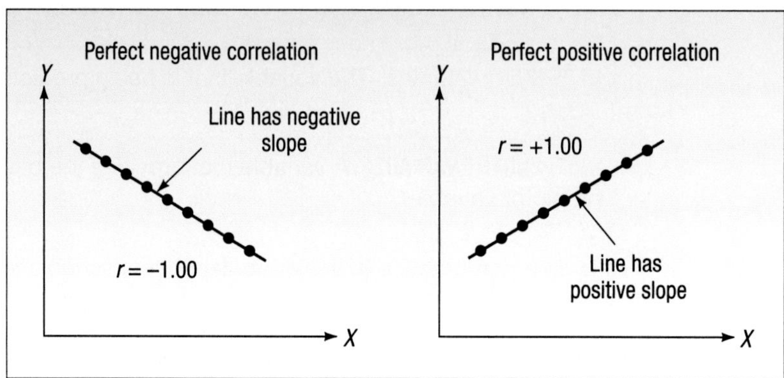

CHART 13–2 Scatter Diagrams Showing Perfect Negative Correlation and Perfect Positive Correlation

If there is absolutely no relationship between the two sets of variables, Pearson's r is zero. A coefficient of correlation r close to 0 (say, .08) shows that the linear relationship is quite weak. The same conclusion is drawn if $r = -.08$. Coefficients of $-.91$ and $+.91$ have equal strength; both indicate very strong correlation between the two variables. Thus, *the strength of the correlation does not depend on the direction (either – or +).*

Scatter diagrams for $r = 0$, a weak r (say, $-.23$), and a strong r (say, $+.87$) are shown in Chart 13–3. Note that if the correlation is weak, there is considerable scatter about a line drawn through the center of the data. For the scatter diagram representing a strong relationship, there is very little scatter about the line. This indicates, in the example shown on the chart, that hours studied is a good predictor of exam score.

Examples of degrees of correlation

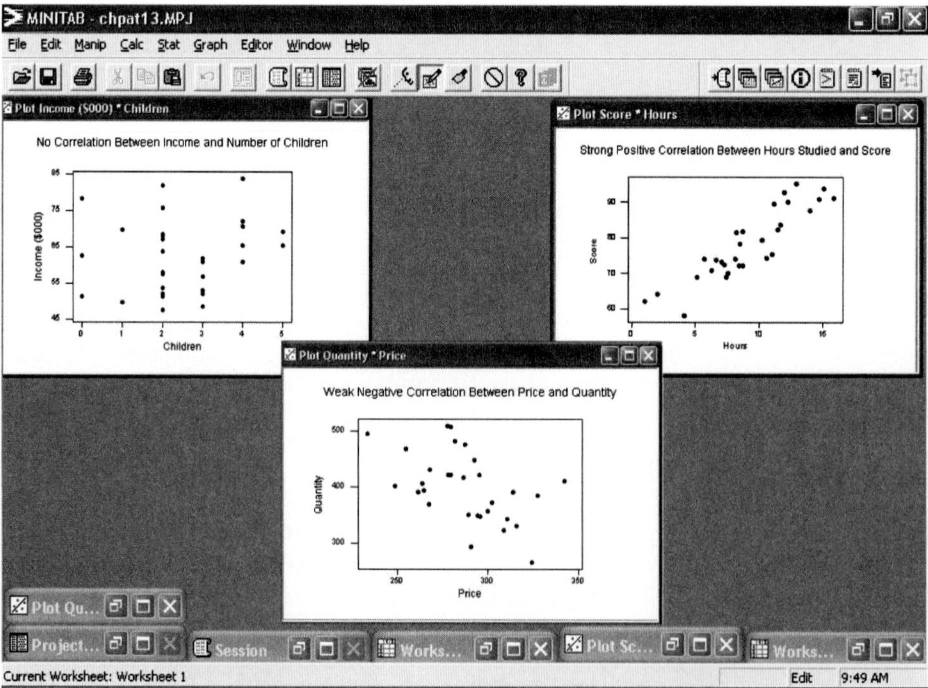

CHART 13–3 Scatter Diagrams Depicting Zero, Weak, and Strong Correlation

The following drawing summarizes the strength and direction of the coefficient of correlation.

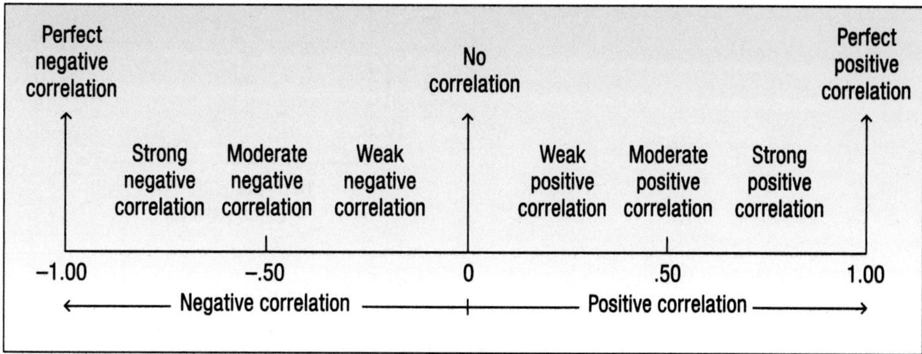

COEFFICIENT OF CORRELATION A measure of the strength of the linear relationship between two variables.

How is the value of the coefficient of correlation determined? We will use the Copier Sales of America data, which are reported in Table 13–2, as an example. We begin with a scatter diagram, similar to Chart 13–2. Draw a vertical line through the data values at the mean of the X-values and a horizontal line at the mean of the Y-values. In Chart 13–4 we've added a vertical line at 22.0 calls ($\bar{X} = \Sigma X/n = 220/10 = 22$) and a horizontal line at 45.0 copiers ($\bar{Y} = \Sigma Y/n = 450/10 = 45.0$). These lines pass through the "center" of the data and divide the scatter diagram into four quadrants. Think of moving the origin from (0, 0) to (22, 45).

TABLE 13–2 Sales Calls and Copiers Sold for 10 Salespeople

Sales Representative	Sales Calls (X)	Copiers Sold (Y)
Tom Keller	20	30
Jeff Hall	40	60
Brian Virost	20	40
Greg Fish	30	60
Susan Welch	10	30
Carlos Ramirez	10	40
Rich Niles	20	40
Mike Kiel	20	50
Mark Reynolds	20	30
Soni Jones	30	70
Total	220	450

Two variables are positively related, when the number of copiers sold is above the mean and the number of sales calls is also above the mean. These points appear in the upper-right quadrant of Chart 13–4 on the next page. Similarly, when the number of copiers sold is less than the mean, so is the number of sales calls. These points fall in the lower-left quadrant of Chart 13–4. For example, the last person on the list in Table 13–2, Soni Jones, made 30 sales calls and sold 70 copiers. These values are above their respective means, so this point is located in the upper-right quadrant. She made 8 ($X - \bar{X} = 30 - 22$) more sales calls than the mean and sold 25 ($Y - \bar{Y} =$

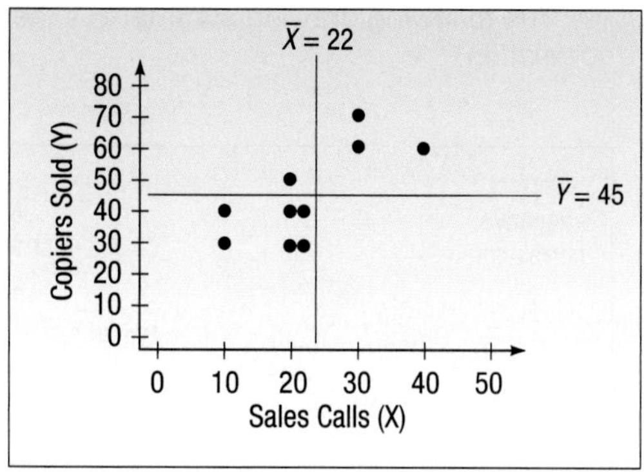

CHART 13–4 Computation of the Coefficient of Correlation

70 − 45) more copiers than the mean. Tom Keller, the first name on the list in Table 13–2, made 20 sales calls and sold 30 copiers. Both of these values are less than their respective mean; hence this point is in the lower-left quadrant. Tom made 2 less sales calls and sold 15 less copiers than the respective means. The deviations from the mean number of sales calls and for the mean number of copiers sold are summarized in Table 13–3 for the 10 sales representatives. The sum of the products of the deviations from the respective means is 900. That is, the term $\Sigma(X - \bar{X})(Y - \bar{Y}) = 900$.

TABLE 13–3 Deviations from the Mean and Their Products

Sales Representative	Calls Y	Sales X	$X - \bar{X}$	$Y - \bar{Y}$	$(X - \bar{X})(Y - \bar{Y})$
Tom Keller	20	30	−2	−15	30
Jeff Hall	40	60	18	15	270
Brian Virost	20	40	−2	−5	10
Greg Fish	30	60	8	15	120
Susan Welch	10	30	−12	−15	180
Carlos Ramirez	10	40	−12	−5	60
Rich Niles	20	40	−2	−5	10
Mike Kiel	20	50	−2	5	−10
Mark Reynolds	20	30	−2	−15	30
Soni Jones	30	70	8	25	200
					900

In both the upper-right and the lower-left quadrants, the product of $(X - \bar{X})(Y - \bar{Y})$ is positive because both of the factors have the same sign. In our example this happens for all sales representatives except Mike Kiel. We can therefore expect the coefficient of correlation to have a positive value.

If the two variables are inversely related, one variable will be above the mean and the other below the mean. Most of the points in this case occur in the upper-left and lower-right quadrants. Now $(X - \bar{X})$ and $(Y - \bar{Y})$ will have opposite signs, so their product is negative. The resulting correlation coefficient is negative.

What happens if there is no linear relationship between the two variables? The points in the scatter diagram will appear in all four quadrants. The negative products of $(X - \bar{X})(Y - \bar{Y})$ offset the positive products, so the sum is near zero. This leads to a correlation coefficient near zero.

Pearson also wanted the correlation coefficient to be unaffected by the units of the two variables. For example, if we had used hundreds of copiers sold instead of the number sold, the coefficient of correlation would be the same. The coefficient of correlation is independent of the scale used if we divide the term $\Sigma(X - \bar{X})(Y - \bar{Y})$ by the sample standard deviations. It is also made independent of the sample size and bounded by the values +1.00 and −1.00 if we divide by $(n - 1)$.

This reasoning leads to the following formula:

CORRELATION COEFFICIENT

$$r = \frac{\Sigma(X - \bar{X})(Y - \bar{Y})}{(n - 1)\, s_x\, s_y} \qquad \textbf{[13–1]}$$

To compute the coefficient of correlation, we use the standard deviations of the sample of 10 sales calls and 10 copiers sold. We could use formula (3–11) to calculate the sample standard deviations or we could use a software package. For the specific Excel and MINITAB commands see the Software Command section at the end of Chapter 3. The following is the Excel output. The standard deviation of the number of sales calls is 9.189 and of the number of copiers sold 14.337.

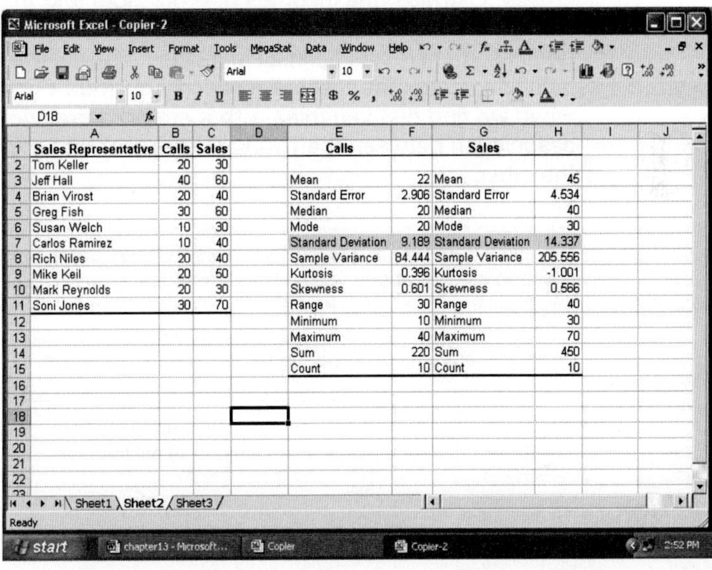

	A	B	C	D	E	F	G	H
1	Sales Representative	Calls	Sales		Calls		Sales	
2	Tom Keller	20	30					
3	Jeff Hall	40	60		Mean	22	Mean	45
4	Brian Virost	20	40		Standard Error	2.906	Standard Error	4.534
5	Greg Fish	30	60		Median	20	Median	40
6	Susan Welch	10	30		Mode	20	Mode	30
7	Carlos Ramirez	10	40		Standard Deviation	9.189	Standard Deviation	14.337
8	Rich Niles	20	40		Sample Variance	84.444	Sample Variance	205.556
9	Mike Keil	20	50		Kurtosis	0.396	Kurtosis	-1.001
10	Mark Reynolds	20	30		Skewness	0.601	Skewness	0.566
11	Soni Jones	30	70		Range	30	Range	40
12					Minimum	10	Minimum	30
13					Maximum	40	Maximum	70
14					Sum	220	Sum	450
15					Count	10	Count	10

We now insert these values into formula (13–1) to determine the coefficient of correlation:

$$r = \frac{\Sigma(X - \bar{X})(Y - \bar{Y})}{(n - 1)\, s_x\, s_y} = \frac{900}{(10 - 1)(9.189)(14.337)} = 0.759$$

How do we interpret a correlation of 0.759? First, it is positive, so we see there is a direct relationship between the number of sales calls and the number of copiers sold. This confirms our reasoning based on the scatter diagram, Chart 13–4. The value of 0.759 is fairly close to 1.00, so we conclude that the association is strong. To put it another way, an increase in calls will likely lead to more sales.

The Coefficient of Determination

In the previous example regarding the relationship between the number of sales calls and the units sold, the coefficient of correlation, 0.759, was interpreted as being "strong." Terms such as *weak, moderate,* and *strong,* however, do not have precise meaning. A measure that has a more easily interpreted meaning is the **coefficient of determination.** It is computed by squaring the coefficient of correlation. In the example, the coefficient of determination, r^2, is 0.576, found by $(0.759)^2$. This is a proportion or a percent; we can say that 57.6 percent of the variation in the number of copiers sold is explained, or accounted for, by the variation in the number of sales calls.

> **COEFFICIENT OF DETERMINATION** The proportion of the total variation in the dependent variable *Y* that is explained, or accounted for, by the variation in the independent variable *X*.

Further discussion of the coefficient of determination is found later in the chapter.

Correlation and Cause

If there is a strong relationship (say, $r = .91$) between two variables, we are tempted to assume that an increase or decrease in one variable *causes* a change in the other variable. For example, it can be shown that the consumption of Georgia peanuts and the consumption of aspirin have a strong correlation. However, this does not indicate that an increase in the consumption of peanuts *caused* the consumption of aspirin to increase. Likewise, the incomes of professors and the number of inmates in mental institutions have increased proportionately. Further, as the population of donkeys has decreased, there has been an increase in the number of doctoral degrees granted. Relationships such as these are called **spurious correlations.** What we can conclude when we find two variables with a strong correlation is that there is a relationship or association between the two variables, not that a change in one causes a change in the other.

Self-Review 13–1

Haverty's Furniture is a family business that has been selling to retail customers in the Chicago area for many years. They advertise extensively on radio, TV, and the Internet emphasizing their low prices and easy credit terms. The owner would like to review the relationship between sales and the amount spent on advertising. Below is information on sales and advertising expense for the last four months.

Month	Advertising Expense ($ million)	Sales Revenue ($ million)
July	2	7
August	1	3
September	3	8
October	4	10

(a) The owner wants to forecast sales on the basis of advertising expense. Which variable is the dependent variable? Which variable is the independent variable?
(b) Draw a scatter diagram.
(c) Determine the coefficient of correlation.
(d) Interpret the strength of the correlation coefficient.
(e) Determine the coefficient of determination. Interpret.

Exercises

1. The following sample observations were randomly selected.

X:	4	5	3	6	10
Y:	4	6	5	7	7

Determine the coefficient of correlation and the coefficient of determination. Interpret.

2. The following sample observations were randomly selected.

X:	5	3	6	3	4	4	6	8
Y:	13	15	7	12	13	11	9	5

Determine the coefficient of correlation and the coefficient of determination. Interpret the association between X and Y.

3. Bi-lo Appliance Stores has outlets in several large metropolitan areas in New England. The general sales manager plans to air a commercial for a digital camera on selected local TV stations prior to a sale starting on Saturday and ending Sunday. She plans to get the information for Saturday–Sunday digital camera sales at the various outlets and pair them with the number of times the advertisement was shown on the local TV stations. The purpose is to find whether there is any relationship between the number of times the advertisement was aired and digital camera sales. The pairings are:

Location of TV Station	Number of Airings	Saturday–Sunday Sales ($ thousands)
Providence	4	15
Springfield	2	8
New Haven	5	21
Boston	6	24
Hartford	3	17

a. What is the dependent variable?
b. Draw a scatter diagram.
c. Determine the coefficient of correlation.
d. Determine the coefficient of determination.
e. Interpret these statistics.

4. The production department of NDB Electronics wants to explore the relationship between the number of employees who assemble a subassembly and the number produced. As an experiment, two employees were assigned to assemble the subassemblies. They produced 15 during a one-hour period. Then four employees assembled them. They produced 25 during a one-hour period. The complete set of paired observations follows.

Number of Assemblers	One-Hour Production (units)
2	15
4	25
1	10
5	40
3	30

The dependent variable is production; that is, it is assumed that the level of production depends upon the number of employees.
a. Draw a scatter diagram.
b. Based on the scatter diagram, does there appear to be any relationship between the number of assemblers and production? Explain.
c. Compute the coefficient of correlation.
d. Evaluate the strength of the relationship by computing the coefficient of determination.

5. The city council of Pine Bluffs is considering increasing the number of police in an effort to reduce crime. Before making a final decision, the council asks the Chief of Police to survey other cities of similar size to determine the relationship between the number of police and the number of crimes reported. The Chief gathered the following sample information.

City	Police	Number of Crimes	City	Police	Number of Crimes
Oxford	15	17	Holgate	17	7
Starksville	17	13	Carey	12	21
Danville	25	5	Whistler	11	19
Athens	27	7	Woodville	22	6

a. If we want to estimate crimes on the basis of the number of police, which variable is the dependent variable and which is the independent variable?
b. Draw a scatter diagram.

c. Determine the coefficient of correlation.
d. Determine the coefficient of determination.
e. Interpret these statistics. Does it surprise you that the relationship is inverse?

6. The owner of Maumee Ford-Mercury wants to study the relationship between the age of a car and its selling price. Listed below is a random sample of 12 used cars sold at the dealership during the last year.

Car	Age (years)	Selling Price ($000)	Car	Age (years)	Selling Price ($000)
1	9	8.1	7	8	7.6
2	7	6.0	8	11	8.0
3	11	3.6	9	10	8.0
4	12	4.0	10	12	6.0
5	8	5.0	11	6	8.6
6	7	10.0	12	6	8.0

a. If we want to estimate selling price on the basis of the age of the car, which variable is the dependent variable and which is the independent variable?
b. Draw a scatter diagram.
c. Determine the coefficient of correlation.
d. Determine the coefficient of determination.
e. Interpret these statistics. Does it surprise you that the relationship is inverse?

Testing the Significance of the Correlation Coefficient

Recall the sales manager of Copier Sales of America found the correlation between the number of sales calls and the number of copiers sold was 0.759. This indicated a strong association between the two variables. However, only 10 salespeople were sampled. Could it be that the correlation in the population is actually 0? This would mean the correlation of 0.759 was due to chance. The population in this example is all the salespeople employed by the firm.

Could the correlation in the population be zero?

Resolving this dilemma requires a test to answer the obvious question: Could there be zero correlation in the population from which the sample was selected? To put it another way, did the computed *r* come from a population of paired observations with zero correlation? To continue our convention of allowing Greek letters to represent a population parameter, we will let ρ represent the correlation in the population. It is pronounced "rho."

We will continue with the illustration involving sales calls and copiers sold. We employ the same hypothesis testing steps described in Chapter 10. The null hypothesis and the alternate hypothesis are:

H_0: $\rho = 0$ (The correlation in the population is zero.)
H_1: $\rho \neq 0$ (The correlation in the population is different from zero.)

From the way H_1 is stated, we know that the test is two-tailed.

The formula for *t* is:

t TEST FOR THE COEFFICIENT OF CORRELATION

$$t = \frac{r\sqrt{n-2}}{\sqrt{1-r^2}} \quad \text{with } n - 2 \text{ degrees of freedom} \qquad [13\text{–}2]$$

Using the .05 level of significance, the decision rule states that if the computed *t* falls in the area between plus 2.306 and minus 2.306, the null hypothesis is not rejected. To locate the critical value of 2.306, refer to Appendix F for $df = n - 2 = 10 - 2 = 8$. See Chart 13–5.

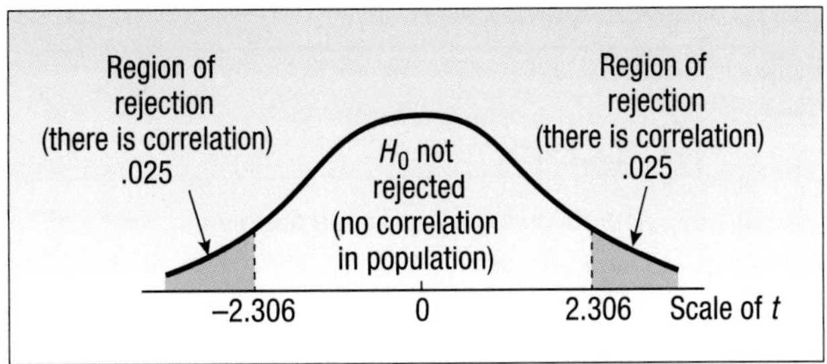

CHART 13–5 Decision Rule for Test of Hypothesis at .05 Significance Level and 8 *df*

Applying formula (13–2) to the example regarding the number of sales calls and units sold:

$$t = \frac{r\sqrt{n-2}}{\sqrt{1-r^2}} = \frac{.759\sqrt{10-2}}{\sqrt{1-.759^2}} = 3.297$$

The computed *t* is in the rejection region. Thus, H_0 is rejected at the .05 significance level. This means the correlation in the population is not zero. From a practical standpoint, it indicates to the sales manager that there is correlation with respect to the number of sales calls made and the number of copiers sold in the population of salespeople.

We can also interpret the test of hypothesis in terms of *p*-values. A *p*-value is the likelihood of finding a value of the test statistic more extreme than the one computed, when H_0 is true. To determine the *p*-value, go to the *t* distribution in Appendix F and find the row for 8 degrees of freedom. The value of the test statistic is 3.297, so in the row for 8 degrees of freedom and a two-tailed test, find the value closest to 3.297. For a two-tailed test at the .02 significance level, the critical value is 2.896, and the critical value at the .01 significance level is 3.355. Because 3.297 is between 2.896 and 3.355 we conclude that the *p*-value is between .01 and .02.

Both MINITAB and Excel will report the correlation between two variables. In addition to the correlation, MINITAB reports the *p*-value for the test of hypothesis that the correlation in the population between the two variables is 0. The MINITAB output showing the results is below. They are the same as those calculated earlier.

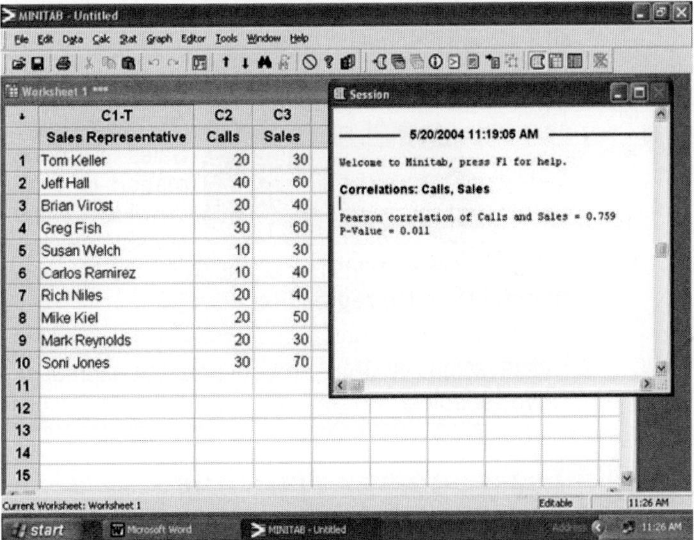

Self-Review 13–2 A sample of 25 mayoral campaigns in cities with populations larger than 50,000 showed that the correlation between the percent of the vote received and the amount spent on the campaign by the candidate was .43. At the .05 significance level, is there a positive association between the variables?

Exercises

7. The following hypotheses are given.

H_0: $\rho \leq 0$
H_1: $\rho > 0$

A random sample of 12 paired observations indicated a correlation of .32. Can we conclude that the correlation in the population is greater than zero? Use the .05 significance level.

8. The following hypotheses are given.

H_0: $\rho \geq 0$
H_1: $\rho < 0$

A random sample of 15 paired observations has a correlation of −.46. Can we conclude that the correlation in the population is less than zero? Use the .05 significance level.

9. The Pennsylvania Refining Company is studying the relationship between the pump price of gasoline and the number of gallons sold. For a sample of 20 stations last Tuesday, the correlation was .78. At the .01 significance level, is the correlation in the population greater than zero?

10. A study of 20 worldwide financial institutions showed the correlation between their assets and pretax profit to be .86. At the .05 significance level, can we conclude that there is positive correlation in the population?

Regression Analysis

In the previous section we developed measures to express the strength and the direction of the relationship between two variables. In this section we wish to develop an equation to express the *linear* (straight line) relationship between two variables. In addition we want to be able to estimate the value of the dependent variable *Y* based on a selected value of the independent variable *X*. The technique used to develop the equation and provide the estimates is called **regression analysis.**

In Table 13–1 we reported the number of sales calls and the number of units sold for a sample of 10 sales representatives employed by Copier Sales of America. Chart 13–1 portrayed this information in a scatter diagram. Now we want to develop a linear equation that expresses the relationship between the number of sales calls and the number of units sold. The equation for the line used to estimate *Y* on the basis of *X* is referred to as the **regression equation.**

REGRESSION EQUATION An equation that expresses the linear relationship between two variables.

Least Squares Principle

The scatter diagram in Chart 13–1 is reproduced in Chart 13–6, with a line drawn with a ruler through the dots to illustrate that a straight line would probably fit the data.

However, the line drawn using a straight edge has one disadvantage: Its position is based in part on the judgment of the person drawing the line. The hand-drawn lines in Chart 13–7 represent the judgments of four people. All the lines except line *A* seem to be reasonable. However, each would result in a different estimate of units sold for a particular number of sales calls.

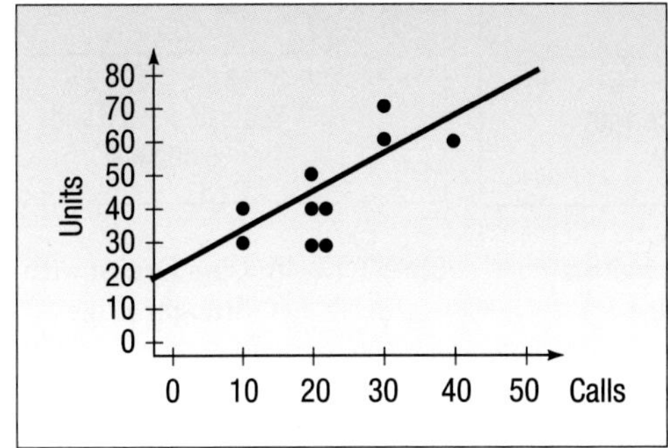

CHART 13–6 Sales Calls and Copiers Sold for 10 Sales Representatives

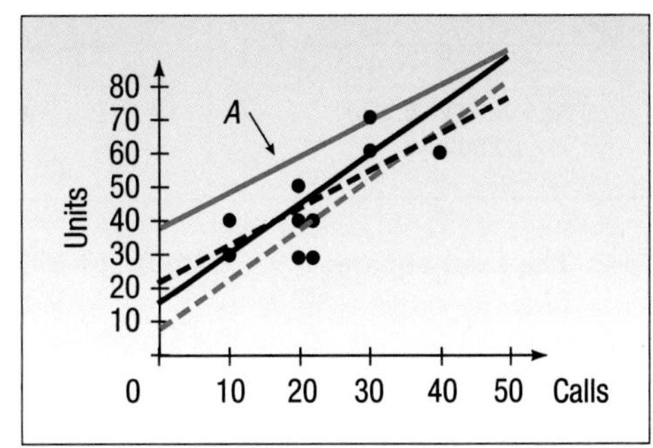

CHART 13–7 Four Lines Superimposed on the Scatter Diagram

Least squares line gives "best" fit; subjective method is unreliable.

Judgment is eliminated by determining the regression line using a mathematical method called the **least squares principle.** This method gives what is commonly referred to as the "best-fitting" line.

> **LEAST SQUARES PRINCIPLE** Determining a regression equation by minimizing the sum of the squares of the vertical distances between the actual *Y* values and the predicted values of *Y*.

To illustrate this concept, the same data are plotted in the three charts that follow. The regression line in Chart 13–8 was determined using the least squares method. It is the best-fitting line because the sum of the squares of the vertical deviations about it is at a minimum. The first plot ($X = 3$, $Y = 8$) deviates by 2 from the line, found by $10 - 8$. The deviation squared is 4. The squared deviation for the plot $X = 4$, $Y = 18$ is 16. The squared deviation for the plot $X = 5$, $Y = 16$ is 4. The sum of the squared deviations is 24, found by $4 + 16 + 4$.

Assume that the lines in Charts 13–9 and 13–10 were drawn with a straight edge. The sum of the squared vertical deviations in Chart 13–9 is 44. For Chart 13–10 it is 132. Both sums are greater than the sum for the line in Chart 13–8, found by using the least squares method.

The equation of a straight line has the form

GENERAL FORM OF LINEAR REGRESSION EQUATION $$Y' = a + bX \quad \textbf{[13–3]}$$

where:

- Y' read *Y* prime, is the predicted value of the *Y* variable for a selected *X* value.
- a is the *Y*-intercept. It is the estimated value of *Y* when $X = 0$. Another way to put it is: *a* is the estimated value of *Y* where the regression line crosses the *Y*-axis when *X* is zero.
- b is the slope of the line, or the average change in Y' for each change of one unit (either increase or decrease) in the independent variable *X*.
- X is any value of the independent variable that is selected.

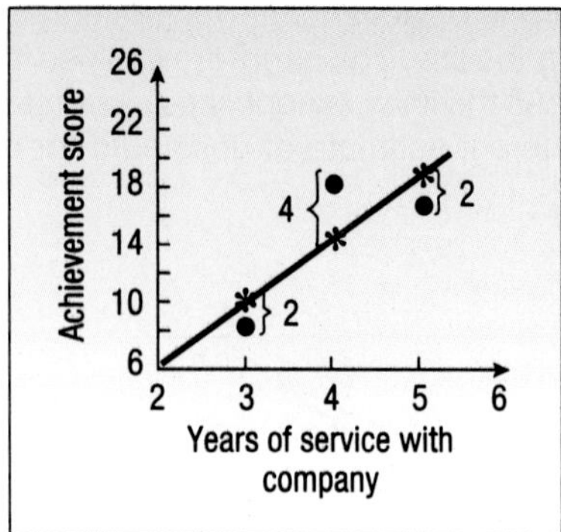

CHART 13–8 The Least Squares Line

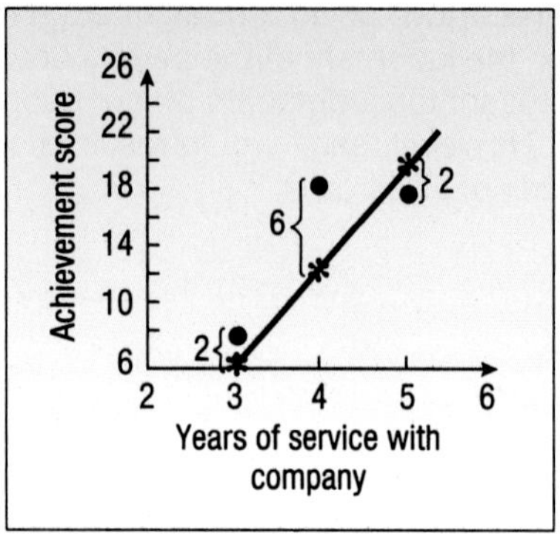

CHART 13–9 Line Drawn with a Straight Edge

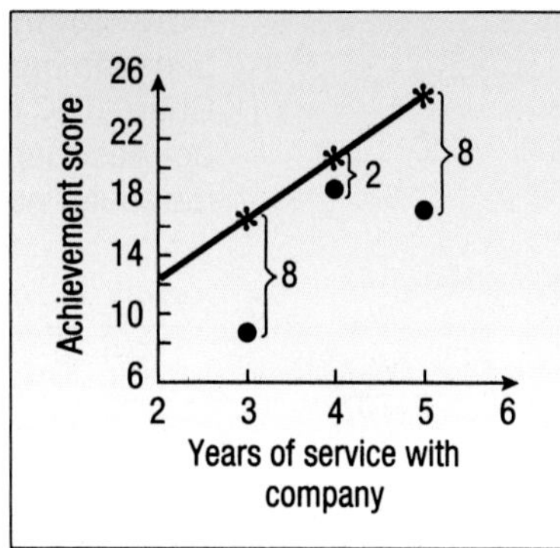

CHART 13–10 Line Drawn with a Straight Edge

The formulas for *a* and *b* are:

SLOPE OF THE REGRESSION LINE	$b = r\frac{s_y}{s_x}$	[13-4]

where:

r is the correlation coefficient.
s_y is the standard deviation of Y (the dependent variable).
s_x is the standard deviation of X (the independent variable).

Y-INTERCEPT	$a = \bar{Y} - b\bar{X}$	[13-5]

where:

$\bar{Y}$ is the mean of Y (the dependent variable).
$\bar{X}$ is the mean of X (the independent variable).

The following example shows the details of determining the slope and intercept values.

EXAMPLE

Recall the example involving Copier Sales of America. The sales manager gathered information on the number of sales calls made and the number of copiers sold for a random sample of 10 sales representatives. As a part of her presentation at the upcoming sales meeting, Ms. Bancer, the sales manager, would like to offer specific information about the relationship between the number of sales calls and the number of copiers sold. Use the least squares method to determine a linear equation to express the relationship between the two variables. What is the expected number of copiers sold by a representative who made 20 calls?

SOLUTION

The calculations necessary to determine the regression equation are:

$$b = r\left(\frac{s_y}{s_x}\right) = .759\left(\frac{14.337}{9.189}\right) = 1.1842$$

$$a = \bar{Y} - b\bar{X} = 45 - (1.1842)22 = 18.9476$$

The standard deviation for the sales calls (X) and the units sold (Y) as well as their respective means can be found in the Excel spreadsheet on page 381. The value of r is calculated just below the spreadsheet.

Statistics in Action

In finance, investors are interested in the tradeoff between returns and risk. One technique to quantify risk is a regression analysis of a company's stock price (dependent variable) and an average measure of the stock market (independent variable). Often the Standard and Poor's (S&P) 500 Index is used to estimate the market. The regression coefficient, called Beta in finance, shows the change in a company's stock price for a one-unit change in the S&P Index. For example, if a stock has a beta of 1.5, then when the S&P index increases by 1%, the stock price will increase by 1.5%. The opposite is also true. If the S&P decreases by 1%, the stock price will decrease by 1.5%. If the beta is 1.0, then a 1% change in the index should show a 1% change in a stock price. If the beta is less than 1.0, then a 1% change in the index shows less than a 1% change in the stock price.

Thus, the regression equation is $Y' = 18.9476 + 1.1842X$. So if a salesperson makes 20 calls, he or she can expect to sell 42.6316 copiers, found by $Y' = 18.9476 + 1.1842X = 18.9476 + 1.1842(20)$. The b value of 1.1842 means that for each additional sales call made the sales representative can expect to increase the number of copiers sold by about 1.2. To put it another way, five additional sales calls in a month will result in about six more copiers being sold, found by $1.1842(5) = 5.921$.

The a value of 18.9476 is the point where the equation crosses the Y-axis. A literal translation is that if no sales calls are made, that is, $X = 0$, 18.9476 copiers will be sold. Note that $X = 0$ is outside the range of values included in the sample and, therefore, should not be used to estimate the number of copiers sold. The sales calls ranged from 10 to 40, so estimates should be made within that range.

Drawing the Line of Regression

The least squares equation, $Y' = 18.9476 + 1.1842X$, can be drawn on the scatter diagram. The first sales representative in the sample is Tom Keller. He made 20 calls. His estimated number of copiers sold is $Y' = 18.9476 + 1.1842(20) = 42.6316$. The plot $X = 20$ and $Y = 42.6316$ is located by moving to 20 on the X-axis and then going vertically to 42.6316. The other points on the regression equation can be determined by substituting the particular value of X into the regression equation.

Sales Representative	Sales Calls (X)	Estimated Sales (Y')	Sales Representative	Sales Calls (X)	Estimated Sales (Y')
Tom Keller	20	42.6316	Carlos Ramirez	10	30.7896
Jeff Hall	40	66.3156	Rich Niles	20	42.6316
Brian Virost	20	42.6316	Mike Kiel	20	42.6316
Greg Fish	30	54.4736	Mark Reynolds	20	42.6316
Susan Welch	10	30.7896	Soni Jones	30	54.4736

All the other points are connected to give the line. See Chart 13–11.

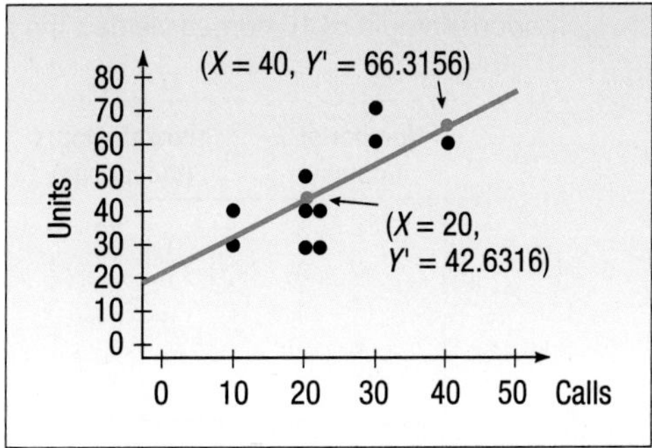

CHART 13–11 The Line of Regression Drawn on the Scatter Diagram

This line has some interesting features. As we have discussed, there is no other line through the data for which the sum of the squared deviations is smaller. In addition, this line will pass through the points represented by the mean of the X values and the mean of the Y values, that is, $\bar{X}$ and $\bar{Y}$. In this example $\bar{X} = 22.0$ and $\bar{Y} = 45.0$.

Self-Review 13–3

Refer to Self-Review 13–1, where the owner of Haverty's Furniture Company was studying the relationship between sales and the amount spent on advertising. The sales information for the last four months is repeated below.

Month	Advertising Expense ($ million)	Sales Revenue ($ million)
July	2	7
August	1	3
September	3	8
October	4	10

(a) Determine the regression equation.
(b) Interpret the values of *a* and *b*.
(c) Estimate sales when $3 million is spent on advertising.

Exercises

11. The following sample observations were randomly selected.

X:	4	5	3	6	10
Y:	4	6	5	7	7

a. Determine the regression equation.
b. Determine the value of Y' when X is 7.

12. The following sample observations were randomly selected.

X:	5	3	6	3	4	4	6	8
Y:	13	15	7	12	13	11	9	5

a. Determine the regression equation.
b. Determine the value of Y' when X is 7.

13. The Bradford Electric Illuminating Company is studying the relationship between kilowatt-hours (thousands) used and the number of rooms in a private single-family residence. A random sample of 10 homes yielded the following.

Number of Rooms	Kilowatt-Hours (thousands)	Number of Rooms	Kilowatt-Hours (thousands)
12	9	8	6
9	7	10	8
14	10	10	10
6	5	5	4
10	8	7	7

a. Determine the regression equation.
b. Determine the number of kilowatt-hours, in thousands, for a six-room house.

14. Mr. James McWhinney, president of Daniel-James Financial Services, believes there is a relationship between the number of client contacts and the dollar amount of sales. To document this assertion, Mr. McWhinney gathered the following sample information. The *X* column indicates the number of client contacts last month, and the *Y* column shows the value of sales ($ thousands) last month for each salesperson sampled.

Salesperson	Contacts (X)	Sales (Y)
Robert Armstrong	14	24
Jack Bender	12	14
Dorothy Brumley	20	28
Carmen Carella	16	30
Annette Perrault	46	80
Mary Jane Duryee	23	30
David Gwyer	48	90
Harvey Lazik	50	85
Ray Osbeck	55	120
Al Montanaro	50	110

a. Determine the regression equation.
b. Determine the estimated sales if 40 contacts are made.

15. A recent article in *Business Week* listed the "Best Small Companies." We are interested in the current results of the companies' sales and earnings. A random sample of 12 companies was selected and the sales and earnings, in millions of dollars, are reported below.

Company	Sales ($ millions)	Earnings ($ millions)	Company	Sales ($ millions)	Earnings ($ millions)
Papa John's International	$89.2	$4.9	Checkmate Electronics	$17.5	$2.6
Applied Innovation	18.6	4.4	Royal Grip	11.9	1.7
Integracare	18.2	1.3	M-Wave	19.6	3.5
Wall Data	71.7	8.0	Serving-N-Slide	51.2	8.2
Davidson Associates	58.6	6.6	Daig	28.6	6.0
Chico's Fas	46.8	4.1	Cobra Golf	69.2	12.8

Let sales be the independent variable and earnings be the dependent variable.
a. Draw a scatter diagram.
b. Compute the coefficient of correlation.
c. Compute the coefficient of determination.
d. Interpret your findings in parts b and c.
e. Determine the regression equation.
f. For a small company with $50.0 million in sales, estimate the earnings.

16. We are studying mutual bond funds for the purpose of investing in several funds. For this particular study, we want to focus on the assets of a fund and its five-year performance. The question is: Can the five-year rate of return be estimated based on the assets of the fund? Nine mutual funds were selected at random, and their assets and rates of return are shown below.

Fund	Assets ($ millions)	Return (%)	Fund	Assets ($ millions)	Return (%)
AARP High Quality Bond	$622.2	10.8	MFS Bond A	$494.5	11.6
Babson Bond L	160.4	11.3	Nichols Income	158.3	9.5
Compass Capital Fixed Income	275.7	11.4	T. Rowe Price Short-term	681.0	8.2
Galaxy Bond Retail	433.2	9.1	Thompson Income B	241.3	6.8
Keystone Custodian B-1	437.9	9.2			

a. Draw a scatter diagram.
b. Compute the coefficient of correlation.
c. Compute the coefficient of determination.
d. Write a brief report of your findings for parts b and c.
e. Determine the regression equation. Use assets as the independent variable.
f. For a fund with $400.0 million in sales, determine the five-year rate of return (in percent).

17. Refer to Exercise 5.
  a. Determine the regression equation.
  b. Estimate the number of crimes for a city with 20 police.
  c. Interpret the regression equation.

18. Refer to Exercise 6.
  a. Determine the regression equation.
  b. Estimate the selling price of a 10-year-old car.
  c. Interpret the regression equation.

The Standard Error of Estimate

Note in the preceding scatter diagram (Chart 13–11) that all of the points do not lie exactly on the regression line. If they all were on the line, there would be no error in estimating the number of units sold. To put it another way, if all the points were on the regression line, units sold could be predicted with 100 percent accuracy. Thus, there would be no error in predicting the Y variable based on an X variable. This is true in the following hypothetical case (see Chart 13–12). Theoretically, if $X = 4$, then an exact Y of 100 could be predicted with 100 percent confidence. Or if $X = 12$, then $Y = 300$. Because there is no difference between the observed values and the predicted values, there is no error in this estimate.

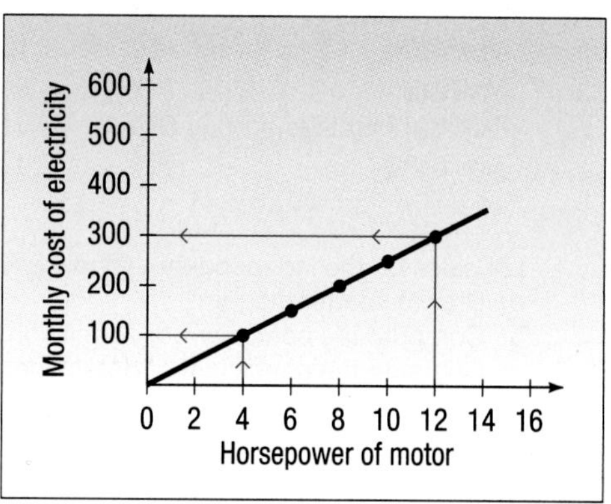

CHART 13–12 Example of Perfect Prediction: Horsepower and Cost of Electricity

Perfect prediction unrealistic in business

Perfect prediction in economics and business is practically impossible. For example, the revenue for the year from gasoline sales (Y) based on the number of automobile registrations (X) as of a certain date could no doubt be closely approximated, but the prediction would not be exact to the nearest dollar, or probably even to the nearest thousand dollars. Even predictions of tensile strength of steel wires based on the outside diameters of the wires are not always exact due to slight differences in the composition of the steel.

What is needed, then, is a measure that describes how precise the prediction of Y is based on X or, conversely, how inaccurate the estimate might be. This measure is called the **standard error of estimate.** The standard error of estimate, symbolized by $s_{y \cdot x}$, is the same concept as the standard deviation discussed in Chapter 3. The standard deviation measures the dispersion around the mean. The standard error of estimate measures the dispersion about the regression line.

> **STANDARD ERROR OF ESTIMATE** A measure of the scatter, or dispersion, of the observed values around the line of regression.

The standard error of estimate is found by the following equation. Note that the equation is quite similar to the one for the standard deviation of a sample.

STANDARD ERROR OF ESTIMATE

$$s_{y \cdot x} = \sqrt{\frac{\Sigma(Y - Y')^2}{n - 2}} \quad \textbf{[13–6]}$$

The standard deviation is based on the squared deviations from the mean, whereas the standard error of estimate is based on squared deviations between each Y and its predicted value, Y'. Remember that the regression line represents all the values of Y'. If $s_{y \cdot x}$ is small, this means that the data are relatively close to the regression line and the regression equation can be used to predict Y with little error. If $s_{y \cdot x}$ is large, this means that the data are widely scattered around the regression line and the regression equation will not provide a precise estimate Y.

EXAMPLE

Recall the example involving Copier Sales of America. The sales manager determined the least squares regression equation to be $Y' = 18.9476 + 1.1842X$, where Y' refers to the predicted number of copiers sold and X the number of sales calls made. Determine the standard error of estimate as a measure of how well the values fit the regression line.

SOLUTION

To find the standard error, we begin by finding the difference between the value, Y, and the value estimated from the regression equation, Y'. Next we square this difference, that is, $(Y - Y')^2$. We do this for each of the n observations and sum the results. That is, we compute $\Sigma(Y - Y')^2$, which is the numerator of formula (13–6). Finally, we divide by the number of observations minus 2. Why minus 2? We lose a degree of freedom each for estimating the intercept value, a, and the slope value, b. The details of the calculations are summarized in Table 13–4.

TABLE 13–4 Computations Needed for the Standard Error of Estimate

Sales Representative	Actual Sales (Y)	Estimated Sales (Y')	Deviation ($Y - Y'$)	Deviation Squared $(Y - Y')^2$
Tom Keller	30	42.6316	−12.6316	159.557
Jeff Hall	60	66.3156	−6.3156	39.887
Brian Virost	40	42.6316	−2.6316	6.925
Greg Fish	60	54.4736	5.5264	30.541
Susan Welch	30	30.7896	−0.7896	0.623
Carlos Ramirez	40	30.7896	9.2104	84.831
Rich Niles	40	42.6316	−2.6316	6.925
Mike Kiel	50	42.6316	7.3684	54.293
Mark Reynolds	30	42.6316	−12.6316	159.557
Soni Jones	70	54.4736	15.5264	241.069
			0.0000	784.211

The standard error of estimate is 9.901, found by using formula (13–6).

$$s_{y \cdot x} = \sqrt{\frac{\Sigma(Y - Y')^2}{n - 2}} = \sqrt{\frac{784.211}{10 - 2}} = 9.901$$

The deviations $(Y - Y')$ are the vertical deviations from the regression line. To illustrate, the 10 deviations from Table 13–4 are shown in Chart 13–13. Note in Table 13–4 that the sum of the signed deviations is zero. This indicates that the positive deviations (above the regression line) are offset by the negative deviations (below the regression line).

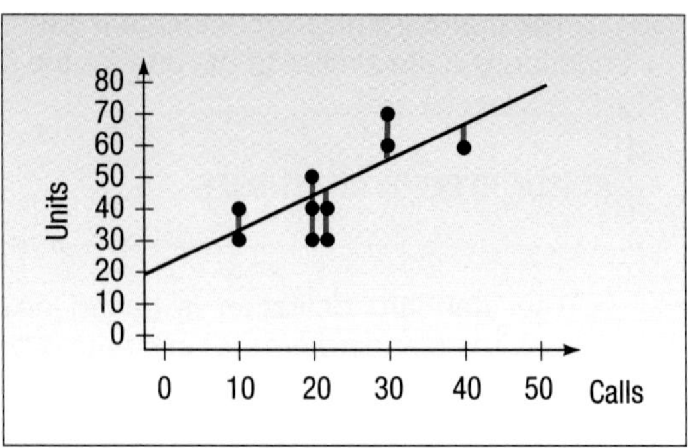

CHART 13–13 Sales Calls and Copiers Sold for 10 Salespeople

Software eases computation when you are finding the least squares regression line, calculating fitted values, or finding the standard error. The Excel output from the Copier Sales of America example is included below. The slope and intercept are in the column "Coefficients" (cells G17 and G18). The fitted values for each sales representative are the column "Predicted Sales" (cells D2:D11). The "Residuals" or differences between the actual and the estimated values are in the next column (cells E2:E11). The standard error of estimate is in cell G7. All of these values are highlighted below.

EXCEL

Microsoft Excel - Copier

	A	B	C	D	E	F	G	H
1	**Sales Representative**	**Calls**	**Sales**	**Predicted Sales**	**Residuals**	**SUMMARY OUTPUT**		
2	Tom Keller	20	30	42.63158	-12.631579			
3	Jeff Hall	40	60	66.31579	-6.315789	Regression Statistics		
4	Brian Virost	20	40	42.63158	-2.631579	Multiple R	0.7590	
5	Greg Fish	30	60	54.47368	5.526316	R Square	0.5761	
6	Susan Welch	10	30	30.78947	-0.789474	Adjusted R Square	0.5231	
7	Carlos Ramirez	10	40	30.78947	9.210526	Standard Error	9.9008	
8	Rich Niles	20	40	42.63158	-2.631579	Observations	10.0000	
9	Mike Keil	20	50	42.63158	7.368421			
10	Mark Reynolds	20	30	42.63158	-12.631579	ANOVA		
11	Soni Jones	30	70	54.47368	15.526316		df	**SS**
12						Regression	1	1065.7
13						Residual	8	784.21
14						Total	9	
15								
16							**Coefficients**	Standard
17						Intercept	18.9474	8.4988
18						Calls	1.1842	0.3591

Thus far we have presented linear regression only as a descriptive tool. In other words it is a simple summary ($Y' = a + bX$) of the relationship between the dependent Y variable and the independent X variable. When our data is a sample taken from a population, we are doing inferential statistics. Then we need to recall the distinction between population parameters and sample statistics. In this case, we "model" the linear relationship in the population by the equation:

$$Y = \alpha + \beta X$$

where:

Y is any value of the dependent variable.
α is the Y-intercept (the value of Y when $X = 0$) in the population.

Statistics in Action

Studies indicate that for both men and women, those who are considered good looking earn higher wages than those who are not. In addition, for men there is a correlation between height and salary. For each additional inch of height, a man can expect to earn an additional $250 per year. So a man 6′6″ tall receives a $3,000 "stature" bonus over his 5′6″ counterpart. Being overweight or underweight is also related to earnings, particularly among women. A study of young women showed the heaviest 10 percent earned about 6 percent less than their lighter counterparts.

β is the slope (the amount by which Y changes when X increases by one unit) of the population line.
X is any value of the independent variable.

Now α and β are population parameters and a and b, respectively, are estimates of those parameters. They are computed from a particular sample taken from the population. Fortunately, the formulas given earlier in the chapter for a and b do not change when we move from using regression as a descriptive tool to regression in statistical inference.

It should be noted that the linear regression equation for the sample of salespeople is only an estimate of the relationship between the two variables for the population. Thus, the values of a and b in the regression equation are usually referred to as the **estimated regression coefficients,** or simply the **regression coefficients.**

Assumptions Underlying Linear Regression

To properly apply linear regression, several assumptions are necessary. Chart 13–14 illustrates these assumptions.

1. For each value of X, there is a group of Y values. These Y values follow the normal distribution.
2. The means of these normal distributions lie on the regression line.
3. The standard deviations of these normal distributions are all the same. The best estimate we have of this common standard deviation is the standard error of estimate ($s_{y \cdot x}$).
4. The Y values are statistically independent. This means that in selecting a sample a particular X does not depend on any other value of X. This assumption is particularly important when data are collected over a period of time. In such situations, the errors for a particular time period are often correlated with those of other time periods.

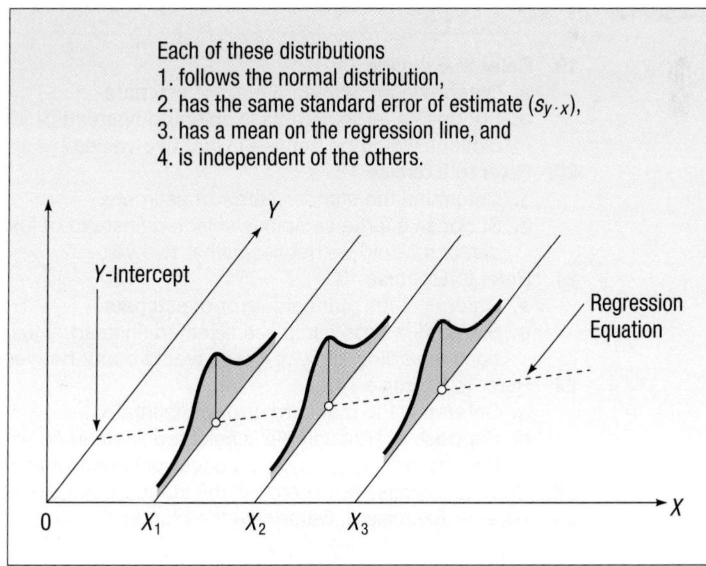

CHART 13–14 Regression Assumptions Shown Graphically

Recall from Chapter 7 that if the values follow a normal distribution, then the mean plus or minus one standard deviation will encompass 68 percent of the observations, the mean plus or minus two standard deviations will encompass 95 percent of the observations, and the mean plus or minus three standard deviations will encompass virtually all of the observations. The same relationship exists between the predicted values Y' and the standard error of estimate ($s_{y \cdot x}$).

1. $Y' \pm s_{y \cdot x}$ will include the middle 68 percent of the observations.
2. $Y' \pm 2s_{y \cdot x}$ will include the middle 95 percent of the observations.
3. $Y' \pm 3s_{y \cdot x}$ will include virtually all the observations.

We can now relate these assumptions to Copier Sales of America, where we studied the relationship between the number of sales calls and the number of copiers sold. Assume that we took a much larger sample than $n = 10$, but that the standard error of estimate was still 9.901. If we drew a parallel line 9.901 units above the regression line and another 9.901 units below the regression line, about 68 percent of the points would fall between the two lines. Similarly, a line 19.802 [$2s_{y \cdot x} = 2(9.901)$] units above the regression line and another 19.802 units below the regression line should include about 95 percent of the data values.

As a rough check, refer to the second column from the right in Table 13–4 on page 393, i.e., the column headed "Deviation." Three of the 10 deviations exceed one standard error of estimate. That is, the deviation of −12.6316 for Tom Keller, −12.6316 for Mark Reynolds, and +15.5264 for Soni Jones all exceed the value of 9.901, which is one standard error from the regression line. All of the values are within 19.802 units of the regression line. To put it another way, 7 of the 10 deviations in the sample are within one standard error of the regression line and all are within two—a good result for a relatively small sample.

Self-Review 13–4 Refer to Self-Reviews 13–1 and 13–3, where the owner of Haverty's Furniture was studying the relationship between sales and the amount spent on advertising. Determine the standard error of estimate.

Exercises

19. Refer to Exercise 11.
 a. Determine the standard error of estimate.
 b. Suppose a large sample is selected (instead of just five). About 68 percent of the predictions would be between what two values?

20. Refer to Exercise 12.
 a. Determine the standard error of estimate.
 b. Suppose a large sample is selected (instead of just eight). About 95 percent of the predictions would be between what two values?

21. Refer to Exercise 13.
 a. Determine the standard error of estimate.
 b. Suppose a large sample is selected (instead of just 10). About 95 percent of the predictions regarding kilowatt-hours would occur between what two values?

22. Refer to Exercise 14.
 a. Determine the standard error of estimate.
 b. Suppose a large sample is selected (instead of just 10). About 95 percent of the predictions regarding sales would occur between what two values?

23. Refer to Exercise 5. Determine the standard error of estimate.

24. Refer to Exercise 6. Determine the standard error of estimate.

Confidence and Prediction Intervals

The standard error of estimate is also used to establish confidence intervals when the sample size is large and the scatter around the regression line approximates the normal distribution. In our example involving the number of sales calls and the number of copiers sold, the sample size is small; hence, we need a correction factor to account for the size of the sample. In addition, when we move away from the mean of the independent variable, our estimates are subject to more variation, and we also need to adjust for this.

We are interested in providing interval estimates of two types. The first, which is called a **confidence interval,** reports the *mean* value of *Y* for a given *X.* The second type of estimate is called a **prediction interval,** and it reports the *range of values* of *Y* for a *particular* value of *X.* To explain further, suppose we estimate the salary of executives in the retail industry based on their years of experience. If we want an interval estimate of the mean salary of *all* retail executives with 20 years of experience, we calculate a confidence interval. If we want an estimate of the salary of Curtis Bender, a particular retail executive with 20 years of experience, we calculate a prediction interval.

To determine the confidence interval for the mean value of *Y* for a given *X,* the formula is:

CONFIDENCE INTERVAL FOR THE MEAN OF *Y*, GIVEN *X*.

$$Y' \pm t s_{y \cdot x} \sqrt{\frac{1}{n} + \frac{(X - \bar{X})^2}{\Sigma(X - \bar{X})^2}} \qquad \textbf{[13–7]}$$

where:

Y' is the predicted value for any selected X value.
X is any selected value of X.
$\bar{X}$ is the mean of the Xs, found by $\Sigma X/n$.
n is the number of observations.
$s_{y \cdot x}$ is the standard error of estimate.
t is the value of t from Appendix F with $n - 2$ degrees of freedom.

We first described the *t* distribution in Chapter 9. In review the concept of *t* was developed by William Gossett in the early 1900s. He noticed that $\bar{X} \pm z(s)$ was not precisely correct for small samples. He observed, for example, for degrees of freedom of 120, that 95 percent of the items fell within $\bar{X} \pm 1.98s$ instead of $\bar{X} \pm 1.96s$. This difference is not too critical, but note what happens as the sample size becomes smaller:

df	*t*
120	1.980
60	2.000
21	2.080
10	2.228
3	3.182

This is logical. The smaller the sample size, the larger the possible error. The increase in the *t* value compensates for this possibility.

EXAMPLE

We return to the Copier Sales of America illustration. Determine a 95 percent confidence interval for all sales representatives who make 25 calls and for Sheila Baker, a West Coast sales representative who made 25 calls.

SOLUTION

We use formula (13–7) to determine a confidence interval. Table 13–5 includes the necessary totals and a repeat of the information of Table 13–2 on page 379.

TABLE 13–5 Calculations Needed for Determining the Confidence Interval and Prediction Interval

Sales Representative	Sales Calls (X)	Copier Sales (Y)	$(X - \bar{X})$	$(X - \bar{X})^2$
Tom Keller	20	30	−2	4
Jeff Hall	40	60	18	324
Brian Virost	20	40	−2	4
Greg Fish	30	60	8	64
Susan Welch	10	30	−12	144
Carlos Ramirez	10	40	−12	144
Rich Niles	20	40	−2	4
Mike Kiel	20	50	−2	4
Mark Reynolds	20	30	−2	4
Soni Jones	30	70	8	64
			0	760

The first step is to determine the number of copiers we expect a sales representative to sell if he or she makes 25 calls. It is 48.5526, found by $Y' = 18.9476 + 1.1842X = 18.9476 + 1.1842(25)$.

To find the t value, we need to first know the number of degrees of freedom. In this case the degrees of freedom is $n - 2 = 10 - 2 = 8$. We set the confidence level at 95 percent. To find the value of t, move down the left-hand column to 8 degrees of freedom, then move across to the column with the 95 percent level of confidence. The value of t is 2.306.

In the previous section we calculated the standard error of estimate to be 9.901. We let $X = 25$, $\bar{X} = \Sigma X/n = 220/10 = 22$, and from Table 13–5 $\Sigma(X - \bar{X})^2 = 760$. Inserting these values in formula (13–7), we can determine the confidence interval.

$$\text{Confidence Interval} = Y' \pm ts_{y \cdot x}\sqrt{\frac{1}{n} + \frac{(X - \bar{X})^2}{\Sigma(X - \bar{X})^2}}$$

$$= 48.5526 \pm 2.306(9.901)\sqrt{\frac{1}{10} + \frac{(25 - 22)^2}{760}}$$

$$= 48.5526 \pm 7.6356$$

Thus, the 95 percent confidence interval for all sales representatives who make 25 calls is from 40.9170 up to 56.1882. To interpret, let's round the values. If a sales representative makes 25 calls, he or she can expect to sell 48.6 copiers. It is likely those sales will range from 40.9 to 56.2 copiers.

To determine the prediction interval for a particular value of Y for a given X, formula (13–7) is modified slightly: A 1 is added under the radical. The formula becomes:

PREDICTION INTERVAL FOR Y, GIVEN X

$$Y' \pm ts_{y \cdot x}\sqrt{1 + \frac{1}{n} + \frac{(X - \bar{X})^2}{\Sigma(X - \bar{X})^2}} \quad \textbf{[13–8]}$$

Suppose we want to estimate the number of copiers sold by Sheila Baker, who made 25 sales calls. The 95 percent prediction interval is determined as follows:

$$\text{Prediction Interval} = Y' \pm ts_{y \cdot x}\sqrt{1 + \frac{1}{n} + \frac{(X - \bar{X})^2}{\Sigma(X - \bar{X})^2}}$$

$$= 48.5526 \pm 2.306(9.901)\sqrt{1 + \frac{1}{10} + \frac{(25 - 22)^2}{760}}$$

$$= 48.5526 \pm 24.0746$$

Thus, the interval is from 24.478 up to 72.627 copiers. We conclude that the number of copiers sold will be between about 24 and 73 for a particular sales representative. This interval is quite large. It is much larger than the confidence interval for all sales representatives who made 25 calls. It is logical, however, that there should be more variation in the sales estimate for an individual than for a group.

The following MINITAB graph shows the relationship between the regression line (in the center), the confidence interval (dashed lines), and the prediction interval (dotted lines). The bands for the prediction interval are always further from the regression line than for the confidence interval. Also, as the values of X move away from the mean number of calls (22) in either the positive or the negative direction the confidence interval and prediction interval bands widen. This is caused by the numerator of the right-hand term under the radical in formulas (13–7) and (13–8). That is, as the term $(X - \bar{X})^2$ increases, the widths of the confidence interval and the prediction interval also increase. To put it another way, there is less precision in our estimates as we move away, in either direction, from the mean of the independent variable.

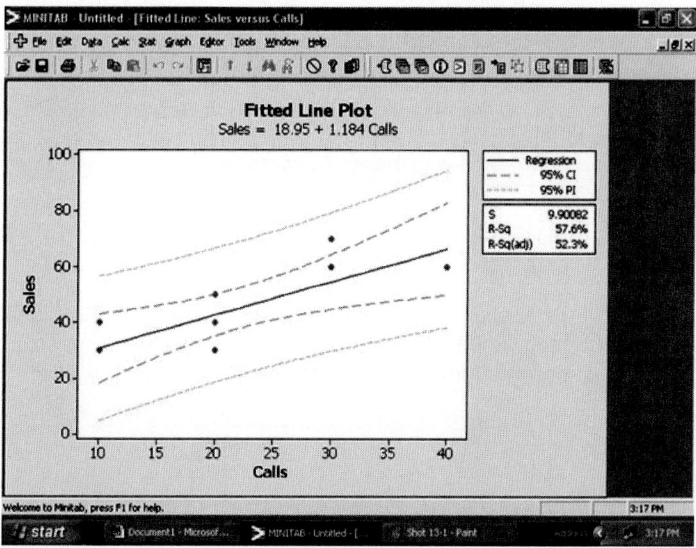

We wish to emphasize again the distinction between a confidence interval and a prediction interval. A confidence interval refers to all cases with a given value of X and is computed by formula (13–7). A prediction interval refers to a particular case for a given value of X and is computed using formula (13–8). The prediction interval will always be wider because of the extra 1 under the radical in the second equation.

Self-Review 13–5

Refer to the sample data in Self-Reviews 13–1, 13–3, and 13–4, where the owner of Haverty's Furniture was studying the relationship between sales and the amount spent on advertising. The sales information for the last four months is repeated below.

Month	Advertising Expense ($ million)	Sales Revenue ($ million)
July	2	7
August	1	3
September	3	8
October	4	10

The regression equation was computed to be $Y' = 1.5 + 2.2X$, and the standard error is 0.9487. Both variables are reported in millions of dollars. Determine the 90 percent confidence interval for the typical sales revenue for a month in which $3 million was spent on advertising.

Exercises

25. Refer to Exercise 11.
 a. Determine the .95 confidence interval for the mean predicted when $X = 7$.
 b. Determine the .95 prediction interval for an individual predicted when $X = 7$.

26. Refer to Exercise 12.
 a. Determine the .95 confidence interval for the mean predicted when $X = 7$.
 b. Determine the .95 prediction interval for an individual predicted when $X = 7$.

27. Refer to Exercise 13.
 a. Determine the .95 confidence interval, in thousands of kilowatt-hours, for the mean of all six-room homes.
 b. Determine the .95 prediction interval, in thousands of kilowatt-hours, for a particular six-room home.

28. Refer to Exercise 14.
 a. Determine the .95 confidence interval, in thousands of dollars, for the mean of all sales personnel who make 40 contacts.
 b. Determine the .95 prediction interval, in thousands of dollars, for a particular salesperson who makes 40 contacts.

More on the Coefficient of Determination

To further examine the basic concept of the coefficient of determination, suppose there is interest in the relationship between years on the job, X, and weekly production, Y. Sample data revealed:

Employee	Years on Job, X	Weekly Production, Y
Gordon	14	6
James	7	5
Ford	3	3
Salter	15	9
Artes	11	7

The sample data were plotted in a scatter diagram. Since the relationship between X and Y appears to be linear, a line was drawn through the plots (see Chart 13–15). The equation is $Y' = 2 + 0.4X$.

Note in Chart 13–15 that if we were to use that line to predict weekly production for an employee, in no case would our prediction be exact. That is, there would be some error in each of our predictions. As an example, for Gordon, who has been with the company 14 years, we would predict weekly production to be 7.6 units; however, he produces only 6 units.

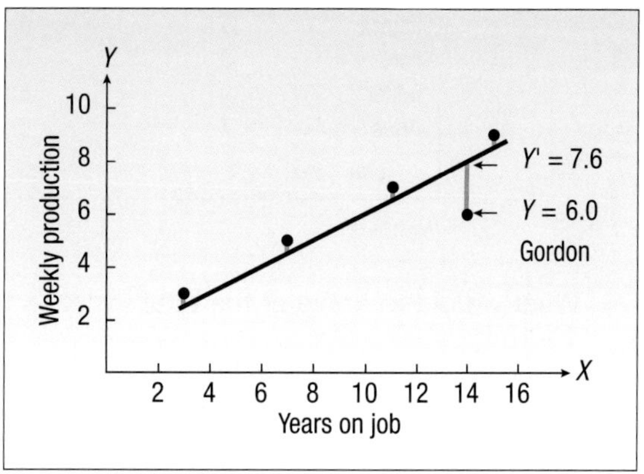

CHART 13–15 Observed Data and the Least Squares Line

Unexplained variation

To measure the overall error in our prediction, every deviation from the line is squared and the squares summed. The predicted point on the line is designated Y', read Y prime, and the observed point is designated Y. For Gordon, $(Y - Y')^2 = (6 - 7.6)^2 = (-1.6)^2 = 2.56$. Logically, this variation cannot be explained by the independent variable, so it is referred to as the *unexplained variation.* Specifically, we cannot explain why Gordon's production of 6 units is 1.6 units below his predicted production of 7.6 units, based on the number of years he has been on the job.

The sum of the squared deviations, $\Sigma(Y - Y')^2$, is 4.00. (See Table 13–6.) The term $\Sigma(Y - Y')^2 = 4.00$ is the variation in Y (production) that cannot be predicted from X. It is the "unexplained" variation in Y.

TABLE 13–6 Computations Needed for the Unexplained Variation

	X	Y	Y'	$Y - Y'$	$(Y - Y')^2$
Gordon	14	6	7.6	−1.6	2.56
James	7	5	4.8	0.2	0.04
Ford	3	3	3.2	−0.2	0.04
Salter	15	9	8.0	1.0	1.00
Artes	11	7	6.4	0.6	0.36
Total	50	30		0.0*	4.00

*Must be 0.

Now suppose *only* the Y values (weekly production, in this problem) are known and we want to predict production for every employee. The actual production figures for the employees are 6, 5, 3, 9, and 7 (from Table 13–6). To make these predictions, we could assign the mean weekly production (6 units, found by $\Sigma Y/n = 30/5 = 6$) to each employee. This would keep the sum of the squared prediction errors at a minimum. (Recall from Chapter 3 that the sum of the squared deviations from the arithmetic mean for a set of numbers is smaller than the sum of the squared deviations from any other value, such as the median.) Table 13–7 shows the necessary calculations. The sum of the squared deviations is 20, as shown in Table 13–7. The value 20 is referred to as the *total variation in Y.*

Total variation in Y

TABLE 13–7 Calculations Needed for the Total Variation in Y

Name	Weekly Production, Y	Mean Weekly Production, $\bar{Y}$	$Y - \bar{Y}$	$(Y - \bar{Y})^2$
Gordon	6	6	0	0
James	5	6	−1	1
Ford	3	6	−3	9
Salter	9	6	3	9
Artes	7	6	1	1
Total			0*	20

*Must be 0.

What we did to arrive at the total variation in Y is shown diagrammatically in Chart 13–16.

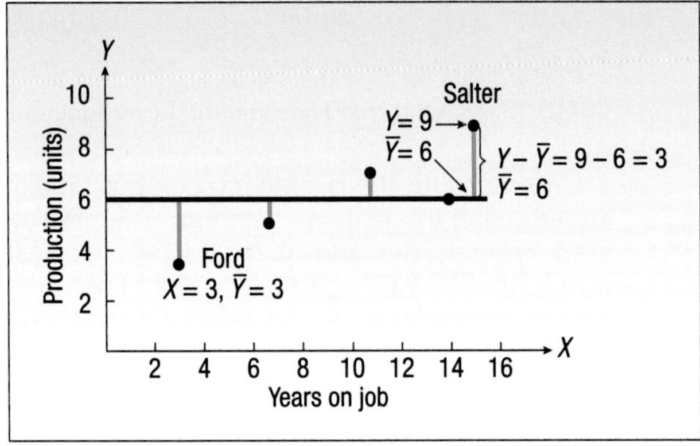

CHART 13–16 Plots Showing Deviations from the Mean of Y

Logically, the total variation in Y can be subdivided into unexplained variation and explained variation. To arrive at the explained variation, since we know the total variation and unexplained variation, we simply subtract: Explained variation = Total variation − Unexplained variation. Dividing the explained variation by the total variation gives the coefficient of determination, r^2, which is a proportion. In terms of a formula:

COEFFICIENT OF DETERMINATION

$$r^2 = \frac{\text{Total variation} - \text{Unexplained variation}}{\text{Total variation}} = \frac{\Sigma(Y - \bar{Y})^2 - \Sigma(Y - Y')^2}{\Sigma(Y - \bar{Y})^2} \quad \textbf{[13–9]}$$

In this problem:

$$r^2 = \frac{20 - 4}{20} = \frac{16}{20} = .80$$

Table 13–7
Table 13–6
Explained variation
Total variation

As mentioned, .80 is a proportion. It is not a probability. We say that 80 percent of the variation in weekly production, *Y*, is determined, or accounted for, by its linear relationship with *X* (years on the job).

As a check, formula (13–1) for the coefficient of correlation could be used. Squaring *r* gives the coefficient of determination. Exercise 29 offers a check on the preceding problem.

Exercises

29. Using the preceding problem, involving years on the job and weekly production, verify that the coefficient of determination is in fact .80.

30. The number of shares of Icom, Inc., turned over during a month, and the price at the end of the month, are listed in the following table. Also given are the *Y*′ values.

Turnover (thousands of shares), *X*	Actual Price, *Y*	Estimated Price, *Y*′
4	$2	$2.7
1	1	0.6
5	4	3.4
3	2	2.0
2	1	1.3

a. Draw a scatter diagram. Plot a line through the dots.
b. Compute the coefficient of determination using formula (13–10).
c. Interpret the coefficient of determination.

The Relationships among the Coefficient of Correlation, the Coefficient of Determination, and the Standard Error of Estimate

In an earlier section, we discussed the standard error of estimate, which measures how close the actual values are to the regression line. When the standard error is small, it indicates that the two variables are closely related. In the calculation of the standard error, the key term is $\Sigma(Y - Y')^2$. If the value of this term is small, then the standard error will also be small.

The correlation coefficient measures the strength of the linear association between two variables. When the points on the scatter diagram appear close to the line, we note that the correlation coefficient tends to be large. Thus, the standard error of estimate and the coefficient of correlation relate the same information but use a different scale to report the strength of the association. However, both measures involve the term $\Sigma(Y - Y')^2$.

We also noted that the square of the correlation coefficient is the coefficient of determination. The coefficient of determination measures the percent of the variation in *Y* that is explained by the variation in *X*.

A convenient vehicle for showing the relationship among these three measures is an ANOVA table. This table is similar to the analysis of variance table developed in Chapter 12. In that chapter, the total variation was divided into two components: that due to the *treatments* and that due to *random error*. The concept is similar in regression analysis. The total variation, $\Sigma(Y - Y')^2$, is divided into two components: (1) that explained by the *regression* (explained by the independent variable) and (2) the *error,* or unexplained variation. These two categories are identified in the first column of the ANOVA table that follows. The column headed "df" refers to the degrees of freedom associated with each category. The total number of degrees of freedom is $n - 1$. The number of degrees of freedom in the regression is 1, since there is only one independent variable. The number of degrees of freedom associated with the error term is $n - 2$. The term "SS" located in the middle of the ANOVA table refers to the sum of squares—the variation. The terms are computed as follows:

$$\text{Regression} = \text{SSR} = \Sigma(Y' - \bar{Y})^2$$

$$\text{Error variation} = \text{SSE} = \Sigma(Y - Y')^2$$

$$\text{Total variation} = \text{SS total} = \Sigma(Y - \bar{Y})^2$$

The format for the ANOVA table is:

Source	df	SS	MS
Regression	1	SSR	SSR/1
Error	$n - 2$	SSE	SSE/($n - 2$)
Total	$n - 1$	SS total*	

*SS total = SSR + SSE.

The coefficient of determination, r^2, can be obtained directly from the ANOVA table by:

COEFFICIENT OF DETERMINATION

$$r^2 = \frac{\text{SSR}}{\text{SS total}} = 1 - \frac{\text{SSE}}{\text{SS total}} \quad \textbf{[13–10]}$$

The term "SSR/SS total" is the proportion of the variation in Y *explained* by the independent variable, X. Note the effect of the SSE term on r^2. As SSE decreases, r^2 will increase. Conversely, as the standard error decreases, the r^2 term increases.

The standard error of estimate can also be obtained from the ANOVA table using the following equation:

STANDARD ERROR OF ESTIMATE

$$s_{y \cdot x} = \sqrt{\frac{\text{SSE}}{n - 2}} \quad \textbf{[13–11]}$$

The Copier Sales of America example is used to illustrate the computations of the coefficient of determination and the standard error of estimate from an ANOVA table.

EXAMPLE

In the Copier Sales of America example we studied the relationship between the number of sales calls made and the number of copiers sold. Use a computer software package to determine the least squares regression equation and the ANOVA table. Identify the regression equation, the standard error of estimate, and the coefficient of determination on the computer output. From the ANOVA table on the computer output, determine the coefficient of determination and the standard error of estimate using formulas (13–10) and (13–11).

SOLUTION

The output from Excel follows.

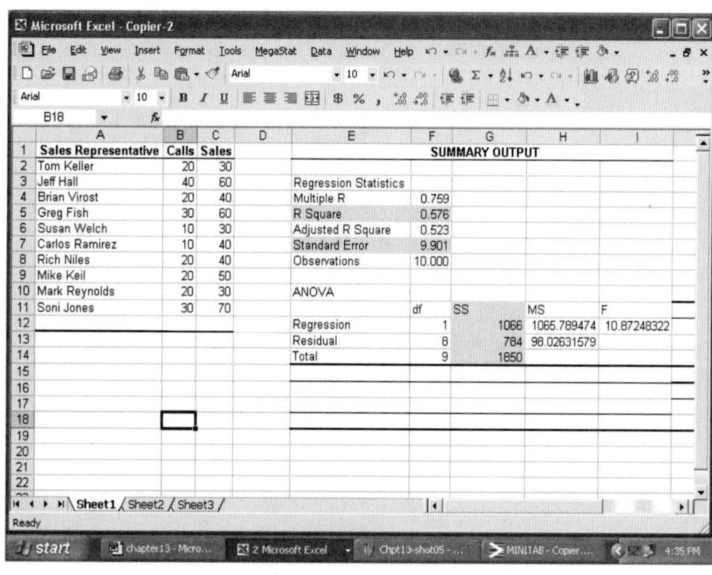

	A	B	C
1	Sales Representative	Calls	Sales
2	Tom Keller	20	30
3	Jeff Hall	40	60
4	Brian Virost	20	40
5	Greg Fish	30	60
6	Susan Welch	10	30
7	Carlos Ramirez	10	40
8	Rich Niles	20	40
9	Mike Keil	20	50
10	Mark Reynolds	20	30
11	Soni Jones	30	70

SUMMARY OUTPUT

Regression Statistics	
Multiple R	0.759
R Square	0.576
Adjusted R Square	0.523
Standard Error	9.901
Observations	10.000

ANOVA

	df	SS	MS	F
Regression	1	1066	1065.789474	10.87248322
Residual	8	784	98.02631579	
Total	9	1850		

From formula (13–10) the coefficient of determination is .576, found by

$$r^2 = \frac{\text{SSR}}{\text{SS total}} = \frac{1{,}066}{1{,}850} = .576$$

This is the same value we computed earlier in the chapter, when we found the coefficient of determination by squaring the coefficient of correlation. Again, the interpretation is that the independent variable, *Calls,* explains 57.6 percent of the variation in the number of copiers sold. If we needed the coefficient of correlation, we could find it by taking the square root of the coefficient of determination:

$$r = \sqrt{r^2} = \sqrt{.576} = .759$$

A problem does remain, and that involves the sign for the coefficient of correlation. Recall that the square root of a value could have either a positive or a negative sign. The sign of the coefficient of correlation will always be the same as that of the slope. That is, *b* and *r* will always have the same sign. In this case the sign is positive, so the coefficient of correlation is .759.

To find the standard error of estimate, we use formula (13–11):

$$s_{y \cdot x} = \sqrt{\frac{\text{SSE}}{n-2}} = \sqrt{\frac{784.2}{10-2}} = 9.901$$

Again, this is the same value calculated earlier in the chapter. These values are identified on the Excel computer output.

Transforming Data

The coefficient of correlation describes the strength of the *linear* relationship between two variables. It could be that two variables are closely related, but this relationship is not linear. Be cautious when you are interpreting the coefficient of correlation. A value of *r* may indicate there is no linear relationship, but it could be there is a relationship of some other nonlinear or curvilinear form. To explain, below is a listing of 13 professional golfers, the amount they earned during the 2002 season, and their mean score per round. (In golf, the objective is to play 18 holes in the least number of strokes. So, lower mean scores are related to the higher earnings.)

Player	Earnings ($000)	Mean score
Tiger Woods	6,912.6	68.56
Phil Michelson	4,312.0	69.58
Fred Funk	2,383.1	69.99
Peter Lonard	1,413.1	70.00
Tim Herron	954.9	70.68
Paul Azinger	769.9	71.54
John Daly	593.0	71.86
Bob May	407.8	71.16
Hal Sutton	320.0	71.95
Jason Hill	150.9	72.68
Bradley Hughes	85.4	71.50
Gary Nicklaus	42.0	72.81
Jack Nicklaus	8.9	74.83

For the above golf data the correlation between the variables, earnings and score, shows a fairly strong negative relationship. The correlation is −0.782, but when we use a scatter diagram to plot the data the relationship appears to be nonlinear. That is, the relationship does not follow a straight line.

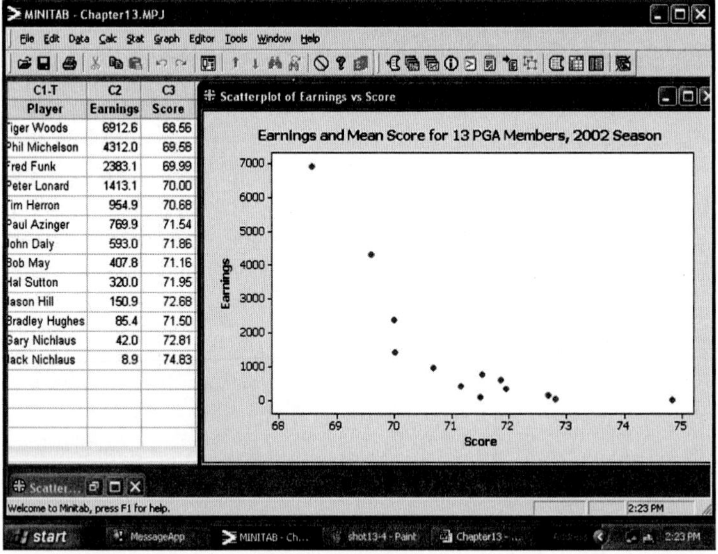

What can we do to explore other (nonlinear) relationships? One possibility is to transform one of the variables. For example, instead of using X as the independent variable we might use its square as the independent variable. Another possibility is to transform the dependent variable.

In the golf-earnings example, changing the scale of the dependent variable is effective. We use MINITAB to determine the log of each golfer's earnings and then find the correlation between the log of earnings and score. The coefficient of correlation increases to −0.943, which means 88.9 percent of the variation in the log of earnings is accounted for by the independent variable score. Clearly as the mean score increases for a golfer, he can expect his earnings to decrease.

There is no commonly accepted procedure to determine which variable to transform or what transformation to use. So experience and trial and error are your guides. The most common types of transformations are:

- Take the log of one of the variables.
- Square one of the variables.
- Take the square root of one of the variables.
- Take the reciprocal of one of the variables.

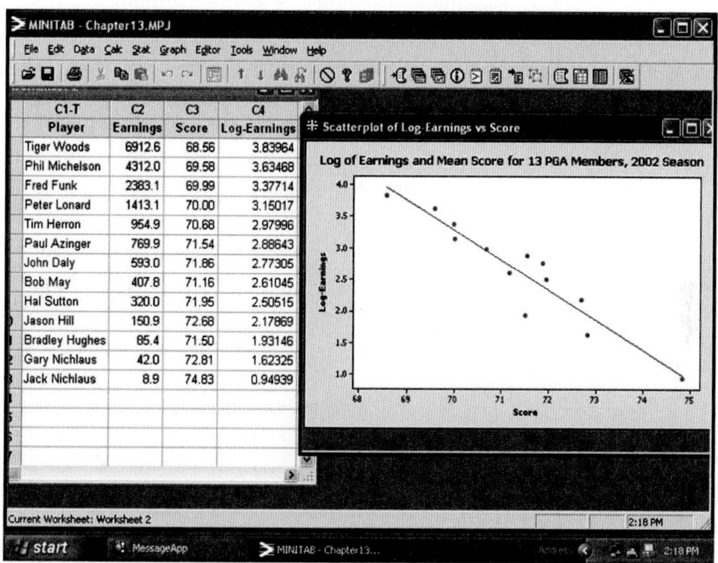

C1-T Player	C2 Earnings	C3 Score	C4 Log-Earnings
Tiger Woods	6912.6	68.56	3.83964
Phil Michelson	4312.0	69.58	3.63468
Fred Funk	2383.1	69.99	3.37714
Peter Lonard	1413.1	70.00	3.15017
Tim Herron	954.9	70.68	2.97996
Paul Azinger	769.9	71.54	2.88643
John Daly	593.0	71.86	2.77305
Bob May	407.8	71.16	2.61045
Hal Sutton	320.0	71.95	2.50515
Jason Hill	150.9	72.68	2.17869
Bradley Hughes	85.4	71.50	1.93146
Gary Nichlaus	42.0	72.81	1.62325
Jack Nichlaus	8.9	74.83	0.94939

Exercises

31. Given the following ANOVA table:

SOURCE	DF	SS	MS	F
Regression	1	1000.0	1000.00	26.00
Error	13	500.0	38.46	
Total	14	1500.0		

a. Determine the coefficient of determination.

b. Assuming a direct relationship between the variables, what is the coefficient of correlation?

c. Determine the standard error of estimate.

32. On the first statistics exam the coefficient of determination between the hours studied and the grade earned was 80 percent. The standard error of estimate was 10. There were 20 students in the class. Develop an ANOVA table.

33. The information listed below shows the relationship between the interest rate on home mortgages and the number of housing starts for selected periods. Observe that the relationship is inverse; that is, as the interest rate declines the number of housing starts increases.

Rate	Starts
11	9000
10	10000
9	24000
8	40000
7	52000
6	65000
5	80000
4	100000
3	130000
2	135000

a. Plot the above data in a scatter diagram. Can you confirm the inverse relationship?
b. Use statistical software to develop a regression equation. What is the coefficient of determination? What do you conclude about the strength of the relationship between the variables?
c. Estimate the number of housing starts when the interest rate is at 11 or 12 percent. Is this a reasonable conclusion?
d. Transform the data on the number of housing starts to the log of the number of starts. Use this transformed variable to develop a regression equation. How does this transformation affect the coefficient of determination? Is the estimated value of the number of housing starts more reasonable when the interest rate is 11 percent? Give the specific evidence.

34. According to basic economics as the demand for a product increases the price will decrease. Listed below is the number of units demanded and the price.

Demand	Price
2	$120.0
5	90.0
8	80.0
12	70.0
16	50.0
21	45.0
27	31.0
35	30.0
45	25.0
60	21.0

a. Determine the correlation between price and demand. Plot the data in a scatter diagram. Does the relationship seem to be linear?
b. Transform the price to a log to the base 10. Plot the log of the price and the demand. Determine the correlation coefficient. Does this seem to improve the relationship between the variables?

Chapter Outline

I. A scatter diagram is a graphic tool to portray the relationship between two variables.
  A. The dependent variable is scaled on the *Y*-axis and is the variable being estimated.
  B. The independent variable is scaled on the *X*-axis and is the variable used as the estimator.

II. The coefficient of correlation measures the strength of the linear association between two variables.
  A. Both variables must be at least the interval scale of measurement.
  B. The coefficient of correlation can range from −1.00 up to 1.00.
  C. If the correlation between two variables is 0, there is no association between them.
  D. A value of 1.00 indicates perfect positive correlation, and −1.00 perfect negative correlation.
  E. A positive sign means there is a direct relationship between the variables, and a negative sign means there is an inverse relationship.

F. It is designated by the letter *r* and found by the following equation:

$$r = \frac{\Sigma(X - \bar{X})(Y - \bar{Y})}{(n - 1)\, s_x s_y} \qquad \textbf{[13–1]}$$

G. The following equation is used to determine whether the correlation in the population is different from 0.

$$t = \frac{r\sqrt{n - 2}}{\sqrt{1 - r^2}} \qquad \textbf{[13–2]}$$

III. The coefficient of determination is the fraction of the variation in one variable that is explained by the variation in the other variable.
  A. It ranges from 0 to 1.0.
  B. It is the square of the coefficient of correlation.

IV. In regression analysis we estimate one variable based on another variable.
  A. The relationship between the variables must be linear.
  B. Both the independent and the dependent variables must be interval or ratio scale.
  C. The least squares criterion is used to determine the regression equation.

V. The least squares regression line is of the form $Y' = a + bX$.
  A. Y' is the estimated value of Y for a selected value of X.
  B. b is the slope of the fitted line.
    1. It shows the amount of change in Y' for a change of one unit in X.
    2. A positive value for b indicates a direct relationship between the two variables, and a negative value an inverse relationship.
    3. The sign of b and the sign of r, the coefficient of correlation, are always the same.
    4. b is computed using the following equation.

$$b = r\frac{s_y}{s_x} \qquad \textbf{[13–4]}$$

  C. a is the constant or intercept.
    1. It is the value of Y' when $X = 0$.
    2. a is computed using the following equation.

$$a = \bar{Y} - b\bar{X} \qquad \textbf{[13–5]}$$

  D. X is the value of the independent variable.

VI. The standard error of estimate measures the variation around the regression line.
  A. It is in the same units as the dependent variable.
  B. It is based on squared deviations from the regression line.
  C. Small values indicate that the points cluster closely about the regression line.
  D. It is computed using the following formula.

$$s_{y \cdot x} = \sqrt{\frac{\Sigma(Y - Y')^2}{n - 2}} \qquad \textbf{[13–6]}$$

VII. Inference about linear regression is based on the following assumptions.
  A. For a given value of X, the values of Y are normally distributed about the line of regression.
  B. The standard deviation of each of the normal distributions is the same for all values of X and is estimated by the standard error of estimate.
  C. The deviations from the regression line are independent, with no pattern to the size or direction.

VIII. There are two types of interval estimates.
  A. In a confidence interval the mean value of Y is estimated for a given value of X.
    1. It is computed from the following formula.

$$Y' \pm t s_{y \cdot x}\sqrt{\frac{1}{n} + \frac{(X - \bar{X})^2}{\Sigma(X - \bar{X})^2}} \qquad \textbf{[13–7]}$$

    2. The width of the interval is affected by the level of confidence, the size of the standard error of estimate, and the size of the sample, as well as the value of the independent variable.
  B. In a prediction interval the individual value of Y is estimated for a given value of X.

1. It is computed from the following formula.

$$Y' \pm ts_{y \cdot x}\sqrt{1 + \frac{1}{n} + \frac{(X - \bar{X})^2}{\Sigma(X - \bar{X})^2}} \quad \textbf{[13–8]}$$

2. The difference between formulas (13–7) and (13–8) is the 1 under the radical.
   a. The prediction interval will be wider than the confidence interval.
   b. The prediction interval is also based on the level of confidence, the size of the standard error of estimate, the size of the sample, and the value of the independent variable.

Pronunciation Key

SYMBOL	MEANING	PRONUNCIATION
ΣXY	Sum of the products of X and Y	*Sum X Y*
ρ	Coefficient of correlation in the population	*Rho*
Y'	Estimated value of Y	*Y prime*
$s_{y \cdot x}$	Standard error of estimate	*s sub y dot x*
r^2	Coefficient of determination	*r square*

Chapter Exercises

35. A regional commuter airline selected a random sample of 25 flights and found that the correlation between the number of passengers and the total weight, in pounds, of luggage stored in the luggage compartment is 0.94. Using the .05 significance level, can we conclude that there is a positive association between the two variables?

36. A sociologist claims that the success of students in college (measured by their GPA) is related to their family's income. For a sample of 20 students, the coefficient of correlation is 0.40. Using the 0.01 significance level, can we conclude that there is a positive correlation between the variables?

37. An Environmental Protection Agency study of 12 automobiles revealed a correlation of 0.47 between the engine size and emissions. At the .01 significance level, can we conclude that there is a positive association between these variables? What is the p-value? Interpret.

38. A sample of 15 financial executives in the pharmaceutical industry revealed the correlation between the number of fat grams an executive consumed the previous day and that executive's cholesterol level was 0.345.

a. Does cholesterol seem to increase for those who consumed more fat? How can you tell?
b. How much of the variation in cholesterol level is accounted for by the number of fat grams consumed?
c. At the .05 significance level is it reasonable to conclude there is a positive association between fat grams consumed and cholesterol level? What is the p-value?

39. A sample of 20 American cities showed the correlation between the population of the city and its unemployment rate was 0.237.

a. Does unemployment rate seem to increase as the size of the population increases? How can you tell?
b. How much of the variation in the unemployment rate is accounted for by the variation in the population?
c. At the .01 significance level, is it reasonable to conclude there is positive association between the unemployment rate and the population?

40. Dr. Megan Boyle wishes to investigate the relationship between stress and job satisfaction. To begin she developed a profile for stress based on assigning points for events such as the death of a spouse, a change in sleeping habits, a change in eating habits, and the addition of a family member. The job satisfaction was also based on assigning points for salary, ability to get along with coworkers, and the job environment. Dr. Boyle sampled 25 workers in the technology sector and found correlation between the stress and job satisfaction was −0.536.

a. Does job satisfaction seem to increase or decrease as stress increases? How can you tell?
b. How much of the variation in stress is accounted for by the variation in job satisfaction?
c. At the .05 significance level, is it reasonable to conclude there is negative association between stress and job satisfaction?

41. What is the relationship between the amount spent per week on food and the size of the family? Do larger families spend more on food? A sample of 10 families in the Chicago area revealed the following figures for family size and the amount spent on food per week.

Family Size	Amount Spent on Food	Family Size	Amount Spent on Food
3	$ 99	3	$111
6	104	4	74
5	151	4	91
6	129	5	119
6	142	3	91

a. Compute the coefficient of correlation.
b. Determine the coefficient of determination.
c. Can we conclude that there is a positive association between the amount spent on food and the family size? Use the .05 significance level.

42. A sample of 12 homes sold last week in St. Paul, Minnesota is selected. Can we conclude that as the size of the home (reported below in thousands of square feet) increases, the selling price (reported in $ thousands) also increases?

Home Size (thousands of square feet)	Selling Price ($ thousands)	Home Size (thousands of square feet)	Selling Price ($ thousands)
1.4	100	1.3	110
1.3	110	0.8	85
1.2	105	1.2	105
1.1	120	0.9	75
1.4	80	1.1	70
1.0	105	1.1	95

a. Compute the coefficient of correlation.
b. Determine the coefficient of determination.
c. Can we conclude that there is a positive association between the size of the home and the selling price? Use the .05 significance level.

43. The manufacturer of Cardio Glide exercise equipment wants to study the relationship between the number of months since the glide was purchased and the length of time the equipment was used last week.

Person	Months Owned	Hours Exercised	Person	Months Owned	Hours Exercised
Rupple	12	4	Massa	2	8
Hall	2	10	Sass	8	3
Bennett	6	8	Karl	4	8
Longnecker	9	5	Malrooney	10	2
Phillips	7	5	Veights	5	5

a. Plot the information on a scatter diagram. Let hours of exercise be the dependent variable. Comment on the graph.
b. Determine the coefficient of correlation. Interpret.
c. At the .01 significance level, can we conclude that there is a negative association between the variables?

44. The following regression equation was computed from a sample of 20 observations:

$$Y' = 15 - 5X$$

SSE was found to be 100 and SS total 400.

a. Determine the standard error of estimate.
b. Determine the coefficient of determination.
c. Determine the coefficient of correlation. (Caution: Watch the sign!)

45. An ANOVA table is:

SOURCE	DF	SS	MS	F
Regression	1	50		
Error				
Total	24	500		

a. Complete the ANOVA table.
b. How large was the sample?
c. Determine the standard error of estimate.
d. Determine the coefficient of determination.

46. Following is a regression equation.

$$Y' = 17.08 + 0.16X$$

This information is also available: $s_{y \cdot x} = 4.05$, $\Sigma(X - \bar{X})^2 = 1030$, and $n = 5$.
a. Estimate the value of Y' when $X = 50$.
b. Develop a 95 percent prediction interval for an individual value of Y for $X = 50$.

47. The National Highway Association is studying the relationship between the number of bidders on a highway project and the winning (lowest) bid for the project. Of particular interest is whether the number of bidders increases or decreases the amount of the winning bid.

Project	Number of Bidders, *X*	Winning Bid ($ millions), *Y*	Project	Number of Bidders, *X*	Winning Bid ($ millions), *Y*
1	9	5.1	9	6	10.3
2	9	8.0	10	6	8.0
3	3	9.7	11	4	8.8
4	10	7.8	12	7	9.4
5	5	7.7	13	7	8.6
6	10	5.5	14	7	8.1
7	7	8.3	15	6	7.8
8	11	5.5			

a. Determine the regression equation. Interpret the equation. Do more bidders tend to increase or decrease the amount of the winning bid?
b. Estimate the amount of the winning bid if there were seven bidders.
c. A new entrance is to be constructed on the Ohio Turnpike. There are seven bidders on the project. Develop a 95 percent prediction interval for the winning bid.
d. Determine the coefficient of determination. Interpret its value.

48. Mr. William Profit is studying companies going public for the first time. He is particularly interested in the relationship between the size of the offering and the price per share. A sample of 15 companies that recently went public revealed the following information.

Company	Size ($ millions), *X*	Price per Share, *Y*	Company	Size ($ millions), *X*	Price per Share, *Y*
1	9.0	10.8	9	160.7	11.3
2	94.4	11.3	10	96.5	10.6
3	27.3	11.2	11	83.0	10.5
4	179.2	11.1	12	23.5	10.3
5	71.9	11.1	13	58.7	10.7
6	97.9	11.2	14	93.8	11.0
7	93.5	11.0	15	34.4	10.8
8	70.0	10.7			

a. Determine the regression equation.

b. Determine the coefficient of determination. Do you think Mr. Profit should be satisfied with using the size of the offering as the independent variable?

49. The Bardi Trucking Co., located in Cleveland, Ohio, makes deliveries in the Great Lakes region, the Southeast, and the Northeast. Jim Bardi, the president, is studying the relationship between the distance a shipment must travel and the length of time, in days, it takes the shipment to arrive at its destination. To investigate, Mr. Bardi selected a random sample of 20 shipments made last month. Shipping distance is the independent variable, and shipping time is the dependent variable. The results are as follows:

Shipment	Distance (miles)	Shipping Time (days)	Shipment	Distance (miles)	Shipping Time (days)
1	656	5	11	862	7
2	853	14	12	679	5
3	646	6	13	835	13
4	783	11	14	607	3
5	610	8	15	665	8
6	841	10	16	647	7
7	785	9	17	685	10
8	639	9	18	720	8
9	762	10	19	652	6
10	762	9	20	828	10

a. Draw a scatter diagram. Based on these data, does it appear that there is a relationship between how many miles a shipment has to go and the time it takes to arrive at its destination?

b. Determine the coefficient of correlation. Can we conclude that there is a positive correlation between distance and time? Use the .05 significance level.

c. Determine and interpret the coefficient of determination.

d. Determine the standard error of estimate.

50. Super Markets, Inc. is considering expanding into the Scottsdale, Arizona, area. Ms. Luann Miller, Director of Planning, must present an analysis of the proposed expansion to the operating committee of the board of directors. As a part of her proposal, she needs to include information on the amount people in the region spend per month for grocery items. She would also like to include information on the relationship between the amount spent for grocery items and income. She gathered the following sample information.

Household	Monthly Amount	Monthly Income	Household	Monthly Amount	Monthly Income
1	$555	$4,388	21	$ 913	$6,688
2	489	4,558	22	918	6,752
3	458	4,793	23	710	6,837
4	613	4,856	24	1,083	7,242
5	647	4,856	25	937	7,263
6	661	4,899	26	839	7,540
7	662	4,899	27	1,030	8,009
8	675	5,091	28	1,065	8,094
9	549	5,133	29	1,069	8,264
10	606	5,304	30	1,064	8,392
11	668	5,304	31	1,015	8,414
12	740	5,304	32	1,148	8,882
13	592	5,346	33	1,125	8,925
14	720	5,495	34	1,090	8,989
15	680	5,581	35	1,208	9,053
16	540	5,730	36	1,217	9,138
17	693	5,943	37	1,140	9,329
18	541	5,943	38	1,265	9,649
19	673	6,156	39	1,206	9,862
20	676	6,603	40	1,145	9,883

a. Let the amount spent be the dependent variable and monthly income the independent variable. Create a scatter diagram, using a software package.
b. Determine the regression equation. Interpret the slope value.
c. Determine the coefficient of correlation. Can you conclude that it is greater than 0?

51. Below is information on the price per share and the dividend for a sample of 30 companies.

Company	Price per Share	Dividend	Company	Price per Share	Dividend
1	$20.00	$ 3.14	16	$57.06	$ 9.53
2	22.01	3.36	17	57.40	12.60
3	31.39	0.46	18	58.30	10.43
4	33.57	7.99	19	59.51	7.97
5	35.86	0.77	20	60.60	9.19
6	36.12	8.46	21	64.01	16.50
7	36.16	7.62	22	64.66	16.10
8	37.99	8.03	23	64.74	13.76
9	38.85	6.33	24	64.95	10.54
10	39.65	7.96	25	66.43	21.15
11	43.44	8.95	26	68.18	14.30
12	49.08	9.61	27	69.56	24.42
13	53.73	11.11	28	74.90	11.54
14	54.41	13.28	29	77.91	17.65
15	55.10	10.22	30	80.00	17.36

a. Calculate the regression equation using selling price based on the annual dividend. Interpret the slope value.
b. Determine the coefficient of determination. Interpret its value.
c. Determine the coefficient of correlation. Can you conclude that it is greater than 0 using the .05 significance level?

52. A highway employee performed a regression analysis of the relationship between the number of construction work-zone fatalities and the number of unemployed people in a state. The regression equation is Fatalities = 12.7 + 0.000114 (Unemp). Some additional output is:

```
Predictor          Coef        SE Coef      T       P
Constant         12.726          8.115   1.57   0.134
Unemp        0.00011386     0.00002896   3.93   0.001

Analysis of Variance
Source            DF       SS       MS        F       P
Regression         1    10354    10354    15.46   0.001
Residual Error    18    12054      670
Total             19    22408
```

a. How many states were in the sample?
b. Determine the standard error of estimate.
c. Determine the coefficient of determination.
d. Determine the coefficient of correlation.
e. At the .05 significance level does the evidence suggest there is a positive association between fatalities and the number unemployed?

53. Regression analysis relating the current market value in dollars to the size in square feet of homes in Greene County has been developed. The computer output follows. The regression equation is: Value = −37,186 + 65.0 Size.

```
Predictor       Coef    SE Coef        T        P
Constant      -37186       4629    -8.03    0.000
Size          64.993      3.047    21.33    0.000

Analysis of Variance
Source            DF           SS           MS        F       P
Regression         1  13548662082  13548662082   454.98   0.000
Residual Error    33    982687392     29778406
Total             34  14531349474
```

a. How many homes were in the sample?
b. Compute the standard error of estimate.
c. Compute the coefficient of determination.
d. Compute the coefficient of correlation.
e. At the .05 significance level does the evidence suggest a positive association between the market value of homes and the size of the home in square feet?

54. The following table shows the mean annual percent return on capital (profitability) and the mean annual percentage sales growth for eight aerospace and defense companies.

Company	Profitability	Growth
Alliant Techsystems	23.1	8.0
Boeing	13.2	15.6
General Dynamics	24.2	31.2
Honeywell	11.1	2.5
L-3 Communications	10.1	35.4
Northrop Grunmman	10.8	6.0
Rockwell Collins	27.3	8.7
United Technologies	20.1	3.2

a. Compute the coefficient of correlation. Conduct a test of hypothesis to determine if it is reasonable to conclude that the population correlation is greater than zero. Use the .05 significance level.
b. Develop the regression equation for profitability based on growth. Comment on the slope value.
c. Use a software package to determine the residual for each observation. Which company has the largest residual?

55. The following data shows the retail price for 12 randomly selected laptop computers along with their corresponding processor speeds.

Computers	Speed	Price
1	2.0	$2,689
2	1.6	1,229
3	1.6	1,419
4	1.8	2,589
5	2.0	2,849
6	1.2	1,349
7	2.0	2,929
8	1.6	1,849
9	2.0	2,819
10	1.6	2,669
11	1.0	1,249
12	1.4	1,159

a. Develop a linear equation that can be used to describe how the price depends on the processor speed.
b. Based on your regression equation, is there one machine that seems particularly over- or underpriced?
c. Compute the correlation coefficient between the two variables. At the .05 significance level conduct a test of hypothesis to determine if the population correlation could be greater than zero.

56. A consumer buying cooperative tested the effective heating area of 20 different electric space heaters with different wattages. Here are the results.

Heater	Wattage	Area	Heater	Wattage	Area
1	1,500	205	11	1,250	116
2	750	70	12	500	72
3	1,500	199	13	500	82
4	1,250	151	14	1,500	206
5	1,250	181	15	2,000	245
6	1,250	217	16	1,500	219
7	1,000	94	17	750	63
8	2,000	298	18	1,500	200
9	1,000	135	19	1,250	151
10	1,500	211	20	500	44

a. Compute the correlation between the wattage and heating area. Is there a direct or an indirect relationship?
b. Conduct a test of hypothesis to determine if it is reasonable that the coefficient is greater than zero. Use the .05 significance level.
c. Develop the regression equation for effective heating based on wattage.
d. Which heater looks like the "best buy" based on the size of the residual?

57. A dog trainer is exploring the relationship between the size of the dog (weight) and its daily food consumption (measured in standard cups). Below is the result of a sample of 18 observations.

Dog	Weight	Consumption
1	41	3
2	148	8
3	79	5
4	41	4
5	85	5
6	111	6
7	37	3
8	111	6
9	41	3
10	91	5
11	109	6
12	207	10
13	49	3
14	113	6
15	84	5
16	95	5
17	57	4
18	168	9

a. Compute the correlation coefficient. Is it reasonable to conclude that the correlation in the population is greater than zero? Use the .05 significance level.
b. Develop the regression equation for cups based on the dog's weight. How much does each additional cup change the estimated weight of the dog?
c. Is one of the dogs a big undereater or overeater?

exercises.com

58. Suppose you want to study the association between the literacy rate in a country, the population, and the country's gross domestic product (GDP). Go to the website of *Information Please Almanac* (http://www.infoplease.com). Select the category **World,** and then select **Countries.** A list of 195 countries starting with Afghanistan and ending with Zimbabwe will appear. Randomly select a sample of about 20 countries. It may be convenient to use a systematic sample. In other words, randomly select 1 of the first 10 countries and then select every tenth country thereafter. Click on each country name and scan the information to find the literacy rate, the population, and the GDP. Compute the correlation among the variables. In other words, find the correlation between: literacy and population, literacy and GDP, and population and GDP. *Warning:* Be careful of the units. Sometimes population is reported in millions, other times in thousands. At the .05 significance level, can we conclude that the correlation is different from zero for each pair of variables?

59. Many real estate companies and rental agencies now publish their listings on the Web. One example is the Dunes Realty Company, located in Garden City and Surfside Beaches in South Carolina. Go to the Web site http://www.dunes.com and select **Vacation Rentals,** then **Beach Home Search.** Then indicate 5 bedroom, accommodations for 14 people, second row (this means it is across the street from the beach), and no pool or floating dock; select a week in July or August; indicate that you are willing to spend $8,000 per week; and then click on **Search the Beach Homes.** The output should include details on the cottages that met your criteria.

a. Determine the correlation between the number of baths in each cottage and the weekly rental price. Can you conclude that the correlation is greater than zero at the .05 significance level? Determine the coefficient of determination.

b. Determine the regression equation using the number of bathrooms as the independent variable and the price per week as the dependent variable. Interpret the regression equation.

c. Calculate the correlation between the number of people the cottage will accommodate and the weekly rental price. At the .05 significance level can you conclude that it is different from zero?

Dataset Exercises

60. Refer to the Real Estate data, which reports information on homes sold in Denver, Colorado, last year.

a. Let selling price be the dependent variable and size of the home the independent variable. Determine the regression equation. Estimate the selling price for a home with an area of 2,200 square feet. Determine the 95 percent confidence interval and the 95 percent prediction interval for the selling price of a home with 2,200 square feet.

b. Let selling price be the dependent variable and distance from the center of the city the independent variable. Determine the regression equation. Estimate the selling price of a home 20 miles from the center of the city. Determine the 95 percent confidence interval and the 95 percent prediction interval for homes 20 miles from the center of the city.

c. Can you conclude that the independent variables "distance from the center of the city" and "selling price" are negatively correlated and that the area of the home and the selling price are positively correlated? Use the .05 significance level. Report the *p*-value of the test.

61. Refer to the Baseball 2003 data, which reports information on the 2003 Major League Baseball season.

a. Let the games won be the dependent variable and total team salary, in millions of dollars, be the independent variable. Can you conclude that there is a positive association between the two variables? Determine the regression equation. Interpret the slope, that is the value of *b*. How many additional wins will an additional $5 million in salary bring?

b. Determine the correlation between games won and ERA and between games won and team batting average. Which has the stronger correlation? Can we conclude that there is a positive correlation between wins and team batting and a negative correlation between wins and ERA? Use the .05 significance level.

c. Assume the number of games won is the dependent variable and attendance the independent variable. Can we conclude that the correlation between these two variables is greater than 0? Use the .05 significance level.

62. Refer to the Wage data, which reports information on annual wages for a sample of 100 workers. Also included are variables relating to industry, years of education, and gender for each worker.
   a. Determine the correlation between the annual wage and the years of education. At the .05 significance level can we conclude there is a positive correlation between the two variables?
   b. Determine the correlation between the annual wage and the years of work experience. At the .05 significance level can we conclude there is a positive correlation between the two variables?
63. Refer to the CIA data, which reports demographic and economic information on 46 countries.
   a. You wish to use the Labor force variable as the independent variable to predict the unemployment rate. Interpret the slope value. Use the appropriate linear regression equation to predict unemployment in the United Arab Emirates.
   b. Find the correlation coefficient between the levels of exports and imports. Use the .05 significance level to test whether there is a positive correlation between these two variables.
   c. Does there appear to be a relationship between the percentage of the population over 65 and the literacy percentage? Support your answer with statistical evidence. Conduct an appropriate test of hypothesis and interpret the result.

Software Commands

1. The MINITAB commands for the output showing the coefficient of correlation on page 385 are:
   a. Enter the sales representative's name in C1, the number of calls in C2, and the sales in C3.
   b. Select **Stat, Basic Statistics,** and **Correlation.**
   c. Select *Calls* and *Sales* as the variables, click on **Display p-values,** and then click **OK.**

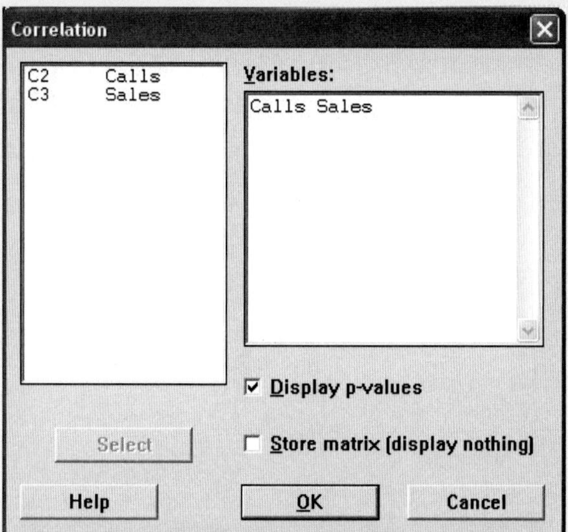

2. The computer commands for the Excel output on page 394 are:
   a. Enter the variable names in row 1 of columns A, B, and C. Enter the data in rows 2 through 11 in the same columns.
   b. Select **Tools, Data Analysis,** and then select **Regression.**
   c. For our spreadsheet we have *Calls* in column B and *Sales* in column C. The **Input Y-Range** is *C1:C11* and the **Input X-Range** is *B1:B11,* click on **Labels,** select *D1* as the **Output Range,** and click **OK.**

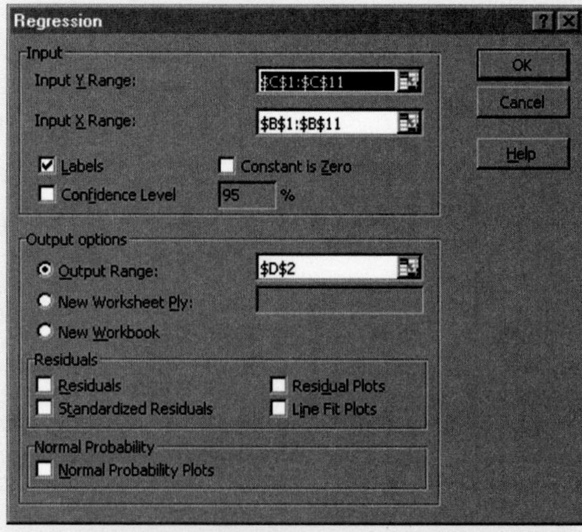

3. The MINITAB commands to the confidence intervals and prediction intervals on page 399 are:
   a. Select **Stat, Regression,** and **Fitted line plot.**
   b. In the next dialog box the **Response (Y)** is Sales and **Predictor (X)** is Calls. Select **Linear** for the type of regression model and then click on **Options.**
   c. In the **Options** dialog box click on **Display confidence and prediction bands,** use the **95.0 for confidence level,** and then in the **Title** box type an appropriate heading, then click **OK** and then **OK** again.

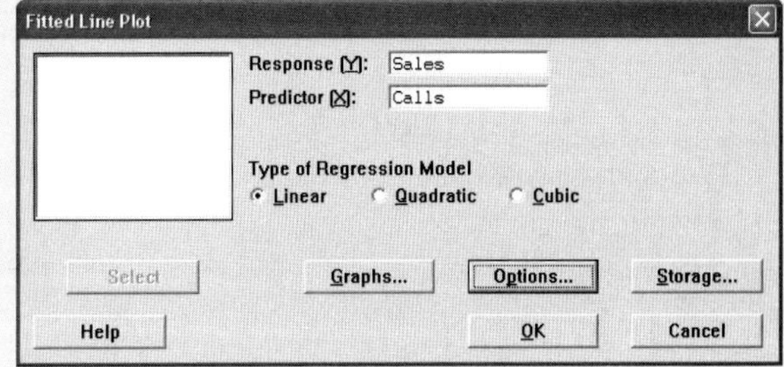

Chapter 13 Answers to Self-Review

13–1 **a.** Advertising expense is the independent variable and sales revenue is the dependent variable.

b.

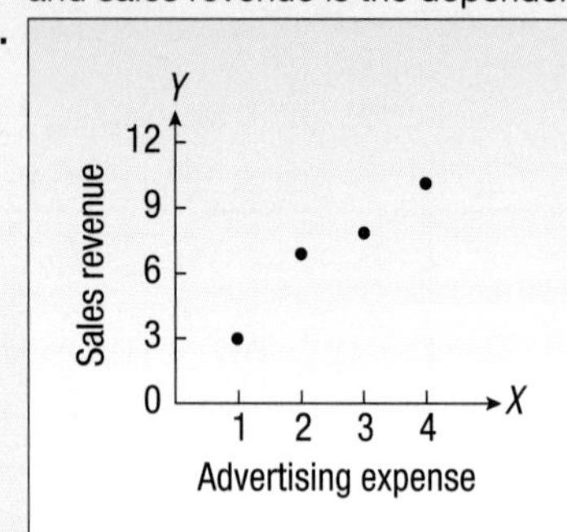

c.

X	Y	$(X-\bar{X})$	$(X-\bar{X})^2$	$(Y-\bar{Y})$	$(Y-\bar{Y})^2$	$(X-\bar{X})(Y-\bar{Y})$
2	7	−0.5	.25	0	0	0
1	3	−1.5	2.25	−4	16	6
3	8	0.5	.25	1	1	0.5
4	10	1.5	2.25	3	9	4.5
10	28		5.00		26	11

$$\bar{X} = \frac{10}{4} = 2.5 \qquad \bar{Y} = \frac{28}{4} = 7$$

$$s_x = \sqrt{\frac{5}{3}} = 1.2909944$$

$$s_y = \sqrt{\frac{26}{3}} = 2.9439203$$

$$r = \frac{\Sigma(X-\bar{X})(Y-\bar{Y})}{(n-1)\,s_x s_y}$$

$$= \frac{11}{(4-1)(1.2909944)(2.9439203)}$$

$$= 0.9648$$

d. There is a strong correlation between the advertising expense and sales.

e. $r^2 = .93$, 93% of the variation in sales is "explained" by variation in advertising.

13–2 H_0: $\rho \le 0$, H_1: $\rho > 0$. H_0 is rejected if $t > 1.714$.

$$t = \frac{.43\sqrt{25-2}}{\sqrt{1-(.43)^2}} = 2.284$$

H_0 is rejected. There is a positive correlation between the percent of the vote received and the amount spent on the campaign.

13–3 **a.** See the calculations in Self-Review 13–1, part (c).

$$b = \frac{rs_y}{s_x} = \frac{(0.9648)(2.9439)}{1.2910} = 2.2$$

$$a = \frac{28}{4} - 2.2\left(\frac{10}{4}\right) = 7 - 5.5 = 1.5$$

b. The slope is 2.2. This indicates that an increase of \$1 million in advertising will result in an increase of \$2.2 million in sales. The intercept is 1.5. If there was no expenditure for advertising, sales would be \$1.5 million.

c. $Y' = 1.5 + 2.2(3) = 8.1$

13–4 0.9487, found by:

Y	Y'	$(Y-Y')$	$(Y-Y')^2$
7	5.9	1.1	1.21
3	3.7	−0.7	.49
8	8.1	−0.1	.01
10	10.3	−0.3	.09
			1.80

$$s_{y\cdot x} = \sqrt{\frac{\Sigma(Y-Y')^2}{n-2}}$$

$$= \sqrt{\frac{1.80}{4-2}} = .9487$$

13–5 Since Y' for an X of 3 is 8.1, found by $Y' = 1.5 + 2.2(3) = 8.1$, then $\bar{X} = 2.5$ and $\Sigma(X-\bar{X})^2 = 5$.

t from Appendix F for $4 - 2 = 2$ degrees of freedom at the .10 level is 2.920.

$$Y' \pm t(s_{y\cdot x})\sqrt{\frac{1}{n} + \frac{(X-\bar{X})^2}{\Sigma(X-\bar{X})^2}}$$

$$= 8.1 \pm 2.920(0.9487)\sqrt{\frac{1}{n} + \frac{(3-2.5)^2}{5}}$$

$$= 8.1 \pm 2.920(0.9487)(0.5477)$$

$$= 6.58 \text{ and } 9.62 \text{ (in \$ millions)}$$

14

Multiple Regression and Correlation Analysis

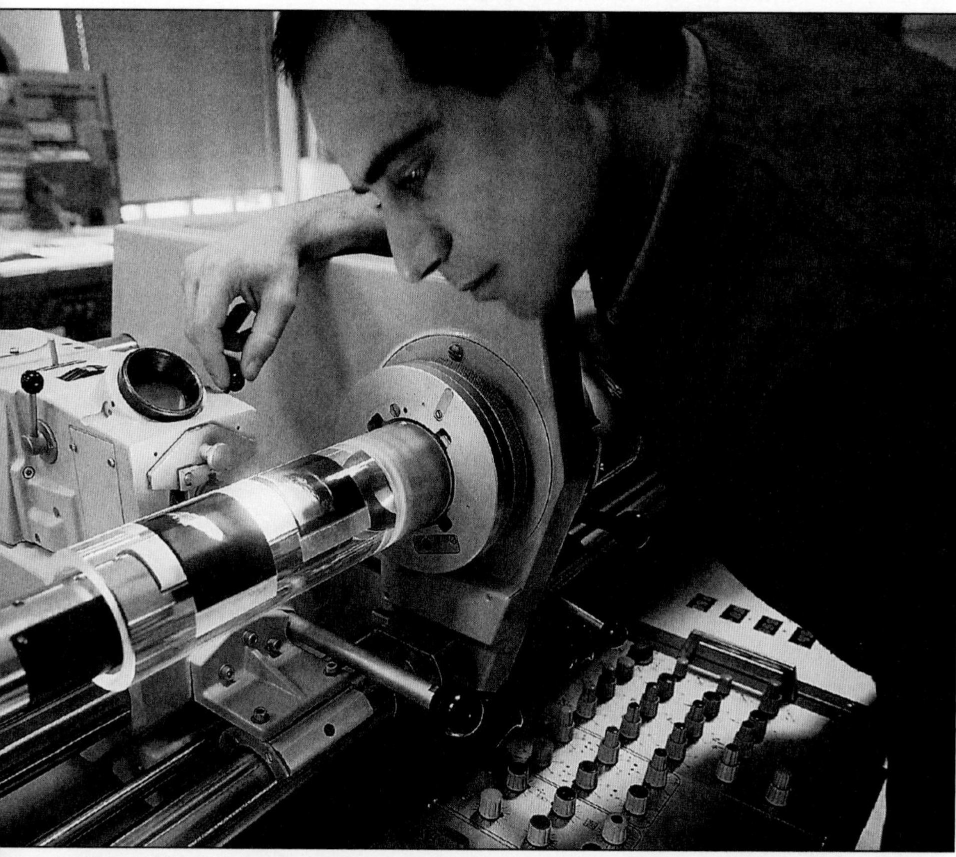

Thompson Photo Works purchased several new, highly sophisticated machines. The production department needed some guidance with respect to qualifications needed by an operator. In order to explore factors needed to estimate performance on the new machines, they explored four variables. (See Goal 1 and Exercise 2.)

GOALS

When you have completed this chapter, you will be able to:

1 **Describe the relationship between several *independent variables* and a *dependent variable* using a *multiple regression equation.***

2 **Compute and interpret the *multiple standard error of estimate* and the *coefficient of determination.***

3 **Interpret a *correlation matrix.***

4 **Set up and interpret an ANOVA table.**

5 **Conduct a test of hypothesis to determine whether regression coefficients differ from zero.**

6 **Conduct a test of hypothesis on each of the regression coefficients.**

Introduction

In Chapter 13 we described the relationship between a pair of interval- or ratio-scaled measurements. We began the chapter by studying the coefficient of correlation, which measures strength of the relationship. A coefficient near plus or minus 1.00 (−.88 or .78, for example) indicates a very strong linear relationship, whereas a value near 0 (−.12 or .18, for example) means that the relationship is weak. Next we developed a procedure to determine a linear equation to express the relationship between the two variables. We referred to this as a *line of regression.* This line describes the relationship between the variables. It also describes the overall pattern of a dependent variable (Y) to a single independent or explanatory variable (X).

In multiple linear correlation and regression we use additional independent variables (denoted $X_1, X_2, \ldots$, and so on) that help us better explain or predict the dependent variable (Y). Almost all of the ideas we saw in simple linear correlation and regression extend to this more general situation. However, the additional independent variables do lead to some new considerations. Multiple regression analysis can be used either as a descriptive or as an inferential technique.

Multiple Regression Analysis

The general descriptive form of a multiple linear equation is shown in formula (14–1). We use k to represent the number of independent variables. So k can be any positive integer.

GENERAL MULTIPLE REGRESSION EQUATION

$$Y' = a + b_1X_1 + b_2X_2 + b_3X_3 + \cdots + b_kX_k \qquad \textbf{[14-1]}$$

where:

a is the intercept, the value of Y when all the X's are zero.

b_j is the amount by which Y changes when that particular X_j increases by one unit with all other values held the same. The subscript $_j$ can assume values between 1 and k, which is the number of independent variables.

When there are only two independent variables, this equation can be portrayed graphically as a plane. Chart 14–1 is a graph of the relationship $Y' = a + b_1X_1 + b_2X_2$ used to summarize or "fit" 10 observations.

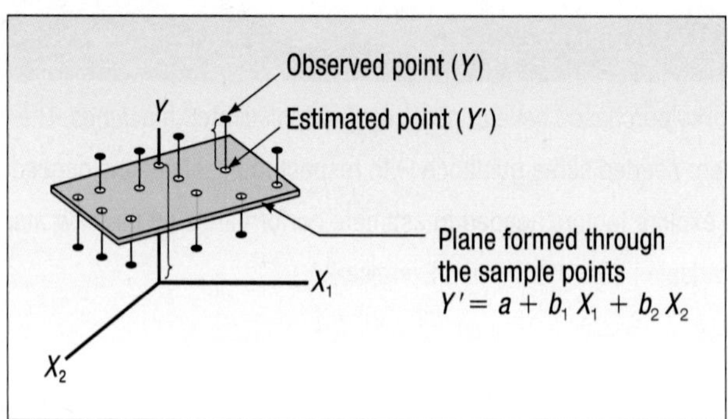

CHART 14–1 Regression Plane with Ten Sample Points

To illustrate the interpretation of the intercept and the two regression coefficients, suppose a vehicle's mileage per gallon of gasoline is directly related to the octane rating of the gasoline being used (X_1) and inversely related to the weight of the automobile (X_2). Assume that the regression equation, calculated using statistical software, is:

$$Y' = 6.3 + 0.2X_1 - 0.001X_2$$

The intercept value of 6.3 indicates the regression equation intersects the Y-axis at 6.3 when both X_1 and X_2 are zero. Of course, this does not make any physical sense to own an automobile that has no (zero) weight and to use gasoline with no octane. It is important to keep in mind that a regression equation is not generally used outside the range of the sample values.

The b_1 of 0.2 indicates that for each increase of 1 in the octane rating of the gasoline, the automobile would travel 2/10 of a mile more per gallon, *regardless of the weight of the vehicle.* That is, the vehicle's weight is held constant. The b_2 value of -0.001 reveals that for each increase of one pound in the vehicle's weight, the number of miles traveled per gallon decreases by 0.001, *regardless of the octane of the gasoline being used.*

As an example, an automobile with 92-octane gasoline in the tank and weighing 2,000 pounds would travel an average 22.7 miles per gallon, found by:

$$Y' = a + b_1X_1 + b_2X_2 = 6.3 + 0.2(92) - 0.001(2{,}000) = 22.7$$

The value of 22.7 is in miles per gallon.

The values for the coefficients in the multiple linear equation are found by using the method of least squares. Recall from the previous chapter that the least squares method makes the sum of the squared differences between the fitted and actual values of Y as small as possible. Because the calculations are very tedious, they are usually performed by a statistical software package, such as Excel or MINITAB. Fortunately, the information reported is fairly standard.

Inferences in Multiple Linear Regression

Thus far, multiple regression analysis has been viewed only as a way to describe the relationship between a dependent variable and several independent variables. However, the least squares method also has the ability to draw inferences or generalizations about the relationship for an entire population. Recall that when you create confidence intervals or perform hypothesis tests as a part of inferential statistics, you view the data as a random sample taken from some population.

In the multiple regression setting, we assume there is an unknown population regression equation that relates the dependent variable to the k independent variables. This is sometimes called a **model** of the relationship. In symbols we write:

$$Y' = \alpha + \beta_1X_1 + \beta_2X_2 + \cdots + \beta_kX_k$$

This equation is analogous to formula (14–1) except the coefficients are now reported as Greek letters. We use the Greek letters to denote *population parameters*. Then under a certain set of assumptions, which will be discussed shortly, the computed values of a and b_j are sample statistics. These sample statistics are point estimates of the corresponding population parameters α and β_j. These point estimates have normally distributed sampling distributions. These sampling distributions are each centered at their respective parameter values. To put it another way, the means of the sampling distributions are equal to the parameter values to be estimated. Thus, by using the properties of the sampling distributions of these statistics, we can make inferences about the population parameters.

We begin the discussion of multiple regression by describing a situation involving three independent variables.

EXAMPLE

Salsberry Realty sells homes along the east coast of the United States. One of the questions most frequently asked by prospective buyers is: If we purchase this home, how much can we expect to pay to heat it during the winter? The research department at Salsberry has been asked to develop some guidelines regarding heating costs for single-family homes. Three variables are thought to relate to the heating costs: (1) the mean daily outside temperature, (2) the number of inches of insulation in the attic, and (3) the age of the furnace. To investigate, Salsberry's research department selected a random sample of 20 recently sold homes. They determined the cost to heat the home last January, as well as the January outside temperature in the region, the number of inches of insulation in the attic, and the age of the furnace. The sample information is reported in Table 14–1.

TABLE 14–1 Factors in January Heating Cost for a Sample of 20 Homes

Home	Heating Cost ($)	Mean Outside Temperature (°F)	Attic Insulation (inches)	Age of Furnace (years)
1	$250	35	3	6
2	360	29	4	10
3	165	36	7	3
4	43	60	6	9
5	92	65	5	6
6	200	30	5	5
7	355	10	6	7
8	290	7	10	10
9	230	21	9	11
10	120	55	2	5
11	73	54	12	4
12	205	48	5	1
13	400	20	5	15
14	320	39	4	7
15	72	60	8	6
16	272	20	5	8
17	94	58	7	3
18	190	40	8	11
19	235	27	9	8
20	139	30	7	5

Statistics in Action

Many studies indicate a woman will earn about 70 percent of what a man would for the same work. Researchers at the University of Michigan Institute for Social Research found that about one-third of the difference can be explained by such social factors as differences in education, seniority, and work interruptions. The remaining two-thirds is not explained by these social factors.

Determine the multiple regression equation. Which variables are the independent variables? Which variable is the dependent variable? Discuss the regression coefficients. What does it indicate if some coefficients are positive and some coefficients are negative? What is the intercept value? What is the estimated heating cost for a home if the mean outside temperature is 30 degrees, there are 5 inches of insulation in the attic, and the furnace is 10 years old?

SOLUTION

The MINITAB and Excel statistical software systems generate the outputs shown below.

MINITAB - Untitled

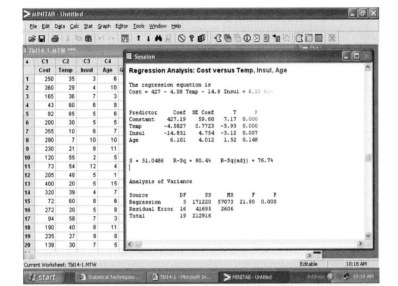

Tbl14-1.MTW ***

	C1 Cost	C2 Temp	C3 Insul	C4 Age
1	250	35	3	6
2	360	29	4	10
3	165	36	7	3
4	43	60	6	9
5	92	65	5	6
6	200	30	5	5
7	355	10	6	7
8	290	7	10	10
9	230	21	9	11
10	120	55	2	5
11	73	54	12	4
12	205	48	5	1
13	400	20	5	15
14	320	39	4	7
15	72	60	8	6
16	272	20	5	8
17	94	58	7	3
18	190	40	8	11
19	235	27	9	8
20	139	30	7	5

Session

Regression Analysis: Cost versus Temp, Insul, Age

```
The regression equation is
Cost = 427 - 4.58 Temp - 14.8 Insul + 6.10 Age

Predictor     Coef   SE Coef      T      P
Constant    427.19     59.60   7.17  0.000
Temp       -4.5827    0.7723  -5.93  0.000
Insul      -14.831     4.754  -3.12  0.007
Age          6.101     4.012   1.52  0.148

S = 51.0486   R-Sq = 80.4%   R-Sq(adj) = 76.7%

Analysis of Variance

Source          DF      SS     MS      F      P
Regression       3  171220  57073  21.90  0.000
Residual Error  16   41695   2606
Total           19  212916
```

Current Worksheet: Tbl14-1.MTW

EXCEL

Microsoft Excel - TBL14-1

	A Cost	B Temp	C Insul	D Age	E Garage
2	250	35	3	6	0
3	360	29	4	10	1
4	165	36	7	3	0
5	43	60	6	9	0
6	92	65	5	6	0
7	200	30	5	5	0
8	355	10	6	7	1
9	290	7	10	10	1
10	230	21	9	11	0
11	120	55	2	5	0
12	73	54	12	4	0
13	205	48	5	1	1
14	400	20	5	15	1
15	320	39	4	7	1
16	72	60	8	6	0
17	272	20	5	8	1
18	94	58	7	3	0
19	190	40	8	11	1
20	235	27	9	8	0
21	139	30	7	5	0

SUMMARY OUTPUT

Regression Statistics	
Multiple R	0.897
R Square	0.804
Adjusted R Square	0.767
Standard Error	51.049
Observations	20.000

ANOVA

	df	SS	MS
Regression	3	171220.473	57073.49
Residual	16	41695.277	2605.95
Total	19	212915.750	

	Coefficients	Standard Error	t Stat
Intercept	427.194	59.6014	7.17
Temp	-4.583	0.7723	-5.93
Insul	-14.831	4.7544	-3.12
Age	6.101	4.0121	1.52

The dependent variable is the January heating cost. There are three independent variables, the mean outside temperature, the number of inches of insulation in the attic, and the age of the furnace.

The general form of a multiple regression equation with three independent variables is:

$$Y' = a + b_1X_1 + b_2X_2 + b_3X_3$$

In this case the estimated multiple regression equation is $Y' = 427 - 4.58X_1 - 14.8X_2 + 6.10X_3$. The intercept value is 427. This is the point where the regression equation crosses the Y-axis. The regression coefficients for the mean outside temperature and the amount of attic insulation are both negative. This is not surprising. As the outside temperature increases, the cost to heat the home will go down. Hence, we would expect an inverse relationship. For each degree the mean temperature increases, we expect the heating cost to decrease \$4.58 per month. So if the mean temperature in Boston is 25 degrees and it is 35 degrees in Philadelphia, all other things being the same, we expect the heating cost would be \$45.80 less in Philadelphia.

The variable "attic insulation" also shows an inverse relationship: the more insulation in the attic, the less the cost to heat the home. So the negative sign for this coefficient is logical. For each additional inch of insulation, we expect the cost to heat the home to decline \$14.80 per month, regardless of the outside temperature or the age of the furnace.

The age of the furnace variable shows a direct relationship. With an older furnace, the cost to heat the home increases. Specifically, for each additional year older the furnace is, we expect the cost to increase \$6.10 per month.

The estimated heating cost for the month is \$276.60 if the mean outside temperature for the month is 30 degrees, there are 5 inches of insulation in the attic, and the furnace is 10 years old.

$$Y' = a + b_1X_1 + b_2X_2 + b_3X_3 = 427 - 4.58(30) - 14.8(5) + 6.10(10) = 276.60$$

Self-Review 14–1

The quality control engineer at Palmer Industries is interested in estimating the tensile strength of steel wire based on its outside diameter and the amount of molybdenum in the steel. As an experiment, she selected 25 pieces of wire, measured the outside diameters, and determined the molybdenum content. Then she measured the tensile strength of each piece. The results of the first four were:

Piece	Tensile Strength (psi), Y	Outside Diameter (mm), X_1	Amount of Molybdenum (units), X_2
A	11	.3	6
B	9	.2	5
C	16	.4	8
D	12	.3	7

Using a statistical software package, the QC engineer determined the multiple regression equation to be $Y' = -0.5 + 20X_1 + 1X_2$.

(a) From the equation, what is the estimated tensile strength of a steel wire having an outside diameter of .35 mm and 6.4 units of molybdenum?
(b) Interpret the value of b_1 in the equation.

Exercises

1. The director of marketing at Reeves Wholesale Products is studying monthly sales. Three independent variables were selected as estimators of sales: regional population, per-capita income, and regional unemployment rate. The regression equation was computed to be (in dollars):

$$Y' = 64{,}100 + 0.394X_1 + 9.6X_1 - 11{,}600X_3$$

a. What is the full name of the equation?
b. Interpret the number 64,100.
c. What are the estimated monthly sales for a particular region with a population of 796,000, per-capita income of \$6,940, and an unemployment rate of 6.0 percent?

2. Thompson Photo Works purchased several new, ...isticated processing machines. The production department needed some guidance ...t to qualifications needed by an operator. Is age a factor? Is the length of service ...or important? In order to explore further the factors needed to estimate performance ...w processing machines, four variables were listed:

X_1 = Length of time an employee was in the industry.
X_2 = Mechanical aptitude test score.
X_3 = Prior on-the... ...ating.
X_4 = Age.

Performance on the new machine is designated Y.

Thirty employees were selected at random. Data were collected for each, and their performances on the new machines were recorded. A few results are:

Name	Performance on New Machine, Y	Length of Time in Industry, X_1	Mechanical Aptitude Score, X_2	Prior On-the-Job Performance, X_3	Age, X_4
Andy Kosin	112	12	312	121	52
Sue Annis	113	2	380	123	27

The equation is:

$$Y' = 11.6 + 0.4X_1 + 0.286X_2 + 0.112X_3 + 0.002X_4$$

a. What is the full designation of the equation?
b. How many dependent variables are there? Independent variables?
c. What is the number 0.286 called?
d. As age increases by one year, how much does estimated performance on the new machine increase?
e. Carl Knox applied for a job at Photo Works. He has been in the business for six years, and scored 280 on the mechanical aptitude test. Carl's prior on-the-job performance rating is 97, and he is 35 years old. Estimate Carl's performance on the new machine.

3. A sample of General Mills employees was studied to determine their degree of satisfaction with their present life. A special index, called the index of satisfaction, was used to measure satisfaction. Six factors were studied, namely, age at the time of first marriage (X_1), annual income (X_2), number of children living (X_3), value of all assets (X_4), status of health in the form of an index (X_5), and the average number of social activities per week—such as bowling and dancing (X_6). Suppose the multiple regression equation is:

$$Y' = 16.24 + 0.017X_1 + 0.0028X_2 + 42X_3 + 0.0012X_4 + 0.19X_5 + 26.8X_6$$

a. What is the estimated index of satisfaction for a person who first married at 18, has an annual income of \$26,500, has three children living, has assets of \$156,000, has an index of health status of 141, and has 2.5 social activities a week on the average?
b. Which would add more to satisfaction, an additional income of \$10,000 a year or two more social activities a week?

4. Cellulon, a manufacturer of home insulation, wants to develop guidelines for builders and consumers regarding the effects (1) of the thickness of the insulation in the attic of a home and (2) of the outdoor temperature on natural gas consumption. In the laboratory they varied the insulation thickness and temperature. A few of the findings are:

Monthly Natural Gas Consumption (cubic feet), Y	Thickness of Insulation (inches), X_1	Outdoor Temperature (°F), X_2
30.3	6	40
26.9	12	40
22.1	8	49

On the basis of the sample results, the regression equation is:

$$Y' = 62.65 - 1.86X_1 - 0.52X_2$$

.. gas can homeowners expect to use per month if they install 6 inches . and the outdoor temperature is 40 degrees F?

a. Ho effect would installing 7 inches of insulation instead of 6 have on the monthly natural gas consumption (assuming the outdoor temperature remains at 40 degrees F)?

c. Why are the regression coefficients b_1 and b_2 negative? Is this logical?

Multiple Standard Error of Estimate

In the Salsberry Realty example we estimated the cost to heat a home during the month of January when the mean outside temperature was 30 degrees, there were 5 inches of attic insulation, and the furnace was 10 years old to be \$276.60. We would expect to find some random error in this estimate. Sometimes a home with these statistics would cost more than \$276.60 to heat and other times less. The error in this estimate is measured by the **multiple standard error of estimate.** The standard error, as it is usually called, is denoted $s_{y \cdot 123}$. The subscripts indicate that three independent variables are being used to estimate the value of Y.

Recall from Chapter 13 the standard error of estimate described the variation around the regression line. A small standard error indicates the points are close to the regression line, whereas a large value indicates the points are scattered about the regression line. The same concept is true in multiple regression. If we have two independent variables, then we can think of the variation around a regression plane. See Chart 14–1 on page 422. If there are more than two independent variables, we do not have a geometric interpretation of the equation, but the standard error is still a measure of the "error" or variability in the prediction.

The formula to compute the standard error is similar to that used in the previous chapter. See formula (13–6) on page 393. The numerator is the sum of the squared differences between the estimated and the actual values of the dependent variable. In the denominator, we adjust for the fact that we are considering several, that is, k, independent variables.

MULTIPLE STANDARD ERROR OF ESTIMATE

$$s_{y \cdot 12 \cdots k} = \sqrt{\frac{\Sigma(Y - Y')^2}{n - (k + 1)}} \qquad \textbf{[14–2]}$$

where:

Y is the observation.
Y' is the value estimated from the regression equation.
n is the number of observations in the sample.
k is the number of independent variables.

In the Salsberry Realty example, $k = 3$.

Again, we use the Salsberry Realty problem to illustrate. The first home had a mean outside temperature of 35 degrees, 3 inches of attic insulation, and a 6-year-old furnace. Substituting these values into the regression equation, the estimated heating cost is \$258.90, determined by $427 - 4.58(35) - 14.80(3) + 6.10(6)$. The Y' values for the other homes are found similarly and are reported in Table 14–2.

The actual heating cost for the first home is \$250, in contrast to the estimated cost of \$258.90. That is, the error in the prediction is $-\$8.90$, found by (\$250 − \$258.90). This difference between the actual heating cost and the estimated heating cost is called the **residual.** To find the multiple standard error of estimate, we determine the residual for each of the sampled homes, square the residual, and then total the squared residuals. The total is reported in the lower right corner of Table 14–2.

In this example $n = 20$ and $k = 3$ (three independent variables), so the multiple standard error of estimate is:

$$s_{y \cdot 123} = \sqrt{\frac{\Sigma(Y - Y')^2}{n - (k + 1)}} = \sqrt{\frac{41{,}695.58}{20 - (3 + 1)}} = 51.05$$

TABLE 14–2 Calculations Needed for the Multiple Standard Error of Estimate

Home	Temperature (°F)	Insulation (inches)	Age (years)	Cost, Y	Y'	$(Y - Y')$	$(Y - Y')^2$
1	35	3	6	$250	258.90	−8.90	79.21
2	29	4	10	360	295.98	64.02	4,098.56
3	36	7	3	165	176.82	−11.82	139.71
4	60	6	9	43	118.30	−75.30	5,670.09
5	65	5	6	92	91.90	0.10	0.01
6	30	5	5	200	246.10	−46.10	2,125.21
7	10	6	7	355	335.10	19.90	396.01
8	7	10	10	290	307.94	−17.94	321.84
9	21	9	11	230	264.72	−34.72	1,205.48
10	55	2	5	120	176.00	−56.00	3,136.00
11	54	12	4	73	26.48	46.52	2,164.11
12	48	5	1	205	139.26	65.74	4,321.75
13	20	5	15	400	352.90	47.10	2,218.41
14	39	4	7	320	231.88	88.12	7,765.13
15	60	8	6	72	70.40	1.60	2.56
16	20	5	8	272	310.20	−38.20	1,459.24
17	58	7	3	94	76.06	17.94	321.84
18	40	8	11	190	192.50	−2.50	6.25
19	27	9	8	235	218.94	16.06	257.92
20	30	7	5	139	216.50	−77.50	6,006.25
Total							41,695.58

How do we interpret the 51.05? It is the typical "error" we make when we use this equation to predict the cost. First, the units are the same as the dependent variable, so the standard error is in dollars. Second, if the errors are normally distributed, about 68 percent of the residuals should be between ±51.05 and about 95 percent should be less than ±2(51.05) or ±102.10. Refer to the second column from the right in Table 14–2, the column headed $(Y - Y')$. Of the 20 residuals reported in this column, 14 are less than ±51.05 and all are less than ±102.10, which is quite close to the guidelines of 68 percent and 95 percent.

In Chapter 13 we used the standard error of estimate to construct confidence intervals and prediction intervals. We will not detail these procedures for multiple regression, but they are available on statistical software systems, such as MINITAB.

Assumptions about Multiple Regression and Correlation

Before continuing our discussion, we list the assumptions underlying both multiple regression and multiple correlation. As noted in several previous chapters, we identify the assumptions because if they are not fully met, the results might be biased. For instance, in selecting a sample, we assume that all the items in the population have a chance of being selected. If our research involves surveying all those who ski, but we ignore those over 40 because we believe they are "too old," we would be biasing the responses toward the younger skiers. It should be mentioned, however, that in practice strict adherence to the following assumptions is not always possible in multiple regression and correlation problems involving the ever-changing business climate. But the statistical techniques discussed in this chapter appear to work well even when one or more of the assumptions are violated. Even if the values in the multiple regression equation are "off" slightly, our estimates based on the equation will be closer than any that could otherwise be made.

Each of the following assumptions will be discussed in more detail as we progress through the chapter.

1. The independent variables and the dependent variable have a linear relationship.
2. The dependent variable is continuous and at least interval scale.
3. The variation in the difference between the actual and the predicted values is the same for all fitted values of Y. That is, $(Y - Y')$ must be approximately the same for all values of Y'. When this is the case, differences exhibit **homoscedasticity.**
4. The residuals, computed by $Y - Y'$, are normally distributed with a mean of 0.
5. Successive observations of the dependent variable are uncorrelated. Violation of this assumption is called **autocorrelation.** Autocorrelation often happens when data are collected successively over periods of time.

Homoscedasticity

Autocorrelation

Statistical tests are available to detect homoscedasticity and autocorrelation. For those interested, these tests are covered in more advanced textbooks such as *Applied Linear Regression Models* by Kutner, Nachtscheim, and Neter (4th ed., 2004, published by McGraw-Hill/Irwin).

The ANOVA Table

As mentioned previously, the multiple regression calculations are lengthy. Fortunately, many software systems are available to perform the calculations. Most of the systems report the results in a fairly standard format. The outputs from MINITAB and Excel shown on page 425 is typical. It includes the regression equation, the standard error of estimate, the coefficient of determination, as well as an analysis of variance table. We have already described the meaning of the regression coefficients in the equation $Y' = 427 - 4.58X_1 - 14.8X_2 + 6.10X_3$. We will discuss the "Coef," "StDev," and "T" (i.e., t ratio) columns later in the chapter. A portion of the output from MINITAB is repeated here.

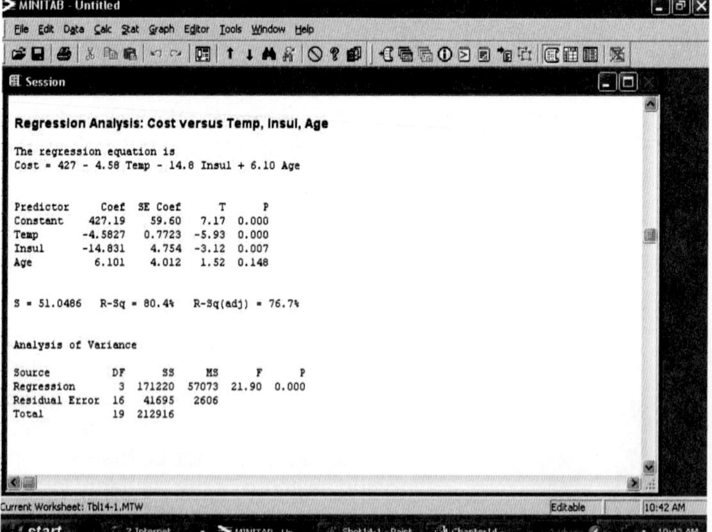

MINITAB - Untitled

File Edit Data Calc Stat Graph Editor Tools Window Help

Session

Regression Analysis: Cost versus Temp, Insul, Age

The regression equation is
Cost = 427 - 4.58 Temp - 14.8 Insul + 6.10 Age

Predictor	Coef	SE Coef	T	P
Constant	427.19	59.60	7.17	0.000
Temp	-4.5827	0.7723	-5.93	0.000
Insul	-14.831	4.754	-3.12	0.007
Age	6.101	4.012	1.52	0.148

S = 51.0486 R-Sq = 80.4% R-Sq(adj) = 76.7%

Analysis of Variance

Source	DF	SS	MS	F	P
Regression	3	171220	57073	21.90	0.000
Residual Error	16	41695	2606		
Total	19	212916			

Current Worksheet: Tbl14-1.MTW

First, let's focus on the analysis of variance table. It is similar to the ANOVA table described in Chapter 12. In that chapter the variation was divided into two components: variance due to the *treatments* and variance due to random *error.* Here the total variance is also divided into two components: variance explained by the **regression,** that is, the independent variables, and the **error variance, residual error,** or unexplained variation. These two categories are identified in the "Source" column of the analysis of variance table. In the example there are 20 observations, so $n = 20$. The *total* number of degrees of freedom is $n - 1$, or $20 - 1 = 19$. The number of degrees of freedom in the "Regression" row is the number of independent variables. We let k represent the number of independent variables, so $k = 3$. The number of degrees of freedom in the "Residual Error" row is $n - (k + 1) = 20 - (3 + 1) = 16$ degrees of freedom.

The heading "SS" in the middle of the ANOVA table refers to the sum of squares, or the variation.

$$\text{Total variation} = \text{SS total} = \Sigma(Y - \bar{Y})^2 = 212{,}916$$
$$\text{Residual error} = \text{SSE} = \Sigma(Y - Y')^2 = 41{,}695$$
$$\text{Regression variation} = \text{SSR} = \Sigma(Y' - \bar{Y})^2 = \text{SS total} - \text{SSE} = 212{,}916 - 41{,}695 = 171{,}220$$

The column headed "MS" (mean square) is determined by dividing the SS term by the *df* term. Thus, MSR, the mean square regression, is equal to SSR/k, and MSE equals SSE/$[n - (k + 1)]$. The general format of the ANOVA table is:

Source	*df*	SS	MS	*F*
Regression	k	SSR	MSR = SSR/k	MSR/MSE
Error	$n - (k + 1)$	SSE	MSE = SSE/$[n - (k + 1)]$	
Total	$n - 1$	SS total		

The **coefficient of multiple determination,** written as R^2, is the percent of the total variation explained by the regression. It is the sum of squares due to the regression, divided by the sum of squares total.

COEFFICIENT OF MULTIPLE DETERMINATION

$$R^2 = \frac{\text{SSR}}{\text{SS total}} \qquad \textbf{[14–3]}$$

$$R^2 = \frac{\text{SSR}}{\text{SS total}} = \frac{171{,}220}{212{,}916} = .804$$

The multiple standard error of estimate may also be found directly from the ANOVA table.

$$s_{y\cdot123} = \sqrt{\frac{\text{SSE}}{n - (k + 1)}} = \sqrt{\frac{41{,}695}{[20-(3+1)]}} = 51.05$$

These values, $R^2 = .804$ and $s_{y\cdot123} = 51.05$, are included in the MINITAB output.

Self-Review 14–2 Refer to the following ANOVA table.

```
SOURCE        DF    SS      MS       F
Regression     4    10    2.50    10.0
Error         20     5    0.25
Total         24    15
```

(a) How large was the sample?
(b) How many independent variables are there?
(c) Compute the coefficient of multiple determination.
(d) Compute the multiple standard error of estimate.

Exercises

5. Refer to the following ANOVA table.

SOURCE	DF	SS	MS	F
Regression	3	21	7.0	2.33
Error	15	45	3.0	
Total	18	66		

a. How large was the sample?
b. How many independent variables are there?
c. Compute the coefficient of multiple determination.
d. Compute the multiple standard error of estimate.

6. Refer to the following ANOVA table.

SOURCE	DF	SS	MS	F
Regression	5	60	12	1.714
Error	20	140	7	
Total	25	200		

a. How large was the sample?
b. How many independent variables are there?
c. Compute the coefficient of multiple determination.
d. Compute the multiple standard error of estimate.

Evaluating the Regression Equation

Earlier in the chapter we described an example in which Salsberry Realty developed, using multiple regression techniques, an equation to express the cost to heat a home during the month of January based on the mean outside temperature, the number of inches of attic insulation, and the age of the furnace. The equation seemed reasonable, but we may wish to verify that the multiple coefficient of determination is significantly larger than zero, evaluate the regression coefficients to see which are not equal to zero, and verify that the regression assumptions are met.

Using a Scatter Diagram

There are three independent variables, designated X_1, X_2, and X_3. The dependent variable, the heating cost, is designated Y. In order to visualize the relationships between the dependent variable and each of the independent variables, we can draw the following scatter diagrams.

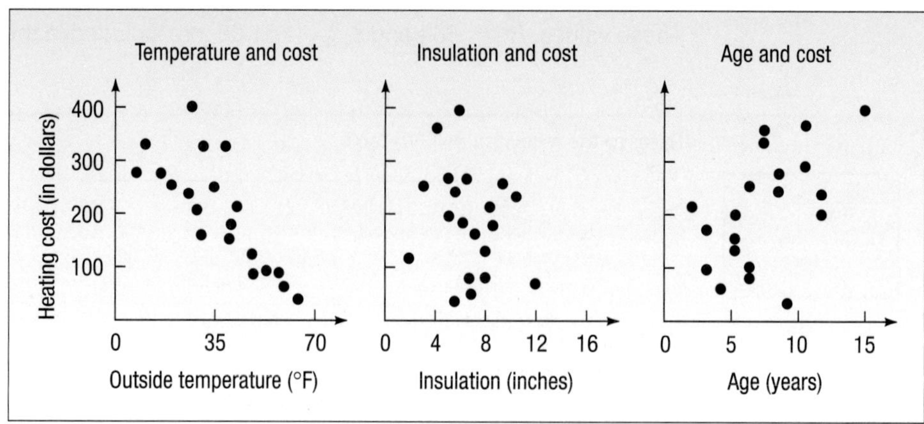

Of the three independent variables, the strongest association is between heating cost and the mean outside temperature. The relationships between cost and temperature and cost and insulation both are inverse. That is, as the independent variable increases, the dependent variable decreases. The relationship between the heating cost and the age of the furnace is direct. As the furnace gets older, it costs more to heat the home.

Correlation Matrix

A correlation matrix is also useful in analyzing the factors involved in the cost to heat a home.

CORRELATION MATRIX A matrix showing the coefficients of correlation between all pairs of variables.

The correlation matrix of the Salsberry Realty example follows. The matrix, which appears on the right-hand side of the output was developed using the Excel software.

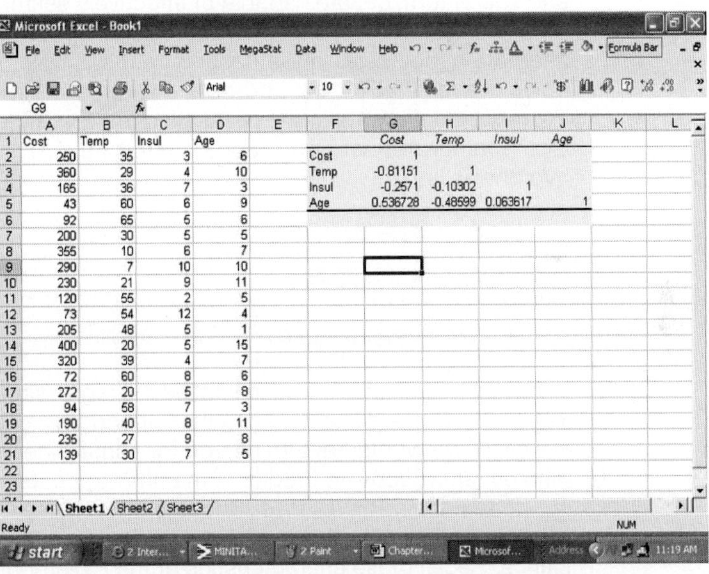

Cost	Temp	Insul	Age
250	35	3	6
360	29	4	10
165	36	7	3
43	60	6	9
92	65	5	6
200	30	5	5
355	10	6	7
290	7	10	10
230	21	9	11
120	55	2	5
73	54	12	4
205	48	5	1
400	20	5	15
320	39	4	7
72	60	8	6
272	20	5	8
94	58	7	3
190	40	8	11
235	27	9	8
139	30	7	5

	Cost	Temp	Insul	Age
Cost	1			
Temp	-0.81151	1		
Insul	-0.2571	-0.10302	1	
Age	0.536728	-0.48599	0.063617	1

Cost is the dependent variable, Y. We are particularly interested in independent variables that have a strong correlation with the dependent variable. We may wish to develop a simpler multiple regression equation using fewer independent variables and the correlation matrix helps us identify which variables may be relatively more important. As indicated in the output, temperature has the strongest correlation with cost, −0.81151. The negative sign indicates the inverse relationship we were expecting. Age has a stronger correlation with cost than insulation and, again as we expected, the correlation between cost and the age of the furnace is direct. It is 0.53673.

A second use of the correlation matrix is to check for **multicollinearity.**

MULTICOLLINEARITY Correlation among the independent variables.

Multicollinearity can distort the standard error of estimate and may, therefore, lead to incorrect conclusions as to which independent variables are statistically significant. In this case, the correlation between the age of the furnace and the temperature is the strongest, but it is not large enough to cause a problem. A common rule of thumb is that correlations among the independent variables between −.70 and .70 do not cause difficulties. The usual remedy for multicollinearity is to drop one of the independent variables that are strongly correlated and recompute the regression equation.

Global Test: Testing the Multiple Regression Model

We can test the ability of the independent variables $X_1, X_2, \ldots, X_k$ to explain the behavior of the dependent variable Y. To put this in question form: Can the dependent variable be estimated without relying on the independent variables? The test used is referred to as the **global test.** Basically, it investigates whether it is possible all the independent variables have zero net regression coefficients. To put it another way, could the amount of explained variation, R^2, occur by chance?

To relate this question to the heating cost example, we will test whether the independent variables (amount of insulation in the attic, mean daily outside temperature, and age of furnace) are capable of effectively estimating home heating costs.

Recall that in testing a hypothesis, we first state the null hypothesis and the alternate hypothesis. In the heating cost example, there are three independent variables. Recall that b_1, b_2, and b_3 are sample net regression coefficients. The corresponding coefficients in the population are given the symbols β_1, β_2, and β_3. We now test whether the net regression coefficients in the population are all zero. The null hypothesis is:

$$H_0: \beta_1 = \beta_2 = \beta_3 = 0$$

The alternate hypothesis is:

$$H_1: \text{Not all the } \beta\text{s are 0.}$$

If the null hypothesis is true, it implies the regression coefficients are all zero and, logically, are of no use in estimating the dependent variable (heating cost). Should that be the case, we would have to search for some other independent variables—or take a different approach—to predict home heating costs.

To test the null hypothesis that the multiple regression coefficients are all zero, we employ the F distribution introduced in Chapter 12. We will use the .05 level of significance. Recall these characteristics of the F distribution:

Characteristics of the F distribution

1. It is positively skewed, with the critical value located in the right tail. The critical value is the point that separates the region where H_0 is not rejected from the region of rejection.
2. It is constructed by knowing the number of degrees of freedom in the numerator and the number of degrees of freedom in the denominator.

The degrees of freedom for the numerator and the denominator may be found in the analysis of variance table. That portion of the table is included on the next page. The top number in the column marked "DF" is 3, indicating that there are 3 degrees of freedom in the numerator. The middle number in the "DF" column (16) indicates that there are 16 degrees of freedom in the denominator. The number 16 is found by $n - (k + 1) = 20 - (3 + 1) = 16$. The number 3 corresponds to the number of independent variables.

MINITAB

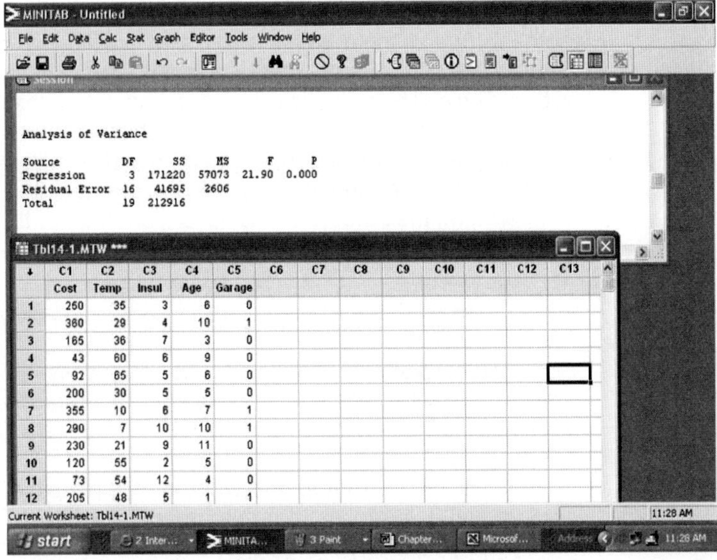

Analysis of Variance

Source	DF	SS	MS	F	P
Regression	3	171220	57073	21.90	0.000
Residual Error	16	41695	2606		
Total	19	212916			

Tbl14-1.MTW ***

↓	C1 Cost	C2 Temp	C3 Insul	C4 Age	C5 Garage
1	250	35	3	6	0
2	360	29	4	10	1
3	165	36	7	3	0
4	43	60	6	9	0
5	92	65	5	6	0
6	200	30	5	5	0
7	355	10	6	7	1
8	290	7	10	10	1
9	230	21	9	11	0
10	120	55	2	5	0
11	73	54	12	4	0
12	205	48	5	1	1

Current Worksheet: Tbl14-1.MTW

The value of F is found from the following equation.

GLOBAL TEST

$$F = \frac{\text{SSR}/k}{\text{SSE}/[n - (k + 1)]} \qquad \textbf{[14–4]}$$

SSR is the sum of the squares "explained by" the regression, SSE the sum of squares error, n the number of observations, and k the number of independent variables. Inserting these values in formula (14–4) gives:

$$F = \frac{\text{SSR}/k}{\text{SSE}/[n - (k + 1)]} = \frac{171{,}220/3}{41{,}695/[20 - (3 + 1)]} = 21.90$$

The critical value of F is found in Appendix G. Using the table for the .05 significance level, move horizontally to 3 degrees of freedom in the numerator, then down to 16 degrees of freedom in the denominator, and read the critical value. It is 3.24. The region where H_0 is not rejected and the region where H_0 is rejected are shown in the following diagram.

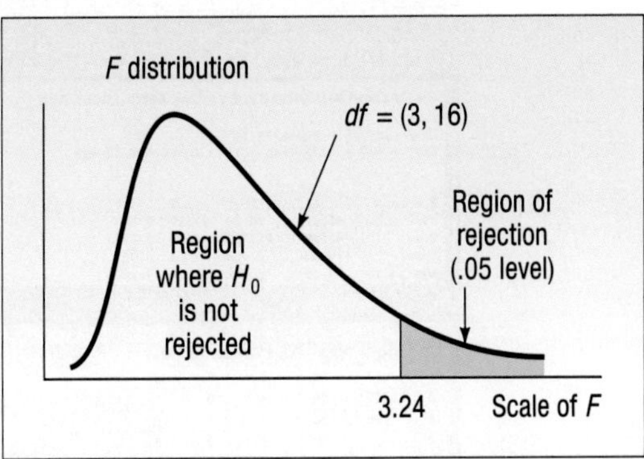

Continuing with the global test, the decision rule is: Do not reject the null hypothesis that all the regression coefficients are 0 if the computed value of F is less than or equal to 3.24. If the computed F is greater than 3.24, reject H_0 and accept the alternate hypothesis, H_1.

The computed value of F is 21.90, which is in the rejection region. The null hypothesis that all the multiple regression coefficients are zero is therefore rejected. The p-value is 0.000 from the above analysis of variance table, so it is quite unlikely that H_0 is true. The null hypothesis is rejected, indicating that not all the regression coefficients are zero. From a practical standpoint, this means that some of the independent variables (amount of insulation, etc.) do have the ability to explain the variation in the dependent variable (heating cost). We expected this decision. Logically, the outside temperature, the amount of insulation, and age of the furnace have a great bearing on heating costs. The global test assures us that they do.

Evaluating Individual Regression Coefficients

So far we have shown that some, but not necessarily all, of the regression coefficients are not equal to zero and thus useful for predictions. The next step is to test the variables *individually* to determine which regression coefficients may be 0 and which are not.

Why is it important to find whether it is possible that any of the βs equal 0? If a β could equal 0, it implies that this particular independent variable is of no value in explaining any variation in the dependent value. If there are coefficients for which H_0 cannot be rejected, we may want to eliminate them from the regression equation.

We will now conduct three separate tests of hypothesis—for temperature, for insulation, and for the age of the furnace.

For temperature:	For insulation:	For furnace age:
H_0: $\beta_1 = 0$	H_0: $\beta_2 = 0$	H_0: $\beta_3 = 0$
H_1: $\beta_1 \neq 0$	H_1: $\beta_2 \neq 0$	H_1: $\beta_3 \neq 0$

We will test the hypotheses at the .05 level. The way the alternate hypothesis is stated indicates that the test is two-tailed.

The test statistic follows the Student t distribution with $n - (k + 1)$ degrees of freedom. The number of sample observations is n. There are 20 homes in the study, so $n = 20$. The number of independent variables is k, which is 3. Thus, there are $n - (k + 1) = 20 - (3 + 1) = 16$ degrees of freedom.

The critical value for t is in Appendix F. For a two-tailed test with 16 degrees of freedom using the .05 significance level, H_0 is rejected if t is less than -2.120 or greater than 2.120. The MINITAB software produced the following output.

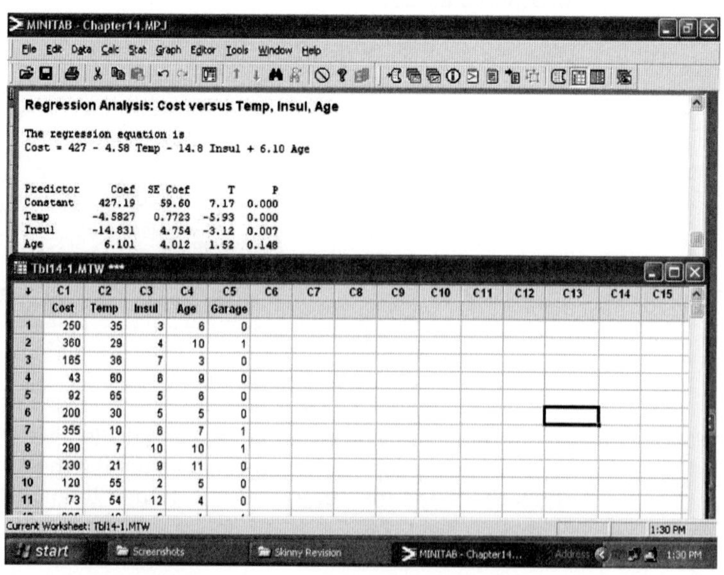

The column headed "Coef" shows the regression coefficients for the multiple regression equation:

$$Y' = 427.19 - 4.5827X_1 - 14.831X_2 + 6.101X_3$$

Interpreting the term $-4.5827X_1$ in the equation: For each degree the temperature increases, it is expected that the heating cost will decrease about \$4.58, holding the two other variables constant.

The column on the MINITAB output labeled "SE Coef" indicates the standard error of the sample regression coefficient. Recall that Salsberry Realty selected a sample of 20 homes along the east coast of the United States. If they were to select a second sample at random and compute the regression coefficients of that sample, the values would not be exactly the same. If they repeated the sampling process many times, however, we could design a sampling distribution of these regression coefficients. The column labeled "SE Coef" estimates the variability of these regression coefficients. The sampling distribution of Coef/SE Coef follows the *t* distribution with $n - (k + 1)$ degrees of freedom. Hence, we are able to test the independent variables individually to determine whether the net regression coefficients differ from zero. The computed *t* ratio is -5.93 for temperature and -3.12 for insulation. Both of these *t* values are in the rejection region to the left of -2.120. Thus, we conclude that the regression coefficients for the temperature and insulation variables are *not* zero. The computed *t* for age of the furnace is 1.52, so we conclude that β_3 could equal 0. The independent variable "age of the furnace" is not a significant predictor of heating cost. It can be dropped from the analysis. We can test individual regression coefficients using the *t* distribution. The formula is:

TESTING INDIVIDUAL REGRESSION COEFFICIENTS

$$t = \frac{b_i - 0}{s_{b_i}} \quad \textbf{[14–5]}$$

The b_i refers to any one of the net regression coefficients and s_{b_i} refers to standard deviation of the net regression coefficient. We include 0 in the equation because the null hypothesis is $\beta_i = 0$.

To illustrate this formula, refer to the test of the regression coefficient for the independent variable Temperature. We let b_1 refer to the net regression coefficient. From the computer output on page 436 it is -4.5827. s_{b_i} is the standard deviation of the sampling distribution of the net regression coefficient for the independent variable Temperature. Again, from the computer output on page 436, it is 0.7723. Inserting these values in formula (14–5):

$$t = \frac{b_1 - 0}{s_{b_1}} = \frac{-4.5827 - 0}{0.7723} = -5.93$$

This is the value found in the "T" column of the output.

In Self-Review 14–3, we run the multiple regression example again using MINITAB, but only two variables—"temperature" and "insulation"—are included. These two variables explained 77.6 percent of the variation in heating cost. Using all three variables—temperature, insulation, and furnace age—a total of 80.4 percent of the variation is explained. The additional variable increased R^2 by only 2.8 percent—a rather small increase for the addition of an independent variable.

At this point we should also develop a strategy for deleting independent variables. In the Salsberry Realty case there were three independent variables and one (age) had a regression coefficient that did not differ from 0. It is clear that we should drop that variable. So we delete that variable and rerun the regression equation. However, in some instances it may not be as clear-cut which variable to delete.

To explain, suppose we developed a multiple regression equation based on five independent variables. We conducted the global test and found that some of the regression coefficients were different from zero. Next, we tested the regression coefficients individually and found that three were significant and two were not. The preferred procedure is to drop the single independent variable with the *smallest absolute* t *value* or *largest* p*-value* and rerun the regression equation with the four remaining variables. Then, on the new regression equation with four independent variables, conduct the individual tests. If there are still regression coefficients that are not significant, again drop the variable with the smallest absolute *t* value. To describe the process in another way, we should delete only one variable at a time. Each time we delete a variable, we need to rerun the regression equation and check the remaining variables.

This process of selecting variables to include in a regression model can be automated, using Excel, MINITAB, Megastat, or other statistical software. Most of the software systems include methods to sequentially remove and/or add independent variables and at the same time provide estimates of the percentage of variation explained (the *R*-square term). Two of the common methods are **stepwise regression** and **best subset regression.** It may take a long time, but in the extreme you could compute every regression between the dependent variable and any possible subset of the independent variables.

Unfortunately, on occasion, the software may work "too hard" to find an equation that fits all the quirks of your particular data set. The resultant equation may not represent the relationship in the population. You will need to use your judgment to choose among the equations presented. Consider whether the results are logical. They should have a simple interpretation and be consistent with your knowledge of the application under study.

Self-Review 14–3

The multiple regression and correlation data for the preceding heating cost example were rerun using only the first two significant independent variables—temperature and insulation. (See the following MINITAB output.)

(a) What is the new multiple regression equation? (Temperature is X_1 and insulation X_2.)
(b) What is the coefficient of multiple determination? Interpret.
(c) How can you tell that these two independent variables are of value in predicting heating costs?
(d) What is the *p*-value of insulation? Interpret.

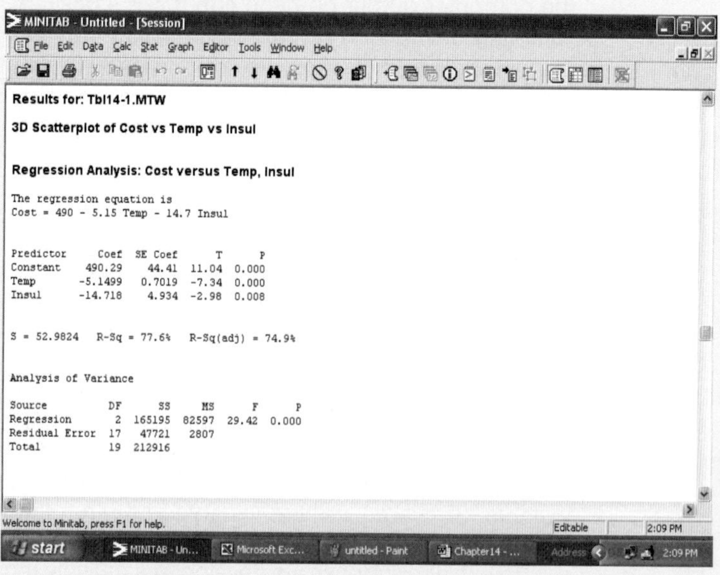

```
MINITAB - Untitled - [Session]

Results for: Tbl14-1.MTW

3D Scatterplot of Cost vs Temp vs Insul

Regression Analysis: Cost versus Temp, Insul

The regression equation is
Cost = 490 - 5.15 Temp - 14.7 Insul

Predictor      Coef  SE Coef      T      P
Constant     490.29    44.41  11.04  0.000
Temp        -5.1499   0.7019  -7.34  0.000
Insul       -14.718    4.934  -2.98  0.008

S = 52.9824   R-Sq = 77.6%   R-Sq(adj) = 74.9%

Analysis of Variance

Source          DF      SS     MS      F      P
Regression       2  165195  82597  29.42  0.000
Residual Error  17   47721   2807
Total           19  212916
```

Qualitative Independent Variables

Statistics in Action

In recent years, multiple regression has been used in a variety of legal proceedings. It is particularly useful in cases alleging discrimination by gender or race. As an example, suppose that a woman alleges that Company X's wage rates are unfair to women. To support the claim, the plaintiff produces data showing that, on the average, women earn less than men. In response, Company X argues that its wage rates are based on experience, training, and skill and that its female employees, on the average, are younger and less experienced than the male employees. In fact, the company might further argue that the current situation is actually due to its recent successful efforts to hire more women.

The three variables used in the Salsberry Realty example were all quantitative; that is, numerical in nature. Frequently we wish to use nominal-scale variables—such as gender, whether the home has a swimming pool, or whether the sports team was the home or the visiting team—in our analysis. These are called *qualitative variables* because they describe a particular quality, such as male or female. To use a qualitative variable in regression analysis, we use a scheme of **dummy variables** in which one of the two possible conditions is coded 0 and the other 1.

DUMMY VARIABLE A variable in which there are only two possible outcomes. For analysis, one of the outcomes is coded a 1 and the other a 0.

For example, we might be interested in estimating an executive's salary on the basis of years of job experience and whether he or she graduated from college. "Graduation from college" can take on only one of two conditions: yes or no. Thus, it is considered a qualitative variable.

Suppose in the Salsberry Realty example that the independent variable "garage" is added. For those homes without an attached garage, 0 is used; for homes with an attached garage, a 1 is used. We will refer to the "garage" variable as X_4. The data from Table 14–3 are entered into the MINITAB system.

TABLE 14–3 Home Heating Costs, Temperature, Insulation, and Presence of a Garage for a Sample of 20 Homes

Cost, Y	Temperature, X_1	Insulation, X_2	Garage, X_4
$250	35	3	0
360	29	4	1
165	36	7	0
43	60	6	0
92	65	5	0
200	30	5	0
355	10	6	1
290	7	10	1
230	21	9	0
120	55	2	0
73	54	12	0
205	48	5	1
400	20	5	1
320	39	4	1
72	60	8	0
272	20	5	1
94	58	7	0
190	40	8	1
235	27	9	0
139	30	7	0

The output from MINITAB is:

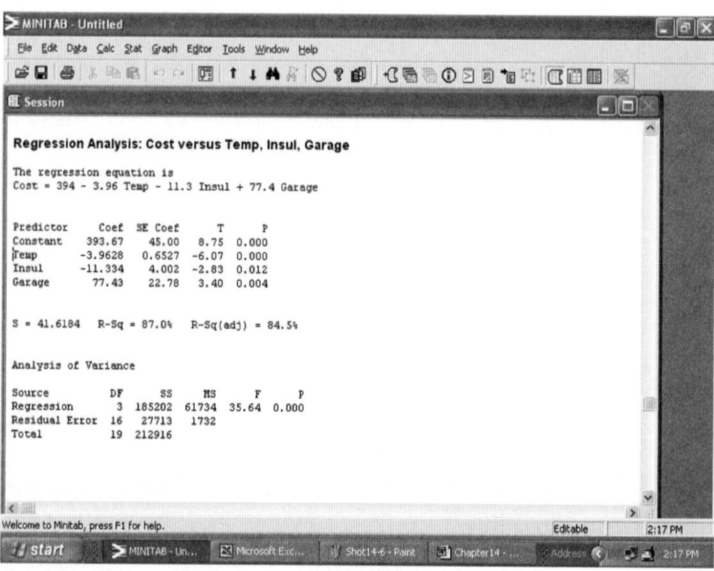

Regression Analysis: Cost versus Temp, Insul, Garage

```
The regression equation is
Cost = 394 - 3.96 Temp - 11.3 Insul + 77.4 Garage

Predictor      Coef  SE Coef      T      P
Constant     393.67    45.00   8.75  0.000
Temp        -3.9628   0.6527  -6.07  0.000
Insul       -11.334    4.002  -2.83  0.012
Garage        77.43    22.78   3.40  0.004

S = 41.6184   R-Sq = 87.0%   R-Sq(adj) = 84.5%

Analysis of Variance

Source          DF      SS     MS      F      P
Regression       3  185202  61734  35.64  0.000
Residual Error  16   27713   1732
Total           19  212916
```

What is the effect of the variable "garage"? Should it be included in the analysis? To show the effect of the variable, suppose we have two houses exactly alike next to each other in Buffalo, New York; one has an attached garage, and the other does not. Both homes have 3 inches of insulation, and the mean January temperature in Buffalo is 20 degrees. For the house without an attached garage, a 0 is substituted for X_4 in the regression equation. The estimated heating cost is \$280.90, found by:

$$Y' = 394 - 3.96X_1 - 11.3X_2 + 77.4X_4$$
$$= 394 - 3.96(20) - 11.3(3) + 77.4(0) = 280.90$$

For the house with an attached garage, a 1 is substituted for X_4 in the regression equation. The estimated heating cost is \$358.30, found by:

$$Y' = 394 - 3.96X_1 - 11.3X_2 + 77.4X_4$$
$$= 394 - 3.96(20) - 11.3(3) + 77.4(1) = 358.30$$

The difference between the estimated heating costs is \$77.40 (\$358.30 − \$280.90). Hence, we can expect the cost to heat a house with an attached garage to be \$77.40 more than the cost for an equivalent house without a garage.

We have shown the difference between the two types of homes to be \$77.40, but is the difference statistically significant? We conduct the following test of hypothesis.

$$H_0: \beta_4 = 0$$
$$H_1: \beta_4 \neq 0$$

The information necessary to answer this question is on the MINITAB output above. The net regression coefficient for the independent variable Garage is 77.43, the standard deviation of the distribution of sampling distribution is 22.78. We identify this as the fourth independent variable, so we use a subscript of 4. Finally, we insert these values in formula (14–5).

$$t = \frac{b_4 - 0}{s_{b_4}} = \frac{77.43 - 0}{22.78} = 3.40$$

There are three independent variables in the analysis, so there are $n - (k + 1) = 20 - (3 + 1) = 16$ degrees of freedom. The critical value from Appendix F is 2.120. The decision rule, using a two-tailed test and the .05 significance level, is to reject H_0

if the computed t is to the left of -2.120 or to the right of 2.120. Since the computed value of 3.40 is to the right of 2.120, the null hypothesis is rejected. It is concluded that the regression coefficient is not zero. The independent variable "garage" should be included in the analysis.

Is it possible to use a qualitative variable with more than two possible outcomes? Yes, but the coding scheme becomes more complex and will require a series of dummy variables. To explain, suppose a company is studying its sales as they relate to advertising expense by quarter for the last 5 years. Let sales be the dependent variable and advertising expense be the first independent variable, X_1. To include the qualitative information regarding the quarter, we use three additional independent variables. For the variable X_2, the five observations referring to the first quarter of each of the 5 years are coded 1 and the other quarters 0. Similarly, for X_3 the five observations referring to the second quarter are coded 1 and the other quarters 0. For X_4 the five observations referring to the third quarter are coded 1 and the other quarters 0. An observation that does not refer to any of the first three quarters must refer to the fourth quarter, so a distinct independent variable referring to this quarter is not necessary.

Exercises

7. Refer to the following information:

Predictor	Coef	StDev
Constant	20.00	10.00
X_1	−1.00	0.25
X_2	12.00	8.00
X_3	−15.00	5.00

SOURCE	DF	SS	MS	F
Regression	3	7,500.00		
Error	18			
Total	21	10,000.0		

a. Complete the ANOVA table.

b. Conduct a global test of hypothesis, using the .05 significance level. Can you conclude that any of the net regression coefficients are different from zero?

c. Conduct a test of hypothesis on each of the regression coefficients. Could you delete any of the variables?

8. Refer to the following information:

Predictor	Coef	StDev
Constant	−150	90
X_1	2000	500
X_2	−25	30
X_3	5	5
X_4	−300	100
X_5	0.60	0.15

SOURCE	DF	SS	MS	F
Regression	5	1,500.0		
Error	15			
Total	20	2,000.0		

a. Complete the ANOVA table.

b. Conduct a global test of hypothesis, using the .05 significance level. Can you conclude that any of the net regression coefficients are different from zero?

c. Conduct a test of hypothesis on each of the regression coefficients. Could you delete any of the variables?

Analysis of Residuals

In an earlier section we describe the assumptions required for regression and correlation analysis. These assumptions are:

1. There is a linear relationship between the dependent variable and the independent variables.
2. The dependent variable is measured as an interval- or ratio-scale variable.
3. Successive observations of the dependent variable are not correlated.
4. The differences between the actual values and estimated values, that is, the residuals, follow the normal distribution.
5. The variation in the residuals is the same for all fitted values of Y'. That is, the distribution of $(Y - Y')$ is the same for all values of Y'.

The last two assumptions can be verified by plotting the residuals. That is, we want to confirm that the residuals follow a normal distribution and that residuals have the same variation whether the Y' value is large or small. We present the necessary data in Table 14–4. The column headed "Actual Cost" is the original heating cost, first presented in Table 14–1. The next column, labeled "Estimated Cost," is the cost to heat the home as estimated from the regression equation. This is also referred to as the fitted value and is Y'. The value for the first home is found by substituting the actual values of the three variables into the regression equation. For example, from Table 14–3, the first home's mean outside temperature was 35 degrees, it had 3 inches of attic insulation, and did not have an attached garage. The actual heating cost was \$250, and the estimated heating cost is \$221.08, found by

$$Y' = 393.67 - 3.96(35) - 11.33(3) + 77.43(0) = 221.08$$

The residual is in the last column. It is 28.92, found by 250 − 221.08. The residuals for the 19 other values are computed similarly.

We can use the last column, the residuals, to verify the normality assumption. The following MINITAB output shows a histogram of the residuals. Both charts indicate

TABLE 14–4 Summary of Actual Costs, Estimated Costs, and Residuals for Salsberry Realty Problem

Home	Actual Cost, Y	Estimated Cost, Y'	Residual $Y - Y'$
1	250	221.08	28.92
2	360	310.94	49.06
3	165	171.80	−6.80
4	43	88.09	−45.09
5	92	79.62	12.38
6	200	218.22	−18.22
7	355	363.52	−8.52
8	290	330.08	−40.08
9	230	208.54	21.46
10	120	153.21	−33.21
11	73	43.87	29.13
12	205	224.37	−19.37
13	400	335.25	64.75
14	320	271.34	48.66
15	72	65.43	6.57
16	272	335.25	−63.25
17	94	84.68	9.32
18	190	222.06	−32.06
19	235	184.78	50.22
20	139	195.56	−56.56

that the distribution of the residuals is somewhat normal, as required in the assumptions. To interpret the output, note that the residuals are tallied into classes with a class interval of 20: −70 up to −50, with a midpoint of −60; −50 up to −30, with a midpoint of −40; and so on. The details of the first three classes are:

Class	Midpoint	Residuals	Count
−70 up to −50	−60	−63.25, −56.56	2
−50 up to −30	−40	−45.09, −40.08, −33.21, −32.06	4
−30 up to −10	−20	−19.37, −18.22	2

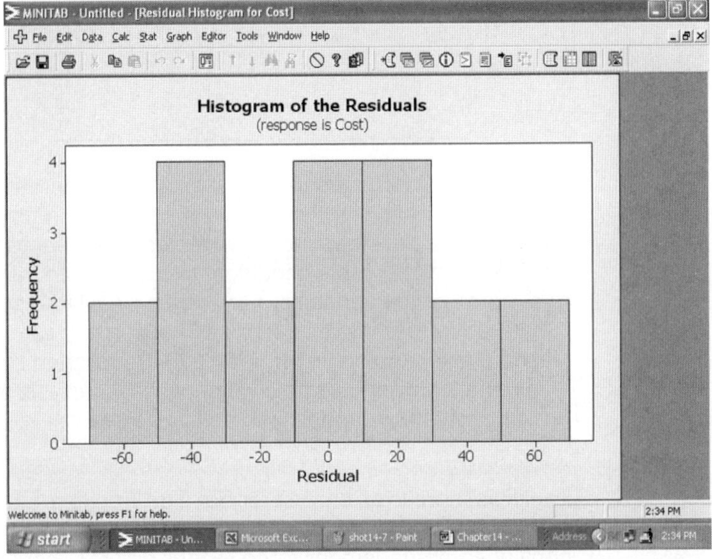

Homoscedasticity

The assumptions for regression analysis also require that the residuals remain constant for all values of Y'. Recall that this condition is called **homoscedasticity.** To check for homoscedasticity, the residuals are plotted against the fitted values of Y. That is, we develop a scatter plot with the values in the Estimated Cost column of Table 14–4 plotted on the horizontal axis and the residuals on the vertical axis. The first plot is 221.08 for X and 28.92 for Y. Because the spread of the residuals is the same for any Y', we conclude that the assumption has not been violated.

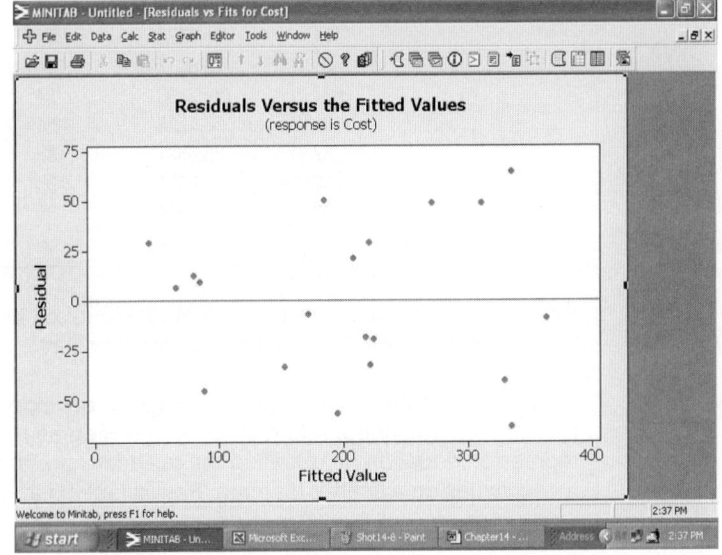

Following are two examples in which the homoscedasticity requirement is not met. Note in the first example, the plot of residuals is funnel-shaped. That is, as the fitted Y values increase, so does the variation in the residuals. In the second example, there is a pattern to the residuals. The residuals seem to take the shape of a polynomial, or a second-degree equation.

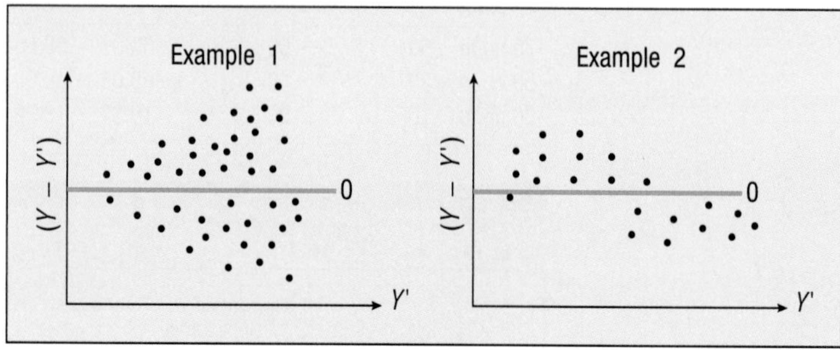

What problems are caused by residuals that fail to show homoscedasticity? The standard deviations of the regression coefficients will be understated (too small), causing potential independent variables to appear to be significant when they may not be. The remedy for this condition is to select other independent variables or to transform some of the variables. For a more detailed discussion of residual analysis, refer to an advanced text, such as *Applied Linear Regression Models* by Kutner, Nachtscheim, and Neter (4th ed., 2004, published by McGraw-Hill/ Irwin).

In the following example we show how analysis of the residuals can lead to an improved regression model.

EXAMPLE

Paul Roseboro is an analyst for Bar Nun Trucking. He is studying the effect of tire pressure on fuel economy (Mpg) for a fleet of 24 sedans used by regional supervisors. He convinced management to have four different cars driven with a tire pressure of 30 pounds per square inch, four at 31, four at 32, and so forth. He obtained the following sample information.

Pressure	Mileage	Pressure	Mileage
30	29.8851	33	37.0772
30	27.5577	33	38.2858
30	27.0726	33	36.1861
30	26.4422	33	40.2397
31	31.7876	34	33.0048
31	29.8017	34	34.6957
31	30.2135	34	35.4852
31	36.1228	34	35.1910
32	35.6521	35	34.3259
32	36.6301	35	32.0578
32	37.7559	35	29.4446
32	35.1194	35	32.4416

Develop an appropriate regression model to relate tire pressure to fuel effectiveness. What appears to be the best level for tire pressure?

SOLUTION

Paul used a statistical software package to develop a regression equation, with tire pressure as the independent variable and Mpg as the dependent variable. From this regression equation he obtained the residuals and the fitted values. Finally he plotted these values on a scatter diagram. Paul is looking at the following plot of the residuals versus the fitted values. What does it show? Are there any problems with the regression assumptions?

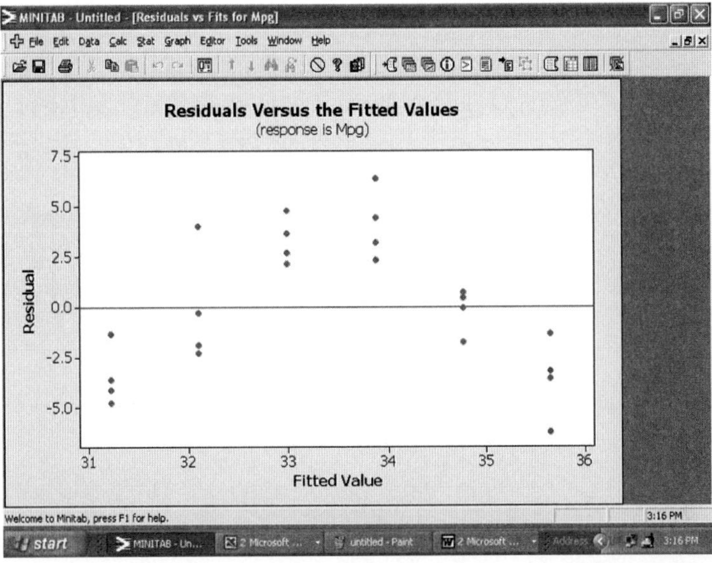

The residuals ($Y - Y'$) are on the vertical axis and fitted values of Y' are on the horizontal axis. It appears that the errors or residuals are not random. Instead, there is a definite pattern to the residuals. They are consistently negative for high and low values of tire pressure and they are consistently positive in the middle of the range.

A data plot with the linear regression equation lends even more insight. Here we have the dependent variable Mpg on the vertical axis and tire pressure on the horizontal axis.

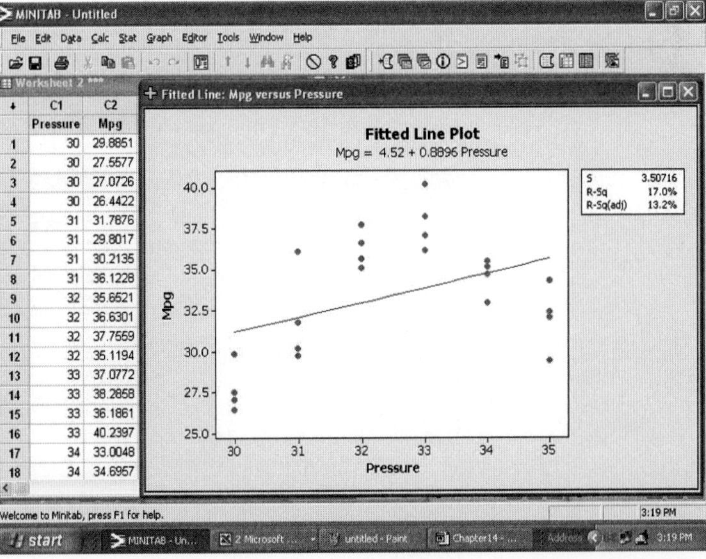

	C1 Pressure	C2 Mpg
1	30	29.8851
2	30	27.5577
3	30	27.0726
4	30	26.4422
5	31	31.7876
6	31	29.8017
7	31	30.2135
8	31	36.1228
9	32	35.6521
10	32	36.6301
11	32	37.7559
12	32	35.1194
13	33	37.0772
14	33	38.2858
15	33	36.1861
16	33	40.2397
17	34	33.0048
18	34	34.6957

The regression equation is Mpg = 4.52 + 0.8896 Pressure. Notice the value of R^2, namely 17 percent (reported in the upper right corner of the output), is rather low. To put it another way, only 17 percent of the variation in mileage is accounted for by the differences in tire pressure. From the plot we can "see" that the relationship between the variables is not linear.

This pattern indicates the relationship may be curvilinear. So Paul decides to fit a quadratic or second-degree equation to the data. His new equation is of the general form:

$$Y' = a + b_1X_1 + b_2X_1^2$$

To create a second independent variable for this analysis, Paul squares each tire pressure. Generally, a variable and its square tend to behave independently of each other. Then he can use multiple regression to determine the second degree equation. In other words, he fits the tire pressure and the tire pressure squared with the Mpg.

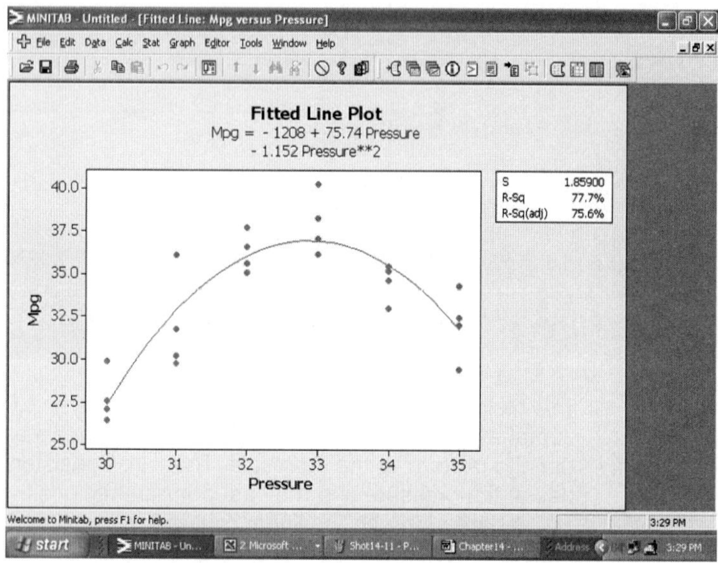

The new regression equation is:

$$\text{Mpg} = -1208 + 75.74 \text{ Pressure} - 1.152 \text{ Pressure**2}$$

The R^2 value has increased to 77.7 percent. That is, the independent variables tire pressure and tire pressure squared now account for nearly 78 percent of the variation in mileage. This is a substantial improvement.

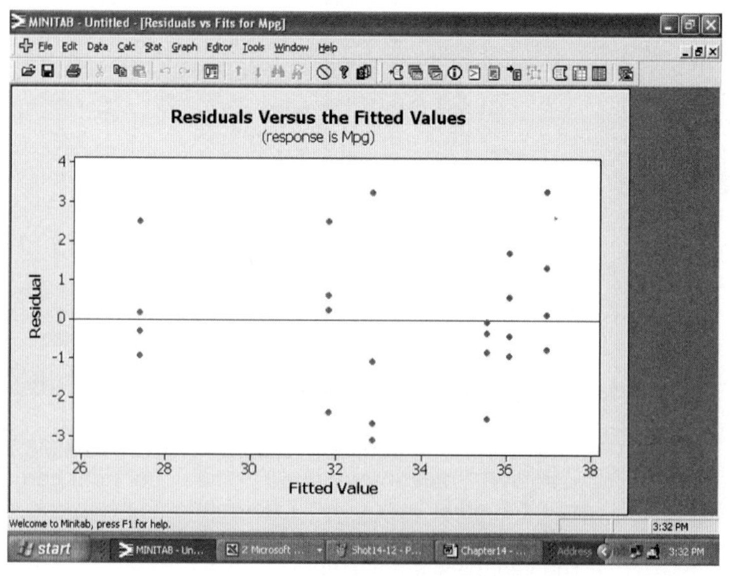

What about the problem with the residuals not being in a random pattern? Paul plots the residuals obtained from the quadratic equation against the variable tire pressure and there seems to be no pattern. The residuals look "more random" now.

What would be the optimum value for the tire pressure? If we look at the scatter plot with the fitted regression equation added, then we can see the mileage increased up to about 33 pounds and then began to decline.

This plot also suggests that the optimum tire pressure should be 33 pounds per square inch. In summary, by using a quadratic equation we were able to increase the explained variation from 17 percent to 78 percent, eliminate the problem with the residuals, and find the most favorable tire pressure of 33 pounds.

Chapter Outline

I. Multiple regression and correlation analysis is based on these assumptions.
- **A.** There is a linear relationship between the independent variables and the dependent variable.
- **B.** The dependent variable is a continuous variable measured on either an interval or ratio scale.
- **C.** The residual variation is the same for all fitted values of Y.
- **D.** The residuals follow the normal distribution.
- **E.** Successive observations of the dependent variable are uncorrelated.

II. The general form of the multiple regression equation is:

$$Y' = a + b_1X_1 + b_2X_2 + \cdots + b_kX_k \qquad \textbf{[14–1]}$$

where Y' is the estimated value, a is the Y-intercept, the b_i refers to the sample regression coefficients, and the X_i refers to the values of the various independent variables.
- **A.** There can be any number of independent variables.
- **B.** The least squares criterion is used to develop the equation.
- **C.** A statistical software package is needed to determine a and the various b values.

III. There are two measures of the effectiveness of the regression equation.
- **A.** The multiple standard error of estimate is similar to the standard deviation.
  1. It is measured in the same units as the dependent variable.
  2. It is difficult to determine what is a large value and what is a small value of the standard error.
- **B.** The coefficient of multiple determination also measures the effectiveness of a set of independent variables.
  1. It reports the fraction of the variation in the dependent variable that is accounted for by the set of independent variables.
  2. It may range from 0 to 1.

IV. An ANOVA table shows the variation in the dependent variable explained by the regression equation and the residual or error variation.

V. A correlation matrix shows all possible simple correlation coefficients between pairs of variables.

VI. A global test is used to investigate whether any of the independent variables have significant regression coefficients.
- **A.** The null hypothesis is: All the regression coefficients are zero.
- **B.** The alternate hypothesis is: At least one regression coefficient is not zero.
- **C.** The test statistic is the F distribution with k (the number of independent variables) degrees of freedom in the numerator and $n - (k + 1)$ degrees of freedom in the denominator, where n is the sample size.
- **D.** The formula to calculate the value of the test statistic for the global test is:

$$F = \frac{\text{SSR}/k}{\text{SSE}/[n - (k + 1)]} \qquad \textbf{[14–4]}$$

VII. The test for individual variables determines which independent variables have nonzero regression coefficients.

A. The variables that have zero regression coefficients are usually dropped from the analysis.

B. The test statistic is the t distribution with $n - (k + 1)$ degrees of freedom.

C. The formula to calculate the value of the test statistic for the individual test is:

$$t = \frac{b_i - 0}{s_{b_i}} \qquad \textbf{[14–5]}$$

VIII. Dummy variables are used to represent qualitative variables and can assume only one of two possible conditions.

IX. A residual is the difference between the actual value of Y and the predicted value of Y.

A. Residuals should be approximately normally distributed. Histograms are useful in checking this requirement.

B. A plot of the residuals and their corresponding Y' values is useful for showing that there are no trends or patterns in the residuals.

Pronunciation Key

SYMBOL	MEANING	PRONUNCIATION
b_1	Regression coefficient for the first independent variable	*b sub 1*
b_k	Regression coefficient for any independent variable	*b sub k*
$s_{y \cdot 12 \cdots k}$	Multiple standard error of estimate	*s sub y dot 1, 2, . . . , k*

Chapter Exercises

9. A multiple regression equation yields the following partial results.

Source	Sum of Squares	*df*
Regression	750	4
Error	500	35

a. What is the total sample size?
b. How many independent variables are being considered?
c. Compute the coefficient of determination.
d. Compute the standard error of estimate.
e. Test the hypothesis that none of the regression coefficients is equal to zero. Let $\alpha = .05$.

10. In a multiple regression equation two independent variables are considered, and the sample size is 25. The regression coefficients and the standard errors are as follows.

$$b_1 = 2.676 \qquad s_{b_1} = 0.56$$

$$b_2 = -0.880 \qquad s_{b_2} = 0.71$$

Conduct a test of hypothesis to determine whether either independent variable has a coefficient equal to zero. Would you consider deleting either variable from the regression equation? Use the .05 significance level.

11. The following output was obtained.
a. What is the sample size?
b. Compute the value of R^2.
c. Compute the multiple standard error of estimate.
d. Conduct a global test of hypothesis to determine whether any of the regression coefficients are significant. Use the .05 significance level.
e. Test the regression coefficients individually. Would you consider omitting any variable(s)? If so, which one(s)? Use the .05 significance level.

Analysis of variance

SOURCE	DF	SS	MS
Regression	5	100	20
Error	20	40	2
Total	25	140	

Predictor	Coef	StDev	t-ratio
Constant	3.00	1.50	2.00
X_1	4.00	3.00	1.33
X_2	3.00	0.20	15.00
X_3	0.20	0.05	4.00
X_4	−2.50	1.00	−2.50
X_5	3.00	4.00	0.75

12. In a multiple regression equation $k = 5$ and $n = 20$, the MSE value is 5.10, and SS total is 519.68. At the .05 significance level, can we conclude that any of the regression coefficients are not equal to 0?

13. The district manager of Jasons, a large discount electronics chain, is investigating why certain stores in her region are performing better than others. She believes that three factors are related to total sales: the number of competitors in the region, the population in the surrounding area, and the amount spent on advertising. From her district, consisting of several hundred stores, she selects a random sample of 30 stores. For each store she gathered the following information.

Y = total sales last year (in \$ thousands).
X_1 = number of competitors in the region.
X_2 = population of the region (in millions).
X_3 = advertising expense (in \$ thousands).

The sample data were run on MINITAB, with the following results.

Analysis of variance

SOURCE	DF	SS	MS
Regression	3	3050.00	1016.67
Error	26	2200.00	84.62
Total	29	5250.00	

Predictor	Coef	StDev	t-ratio
Constant	14.00	7.00	2.00
X_1	−1.00	0.70	−1.43
X_2	30.00	5.20	5.77
X_3	0.20	0.08	2.50

a. What are the estimated sales for the Bryne Store, which has four competitors, a regional population of 0.4 (400,000), and advertising expense of 30 ($30,000)?
b. Compute the R^2 value.
c. Compute the multiple standard error of estimate.
d. Conduct a global test of hypothesis to determine whether any of the regression coefficients are not equal to zero. Use the .05 level of significance.
e. Conduct tests of hypotheses to determine which of the independent variables have significant regression coefficients. Which variables would you consider eliminating? Use the .05 significance level.

14. Suppose that the sales manager of a large automotive parts distributor wants to estimate as early as April the total annual sales of a region. On the basis of regional sales, the total sales for the company can also be estimated. If, based on past experience, it is found that the April estimates of annual sales are reasonably accurate, then in future years the April forecast could be used to revise production schedules and maintain the correct inventory at the retail outlets.

Several factors appear to be related to sales, including the number of retail outlets in the region stocking the company's parts, the number of automobiles in the region registered as of April 1, and the total personal income for the first quarter of the year. Five independent variables were finally selected as being the most important (according to the sales manager). Then the data were gathered for a recent year. The total annual sales for that year for each region were also recorded. Note in the following table that for region 1 there were 1,739 retail outlets stocking the company's automotive parts, there were 9,270,000 registered automobiles in the region as of April 1, and sales for that year were $37,702,000.

Annual Sales ($ millions), Y	Number of Retail Outlets, X_1	Number of Automobiles Registered (millions), X_2	Personal Income ($ billions), X_3	Average Age of Automobiles (years), X_4	Number of Supervisors, X_5
37.702	1,739	9.27	85.4	3.5	9.0
24.196	1,221	5.86	60.7	5.0	5.0
32.055	1,846	8.81	68.1	4.4	7.0
3.611	120	3.81	20.2	4.0	5.0
17.625	1,096	10.31	33.8	3.5	7.0
45.919	2,290	11.62	95.1	4.1	13.0
29.600	1,687	8.96	69.3	4.1	15.0
8.114	241	6.28	16.3	5.9	11.0
20.116	649	7.77	34.9	5.5	16.0
12.994	1,427	10.92	15.1	4.1	10.0

a. Consider the following correlation matrix. Which single variable has the strongest correlation with the dependent variable? The correlations between the independent variables "outlets" and "income" and between "cars" and "outlets" are fairly strong. Could this be a problem? What is this condition called?

```
          sales    outlets      cars    income      age
outlets   0.899
cars      0.605      0.775
income    0.964      0.825     0.409
age      -0.323     -0.489    -0.447    -0.349
bosses    0.286      0.183     0.395     0.155    0.291
```

b. The following regression equation was obtained using the five independent variables. What percent of the variation is explained by the regression equation?

```
The regression equation is
sales = -19.7 - 0.00063 outlets + 1.74 cars + 0.410 income +
        2.04 age - 0.034 bosses

        Predictor         Coef        StDev     t-ratio
        Constant       -19.672        5.422       -3.63
        outlets      -0.000629     0.002638       -0.24
        cars            1.7399       0.5530        3.15
        income         0.40994      0.04385        9.35
        age             2.0357       0.8779        2.32
        bosses         -0.0344       0.1880       -0.18

Analysis of Variance
        SOURCE              DF           SS          MS
        Regression           5      1593.81      318.76
        Error                4         9.08        2.27
        Total                9      1602.89
```

c. Conduct a global test of hypothesis to determine whether any of the regression coefficients are not zero. Use the .05 significance level.
d. Conduct a test of hypothesis on each of the independent variables. Would you consider eliminating "outlets" and "bosses"? Use the .05 significance level.
e. The regression has been rerun below with "outlets" and "bosses" eliminated. Compute the coefficient of determination. How much has R^2 changed from the previous analysis?

```
The regression equation is
sales = −18.9 + 1.61 cars + 0.400 income + 1.96 age

      Predictor          Coef        StDev      t-ratio
      Constant        −18.924        3.636        −5.20
      Cars             1.6129       0.1979         8.15
      Income          0.40031      0.01569        25.52
      Age              1.9637       0.5846         3.36

Analysis of Variance
      SOURCE            DF          SS         MS
      Regression         3     1593.66     531.22
      Error              6        9.23       1.54
      Total              9     1602.89
```

f. Following is a histogram of the residuals. Does the normality assumption appear reasonable?

```
Histogram of residual N = 10

Midpoint  Count
 −1.5   1    *
 −1.0   1    *
 −0.5   2   **
 −0.0   2   **
  0.5   2   **
  1.0   1    *
  1.5   1    *
```

g. Following is a plot of the fitted values of Y (i.e., Y') and the residuals. Do you see any violations of the assumptions?

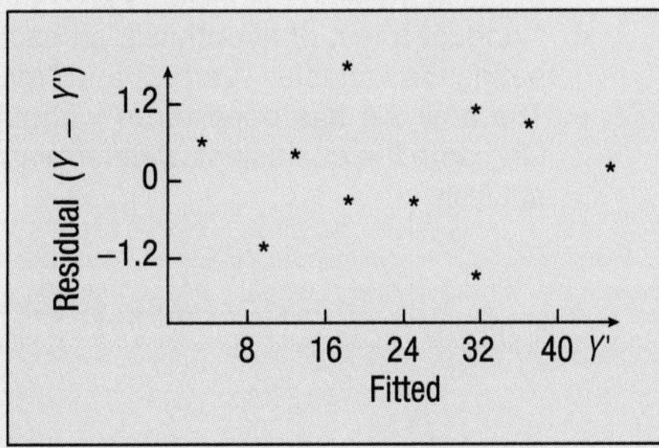

15. The administrator of a new paralegal program at Seagate Technical College wants to estimate the grade point average in the new program. He thought that high school GPA, the verbal score on the Scholastic Aptitude Test (SAT), and the mathematics score on the SAT would be good predictors of paralegal GPA. The data on nine students are:

Student	High School GPA	SAT Verbal	SAT Math	Paralegal GPA
1	3.25	480	410	3.21
2	1.80	290	270	1.68
3	2.89	420	410	3.58
4	3.81	500	600	3.92
5	3.13	500	490	3.00
6	2.81	430	460	2.82
7	2.20	320	490	1.65
8	2.14	530	480	2.30
9	2.63	469	440	2.33

a. Consider the following correlation matrix. Which variable has the strongest correlation with the dependent variable? Some of the correlations among the independent variables are strong. Does this appear to be a problem?

```
          legal      gpa     verbal
gpa       0.911
verbal    0.616     0.609
math      0.487     0.636     0.599
```

b. Consider the following output. Compute the coefficient of multiple determination.

```
The regression equation is
legal = −0.411 + 1.20 gpa + 0.00163 verbal − 0.00194 math

Predictor          Coef           StDev        t-ratio
Constant        −0.4111          0.7823          −0.53
gpa              1.2014          0.2955           4.07
verbal         0.001629        0.002147           0.76
math          −0.001939        0.002074          −0.94

Analysis of Variance
SOURCE         DF        SS          MS
Regression      3      4.3595      1.4532
Error           5      0.7036      0.1407
Total           8      5.0631
```

c. Conduct a global test of hypothesis from the preceding output. Does it appear that any of the regression coefficients are not equal to zero?

d. Conduct a test of hypothesis on each independent variable. Would you consider eliminating the variables "verbal" and "math"? Let $\alpha = .05$.

e. The analysis has been rerun without "verbal" and "math." See the following output. Compute the coefficient of determination. How much has R^2 changed from the previous analysis?

```
The regression equation is
legal = − 0.454 + 1.16 gpa

  Predictor        Coef       StDev      t-ratio
  Constant      −0.4542      0.5542       −0.82
  gpa            1.1589      0.1977        5.86

Analysis of Variance
SOURCE         DF        SS        MS
Regression      1     4.2061    4.2061
Error           7     0.8570    0.1224
Total           8     5.0631
```

f. Following is a histogram of the residuals. Does the normality assumption for the residuals seem reasonable?

```
Histogram of residual N = 9

Midpoint        Count
  -0.4            1   *
  -0.2            3   ***
   0.0            3   ***
   0.2            1   *
   0.4            0
   0.6            1   *
```

g. Following is a plot of the residuals and the Y' values. Do you see any violation of the assumptions?

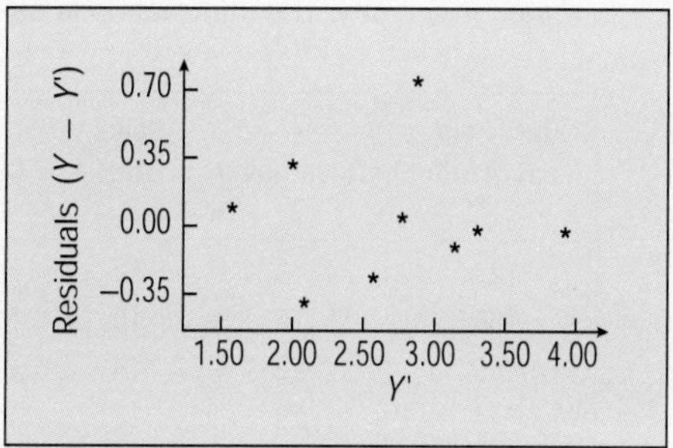

The following problems require a software package.

16. Mike Wilde is president of the teachers' union for Otsego School District. In preparing for upcoming negotiations, he would like to investigate the salary structure of classroom teachers in the district. He believes there are three factors that affect a teacher's salary: years of experience, a rating of teaching effectiveness given by the principal, and whether the teacher has a master's degree. A random sample of 20 teachers resulted in the following data.

Salary ($ thousands) Y	Years of Experience X_1	Principal's Rating X_2	Master's Degree* X_3	Salary ($ thousands) Y	Years of Experience X_1	Principal's Rating X_2	Master's Degree* X_3
21.1	8	35	0	15.7	1	30	0
23.6	5	43	0	20.6	5	44	0
19.3	2	51	1	41.8	23	84	1
33.0	15	60	1	36.7	17	76	0
28.6	11	73	0	28.4	12	68	1
35.0	14	80	1	23.6	14	25	0
32.0	9	76	0	31.8	8	90	1
26.8	7	54	1	20.7	4	62	0
38.6	22	55	1	22.8	2	80	1
21.7	3	90	1	32.8	8	72	0

*1 = yes, 0 = no.

a. Develop a correlation matrix. Which independent variable has the strongest correlation with the dependent variable? Does it appear there will be any problems with multicollinearity?

b. Determine the regression equation. What salary would you estimate for a teacher with five years' experience, a rating by the principal of 60, and no master's degree?

c. Conduct a global test of hypothesis to determine whether any of the net regression coefficients differ from zero. Use the .05 significance level.

d. Conduct a test of hypothesis for the individual regression coefficients. Would you consider deleting any of the independent variables? Use the .05 significance level.

e. If your conclusion in part (d) was to delete one or more independent variables, run the analysis again without those variables.

f. Determine the residuals for the equation of part (e). Use a histogram to verify that the distribution of the residuals is approximately normal.

g. Plot the residuals computed in part (f) in a scatter diagram with the residuals on the Y-axis and the Y' values on the X-axis. Does the plot reveal any violations of the assumptions of regression?

17. The district sales manager for a major automobile manufacturer is studying car sales. Specifically, he would like to determine what factors affect the number of cars sold at a dealership. To investigate, he randomly selects 12 dealers. From these dealers he obtains the number of cars sold last month, the minutes of radio advertising purchased last month, the number of full-time salespeople employed in the dealership, and whether the dealer is located in the city. The information is as follows:

Cars Sold Last Month Y	Advertising X_1	Sales Force X_2	City X_3	Cars Sold Last Month Y	Advertising X_1	Sales Force X_2	City X_3
127	18	10	Yes	161	25	14	Yes
138	15	15	No	180	26	17	Yes
159	22	14	Yes	102	15	7	No
144	23	12	Yes	163	24	16	Yes
139	17	12	No	106	18	10	No
128	16	12	Yes	149	25	11	Yes

a. Develop a correlation matrix. Which independent variable has the strongest correlation with the dependent variable? Does it appear there will be any problems with multicollinearity?

b. Determine the regression equation. How many cars would you expect to be sold by a dealership employing 20 salespeople, purchasing 15 minutes of advertising, and located in a city?

c. Conduct a global test of hypothesis to determine whether any of the net regression coefficients differ from zero. Let $\alpha = .05$.

d. Conduct a test of hypothesis for the individual regression coefficients. Would you consider deleting any of the independent variables? Let $\alpha = .05$.

e. If your conclusion in part (d) was to delete one or more independent variables, run the analysis again without those variables.

f. Determine the residuals for the equation of part (e). Use a histogram to verify that the distribution of the residuals is approximately normal.

g. Plot the residuals computed in part (f) in a scatter diagram with the residuals on the Y-axis and the Y' values on the X-axis. Does the plot reveal any violations of the assumptions of regression?

18. Fran's Convenience Marts are located throughout metropolitan Erie, Pennsylvania. Fran, the owner, would like to expand into other communities in northwestern Pennsylvania and southwestern New York, such as Jamestown, Corry, Meadville, and Warren. As part of her presentation to the local bank, she would like to better understand the factors that make a particular outlet profitable. She must do all the work herself, so she will not be able to study all her outlets. She selects a random sample of 15 marts and records the average daily sales (Y), the floor space (area), the number of parking spaces, and the median income of families in that ZIP code region for each. The sample information is reported on the next page.

Sampled Mart	Daily Sales	Store Area	Parking Spaces	Income ($ thousands)
1	$1,840	532	6	44
2	1,746	478	4	51
3	1,812	530	7	45
4	1,806	508	7	46
5	1,792	514	5	44
6	1,825	556	6	46
7	1,811	541	4	49
8	1,803	513	6	52
9	1,830	532	5	46
10	1,827	537	5	46
11	1,764	499	3	48
12	1,825	510	8	47
13	1,763	490	4	48
14	1,846	516	8	45
15	1,815	482	7	43

a. Determine the regression equation.
b. What is the value of R^2? Comment on the value.
c. Conduct a global hypothesis test to determine if any of the independent variables are different from zero.
d. Conduct individual hypothesis tests to determine if any of the independent variables can be dropped.
e. If variables are dropped, recompute the regression equation and R^2.

19. How important is GPA in determining the starting salary of recent business school graduates? Does graduating from a business school increase the starting salary? The Director of Undergraduate Studies at a major university wanted to study these questions. She gathered the following sample information on 15 graduates last spring to investigate these questions.

Student	Salary	GPA	Business
1	$31.5	3.245	0
2	33.0	3.278	0
3	34.1	3.520	1
4	35.4	3.740	1
5	34.2	3.520	1
6	34.0	3.421	1
7	34.5	3.410	1
8	35.0	3.630	1
9	34.7	3.355	1
10	32.5	3.080	0
11	31.5	3.025	0
12	32.2	3.146	0
13	34.0	3.465	1
14	32.8	3.245	0
15	31.8	3.025	0

The salary is reported in $000, GPA on the traditional 4-point scale. A 1 indicates the student graduated from a school of business; a 0 indicates that the student graduated from one of the other schools.

a. Develop a correlation matrix. Do you see any problems with multicollinearity?
b. Determine the regression equation. Discuss the regression equation. How much does graduating from a college of business add to a starting salary? What starting salary would you estimate for a student with a GPA of 3.00 who graduated from a college of business?

c. What is the value of R^2? Can we conclude that this value is greater than 0?
d. Would you consider deleting either of the independent variables?
e. Plot the residuals in a histogram. Is there any problem with the normality assumption?
f. Plot the fitted values against the residuals. Does this plot indicate any problems with homoscedasticity?

20. A mortgage department of a large bank is studying its recent loans. Of particular interest is how such factors as the value of the home (in thousands of dollars), education level of the head of the household, age of the head of the household, current monthly mortgage payment (in dollars), and gender of the head of the household (male = 1, female = 0) relate to the family income. Are these variables effective predictors of the income of the household? A random sample of 25 recent loans is obtained.

Income ($ thousands)	Value ($ thousands)	Years of Education	Age	Mortgage Payment	Gender
$40.3	$190	14	53	$230	1
39.6	121	15	49	370	1
40.8	161	14	44	397	1
40.3	161	14	39	181	1
40.0	179	14	53	378	0
38.1	99	14	46	304	0
40.4	114	15	42	285	1
40.7	202	14	49	551	0
40.8	184	13	37	370	0
37.1	90	14	43	135	0
39.9	181	14	48	332	1
40.4	143	15	54	217	1
38.0	132	14	44	490	0
39.0	127	14	37	220	0
39.5	153	14	50	270	1
40.6	145	14	50	279	1
40.3	174	15	52	329	1
40.1	177	15	47	274	0
41.7	188	15	49	433	1
40.1	153	15	53	333	1
40.6	150	16	58	148	0
40.4	173	13	42	390	1
40.9	163	14	46	142	1
40.1	150	15	50	343	0
38.5	139	14	45	373	0

a. Determine the regression equation.
b. What is the value of R^2? Comment on the value.
c. Conduct a global hypothesis test to determine whether any of the independent variables are different from zero.
d. Conduct individual hypothesis tests to determine whether any of the independent variables can be dropped.
e. If variables are dropped, recompute the regression equation and R^2.

21. Fred G. Hire is the manager of human resources at Crescent Tool and Die, Inc. As part of his yearly report to the CEO, he is required to present an analysis of the salaried employees. Because there are over 1,000 employees, he does not have the staff to gather information on each salaried employee, so he selects a random sample of 30. For each employee, he records monthly salary; service at Crescent, in months; gender (1 = male, 0 = female); and

whether the employee has a technical or clerical job. Those working technical jobs are coded 1, and those who are clerical 0.

Sampled Employee	Monthly Salary	Length of Service	Age	Gender	Job
1	$1,769	93	42	1	0
2	1,740	104	33	1	0
3	1,941	104	42	1	1
4	2,367	126	57	1	1
5	2,467	98	30	1	1
6	1,640	99	49	1	1
7	1,756	94	35	1	0
8	1,706	96	46	0	1
9	1,767	124	56	0	0
10	1,200	73	23	0	1
11	1,706	110	67	0	1
12	1,985	90	36	0	1
13	1,555	104	53	0	0
14	1,749	81	29	0	0
15	2,056	106	45	1	0
16	1,729	113	55	0	1
17	2,186	129	46	1	1
18	1,858	97	39	0	1
19	1,819	101	43	1	1
20	1,350	91	35	1	1
21	2,030	100	40	1	0
22	2,550	123	59	1	0
23	1,544	88	30	0	0
24	1,766	117	60	1	1
25	1,937	107	45	1	1
26	1,691	105	32	0	1
27	1,623	86	33	0	0
28	1,791	131	56	0	1
29	2,001	95	30	1	1
30	1,874	98	47	1	0

a. Determine the regression equation, using salary as the dependent variable and the other four variables as independent variables.
b. What is the value of R^2? Comment on this value.
c. Conduct a global test of hypothesis to determine whether any of the independent variables are different from 0.
d. Conduct an individual test to determine whether any of the independent variables can be dropped.
e. Rerun the regression equation, using only the independent variables that are significant. How much more does a man earn per month than a woman? Does it make a difference whether the employee has a technical or a clerical job?

22. Many regions along the coast in North and South Carolina and Georgia have experienced rapid population growth over the last 10 years. It is expected that the growth will continue over the next 10 years. This has resulted in many of the large grocery store chains building new stores in the region. The Kelley's Super Grocery Stores, Inc. chain is no exception. The director of planning for Kelley's Super Grocery Stores wants to study adding more stores in this region. He believes there are two main factors that indicate the amount families spend on groceries. The first is their income and the other is the number of people in the family. The director gathered the following sample information.

Family	Food	Income	Size
1	$5.04	$73.98	4
2	4.08	54.90	2
3	5.76	94.14	4
4	3.48	52.02	1
5	4.20	65.70	2
6	4.80	53.64	4
7	4.32	79.74	3
8	5.04	68.58	4
9	6.12	165.60	5
10	3.24	64.80	1
11	4.80	138.42	3
12	3.24	125.82	1
13	6.60	77.58	7
14	4.92	171.36	2
15	6.60	82.08	9
16	5.40	141.30	3
17	6.00	36.90	5
18	5.40	56.88	4
19	3.36	71.82	1
20	4.68	69.48	3
21	4.32	54.36	2
22	5.52	87.66	5
23	4.56	38.16	3
24	5.40	43.74	7
25	4.80	48.42	5

Food and income are reported in thousands of dollars per year, and the variable "Size" refers to the number of people in the household.

a. Develop a correlation matrix. Do you see any problems with multicollinearity?

b. Determine the regression equation. Discuss the regression equation. How much does an additional family member add to the amount spent on food?

c. What is the value of R^2? Can we conclude that this value is greater than 0?

d. Would you consider deleting either of the independent variables?

e. Plot the residuals in a histogram. Is there any problem with the normality assumption?

f. Plot the fitted values against the residuals. Does this plot indicate any problems with homoscedasticity?

23. An investment advisor is studying the relationship between a common stock's price to earnings ratio (P/E) and factors that she thinks would influence it. She has the following data on the earnings per share (EPS) and the dividend percentage (Yield) for a sample of 20 stocks.

Stock	P/E	EPS	Yield	Stock	P/E	EPS	Yield
1	20.79	2.46	1.42	11	1.35	2.93	2.59
2	3.03	2.69	4.05	12	25.43	2.07	1.04
3	44.46	−0.28	4.16	13	22.14	2.19	3.52
4	41.72	−0.45	1.27	14	24.21	−0.83	1.56
5	18.96	1.60	3.39	15	30.91	2.29	2.23
6	18.42	2.32	3.86	16	35.79	1.64	3.36
7	34.82	0.81	4.56	17	18.99	3.07	1.98
8	30.43	2.13	1.62	18	30.21	1.71	3.07
9	29.97	2.22	5.10	19	32.88	0.35	2.21
10	10.86	1.44	1.17	20	15.19	5.02	3.50

a. Develop a multiple linear regression with P/E as the dependent variable.

b. Are either of the two independent variables an effective predictor of P/E?

c. Interpret the regression coefficients.

d. Do any of these stocks look particularly undervalued?
e. Plot the residuals and check the normality assumption. Plot the fitted values against the residuals.
f. Does there appear to be any problems with homoscedasticity?
g. Develop a correlation matrix. Do any of the correlations indicate multicollinearity?

24. Listed below is recent data from the United States Bureau of Labor Statistics on the percent changes in Output/Hour, Unit Labor Costs, and Real Hourly Compensation for nonfarm payrolls in the United States.

Year	Quarter	Output/Hour	Labor Cost	Compensation
1997	1	1.1	1.1	−0.1
1997	2	4.5	−2.6	0.9
1997	3	3.0	0.7	2.0
1997	4	0.5	5.6	0.8
1998	1	4.9	2.0	6.2
1998	2	0.6	5.1	4.6
1998	3	1.9	2.7	3.0
1998	4	4.3	−0.4	2.0
1999	1	2.4	4.8	5.5
1999	2	−0.8	1.3	−2.2
1999	3	3.7	0.0	0.8
1999	4	6.3	−0.5	2.5
2000	1	0.2	14.9	10.7
2000	2	6.0	−3.6	−0.7
2000	3	0.6	8.0	4.9
2000	4	1.7	1.4	0.2
2001	1	−1.5	4.3	−0.9
2001	2	−0.1	0.3	−2.9
2001	3	2.1	−1.1	0.3
2001	4	7.3	−5.4	1.8
2002	1	8.6	−5.3	1.4
2002	2	1.7	2.2	0.5
2002	3	5.1	−0.2	3.0

a. Develop a multiple regression equation with output and labor as independent variables and compensation as the dependent variable.
b. Conduct a global test. Can we conclude the value of R^2 is greater than zero?
c. Test each variable for significance. Should any be dropped?
d. Plot the residuals and verify the normality assumption.
e. Plot the fitted value against the residuals. Is there a problem with homoscedasticity?
f. Construct a correlation matrix. Is there a problem with multicollinearity?

exercises.com

25. The National Institute of Standards and Technology provides several datasets to allow any user to test the accuracy of their statistical software. Go to the website: http://www.itl.nist.gov/div898/strd. Select the **Dataset Archives** section and, within that, the **Linear Regression** section. You will find the names of 11 small data sets stored in ASCII format on this page. Select one and run the data through your statistical software. Compare your results with the "official" results of the federal government.

26. As described in the examples in Chapters 12 and 13, many real estate companies and rental agencies now publish their listings on the Web. One example is the Dunes Realty Company, located in Garden City and Surfside Beaches in South Carolina. Go to the website http://www.dunes.com, select **Vacation Rentals,** then **Beach Home Search,** then indicate 5 bedroom, accommodations for 14 people, oceanfront, and no pool or floating dock, select a week, indicate that you are willing to spend $8,000 per week, and then click on **Search Beach Homes.** The output should include details on the cottages that met your criteria. Develop a multiple linear regression equation using the rental price per week as the dependent variable and number of bedrooms, number of bathrooms, and how many people the cottage will accommodate as independent variables. Analyze the regression equations. Would you consider deleting any independent variables? What is the coefficient of determination? If you delete any of the variables, rerun the regression equation and discuss the new equation.

Dataset Exercises

27. Refer to the Real Estate data which reports information on homes sold in the Denver, Colorado, area during the last year. Use the selling price of the home as the dependent variable and determine the regression equation with number of bedrooms, size of the house, whether there is a pool, whether there is an attached garage, distance from the center of the city, and number of bathrooms as independent variables.
   a. Write out the regression equation. Discuss each of the variables. For example, are you surprised that the regression coefficient for distance from the center of the city is negative? How much does a garage or a swimming pool add to the selling price of a home?
   b. Determine the value of R^2. Interpret.
   c. Develop a correlation matrix. Which independent variables have strong or weak correlations with the dependent variable? Do you see any problems with multicollinearity?
   d. Conduct the global test on the set of independent variables. Interpret.
   e. Conduct a test of hypothesis on each of the independent variables. Would you consider deleting any of the variables? If so, which ones?
   f. Rerun the analysis until only significant net regression coefficients remain in the analysis. Identify these variables.
   g. Develop a histogram of the residuals from the final regression equation developed in part (f). Is it reasonable to conclude that the normality assumption has been met?
   h. Plot the residuals against the fitted values from the final regression equation developed in part (f) against the fitted values of Y. Plot the residuals on the vertical axis and the fitted values on the horizontal axis.

28. Refer to the Baseball 2003 data, which reports information on the 30 Major League Baseball teams for the 2003 season. Let the number of games won be the dependent variable and the following variables be independent variables: team batting average, number of stolen bases, number of errors committed, team ERA, number of home runs, and whether the team's home field is natural grass or artificial turf.
   a. Write out the regression equation. Discuss each of the variables. For example, are you surprised that the regression coefficient for ERA is negative? How many wins does playing on natural grass for a home field add to or subtract from the total wins for the season?
   b. Determine the value of R^2. Interpret.
   c. Develop a correlation matrix. Which independent variables have strong or weak correlations with the dependent variable? Do you see any problems with multicollinearity?
   d. Conduct a global test on the set of independent variables. Interpret.
   e. Conduct a test of hypothesis on each of the independent variables. Would you consider deleting any of the variables? If so, which ones?
   f. Rerun the analysis until only significant net regression coefficients remain in the analysis. Identify these variables.
   g. Develop a histogram of the residuals from the final regression equation developed in part (f). Is it reasonable to conclude that the normality assumption has been met?
   h. Plot the residuals against the fitted values from the final regression equation developed in part (f) against the fitted values of Y. Plot the residuals on the vertical axis and the fitted values on the horizontal axis.

29. Refer to the Wage data, which reports information on annual wages for a sample of 100 workers. Also included are variables relating to industry, years of education, and gender for each worker. Determine the regression equation using annual wage as the dependent variable and years of education, gender, years of work experience, age in years, and whether or not the worker was a union member.
   a. Write out the regression equation. Discuss each variable.
   b. Determine and interpret the R^2 value.
   c. Develop a correlation matrix. Which independent variables have strong or weak correlations with the dependent variable? Do you see any problems with multicollinearity?
   d. Conduct a global test of hypothesis on the set of independent variables. Interpret your findings. Is it reasonable to continue with the analysis or should you stop here?

e. Conduct a test of hypothesis on each of the independent variables. Would you consider deleting any of these variables? If so, which ones?
f. Rerun the analysis deleting any of the independent variables that are not significant. Delete the variables one at a time.
g. Develop a histogram of the residuals from the final regression equation. Is it reasonable to conclude that the normality assumption has been met?
h. Plot the residuals against the fitted values from the final regression equation. Plot the residuals on the vertical axis and the fitted values on the horizontal axis.

30. Refer to the CIA data, which reports demographic and economic information on 46 countries. Let unemployment be the dependent variable and percent of the population over 65, life expectancy, and literacy be the independent variables.

a. Determine the regression equation using a software package. Write out the regression equation.
b. What is the value of the coefficient of determination?
c. Check the independent variables for multicollinearity.
d. Conduct a global test on the set of independent variables.
e. Test each of the independent variables to determine if they differ from zero.
f. Would you delete any of the independent variables? If so, rerun the regression analysis and report the new equation.
g. Make a histogram of the residuals from your final regression equation. Is it reasonable to conclude that the residuals follow a normal distribution?
h. Plot the residuals versus the fitted values and check. Are there any problems?

Software Commands

1. The MINITAB commands for the multiple regression output on page 425 are:
   a. Import the data from the CD. The file name is Tbl14–1.
   b. Select **Stat, Regression,** and then click on **Regression.**
   c. Select *Cost* as the **Response** variable, and *Temp, Insulation,* and *Age* as the **Predictors,** then click on **OK.**

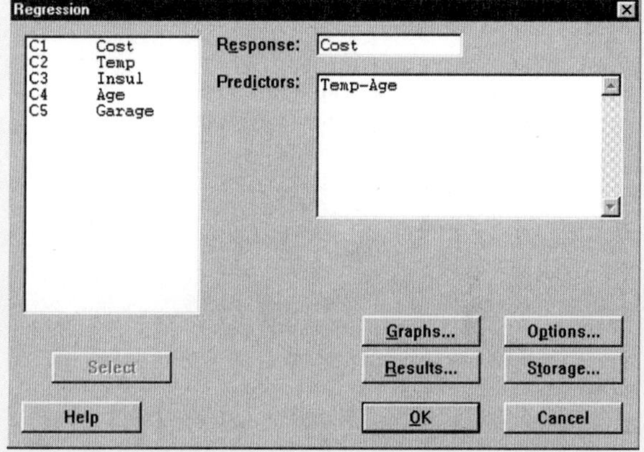

2. The Excel commands to produce the multiple regression output on page 425 are:
   a. Import the data from the CD. The file name is Tbl14.
   b. Select **Tools,** then **Data Analysis,** highlight **Regression,** and click **OK.**
   c. Make the **Input Y Range** *A1:A21,* the **Input X Range** *B1:D21,* check the **Labels** box, the **Output Range** is *F1,* click **OK.**

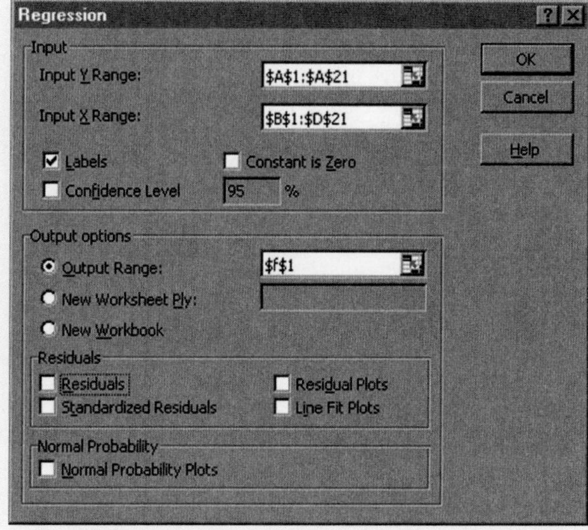

3. The Excel commands to develop the correlation matrix on page 433 are:
   a. Import the data from the CD. The file name is Tbl14–1.
   b. Select **Tools, Data Analysis,** then hit **Enter.** Select the command **Correlation** and then hit **OK.**
   c. The **Input Range** is *A1:D21,* grouped by **Columns,** check the **Labels** box, select the **Output Range** as *G1,* and click **OK.**

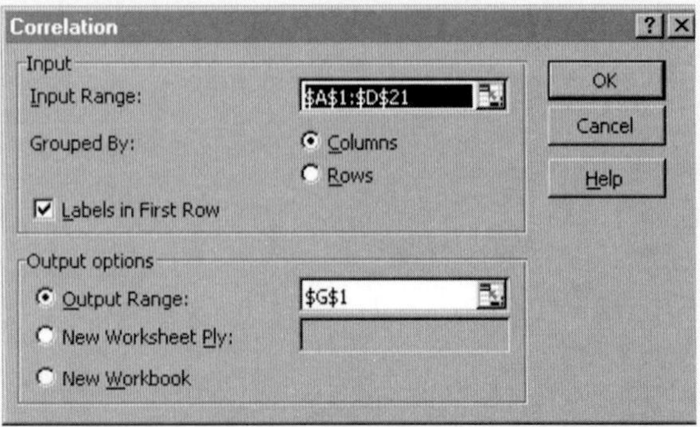

4. The MINITAB commands for the multiple regression output on page 436 are:
   a. Import the data from the CD. The file name is Tbl14–1.
   b. Select **Stat, Regression,** and then click on **Regression.**
   c. Select *Cost* as the **Response** variable, and *Temp, Insulation,* and *Age* as the **Predictors,** then click on **OK.**
   d. Click on **Storage,** then check **Residuals** and **Fits,** and click **OK** in both dialog boxes.

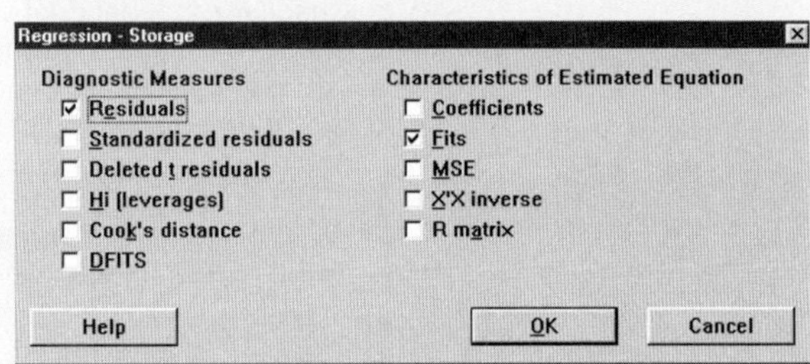

5. The MINITAB commands for the fitted regression on page 446 are:
   a. Import the data from the CD.
   b. Select **Stat, Regression,** and then click on **Fitted Line Plot.**
   c. Select Mpg as the **Response (*Y*)** and Pressure as the **Predictor (*X*),** and then select Quadratic as the **Type of Regression Model** and click on **OK.**

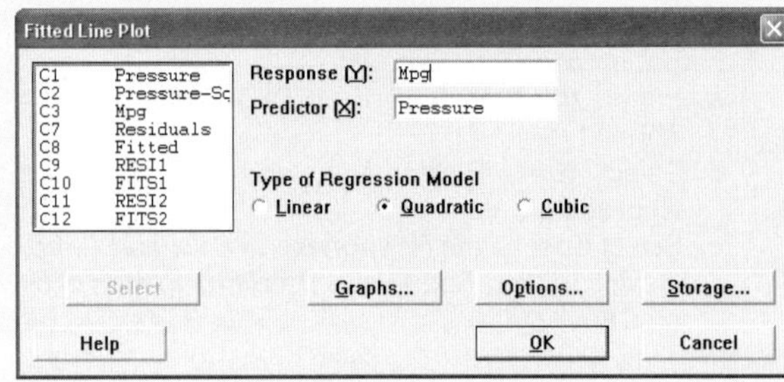

Chapter 14 Answers to Self-Review

14–1 a. 12.9 psi, found by $Y' = -0.5 + 20(.35) + 1(6.4)$.

b. The b_1 of 20 indicates that the tensile strength of the wire will increase 20 psi for each increase of 1 mm in outside diameter, with the amount of molybdenum held constant. That is, tensile strength will increase 20 psi regardless of the amount of molybdenum in the wire.

14–2 a. $n = 25$

b. 4

c. $R^2 = \frac{10}{15} = 0.667$

d. $s_{y \cdot 1234} = \sqrt{\frac{5}{20}} = 0.50$

14–3 a. $Y' = 490 - 5.15X_1 - 14.7X_2$

b. .776. A total of 77.6 percent of the variation in heating cost is explained by temperature and insulation.

c. The results of the global test indicate that at least one of the regression coefficients is not zero. To arrive at that conclusion, we first stated the null hypothesis as H_0: $\beta_1 = \beta_2 = 0$. The critical value of F is 3.59, and the computed value 29.4, found by 82,597/2,807. Since 29.4 lies in the region of rejection beyond 3.59, we reject H_0.

d. The p-value is .008. The probability of a t value less than -2.98 or greater than 2.98, with 17 degrees of freedom, is .008.

15

Chi-Square Applications

GOALS

When you have completed this chapter, you will be able to:

1 List the characteristics of the chi-square distribution.

2 Conduct a test of hypothesis comparing an observed set of frequencies to an expected distribution.

3 Conduct a test of hypothesis to determine whether two classification criteria are related.

Recently a large retailer studied the relationship between the importance a store manager placed on advertising and the size of the store. The study showed the following results:

	Important	Not Important
Small	40	52
Medium	106	47
Large	67	32

What is your conclusion? Use the .05 significance level. (See Goal 3 and Exercise 24.).

Introduction

Chapters 9 through 12 discuss hypothesis tests for data of interval or ratio scale, such as weights of steel ingots, incomes of minorities, and years of employment. We conduct hypothesis tests about a single population mean, two population means, and three or more population means. For these tests we assume the populations follow the normal distribution. However, there are tests available in which no assumption regarding the shape of the population is necessary. There are also tests exclusively for data of nominal scale of measurement. Recall from Chapter 1 that nominal data is the "lowest" or most primitive. For this type of measurement, data are classified into categories where there is no natural order. Examples include gender of Congressional representatives, state of birth of students, or brand of peanut butter purchased. In this chapter we introduce a new test statistic, the chi-square statistic. We can use it for data measured with a nominal scale.

Goodness-of-Fit Test: Equal Expected Frequencies

The goodness-of-fit test is one of the most commonly used statistical tests. The first illustration of this test involves the case in which the expected cell frequencies are equal.

As the full name implies, the purpose of the goodness-of-fit test is to compare an observed distribution to an expected distribution. An example will describe the hypothesis-testing situation.

EXAMPLE

Ms. Jan Kilpatrick is the marketing manager for a manufacturer of sports cards. She plans to begin a series of cards with pictures and playing statistics of former Major League Baseball players. One of the problems is the selection of the former players. At the baseball card show at the Southwyck Mall last weekend, she set up a booth and offered cards of the following six Hall of Fame baseball players: Tom Seaver, Nolan Ryan, Ty Cobb, George Brett, Hank Aaron, and Johnny Bench. At the end of the day she sold a total of 120 cards. The number of cards sold for each old-time player is shown in Table 15–1. Can she conclude the sales are not the same for each player?

TABLE 15–1 Number of Cards Sold for Each Player

Player	Cards Sold
Tom Seaver	13
Nolan Ryan	33
Ty Cobb	14
George Brett	7
Hank Aaron	36
Johnny Bench	17
Total	120

SOLUTION

If there is no significant difference in the popularity of the players, we would expect that the observed frequencies (f_o) would be equal—or nearly equal. That is, we would expect to sell as many cards for Tom Seaver as for Nolan Ryan. Thus, any discrepancy in the observed and expected frequencies could be attributed to sampling (chance).

What about the level of measurement in this problem? Notice when a card is sold, the "measurement" of the card is based on the player's name. There is no natural order to the players. Therefore, a nominal scale is used to evaluate each observation.

Because there are 120 cards in the sample, we expect that 20 (f_e) cards, i.e., the expected frequency f_e, will fall in each of the six categories (Table 15–2). These categories are called **cells.** An examination of the set of observed frequencies or Cards Sold in Table 15–2 indicates that the card for George Brett is sold rather infrequently, whereas the cards for Hank Aaron and Nolan Ryan are sold more often. Is the difference in sales due to chance, or can we conclude that there is a preference for the cards of certain players?

TABLE 15–2 Observed and Expected Frequencies for the 120 Cards Sold

Player	Cards Sold, f_o	Expected Number Sold, f_e
Tom Seaver	13	20
Nolan Ryan	33	20
Ty Cobb	14	20
George Brett	7	20
Hank Aaron	36	20
Johnny Bench	17	20
Total	120	120

We will use the same systematic five-step hypothesis-testing procedure followed in previous chapters.

Step 1: State the null hypothesis and the alternate hypothesis. The null hypothesis, H_0, is that there is no difference between the set of observed frequencies and the set of expected frequencies; that is, any difference between the two sets of frequencies can be attributed to sampling (chance). The alternate hypothesis, H_1, is that there is a difference between the observed and expected sets of frequencies. If H_0 is rejected and H_1 is accepted, it means that sales are not equally distributed among the six categories (cells).

Step 2: Select the level of significance. We selected the .05 level, which is the same as the Type I error probability. Thus, the probability is .05 that a true null hypothesis will be rejected.

Step 3: Select the test statistic. The test statistic follows the chi-square distribution, designated as χ^2:

CHI-SQUARE TEST STATISTIC

$$\chi^2 = \Sigma\left[\frac{(f_o - f_e)^2}{f_e}\right] \qquad [15\text{–}1]$$

with $k - 1$ degrees of freedom, where:

k is the number of categories.
f_o is an observed frequency in a particular category.
f_e is an expected frequency in a particular category.

We will examine the characteristics of the chi-square distribution in more detail shortly.

Step 4: Formulate the decision rule. Recall the decision rule in hypothesis testing requires finding a number that separates the region where we do not reject H_0 from the region of rejection. This number is called the *critical*

Statistics in Action

For many years, researchers and statisticians believed that all variables were normally distributed. In fact, it was generally assumed to be a universal law. However, Karl Pearson observed that experimental data were not always normally distributed but there was no way to prove his observations were correct. To solve this problem, Pearson discovered the chi-square statistic that basically compares an observed frequency distribution with an assumed normal distribution. His discovery proved that all variables were not normally distributed.

value. As we will soon see, the chi-square distribution is really a family of distributions. Each distribution has a slightly different shape, depending on the number of degrees of freedom. The number of degrees of freedom in this type of problem is found by $k - 1$, where k is the number of categories. In this particular problem there are six. Since there are six categories, there are $k - 1 = 6 - 1 = 5$ degrees of freedom. As noted, a category is called a *cell,* so there are six cells. The critical value for 5 degrees of freedom and the .05 level of significance is found in Appendix B. A portion of that table is shown in Table 15–3. The critical value is 11.070, found by locating 5 degrees of freedom in the left margin and then moving horizontally (to the right) and reading the critical value in the .05 column.

TABLE 15–3 A Portion of the Chi-Square Table

Degrees of Freedom	Right-Tail Area, α			
df	.10	.05	.02	.01
1	2.706	3.841	5.412	6.635
2	4.605	5.991	7.824	9.210
3	6.251	7.815	9.837	11.345
4	7.779	9.488	11.668	13.277
5	9.236	11.070	13.388	15.086

The decision rule is to reject H_0 if the computed value of chi-square is greater than 11.070. If it is less than or equal to 11.070, do not reject H_0. Chart 15–1 shows the decision rule.

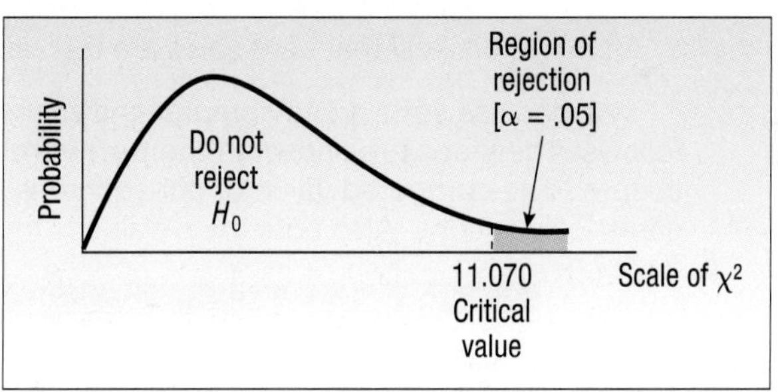

CHART 15–1 Chi-Square Probability Distribution for 5 Degrees of Freedom, Showing the Region of Rejection, .05 Level of Significance

The decision rule indicates that if there are large differences between the observed and expected frequencies, resulting in a computed χ^2 of more than 11.070, the null hypothesis should be rejected. However, if the differences between f_o and f_e are small, the computed χ^2 value will be 11.070 or less, and the null hypothesis should not be rejected. The reasoning is that such small differences between the observed and expected frequencies are probably due to chance. Remember, the 120 observations are a sample of the population.

Step 5: Compute the value of chi-square and make a decision. Of the 120 cards sold in the sample, we counted the number of times Tom Seaver and Nolan Ryan, and each of the others were sold. The counts were reported in Table 15–1. The calculations for chi-square follow. (Note again that the expected frequencies are the same for each cell.)

Column 1: Determine the differences between each f_o and f_e. That is, $(f_o - f_e)$. The sum of these differences always is zero.

Column 2: Square the difference between each observed and expected frequency, that is, $(f_o - f_e)^2$.

Column 3: Divide the result for each observation by the expected frequency. That is, $\frac{(f_o - f_e)^2}{f_e}$. Finally, sum these values.

The result is the value of χ^2, which is 34.40.

Baseball Player	f_o	f_e	(1) $(f_o - f_e)$	(2) $(f_o - f_e)^2$	(3) $\frac{(f_o - f_e)^2}{f_e}$
Tom Seaver	13	20	−7	49	49/20 = 2.45
Nolan Ryan	33	20	13	169	169/20 = 8.45
Ty Cobb	14	20	−6	36	36/20 = 1.80
George Brett	7	20	−13	169	169/20 = 8.45
Hank Aaron	36	20	16	256	256/20 = 12.80
Johnny Bench	17	20	−3	9	9/20 = 0.45
			0 (Must be)		34.40 (χ^2)

The computed χ^2 of 34.40 is in the rejection region beyond the critical value of 11.070. The decision, therefore, is to reject H_0 at the .05 level and to accept H_1. The difference between the observed and the expected frequencies is not due to chance. Rather, the differences between f_o and f_e are large enough to be considered significant. The chance these differences are due to sampling error is very small. So we conclude that it is unlikely that card sales are the same among the six players.

We can use software to compute the value of chi-square. The output of MegaStat follows. The steps are shown in the **Software Commands** section at the end of the chapter. The computed value of chi-square is 34.40, the same value obtained in our earlier calculations. Also note the *p*-value is much less than .05 (.00000198).

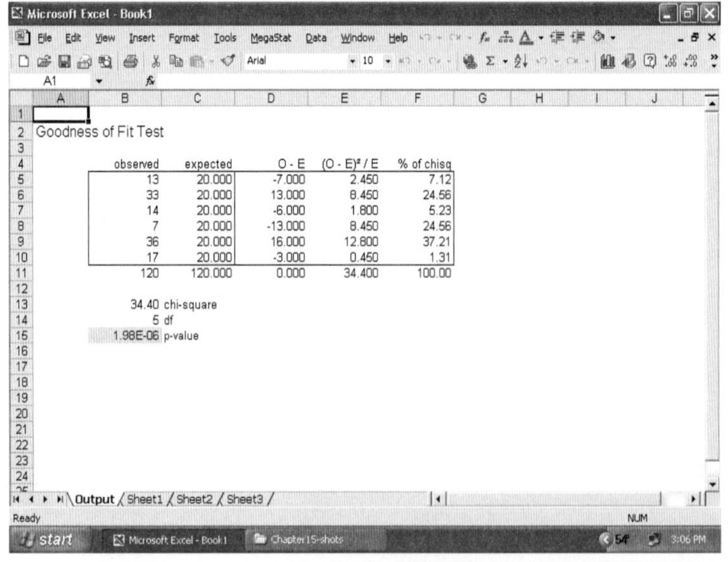

Goodness of Fit Test

observed	expected	O - E	(O - E)² / E	% of chisq
13	20.000	-7.000	2.450	7.12
33	20.000	13.000	8.450	24.56
14	20.000	-6.000	1.800	5.23
7	20.000	-13.000	8.450	24.56
36	20.000	16.000	12.800	37.21
17	20.000	-3.000	0.450	1.31
120	120.000	0.000	34.400	100.00

34.40 chi-square
5 df
1.98E-06 p-value

The chi-square distribution, which is used as the test statistic in this chapter, has the following characteristics.

1. **Chi-square values are never negative.** This is because the difference between f_o and f_e is squared, that is, $(f_o - f_e)^2$.
2. **There is a family of chi-square distributions.** There is a chi-square distribution for 1 degree of freedom, another for 2 degrees of freedom, another for 3 degrees of freedom, and so on. In this type of problem the number of degrees of freedom is determined by $k - 1$, where k is the number of categories. Therefore, the shape of the chi-square distribution does *not* depend on the size of the sample, but on the number of categories used. For example, if 200 employees of an airline were classified into one of three categories—flight personnel, ground support, and administrative personnel—there would be $k - 1 = 3 - 1 = 2$ degrees of freedom.
3. **The chi-square distribution is positively skewed.** However, as the number of degrees of freedom increases, the distribution begins to approximate the normal distribution. Chart 15–2 shows the distributions for selected degrees of freedom. Notice that for 10 degrees of freedom the curve is approaching a normal distribution.

Shape of χ^2 distribution approaches normal distribution as *df* becomes larger

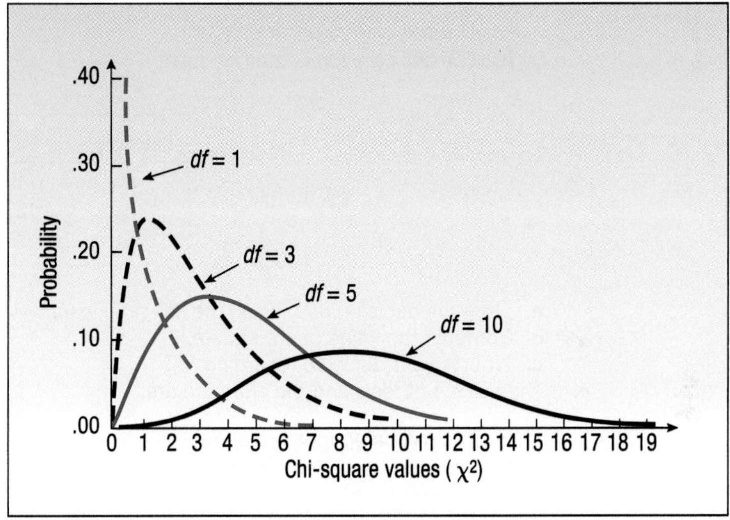

CHART 15–2 Chi-Square Distributions for Selected Degrees of Freedom

Self-Review 15–1

The human resources director at Georgetown Paper, Inc. is concerned about absenteeism among hourly workers. She decides to sample the records to determine whether absenteeism is distributed evenly throughout the six-day workweek. The null hypothesis to be tested is: Absenteeism is distributed evenly throughout the week. The sample results are:

	Number Absent		Number Absent
Monday	12	Thursday	10
Tuesday	9	Friday	9
Wednesday	11	Saturday	9

Use the .01 significance level and the five-step hypothesis testing procedure.

(a) What are the numbers 12, 9, 11, 10, 9, and 9 called?
(b) How many categories (cells) are there?
(c) What is the *expected* frequency for each day?

(d) How many degrees of freedom are there?
(e) What is the chi-square critical value at the 1 percent significance level?
(f) Compute the χ^2 test statistic.
(g) What is the decision regarding the null hypothesis?
(h) Specifically, what does this indicate to the human resources director?

Exercises

1. In a particular chi-square goodness-of-fit test there are four categories and 200 observations. Use the .05 significance level.
   a. How many degrees of freedom are there?
   b. What is the critical value of chi-square?
2. In a particular chi-square goodness-of-fit test there are six categories and 500 observations. Use the .01 significance level.
   a. How many degrees of freedom are there?
   b. What is the critical value of chi-square?
3. The null hypothesis and the alternate are:

   H_0: The cell categories are equal.
   H_1: The cell categories are not equal.

Category	f_o
A	10
B	20
C	30

   a. State the decision rule, using the .05 significance level.
   b. Compute the value of chi-square.
   c. What is your decision regarding H_0?
4. The null hypothesis and the alternate are:

   H_0: The cell categories are equal.
   H_1: The cell categories are not equal.

Category	f_o
A	10
B	20
C	30
D	20

   a. State the decision rule, using the .05 significance level.
   b. Compute the value of chi-square.
   c. What is your decision regarding H_0?
5. A six-sided die is rolled 30 times and the numbers 1 through 6 appear as shown in the following frequency distribution. At the .10 significance level, can we conclude that the die is fair?

Outcome	Frequency	Outcome	Frequency
1	3	4	3
2	6	5	9
3	2	6	7

6. Classic Golf, Inc. manages five courses in the Jacksonville, Florida, area. The Director wishes to study the number of rounds of golf played per weekday at the five courses. He gathered the following sample information.

Day	Rounds
Monday	124
Tuesday	74
Wednesday	104
Thursday	98
Friday	120

At the .05 significance level, is there a difference in the number of rounds played by day of the week?

7. A group of department store buyers viewed a new line of dresses and gave their opinions of them. The results were:

Opinion	Number of Buyers	Opinion	Number of Buyers
Outstanding	47	Good	39
Excellent	45	Fair	35
Very good	40	Undesirable	34

Because the largest number (47) indicated the new line is outstanding, the head designer thinks that this is a mandate to go into mass production of the dresses. The head sweeper (who somehow became involved in this) believes that there is not a clear mandate and claims that the opinions are evenly distributed among the six categories. He further states that the slight differences among the various counts are probably due to chance. Test the null hypothesis that there is no significant difference among the opinions of the buyers. Test at the .01 level of risk. Follow a formal approach; that is, state the null hypothesis, the alternate hypothesis, and so on.

8. The safety director of Honda USA took samples at random from the file of minor work-related accidents and classified them according to the time the accident took place.

Time	Number of Accidents	Time	Number of Accidents
8 up to 9 A.M.	6	1 up to 2 P.M.	7
9 up to 10 A.M.	6	2 up to 3 P.M.	8
10 up to 11 A.M.	20	3 up to 4 P.M.	19
11 up to 12 P.M.	8	4 up to 5 P.M.	6

Using the goodness-of-fit test and the .01 level of significance, determine whether the accidents are evenly distributed throughout the day. Write a brief explanation of your conclusion.

Goodness-of-Fit Test: Unequal Expected Frequencies

The expected frequencies (f_e) in the previous distribution involving baseball cards were all equal (20). According to the null hypothesis, it was expected that a card of Tom Seaver would appear 20 times at random, a card of Johnny Bench would appear 20 times out of 120 trials, and so on. The chi-square test can also be used if the expected frequencies are not equal.

Expected frequencies not equal in this problem

The following example illustrates the case of unequal frequencies and also gives a practical use of the chi-square goodness-of-fit test—namely, to find whether a local experience differs from the national experience.

EXAMPLE

The American Hospital Administrators Association (AHAA) reports the following information concerning the number of times senior citizens are admitted to a hospital during a one-year period. Forty percent are not admitted; 30 percent are admitted once; 20 percent are admitted twice, and the remaining 10 percent are admitted three or more times.

A survey of 150 residents of Bartow Estates, a community devoted to active seniors located in Central Florida, revealed 55 residents were not admitted during the last year, 50 were admitted to a hospital once, 32 were admitted twice, and the rest of those in the survey were admitted three or more times. Can we conclude the survey at Bartow Estates is consistent with the information suggested by the AHAA? Use the .05 significance level.

SOLUTION

We begin by organizing the above information into Table 15–4. Clearly, we cannot compare percentages given in the study by the AHAA to the frequencies reported for the Bartow Estates. However, these percentages can be converted to expected frequencies, f_e. According to the AHAA, 40 percent of those surveyed should not require hospitalization. Thus, if there is no difference between the national experience and those of Bartow Estates, then 40 percent of the 150 seniors surveyed (60 residents) would not have been hospitalized. Further, 30 percent of those surveyed were admitted once (45 residents), and so on. The observed frequencies for Bartow residents and the expected frequencies based on the percents in the national study are given in Table 15–4.

Statistics in Action

Many state governments operate lotteries to help fund education. In many lotteries, numbered balls are mixed and selected by a machine. In a "Select Three" game, numbered balls are selected randomly from three groups of balls numbered zero through nine. Randomness would predict that the frequency of each number is equal. How would you prove that the selection machine ensured randomness? A chi-square, goodness-of-fit test could be used to prove or disprove randomness.

TABLE 15–4 Summary of Study by AHAA and a Survey of Bartow Estates Residents

Number of Times Admitted	AHAA Percent of Total	Number of Bartow Residents (f_o)	Expected Number of Residents (f_e)
0	40	55	60
1	30	50	45
2	20	32	30
3 or more	10	13	15
Total	100	150	150

The null hypothesis and the alternate hypotheses are:

H_0: There is no difference between local and national experience for hospital admissions.

H_1: There is a difference between local and national experience for hospital admissions.

To find the decision rule we use Appendix B. There are four admitting categories, so the degrees of freedom are $df = 4 - 1 = 3$. The critical value of 7.815 is found by moving down the column headed .05 to the row of 3 degrees of freedom. Therefore, the decision rule is to reject the null hypothesis if $\chi^2 > 7.815$. The decision rule is portrayed in Chart 15–3.

Now to compute the chi-square test statistic:

Number of Times Admitted	(f_o)	(f_e)	$f_o - f_e$	$(f_o - f_e)^2/f_e$
0	55	60	−5	0.4167
1	50	45	5	0.5556
2	32	30	2	0.1333
3 or more	13	15	−2	0.2667
Total	150	150	0	1.3723

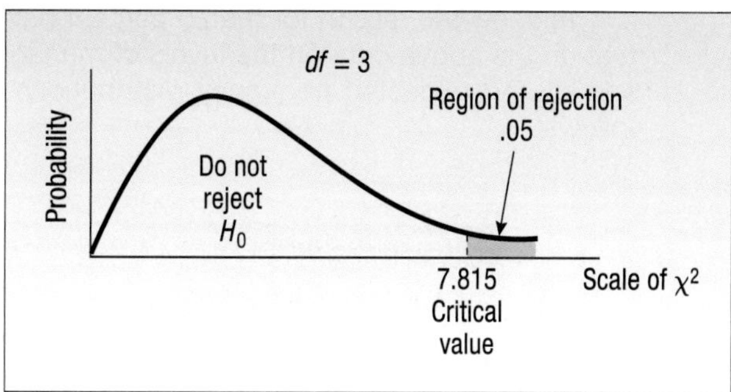

CHART 15–3 Decision Criteria for the Bartow Estates Research Study

The computed value of χ^2 (1.3723) lies to the left of 7.815. Thus, we cannot reject the null hypothesis. We conclude that there is no evidence of a difference between the experience at Bartow Estates and that reported by the AHAA.

Limitations of Chi-Square

Be careful in applying χ^2 to some problems.

If there is an unusually small expected frequency in a cell, chi-square (if applied) might result in an erroneous conclusion. This can happen because f_e appears in the denominator, and dividing by a very small number makes the quotient quite large! Two generally accepted rules regarding small cell frequencies are:

1. If there are only two cells, the *expected* frequency in each cell should be 5 or more. The computation of chi-square would be permissible in the following problem, involving a minimum f_e of 6.

Individual	f_o	f_e
Literate	643	642
Illiterate	7	6

2. For more than two cells, chi-square should *not* be used if more than 20 percent of the f_e cells have expected frequencies less than 5. According to this rule, it would not be appropriate to use the goodness-of-fit test on the following data. Three of the seven cells, or 43 percent, have expected frequencies (f_e) of less than 5.

Level of Management	f_o	f_e
Foreman	30	32
Supervisor	110	113
Manager	86	87
Middle management	23	24
Assistant vice president	5	2
Vice president	5	4
Senior vice president	4	1
Total	263	263

To show the reason for the 20 percent policy, we conducted the goodness-of-fit test on the above data on the levels of management. The hypothesis is that the observed and expected frequency distributions are the same. The MegaStat output follows.

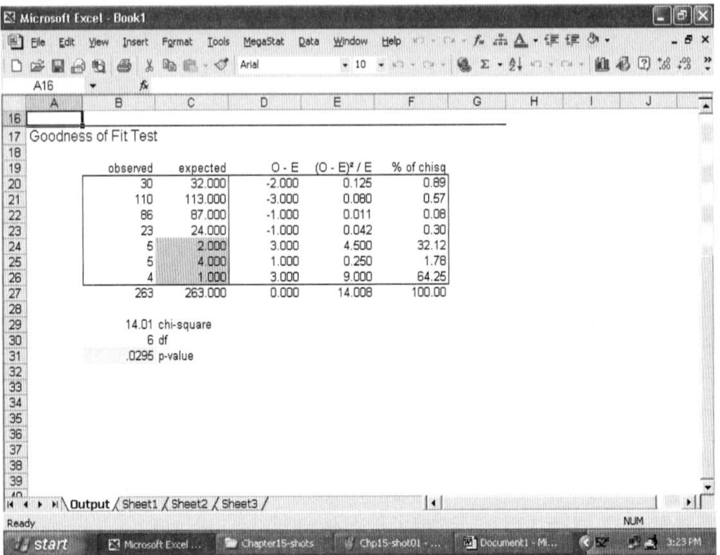

Goodness of Fit Test

observed	expected	O - E	(O - E)² / E	% of chisq
30	32.000	-2.000	0.125	0.89
110	113.000	-3.000	0.080	0.57
86	87.000	-1.000	0.011	0.08
23	24.000	-1.000	0.042	0.30
5	2.000	3.000	4.500	32.12
5	4.000	1.000	0.250	1.78
4	1.000	3.000	9.000	64.25
263	263.000	0.000	14.008	100.00

14.01 chi-square
6 df
.0295 p-value

For this test at the .05 significance level, H_0 is rejected if the computed value of chi-square is greater than 12.592. The computed value is 14.01 with a p-value of .0295. So we reject the null hypothesis that the observed and expected distributions are the same. However, the relatively small frequencies for the three vice presidents may inflate the computed chi-square value. Examine the MegaStat output. More than 98 percent of the computed chi-square value is accounted for by the three vice president categories ([4.500 + .250 + 9.000]/14.008 = 0.9815). Logically, too much weight is being given to these categories.

The dilemma can be resolved by combining categories if it is logical to do so. In the above example we combine the three vice-presidential categories, which satisfies the 20 percent rule.

Level of Management	f_o	f_e
Foreman	30	32
Supervisor	110	113
Manager	86	87
Middle management	23	24
Vice president	14	7
Total	263	263

The computed value of chi-square with the revised categories is 7.26 and the p-value is .1229. See the output on the next page. This value is less than the critical value of 9.488 for the .05 significance level. The null hypothesis is, therefore, not rejected at the .05 significance level. This indicates there is no evidence of a significant difference between the observed distribution and the expected distribution.

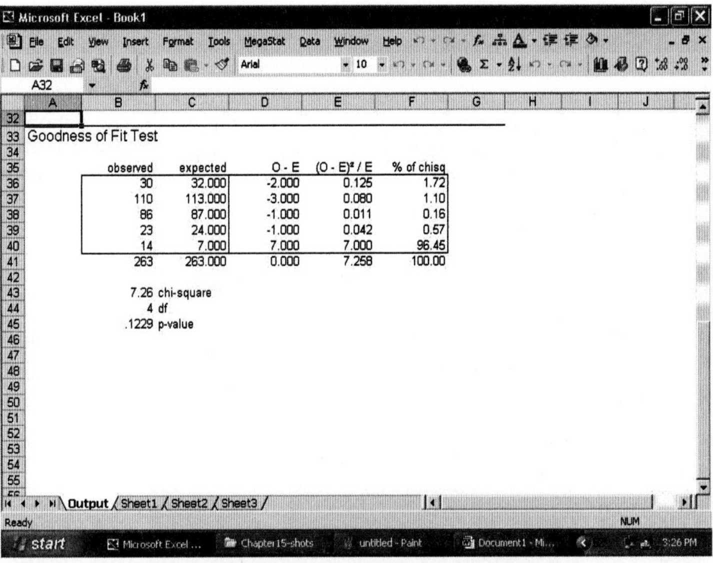

observed	expected	O - E	(O - E)²/E	% of chisq
30	32.000	-2.000	0.125	1.72
110	113.000	-3.000	0.080	1.10
86	87.000	-1.000	0.011	0.16
23	24.000	-1.000	0.042	0.57
14	7.000	7.000	7.000	96.45
263	263.000	0.000	7.258	100.00

7.26 chi-square
4 df
.1229 p-value

Self-Review 15–2

The American Accounting Association classifies accounts receivable as "current," "late," and "not collectible." Industry figures show that 60 percent of accounts receivable are current, 30 percent are late, and 10 percent are not collectible. Massa and Barr, attorneys in Greenville, Ohio, has 500 accounts receivable: 320 are current, 120 are late, and 60 are not collectible. Are these numbers in agreement with the industry distribution? Use the .05 significance level.

Exercises

9. The following hypotheses are given:

H_0: Forty percent of the observations are in category A, 40 percent are in B, and 20 percent are in C.

H_1: The observations are not as described in H_0.

We took a sample of 60, with the following results.

Category	f_o
A	30
B	20
C	10

a. State the decision rule using the .01 significance level.
b. Compute the value of chi-square.
c. What is your decision regarding H_0?

10. The chief of security for the Mall of the Dakotas was directed to study the problem of missing goods. He selected a sample of 100 boxes that had been tampered with and ascertained that for 60 of the boxes, the missing pants, shoes, and so on were attributed to shoplifting. For 30 other boxes employees had stolen the goods, and for the remaining 10 boxes he blamed poor inventory control. In his report to the mall management, can he say that shoplifting is *twice* as likely to be the cause of the loss as compared with either employee theft or poor inventory control and that employee theft and poor inventory control are equally likely? Use the .02 significance level.

11. The credit card department of Carolina Bank knows from experience that 5 percent of the card holders have had some high school, 15 percent have completed high school, 25 percent have had some college, and 55 percent have completed college. Of the 500 card holders whose cards have been called in for failure to pay their charges this month, 50 had some high school, 100 had completed high school, 190 had some college, and 160 had completed college. Can we conclude that the distribution of card holders who do not pay their charges is different from all others? Use the .01 significance level.
12. For many years TV executives used the guideline that 30 percent of the audience were watching each of the prime-time networks, that is ABC, NBC and CBS, and 10 percent were watching cable stations on a weekday night. A random sample of 500 viewers in the Tampa–St. Petersburg, Florida, area last Monday night showed that 165 homes were tuned in to the ABC affiliate, 140 to the CBS affiliate, 125 to the NBC affiliate, and the remainder were viewing a cable station. At the .05 significance level, can we conclude that the guideline is still reasonable?

Contingency Table Analysis

In Chapter 4 we discuss bivariate data, where we study the relationship between two variables. We describe a contingency table which simultaneously summarizes two nominal-scale variables of interest. For example, a sample of students enrolled in the School of Business is classified by gender (male or female) and major (accounting, management, finance, marketing, or quantitative methods). This classification is based on the nominal scale, because there is no natural order to the classifications.

We discussed contingency tables earlier, in Chapter 5. On page 138, we illustrated the relationship between the loyalty to the company and the length of employment. Are older employees likely to be more loyal or less to the company?

We can use the chi-square statistic to formally test for a relationship between two nominal-scaled variables. To put it another way, is one variable *independent* of the other? Here are some examples where we are interested in testing whether two variables are related.

- The Ford Motor Company operates an assembly plant in Dearborn, Michigan. The plant operates three shifts per day, 5 days a week. The quality control manager wishes to compare the quality level on the three shifts. Vehicles are classified by quality level (acceptable, unacceptable) and shift (day, afternoon, night). Is there a difference in the quality level on the three shifts? That is, is the quality of the product related to the shift when it was manufactured? Or, is the quality of the product independent of the shift on which it was manufactured?
- A sample of 100 drivers who were stopped for speeding violations was classified by gender and whether or not they were wearing a seat belt. For this sample, is wearing a seatbelt related to gender?
- Does a male released from federal prison make a different adjustment to civilian life if he returns to his hometown or if he goes elsewhere to live? The two variables are adjustment to civilian life and place of residence. Note that both variables are measured on the nominal scale.

EXAMPLE

The Federal Correction Agency is investigating the last question cited above: Does a male released from federal prison make a different adjustment to civilian life if he returns to his hometown or if he goes elsewhere to live? To put it another way, is there a relationship between adjustment to civilian life and place of residence after release from prison?

SOLUTION

As before, the first step in hypothesis testing is to state the null and alternate hypotheses.

H_0: There is no relationship between adjustment to civilian life and where the individual lives after being released from prison.
H_1: There is a relationship between adjustment to civilian life and where the individual lives after being released from prison.

The .01 level of significance will be used to test the hypothesis.

The agency's psychologists interviewed 200 randomly selected former prisoners. Using a series of questions, the psychologists classified the adjustment of each individual to civilian life as outstanding, good, fair, or unsatisfactory. The classifications for the 200 former prisoners were tallied as follows. Joseph Camden, for example, returned to his hometown and has shown outstanding adjustment to civilian life. His case is one of the 27 tallies in the upper left box.

Residence after Release from Prison	Adjustment to Civilian Life			
	Outstanding	Good	Fair	Unsatisfactory
Hometown	𝍸 𝍸 𝍸 𝍸 𝍸 ||	𝍸 𝍸 𝍸 𝍸 𝍸 𝍸 𝍸	𝍸 𝍸 𝍸 𝍸 𝍸 𝍸 |||	𝍸 𝍸 𝍸 𝍸 𝍸
Not hometown	𝍸 𝍸 𝍸	𝍸 𝍸 𝍸	𝍸 𝍸 𝍸 𝍸 𝍸 ||	𝍸 𝍸 𝍸 𝍸 𝍸

Contingency table consists of count data.

The tallies in each box, or *cell,* were counted. The counts are given in the following **contingency table.** (See Table 15–5.) In this case, the Federal Correction Agency wondered whether adjustment to civilian life is *contingent on* or related to where the prisoner goes after release from prison.

TABLE 15–5 Adjustment to Civilian Life and Place of Residence

Residence after Release from Prison	Adjustment to Civilian Life				
	Outstanding	Good	Fair	Unsatisfactory	Total
Hometown	27	35	33	25	120
Not hometown	13	15	27	25	80
Total	40	50	60	50	200

Once we know how many rows (2) and columns (4) there are in the contingency table, we can determine the critical value and the decision rule. For a chi-square test of significance where two traits are classified in a contingency table, the degrees of freedom are found by:

$$df = (\text{number of rows} - 1)(\text{number of columns} - 1) = (r - 1)(c - 1)$$

In this problem:

$$df = (r - 1)(c - 1) = (2 - 1)(4 - 1) = 3$$

To find the critical value for 3 degrees of freedom and the .01 level (selected earlier), refer to Appendix B. It is 11.345. The decision rule is to reject the null hypothesis if the computed value of χ^2 is greater than 11.345. The decision rule is portrayed graphically in Chart 15–4.

Statistics in Action

A study of 1,000 Americans over the age of 24 showed that 28 percent never married. Of those, 22 percent completed college. Twenty-three percent of the 1,000 married and completed college. Can we conclude for the information given that being married is related to completing college? The study indicated that the two variables were related, that the computed value of the chi-square statistic was 9.368. Can you duplicate these results?

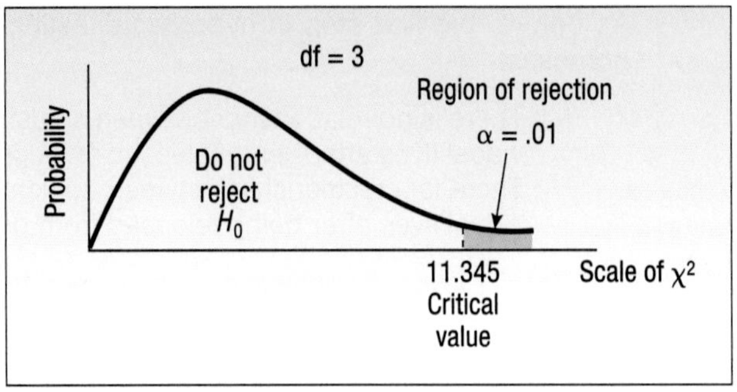

CHART 15–4 Chi-Square Distribution for 3 Degrees of Freedom

Next we find the computed value of χ^2. The observed frequencies, f_o, are shown in Table 15–5. How are the corresponding expected frequencies, f_e, determined? Note in the "Total" column of Table 15–5 that 120 of the 200 former prisoners (60 percent) returned to their hometowns. *If there were no relationship* between adjustment and residency after release from prison, we would expect 60 percent of the 40 ex-prisoners who made outstanding adjustment to civilian life to reside in their hometowns. Thus, the expected frequency f_e for the upper left cell is $.60 \times 40 = 24$. Likewise, if there were no relationship between adjustment and present residence, we would expect 60 percent of the 50 ex-prisoners (30) who had "good" adjustment to civilian life to reside in their hometowns.

Further, notice that 80 of the 200 ex-prisoners studied (40 percent) did not return to their hometowns to live. Thus, of the 60 considered by the psychologists to have made "fair" adjustment to civilian life, $.40 \times 60$, or 24, would be expected not to return to their hometowns.

The expected frequency for any cell can be determined by

EXPECTED FREQUENCY

$$f_e = \frac{(\text{Row total})(\text{Column total})}{\text{Grand total}} \qquad [15\text{–}2]$$

From this formula, the expected frequency for the upper left cell in Table 15–5 is:

$$\text{Expected frequency} = \frac{(\text{Row total})(\text{Column total})}{\text{Grand total}} = \frac{(120)(40)}{200} = 24$$

The observed frequencies, f_o, and the expected frequencies, f_e, for all of the cells in the contingency table are listed in Table 15–6.

TABLE 15–6 Observed and Expected Frequencies

Residence after Release from Prison	Adjustment to Civilian Life: Outstanding		Good		Fair		Unsatisfactory		Total	
	f_o	f_e	f_o	f_e	f_o	f_e	f_o	f_e	f_o	f_e
Hometown	27	24	35	30	33	36	25	30	120	120
Not hometown	13	16	15	20	27	24	25	20	80	80
Total	40	40	50	50	60	60	50	50	200	200
	Must be equal			(80)(50)/200					Must be equal	

Recall that the computed value of chi-square using formula (15–1) is found by:

$$\chi^2 = \Sigma\left[\frac{(f_o - f_e)^2}{f_e}\right]$$

Starting with the upper left cell:

$$\chi^2 = \frac{(27-24)^2}{24} + \frac{(35-30)^2}{30} + \frac{(33-36)^2}{36} + \frac{(25-30)^2}{30}$$

$$+ \frac{(13-16)^2}{16} + \frac{(15-20)^2}{20} + \frac{(27-24)^2}{24} + \frac{(25-20)^2}{20}$$

$$= 0.375 + 0.833 + 0.250 + 0.833 + 0.563 + 1.250 + 0.375 + 1.250$$

$$= 5.729$$

Because the computed value of chi-square (5.729) lies in the region to the left of 11.345, the null hypothesis is not rejected at the .01 significance level. We conclude there is no evidence of a relationship between adjustment to civilian life and where the prisoner resides after being released from prison. For the Federal Correction Agency's advisement program, adjustment to civilian life is not related to where the ex-prisoner lives.

The following output is from the MINITAB system.

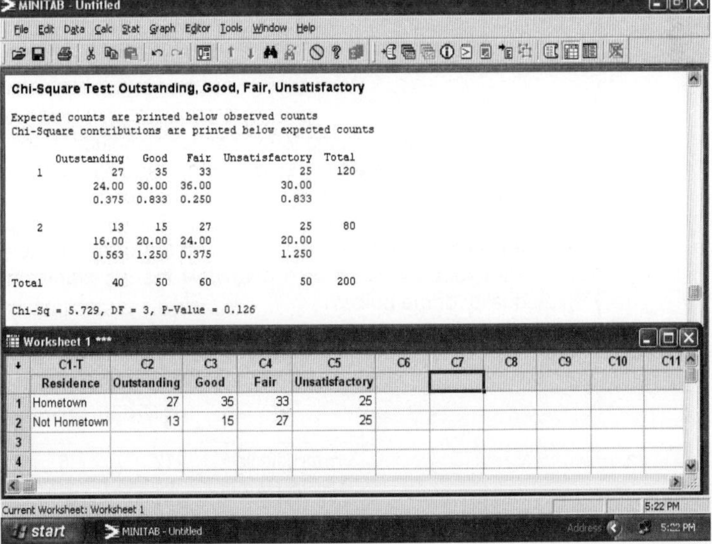

Observe that the value of chi-square is the same as that computed earlier. In addition, the *p*-value is reported, .126. So the probability of finding a value of the test statistic as large or larger is .126 when the null hypothesis is true. The *p*-value also results in the same decision, do not reject the null hypothesis.

Self-Review 15–3

A social scientist sampled 140 people and classified them according to income level and whether or not they played a state lottery in the last month. The sample information is reported below. Is it reasonable to conclude that playing the lottery is related to income level? Use the .05 significance level.

	Income			
	Low	**Middle**	**High**	**Total**
Played	46	28	21	95
Did not play	14	12	19	45
Total	60	40	40	140

(a) What is this table called?
(b) State the null hypothesis and the alternate hypothesis.
(c) What is the decision rule?
(d) Determine the value of chi-square.
(e) Make a decision on the null hypothesis. Interpret the result.

Exercises

13. The director of advertising for the *Carolina Sun Times,* the largest newspaper in the Carolinas, is studying the relationship between the type of community in which a subscriber resides and the section of the newspaper he or she reads first. For a sample of readers, she collected the following sample information.

	National News	**Sports**	**Comics**
City	170	124	90
Suburb	120	112	100
Rural	130	90	88

At the .05 significance level, can we conclude there is a relationship between the type of community where the person resides and the section of the paper read first?

14. Four brands of light bulbs are being considered for use in the final assembly area of the Saturn plant in Spring Hill, Tennessee. The director of purchasing asked for samples of 100 from each manufacturer. The numbers of acceptable and unacceptable bulbs from each manufacturer are shown below. At the .05 significance level, is there a difference in the quality of the bulbs?

	Manufacturer			
	A	**B**	**C**	**D**
Unacceptable	12	8	5	11
Acceptable	88	92	95	89
Total	100	100	100	100

15. The Quality Control Department at Food Town, Inc., a grocery chain in upstate New York, conducts a monthly check on the comparison of scanned prices to posted prices. The chart below summarizes the results of a sample of 500 items last month. Company management would like to know whether there is any relationship between error rates on regular priced items and specially priced items. Use the .01 significance level.

	Regular Price	Advertised Special Price
Undercharge	20	10
Overcharge	15	30
Correct price	200	225

16. The use of cellular phones in automobiles has increased dramatically in the last few years. Of concern to traffic experts, as well as manufacturers of cellular phones, is the effect on accident rates. Is someone who is using a cellular phone more likely to be involved in a traffic accident? What is your conclusion from the following sample information? Use the .05 significance level.

	Had Accident in the Last Year	Did Not Have an Accident in the Last Year
Cellular phone in use	25	300
Cellular phone not in use	50	400

Chapter Outline

I. The characteristics of the chi-square distribution are:
- **A.** The value of chi-square is never negative.
- **B.** The chi-square distribution is positively skewed.
- **C.** There is a family of chi-square distributions.
  1. Each time the degrees of freedom change, a new distribution is formed.
  2. As the degrees of freedom increase, the distribution approaches the normal distribution.

II. A goodness-of-fit test will show whether an observed set of frequencies could have come from a hypothesized population distribution.
- **A.** The degrees of freedom are $k - 1$, where k is the number of categories.
- **B.** The formula for computing the value of chi-square is

$$\chi^2 = \Sigma\left[\frac{(f_o - f_e)^2}{f_e}\right] \quad \textbf{[15–1]}$$

III. A contingency table is used to test whether two traits or characteristics are related.
- **A.** Each observation is classified according to two traits.
- **B.** The expected frequency is determined as follows:

$$f_e = \frac{\text{(Row total)(Column total)}}{\text{Grand total}} \quad \textbf{[15–2]}$$

- **C.** The degrees of freedom are found by:

$$df = (\text{Rows} - 1)(\text{Columns} - 1)$$

- **D.** The usual hypothesis testing procedure is used.

Pronunciation Key

SYMBOL	MEANING	PRONUNCIATION
χ^2	Probability distribution	*ki square*
f_o	Observed frequency	*f sub oh*
f_e	Expected frequency	*f sub e*

Chapter Exercises

17. Vehicles heading west on Front Street may turn right, left, or go straight ahead at Elm Street. The city traffic engineer believes that half of the vehicles will continue straight through the intersection. Of the remaining half, equal proportions will turn right and left. Two hundred vehicles were observed, with the following results. Can we conclude that the traffic engineer is correct? Use the .10 significance level.

	Straight	Right Turn	Left Turn
Frequency	112	48	40

18. The publisher of a sports magazine plans to offer new subscribers one of three gifts: a sweatshirt with the logo of their favorite team, a coffee cup with the logo of their favorite team, or a pair of earrings also with the logo of their favorite team. In a sample of 500 new subscribers, the number selecting each gift is reported below. At the .05 significance level, is there a preference for the gifts or should we conclude that the gifts are equally well liked?

Gift	Frequency
Sweatshirt	183
Coffee cup	175
Earrings	142

19. In the Tidewater Virginia TV market there are three commercial television stations, each with its own evening news program from 6:00 to 6:30 P.M. According to a report in this morning's local newspaper, a random sample of 150 viewers last night revealed 53 watched the news on WNAE (channel 5), 64 watched on WRRN (channel 11), and 33 on WSPD (channel 13). At the .05 significance level, is there a difference in the proportion of viewers watching the three channels?
20. A recent survey suggested that 55 percent of all adults favored legislation requiring restaurants to include information on their menus regarding calories, fat, and carbohydrates of the menu items. The same survey indicated that 28 percent of all adult respondents were opposed to such legislation. The remainder of those surveyed was unsure of the need. A sample of 450 young adults revealed 220 favored the proposed legislation, 158 opposed it, and the remaining 72 were unsure. At the .05 significance level is it reasonable to conclude the position of young adults regarding adding dietary information to restaurant menus is different from the total population?
21. The owner of a mail-order catalog would like to compare her sales with the geographic distribution of the population. According to the United States Bureau of the Census, 21 percent of the population lives in the Northeast, 24 percent in the Midwest, 35 percent in the South, and 20 percent in the West. Listed below is a breakdown of a sample of 400 orders randomly selected from those shipped last month. At the .01 significance level, does the distribution of the orders reflect the population?

Region	Frequency
Northeast	68
Midwest	104
South	155
West	73
Total	400

22. The Banner Mattress and Furniture Company wishes to study the number of credit applications received per day for the last 300 days. The information is reported in the following table.

Number of Credit Applications	Frequency (Number of Days)
0	50
1	77
2	81
3	48
4	31
5 or more	13

To interpret, there were 50 days on which no credit applications were received, 77 days on which only one application was received, and so on. Would it be reasonable to conclude that the population distribution is Poisson with a mean of 2.0? Use the .05 significance level. *Hint:* To find the expected frequencies use the Poisson distribution with a mean of 2.0. Find the probability of exactly one success given a Poisson distribution with a mean of 2.0. Multiply this probability by 300 to find the expected frequency for the number of days in which there was exactly one application. Determine the expected frequency for the other days in a similar manner.

23. In the early 2000s the Deep Down Mining Company implemented new safety guidelines. Prior to these new guidelines, management expected no accidents in 40 percent of the months, one accident in 30 percent of the months, two accidents in 20 percent of the months, and three accidents in 10 percent of the months. Over the last 10 years, or 120 months, there have been 46 months in which there were no accidents, 40 months in which there was one accident, 22 months in which there were two accidents, and 12 months in which there were 3 accidents. At the .05 significance level can the management at Deep Down conclude that there has been a change in the monthly accident distribution?

24. A recent study by a large retailer designed to determine whether there was a relationship between the importance a store manager placed on advertising and the size of the store revealed the following sample information:

	Important	Not Important
Small	40	52
Medium	106	47
Large	67	32

What is your conclusion? Use the .05 significance level.

25. Two hundred managers employed in the lumber industry were randomly selected and interviewed regarding their concern about environmental issues. The response of each person was tallied into one of three categories: no concern, some concern, and great concern. The results were:

Level of Management	No Concern	Some Concern	Great Concern
Top management	15	13	12
Middle management	20	19	21
Supervisor	7	7	6
Group leader	28	21	31

Use the .01 significance level to determine whether there is a relationship between management level and environmental concern.

26. A study regarding the relationship between age and the amount of pressure sales personnel feel in relation to their jobs revealed the following sample information. At the .01 significance level, is there a relationship between job pressure and age?

Age (years)	Degree of Job Pressure Low	Medium	High
Less than 25	20	18	22
25 up to 40	50	46	44
40 up to 60	58	63	59
60 and older	34	43	43

27. The claims department at the Wise Insurance Company believes that younger drivers have more accidents and, therefore, should be charged higher insurance rates. Investigating a sample of 1,200 Wise policyholders revealed the following breakdown on whether a claim had been filed in the last three years and the age of the policyholder. Is it reasonable to conclude that there is a relationship between the age of the policyholder and whether or not the person filed a claim? Use the .05 significance level.

Age Group	No Claim	Claim
16 up to 25	170	74
25 up to 40	240	58
40 up to 55	400	44
55 or older	190	24
Total	1,000	200

28. Is it proper to respond with an email after a job interview thanking the prospective employer for the interview? This question was asked of sample of 200 human resource professionals and 250 technical personnel who were a part of the interview process. The results are reported below. At the .01 significance level is it reasonable to conclude that human resource and technical personnel differ on whether an email response is appropriate?

Email response	Human resource	Technical
Very appropriate	35	98
Somewhat appropriate	95	114
Somewhat inappropriate	40	22
Very inappropriate	30	16
Total	200	250

exercises.com

29. Did you ever purchase a bag of M&M's candies and wonder about the distribution of colors? You can go to the website http://www.m-ms.com/us/about/index.jsp and click on **Products,** then **Peanut,** and find the percentage breakdown according to the manufacturer as well as a brief history of the product. Did you know that at one time all M&M's peanuts were brown and there were not really peanuts inside but legumes? For M&M's peanuts, 23 percent are blue, 15 percent are yellow, 12 percent are red, 15 percent are green, 12 percent are brown, and 23 percent are orange. A 9.40-ounce bag purchased at the Student Store at Coastal Carolina University on May 19, 2004, had 10 brown, 25 yellow, 19 red, 20 blue, 21 orange, and 25 green candies. Is it reasonable to conclude the actual distribution agrees with the expected distribution? Use the .01 significance level. Conduct your own trial. Be sure to share with your instructor!

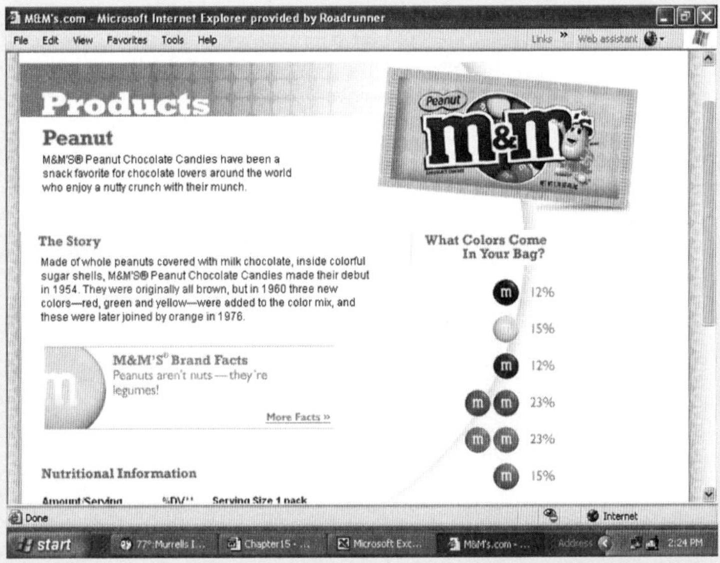

30. As described in earlier chapters, many real estate companies and rental agencies now publish their listings on the World Wide Web. One example is the Dunes Realty Company located in Garden City, South Carolina and Surfside Beach, South Carolina. Go to the website http://www.dunes.com and click on **Vacation Rentals,** select **Beach House Search,** then indicate at least 5 bedrooms, accommodations for at least 14 people, oceanfront, and no pool or floating dock; select a period in the next month; indicate that you are willing to spend up to $8,000 per week; and finally click on **Search the Cottages.** Sort the cottages offered into a contingency table by the number of bathrooms and whether the rental price is less than $2,000 for the week or $2,000 or more. You may need to combine some of the cells. Conduct a statistical test to determine if the number of bedrooms is related to the cost. Use the .05 significance level.

Dataset Exercises

31. Refer to the Real Estate data, which reports information on homes sold in the Denver, Colorado, area last year.
    a. Develop a contingency table that shows whether a home has a pool and the township in which the house is located. Is there an association between the variables "pool" and "township"? Use the .05 significance level.
    b. Develop a contingency table that shows whether a home has an attached garage and the township in which the home is located. Is there an association between the variables "attached garage" and "township"? Use the .05 significance level.
32. Refer to the Baseball 2003 data, which reports information on the 30 Major League Baseball teams for the 2003 season. Set up a variable that divides the teams into two groups, those that had a winning season and those that did not. There are 162 games in the season, so define a winning season as having won 81 or more games. Next, divide the teams into two salary groups. Let the 15 teams with the largest salaries be in one group and the 15 teams with the smallest salaries in the other. At the .05 significance level is there a relationship between salaries and winning?
33. Refer to the Wage data, which reports information on annual wages for a sample of 100 workers. Also included are variables relating to industry, years of education, and gender for each worker. Develop a table showing the industry of employment by gender. At the .05 significance level is it reasonable to conclude that industry of employment and gender are related?
34. Refer to the CIA data, which reports demographic and economic information on 46 countries.
    a. Develop a contingency table that shows G-20 membership versus level of petroleum activity. Is there a significant association at the .05 level of significance between these variables?

b. Group the countries into "young" (percent of population over 65 is less than 10) and "old" (percent of population over 65 is more than 10). Then develop a contingency table between this "age" variable and the level of petroleum activity. At the .05 level of significance can we conclude these variables are related?

Software Commands

1. The MegaStat commands to create the chi-square goodness-of-fit test on page 468 are:
   a. Enter the information from Table 15–1 into a worksheet as shown.
   b. Select **MegaStat, Chi-Square/Crosstabs,** and **Goodness-of-fit** and hit **Enter.**
   c. In the dialog box select *B2:B7* as the **Observed values,** *C2:C7* as the **Expected values,** and enter *0* as the **Number of parameters estimated from the data.** Click on **OK.**

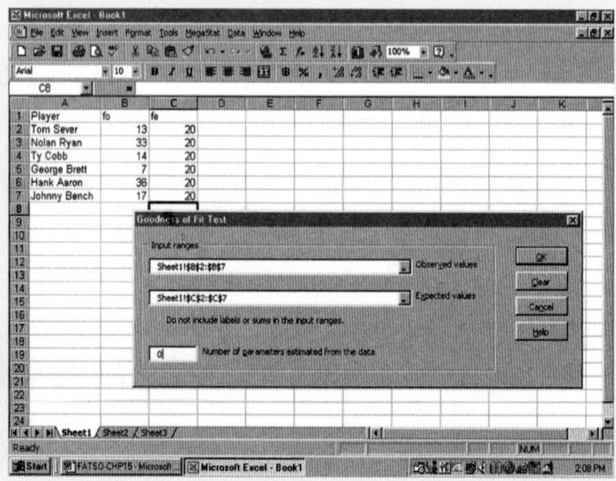

2. The MegaStat commands to create the chi-square goodness-of-fit tests on pages 474 and 475 are the same except for the number of items in the observed and expected frequency columns. Only one dialog box is shown.
   a. Enter the Levels of Management information shown on page 473.
   b. Select **MegaStat, Chi-Square/Crosstabs,** and **Goodness-of-fit** and hit **Enter.**
   c. In the dialog box select *B2:B8* as the **Observed values,** *C2:C8* as the **Expected values,** and enter *0* as the **Number of parameters estimated from the data.** Click on **OK.**

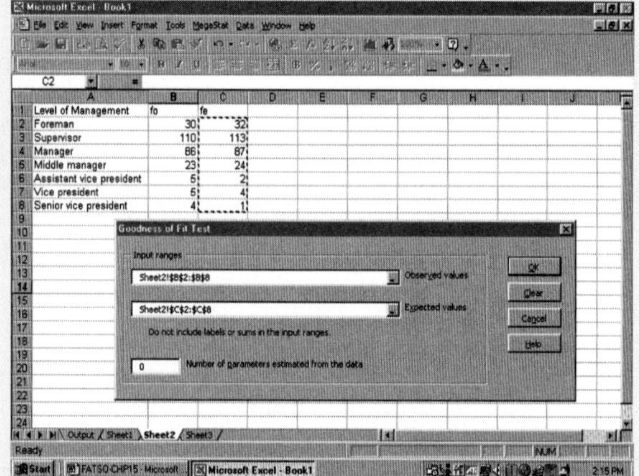

3. The MINITAB commands for the chi-square analysis on page 479 are:
   a. Enter the names of the variables in the first row and the data in the next two rows.
   b. Select **Stat, Table,** and then click on **Chi-square test** and hit **Enter.**
   c. In the dialog box select the columns labeled *Outstanding* to *Unsatisfactory* and click **OK.**

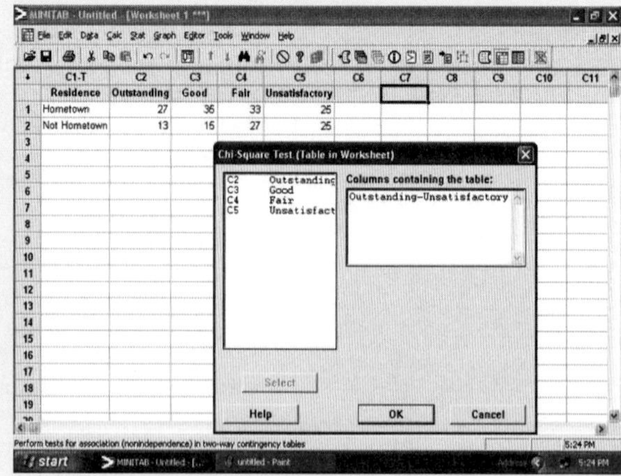

Chapter 15 Answers to Self-Review

15–1 **a.** Observed frequencies.
b. Six (six days of the week).
c. 10. Total observed frequencies ÷ 6 = 60/6 = 10.
d. 5; $k - 1 = 6 - 1 = 5$.
e. 15.086 (from the chi-square table in Appendix B).
f.

$$\chi^2 = \Sigma\left[\frac{(f_o - f_e)^2}{f_e}\right] = \frac{(12 - 10)^2}{10} + \cdots + \frac{(9 - 10)^2}{10} = 0.8$$

g. We do not reject H_0.
h. Absenteeism is distributed evenly throughout the week. The observed differences are due to sampling error.

15–2 H_0: $P_C = .60$, $P_L = .30$, and $P_U = .10$.
H_1: Distribution is not as above.
Reject H_0 if $\chi^2 > 5.991$.

Category	f_o	f_e	$\frac{(f_o - f_e)^2}{f_e}$
Current	320	300	1.33
Late	120	150	6.00
Uncollectible	60	50	2.00
	500	500	9.33

Reject H_0. The accounts receivable data does not reflect the national average.

15–3 **a.** Contingency table
b. H_0: There is no relationship between income and whether the person played the lottery.
H_1: There is a relationship between income and whether the person played the lottery.
c. Reject H_0 if χ^2 is greater than 5.991.
d.

$$\chi^2 = \frac{(46 - 40.71)^2}{40.71} + \frac{(28 - 27.14)^2}{27.14} + \frac{(21 - 27.14)^2}{27.14}$$

$$+ \frac{(14 - 19.29)^2}{19.29} + \frac{(12 - 12.86)^2}{12.86} + \frac{(19 - 12.86)^2}{12.86}$$

$$= 6.544$$

e. Reject H_0. There is a relationship between income level and playing the lottery.

Appendixes

TABLES

A Binomial Probability Distribution

B Critical Values of Chi-Square

C Poisson Distribution

D Areas under the Normal Curve

E Table of Random Numbers

F Student's *t* Distribution

G Critical Values of the *F* Distribution

H Wilcoxon *T* Values

I Factors for Control Charts

DATASETS

J Dataset 1—Real Estate

K Dataset 2—Major League Baseball

L Dataset 3—Wages and Wage Earners

M Dataset 4—CIA International Economic and Demographic Data

N Whitner Autoplex

SOFTWARE

O Getting Started with MegaStat

P Visual Statistics

Appendix A

Binomial Probability Distribution

n = 1

Probability

x	0.05	0.10	0.20	0.30	0.40	0.50	0.60	0.70	0.80	0.90	0.95
0	0.950	0.900	0.800	0.700	0.600	0.500	0.400	0.300	0.200	0.100	0.050
1	0.050	0.100	0.200	0.300	0.400	0.500	0.600	0.700	0.800	0.900	0.950

n = 2

Probability

x	0.05	0.10	0.20	0.30	0.40	0.50	0.60	0.70	0.80	0.90	0.95
0	0.903	0.810	0.640	0.490	0.360	0.250	0.160	0.090	0.040	0.010	0.003
1	0.095	0.180	0.320	0.420	0.480	0.500	0.480	0.420	0.320	0.180	0.095
2	0.003	0.010	0.040	0.090	0.160	0.250	0.360	0.490	0.640	0.810	0.903

n = 3

Probability

x	0.05	0.10	0.20	0.30	0.40	0.50	0.60	0.70	0.80	0.90	0.95
0	0.857	0.729	0.512	0.343	0.216	0.125	0.064	0.027	0.008	0.001	0.000
1	0.135	0.243	0.384	0.441	0.432	0.375	0.288	0.189	0.096	0.027	0.007
2	0.007	0.027	0.096	0.189	0.288	0.375	0.432	0.441	0.384	0.243	0.135
3	0.000	0.001	0.008	0.027	0.064	0.125	0.216	0.343	0.512	0.729	0.857

n = 4

Probability

x	0.05	0.10	0.20	0.30	0.40	0.50	0.60	0.70	0.80	0.90	0.95
0	0.815	0.656	0.410	0.240	0.130	0.063	0.026	0.008	0.002	0.000	0.000
1	0.171	0.292	0.410	0.412	0.346	0.250	0.154	0.076	0.026	0.004	0.000
2	0.014	0.049	0.154	0.265	0.346	0.375	0.346	0.265	0.154	0.049	0.014
3	0.000	0.004	0.026	0.076	0.154	0.250	0.346	0.412	0.410	0.292	0.171
4	0.000	0.000	0.002	0.008	0.026	0.063	0.130	0.240	0.410	0.656	0.815

n = 5

Probability

x	0.05	0.10	0.20	0.30	0.40	0.50	0.60	0.70	0.80	0.90	0.95
0	0.774	0.590	0.328	0.168	0.078	0.031	0.010	0.002	0.000	0.000	0.000
1	0.204	0.328	0.410	0.360	0.259	0.156	0.077	0.028	0.006	0.000	0.000
2	0.021	0.073	0.205	0.309	0.346	0.313	0.230	0.132	0.051	0.008	0.001
3	0.001	0.008	0.051	0.132	0.230	0.313	0.346	0.309	0.205	0.073	0.021
4	0.000	0.000	0.006	0.028	0.077	0.156	0.259	0.360	0.410	0.328	0.204
5	0.000	0.000	0.000	0.002	0.010	0.031	0.078	0.168	0.328	0.590	0.774

Appendix A

Binomial Probability Distribution (*continued*)

$n = 6$

Probability

x	0.05	0.10	0.20	0.30	0.40	0.50	0.60	0.70	0.80	0.90	0.95
0	0.735	0.531	0.262	0.118	0.047	0.016	0.004	0.001	0.000	0.000	0.000
1	0.232	0.354	0.393	0.303	0.187	0.094	0.037	0.010	0.002	0.000	0.000
2	0.031	0.098	0.246	0.324	0.311	0.234	0.138	0.060	0.015	0.001	0.000
3	0.002	0.015	0.082	0.185	0.276	0.313	0.276	0.185	0.082	0.015	0.002
4	0.000	0.001	0.015	0.060	0.138	0.234	0.311	0.324	0.246	0.098	0.031
5	0.000	0.000	0.002	0.010	0.037	0.094	0.187	0.303	0.393	0.354	0.232
6	0.000	0.000	0.000	0.001	0.004	0.016	0.047	0.118	0.262	0.531	0.735

$n = 7$

Probability

x	0.05	0.10	0.20	0.30	0.40	0.50	0.60	0.70	0.80	0.90	0.95
0	0.698	0.478	0.210	0.082	0.028	0.008	0.002	0.000	0.000	0.000	0.000
1	0.257	0.372	0.367	0.247	0.131	0.055	0.017	0.004	0.000	0.000	0.000
2	0.041	0.124	0.275	0.318	0.261	0.164	0.077	0.025	0.004	0.000	0.000
3	0.004	0.023	0.115	0.227	0.290	0.273	0.194	0.097	0.029	0.003	0.000
4	0.000	0.003	0.029	0.097	0.194	0.273	0.290	0.227	0.115	0.023	0.004
5	0.000	0.000	0.004	0.025	0.077	0.164	0.261	0.318	0.275	0.124	0.041
6	0.000	0.000	0.000	0.004	0.017	0.055	0.131	0.247	0.367	0.372	0.257
7	0.000	0.000	0.000	0.000	0.002	0.008	0.028	0.082	0.210	0.478	0.698

$n = 8$

Probability

x	0.05	0.10	0.20	0.30	0.40	0.50	0.60	0.70	0.80	0.90	0.95
0	0.663	0.430	0.168	0.058	0.017	0.004	0.001	0.000	0.000	0.000	0.000
1	0.279	0.383	0.336	0.198	0.090	0.031	0.008	0.001	0.000	0.000	0.000
2	0.051	0.149	0.294	0.296	0.209	0.109	0.041	0.010	0.001	0.000	0.000
3	0.005	0.033	0.147	0.254	0.279	0.219	0.124	0.047	0.009	0.000	0.000
4	0.000	0.005	0.046	0.136	0.232	0.273	0.232	0.136	0.046	0.005	0.000
5	0.000	0.000	0.009	0.047	0.124	0.219	0.279	0.254	0.147	0.033	0.005
6	0.000	0.000	0.001	0.010	0.041	0.109	0.209	0.296	0.294	0.149	0.051
7	0.000	0.000	0.000	0.001	0.008	0.031	0.090	0.198	0.336	0.383	0.279
8	0.000	0.000	0.000	0.000	0.001	0.004	0.017	0.058	0.168	0.430	0.663

Binomial Probability Distribution (*continued*)

n = 9

Probability

x	0.05	0.10	0.20	0.30	0.40	0.50	0.60	0.70	0.80	0.90	0.95
0	0.630	0.387	0.134	0.040	0.010	0.002	0.000	0.000	0.000	0.000	0.000
1	0.299	0.387	0.302	0.156	0.060	0.018	0.004	0.000	0.000	0.000	0.000
2	0.063	0.172	0.302	0.267	0.161	0.070	0.021	0.004	0.000	0.000	0.000
3	0.008	0.045	0.176	0.267	0.251	0.164	0.074	0.021	0.003	0.000	0.000
4	.001	0.007	0.066	0.172	0.251	0.246	0.167	0.074	0.017	0.001	0.000
5	0.000	0.001	0.017	0.074	0.167	0.246	0.251	0.172	0.066	0.007	0.001
6	0.000	0.000	0.003	0.021	0.074	0.164	0.251	0.267	0.176	0.045	0.008
7	0.000	0.000	0.000	0.004	0.021	0.070	0.161	0.267	0.302	0.172	0.063
8	0.000	0.000	0.000	0.000	0.004	0.018	0.060	0.156	0.302	0.387	0.299
9	0.000	0.000	0.000	0.000	0.000	0.002	0.010	0.040	0.134	0.387	0.630

n = 10

Probability

x	0.05	0.10	0.20	0.30	0.40	0.50	0.60	0.70	0.80	0.90	0.95
0	0.599	0.349	0.107	0.028	0.006	0.001	0.000	0.000	0.000	0.000	0.000
1	0.315	0.387	0.268	0.121	0.040	0.010	0.002	0.000	0.000	0.000	0.000
2	0.075	0.194	0.302	0.233	0.121	0.044	0.011	0.001	0.000	0.000	0.000
3	0.010	0.057	0.201	0.267	0.215	0.117	0.042	0.009	0.001	0.000	0.000
4	0.001	0.011	0.088	0.200	0.251	0.205	0.111	0.037	0.006	0.000	0.000
5	0.000	0.001	0.026	0.103	0.201	0.246	0.201	0.103	0.026	0.001	0.000
6	0.000	0.000	0.006	0.037	0.111	0.205	0.251	0.200	0.088	0.011	0.001
7	0.000	0.000	0.001	0.009	0.042	0.117	0.215	0.267	0.201	0.057	0.010
8	0.000	0.000	0.000	0.001	0.011	0.044	0.121	0.233	0.302	0.194	0.075
9	0.000	0.000	0.000	0.000	0.002	0.010	0.040	0.121	0.268	0.387	0.315
10	0.000	0.000	0.000	0.000	0.000	0.001	0.006	0.028	0.107	0.349	0.599

n = 11

Probability

x	0.05	0.10	0.20	0.30	0.40	0.50	0.60	0.70	0.80	0.90	0.95
0	0.569	0.314	0.086	0.020	0.004	0.000	0.000	0.000	0.000	0.000	0.000
1	0.329	0.384	0.236	0.093	0.027	0.005	0.001	0.000	0.000	0.000	0.000
2	0.087	0.213	0.295	0.200	0.089	0.027	0.005	0.001	0.000	0.000	0.000
3	0.014	0.071	0.221	0.257	0.177	0.081	0.023	0.004	0.000	0.000	0.000
4	0.001	0.016	0.111	0.220	0.236	0.161	0.070	0.017	0.002	0.000	0.000
5	0.000	0.002	0.039	0.132	0.221	0.226	0.147	0.057	0.010	0.000	0.000
6	0.000	0.000	0.010	0.057	0.147	0.226	0.221	0.132	0.039	0.002	0.000
7	0.000	0.000	0.002	0.017	0.070	0.161	0.236	0.220	0.111	0.016	0.001
8	0.000	0.000	0.000	0.004	0.023	0.081	0.177	0.257	0.221	0.071	0.014
9	0.000	0.000	0.000	0.001	0.005	0.027	0.089	0.200	0.295	0.213	0.087
10	0.000	0.000	0.000	0.000	0.001	0.005	0.027	0.093	0.236	0.384	0.329
11	0.000	0.000	0.000	0.000	0.000	0.000	0.004	0.020	0.086	0.314	0.569

Binomial Probability Distribution (*continued*)

$n = 12$

Probability

x	0.05	0.10	0.20	0.30	0.40	0.50	0.60	0.70	0.80	0.90	0.95
0	0.540	0.282	0.069	0.014	0.002	0.000	0.000	0.000	0.000	0.000	0.000
1	0.341	0.377	0.206	0.071	0.017	0.003	0.000	0.000	0.000	0.000	0.000
2	0.099	0.230	0.283	0.168	0.064	0.016	0.002	0.000	0.000	0.000	0.000
3	0.017	0.085	0.236	0.240	0.142	0.054	0.012	0.001	0.000	0.000	0.000
4	0.002	0.021	0.133	0.231	0.213	0.121	0.042	0.008	0.001	0.000	0.000
5	0.000	0.004	0.053	0.158	0.227	0.193	0.101	0.029	0.003	0.000	0.000
6	0.000	0.000	0.016	0.079	0.177	0.226	0.177	0.079	0.016	0.000	0.000
7	0.000	0.000	0.003	0.029	0.101	0.193	0.227	0.158	0.053	0.004	0.000
8	0.000	0.000	0.001	0.008	0.042	0.121	0.213	0.231	0.133	0.021	0.002
9	0.000	0.000	0.000	0.001	0.012	0.054	0.142	0.240	0.236	0.085	0.017
10	0.000	0.000	0.000	0.000	0.002	0.016	0.064	0.168	0.283	0.230	0.099
11	0.000	0.000	0.000	0.000	0.000	0.003	0.017	0.071	0.206	0.377	0.341
12	0.000	0.000	0.000	0.000	0.000	0.000	0.002	0.014	0.069	0.282	0.540

$n = 13$

Probability

x	0.05	0.10	0.20	0.30	0.40	0.50	0.60	0.70	0.80	0.90	0.95
0	0.513	0.254	0.055	0.010	0.001	0.000	0.000	0.000	0.000	0.000	0.000
1	0.351	0.367	0.179	0.054	0.011	0.002	0.000	0.000	0.000	0.000	0.000
2	0.111	0.245	0.268	0.139	0.045	0.010	0.001	0.000	0.000	0.000	0.000
3	0.021	0.100	0.246	0.218	0.111	0.035	0.006	0.001	0.000	0.000	0.000
4	0.003	0.028	0.154	0.234	0.184	0.087	0.024	0.003	0.000	0.000	0.000
5	0.000	0.006	0.069	0.180	0.221	0.157	0.066	0.014	0.001	0.000	0.000
6	0.000	0.001	0.023	0.103	0.197	0.209	0.131	0.044	0.006	0.000	0.000
7	0.000	0.000	0.006	0.044	0.131	0.209	0.197	0.103	0.023	0.001	0.000
8	0.000	0.000	0.001	0.014	0.066	0.157	0.221	0.180	0.069	0.006	0.000
9	0.000	0.000	0.000	0.003	0.024	0.087	0.184	0.234	0.154	0.028	0.003
10	0.000	0.000	0.000	0.001	0.006	0.035	0.111	0.218	0.246	0.100	0.021
11	0.000	0.000	0.000	0.000	0.001	0.010	0.045	0.139	0.268	0.245	0.111
12	0.000	0.000	0.000	0.000	0.000	0.002	0.011	0.054	0.179	0.367	0.351
13	0.000	0.000	0.000	0.000	0.000	0.000	0.001	0.010	0.055	0.254	0.513

Binomial Probability Distribution (*concluded*)

$n = 14$

Probability

x	0.05	0.10	0.20	0.30	0.40	0.50	0.60	0.70	0.80	0.90	0.95
0	0.488	0.229	0.044	0.007	0.001	0.000	0.000	0.000	0.000	0.000	0.000
1	0.359	0.356	0.154	0.041	0.007	0.001	0.000	0.000	0.000	0.000	0.000
2	0.123	0.257	0.250	0.113	0.032	0.006	0.001	0.000	0.000	0.000	0.000
3	0.026	0.114	0.250	0.194	0.085	0.022	0.003	0.000	0.000	0.000	0.000
4	0.004	0.035	0.172	0.229	0.155	0.061	0.014	0.001	0.000	0.000	0.000
5	0.000	0.008	0.086	0.196	0.207	0.122	0.041	0.007	0.000	0.000	0.000
6	0.000	0.001	0.032	0.126	0.207	0.183	0.092	0.023	0.002	0.000	0.000
7	0.000	0.000	0.009	0.062	0.157	0.209	0.157	0.062	0.009	0.000	0.000
8	0.000	0.000	0.002	0.023	0.092	0.183	0.207	0.126	0.032	0.001	0.000
9	0.000	0.000	0.000	0.007	0.041	0.122	0.207	0.196	0.086	0.008	0.000
10	0.000	0.000	0.000	0.001	0.014	0.061	0.155	0.229	0.172	0.035	0.004
11	0.000	0.000	0.000	0.000	0.003	0.022	0.085	0.194	0.250	0.114	0.026
12	0.000	0.000	0.000	0.000	0.001	0.006	0.032	0.113	0.250	0.257	0.123
13	0.000	0.000	0.000	0.000	0.000	0.001	0.007	0.041	0.154	0.356	0.359
14	0.000	0.000	0.000	0.000	0.000	0.000	0.001	0.007	0.044	0.229	0.488

$n = 15$

Probability

x	0.05	0.10	0.20	0.30	0.40	0.50	0.60	0.70	0.80	0.90	0.95
0	0.463	0.206	0.035	0.005	0.000	0.000	0.000	0.000	0.000	0.000	0.000
1	0.366	0.343	0.132	0.031	0.005	0.000	0.000	0.000	0.000	0.000	0.000
2	0.135	0.267	0.231	0.092	0.022	0.003	0.000	0.000	0.000	0.000	0.000
3	0.031	0.129	0.250	0.170	0.063	0.014	0.002	0.000	0.000	0.000	0.000
4	0.005	0.043	0.188	0.219	0.127	0.042	0.007	0.001	0.000	0.000	0.000
5	0.001	0.010	0.103	0.206	0.186	0.092	0.024	0.003	0.000	0.000	0.000
6	0.000	0.002	0.043	0.147	0.207	0.153	0.061	0.012	0.001	0.000	0.000
7	0.000	0.000	0.014	0.081	0.177	0.196	0.118	0.035	0.003	0.000	0.000
8	0.000	0.000	0.003	0.035	0.118	0.196	0.177	0.081	0.014	0.000	0.000
9	0.000	0.000	0.001	0.012	0.061	0.153	0.207	0.147	0.043	0.002	0.000
10	0.000	0.000	0.000	0.003	0.024	0.092	0.186	0.206	0.103	0.010	0.001
11	0.000	0.000	0.000	0.001	0.007	0.042	0.127	0.219	0.188	0.043	0.005
12	0.000	0.000	0.000	0.000	0.002	0.014	0.063	0.170	0.250	0.129	0.031
13	0.000	0.000	0.000	0.000	0.000	0.003	0.022	0.092	0.231	0.267	0.135
14	0.000	0.000	0.000	0.000	0.000	0.000	0.005	0.031	0.132	0.343	0.366
15	0.000	0.000	0.000	0.000	0.000	0.000	0.000	0.005	0.035	0.206	0.463

Appendix B

Critical Values of Chi-Square

This table contains the values of χ^2 that correspond to a specific right-tail area and specific number of degrees of freedom.

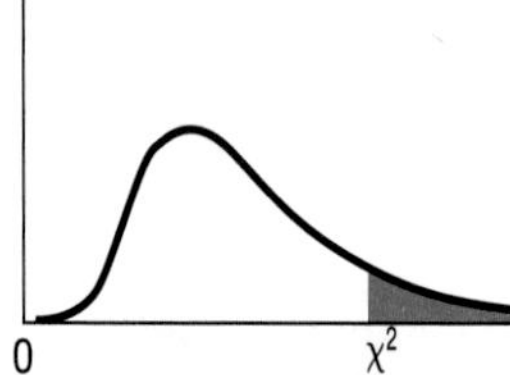

Example: With 17 *df* and a .02 area in the upper tail, $\chi^2 = 30.995$

Degrees of Freedom, *df*	Right-Tail Area			
	0.10	**0.05**	**0.02**	**0.01**
1	2.706	3.841	5.412	6.635
2	4.605	5.991	7.824	9.210
3	6.251	7.815	9.837	11.345
4	7.779	9.488	11.668	13.277
5	9.236	11.070	13.388	15.086
6	10.645	12.592	15.033	16.812
7	12.017	14.067	16.622	18.475
8	13.362	15.507	18.168	20.090
9	14.684	16.919	19.679	21.666
10	15.987	18.307	21.161	23.209
11	17.275	19.675	22.618	24.725
12	18.549	21.026	24.054	26.217
13	19.812	22.362	25.472	27.688
14	21.064	23.685	26.873	29.141
15	22.307	24.996	28.259	30.578
16	23.542	26.296	29.633	32.000
17	24.769	27.587	30.995	33.409
18	25.989	28.869	32.346	34.805
19	27.204	30.144	33.687	36.191
20	28.412	31.410	35.020	37.566
21	29.615	32.671	36.343	38.932
22	30.813	33.924	37.659	40.289
23	32.007	35.172	38.968	41.638
24	33.196	36.415	40.270	42.980
25	34.382	37.652	41.566	44.314
26	35.563	38.885	42.856	45.642
27	36.741	40.113	44.140	46.963
28	37.916	41.337	45.419	48.278
29	39.087	42.557	46.693	49.588
30	40.256	43.773	47.962	50.892

Appendix C

Poisson Distribution

x	μ 0.1	0.2	0.3	0.4	0.5	0.6	0.7	0.8	0.9
0	0.9048	0.8187	0.7408	0.6703	0.6065	0.5488	0.4966	0.4493	0.4066
1	0.0905	0.1637	0.2222	0.2681	0.3033	0.3293	0.3476	0.3595	0.3659
2	0.0045	0.0164	0.0333	0.0536	0.0758	0.0988	0.1217	0.1438	0.1647
3	0.0002	0.0011	0.0033	0.0072	0.0126	0.0198	0.0284	0.0383	0.0494
4	0.0000	0.0001	0.0003	0.0007	0.0016	0.0030	0.0050	0.0077	0.0111
5	0.0000	0.0000	0.0000	0.0001	0.0002	0.0004	0.0007	0.0012	0.0020
6	0.0000	0.0000	0.0000	0.0000	0.0000	0.0000	0.0001	0.0002	0.0003
7	0.0000	0.0000	0.0000	0.0000	0.0000	0.0000	0.0000	0.0000	0.0000

x	μ 1.0	2.0	3.0	4.0	5.0	6.0	7.0	8.0	9.0
0	0.3679	0.1353	0.0498	0.0183	0.0067	0.0025	0.0009	0.0003	0.0001
1	0.3679	0.2707	0.1494	0.0733	0.0337	0.0149	0.0064	0.0027	0.0011
2	0.1839	0.2707	0.2240	0.1465	0.0842	0.0446	0.0223	0.0107	0.0050
3	0.0613	0.1804	0.2240	0.1954	0.1404	0.0892	0.0521	0.0286	0.0150
4	0.0153	0.0902	0.1680	0.1954	0.1755	0.1339	0.0912	0.0573	0.0337
5	0.0031	0.0361	0.1008	0.1563	0.1755	0.1606	0.1277	0.0916	0.0607
6	0.0005	0.0120	0.0504	0.1042	0.1462	0.1606	0.1490	0.1221	0.0911
7	0.0001	0.0034	0.0216	0.0595	0.1044	0.1377	0.1490	0.1396	0.1171
8	0.0000	0.0009	0.0081	0.0298	0.0653	0.1033	0.1304	0.1396	0.1318
9	0.0000	0.0002	0.0027	0.0132	0.0363	0.0688	0.1014	0.1241	0.1318
10	0.0000	0.0000	0.0008	0.0053	0.0181	0.0413	0.0710	0.0993	0.1186
11	0.0000	0.0000	0.0002	0.0019	0.0082	0.0225	0.0452	0.0722	0.0970
12	0.0000	0.0000	0.0001	0.0006	0.0034	0.0113	0.0263	0.0481	0.0728
13	0.0000	0.0000	0.0000	0.0002	0.0013	0.0052	0.0142	0.0296	0.0504
14	0.0000	0.0000	0.0000	0.0001	0.0005	0.0022	0.0071	0.0169	0.0324
15	0.0000	0.0000	0.0000	0.0000	0.0002	0.0009	0.0033	0.0090	0.0194
16	0.0000	0.0000	0.0000	0.0000	0.0000	0.0003	0.0014	0.0045	0.0109
17	0.0000	0.0000	0.0000	0.0000	0.0000	0.0001	0.0006	0.0021	0.0058
18	0.0000	0.0000	0.0000	0.0000	0.0000	0.0000	0.0002	0.0009	0.0029
19	0.0000	0.0000	0.0000	0.0000	0.0000	0.0000	0.0001	0.0004	0.0014
20	0.0000	0.0000	0.0000	0.0000	0.0000	0.0000	0.0000	0.0002	0.0006
21	0.0000	0.0000	0.0000	0.0000	0.0000	0.0000	0.0000	0.0001	0.0003
22	0.0000	0.0000	0.0000	0.0000	0.0000	0.0000	0.0000	0.0000	0.0001

Appendix D

Areas under the Normal Curve

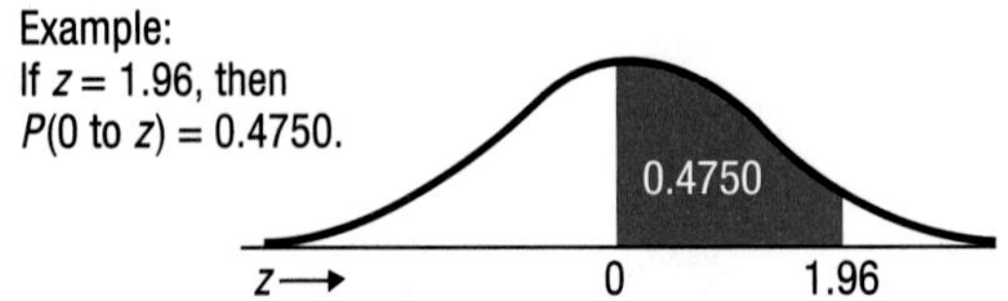

z	0.00	0.01	0.02	0.03	0.04	0.05	0.06	0.07	0.08	0.09
0.0	0.0000	0.0040	0.0080	0.0120	0.0160	0.0199	0.0239	0.0279	0.0319	0.0359
0.1	0.0398	0.0438	0.0478	0.0517	0.0557	0.0596	0.0636	0.0675	0.0714	0.0753
0.2	0.0793	0.0832	0.0871	0.0910	0.0948	0.0987	0.1026	0.1064	0.1103	0.1141
0.3	0.1179	0.1217	0.1255	0.1293	0.1331	0.1368	0.1406	0.1443	0.1480	0.1517
0.4	0.1554	0.1591	0.1628	0.1664	0.1700	0.1736	0.1772	0.1808	0.1844	0.1879
0.5	0.1915	0.1950	0.1985	0.2019	0.2054	0.2088	0.2123	0.2157	0.2190	0.2224
0.6	0.2257	0.2291	0.2324	0.2357	0.2389	0.2422	0.2454	0.2486	0.2517	0.2549
0.7	0.2580	0.2611	0.2642	0.2673	0.2704	0.2734	0.2764	0.2794	0.2823	0.2852
0.8	0.2881	0.2910	0.2939	0.2967	0.2995	0.3023	0.3051	0.3078	0.3106	0.3133
0.9	0.3159	0.3186	0.3212	0.3238	0.3264	0.3289	0.3315	0.3340	0.3365	0.3389
1.0	0.3413	0.3438	0.3461	0.3485	0.3508	0.3531	0.3554	0.3577	0.3599	0.3621
1.1	0.3643	0.3665	0.3686	0.3708	0.3729	0.3749	0.3770	0.3790	0.3810	0.3830
1.2	0.3849	0.3869	0.3888	0.3907	0.3925	0.3944	0.3962	0.3980	0.3997	0.4015
1.3	0.4032	0.4049	0.4066	0.4082	0.4099	0.4115	0.4131	0.4147	0.4162	0.4177
1.4	0.4192	0.4207	0.4222	0.4236	0.4251	0.4265	0.4279	0.4292	0.4306	0.4319
1.5	0.4332	0.4345	0.4357	0.4370	0.4382	0.4394	0.4406	0.4418	0.4429	0.4441
1.6	0.4452	0.4463	0.4474	0.4484	0.4495	0.4505	0.4515	0.4525	0.4535	0.4545
1.7	0.4554	0.4564	0.4573	0.4582	0.4591	0.4599	0.4608	0.4616	0.4625	0.4633
1.8	0.4641	0.4649	0.4656	0.4664	0.4671	0.4678	0.4686	0.4693	0.4699	0.4706
1.9	0.4713	0.4719	0.4726	0.4732	0.4738	0.4744	0.4750	0.4756	0.4761	0.4767
2.0	0.4772	0.4778	0.4783	0.4788	0.4793	0.4798	0.4803	0.4808	0.4812	0.4817
2.1	0.4821	0.4826	0.4830	0.4834	0.4838	0.4842	0.4846	0.4850	0.4854	0.4857
2.2	0.4861	0.4864	0.4868	0.4871	0.4875	0.4878	0.4881	0.4884	0.4887	0.4890
2.3	0.4893	0.4896	0.4898	0.4901	0.4904	0.4906	0.4909	0.4911	0.4913	0.4916
2.4	0.4918	0.4920	0.4922	0.4925	0.4927	0.4929	0.4931	0.4932	0.4934	0.4936
2.5	0.4938	0.4940	0.4941	0.4943	0.4945	0.4946	0.4948	0.4949	0.4951	0.4952
2.6	0.4953	0.4955	0.4956	0.4957	0.4959	0.4960	0.4961	0.4962	0.4963	0.4964
2.7	0.4965	0.4966	0.4967	0.4968	0.4969	0.4970	0.4971	0.4972	0.4973	0.4974
2.8	0.4974	0.4975	0.4976	0.4977	0.4977	0.4978	0.4979	0.4979	0.4980	0.4981
2.9	0.4981	0.4982	0.4982	0.4983	0.4984	0.4984	0.4985	0.4985	0.4986	0.4986
3.0	0.4987	0.4987	0.4987	0.4988	0.4988	0.4989	0.4989	0.4989	0.4990	0.4990

Appendix E

Table of Random Numbers

02711	08182	75997	79866	58095	83319	80295	79741	74599	84379
94873	90935	31684	63952	09865	14491	99518	93394	34691	14985
54921	78680	06635	98689	17306	25170	65928	87709	30533	89736
77640	97636	37397	93379	56454	59818	45827	74164	71666	46977
61545	00835	93251	87203	36759	49197	85967	01704	19634	21898
17147	19519	22497	16857	42426	84822	92598	49186	88247	39967
13748	04742	92460	85801	53444	65626	58710	55406	17173	69776
87455	14813	50373	28037	91182	32786	65261	11173	34376	36408
08999	57409	91185	10200	61411	23392	47797	56377	71635	08601
78804	81333	53809	32471	46034	36306	22498	19239	85428	55721
82173	26921	28472	98958	07960	66124	89731	95069	18625	92405
97594	25168	89178	68190	05043	17407	48201	83917	11413	72920
73881	67176	93504	42636	38233	16154	96451	57925	29667	30859
46071	22912	90326	42453	88108	72064	58601	32357	90610	32921
44492	19686	12495	93135	95185	77799	52441	88272	22024	80631
31864	72170	37722	55794	14636	05148	54505	50113	21119	25228
51574	90692	43339	65689	76539	27909	05467	21727	51141	72949
35350	76132	92925	92124	92634	35681	43690	89136	35599	84138
46943	36502	01172	46045	46991	33804	80006	35542	61056	75666
22665	87226	33304	57975	03985	21566	65796	72915	81466	89205
39437	97957	11838	10433	21564	51570	73558	27495	34533	57808
77082	47784	40098	97962	89845	28392	78187	06112	08169	11261
24544	25649	43370	28007	06779	72402	62632	53956	24709	06978
27503	15558	37738	24849	70722	71859	83736	06016	94397	12529
24590	24545	06435	52758	45685	90151	46516	49644	92686	84870
48155	86226	40359	28723	15364	69125	12609	57171	86857	31702
20226	53752	90648	24362	83314	00014	19207	69413	97016	86290
70178	73444	38790	53626	93780	18629	68766	24371	74639	30782
10169	41465	51935	05711	09799	79077	88159	33437	68519	03040
81084	03701	28598	70013	63794	53169	97054	60303	23259	96196
69202	20777	21727	81511	51887	16175	53746	46516	70339	62727
80561	95787	89426	93325	86412	57479	54194	52153	19197	81877
08199	26703	95128	48599	09333	12584	24374	31232	61782	44032
98883	28220	39358	53720	80161	83371	15181	11131	12219	55920
84568	69286	76054	21615	80883	36797	82845	39139	90900	18172
04269	35173	95745	53893	86022	77722	52498	84193	22448	22571
10538	13124	36099	13140	37706	44562	57179	44693	67877	01549
77843	24955	25900	63843	95029	93859	93634	20205	66294	41218
12034	94636	49455	76362	83532	31062	69903	91186	65768	55949
10524	72829	47641	93315	80875	28090	97728	52560	34937	79548
68935	76632	46984	61772	92786	22651	07086	89754	44143	97687
89450	65665	29190	43709	11172	34481	95977	47535	25658	73898
90696	20451	24211	97310	60446	73530	62865	96574	13829	72226
49006	32047	93086	00112	20470	17136	28255	86328	07293	38809
74591	87025	52368	59416	34417	70557	86746	55809	53628	12000
06315	17012	77103	00968	07235	10728	42189	33292	51487	64443
62386	09184	62092	46617	99419	64230	95034	85481	07857	42510
86848	82122	04028	36959	87827	12813	08627	80699	13345	51695
65643	69480	46598	04501	40403	91408	32343	48130	49303	90689
11084	46534	78957	77353	39578	77868	22970	84349	09184	70603

Appendix F

Student's *t* Distribution

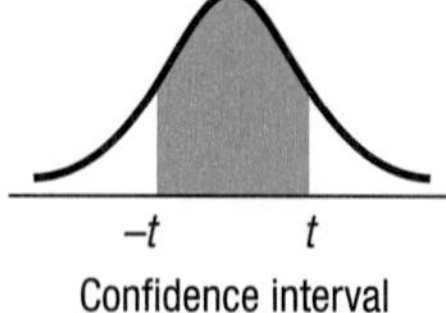

Confidence interval

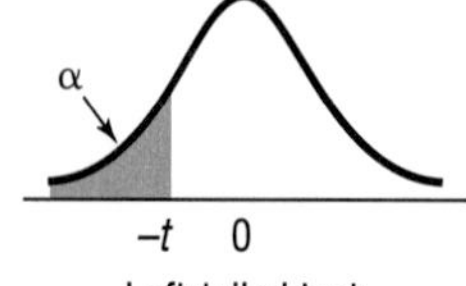

Left-tailed test

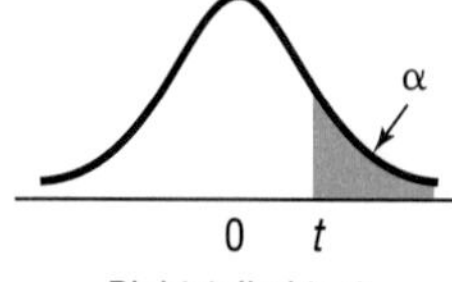

Right-tailed test

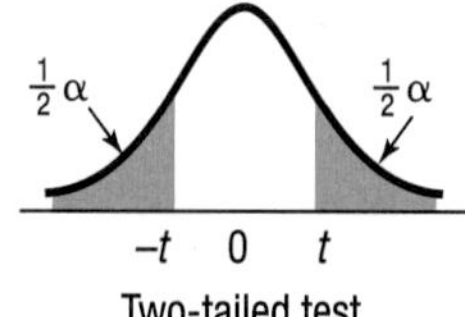

Two-tailed test

	Confidence Intervals					
	80%	90%	95%	98%	99%	99.9%
	Level of Significance for One-Tailed Test, α					
df	0.100	0.050	0.025	0.010	0.005	0.0005
	Level of Significance for Two-Tailed Test, α					
	0.20	0.10	0.05	0.02	0.01	0.001
1	3.078	6.314	12.706	31.821	63.657	636.619
2	1.886	2.920	4.303	6.965	9.925	31.599
3	1.638	2.353	3.182	4.541	5.841	12.924
4	1.533	2.132	2.776	3.747	4.604	8.610
5	1.476	2.015	2.571	3.365	4.032	6.869
6	1.440	1.943	2.447	3.143	3.707	5.959
7	1.415	1.895	2.365	2.998	3.499	5.408
8	1.397	1.860	2.306	2.896	3.355	5.041
9	1.383	1.833	2.262	2.821	3.250	4.781
10	1.372	1.812	2.228	2.764	3.169	4.587
11	1.363	1.796	2.201	2.718	3.106	4.437
12	1.356	1.782	2.179	2.681	3.055	4.318
13	1.350	1.771	2.160	2.650	3.012	4.221
14	1.345	1.761	2.145	2.624	2.977	4.140
15	1.341	1.753	2.131	2.602	2.947	4.073
16	1.337	1.746	2.120	2.583	2.921	4.015
17	1.333	1.740	2.110	2.567	2.898	3.965
18	1.330	1.734	2.101	2.552	2.878	3.922
19	1.328	1.729	2.093	2.539	2.861	3.883
20	1.325	1.725	2.086	2.528	2.845	3.850
21	1.323	1.721	2.080	2.518	2.831	3.819
22	1.321	1.717	2.074	2.508	2.819	3.792
23	1.319	1.714	2.069	2.500	2.807	3.768
24	1.318	1.711	2.064	2.492	2.797	3.745
25	1.316	1.708	2.060	2.485	2.787	3.725
26	1.315	1.706	2.056	2.479	2.779	3.707
27	1.314	1.703	2.052	2.473	2.771	3.690
28	1.313	1.701	2.048	2.467	2.763	3.674
29	1.311	1.699	2.045	2.462	2.756	3.659
30	1.310	1.697	2.042	2.457	2.750	3.646
40	1.303	1.684	2.021	2.423	2.704	3.551
60	1.296	1.671	2.000	2.390	2.660	3.460
120	1.289	1.658	1.980	2.358	2.617	3.373
∞	1.282	1.645	1.960	2.326	2.576	3.291

Appendix G

Critical Values of the *F* Distribution at a 5 Percent Level of Significance

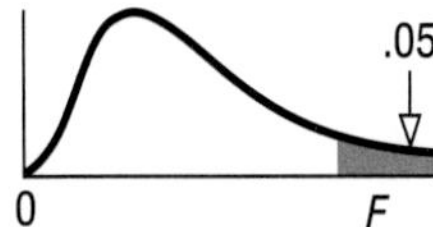

Degrees of Freedom for the Denominator	Degrees of Freedom for the Numerator															
	1	**2**	**3**	**4**	**5**	**6**	**7**	**8**	**9**	**10**	**12**	**15**	**20**	**24**	**30**	**40**
1	161	200	216	225	230	234	237	239	241	242	244	246	248	249	250	251
2	18.5	19.0	19.2	19.2	19.3	19.3	19.4	19.4	19.4	19.4	19.4	19.4	19.4	19.5	19.5	19.5
3	10.1	9.55	9.28	9.12	9.01	8.94	8.89	8.85	8.81	8.79	8.74	8.70	8.66	8.64	8.62	8.59
4	7.71	6.94	6.59	6.39	6.26	6.16	6.09	6.04	6.00	5.96	5.91	5.86	5.80	5.77	5.75	5.72
5	6.61	5.79	5.41	5.19	5.05	4.95	4.88	4.82	4.77	4.74	4.68	4.62	4.56	4.53	4.50	4.46
6	5.99	5.14	4.76	4.53	4.39	4.28	4.21	4.15	4.10	4.06	4.00	3.94	3.87	3.84	3.81	3.77
7	5.59	4.74	4.35	4.12	3.97	3.87	3.79	3.73	3.68	3.64	3.57	3.51	3.44	3.41	3.38	3.34
8	5.32	4.46	4.07	3.84	3.69	3.58	3.50	3.44	3.39	3.35	3.28	3.22	3.15	3.12	3.08	3.04
9	5.12	4.26	3.86	3.63	3.48	3.37	3.29	3.23	3.18	3.14	3.07	3.01	2.94	2.90	2.86	2.83
10	4.96	4.10	3.71	3.48	3.33	3.22	3.14	3.07	3.02	2.98	2.91	2.85	2.77	2.74	2.70	2.66
11	4.84	3.98	3.59	3.36	3.20	3.09	3.01	2.95	2.90	2.85	2.79	2.72	2.65	2.61	2.57	2.53
12	4.75	3.89	3.49	3.26	3.11	3.00	2.91	2.85	2.80	2.75	2.69	2.62	2.54	2.51	2.47	2.43
13	4.67	3.81	3.41	3.18	3.03	2.92	2.83	2.77	2.71	2.67	2.60	2.53	2.46	2.42	2.38	2.34
14	4.60	3.74	3.34	3.11	2.96	2.85	2.76	2.70	2.65	2.60	2.53	2.46	2.39	2.35	2.31	2.27
15	4.54	3.68	3.29	3.06	2.90	2.79	2.71	2.64	2.59	2.54	2.48	2.40	2.33	2.29	2.25	2.20
16	4.49	3.63	3.24	3.01	2.85	2.74	2.66	2.59	2.54	2.49	2.42	2.35	2.28	2.24	2.19	2.15
17	4.45	3.59	3.20	2.96	2.81	2.70	2.61	2.55	2.49	2.45	2.38	2.31	2.23	2.19	2.15	2.10
18	4.41	3.55	3.16	2.93	2.77	2.66	2.58	2.51	2.46	2.41	2.34	2.27	2.19	2.15	2.11	2.06
19	4.38	3.52	3.13	2.90	2.74	2.63	2.54	2.48	2.42	2.38	2.31	2.23	2.16	2.11	2.07	2.03
20	4.35	3.49	3.10	2.87	2.71	2.60	2.51	2.45	2.39	2.35	2.28	2.20	2.12	2.08	2.04	1.99
21	4.32	3.47	3.07	2.84	2.68	2.57	2.49	2.42	2.37	2.32	2.25	2.18	2.10	2.05	2.01	1.96
22	4.30	3.44	3.05	2.82	2.66	2.55	2.46	2.40	2.34	2.30	2.23	2.15	2.07	2.03	1.98	1.94
23	4.28	3.42	3.03	2.80	2.64	2.53	2.44	2.37	2.32	2.27	2.20	2.13	2.05	2.01	1.96	1.91
24	4.26	3.40	3.01	2.78	2.62	2.51	2.42	2.36	2.30	2.25	2.18	2.11	2.03	1.98	1.94	1.89
25	4.24	3.39	2.99	2.76	2.60	2.49	2.40	2.34	2.28	2.24	2.16	2.09	2.01	1.96	1.92	1.87
30	4.17	3.32	2.92	2.69	2.53	2.42	2.33	2.27	2.21	2.16	2.09	2.01	1.93	1.89	1.84	1.79
40	4.08	3.23	2.84	2.61	2.45	2.34	2.25	2.18	2.12	2.08	2.00	1.92	1.84	1.79	1.74	1.69
60	4.00	3.15	2.76	2.53	2.37	2.25	2.17	2.10	2.04	1.99	1.92	1.84	1.75	1.70	1.65	1.59
120	3.92	3.07	2.68	2.45	2.29	2.18	2.09	2.02	1.96	1.91	1.83	1.75	1.66	1.61	1.55	1.50
∞	3.84	3.00	2.60	2.37	2.21	2.10	2.01	1.94	1.88	1.83	1.75	1.67	1.57	1.52	1.46	1.39

Appendix G

Critical Values of the *F* Distribution at a 1 Percent Level of Significance (*concluded*)

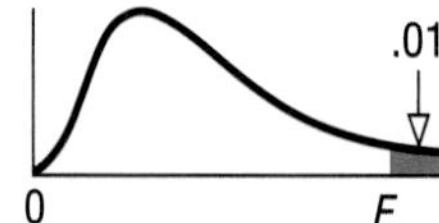

Degrees of Freedom for the Denominator	Degrees of Freedom for the Numerator															
	1	2	3	4	5	6	7	8	9	10	12	15	20	24	30	40
1	4052	5000	5403	5625	5764	5859	5928	5981	6022	6056	6106	6157	6209	6235	6261	6287
2	98.5	99.0	99.2	99.2	99.3	99.3	99.4	99.4	99.4	99.4	99.4	99.4	99.4	99.5	99.5	99.5
3	34.1	30.8	29.5	28.7	28.2	27.9	27.7	27.5	27.3	27.2	27.1	26.9	26.7	26.6	26.5	26.4
4	21.2	18.0	16.7	16.0	15.5	15.2	15.0	14.8	14.7	14.5	14.4	14.2	14.0	13.9	13.8	13.7
5	16.3	13.3	12.1	11.4	11.0	10.7	10.5	10.3	10.2	10.1	9.89	9.72	9.55	9.47	9.38	9.29
6	13.7	10.9	9.78	9.15	8.75	8.47	8.26	8.10	7.98	7.87	7.72	7.56	7.40	7.31	7.23	7.14
7	12.2	9.55	8.45	7.85	7.46	7.19	6.99	6.84	6.72	6.62	6.47	6.31	6.16	6.07	5.99	5.91
8	11.3	8.65	7.59	7.01	6.63	6.37	6.18	6.03	5.91	5.81	5.67	5.52	5.36	5.28	5.20	5.12
9	10.6	8.02	6.99	6.42	6.06	5.80	5.61	5.47	5.35	5.26	5.11	4.96	4.81	4.73	4.65	4.57
10	10.0	7.56	6.55	5.99	5.64	5.39	5.20	5.06	4.94	4.85	4.71	4.56	4.41	4.33	4.25	4.17
11	9.65	7.21	6.22	5.67	5.32	5.07	4.89	4.74	4.63	4.54	4.40	4.25	4.10	4.02	3.94	3.86
12	9.33	6.93	5.95	5.41	5.06	4.82	4.64	4.50	4.39	4.30	4.16	4.01	3.86	3.78	3.70	3.62
13	9.07	6.70	5.74	5.21	4.86	4.62	4.44	4.30	4.19	4.10	3.96	3.82	3.66	3.59	3.51	3.43
14	8.86	6.51	5.56	5.04	4.69	4.46	4.28	4.14	4.03	3.94	3.80	3.66	3.51	3.43	3.35	3.27
15	8.68	6.36	5.42	4.89	4.56	4.32	4.14	4.00	3.89	3.80	3.67	3.52	3.37	3.29	3.21	3.13
16	8.53	6.23	5.29	4.77	4.44	4.20	4.03	3.89	3.78	3.69	3.55	3.41	3.26	3.18	3.10	3.02
17	8.40	6.11	5.18	4.67	4.34	4.10	3.93	3.79	3.68	3.59	3.46	3.31	3.16	3.08	3.00	2.92
18	8.29	6.01	5.09	4.58	4.25	4.01	3.84	3.71	3.60	3.51	3.37	3.23	3.08	3.00	2.92	2.84
19	8.18	5.93	5.01	4.50	4.17	3.94	3.77	3.63	3.52	3.43	3.30	3.15	3.00	2.92	2.84	2.76
20	8.10	5.85	4.94	4.43	4.10	3.87	3.70	3.56	3.46	3.37	3.23	3.09	2.94	2.86	2.78	2.69
21	8.02	5.78	4.87	4.37	4.04	3.81	3.64	3.51	3.40	3.31	3.17	3.03	2.88	2.80	2.72	2.64
22	7.95	5.72	4.82	4.31	3.99	3.76	3.59	3.45	3.35	3.26	3.12	2.98	2.83	2.75	2.67	2.58
23	7.88	5.66	4.76	4.26	3.94	3.71	3.54	3.41	3.30	3.21	3.07	2.93	2.78	2.70	2.62	2.54
24	7.82	5.61	4.72	4.22	3.90	3.67	3.50	3.36	3.26	3.17	3.03	2.89	2.74	2.66	2.58	2.49
25	7.77	5.57	4.68	4.18	3.85	3.63	3.46	3.32	3.22	3.13	2.99	2.85	2.70	2.62	2.54	2.45
30	7.56	5.39	4.51	4.02	3.70	3.47	3.30	3.17	3.07	2.98	2.84	2.70	2.55	2.47	2.39	2.30
40	7.31	5.18	4.31	3.83	3.51	3.29	3.12	2.99	2.89	2.80	2.66	2.52	2.37	2.29	2.20	2.11
60	7.08	4.98	4.13	3.65	3.34	3.12	2.95	2.82	2.72	2.63	2.50	2.35	2.20	2.12	2.03	1.94
120	6.85	4.79	3.95	3.48	3.17	2.96	2.79	2.66	2.56	2.47	2.34	2.19	2.03	1.95	1.86	1.76
∞	6.63	4.61	3.78	3.32	3.02	2.80	2.64	2.51	2.41	2.32	2.18	2.04	1.88	1.79	1.70	1.59

Appendix H

Wilcoxon *T* Values

	2α						
	.15	.10	.05	.04	.03	.02	.01
	α						
n	.075	.050	.025	.020	.015	.010	.005
4	0						
5	1	0					
6	2	2	0	0			
7	4	3	2	1	0	0	
8	7	5	3	3	2	1	0
9	9	8	5	5	4	3	1
10	12	10	8	7	6	5	3
11	16	13	10	9	8	7	5
12	19	17	13	12	11	9	7
13	24	21	17	16	14	12	9
14	28	25	21	19	18	15	12
15	33	30	25	23	21	19	15
16	39	35	29	28	26	23	19
17	45	41	34	33	30	27	23
18	51	47	40	38	35	32	27
19	58	53	46	43	41	37	32
20	65	60	52	50	47	43	37
21	73	67	58	56	53	49	42
22	81	75	65	63	59	55	48
23	89	83	73	70	66	62	54
24	98	91	81	78	74	69	61
25	108	100	89	86	82	76	68
26	118	110	98	94	90	84	75
27	128	119	107	103	99	92	83
28	138	130	116	112	108	101	91
29	150	140	126	122	117	110	100
30	161	151	137	132	127	120	109
31	173	163	147	143	137	130	118
32	186	175	159	154	148	140	128
33	199	187	170	165	159	151	138
34	212	200	182	177	171	162	148
35	226	213	195	189	182	173	159
40	302	286	264	257	249	238	220
50	487	466	434	425	413	397	373
60	718	690	648	636	620	600	567
70	995	960	907	891	872	846	805
80	1,318	1,276	1,211	1,192	1,168	1,136	1,086
90	1,688	1,638	1,560	1,537	1,509	1,471	1,410
100	2,105	2,045	1,955	1,928	1,894	1,850	1,779

Appendix I

Factors for Control Charts

Number of Items in Sample	Chart for Averages	Chart for Ranges		
	Factors for Control Limits	Factors for Central Line	Factors for Control Limits	
n	A_2	d_2	D_3	D_4
2	1.880	1.128	0	3.267
3	1.023	1.693	0	2.575
4	.729	2.059	0	2.282
5	.577	2.326	0	2.115
6	.483	2.534	0	2.004
7	.419	2.704	.076	1.924
8	.373	2.847	.136	1.864
9	.337	2.970	.184	1.816
10	.308	3.078	.223	1.777
11	.285	3.173	.256	1.744
12	.266	3.258	.284	1.716
13	.249	3.336	.308	1.692
14	.235	3.407	.329	1.671
15	.223	3.472	.348	1.652

SOURCE: Adapted from American Society for Testing and Materials, *Manual on Quality Control of Materials,* 1951, Table B2, p. 115. For a more detailed table and explanation, see Acheson, J. Duncan, *Quality Control and Industrial Statistics,* 3d ed. (Homewood, Ill.: Richard D. Irwin, 1974), Table M, p. 927.

Appendix J

Dataset 1—Real Estate

x_1 = Selling price in \$000
x_2 = Number of bedrooms
x_3 = Size of the home in square feet
x_4 = Pool (1 = yes, 0 = no)
x_5 = Distance from the center of the city
x_6 = Township
x_7 = Garage attached (1 = yes, 0 = no)
x_8 = Number of bathrooms

x_1	x_2	x_3	x_4	x_5	x_6	x_7	x_8
263.1	4	2,300	1	17	5	1	2
182.4	4	2,100	0	19	4	0	2
242.1	3	2,300	0	12	3	0	2
213.6	2	2,200	0	16	2	0	2.5
139.9	2	2,100	0	28	1	0	1.5
245.4	2	2,100	1	12	1	1	2
327.2	6	2,500	0	15	3	1	2
271.8	2	2,100	0	9	2	1	2.5
221.1	3	2,300	1	18	1	0	1.5
266.6	4	2,400	0	13	4	1	2
292.4	4	2,100	0	14	3	1	2
209	2	1,700	0	8	4	1	1.5
270.8	6	2,500	0	7	4	1	2
246.1	4	2,100	0	18	3	1	2
194.4	2	2,300	0	11	3	0	2
281.3	3	2,100	0	16	2	1	2
172.7	4	2,200	1	16	3	0	2
207.5	5	2,300	1	21	4	0	2.5
198.9	3	2,200	1	10	4	1	2
209.3	6	1,900	1	15	4	1	2
252.3	4	2,600	0	8	4	1	2
192.9	4	1,900	1	14	2	1	2.5
209.3	5	2,100	0	20	5	0	1.5
345.3	8	2,600	0	9	4	1	2
326.3	6	2,100	0	11	5	1	3
173.1	2	2,200	1	21	5	1	1.5
187	2	1,900	0	26	4	0	2
257.2	2	2,100	0	9	4	1	2
233	3	2,200	0	14	3	1	1.5
180.4	2	2,000	0	11	5	0	2
234	2	1,700	0	19	3	1	2
207.1	2	2,000	0	11	5	1	2
247.7	5	2,400	0	16	2	1	2
166.2	3	2,000	1	16	2	1	2
177.1	2	1,900	0	10	5	1	2

Appendix J

Dataset 1—Real Estate (*continued*)

x_1	x_2	x_3	x_4	x_5	x_6	x_7	x_8
182.7	4	2,000	1	14	4	0	2.5
216	4	2,300	0	19	2	0	2
312.1	6	2,600	0	7	5	1	2.5
199.8	3	2,100	0	19	3	1	2
273.2	5	2,200	0	16	2	1	3
206	3	2,100	1	9	3	0	1.5
232.2	3	1,900	1	16	1	1	1.5
198.3	4	2,100	1	19	1	1	1.5
205.1	3	2,000	1	20	4	0	2
175.6	4	2,300	1	24	4	1	2
307.8	3	2,400	1	21	2	1	3
269.2	5	2,200	0	8	5	1	3
224.8	3	2,200	0	17	1	1	2.5
171.6	3	2,000	1	16	4	0	2
216.8	3	2,200	0	15	1	1	2
192.6	6	2,200	1	14	1	0	2
236.4	5	2,200	0	20	3	1	2
172.4	3	2,200	0	23	3	0	2
251.4	3	1,900	0	12	2	1	2
246	6	2,300	0	7	3	1	3
147.4	6	1,700	1	12	1	0	2
176	4	2,200	0	15	1	1	2
228.4	3	2,300	0	17	5	1	1.5
166.5	3	1,600	1	19	3	0	2.5
189.4	4	2,200	0	24	1	1	2
312.1	7	2,400	0	13	3	1	3
289.8	6	2,000	0	21	3	1	3
269.9	5	2,200	1	11	4	1	2.5
154.3	2	2,000	0	13	2	0	2
222.1	2	2,100	0	9	5	1	2
209.7	5	2,200	1	13	2	1	2
190.9	3	2,200	1	18	3	1	2
254.3	4	2,500	1	15	3	1	2
207.5	3	2,100	1	10	2	0	2
209.7	4	2,200	1	19	2	1	2
294	2	2,100	0	13	2	1	2.5
176.3	2	2,000	1	17	3	0	2
294.3	7	2,400	0	8	4	1	2
224	3	1,900	1	6	1	1	2
125	2	1,900	0	18	4	0	1.5
236.8	4	2,600	1	17	5	1	2
164.1	4	2,300	0	19	4	0	2
217.8	3	2,500	0	12	3	0	2
192.2	2	2,400	0	16	2	0	2.5
125.9	2	2,400	0	28	1	0	1.5

Appendix J

Dataset 1—Real Estate (*concluded*)

X_1	X_2	X_3	X_4	X_5	X_6	X_7	X_8
220.9	2	2,300	1	12	1	1	2
294.5	6	2,700	0	15	3	1	2
244.6	2	2,300	0	9	2	1	2.5
199	3	2,500	1	18	1	0	1.5
240	4	2,600	0	13	4	1	2
263.2	4	2,300	0	14	3	1	2
188.1	2	1,900	0	8	4	1	1.5
243.7	6	2,700	0	7	4	1	2
221.5	4	2,300	0	18	3	1	2
175	2	2,500	0	11	3	0	2
253.2	3	2,300	0	16	2	1	2
155.4	4	2,400	1	16	3	0	2
186.7	5	2,500	1	21	4	0	2.5
179	3	2,400	1	10	4	1	2
188.3	6	2,100	1	15	4	1	2
227.1	4	2,900	0	8	4	1	2
173.6	4	2,100	1	14	2	1	2.5
188.3	5	2,300	0	20	5	0	1.5
310.8	8	2,900	0	9	4	1	2
293.7	6	2,400	0	11	5	1	3
179	3	2,400	0	8	4	1	2
188.3	6	2,100	1	14	2	1	2.5
227.1	4	2,900	0	20	5	0	1.5
173.6	4	2,100	0	9	4	1	2
188.3	5	2,300	0	11	5	1	3

Appendix K

Dataset 2—Major League Baseball

x_1 = Team
x_2 = League (American = 1, National = 0)
x_3 = Built (Year Stadium Was Built)
x_4 = Size (Stadium Capacity)
x_5 = Salary (Total 2003 Team Salary $ Mil)
x_6 = Attendance (Total 2003 Team Attendance in 000)
x_7 = Wins (Number of Wins in 2003)
x_8 = ERA (Earned Run Average)
x_9 = Batting (Team Batting Average)
x_{10} = HR (Number of Home Runs for the Team)
x_{11} = Surface (Natural = 0, Artificial = 1)
x_{12} = Stolen (Stolen Bases)
x_{13} = Errors (Team Errors)
x_{14} = Year
x_{15} = Average (Average Player Salary)

Team x_1	League x_2	Built x_3	Size x_4	Salary x_5	Attendance x_6	Wins x_7	ERA x_8	Batting x_9	HR x_{10}	Surface x_{11}	Stolen x_{12}	Errors x_{13}	Year x_{14}	Average x_{15}
Boston	1	1912	33,871	99.9	2,724.2	95	4.48	0.289	238	0	88	113	1989	512,930
New York Yankees	1	1923	57,746	152.7	3,465.6	101	4.02	0.271	230	0	98	114	1990	578,930
Oakland	1	1966	43,662	50.3	2,216.6	96	3.63	0.254	176	0	48	107	1991	891,188
Baltimore	1	1992	48,262	73.3	2,454.5	71	4.76	0.268	152	0	89	105	1992	1,084,408
Anaheim	1	1966	45,050	79.0	3,061.1	77	4.28	0.268	150	0	129	105	1993	1,120,254
Cleveland	1	1994	43,368	48.6	1,730.0	68	4.21	0.254	158	0	86	126	1994	1,188,679
Chicago White Sox	1	1991	44,321	51.0	1,939.5	86	4.17	0.263	220	0	77	93	1995	1,071,029
Toronto	1	1989	50,516	51.3	1,799.5	86	4.69	0.279	190	1	37	117	1996	1,176,967
Minnesota	1	1982	48,678	55.5	1,946.0	90	4.41	0.277	155	1	94	87	1997	1,383,578
Tampa Bay	1	1990	44,027	19.6	1,058.7	63	4.93	0.265	137	1	142	103	1998	1,441,406
Texas	1	1994	52,000	103.5	2,094.4	71	5.67	0.268	239	0	65	94	1999	1,720,050
Detroit	1	2000	40,000	49.2	1,368.2	43	5.3	0.240	153	0	98	138	2000	1,988,034
Seattle	1	1999	45,611	87.0	3,268.5	93	3.76	0.271	139	0	108	65	2001	2,264,403
Kansas City	1	1973	40,529	40.5	1,779.9	83	5.05	0.274	162	0	120	108	2002	2,383,235
Atlanta	0	1993	50,062	106.2	2,401.1	101	4.1	0.284	235	0	68	121	2003	2,555,476
Arizona	0	1998	49,075	90.7	2,805.5	84	3.84	0.263	152	0	76	107		
Houston	0	2000	42,000	71.0	2,454.2	87	3.86	0.263	191	0	66	95		
Cincinnati	0	1970	52,953	59.4	2,355.3	89	5.09	0.245	182	0	80	141		
New York Mets	0	1964	55,775	117.2	2,140.6	66	4.48	0.247	124	0	70	118		
Pittsburgh	0	2001	38,127	54.8	1,636.8	75	4.64	0.267	163	0	86	123		
Los Angeles	0	1962	56,000	105.9	3,138.6	95	3.16	0.243	124	0	80	119		
San Diego	0	1967	53,166	45.2	2,030.1	64	4.87	0.261	128	0	76	102		
Montreal	0	1976	46,500	51.9	1,025.6	93	4.01	0.258	144	1	100	102		
San Francisco	0	2000	40,800	82.9	3,264.9	100	3.73	0.264	180	0	53	80		
St. Louis	0	1966	49,625	83.8	2,910.4	95	4.6	0.279	196	0	82	77		
Florida	0	1987	42,531	48.8	1,303.2	91	4.04	0.266	157	0	150	78		
Philadelphia	0	1971	62,411	70.8	2,259.9	96	4.04	0.261	166	1	72	97		
Milwaukee	0	2001	42,400	40.6	1,700.4	68	5.02	0.256	196	0	99	114		
Chicago Cubs	0	1914	38,957	79.9	2,962.8	88	3.83	0.259	172	0	73	106		
Colorado	0	1995	50,381	67.2	2,334.1	74	5.2	0.267	198	0	63	116		

Appendix L

Dataset 3—Wages and Wage Earners

x_1 = Annual wage in dollars
x_2 = Industry (1 = Manufacturing, 2 = Construction, 0 = Other)
x_3 = Occupation (1 = Mgmt., 2 = Sales, 3 = Clerical, 4 = Service, 5 = Prof., 0 = Other)
x_4 = Years of education
x_5 = Southern resident (1 = Yes, 0 = No)
x_6 = Non-white (1 = Yes, 0 = No)
x_7 = Hispanic (1 = Yes, 0 = No)
x_8 = Female (1 = Yes, 0 = No)
x_9 = Years of Work Experience
x_{10} = Married (1 = Yes, 0 = No)
x_{11} = Age in years
x_{12} = Union member (1 = Yes, 0 = No)

Row	Wage x_1	Industry x_2	Occupation x_3	Education x_4	South x_5	Non-white x_6	Hispanic x_7
1	19,388	1	0	6	1	0	0
2	49,898	2	0	12	0	0	0
3	28,219	0	3	12	1	0	0
4	83,601	0	5	17	0	0	1
5	29,736	0	4	8	0	0	1
6	50,235	1	0	16	0	0	0
7	45,976	0	2	12	0	0	0
8	33,411	1	2	12	1	0	0
9	21,716	0	5	12	0	0	0
10	37,664	0	5	18	0	0	0
11	26,820	0	5	18	0	0	0
12	29,977	0	4	16	0	1	0
13	33,959	0	5	17	0	0	0
14	11,780	0	2	11	0	0	0
15	10,997	0	4	14	0	1	0
16	17,626	0	3	12	0	0	0
17	22,133	0	5	16	0	0	0
18	21,994	0	1	12	0	0	0
19	29,390	0	0	13	0	0	0
20	32,138	0	4	14	0	0	0
21	30,006	1	3	16	0	0	0
22	68,573	0	5	16	1	0	0
23	17,694	0	4	8	0	0	0
24	26,795	0	0	7	1	0	0
25	19,981	0	4	4	0	0	0
26	14,476	0	5	12	0	0	0
27	19,452	0	4	13	0	1	0
28	28,168	1	0	13	0	0	0
29	19,306	0	5	9	1	1	0
30	13,318	1	0	11	1	0	0

Dataset 3—Wages and Wage Earners (*continued*)

Row	Wage x_1	Industry x_2	Occupation x_3	Education x_4	South x_5	Non-white x_6	Hispanic x_7
31	25,166	0	4	12	0	0	0
32	18,121	1	3	12	0	0	0
33	13,162	1	0	12	0	1	0
34	32,094	0	3	12	1	0	0
35	16,667	0	3	12	1	0	0
36	50,171	0	5	12	0	0	0
37	31,691	1	0	12	0	0	0
38	36,178	0	3	12	0	0	0
39	15,234	0	1	12	1	0	1
40	16,817	0	3	12	1	0	0
41	22,485	0	3	12	0	0	0
42	30,308	0	4	12	0	0	0
43	11,702	0	2	14	1	0	0
44	11,186	0	0	12	0	0	0
45	12,285	0	1	12	0	0	0
46	19,284	1	4	16	0	0	0
47	11,451	1	0	12	0	0	0
48	57,623	0	1	15	0	0	0
49	25,670	0	3	13	0	0	0
50	83,443	0	5	17	0	0	0
51	49,974	1	1	16	0	1	0
52	46,646	2	0	5	1	0	0
53	31,702	0	3	12	1	0	0
54	13,312	0	4	12	1	0	0
55	44,543	0	2	18	0	0	0
56	15,013	0	4	16	0	0	0
57	33,389	0	1	14	0	1	0
58	60,626	0	5	18	0	0	0
59	24,509	0	5	14	0	0	1
60	20,852	1	0	12	0	0	0
61	30,133	2	0	10	0	0	0
62	31,799	0	3	12	0	0	0
63	16,796	0	4	12	0	0	0
64	20,793	0	0	12	1	0	0
65	29,407	0	4	10	1	0	0
66	29,191	0	0	12	0	0	0
67	15,957	0	2	12	1	0	0
68	34,484	0	3	13	1	0	0
69	35,185	1	3	14	0	0	0
70	26,614	1	0	12	0	0	0
71	41,780	0	0	12	1	0	0
72	55,777	0	1	14	1	0	0
73	15,160	0	4	8	1	0	0
74	66,738	0	0	9	1	0	0
75	33,351	0	5	16	1	0	0

Appendix L

Dataset 3—Wages and Wage Earners (*continued*)

Row	Wage x_1	Industry x_2	Occupation x_3	Education x_4	South x_5	Non-white x_6	Hispanic x_7
76	33,498	0	1	10	0	0	0
77	29,809	0	4	8	0	1	0
78	15,193	1	0	12	0	0	0
79	23,027	0	4	14	0	1	0
80	75,165	0	1	15	0	0	0
81	18,752	0	4	11	0	0	0
82	83,569	0	1	18	0	0	0
83	32,235	0	3	12	0	0	0
84	20,852	0	0	12	1	0	0
85	13,787	0	4	11	0	0	0
86	34,746	0	3	14	1	0	0
87	17,690	0	1	12	1	1	0
88	52,762	0	5	18	0	0	0
89	60,152	0	5	16	1	0	0
90	33,461	0	1	16	0	0	1
91	13,481	0	4	12	1	0	1
92	9,879	0	3	12	1	0	0
93	16,789	0	3	13	1	0	0
94	31,304	0	1	16	0	0	0
95	37,771	0	5	15	0	0	0
96	50,187	0	3	12	0	0	0
97	39,888	0	3	12	1	0	0
98	19,227	0	3	12	0	0	0
99	32,786	1	0	11	1	0	0
100	28,440	0	4	12	0	0	0

Appendix L

Dataset 3—Wages and Wage Earners (*concluded*)

Row	Female x_8	Experience x_9	Married x_{10}	Age x_{11}	Union x_{12}
1	0	45	1	57	0
2	0	33	1	51	1
3	0	12	1	30	0
4	0	18	1	41	0
5	0	47	1	61	1
6	0	12	1	34	0
7	0	43	1	61	1
8	0	20	1	38	0
9	1	11	0	29	0
10	0	19	1	43	0
11	0	33	0	57	1
12	1	6	1	28	0
13	1	26	1	49	1
14	1	33	1	50	0
15	0	0	0	20	0
16	1	45	1	63	0
17	1	10	0	32	1
18	1	24	1	42	0
19	0	18	1	37	0
20	0	22	1	42	1
21	1	27	1	49	0
22	0	14	1	36	1
23	1	38	1	52	0
24	0	44	1	57	0
25	0	54	1	64	0
26	1	3	1	21	0
27	0	3	0	22	0
28	0	17	0	36	0
29	1	34	1	49	1
30	1	25	1	42	1
31	1	10	0	28	0
32	1	18	1	36	0
33	0	6	0	24	1
34	1	14	1	32	0
35	0	4	0	22	0
36	0	39	1	57	1
37	0	13	0	31	0
38	1	40	1	58	0
39	1	4	0	22	0
40	1	26	0	44	0
41	0	22	0	40	0
42	0	10	1	28	0
43	1	6	1	26	0
44	0	0	0	18	0
45	1	42	1	60	0
46	0	3	0	25	0
47	1	8	1	26	0
48	0	31	1	52	0
49	1	8	0	27	1
50	1	5	0	28	0
51	0	26	1	48	1
52	0	44	1	55	0
53	1	39	1	57	0
54	1	9	1	27	0
55	0	10	1	34	0
56	0	21	1	43	0
57	0	22	0	42	0
58	0	7	1	31	0
59	1	15	0	35	0
60	1	38	1	56	0
61	0	27	1	43	0
62	1	25	0	43	0
63	1	14	1	32	0
64	1	6	0	24	0
65	0	19	0	35	0
66	0	9	0	27	0
67	1	10	0	28	0
68	1	28	0	47	0
69	1	12	1	32	0
70	1	19	1	37	0
71	0	9	1	27	0
72	0	21	1	41	0
73	1	45	0	59	0
74	0	29	1	44	0
75	1	4	1	26	0
76	0	20	1	36	0
77	1	29	0	43	0
78	1	15	0	33	0
79	0	34	1	54	1
80	0	12	1	33	0
81	1	45	0	62	1
82	0	29	1	53	0
83	1	38	1	56	0
84	0	1	0	19	0
85	0	4	1	21	0
86	1	15	1	35	0
87	0	14	1	32	0
88	0	7	1	31	0
89	0	38	1	60	0
90	0	7	1	29	1
91	0	7	0	25	0
92	1	28	1	46	0
93	1	6	1	25	0
94	1	26	1	48	0
95	0	5	0	26	0
96	1	24	1	42	0
97	0	5	0	23	0
98	1	15	1	33	0
99	0	37	1	54	1
100	1	24	1	42	0

Appendix M

Dataset 4—CIA International Economic and Demographic Data

x_1 = Country name
x_2 = Total area (square kilometers)
x_3 = Member of the G-20, group of industrial nations to promote international financial stability (0 = nonmember, 1 = member)
x_4 = Country has petroleum as a natural resource [0 = no, 1 = petroleum is a natural resource, 2 = country is a member of OPEC (Organization of Petroleum Exporting Countries)]
x_5 = Population (expressed in thousands)
x_6 = Percent of population aged 65 years and over
x_7 = Life expectancy at birth
x_8 = Literacy: percent of population age 15 or more that can read and write
x_9 = Gross Domestic Product per capita expressed in thousands
x_{10} = Labor force (expressed in millions)
x_{11} = Percent unemployment
x_{12} = Exports expressed in billions of dollars
x_{13} = Imports expressed in billions of dollars
x_{14} = Number of mobile or cellular phones expressed in millions

Country x_1	Area (km^2) x_2	G-20 x_3	Petroleum x_4	Pop (1,000s) x_5	65 & over x_6	Life Expectancy x_7
Algeria	2,381,740	0	2	31,736	4.07	69.95
Argentina	2,766,890	1	1	37,385	10.42	75.26
Australia	7,686,850	1	1	19,357	12.5	79.87
Austria	83,858	0	0	8,150	15.38	77.84
Belgium	30,510	0	0	10,259	16.95	77.96
Brazil	8,511,965	1	1	174,469	5.45	63.24
Canada	9,976,140	1	1	31,592	12.77	79.56
China	9,596,960	1	1	1,273,111	7.11	71.62
Czech Republic	79	0	0	10,264	13.92	74.73
Denmark	43,094	0	1	5,352	14.85	76.72
Finland	337,030	0	0	5,175	15.03	77.58
France	547,030	1	0	59,551	16.13	78.9
Germany	357,021	1	0	83,029	16.61	77.61
Greece	131,940	0	1	10,623	17.72	78.59
Hungary	93,030	0	0	10,106	14.71	71.63
Iceland	103,000	0	0	278	11.81	79.52
India	3,287,590	1	1	1,029,991	4.68	62.68
Indonesia	1,919,440	1	2	228,437	4.63	68.27
Iran	1,648,000	0	2	66,129	4.65	69.95
Iraq	437,072	0	2	23,332	3.08	66.95
Ireland	70,280	0	0	3,840	11.35	76.99
Italy	301,230	1	0	57,680	18.35	79.14
Japan	377,835	1	0	126,771	17.35	80.8
Kuwait	17,820	0	2	2,041	2.42	76.27
Libya	1,759,540	0	2	5,240	3.95	75.65

Appendix M

Dataset 4—CIA International Economic and Demographic Data (*continued*)

Country X_1	Area (km²) X_2	G-20 X_3	Petroleum X_4	Pop (1,000s) X_5	65 & over X_6	Life Expectancy X_7
Luxembourg	2,586	0	0	443	14.06	77.3
Mexico	1,972,550	1	1	101,879	4.4	71.76
Netherlands	41,526	0	1	15,981	13.72	78.43
New Zealand	286,680	0	0	3,864	11.53	77.99
Nigeria	923,768	0	2	126,635	2.82	51.07
Norway	324,220	0	1	4,503	15.1	78.79
Poland	312,685	0	0	38,634	12.44	73.42
Portugal	92,391	0	0	10,066	15.62	75.94
Qatar	11,437	0	2	769	2.48	72.62
Russia	17,075,200	1	1	145,470	12.81	67.34
Saudi Arabia	1,960,582	1	2	22,757	2.68	68.09
South Africa	1,219,912	1	0	43,586	4.88	48.09
South Korea	98,480	1	0	47,904	7.27	74.65
Spain	504,782	0	0	40,038	17.18	78.93
Sweden	449,964	0	0	8,875	17.28	79.71
Switzerland	41,290	0	0	7,283	15.3	79.73
Turkey	780,580	1	0	66,494	6.13	71.24
United Arab Emirates	82,880	0	2	2,407	2.4	74.29
United Kingdom	244,820	1	1	59,648	15.7	77.82
United States	9,629,091	1	1	278,059	12.61	77.26
Venezuela	912,050	0	2	23,917	4.72	73.31

Appendix M

Dataset 4—CIA International Economic and Demographic Data (*concluded*)

Country X_1	Literacy % X_8	GDP/cap X_9	Labor force X_{10}	Unemployment X_{11}	Exports X_{12}	Imports X_{13}	Cell Phones X_{14}
Algeria	61.6	5.5	9.1	30	19.6	9.2	0.034
Argentina	96.2	12.9	15	15	26.5	25.2	3
Australia	100	23.2	9.5	6.4	69	77	6.4
Austria	98	25	3.7	5.4	63.2	65.6	4.5
Belgium	98	25.3	4.34	8.4	181.4	166	1
Brazil	83.3	6.5	79	7.1	55.1	55.8	4.4
Canada	97	24.8	16.1	6.8	272.3	238.2	4.2
China	81.5	3.6	700	10	232	197	65
Czech Republic	99.9	12.9	5.2	8.7	28.3	31.4	4.3
Denmark	100	25.5	2.9	5.3	50.8	43.6	1.4
Finland	100	22.9	2.6	9.8	44.4	32.7	2.2
France	99	24.4	25	9.7	325	320	11.1
Germany	99	23.4	40.5	9.9	578	505	15.3
Greece	95	17.2	4.32	11.3	15.8	33.9	0.937
Hungary	99	11.2	4.2	9.4	25.2	27.6	1.3
Iceland	100	24.8	0.16	2.7	2	2.2	0.066
India	52	2.2	*	*	43.1	60.8	2.93
Indonesia	83.8	2.9	99	17.5	64.7	40.4	1
Iran	72.1	6.3	17.3	14	25	15	0.265
Iraq	58	2.5	4.4	*	21.8	13.8	0
Ireland	98	21.6	1.82	4.1	73.5	45.7	2
Italy	98	22.1	23.4	10.4	241.1	231.4	20.5
Japan	99	24.9	67.7	4.7	450	355	63.9
Kuwait	78.6	15	1.3	1.8	23.2	7.6	0.21
Libya	76.2	8.9	1.5	30	13.9	7.6	0
Luxembourg	100	36.4	0.248	2.7	7.6	10	0.215
Mexico	89.6	9.1	39.8	2.2	168	176	2
Netherlands	99	24.4	7.2	2.6	210.3	201.2	4.1
New Zealand	99	17.7	1.88	6.3	14.6	14.3	0.6
Nigeria	57.1	0.95	66	28	22.2	10.7	0.027
Norway	100	27.7	2.4	3	59.2	35.2	2
Poland	99	8.5	17.2	12	28.4	42.7	1.8
Portugal	87.4	15.8	5	4.3	26.1	41	3
Qatar	79	20.3	0.233	*	9.8	3.8	0.043
Russia	98	7.7	66	10.5	105.1	44.2	2.5
Saudi Arabia	62.8	10.5	7	*	81.2	30.1	1
South Africa	81.1	8.5	17	30	30.8	27.6	2
South Korea	98	16.1	22	4.1	172.6	160.5	27
Spain	97	18	17	14	120.5	153.9	8.4
Sweden	99	22.2	4.4	6	95.5	80	3.8
Switzerland	99	28.6	3.9	1.9	91.3	91.6	2
Turkey	85	6.8	23	5.6	26.9	55.7	12.1
United Arab Emirates	79.2	22.8	1.4	*	46	34	1
United Kingdom	99	22.8	29.2	5.5	282	324	13
United States	97	36.2	140.9	4	776	1,223	69
Venezuela	91.1	6.2	9.9	14	32.8	14.7	2

Appendix N

Whitner Autoplex

x_1 = Selling price
x_2 = Selling price ($000)
x_3 = Age of buyer
x_4 = Domestic (0), Imported (1)

Price x_1	Price ($000) x_2	Age x_3	Type x_4
23,197	23.197	46	0
23,372	23.372	48	0
20,454	20.454	40	1
23,591	23.591	40	0
26,651	26.651	46	1
27,453	27.453	37	1
17,266	17.266	32	1
18,021	18.021	29	1
28,683	28.683	38	1
30,872	30.872	43	0
19,587	19.587	32	0
23,169	23.169	47	0
35,851	35.851	56	0
19,251	19.251	42	1
20,047	20.047	28	1
24,285	24.285	56	0
24,324	24.324	50	1
24,609	24.609	31	1
28,670	38.67	51	1
15,546	15.546	26	1
15,935	15.935	25	1
19,873	19.873	45	1
25,251	25.251	56	1
25,277	25.277	47	0
28,034	28.034	38	1
24,533	24.533	51	0
27,443	27.443	39	0
19,889	19.889	44	1
20,004	20.004	46	1
17,357	17.357	28	1
20,155	20.155	33	1
19,688	19.688	35	1
23,657	23.657	35	0
26,613	26.613	42	1
20,895	20.895	35	0
20,203	20.203	36	1
23,765	23.765	48	0
25,783	25.783	53	1
26,661	26.661	46	1
32,277	32.277	55	0

Price x_1	Price ($000) x_2	Age x_3	Type x_4
20,642	20.642	39	1
21,981	21.981	43	1
24,052	24.052	56	0
25,799	25.799	44	0
15,794	15.794	30	1
18,263	18.263	39	1
35,925	35.925	53	0
17,399	17.399	29	1
17,968	17.968	30	1
20,356	20.356	44	0
21,442	21.442	41	1
21,722	21.722	41	0
19,331	19.331	35	1
22,817	22.817	51	1
19,766	19.766	44	1
20,633	20.633	51	1
20,962	20.962	49	1
22,845	22.845	41	1
26,285	26.285	44	0
27,896	27.896	37	0
29,076	29.076	42	1
32,492	32.492	51	0
18,890	18.89	31	1
21,740	21.74	39	0
22,374	22.374	53	0
24,571	24.571	55	1
25,449	25.449	40	0
28,337	28.337	46	0
20,642	20.642	35	1
23,613	23.613	47	1
24,220	24.22	58	1
30,655	30.655	51	0
22,442	22.442	41	1
17,891	17.891	33	1
20,818	20.818	46	1
26,237	26.237	47	0
20,445	20.445	34	1
21,556	21.556	43	1
21,639	21.639	37	1
24,296	24.296	47	0

Appendix O

Getting Started with MegaStat*

MegaStat is an Excel add-in that performs statistical analysis within an Excel workbook. After it is installed, it appears on the Excel menu and works like any other Excel option.

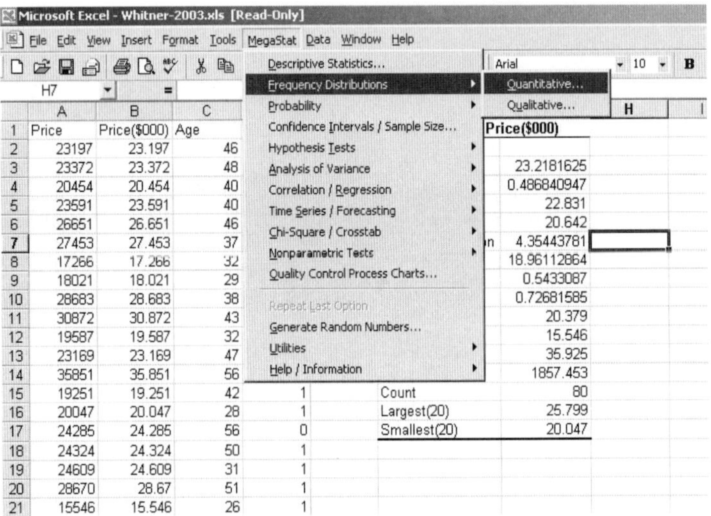

Basic Procedures

When you click on MegaStat, the main Excel menu appears (see chart above). Most of the menu options display submenus. If a menu item is followed by an ellipsis (. . .), clicking it will display the dialog box for that option.

A dialog box allows you to specify the data to be used and other inputs and options. The chart below shows a typical dialog box. After you select the data and options, click OK; the dialog box disappears and MegaStat performs the analysis.

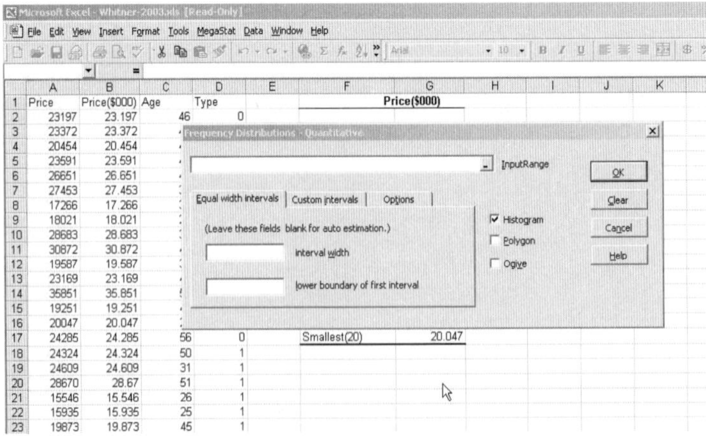

*Written by J. B. Orris, Ph.D., Butler University. MegaStat is copyrighted and is a registered trademark of J. B. Orris. This document was written for version 9.0 of MegaStat; however, most of it will be relevant for other versions.

Buttons

Each dialog box has four buttons down the right-hand side. See the picture on the previous page.

OK This button could also be labeled "Calculate," "Go," "Execute," or "Do it." It tells MegaStat that you are done specifying inputs and you are turning control over to the software. First the software validates your input values, then disappears and performs the analysis and finally displays the output worksheet. When the dialog box disappears, it is still in memory and will contain the same inputs if it is recalled later.

Clear This button removes all input values and resets any default options on the form.

Cancel This button could be labeled "Never mind." It simply hides the dialog box. The dialog box is not cleared or removed from memory. Userforms do not take much memory and there is no problem with having several of them in memory. However, if you really want to unload the form, click the "X" in the upper right corner of the form.

Help This button displays context sensitive help for the active userform. If you want to see the full Help System, use the Help selection on the main menu.

Data Selection Most MegaStat dialog boxes have fields where you select input ranges that contain the data to be used. Input ranges can be selected in four ways:

1. *Pointing and dragging with the mouse (the most common method).* Since the dialog box pops up on the screen, it may block some of your data. You can move dialog boxes around on the screen by placing the mouse pointer over the title bar (colored area at the top), clicking, and holding the left mouse button while dragging the dialog box to a new location. You can even drag it partially off the screen.
2. *Using MegaStat's AutoExpand feature.* AutoExpand allows rapid data selection without having to drag through the entire column of data. Here is how it works:
   - Make sure the input box has the focus. (Click in it or tab to it.) An input box had the focus when the insertion pointer is blinking in it.
   - Select one row of data by clicking in one cell of the column you want. If more than one column is being selected, drag the mouse across the columns.
   - Right-click over the input field or left-click the label next to the input box. The data range will expand to include all of the rows in the region where you selected one row.
3. *Typing the name of a named range.* If you have previously identified a range of cells using Excel's name box, you may use that name to specify a data range in a MegaStat userform. This method can be very useful if you are using the same data for several different statistical procedures.
4. *Typing a range address.* You may type in any valid Excel range address, e.g., B5:B43. This is the least efficient way to specify data ranges, but it certainly works.

Data Labels

For most procedures the first cell in each input range can be a label. *If the first cell in a range is text, it is considered a label; if the first cell is a numeric value, it is considered data.* If you want to use numbers as variable labels, you must enter the numbers as text by preceding them with a single quote mark, e.g., '2. Even though Excel stores times and dates as numbers, MegaStat will recognize them as labels if they are formatted as time/date values.

If data labels are not part of the input range, the program automatically uses the cell immediately above the data range as a label if it contains a text value.

If an option can consider the entire first row (or column) of an input range as labels, any numeric value in the row will cause the entire row to be treated as data.

Output

When you click OK on a MegaStat dialog box, it performs some statistical analysis and needs a place to put its output. It looks for a worksheet named Output. If it finds one, it goes to the end of it and appends its output; if it doesn't find an Output worksheet, it creates one. MegaStat will never make any changes to the user's worksheets; it sends output only to its Output sheet.

MegaStat makes a good attempt at formatting the output, but it is important to remember that the Output sheet is just a standard Excel worksheet and can be modified in any way by the user. You can adjust column widths and change any formatting that you think needs improvement. You can insert, delete, and modify cells. You can copy all or part of the output to another worksheet or to another application such as a word processor.

MegaStat charts get their values from cells on the Output sheet (or one of your worksheets in the case of the scatter plot). You can click a chart and select "Source Data" to see what values are being displayed.

When you click a chart, the MegaStat menu item will disappear from the main menu bar since the Chart menu becomes active. Click outside the chart to bring back the main menu that contains the MegaStat menu item.

Repeat Last Option

Once you have performed a MegaStat option, this menu selection will allow you to redisplay the last dialog box without having to go through the menu selections. This can be handy if you need to make a change or when you need to repeat the same operation with the different data sets.

Deactivate MegaStat

This option is used to remove the "MegaStat" item from the main menu bar. It does not delete any files or uninstall MegaStat. To restore the "MegaStat" menu item, click on Excel's main menu bar, then click on Tools and select Add-Ins. In the Add-Ins dialog box check MegaStat and click on OK.

Uninstall MegaStat

This menu item does not actually uninstall MegaStat. It displays a dialog box prompting you on how to start the uninstallation process.

Uninstalling is the process of removing the installed MegaStat files from your system. It does not remove any data files nor does it remove the file you used to install MegaStat. You may delete the installation file (MegaStat_Setup.exe) if it is still on your system.

Help/Information

The Help option displays the full MegaStat help program, shown below.

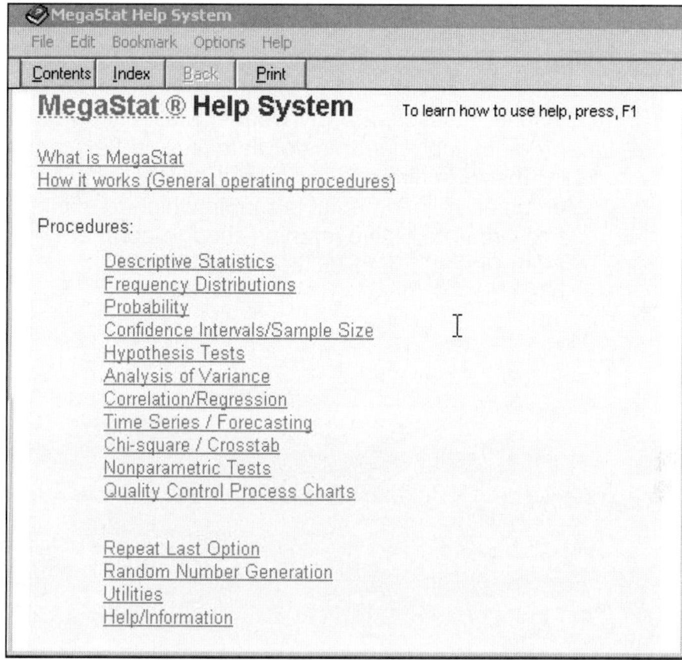

The "How it works (General operating procedures)" section contains all of the information in this tutorial. You can click specific topics or search for a particular item by clicking on **Index.**

Appendix P

Visual Statistics

Visual Statistics, 2.0, by Doane, Mathieson, and Tracy is a package of 21 software programs and hundreds of data files and examples designed for teaching and learning basic statistics. The modules of Visual Statistics provide an interactive, highly graphical, experimental format in which to explore statistics. The software and worktext promote active learning though competency building exercises, individual and team projects, and built-in databases. Over 400 data sets are included within the package.

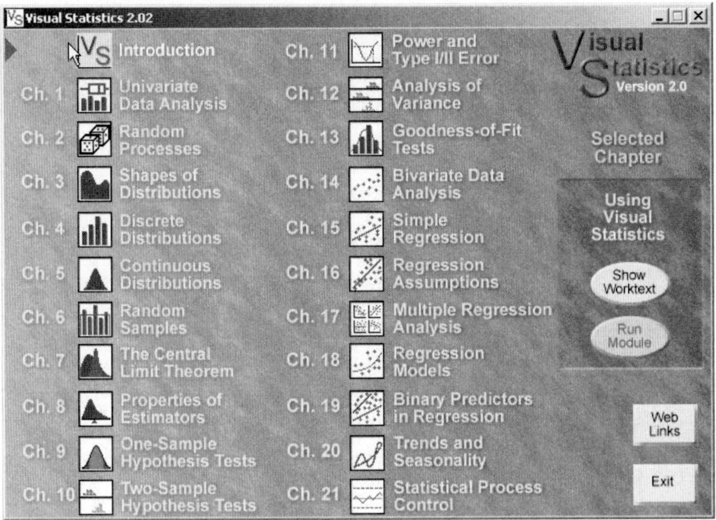

Main Menu

To start Visual Statistics, click on the link on your student CD-ROM menu and follow the installation instructions. Open the cover and you will see a menu like the one shown above. From this menu you can: (1) view a chapter in the worktext (the Show Worktext button); (2) run a software module (the Run Module button); (3) exit Visual Statistics (the Exit button).

Selecting a Program

To select a program, click on the chapter number or icon, then click run module. (Note: You will need to have your Student CD-ROM in the CD drive for the programs to run.)

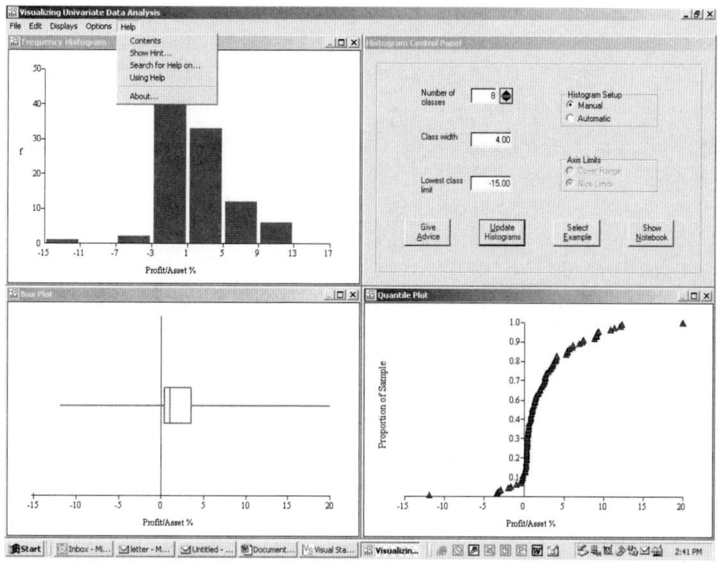

Each program is designed to be as directly interactive as possible, with live graphics and control buttons built into the main screen for that program.

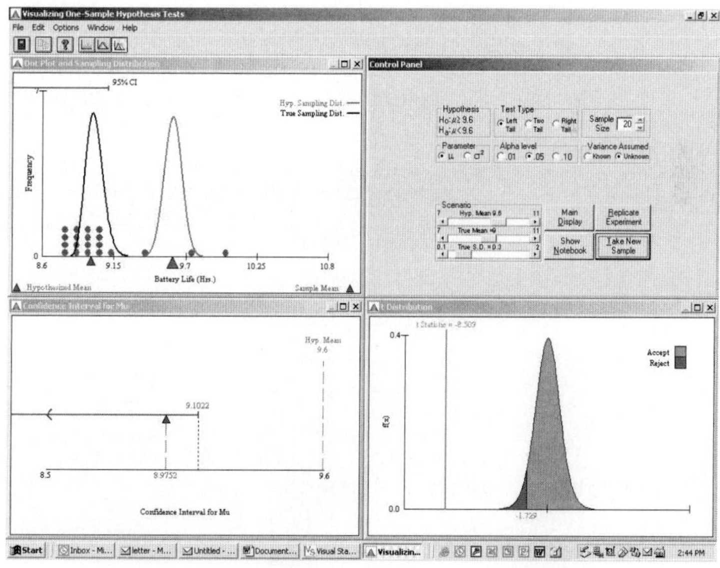

These are just a few examples.

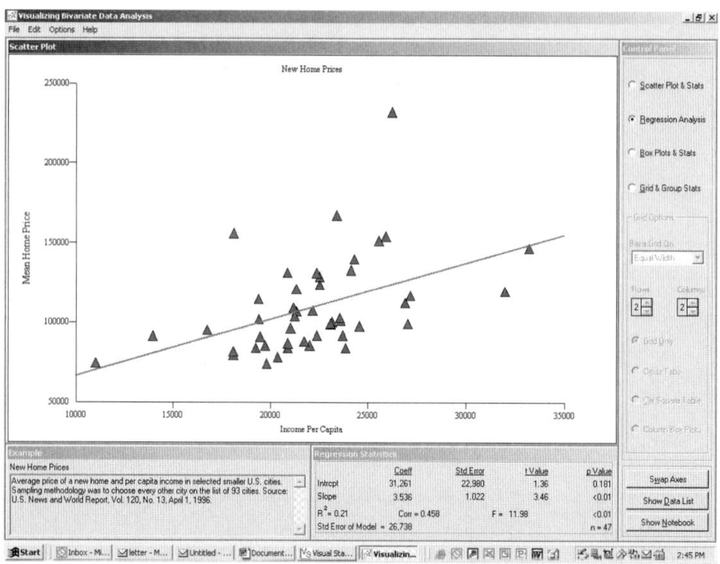

Selecting a Chapter

To select a chapter, click on its chapter number, its icon, or its title. When you click the chapter, a comet will streak across the screen to the Selected Chapter panel on the right, and the Show Worktext and Run Module buttons will appear in the panel. Each software module corresponds to a chapter in the worktext. The chapter's learning exercises will require that you run the corresponding software module.

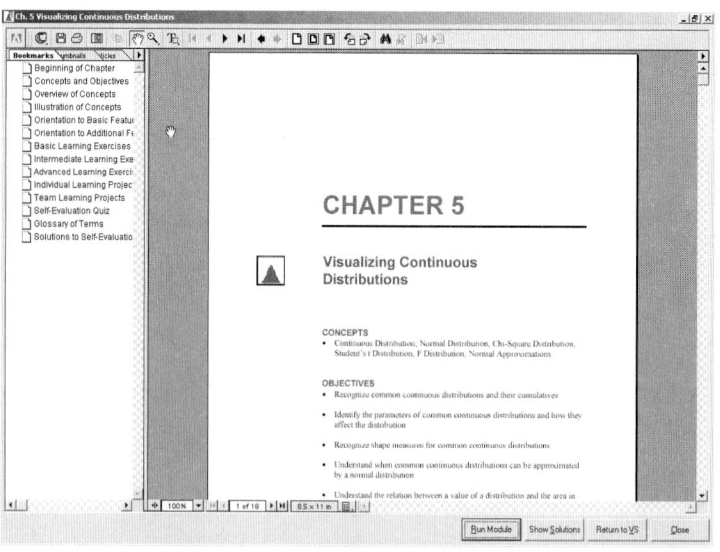

The Worktext

The worktext has one chapter for each module. Each chapter in the worksheet contains:

- A list of concepts and learning objectives
- An overview of concepts and illustrations of concepts
- An orientation to software features
- Structured learning exercises (basic, intermediate, and advanced)
- Suggested independent projects (team, individual)
- A bank of self-test questions
- A glossary of terms
- Answers to the self-test questions

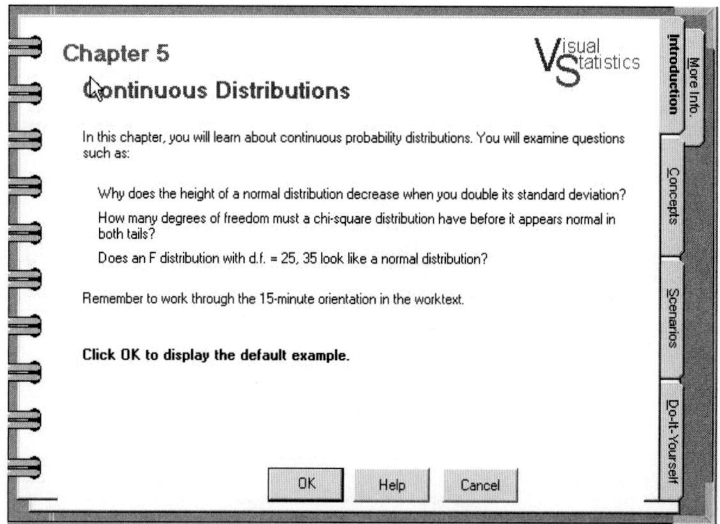

The Notebook

Every Visual Statistics module starts with the Notebook. There is a different Notebook for each module, but they all work the same way. Click on the tabs to see each of the notebook "pages." The main purpose of the Notebook is to let you choose the type of data you want to review.

- *Examples*—examples are real data sets that have been selected to illustrate the concepts of the module.
- *Databases*—a database contains many variables. You select the ones you wish to analyze.
- *Data Editor*—lets you create your own data sets.
- *Scenarios*—allows you to experiment with the process that generates data sets.
- *Templates*—allows you to generate data conforming to a particular shape.
- *Do-It-Yourself*—gives you control over the process generating the data.

Help

Each module has a Help section on the menu bar. Click on **Help** and an Index will appear for the topics where help is available in that module.

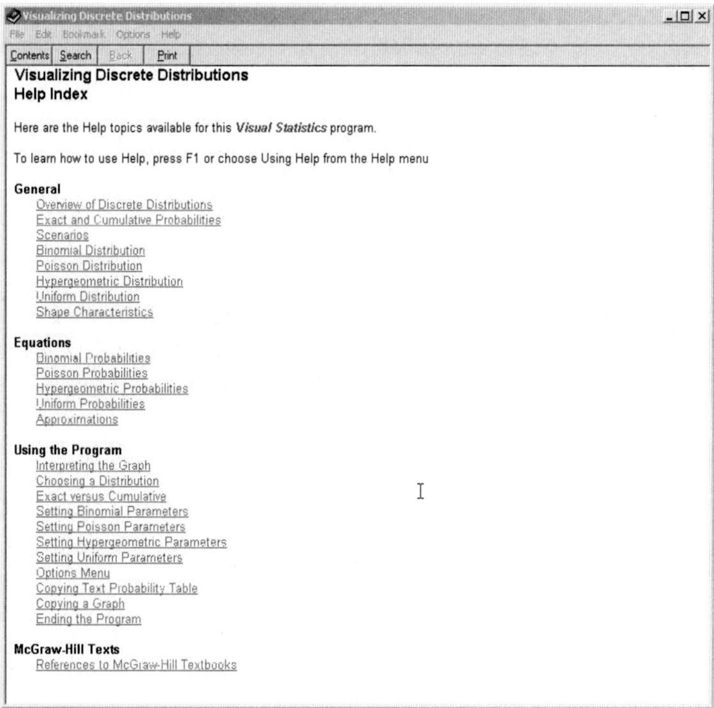

Answers

to Odd-Numbered Chapter Exercises

CHAPTER 1

1. a. Interval
   b. Ratio
   c. Interval
   d. Nominal
   e. Ordinal
   f. Ratio
3. Answers will vary.
5. Qualitative data is not numerical, whereas quantitative data is numerical. Examples will vary by student.
7. Nominal, ordinal, interval, and ratio. Examples will vary.
9. A classification is exhaustive if every object appears in some category.
11. According to the sample information 120/300 or 40% would accept a job transfer.
13. Discrete variables can assume only certain values, but continuous variables can assume any values within some range. Examples will vary.
15. Answers will vary.
17. a. Grass or artificial turf field is a qualitative variable, the others are quantitative.
    b. Grass or artificial turf field is a nominal-level variable, the others are ratio-level variables.
19. a. All variables are quantitative except G-20 and Petroleum.
    b. All variables are ratio except G-20 and Petroleum.

CHAPTER 2

1. $2^5 = 32, 2^6 = 64$ Therefore, 6 classes.
3. $2^7 = 128, 2^8 = 256$ Suggests 8 classes.

   $i \geq \frac{567 - 235}{8} = 41.5$ Use interval of 45.
5. a. $2^4 = 16$ Suggests 5 classes.

   b. $i \geq \frac{31 - 25}{5} = 1.2$ Use interval of 1.5.

   c. 24

   d.

Patients	f	Relative frequency
24.0 up to 25.5	2	0.125
25.5 up to 27.0	4	0.250
27.0 up to 28.5	8	0.500
28.5 up to 30.0	0	0.000
30.0 up to 31.5	2	0.125
Total	16	1.000

   e. The largest concentration is in the 27 up to 28.5 class (8).
7. a.

Number of Visits	f
0 up to 3	9
3 up to 6	21
6 up to 9	13
9 up to 12	4
12 up to 15	3
15 up to 18	1
Total	51

   b. The largest group of shoppers (21) shop at the BiLo Supermarket 3, 4, or 5 times during a month period. Some customers visit the store only 1 time during the month, but others shop as many as 15 times.

   c.

Number of Visits	Percent of Total
0 up to 3	17.65
3 up to 6	41.18
6 up to 9	25.49
9 up to 12	7.84
12 up to 15	5.88
15 up to 18	1.96
Total	100.00

9. a. Histogram
   b. 100
   c. 5
   d. 28
   e. 0.28
   f. 12.5
   g. 13
11. a. 50
    b. 1.5 thousand miles, or 1,500 miles.
    c.

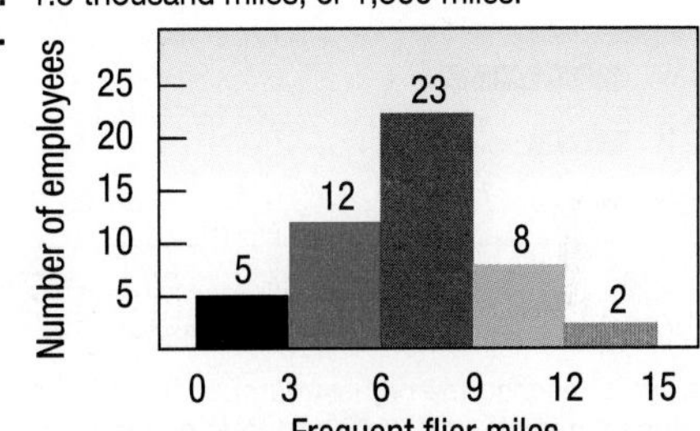

   d. $X = 1.5, Y = 5$

   e.

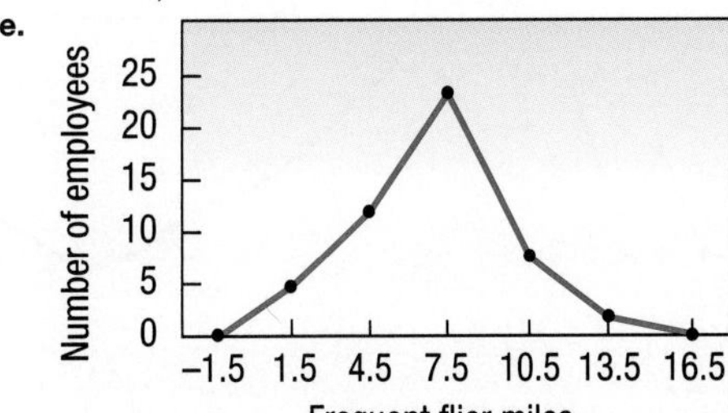

   f. For the 50 employees about half traveled between 6,000 and 9,000 miles. Five employees traveled less than 3,000 miles, and 2 traveled more than 12,000 miles.
13. a. 40
    b. 5
    c. 11 or 12
    d. About $18/hr
    e. About $9/hr
    f. About 75%

15. **a.** 5

b.

Frequent Flier Miles	*f*	CF
0 up to 3	5	5
3 up to 6	12	17
6 up to 9	23	40
9 up to 12	8	48
12 up to 15	2	50

c.

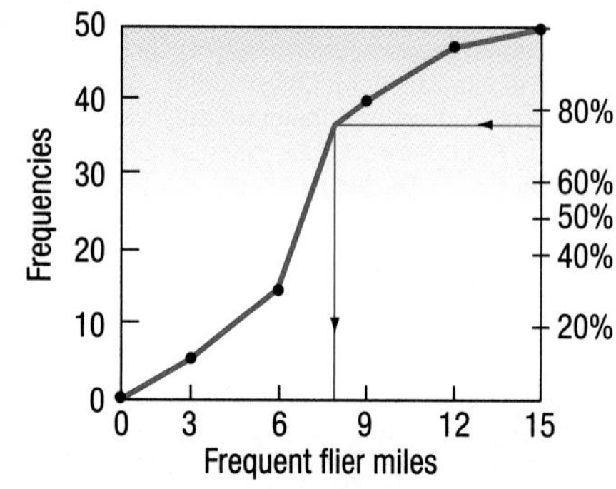

d. About 8.7 thousands of miles

17. Maxwell Heating & Air Conditioning far exceeds the other corporations in sales. Mancell Electric & Plumbing and Mizelle Roofing & Sheet Metal are the two corporations with the least amount of fourth quarter sales.

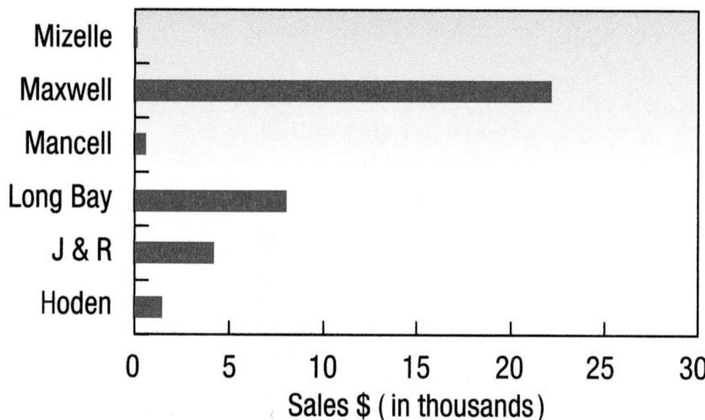

19. Homicides reached the highest number in 1993. They decreased steadily until 2000 and then began to increase again until a decline in 2003.

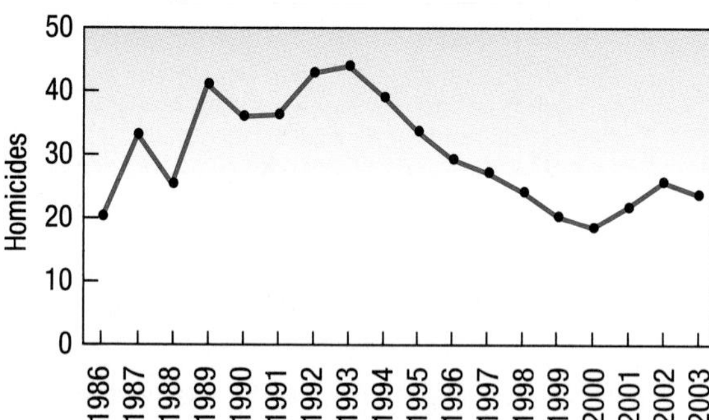

21. **Population Growth in the United States**
Population in the United States has increased steadily since 1950.

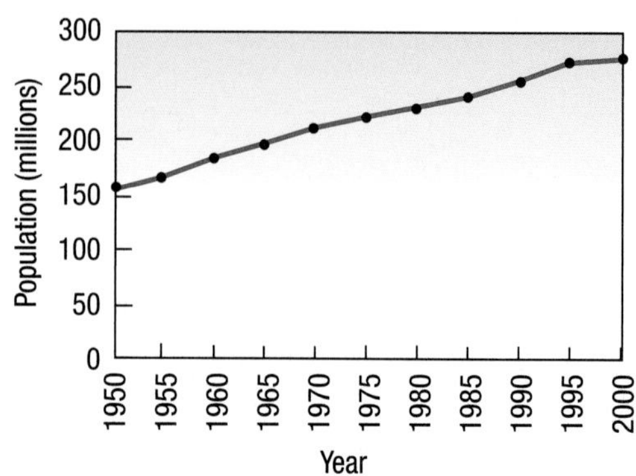

23. $2^6 = 64$ and $2^7 = 128$. Suggest 7 classes.

25. **a.** 5, because $2^4 = 16 < 25$ and $2^5 = 32 > 25$.

b. $i \geq \dfrac{48 - 16}{5} = 6.4$ Use interval of 7.

c. 15

d.

Class	Frequency	
15 up to 22	III	3
22 up to 29	~~IIII~~ III	8
29 up to 36	~~IIII~~ II	7
36 up to 43	~~IIII~~	5
43 up to 50	II	2
		25

e. It is fairly symmetric, with most of the values between 22 and 36.

27. **a.** 56
b. 10 (found by 60 − 50)
c. 55
d. 17

29. **a.** \$36.60, found by (\$265 − \$82)/5.
b. \$40.
c.

\$ 80 up to \$120	8
120 up to 160	19
160 up to 200	10
200 up to 240	6
240 up to 280	1
Total	44

d. The purchases ranged from a low of about \$80 to a high of about \$280. The concentration is in the \$120 up to \$160 class.

31.

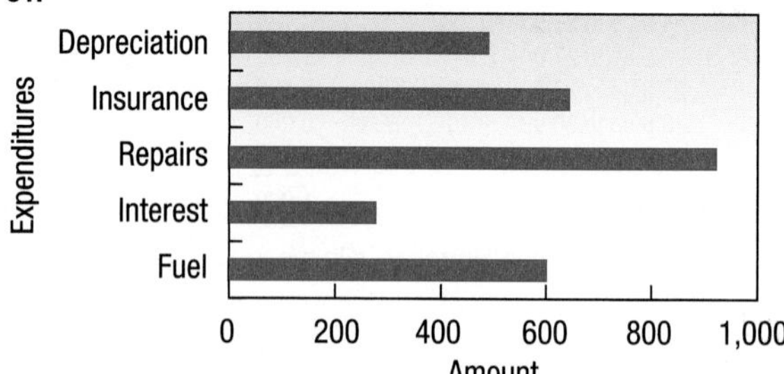

33.

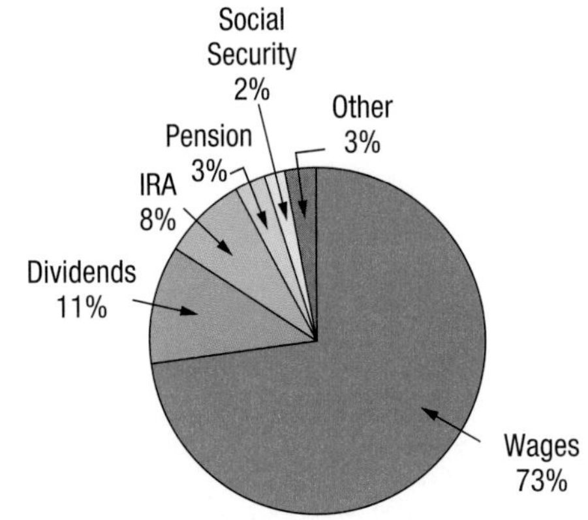

SC Income	Percent	Cumulative
Wages	73	73
Dividends	11	84
IRA	8	92
Pensions	3	95
Social Security	2	97
Other	3	100

By far the largest part of income in South Carolina is earned income. Almost three-fourths of the adjusted gross income comes from wages and salaries. Dividends and IRAs each contribute roughly another ten percent.

35. **a.** Since $2^6 = 64 < 70 < 128 = 2^7$, 7 classes are recommended. The interval should be at least $(1{,}002.2 - 3.3)/7 = 142.7$. Use 150 as a convenient value.

b.

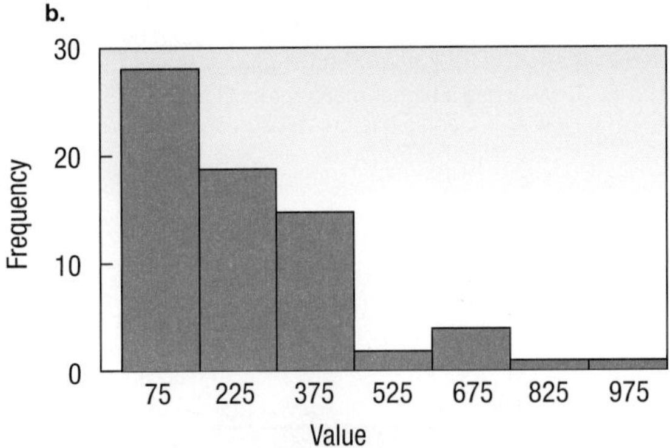

37.

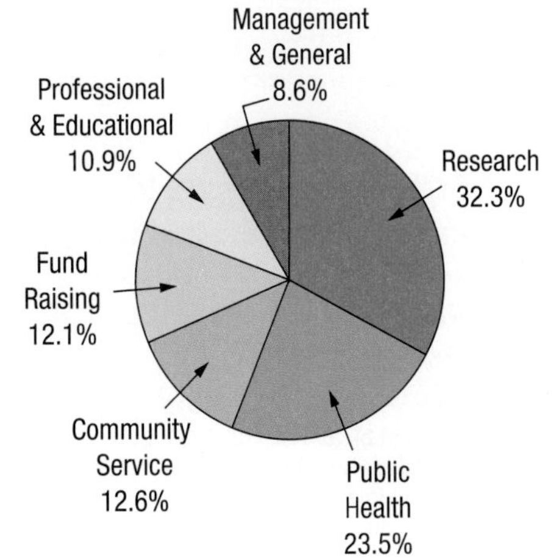

More than half of the expenses are concentrated in the categories Research and Public Health Education.

39.

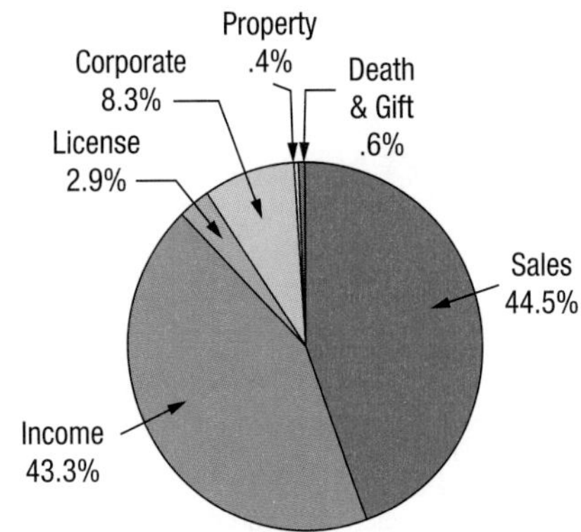

Sales tax and income tax dominate the total revenues for the state of Georgia.

41. There are 50 observations, so the recommended number of classes is 6. However, there are several states that have many more farms than the others, so it may be useful to have an open-ended class. One possible frequency distribution is:

Farms in USA	Frequency
0 up to 20	16
20 up to 40	13
40 up to 60	8
60 up to 80	6
80 up to 100	4
100 or more	3
Total	50

Twenty-nine of the 50 states, or 58 percent, have fewer than 40,000 farms. There are three states that have more than 100,000 farms.

43. Total vehicle sales increased from 13,896,000 in 1993 to 16,634,700 in 2003. This is an increase of 2,738,700 vehicles or 19.7%. In 1993 light-duty trucks accounted for 38.7% of vehicle sales, by 2003 this increased to 54.3% of sales.

45. Wages paid by software companies grew from \$0.4 billion to \$1.65 billion per quarter between 1994 and 2002. Those paid by aerospace manufacturers remained fairly constant between \$1 and \$1.5 billion. Software surpassed aerospace in 1998.

47. **a.** $i \geq \dfrac{345.3 - 124.0}{7} = 31.47$. Use interval of 35.

Selling Price ($000)	*F*	*CF*
110 up to 145	3	3
145 up to 180	19	22
180 up to 215	31	53
215 up to 250	25	78
250 up to 285	14	92
285 up to 320	10	102
320 up to 355	3	105

1. Most homes (53%) are in the 180 up to 250 range.
2. The largest value is near 355; the smallest, near 110.

b.

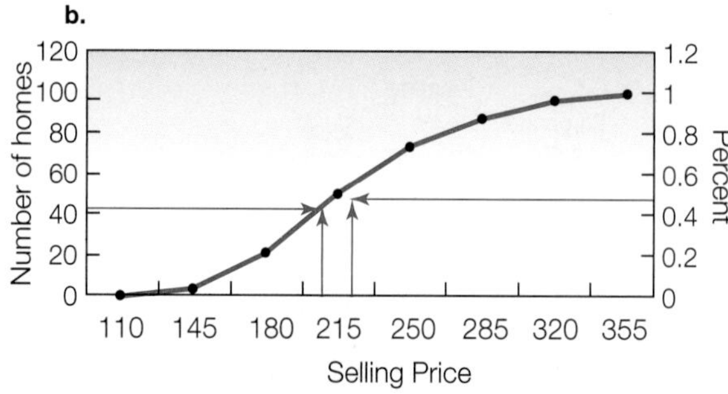

1. About 42 homes sold for less than 200.
2. About 55% of the homes sold for less than 220. So 45% sold for more.
3. Less than 1% of the homes sold for less than 125.

c. The selling price ranges from about \$120,000 up to about \$360,000. A typical home sold for about \$210,000.

49.

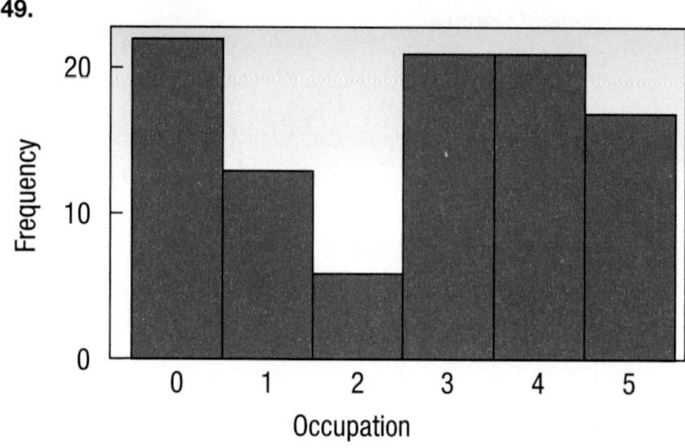

Occupational category 2 has fewer members (5 or 6), and all the others are around 19.

CHAPTER 3

1. $\mu = 5.4$, found by 27/5.

3. **a.** $\bar{X} = 7.0$, found by 28/4.
b. $(5 - 7) + (9 - 7) + (4 - 7) + (10 - 7) = 0$

5. $\bar{X} = 14.58$, found by 43.74/3.

7. **a.** 15.4, found by 154/10.
b. Population parameter, since it includes all the salespersons at Moody Insurance.

9. **a.** \$54.55, found by \$1,091/20.
b. A sample statistic—assuming that the power company serves more than 20 customers.

11. \$22.91, found by $\dfrac{300(\$20) + 400(\$25) + 400(\$23)}{300 + 400 + 400}$

13. $\bar{X}_w = \dfrac{.802(1.749) + .152(1.849) + .046(1.949)}{.802 + .152 + .046} = 1.773$

15. **a.** No mode
b. The given value would be the mode.
c. 3 and 4 bimodal.

17. Median = 5, Mode = 5

19. **a.** Median = 2.9
b. 2.9

21. **a.** $\bar{X} = 7.75$, found by 93/12.
b. 7.65, found by (7.8 + 7.5)/2 and 8.6 (Jan and Dec).
c. 8.6, found by 34.4/4 and 8.6. It is somewhat higher.

23. 12.8 percentage increase, found by
$\sqrt[5]{(1.08)(1.12)(1.14)(1.26)(1.05)} = 1.128.$

25. 12.28 percentage increase, found by
$\sqrt[5]{(1.094)(1.138)(1.117)(1.119)(1.147)} = 1.1228.$

27. 2.53%, found by $\sqrt[11]{\dfrac{184.6}{140.3}} - 1.$

29. 10.76%, found by $\sqrt[5]{\dfrac{70}{42}} - 1.$

31. **a.** 7, found by 10 − 3.
b. 6, found by 30/5.
c. 2.4, found by 12/5.
d. The difference between the highest number sold (10) and the smallest number sold (3) is 7. On average, the number of service reps on duty deviates by 2.4 from the mean of 6.

33. **a.** 30, found by 54 − 24.
b. 38, found by 380/10.
c. 7.2, found by 72/10.
d. The difference of 54 and 24 is 30. On average, the number of minutes required to install a door deviates 7.2 minutes from the mean of 38 minutes.

35. **a.** 15, found by 41 − 26.
b. 33.9, found by 339/10.
c. 4.12, found by 41.2/10.
d. The ratings deviate 4.12 from the mean of 33.9 on average.

37. **a.** 5
b. 4.4, found by

$$\frac{(8 - 5)^2 + (3 - 5)^2 + (7 - 5)^2 + (3 - 5)^2 + (4 - 5)^2}{5}$$

39. **a.** \$2.77
b. 1.26, found by

$$\frac{(2.68 - 2.77)^2 + (1.03 - 2.77)^2 + (2.26 - 2.77)^2 + (4.30 - 2.77)^2 + (3.58 - 2.77)^2}{5}$$

41. **a.** Range: 7.3, found by 11.6 − 4.3. Arithmetic mean: 6.94, found by 34.7/5. Variance: 6.5944, found by 32.972/5. Standard deviation: 2.568, found by $\sqrt{6.5944}$.
b. Dennis has a higher mean return (11.76 > 6.94). However, Dennis has greater spread in their returns on equity (16.89 > 6.59).

43. **a.** $\bar{X} = 4$

$$s^2 = \frac{(7 - 4)^2 + \cdots + (3 - 4)^2}{5 - 1}$$

$$s^2 = \frac{22}{5 - 1} = 5.50$$

b. $s = 2.3452$

45. **a.** $\bar{X} = 38$

$$s^2 = \frac{(28 - 38)^2 + \cdots + (42 - 38)^2}{10 - 1}$$

$$s^2 = \frac{744}{10 - 1} = 82.6667$$

b. $s = 9.0921$

47. **a.** $\bar{X} = \dfrac{951}{10} = 95.1$

$$s^2 = \frac{(101 - 95.1)^2 + \cdots + (88 - 95.1)^2}{10 - 1}$$

$$= \frac{1112.9}{9} = 123.66$$

b. $s = \sqrt{123.66} = 11.12$

49. About 69%, found by $1 - 1/(1.8)^2$.

51. **a.** About 95%.
b. 47.5%, 2.5%.

53. **a.** Mean = 5, found by (6 + 4 + 3 + 7 + 5)/5. Median is 5, found by rearranging the values and selecting the middle value.
b. Population, because all partners were included.

c. $\Sigma(X - \mu) = (6 - 5) + (4 - 5) + (3 - 5) + (7 - 5) + (5 - 5) = 0.$

55. $\bar{X} = \dfrac{545}{16} = 34.06$

Median = 37.50

57. 370.08, found by 18,504/50.

59. $\bar{X}_w = \dfrac{\$5.00(270) + \$6.50(300) + \$8.00(100)}{270 + 300 + 100} = \$6.12$

61. $\bar{X}_w = \dfrac{[15{,}300(4.5) + 10{,}400(3.0) + 150{,}600(10.2)]}{176{,}300} = 9.28$

63. $\text{GM} = \sqrt[21]{\dfrac{6{,}286{,}800}{5{,}164{,}900}} - 1 = 1.0094 - 1.0 = .0094$

65. **a.** 55, found by 72 − 17.
b. 14.4, found by 144/10, where $\bar{X} = 43.2$.
c. 17.6245.

67. **a.** There were 13 flights, so all items are considered.
b. $\mu = \dfrac{2{,}259}{13} = 173.77$

Median = 195

c. Range = 301 − 7 = 294

$\sigma = \sqrt{\dfrac{133{,}846.3}{13}} = 101.47$

69. **a.** $\bar{X} = \dfrac{273}{30} = 9.1$, median = 9.
b. Range = 18 − 4 = 14

$s = \sqrt{\dfrac{368.7}{30 - 1}} = 3.57$

71. Answers will vary.

73. From statistical software:
a. $n = 105$
$\bar{X} = 221.10$
$s = 47.11$
median = 213.60, the distribution is symmetric about \$220,000.
b. $n = 105$
$\bar{X} = 2{,}223.8$
$s = 248.7$
median = 2,200, the distribution is symmetric about 2,200 square feet.

75. From statistical software:
a. $n = 46$
$\bar{X} = 73.81$
$s = 6.90$
median = 76.11
b. $n = 46$
$\bar{X} = 16.58$
$s = 9.27$
median = 17.45
No outliers. Symmetric distribution.

CHAPTER 4

1. **a.** dot plot
b. 15
c. 1 and 7, range is 6
d. 9 of 15 values are 2 or 3.

3. Median = 53, found by $(11 + 1)(\frac{1}{2})$ ∴ 6th value in from lowest.
$Q_1 = 49$, found by $(11 + 1)(\frac{1}{4})$ ∴
3rd value in from lowest.
$Q_3 = 55$, found by $(11 + 1)(\frac{3}{4})$ ∴ 9th value in from lowest.

5. **a.** $Q_1 = 33.25$, $Q_3 = 50.25$
b. $D_2 = 27.8$, $D_8 = 52.6$
c. $P_{67} = 47$

7. **a.** 350
b. $Q_1 = 175$, $Q_3 = 930$
c. 930 − 175 = 755
d. Less than 0, or more than about 2,060.
e. There are no outliers.
f. The distribution is positively skewed.

9.

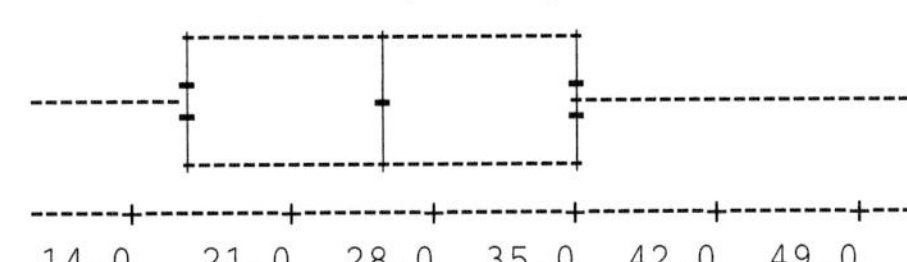

The distribution is somewhat positively skewed. Note that the dashed line above 35 is longer than below 18.

11. **a.** The mean is 30.8, found by 154/5. The median is 31.0, and the standard deviation is 3.96, found by

$$\sqrt{\frac{62.8}{4}}.$$

b. −0.15, found by $\dfrac{3(30.8 - 31.0)}{3.96}$.

c.

Salary	$\left(\dfrac{X - \bar{X}}{s}\right)$	$\left(\dfrac{X - \bar{X}}{s}\right)^3$
36	1.313131	2.264250504
26	−1.212121	−1.780894343
33	0.555556	0.171467764
28	−0.707071	−0.353499282
31	0.050505	0.000128826
		0.301453469

0.125, found by $[5/(4 \times 3)] \times 0.301$.

13. **a.** The mean is 21.93, found by 328.9/15. The median is 15.8, and the standard deviation is 21.18, found by

$$\sqrt{\frac{6282.9893}{14}}.$$

b. 0.868, found by $[3(21.93 - 15.8)]/21.18$.
c. 2.444, found by $[15/(14 \times 13)] \times 29.658$.

15.

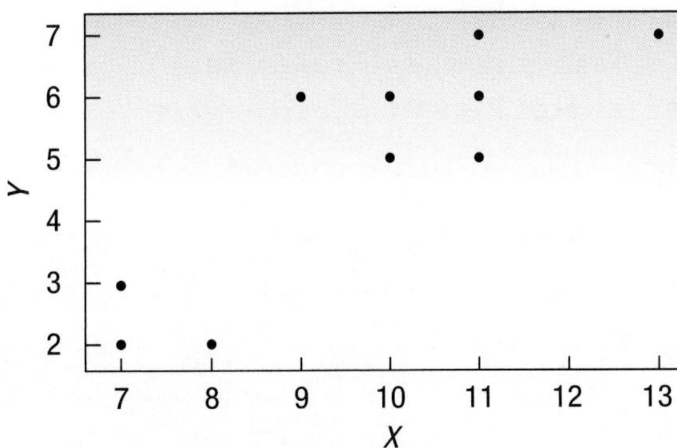

There is a positive relationship between the variables.

17. **a.** Both variables are nominal scale.
b. Contingency table.
c. Men are about twice as likely to order a dessert. From the table 32% of the men ordered dessert, but only 15 percent of the women.

19. **a.** Dot plot
b. 15
c. 5

21. **a.** $L_{50} = (20 + 1)\frac{50}{100} = 10.50$

Median $= \dfrac{83.7 + 85.6}{2} = 84.65$

$L_{25} = (21)(.25) = 5.25$
$Q_1 = 66.6 + .25(72.9 - 66.6) = 68.175$

$L_{75} = 21(.75) = 15.75$
$Q_3 = 87.1 + .75(90.2 - 87.1) = 89.425$

b. $L_{26} = 21(.26) = 5.46$
$P_{26} = 66.6 + .46(72.9 - 66.6) = 69.498$
$L_{83} = 21(.83) = 17.43$
$P_{83} = 93.3 + .43(98.6 - 93.3) = 95.579$

c.

```
              -------------------------
------------I                +  I-----------------
              -------------------------

------+---------+--------+--------+--------+--------C20
  64.0      72.0      80.0      88.0      96.0
```

23. **a.** $Q_1 = 26.25$, $Q_3 = 35.75$, median $= 31.50$.

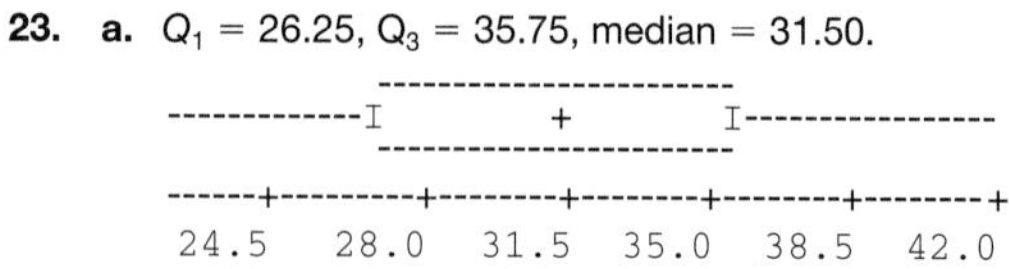

b. $Q_1 = 33.25$, $Q_3 = 38.75$, median $= 37.50$.

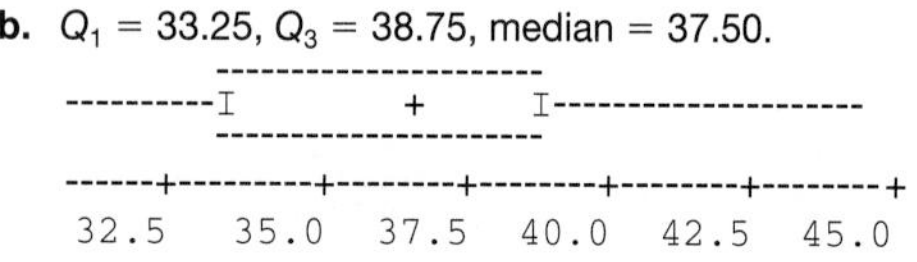

c. The median time for public transportation is about 6 minutes less. There is more variation in public transportation. The difference between Q_1 and Q_3 is 9.5 minutes for public transportation and 5.5 minutes for private transportation.

25. The distribution is positively skewed. The first quartile is approx. \$20 and the third quartile is approx. \$90. There is one outlier located at \$255. The median is about \$50.

27. $Q_1 = 44.25$, $Q_3 = 68.5$, and the median is 55.50. The distribution is approximately symmetric. The box plot is as follows.

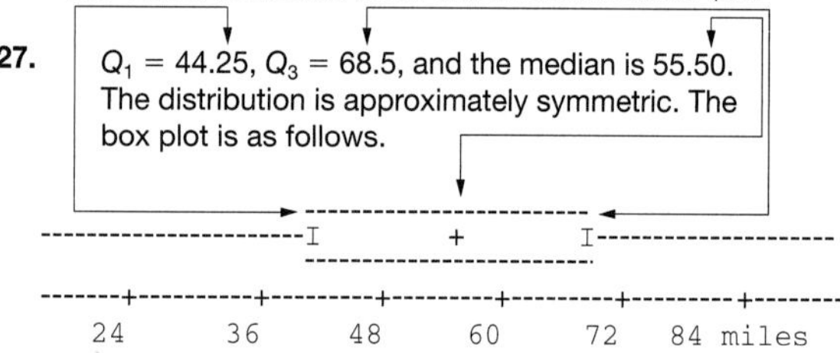

The above results are found using MINITAB.

29. $sk = 0.065$ or $sk = \dfrac{3(7.7143 - 8.0)}{3.9036} = -0.22$

31.

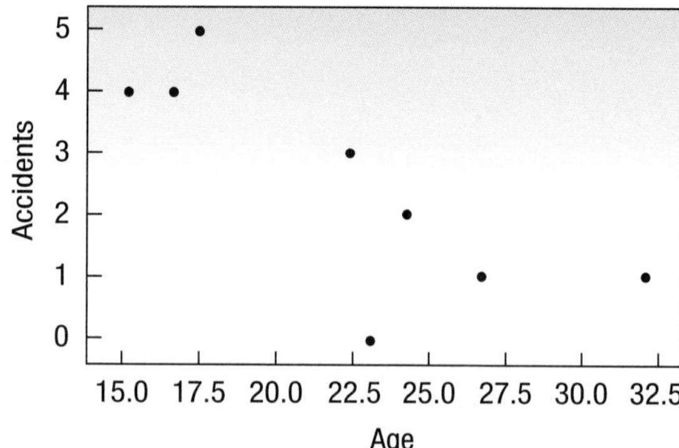

As age increases the number of accidents decreases.

33. 40% of the Democrats favor gun control and 36% of the Republicans favor it.

35. Answer based on data through Superbowl XXVII.
$\bar{X} = 15.87$, $s = 10.65$, $Q_1 = 7.00$, median $= 15.50$, $Q_3 = 21.75$. One outlier, XXIV, point difference of 45.

37. **a.** Age = 2004 − year built. $\bar{X} = 26.13$, $s = 24.72$, min = 3, $Q_1 = 8.25$, median = 16, $Q_3 = 38$, max = 92. There are 3 outliers, Wrigley Field (Cubs), Yankee Stadium, and Fenway Park (Red Sox). Box plot not shown.

b. For the variable salary $\bar{X} = 70.94$, $s = 28.06$, min = 19.63, $Q_1 = 49.99$, median = 68.98, $Q_3 = 84.58$, max = 152.75. The New York Yankees' salary is an outlier. Box plot not shown.

c. Positive association between wins and salary.

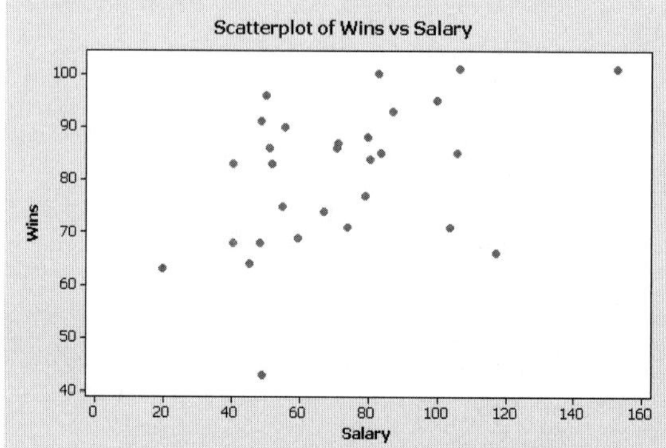

d. The number of wins range from 43 wins (Detroit) to 101 wins (two teams, New York Yankees and Atlanta Braves.)

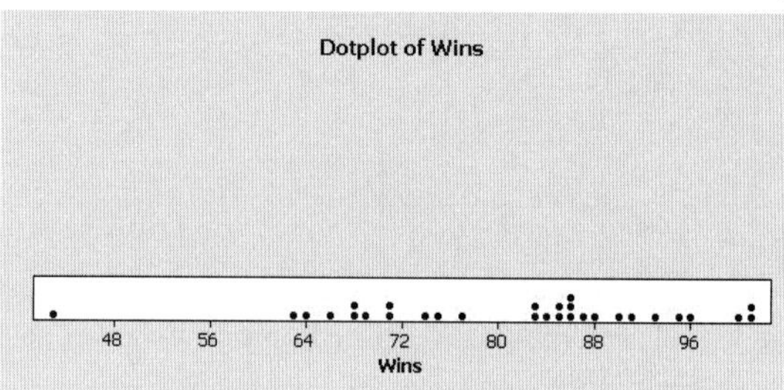

39. **a.** The first quartile is 71.53 years and the third is 78.47 years. The distribution is negatively skewed with two outliers (Nigeria and South Africa at 48 and 51).

b. The first quartile is 8.3 and the third quartile is 24.4. The distribution is symmetric with no outliers.

CHAPTER 5

1.

	Person	
Outcome	1	2
1	A	A
2	A	F
3	F	A
4	F	F

3. **a.** .176, found by $\frac{6}{34}$.
b. Empirical.

5. **a.** Empirical.
b. Classical.
c. Classical.
d. Empirical, based on seismological data.

7. **a.** The survey of 40 people about environmental issues.
b. 26 or more respond yes, for example.
c. 10/40 = .25
d. Empirical.
e. The events are not equally likely, but they are mutually exclusive.

9. **a.** Answers will vary. Here are some possibilities: 123, 124, 125, 999.
b. $(1/10)^3$
c. Classical.

11. $P(A \text{ or } B) = P(A) + P(B) = .30 + .20 = .50$
$P(\text{neither}) = 1 - .50 = .50$.

13. **a.** $102/200 = .51$
b. .49, found by $61/200 + 37/200 = .305 + .185$. Special rule of addition.

15. $P(\text{above } C) = .25 + .50 = .75$

17. $P(A \text{ or } B) = P(A) + P(B) - P(A \text{ and } B) = .20 + .30 - .15 = .35$

19. When two events are mutually exclusive, it means that if one occurs the other event cannot occur. Therefore, the probability of their joint occurrence is zero.

21. **a.** .65, found by $.35 + .40 - .10$.
b. A joint probability.
c. No, an executive might read more than one magazine.

23. $P(A \text{ and } B) = P(A) \times P(B|A) = .40 \times .30 = .12$

25. .90, found by $(.80 + .60) - .5$.
.10, found by $(1 - .90)$.

27. **a.** $P(A_1) = 3/10 = .30$
b. $P(B_1|A_2) = 1/3 = .33$
c. $P(B_2 \text{ and } A_3) = 1/10 = .10$

29. **a.** A contingency table.
b. .27, found by $300/500 \times 135/300$.
c. The tree diagram would appear as:

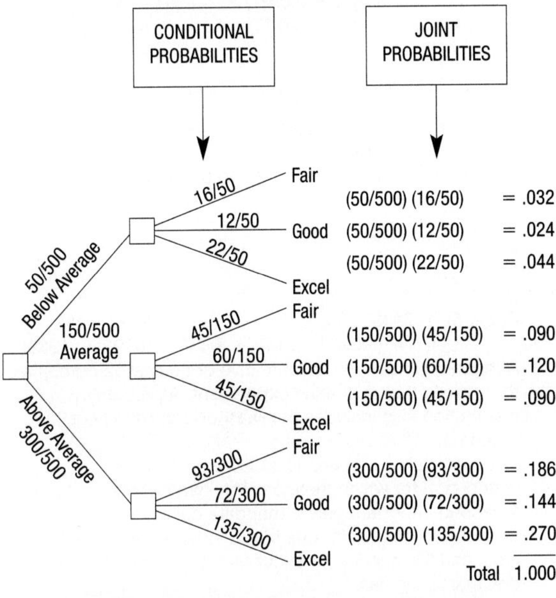

31. Probability the first presentation wins $= 3/5 = .60$.
Probability the second presentation wins $= (2/5)(3/4) = .30$.
Probability the third presentation wins $= (2/5)(1/4)(3/3) = .10$.

33. **a.** 78,960,960
b. 840, found by (7)(6)(5)(4). That is 7!/3!.
c. 10, found by 5!/3!2!.

35. ${}_{20}C_4 = 4845$.

37. 120, found by 5!.

39. 10,897,286,400, found by
${}_{15}P_{10} = (15)(14)(13)(12)(11)(10)(9)(8)(7)(6)$.

41. **a.** Asking teenagers to compare their reactions to a newly developed soft drink.
b. Answers will vary. One possibility is more than half of the respondents like it.

43. Subjective.

45. **a.** The likelihood an event will occur, assuming that another event has already occurred.
b. The collection of one or more outcomes of an experiment.
c. A measure of the likelihood that two or more events will happen concurrently.

47. **a.** .8145, found by $(.95)^4$.
b. Special rule of multiplication.
c. $P(A \text{ and } B \text{ and } C \text{ and } D) = P(A) \times P(B) \times P(C) \times P(D)$.

49. **a.** .08, found by $.80 \times .10$.
b. No; 90% of females attended college, 78% of males.
c.

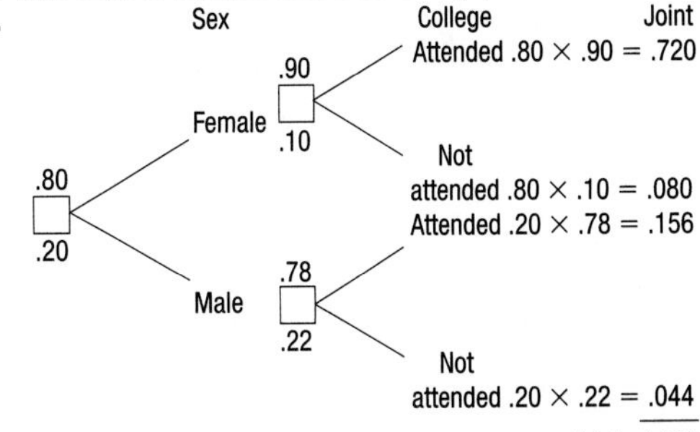

d. Yes, because all the possible outcomes are shown on the tree diagram.

51. **a.** 0.57, found by 57/100.
b. 0.97, found by (57/100) + (40/100).
c. Yes, because an employee cannot be both.
d. 0.03, found by $1 - 0.97$.

53. **a.** 0.4096, found by $(0.8)^4$.
b. 0.0016, found by $(0.2)^4$.
c. 0.9984, found by $1 - 0.0016$.

55. **a.** 0.9039, found by $(0.98)^5$.
b. 0.0961, found by $1 - 0.9039$.

57. **a.** 0.0333, found by (4/10)(3/9)(2/8).
b. 0.1667, found by (6/10)(5/9)(4/8).
c. 0.8333, found by $1 - 0.1667$.
d. Dependent

59. **a.** 0.3818, found by (9/12)(8/11)(7/10).
b. 0.6182, found by $1 - 0.3818$.

61. **a.** 0.5467, found by 82/150.
b. 0.76, found by (39/150) + (75/150).
c. 0.6267, found by $82/150 + 39/150 - 27/150$. General rule of addition.
d. 0.3293, found by 27/82.
e. 0.2972, found by (82/150)(81/149).

63. **a.** $\frac{6}{50} = .12$
b. $\frac{44}{50} = .88$
c. $.88^3 = .6815$
d. .3185

65. Yes. 256 is found by 2^8.

67. .9744, found by $1 - (.40)^4$.

69. **a.** .185, found by (.15)(.95) + (.05)(.85).
b. .0075, found by (.15)(.05).

71. **a.** $P(F \text{ and } > 60) = .25$, found by solving with the general rule of multiplication:
$P(F) \cdot P(>60|F) = (.5)(.5)$
b. 0
c. .3333, found by 1/3.

73. $26^4 = 456{,}976$

75. 1/3, 628,800

77. Answers will vary.

79.

	Attendance			
	< 2.00	2.00 up to 3.00	3.0 or more	Total
Losing	5	6	1	12
Winning	6	8	4	18
Total	11	14	5	30

a. **1.** $P(\text{win}) = \frac{18}{30} = 0.60$

2. $P(\text{win or} > 3.0) = \frac{18}{30} + \frac{5}{30} - \frac{4}{30} = 0.6333$

3. $P(\text{win}|>3.0) = \frac{4}{5} = 0.80$

4. $P(\text{losing and} <2.00) = \frac{5}{30} = .1667$

b.

	Natural	Turf	Total
Losing	11	1	12
Winning	14	4	18
Total	25	5	30

1. $P(\text{natural}) = \frac{25}{30} = 0.8333$

2. $P(\text{winning}|\text{natural}) = \frac{14}{25} = 0.56$

3. $P(\text{winning}|\text{turf}) = \frac{4}{5} = 0.80$

4. $P(\text{winning or turf}) = \frac{18}{30} + \frac{5}{30} - \frac{4}{30} = \frac{19}{30} = 0.6333$

CHAPTER 6

1. $\mu = 0(.20) + 1(.40) + 2(.30) + 3(.10) = 1.3$

$\sigma^2 = (0 - 1.3)^2(.2) + (1 - 1.3)^2(.4)$
$+ (2 - 1.3)^2(.3) + (3 - 1.3)^2(.1)$
$= .81$

3. a. The second, or middle, one.
b. .2, .4, .9
c. $\mu = 14.5$, variance $= 27.25$, found by:

$\mu = 5(.1) + 10(.3) + 15(.2) + 20(.4) = 14.5$
$\sigma^2 = (5 - 14.5)^2(.1) + (10 - 14.5)^2(.3)$
$+ (15 - 14.5)^2(.2) + (20 + 14.5)^2(.4)$
$= 27.25$
$\sigma = 5.22$, found by $\sqrt{27.25}$

5. $\mu = 0(.3) + 1(.4) + 2(.2) + 3(.1) = 1.1$

$\sigma^2 = (0 - 1.1)^2(.3) + (1 - 1.1)^2(.4)$
$+ (2 - 1.1)^2(.2) + (3 - 1.1)^2(.1) = 0.89$
$\sigma = .943.$

7. a. .20
b. .55
c. .95
d. $\mu = 0(.45) + 10(.30) + 100(.20) + 500(.05) = 48.0$

$\sigma^2 = (0 - 48)^2(.45) + (10 - 48)^2(.3)$
$+ (100 - 48)^2(.2) + (500 - 48)^2(.05) = 12{,}226$
$\sigma = 110.57$, found by $\sqrt{12{,}226}$

9. a. $P(2) = \frac{4!}{2!(4-2)!} = (.25)^2(.75)^{4-2} = .2109$

b. $P(3) = \frac{4!}{3!(4-3)!} = (.25)^3(.75)^{4-3} = .0469$

11. a.

X	$P(X)$
0	.064
1	.288
2	.432
3	.216

b. $\mu = 1.8$
$\sigma^2 = 0.72$
$\sigma = \sqrt{0.72} = .8485$

13. a. .2668, found by $P(2) = \frac{9!}{(9-2)!2!}(.3)^2(.7)^7$.

b. .1715, found by $P(4) = \frac{9!}{(9-4)!4!}(.3)^4(.7)^5$.

c. .0404, found by $P(0) = \frac{9!}{(9-0)!0!}(.3)^0(.7)^9$.

15. a. .2824, found by $P(0) = \frac{12!}{(12-0)!0!}(.10)^0(.9)^{12}$.

b. .3765, found by $P(1) = \frac{12!}{(12-1)!1!}(.10)^1(.9)^{11}$.

c. .2301, found by $P(2) = \frac{12!}{(12-2)!2!}(.10)^2(.9)^{10}$.

d. $\mu = 1.2$, found by 12(.10).
$\sigma = 1.0392$, found by $\sqrt{1.08}$.

17. a. 0.1858, found by $\frac{15!}{2!13!}(0.23)^2(0.77)^{13}$.

b. 0.1416, found by $\frac{15!}{5!10!}(0.23)^5(0.77)^{10}$.

c. 3.45, found by (0.23)(15).

19. a. 0.296, found by using Appendix A with n of 8, π of 0.30, and x of 2.
b. $P(x \leq 2) = 0.058 + 0.198 + 0.296 = 0.552$
c. 0.448, found by $P(x \geq 3) = 1 - P(x \leq 2) = 1 - 0.552$.

21. a. 0.387, found from Appendix A with n of 9, π of 0.90, and x of 9.
b. $P(X < 5) = 0.001$
c. 0.992, found by 1 − 0.008.
d. 0.947, found by 1 − 0.053.

23. a. $\mu = 10.5$, found by 15(0.7) and $\sigma = \sqrt{15(0.7)(0.3)} =$ 1.7748.

b. 0.2061, found by $\frac{15!}{10!5!}(0.7)^{10}(0.3)^5$.

c. 0.4247, found by 0.2061 + 0.2186.
d. 0.5154, found by
0.2186 + 0.1700 + 0.0916 + 0.0305 + 0.0047.

25. a. .6703
b. .3297

27. a. .0613
b. .0803

29. $\mu = 6$
$P(X \geq 5) = .7149$
$= 1 - (.0025 + .0149 + .0446 + .0892 + .1339)$

31. A random variable is a quantitative or qualitative outcome that results from a chance experiment. A probability distribution also includes the likelihood of each possible outcome.

33. The binomial distribution is a discrete probability distribution for which there are only two possible outcomes. A second important part is that data collected are a result of counts. Additionally, one trial is independent from the next, and the chance for success remains the same from one trial to the next.

35. $\mu = 0(.1) + 1(.2) + 2(.3) + 3(.4) = 2.00$

$\sigma^2 = (0 - 2)^2(.1) + \cdots + (3 - 2)^2(.40) = 1.0$
$\sigma = 1$

37. $\mu = 0(.4) + 1(.2) + 2(.2) + 3(.1) + 4(.1) = 1.3$

$\sigma^2 = (0 - 1.30)^2(.4) + \cdots + (4 - 1.30)^2(.1) = 1.81$
$\sigma = 1.3454$

39. a. $\mu = n\pi = 10(.33) = 3.3$

b. $P(x = 3) = {}_{10}C_3(.33)^3(.67)^7$
$= (120)(.035937)(.060607)$
$= .2614$

c. $P(x = 3) = {}_{10}C_3(.19)^3(.81)^7$
$= (210)(.006859)(.228768)$
$= .1883$

d. $P(x \geq 1) = 1 - P(x = 0)$
$= 1 - [{}_{10}C_0(.19)^0(.81)^{10}]$
$= 1 - .1216$
$= .8784$

41. **a.** 6, found by 0.4×15.

b. 0.0245, found by $\frac{15!}{10!5!}(0.4)^{10}(0.6)^5$

c. 0.0338, found by $0.0245 + 0.0074 + 0.0016 + 0.0003 + 0.0000$.

d. 0.0093, found by $0.0338 - 0.0245$.

43. **a.** $\mu = 20(0.075) = 1.5$

$\sigma = \sqrt{20(0.075)(0.925)} = 1.1779$

b. 0.2103, found by $\frac{20!}{0!20!}(0.075)^0(0.925)^{20}$.

c. 0.7897, found by $1 - 0.2103$.

45. **a.** 0.1311, found by $\frac{16!}{4!12!}(0.15)^4(0.85)^{12}$.

b. 2.4, found by (0.15)(16).

c. 0.2100, found by $1 - 0.0743 - 0.2097 - 0.2775 = 0.2285$.

47. **a.**

0	0.0002
1	0.0019
2	0.0116
3	0.0418
4	0.1020
5	0.1768
6	0.2234
7	0.2075
8	0.1405
9	0.0676
10	0.0220
11	0.0043
12	0.0004

b. $\mu = 12(0.52) = 6.24$

$\sigma = \sqrt{12(0.52)(0.48)} = 1.7307$

c. 0.1768

d. 0.3343, found by $0.0002 + 0.0019 + 0.0116 + 0.0418 + 0.1020 + 0.1768$.

49. **a.** .0498

b. .7746, found by $(1 - .0498)^5$.

51. $\mu = 4.0$, from Appendix C.

a. .0183

b. .1954

c. .6289

d. .5665

53. **a.** 0.1733, found by $\frac{(3.1)^4e^{-3.1}}{4!}$.

b. 0.0450, found by $\frac{(3.1)^0e^{-3.1}}{0!}$.

c. 0.9550, found by $1 - 0.0450$.

55. $P(2) = .0001539$, found by

$$\frac{\left(\frac{2}{113}\right)^2 e^{-2/113}}{2!}$$

$P(0) = 0.9824566$, found by

$$\frac{\left(\frac{2}{113}\right)^0 e^{-2/113}}{0!}$$

57. Let $\mu = n\pi = 155(1/3709) = 0.042$

$$P(5) = \frac{0.042^5e^{-0.042}}{0!} = 0.000000001$$

Very unlikely!

59. **a.** $\mu = 15(.67) = 10.05$

b. $P(x = 8) = {}_{15}C_8(.67)^8(.33)^7$
$= (6435)(.040606)(.000426)$
$= .1114$

c. $P(x \geq 8) = .1111 + .1759 + \cdots + .0025$
$= .9163$

CHAPTER 7

1. **a.** $b = 10, a = 6$

b. $\mu = \frac{6 + 10}{2} = 8$

c. $\sigma = \sqrt{\frac{(10 - 6)^2}{12}} = 1.1547$

d. $\text{Area} = \frac{1}{(10 - 6)} \cdot \frac{(10 - 6)}{1} = 1$

e. $P(X > 7) = \frac{1}{(10 - 6)} \cdot \frac{10 - 7}{1} = \frac{3}{4} = .75$

f. $P(7 \leq x \leq 9) = \frac{1}{(10 - 6)} \frac{(9 - 7)}{1} = \frac{2}{4} = .50$

3. **a.**

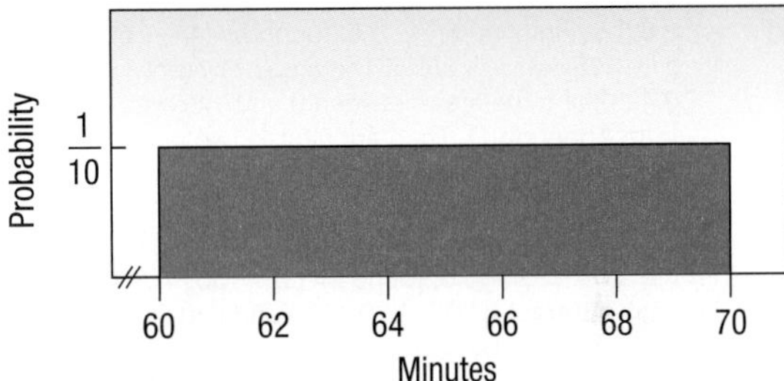

b. $\mu = \frac{60 + 70}{2} = 65$

$\sigma = \sqrt{\frac{(70 - 60)^2}{12}} = 2.8868$

$\sigma^2 = 8.3333$

c. $P(X < 68) = \frac{1}{(70 - 60)}\left(\frac{68 - 60}{1}\right) = .80$

d. $P(X > 64) = \frac{1}{(70 - 60)} \cdot \left(\frac{70 - 64}{1}\right) = .60$

5. **a.** 0.50 and 3.00

b. $\mu = \frac{0.50 + 3.00}{2} = 1.75$

$\sigma = \sqrt{\frac{(3.00 - 0.50)^2}{12}} = 0.7217$

c. $P(x \leq 1) = \frac{1}{(3.00 - 0.50)} \cdot (1.00 - 0.50) = \frac{.50}{2.50} = 0.20$

d. $P(x = 0) = 0$

e. $P(x > 1.50) = \frac{1}{(3.00 - 0.50)}(3.00 - 1.50) = \frac{1.50}{2.50} = 0.60$

7. The actual shape of a normal distribution depends on its mean and standard deviation. Thus, there is a normal distribution, and an accompanying normal curve, for a mean of 7 and a standard deviation of 2. There is another normal curve for a mean of \$25,000 and a standard deviation of \$1,742, and so on.

9. **a.** 490 and 510, found by $500 \pm 1(10)$.

b. 480 and 520, found by $500 \pm 2(10)$.

c. 470 and 530, found by $500 \pm 3(10)$.

11. $z_{Rob} = \frac{\$50,000 - \$60,000}{\$5000} = -2$

$z_{Rachel} = \frac{\$50,000 - \$35,000}{\$8000} = 1.875$

Adjusting for their industries, Rob is well below average and Rachel well above.

13. **a.** 1.25, found by $z = \frac{25 - 20}{4.0} = 1.25$.
b. 0.3944, found in Appendix D.
c. 0.3085, found by $z = \frac{18 - 20}{2.5} = -0.5$.
Find 0.1915 in Appendix D for $z = -0.5$.
Then $0.5000 - 0.1915 = 0.3085$.

15. **a.** 0.3413, found by $z = \frac{\$24 - \$20.50}{\$3.50} = 1.00$.
Then find 0.3413 in Appendix D for $z = 1$.
b. 0.1587, found by $0.5000 - 0.3413 = 0.1587$.
c. 0.3336, found by $z = \frac{\$19.00 - \$20.50}{\$3.50} = -0.43$.
Find 0.1664 in Appendix D, for $z = -0.43$,
then $0.5000 - 0.1664 = 0.3336$.

17. **a.** 0.8276: First find $z = -1.5$, found by $(44 - 50)/4$ and $z = 1.25 = (55 - 50)/4$. The area between -1.5 and 0 is 0.4332 and the area between 0 and 1.25 is 0.3944, both from Appendix D. Then adding the two areas we find that $0.4332 + 0.3944 = 0.8276$.
b. 0.1056, found by $0.5000 - 0.3994$, where $z = 1.25$.
c. 0.2029: Recall that the area for $z = 1.25$ is 0.3944, and the area for $z = 0.5$, found by $(52 - 50)/4$, is 0.1915. Then subtract $0.3944 - 0.1915$ and find 0.2029.

19. **a.** 0.1525, found by subtracting $0.4938 - 0.3413$, which are the areas associated with z values of 2.5 and 1, respectively.
b. 0.0062, found by $0.5000 - 0.4938$.
c. 0.9710, found by recalling that the area of the z value of 2.5 is 0.4938. Then find $z = -2.00$, found by $(6.8 - 7.0)/0.1$. Thus, $0.4938 + 0.4772 = 0.9710$.

21. **a.** 0.0764, found by $z = (20 - 15)/3.5 = 1.43$, then $0.5000 - 0.4236 = 0.0764$.
b. 0.9236, found by $0.5000 + 0.4236$, where $z = 1.43$.
c. 0.1185, found by $z = (12 - 15)/3.5 = -0.86$.
The area under the curve is 0.3051, then
$z = (10 - 15)/3.5 = -1.43$. The area is 0.4236.
Finally, $0.4236 - 0.3051 = 0.1185$.

23. $X = 56.60$, found by adding 0.5000 (the area left of the mean) and then finding a z value that forces 45 percent of the data to fall inside the curve.
Solving for X: $1.65 = (X - 50)/4 = 56.60$.

25. 7.233: Find a z value where 0.4900 of area is between 0 and z. That value is $z = 2.33$.
Then solve for X: $(X - 7)/0.1$, so $X = 7.233$.

27. \$1,630, found by \$2,100 − 1.88(\$250).

29. **a.** $\mu = \frac{11.96 + 12.05}{2} = 12.005$

b. $\sigma = \sqrt{\frac{(12.05 - 11.96)^2}{12}} = .0260$

c. $P(X < 12) = \frac{1}{(12.05 - 11.96)} \frac{12.00 - 11.96}{1}$

$= \frac{.04}{.09} = .44$

d. $P(X > 11.98) = \frac{1}{(12.05 - 11.96)}\left(\frac{12.05 - 11.98}{1}\right)$

$= \frac{.07}{.09} = .78$

e. All cans have more than 11.00 ounces, so the probability is 100%.

31. **a.** $\mu = \frac{4 + 10}{2} = 7$

b. $\sigma = \sqrt{\frac{(10 - 4)^2}{12}} = 1.732$

c. $P(X < 6) = \frac{1}{(10 - 4)} \cdot \left(\frac{6 - 4}{1}\right) = \frac{2}{6} = .33$

d. $P(X > 5) = \frac{1}{(10 - 4)} \cdot \left(\frac{10 - 5}{1}\right) = \frac{5}{6} = .83$

33. **a.** 0.5000, because $z = \frac{30 - 490}{90} = -5.11$.
b. 0.2514, found by $0.5000 - 0.2486$.
c. 0.6374, found by $0.2486 + 0.3888$.
d. 0.3450, found by $0.3888 - 0.0438$.

35. **a.** 0.3015, found by $0.5000 - 0.1985$.
b. 0.2579, found by $0.4564 - 0.1985$.
c. 0.0011, found by $0.5000 - 0.4989$.
d. 1,818, found by 1,280 + 1.28(420).

37. **a.** $P(z < 40) = \frac{40 - 34}{4.5} = 1.33$

$P(z < 1.33) = .5000 + .4082 = .9082$

b. $P(z > 25) = \frac{25 - 29}{5.1} = -0.78$

$P(z > -0.78) = .2823 + .5000 = .7823$

c. For women: $P(z > 2.33) = .0100$

$2.33 = \frac{x - 34}{4.5}$

$x = 34 + 2.33(4.5) = 44.485$

For men:

$2.33 = \frac{x - 29}{5.1}$

$x = 29 + 2.33(5.1) = 40.883$

39. **a.** $z = \frac{860 - 1{,}000}{50} = -2.80$

$.5000 - .4974 = .0026$

b. $z = \frac{1{,}055 - 1{,}000}{50} = 1.10$

$.4772 - .3643 = .1129$

c. $.4974 + .3643 = .8617$

41. About 4,099 units, found by solving for X.
$1.65 = (X - 4{,}000)/60$

43. **a.** 15.39%, found by $(8 - 10.3)/2.25 = -1.02$, then $0.5000 - 0.3461 = 0.1539$.
b. 17.31%, found by:
$z = (12 - 10.3)/2.25 = 0.76$. Area is 0.2764.
$z = (14 - 10.3)/2.25 = 1.64$. Area is 0.4495.
The area between 12 and 14 is 0.1731, found by $0.4495 - 0.2764$.
c. Yes, but it is rather remote. Reasoning: On 99.73 percent of the days, returns are between 3.55 and 17.05, found by $10.3 \pm 3(2.25)$. Thus, the chance of less than 3.55 returns is rather remote.

45. **a.** $1.65 = (45 - \mu)/5$ $\quad \mu = 36.75$
b. $1.65 = (45 - \mu)/10$ $\quad \mu = 28.5$
c. $z = (30 - 28.5)/10 = 0.15$,
then $0.5000 + 0.0596 = 0.5596$.

47. **a.** 21.19 percent found by $z = (9.00 - 9.20)/0.25 = -0.80$; so $0.5000 - 0.2881 = 0.2119$.
b. Increase the mean. $z = (9.00 - 9.25)/0.25 = -1.00$; $P = 0.5000 - 0.3413 = 0.1587$.
Reduce the standard deviation. $\sigma = (9.00 - 9.20)/0.15 = -1.33$; $P = 0.5000 - 0.4082 = 0.0918$.
Reducing the standard deviation is better because a smaller percent of the hams will be below the limit.

49. **a.** $z = (60 - 52)/5 = 1.60$, so $0.5000 - 0.4452 = 0.0548$.

b. Let $z = 0.67$, so $0.67 = (X - 52)/5$ and $X = 55.35$, set mileage at 55,350.
c. $z = (45 - 52)/5 = -1.40$, so $0.5000 - 0.4192 = 0.0808$.

51. $\frac{470 - \mu}{\sigma} = 0.25 \quad \frac{500 - \mu}{\sigma} = 1.28 \quad \sigma = 29{,}126$ and $\mu = 462{,}718$

53. $\mu = 150(0.15) = 22.5 \quad \sigma = \sqrt{150(0.15)(0.85)} = 4.37$
$z = (29.5 - 22.5)/4.37 = 1.60$
$P(z > 1.60) = .5000 - 0.4452 = 0.0548$

55. *Note:* Be careful of the units; 3500 is 3.5 million.

a. $z = \frac{3500 - 2254}{665} = 1.87$
$P(z > 1.87) = .5000 - .4693 = .0307$
Expected number of teams = (.0307)(30) = .921
There were no teams with attendance of more than 3.5, or 3500.

b. $z = \frac{50.0 - 70.94}{28.06} = -0.75$
$P(z > -0.75) = .5000 + .2734 = .7734$
Expected number of teams is .7734(30) = 23.2. There are 23 teams with salaries of at least 50.0 million, so the approximation is accurate.

CHAPTER 8

1. a. 303 Louisiana, 5155 S. Main, 3501 Monroe, 2652 W. Central
b. Answers will vary.
c. 630 Dixie Hwy, 835 S. McCord Rd, 4624 Woodville Rd
d. Answers will vary.

3. a. Bob Schmidt Chevrolet
Great Lakes Ford Nissan
Grogan Towne Chrysler
Southside Lincoln Mercury
Rouen Chrysler Jeep Eagle
b. Answers will vary.
c. Answers will vary.
d. York Automotive, Thayer Chevrolet Geo Toyota
Franklin Park Lincoln Mercury
Mathews Ford Oregon, Inc.
Valiton Chrysler

5. a.

Sample	Values	Sum	Mean
1	12, 12	24	12
2	12, 14	26	13
3	12, 16	28	14
4	12, 14	26	13
5	12, 16	28	14
6	14, 16	30	15

b. $\mu_{\bar{X}} = (12 + 13 + 14 + 13 + 14 + 15)/6 = 13.5$
$\mu = (12 + 12 + 14 + 16)/4 = 13.5$
c. More dispersion with population data compared to the sample means. The sample means vary from 12 to 15, whereas the population varies from 12 to 16.

7. a.

Sample	Values	Sum	Mean
1	12, 12, 14	38	12.66
2	12, 12, 15	39	13.00
3	12, 12, 20	44	14.66
4	14, 15, 20	49	16.33
5	12, 14, 15	41	13.66
6	12, 14, 15	41	13.66
7	12, 15, 20	47	15.66
8	12, 15, 20	47	15.66
9	12, 14, 20	46	15.33
10	12, 14, 20	46	15.33

b. $\mu_{\bar{X}} = \frac{(12.66 + \cdots + 15.33 + 15.33)}{10} = 14.6$
$\mu = (12 + 12 + 14 + 15 + 20)/5 = 14.6$

c. The dispersion of the population is greater than that of the sample means. The sample means vary from 12.66 to 16.33, whereas the population varies from 12 to 20.

9. a. 20, found by ${}_6C_3$
b.

Sample	Cases	Sum	Mean
Ruud, Wu, Sass	3, 6, 3	12	4.00
Ruud, Sass, Flores	3, 3, 3	9	3.00
⋮	⋮	⋮	⋮
Sass, Flores, Schueller	3, 3, 1	7	2.33

c. $\mu_{\bar{X}} = 2.67$, found by $\frac{53.33}{20}$.
$\mu = 2.67$, found by $(3 + 6 + 3 + 3 + 0 + 1)/6$.
They are equal.

d.
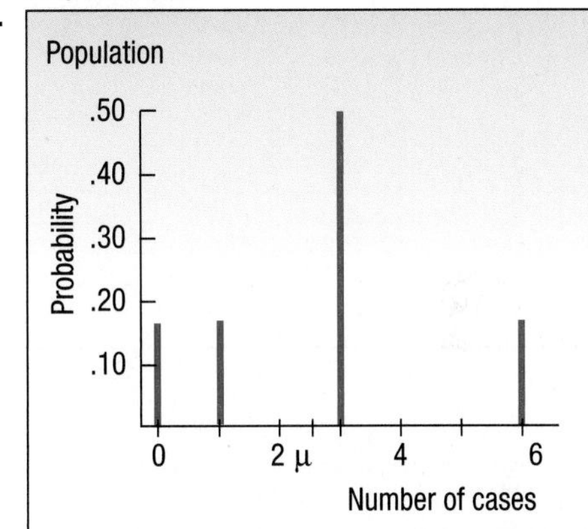

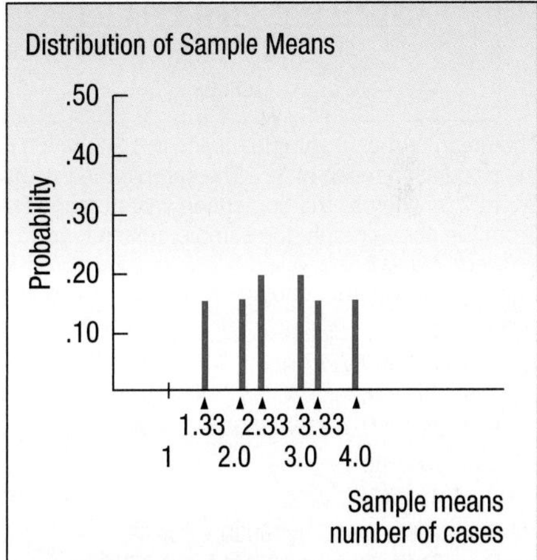

Sample Mean	Number of Means	Probability
1.33	3	.1500
2.00	3	.1500
2.33	4	.2000
3.00	4	.2000
3.33	3	.1500
4.00	3	.1500
	20	1.0000

The population has more dispersion than the sample means. The sample means vary from 1.33 to 4.0. The population varies from 0 to 6.

11. **a.**

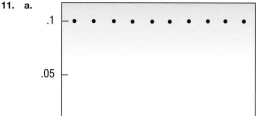

$$\mu = \frac{0 + 1 + \cdots + 9}{10} = 4.5$$

b.

Sample	Sum	$\bar{X}$
1	11	2.2
2	31	6.2
3	21	4.2
4	24	4.8
5	21	4.2
6	20	4.0
7	23	4.6
8	29	5.8
9	35	7.0
10	27	5.4

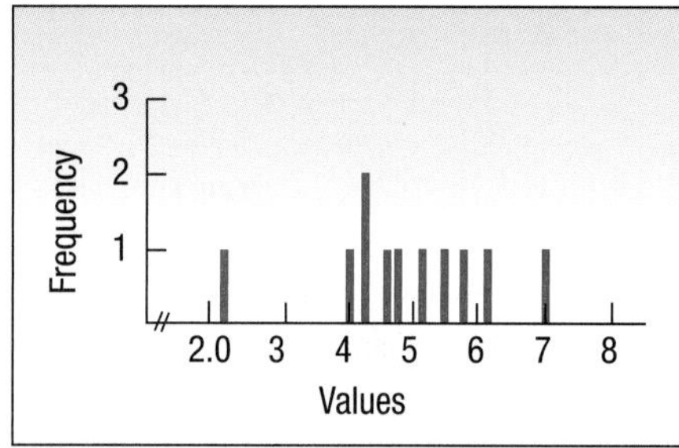

The mean of the 10 sample means is 4.84, which is close to the population mean of 4.5. The sample means range from 2.2 to 7.0, whereas the population values range from 0 to 9. From the above graph, the sample means tend to cluster between 4 and 5.

13. Answers will vary depending on the coins in your possession.

15. **a.** $z = \frac{63 - 60}{12/\sqrt{9}} = 0.75$

$P = .2266$, found by $.5000 - .2734$.

b. $z = \frac{56 - 60}{12/\sqrt{9}} = -1.00$

$P = .1587$, found by $.5000 - .3413$.

c. $P = .6147$, found by $0.3413 + 0.2734$.

17. $z = \frac{1{,}950 - 2{,}200}{250/\sqrt{50}} = -7.07$

The probability is virtually one.

19. **a.** Formal Man, Summit Stationers, Bootleggers, Leather Ltd, Petries.

b. Answers may vary.

c. Elder-Beerman, Frederick's of Hollywood, Summit Stationers, Lion Store, Leather Ltd., Things Remembered, County Seat, Coach House Gifts, Regis Hairstylists

21. The difference between a sample statistic and the population parameter is the sampling error. Yes, the difference could be zero, indicating the sample statistic and the population parameter are the same.

23. The results from the market research firm that selected customers who plan to buy a computer.

25. **a.** We selected 60, 104, 75, 72, and 48. Answers will vary.

b. We selected the third observation. So the sample consists of 75, 72, 68, 82, 48. Answers will vary.

c. Number the first 20 motels from 00 to 19. Randomly select three numbers. Then number the last five numbers 20 to 24. Randomly select two numbers from that group.

27. **a.** 15, found by ${}_6C_2$.

b.

Sample	Value	Sum	Mean
1	79, 64	143	71.5
2	79, 84	163	81.5
⋮	⋮	⋮	⋮
15	92, 77	169	84.5
			1,195.0

c. $\mu_{\bar{X}} = 79.67$, found by 1,195/15.

$\mu = 79.67$, found by 478/6.

They are equal.

d. No. The student is not graded on all available information. He/she is as likely to get a lower grade based on the sample as a higher grade.

29. **a.** 10, found by ${}_5C_2$.

b.

Number of Shutdowns	Mean	Number of Shutdowns	Mean
4, 3	3.5	3, 3	3.0
4, 5	4.5	3, 2	2.5
4, 3	3.5	5, 3	4.0
4, 2	3.0	5, 2	3.5
3, 5	4.0	3, 2	2.5

Sample Mean	Frequency	Probability
2.5	2	.20
3.0	2	.20
3.5	3	.30
4.0	2	.20
4.5	1	.10
	10	1.00

c. $\mu_{\bar{X}} = (3.5 + 4.5 + \cdots + 2.5)/10 = 3.4$

$\mu = (4 + 3 + 5 + 3 + 2)/5 = 3.4$

The two means are equal.

d. The population values are relatively uniform in shape. The distribution of sample means tends toward normality.

31. **a.** The distribution will be normal.

b. $\sigma_{\bar{X}} = \frac{5.5}{\sqrt{25}} = 1.1$

c. $z = \frac{36 - 35}{5.5/\sqrt{25}} = 0.91$

$P = 0.1814$, found by $0.5000 - 0.3186$.

d. $z = \frac{34.5 - 35}{5.5/\sqrt{25}} = -0.45$

$P = 0.6736$, found by $0.5000 + 0.1736$.

e. 0.4922, found by $0.3186 + 0.1736$.

33. $z = \frac{\$335 - \$350}{\$45/\sqrt{40}} = -2.11$

$P = 0.9826$, found by $0.5000 + 0.4826$.

35. $z = \frac{25.1 - 24.8}{2.5/\sqrt{60}} = 0.93$

$P = 0.8238$, found by $0.5000 + 0.3238$.

37. Between 5,954 and 6,046, found by $6{,}000 \pm 1.96(150/\sqrt{40})$.

39. $z = \frac{900 - 947}{205/\sqrt{60}} = -1.78$

$P = 0.0375$, found by $0.5000 - 0.4625$.

41. a. Alaska, Ohio, New Jersey, Texas, Utah, Florida, Vermont, and Connecticut.
    b. Maine, Maryland, Michigan, Missouri, Florida, South Carolina, Oklahoma, Wyoming, and Washington.
    c. Answers will vary depending on random numbers selected.
43. Answers will vary.
45. Answers will vary.

CHAPTER 9

1. 51.314 and 58.686, found by $55 \pm 2.58(10/\sqrt{49})$.
3. a. 1.581, found by $\sigma_{\bar{x}} = 5/\sqrt{10}$.
   b. The population is normally distributed and the population variance is known.
   c. 16.901 and 23.099, found by 20 ± 3.099.
5. a. $20. It is our best estimate of the population mean.
   b. $18.60 and $21.40, found by $\$20 \pm 1.96(\$5/\sqrt{49})$. About 95 percent of the intervals similarly constructed will include the population mean.
7. a. 8.60 gallons.
   b. 7.83 and 9.37, found by $8.60 \pm 2.58(2.30/\sqrt{60})$.
   c. If 100 such intervals were determined, the population mean would be included in about 99 intervals.
9. a. 2.201
   b. 1.729
   c. 3.499
11. a. The population mean is unknown, but the best estimate is 20, the sample mean.
    b. Use the *t* distribution as the standard deviation is unknown and the sample size is small. However, assume the population is normally distributed.
    c. 2.093
    d. Between 19.06 and 20.94, found by $20 \pm 2.093(2/\sqrt{20})$.
    e. Neither value is reasonable, because they are not inside the interval.
13. Between 95.39 and 101.81, found by $98.6 \pm 1.833(5.54/\sqrt{10})$.
15. a. 0.8, found by 80/100.
    b. 0.04, found by $\sqrt{\dfrac{0.8(1-0.8)}{100}}$.
    c. Between 0.72 and 0.88, found by
    $$0.8 \pm 1.96\left(\sqrt{\frac{0.8(1-0.8)}{100}}\right).$$
    d. We are reasonably sure the population proportion is between 72 and 88 percent.
17. a. 0.625, found by 250/400.
    b. 0.0242, found by $\sqrt{\dfrac{0.625(1-0.625)}{400}}$.
    c. Between 0.563 and 0.687, found by
    $$0.625 \pm 2.58\left(\sqrt{\frac{0.625(1-0.625)}{400}}\right).$$
    d. We are reasonably sure the population proportion is between 56 and 69 percent.
19. 33.465 and 36.535, found by
    $$35 \pm 1.96\left(\frac{5}{\sqrt{36}}\right)\sqrt{\frac{300-36}{300-1}}.$$
21. 1.689 up to 2.031, found by
    $$1.86 \pm 2.58\left(\frac{0.50}{\sqrt{50}}\right)\sqrt{\frac{400-50}{400-1}}.$$
23. 97, found by $n = \left(\dfrac{1.96 \times 10}{2}\right)^2 = 96.04$.
25. 196, found by $n = 0.15(0.85)\left(\dfrac{1.96}{0.05}\right)^2 = 195.9216$.
27. 554, found by $n = \left(\dfrac{1.96 \times 3}{0.25}\right)^2 = 553.19$.
29. a. 577, found by $n = 0.60(0.40)\left(\dfrac{1.96}{0.04}\right)^2 = 576.24$.
    b. 601, found by $n = 0.50(0.50)\left(\dfrac{1.96}{0.04}\right)^2 = 600.25$.
31. 6.14 years to 6.86 years, found by $6.5 \pm 1.96(1.7/\sqrt{85})$.
33. a. Between $2.018 and 2.040, found by
    $$2.029 \pm 2.58\frac{.03}{\sqrt{50}} = 2.029 \pm .011.$$
    b. $1.50 is not reasonable because it is not in the interval.
35. a. Population mean is unknown.
    b. $8.32 \pm 1.65\dfrac{3.07}{\sqrt{40}} = 8.32 \pm .80$.
    c. The limits of the confidence interval are 7.52 and 9.12. Ten is not in the interval, therefore the claim of a mean of 10 years is not reasonable.
37. a. 65.61 up to 71.59 hours, found by $68.6 \pm 2.58(8.2/\sqrt{50})$.
    b. The value suggested by the NCAA is included in the confidence interval. Therefore, it is reasonable.
    c. Changing the confidence interval to 95 would reduce the width of the interval. The value of 2.58 would change to 1.96.
39. 61, found by $1.96(16/\sqrt{n}) = 4$.
41. Between $13,734 up to $15,028, found by $14{,}381 \pm 1.711(1{,}892/\sqrt{25})$. 15,000 is reasonable because it is inside of the confidence interval.
43. a. $62.583, found by $751/12.
    b. Between $60.54 and $64.63, found by $62.583 \pm 1.796(3.94/\sqrt{12})$.
    c. $60 is not reasonable, because it is outside of the confidence interval.
45. a. 89.4667, found by 1,342/15.
    b. Between 84.99 and 93.94, found by $89.4667 \pm 2.145(8.08/\sqrt{15})$.
    c. Yes, because even the lower limit of the confidence interval is above 80.
47. Between 0.648 and 0.752, found by $.7 \pm 2.58$
    $$\left(\sqrt{\frac{0.7(1-0.7)}{500}}\right)\left(\sqrt{\frac{20{,}000-500}{20{,}000-1}}\right)$$
    Yes, because even the lower limit of the confidence interval is above 0.500.
49. $52.56 and $55.44, found by $\$54.00 \pm 1.96$
    $$\frac{\$4.50}{\sqrt{35}}\sqrt{\frac{(500-35)}{500-1}}$$
51. 369, found by $n = 0.60(1-0.60)(1.96/0.05)^2$.
53. 97, found by $[(1.96 \times 500)/100]^2$.
55. a. 708.13, rounded up to 709, found by $0.21(1-0.21)(1.96/0.03)^2$.
    b. 1,068, found by $0.50(0.50)(1.96/0.03)^2$.
57. Between 0.573 and 0.653, found by $.613 \pm 2.58$
    $\left(\sqrt{\dfrac{0.613(1-0.613)}{1{,}000}}\right)$. Yes, because even the lower limit of the confidence interval is above 0.500.
59. Between 12.69 and 14.11, found by $13.4 \pm 1.96(6.8/\sqrt{352})$.

61. Answers will vary.

63. **a.** For selling price: 212.09 up to 230.11, found by $221.1 \pm (1.96)(47.11/\sqrt{105}) = 221.1 \pm 9.01$.

b. For distance: 13.697 up to 15.561, found by $14.629 \pm (1.96)(4.874/\sqrt{105}) = 14.629 \pm 0.932$.

c. For garage: 0.5867 up to 0.7657, found by 0.6762 ±

$$(1.96)\sqrt{\frac{0.6762(1 - 0.6762)}{105}} = 0.6762 \pm 0.0895$$

65. **a.** $\$30{,}833 \pm 1.96\ \frac{\$16{,}947}{\sqrt{100}} = \$30{,}833 \pm 3322$,

so the limits are $27,511 and $34,155. It is not reasonable that the population mean is $35,000.

b. $12.73 \pm 1.96\ \frac{\$2{,}792}{\sqrt{100}} = \$12.73 \pm 0.55$, so the limits are 12.18 and 13.28. The population mean could be 13 years.

c. $39.11 \pm 1.96\ \frac{12.57}{\sqrt{100}} = 39.11 \pm 2.46$, so the limits are 36.65 and 41.57. The mean age of the worker could be 40 years.

CHAPTER 10

1. **a.** Two-tailed.

b. Reject H_0 and accept H_1 when z does not fall in the region from −1.96 and 1.96.

c. −1.2, found by $z = (49 - 50)/(5/\sqrt{36}) = -1.2$

d. Fail to reject H_0.

e. $p = .2302$, found by 2(.5000 − .3849). A 23.02 percent chance of finding a z value this large when H_0 is true.

3. **a.** One-tailed.

b. Reject H_0 and accept H_1 when $z > 1.65$.

c. 1.2, found by $z = (21 - 20)/(5/\sqrt{36}) = 1.2$

d. Fail to reject H_0 at the .05 significance level.

e. $p = .1151$, found by .5000 − .3849. An 11.51 percent chance of finding a z value this large or larger.

5. **a.** H_0: $\mu = 60{,}000$ H_1: $\mu \neq 60{,}000$

b. Reject H_0 if $z < -1.96$ or $z > 1.96$.

c. −0.69, found by:

$$z = \frac{59{,}500 - 60{,}000}{5.000 / \sqrt{48}} = -0.69$$

d. Do not reject H_0.

e. $p = .4902$, found by 2(.5000 − .2549). Crosset's experience is not different from that claimed by the manufacturer. If H_0 is true, the probability of finding a value more extreme than this is .4902.

7. **a.** H_0: $\mu \geq 6.8$ H_1: $\mu < 6.8$

b. Reject H_0 if $z < -1.65$

c. $z = \frac{6.2 - 6.8}{0.5/\sqrt{36}} = -7.2$

d. H_0 is rejected.

e. $p = 0$. The mean number of DVDs watched is less than 6.8 per month. If H_0 is true, there is virtually no chance of getting a statistic this small.

9. **a.** H_0 is rejected if $z > 1.65$.

b. 1.09, found by $z = (0.75 - 0.70) / \sqrt{(0.70 \times 0.30)/100}$.

c. H_0 is not rejected.

11. **a.** H_0: $\pi \leq 0.52$ H_1: $\pi > 0.52$

b. H_0 is rejected if $z > 2.33$.

c. 1.62, found by $z = (.5667 - .52) / \sqrt{(0.52 \times 0.48)/300}$.

d. H_0 is not rejected. We cannot conclude that the proportion of men driving on the Ohio Turnpike is larger than 0.52.

13. **a.** H_0: $\pi \geq 0.90$ H_1: $\pi < 0.90$

b. H_0 is rejected if $z < -1.28$.

c. −2.67, found by $z = (0.82 - 0.90) / \sqrt{(0.90 \times 0.10)/100}$.

d. H_0 is rejected. Fewer than 90 percent of the customers receive their orders in less than 10 minutes.

15. **a.** Reject H_0 when $t > 1.833$.

b. $t = \frac{12 - 10}{(3/\sqrt{10})} = 2.108$

c. Reject H_0. The mean is greater than 10.

17. H_0: $\mu \leq 40$ H_1: $\mu > 40$
Reject H_0 if $t > 1.703$.

$$t = \frac{42 - 40}{(2.1/\sqrt{28})} = 5.040$$

Reject H_0 and conclude that the mean number of calls is greater than 40 per week.

19. H_0: $\mu \leq 22{,}100$ H_1: $\mu > 22{,}100$
Reject H_0 if $t > 1.740$.

$$t = \frac{23{,}400 - 22{,}100}{(1{,}500/\sqrt{18})} = 3.680$$

Reject H_0 and conclude that the mean life of the spark plugs is greater than 22,100 miles.

21. **a.** Reject H_0 if $t < -3.747$.

b. $\overline{X} = 17$ and $s = \sqrt{\frac{50}{5-1}} = 3.536$

$$t = \frac{17 - 20}{(3.536/\sqrt{5})} = -1.90$$

c. Do not reject H_0. We cannot conclude the population mean is less than 20.

d. Between .05 and .10, about .065.

23. H_0: $\mu \leq 4.35$ H_1: $\mu > 4.35$
Reject H_0 if $t > 2.821$.

$$t = \frac{4.368 - 4.35}{(0.0339/\sqrt{10})} = 1.68$$

Do not reject H_0. The additive did not increase the mean weight of the chickens. The p-value is between 0.10 and 0.05.

25. H_0: $\mu \leq 4.0$ H_1: $\mu > 4.0$
Reject H_0 if $t > 1.796$.

$$t = \frac{4.50 - 4.0}{(2.68/\sqrt{12})} = 0.65$$

Do not reject H_0. The mean number of fish caught has not been shown to be greater than 4.0. The p-value is greater than 0.10.

27. H_0: $\mu \geq 10$ H_1: $\mu < 10$
Reject H_0 if $z < -1.65$.

$$z = \frac{9.0 - 10.0}{2.8/\sqrt{50}} = -2.53$$

Reject H_0. The mean weight loss is less than 10 pounds. p-value = 0.5000 − 0.4943 = 0.0057

29. H_0: $\mu \geq 7.0$ H_1: $\mu < 7.0$
Assuming a 5% significance level, reject H_0 if $z < -1.65$.

$$z = \frac{6.8 - 7.0}{0.9/\sqrt{50}} = -1.57$$

Do not reject H_0. West Virginia students are not sleeping less than 7 hours. p-value = .5000 − .4418 = .0582.

31. H_0: $\mu = \$45{,}000$ H_1: $\mu \neq \$45{,}000$
Reject H_0 if $z < 1.65$ or $z > 1.65$.

$$z = \frac{45{,}500 - 45{,}000}{\$3{,}000/\sqrt{120}} = 1.83$$

Reject H_0. We can conclude that the mean salary is not $45,000. p-value = 0.0672, found by 2(0.5000 − 0.4664).

33. H_0: $\mu \leq \$2.10$ H_1: $\mu > \$2.10$
Reject H_0 if $z > 1.65$.

$$z = \frac{\$2.12 - \$2.10}{\$0.05/\sqrt{35}} = 2.37$$

Reject H_0. The mean price of gasoline is greater than \$2.10. The p-value = 0.5000 − 0.4911 = 0.0089.

35. H_0: $\pi \le 0.60$ H_1: $\pi > 0.60$
H_0 is rejected if $z > 2.33$.

$$z = \frac{0.70 - 0.60}{\sqrt{(0.60 \times 0.40)/200}} = 2.89$$

H_0 is rejected. Ms. Dennis is correct. More than 60% of the accounts are more than 3 months old.

37. H_0: $\pi \le 0.44$ H_1: $\pi > 0.44$
H_0 is rejected if $z > 1.65$.

$$z = \frac{0.480 - 0.44}{\sqrt{(0.44 \times 0.56)/1{,}000}} = 2.55$$

H_0 is rejected. We conclude that there has been an increase in the proportion of people wanting to go to Europe.

39. H_0: $\pi \le 0.20$ H_1: $\pi > 0.20$
H_0 is rejected if $z > 2.33$.

$$z = \frac{(56/200) - 0.20}{\sqrt{(0.20 \times 0.80)/200}} = 2.83$$

H_0 is rejected. More than 20 percent of the owners move during a particular year.
p-value = 0.5000 − 0.4977 = 0.0023.

41. H_0: $\mu \le 14$ H_1: $\mu > 14$
Reject H_0 if $t > 2.821$
$\bar{X} = 15.66$, $s = 1.5436$

$$t = \frac{15.66 - 14.0}{1.5436/\sqrt{10}} = \frac{1.66}{0.4881} = 3.401$$

Reject H_0. The mean rate charged is greater than 14.0 percent.

43. H_0: $\mu = 3.1$ H_1: $\mu \ne 3.1$
Reject H_0 if $t < -2.201$ or $t > 2.201$

$$\bar{X} = \frac{41.1}{12} = 3.425$$

$$s = \sqrt{\frac{4.0625}{12 - 1}} = .6077$$

$$t = \frac{3.425 - 3.1}{.6077/\sqrt{12}} = 1.853$$

Do not reject H_0. Cannot show a difference between senior citizens and the national average. p-value is about 0.09.

45. H_0: $\mu \ge 6.5$ H_1: $\mu < 6.5$
Reject H_0 if $t < -2.718$.
$\bar{X} = 5.1667$ $s = 3.1575$

$$t = \frac{5.1667 - 6.5}{3.1575/\sqrt{12}} = -1.463$$

Do not reject H_0. The p-value is greater than 0.05.

47. H_0: $\mu = 0$ H_1: $\mu \ne 0$
Reject H_0 if $t < -2.110$ or $t > 2.110$.
$\bar{X} = -0.2322$ $s = 0.3120$

$$t = \frac{-0.2322 - 0}{0.3120/\sqrt{18}} = -3.158$$

Reject H_0. The mean gain or loss does not equal 0. The p-value is less than 0.01, but greater than 0.001.

49. H_0: $\mu \le 100$ H_1: $\mu > 100$
Reject H_0 if $t > 1.761$.

$$\bar{X} = \frac{1641}{15} = 109.4$$

$$s = \sqrt{\frac{1{,}389.6}{15 - 1}} = 9.9628$$

$$t = \frac{109.4 - 100}{9.9628/\sqrt{15}} = 3.654$$

Reject H_0. The mean number with the scanner is greater than 100. p-value is 0.001.

51. H_0: $\pi = 0.50$ H_1: $\pi \ne 0.50$
Reject H_0 if z is not between −1.96 and 1.96.

$$z = \frac{0.482 - 0.500}{\sqrt{(0.5)(0.5)/1{,}002}} = -1.14$$

Do not reject the null. The nation may be evenly divided.

53. Answers will vary.

55. *Note:* Using t distribution as test statistic.

a. H_0: $\mu = 80.0$ H_1: $\mu \ne 80$
Reject H_0 if $t < -2.045$ or $t > 2.045$
$\bar{X} = 70.9387$, $s = 28.0606$

$$t = \frac{70.9387 - 80.00}{28.0606/\sqrt{30}} = -1.769$$

Do not reject H_0. We cannot conclude that the mean is different from 80.

b. H_0: $\mu \le 2000$ H_1: $\mu > 2000$
Reject H_0 if $t > 1.699$
$\bar{X} = 2254.34$, $s = 665.23$

$$t = \frac{2254.34 - 2000}{665.23/\sqrt{30}} = 2.094$$

Reject H_0. The mean attendance is greater than 2000.

57. **a.** H_0: $\mu \le 4.0$ H_1: $\mu > 4.0$
Reject H_0 if $z > 1.65$

$$z = \frac{8.12 - 4.0}{16.43/\sqrt{46}} = 1.70$$

Reject H_0. The mean number of cell phones is greater than 4.0. p-value = .5000 − .4554 = .0446

b. H_0: $\mu \ge 50$ H_1: $\mu < 50$
Reject H_0 if $z < -1.65$. Note there is one missing value, so $n = 45$.

$$z = \frac{36.0 - 50.0}{105.5/\sqrt{45}} = 1.70$$

Do not reject H_0. The mean size of the labor force is not less than 50. The p-value is .5000 − .3159 = .1841.

CHAPTER 11

1. **a.** Two-tailed test.

b. Reject H_0 if $z < -2.05$ or $z > 2.05$.

c. $$z = \frac{102 - 99}{\sqrt{\frac{5^2}{40} + \frac{6^2}{50}}} = 2.59$$

d. Reject H_0 and accept H_1.

e. p-value = .0096, found by 2(.5000 − .4952).

3. **Step 1** H_0: $\mu_1 \ge \mu_2$ H_1: $\mu_1 < \mu_2$
Step 2 The .05 significance level was chosen.
Step 3 Reject H_0 and accept H_1 if $z < -1.65$.
Step 4 −0.94, found by:

$$z = \frac{7.6 - 8.1}{\sqrt{\frac{(2.3)^2}{40} + \frac{(2.9)^2}{55}}} = -0.94$$

Step 5 Fail to reject H_0. Babies using the Gibbs brand did not gain less weight. p-value = .1736, found by .5000 − .3264.

5. Two-tailed test, because we are trying to show that a difference exists between the two means.
Reject H_0 if $z < -2.58$ or $z > 2.58$.

$$z = \frac{31.4 - 34.9}{\sqrt{\frac{(5.1)^2}{32} + \frac{(6.7)^2}{49}}} = -2.66$$

Reject H_0 at the .01 level. There is a difference in the mean turnover rate. p-value = 2(.5000 − .4961) = .0078

7. a. H_0 is rejected if $z > 1.65$.
b. 0.64, found by $p_c = \dfrac{70 + 90}{100 + 150}$.
c. 1.61, found by

$$z = \frac{0.70 - 0.60}{\sqrt{[(0.64 \times 0.36)/100] + [(0.64 \times 0.36)/150]}}$$

d. H_0 is not rejected.

9. a. $H_0: \pi_1 = \pi_2 \quad H_1: \pi_1 \neq \pi_2$
b. H_0 is rejected if $z < -1.96$ or $z > 1.96$.
c. $p_c = \dfrac{24 + 40}{400 + 400} = 0.08$
d. -2.09, found by

$$z = \frac{0.06 - 0.10}{\sqrt{[(0.08 \times 0.92)/400] + [(0.08 \times 0.92)/400]}}.$$

e. H_0 is rejected. The proportion infested is not the same in the two fields.

11. $H_0: \pi_d \leq \pi_r \quad H_1: \pi_d > \pi_r$
H_0 is rejected if $z > 2.05$.

$$p_c = \frac{168 + 200}{800 + 1{,}000} = 0.2044$$

$$z = \frac{0.21 - 0.20}{\sqrt{\dfrac{(0.2044)(0.7956)}{800} + \dfrac{(0.2044)(0.7956)}{1{,}000}}} = 0.52$$

H_0 is not rejected. There is no difference in the proportion of Democrats and Republicans who favor lowering the standards.

13. a. Reject H_0 if $t > 2.120$ or $t < -2.120$.
$df = 10 + 8 - 2 = 16$
b. $s_p^2 = \dfrac{(10 - 1)(4)^2 + (8 - 1)(5)^2}{10 + 8 - 2} = 19.9375$
c. $t = \dfrac{23 - 26}{\sqrt{19.9375\left(\dfrac{1}{10} + \dfrac{1}{8}\right)}} = -1.416$
d. Do not reject H_0.
e. p-value is greater than 0.10 and less than 0.20.

15. $H_0: \mu_w \leq \mu_m \quad H_1: \mu_w > \mu_m$
$df = 9 + 7 - 2 = 14$
Reject H_0 if $t > 2.624$.

$$s_p^2 = \frac{(7 - 1)(6.88)^2 + (9 - 1)(9.49)^2}{7 + 9 - 2} = 71.749$$

$$t = \frac{79 - 78}{\sqrt{71.749\left(\dfrac{1}{7} + \dfrac{1}{9}\right)}} = 0.234$$

Do not reject H_0. There is no difference in the mean grades.

17. $H_0: \mu_s \leq \mu_a \quad H_1: \mu_s > \mu_a$
$df = 6 + 7 - 2 = 11$
Reject H_0 if $t > 1.363$.

$$s_p^2 = \frac{(6 - 1)(12.2)^2 + (7 - 1)(15.8)^2}{6 + 7 - 2} = 203.82$$

$$t = \frac{142.5 - 130.3}{\sqrt{203.82\left(\dfrac{1}{6} + \dfrac{1}{7}\right)}} = 1.536$$

Reject H_0. The mean daily expenses are greater for the sales staff. The p-value is between 0.05 and 0.10.

19. a. Reject H_0 if $t > 2.353$.
b. $\bar{d} = \dfrac{12}{4} = 3.00 \qquad s_d = \sqrt{\dfrac{2}{3}} = 0.816$
c. $t = \dfrac{3.00}{0.816/\sqrt{4}} = 7.35$
d. Reject H_0. There are more defective parts produced on the day shift.
e. p-value is less than 0.005, but greater than 0.0005.

21. $H_0: \mu_d \leq 0 \quad H_d: \mu_d > 0$
$\bar{d} = 25.917$
$s_d = 40.791$
Reject H_0 if $t > 1.796$

$$t = \frac{25.917}{40.791/\sqrt{12}} = 2.20$$

Reject H_0. The incentive plan resulted in an increase in daily income. The p-value is about .025.

23. $H_0: \mu_M = \mu_W \quad H_1: \mu_M \neq \mu_W$
Reject H_0 if $z < -2.33$ or $z > 2.33$.

$$z = \frac{24.51 - 22.69}{\sqrt{\dfrac{(4.48)^2}{35} + \dfrac{(3.86)^2}{40}}} = 1.87$$

Do not reject H_0. There is no difference in the number of times men and women buy take-out dinner in a month. p-value $= 2(.5000 - .4693) = .0614$.

25. $H_0: \mu_1 = \mu_2 \quad H_1: \mu_1 \neq \mu_2$
Reject H_0 if $z < -1.96$ or $z > 1.96$.

$$z = \frac{4.77 - 5.02}{\sqrt{\dfrac{(1.05)^2}{40} + \dfrac{(1.23)^2}{50}}} = -1.04$$

H_0 is not rejected. There is no difference in the mean number of calls. p-value $= 2(0.5000 - 0.3508) = 0.2984$.

27. $H_0: \mu_B \leq \mu_A \quad H_1: \mu_B > \mu_A$
Reject H_0 if $z > 1.65$.

$$z = \frac{\$61{,}000 - \$57{,}000}{\sqrt{\dfrac{(\$7{,}100)^2}{30} + \dfrac{(\$9{,}200)^2}{40}}} = \frac{\$4000.00}{\$1948.42} = 2.05$$

Reject H_0. The mean income is larger for Plan B. The p-value $= .5000 - .4798 = .0202$. The skewness does not matter because of the sample sizes.

29. $H_0: \pi_1 \leq \pi_2 \quad H_1: \pi_1 > \pi_2$
Reject H_0 if $z > 1.65$.

$$p_c = \frac{180 + 261}{200 + 300} = 0.882$$

$$z = \frac{0.90 - 0.87}{\sqrt{\dfrac{0.882(0.118)}{200} + \dfrac{0.882(0.118)}{300}}} = 1.019$$

H_0 is not rejected. There is no difference in the proportions that found relief with the new and the old drugs.

31. $H_0: \pi_1 \leq \pi_2 \quad H_1: \pi_1 > \pi_2$
If $z > 2.33$, reject H_0.

$$p_c = \frac{990 + 970}{1{,}500 + 1{,}600} = 0.63$$

$$z = \frac{.6600 - .60625}{\sqrt{\dfrac{.63(.37)}{1{,}500} + \dfrac{.63(.37)}{1{,}600}}} = 3.10$$

Reject the null hypothesis. We can conclude the proportion of men who believe the division is fair is greater.

33. $H_0: \mu_n = \mu_s \quad H_1: \mu_n \neq \mu_s$
Reject H_0 if $t < -2.086$ or $t > 2.086$.

$$s_p^2 = \frac{(10 - 1)(10.5)^2 + (12 - 1)(14.25)^2}{10 + 12 - 2} = 161.2969$$

$$t = \frac{83.55 - 78.8}{\sqrt{161.2969\left(\dfrac{1}{10} + \dfrac{1}{12}\right)}} = 0.874$$

Do not reject H_0. There is no difference in the mean number of hamburgers sold at the two locations.

35. $H_0: \mu_1 = \mu_2 \quad H_1: \mu_1 \neq \mu_2$
Reject H_0 if $t > 2.819$ or $t < -2.819$.

$$s_p^2 = \frac{(10-1)(2.33)^2 + (14-1)(2.55)^2}{10+14-2} = 6.06$$

$$t = \frac{15.87 - 18.29}{\sqrt{6.06\left(\frac{1}{10}+\frac{1}{14}\right)}} = -2.374$$

Do not reject H_0. There is no difference in the mean amount purchased.

37. $H_0: \mu_1 \leq \mu_2 \quad H_1: \mu_1 > \mu_2$
Reject H_0 if $t > 2.567$.

$$s_p^2 = \frac{(8-1)(2.2638)^2 + (11-1)(2.4606)^2}{8+11-2} = 5.672$$

$$t = \frac{10.375 - 5.636}{\sqrt{5.672\left(\frac{1}{8}+\frac{1}{11}\right)}} = 4.28$$

Reject H_0. The mean number of transactions by the young adults is more than for the senior citizens.

39. $H_0: \mu_1 \leq \mu_2 \quad H_1: \mu_1 > \mu_2$
Reject H_0 if $t > 2.650$.
$\bar{X}_1 = 125.125 \quad s_1 = 15.094$
$\bar{X}_2 = 117.714 \quad s_2 = 19.914$

$$s_p^2 = \frac{(8-1)(15.094)^2 + (7-1)(19.914)^2}{8+7-2} = 305.708$$

$$t = \frac{125.125 - 117.714}{\sqrt{305.708\left(\frac{1}{8}+\frac{1}{7}\right)}} = 0.819$$

H_0 is not rejected. There is no difference in the mean number sold at the regular price and the mean number sold at reduced price.

41. $H_0: \mu_d \leq 0 \quad H_1: \mu_d > 0$
Reject H_0 if $t > 1.895$.
$\bar{d} = 1.75 \quad s_d = 2.9155$

$$t = \frac{1.75}{2.9155/\sqrt{8}} = 1.698$$

Do not reject H_0. There is no difference in the mean number of absences. The p-value is greater than 0.05 but less than .10.

43. $H_0: \mu_1 = \mu_2 \quad H_1: \mu_1 \neq \mu_2$
If z is not between -1.96 and 1.96, reject H_0.

$$z = \frac{150 - 180}{\sqrt{\frac{(40)^2}{75}+\frac{(30)^2}{120}}} = -5.59$$

Reject the null hypothesis. The population means are different.

45. $H_0: \mu_d \leq 0 \quad H_1: \mu_d > 0$
Reject H_0 if $t > 1.895$.
$\bar{d} = 3.11 \quad s_d = 2.91$

$$t = \frac{3.11}{2.91/\sqrt{8}} = 3.02$$

Reject H_0. The mean is lower.

47. $H_0: \mu_O = \mu_R$, $H_1: \mu_O = \mu_R$
$df = 25 + 28 - 2 = 51$
Reject H_0 if $t - 2.008$ or $t > 2.008$
$\bar{X}_O = 86.24$, $s_O = 23.43$
$\bar{X}_R = 92.04$, $s_R = 24.12$

$$s_p^2 = \frac{(25-1)(23.43)^2 + (28-1)(24.12)^2}{25+28-2} = 566.335$$

$$t = \frac{86.24 - 92.04}{\sqrt{566.335\left(\frac{1}{25}+\frac{1}{28}\right)}} = -0.886$$

Do not reject H_0. There is no difference in the mean number of cars in the two lots.

49. Answers will vary.

51. **a.** μ_1 = with pool $\quad \mu_2$ = without pool
$H_0: \mu_1 = \mu_2 \quad H_1: \mu_1 \neq \mu_2$
Reject H_0 if $t > 2.000$ or $t < -2.000$.
$\bar{X}_1 = 202.8 \quad s_1 = 33.7 \quad n_1 = 38$
$\bar{X}_2 = 231.5 \quad s_2 = 50.46 \quad n_2 = 67$

$$s_p^2 = \frac{(38-1)(33.7)^2 + (67-1)(50.46)^2}{38+67-2} = 2{,}041.05$$

$$t = \frac{202.8 - 231.5}{\sqrt{2{,}041.05\left(\frac{1}{38}+\frac{1}{67}\right)}} = -3.12$$

Reject H_0. There is a difference in mean selling price for homes with and without a pool.

b. μ_1 = without garage $\quad \mu_2$ = with garage
$H_0: \mu_1 = \mu_2 \quad H_1: \mu_1 \neq \mu_2$
Reject H_0 if $t > 2.000$ or $t < -2.000$.
$\alpha = 0.05 \quad df = 34 + 71 - 2 = 103$
$\bar{X}_1 = 185.45 \quad s_1 = 28.00$
$\bar{X}_2 = 238.18 \quad s_2 = 44.88$

$$s_p^2 = \frac{(34-1)(28.00)^2 + (71-1)(44.88)^2}{103} = 1{,}620.07$$

$$t = \frac{185.45 - 238.18}{\sqrt{1{,}620.7\left(\frac{1}{34}+\frac{1}{71}\right)}} = -6.28$$

Reject H_0. There is a difference in mean selling price for homes with and without a garage.

c. $H_0: \mu_1 = \mu_2 \quad H_1: \mu_1 \neq \mu_2$
Reject H_0 if $t > 2.036$ or $t < -2.036$.
$\bar{X}_1 = 196.91 \quad s_1 = 35.78 \quad n_1 = 15$
$\bar{X}_2 = 227.45 \quad s_2 = 44.19 \quad n_2 = 20$

$$s_p^2 = \frac{(15-1)(35.78)^2 + (20-1)(44.19)^2}{15+20-2} = 1{,}667.43$$

$$t = \frac{196.91 - 227.45}{\sqrt{1{,}667.43\left(\frac{1}{15}+\frac{1}{20}\right)}} = -2.19$$

Reject H_0. There is a difference in mean selling price for homes in Township 1 and Township 2.

d. $H_0: \pi_1 = \pi_2 \quad H_1: \pi_1 \neq \pi_2$
If z is not between -1.96 and 1.96, reject H_0.

$$p_c = \frac{24+43}{52+53} = 0.64$$

$$z = \frac{0.462 - 0.811}{\sqrt{0.64 \times 0.36 / 52 + 0.64 \times 0.36 / 53}} = -3.73$$

Reject the null hypothesis. There is a difference.

53. **a.** $H_0: \mu_s = \mu_{ns} \quad H_1: \mu_s \neq \mu_{ns}$
Reject H_0 if $z < -1.96$ or $z > 1.96$

$$z = \frac{\$31{,}798 - \$28{,}876}{\sqrt{\frac{(17{,}403)^2}{67}+\frac{(16{,}062)^2}{33}}} = 0.83$$

Do not reject H_0. No difference in the mean wages.

b. $H_0: \mu_w = \mu_n \quad H_1: \mu_w \neq \mu_{nw}$
Note, because one sample is less than 30, use t and pool variances. Also answer reported in \$000.

$$s_p^2 = \frac{(90-1)(17.358)^2 + (10-1)(11.536)^2}{90+10-2} = 285.85$$

$$t = \frac{31.517 - 24.678}{\sqrt{285.85\left(\frac{1}{90}+\frac{1}{10}\right)}} = 1.214$$

Reject H_0 if $t < -1.99$ or $t > 1.99$.
Do not reject H_0. No difference in the mean wages

c. H_0: $\mu_h = \mu_{nh}$ H_1: $\mu_h \neq \mu_{nh}$
Reject H_0 if $t < -1.99$ or $t > 1.99$.
Because one sample is less than 30, use t. Answer reported in $000.

$$s_p^2 = \frac{(94-1)(16.413)^2 + (6-1)(25.843)^2}{94+6-2} = 289.72$$

$$t = \frac{30.674 - 33.337}{\sqrt{289.72\left(\frac{1}{96} + \frac{1}{6}\right)}} = -0.37$$

Do not reject H_0. No difference in the mean wages

d. H_0: $\mu_m = \mu_f$ H_1: $\mu_m \neq \mu_f$
Reject H_0 if $z < -1.96$ or $z > 1.96$

$$z = \frac{\$36{,}493 - \$24{,}452}{\sqrt{\frac{(18{,}448)^2}{53} + \frac{(12{,}446)^2}{47}}} = 3.86$$

Reject H_0. There is a difference in the mean wages for men and women.

e. H_0: $\mu_m = \mu_{nm}$ H_1: $\mu_m \neq \mu_{nm}$
Reject H_0 if $z < -1.96$ or $z > 1.96$

$$z = \frac{\$24{,}864 - \$33{,}773}{\sqrt{\frac{(13{,}055)^2}{33} + \frac{(17{,}933)^2}{67}}} = -2.822$$

Reject H_0. There is a difference in the mean wages of the two groups.

CHAPTER 12

1. 9.01, from Appendix G.

3. Reject H_0 if $F > 10.5$, where degrees of freedom in the numerator are 7 and 5 in the denominator. Computed $F = 2.04$, found by:

$$F = \frac{s_1^2}{s_2^2} = \frac{(10)^2}{(7)^2} = 2.04$$

Do not reject H_0. There is no difference in the variations of the two populations.

5. H_0: $\sigma_1^2 = \sigma_2^2$ H_1: $\sigma_1^2 \neq \sigma_2^2$
Reject H_0 where $F > 3.10$. (3.10 is about halfway between 3.14 and 3.07) Computed $F = 1.44$, found by:

$$F = \frac{(12)^2}{(10)^2} = 1.44$$

Do not reject H_0. There is no difference in the variations of the two populations.

7. a. H_0: $\mu_1 = \mu_2 = \mu_3$; H_1: Treatment means are not all the same.

b. Reject H_0 if $F > 4.26$.

c & d.

Source	SS	df	MS	F
Treatment	62.17	2	31.08	21.94
Error	12.75	9	1.42	
Total	74.92	11		

e. Reject H_0. The treatment means are not all the same.

9. H_0: $\mu_1 = \mu_2 = \mu_3$; H_1: Treatment means are not all the same. Reject H_0 if $F > 4.26$.

Source	SS	df	MS	F
Treatment	276.50	2	138.25	14.18
Error	87.75	9	9.75	
Total	364.25	11		

Reject H_0. The treatment means are not all the same.

11. a. H_0: $\mu_1 = \mu_2 = \mu_3$; H_1: Not all means are the same.

b. Reject H_0 if $F > 4.26$.

c. SST = 107.20, SSE = 9.47, SS total = 116.67.

d.

Source	SS	df	MS	F
Treatment	107.20	2	53.600	50.96
Error	9.47	9	1.052	
Total	116.67	11		

e. Since $50.96 > 4.26$, H_0 is rejected. At least one of the means differs.

f. $(\bar{X}_1 - \bar{X}_2) \pm t\sqrt{\text{MSE}(1/n_1 + 1/n_2)}$

$= (9.667 - 2.20) \pm 2.262\sqrt{1.052(1/3 + 1/5)}$

$= 7.467 \pm 1.69$

$= [5.777, 9.157]$

Yes, we can conclude that treatments 1 and 2 have different means.

13. H_0: $\mu_1 = \mu_2 = \mu_3 = \mu_4$; H_1: Not all means are equal. H_0 is rejected if $F > 3.71$.

Source	SS	df	MS	F
Treatment	32.33	3	10.77	2.36
Error	45.67	10	4.567	
Total	78.00	13		

Because 2.36 is less than 3.71, H_0 is not rejected. There is no difference in the mean number of weeks.

15. H_0: $\sigma_1^2 \leq \sigma_2^2$; H_1: $\sigma_1^2 > \sigma_2^2$, $df_1 = 21 - 1 = 20$; $df_2 = 18 - 1 = 17$. H_0 is rejected if $F > 3.16$.

$$F = \frac{(45{,}600)^2}{(21{,}330)^2} = 4.57$$

Reject H_0. There is more variation in the selling price of oceanfront homes.

17. Sharkey: $n = 7$ $s_s = 14.79$
White: $n = 8$ $s_w = 22.95$

H_0: $\sigma_w^2 \leq \sigma_s^2$; H_1: $\sigma_w^2 > \sigma_s^2$, $df_s = 7 - 1 = 6$; $df_w = 8 - 1 = 7$. Reject H_0 if $F > 8.26$.

$$F = \frac{(22.95)^2}{(14.79)^2} = 2.41$$

Cannot reject H_0. There is no difference in the variation of the monthly sales.

19. a. H_0: $\mu_1 = \mu_2 = \mu_3 = \mu_4$
H_1: Treatment means are not all equal.

b. $\alpha = .05$ Reject H_0 if $F > 3.10$.

c.

Source	SS	df	MS	F
Treatment	50	4 − 1 = 3	50/3	1.67
Error	200	24 − 4 = 20	10	
Total	250	24 − 1 = 23		

d. Do not reject H_0.

21. H_0: $\mu_1 = \mu_2 = \mu_3$; H_1: Not all treatment means are equal. H_0 is rejected if $F > 3.89$.

Source	SS	df	MS	F
Treatment	63.33	2	31.667	13.38
Error	28.40	12	2.367	
Total	91.73	14		

H_0 is rejected. There is a difference in the treatment means.

23. H_0: $\mu_1 = \mu_2 = \mu_3 = \mu_4$; H_1: Not all means are equal. H_0 is rejected if $F > 3.10$

Source	SS	df	MS	F
Treatment	87.79	3	29.26	9.12
Error	64.17	20	3.21	
Total	151.96	23		

Because computed F of 9.12 > 3.10, the null hypothesis of no difference is rejected at the .05 level.

25. **a.** H_0: $\mu_1 = \mu_2$; H_1: $\mu_1 \neq \mu_2$. Critical value of F = 4.75.

Source	SS	df	MS	F
Treatment	219.43	1	219.43	23.10
Error	114.00	12	9.5	
Total	333.43	13		

b. $$t = \frac{19 - 27}{\sqrt{9.5\left(\frac{1}{6} + \frac{1}{8}\right)}} = -4.806$$

Then $t^2 = F$. That is $(-4.806)^2 = 23.10$.

c. H_0 is rejected. There is a difference in the mean scores.

27. The null hypothesis is rejected because the F statistic (8.26) is greater than the critical value (5.61) at the .01 significance level. The p-value (.0019) is also less than the significance level. The mean gasoline mileages are not the same.

29. **a.** The null hypothesis of equal population means is not rejected because the F statistic (3.41) is less than the critical value (5.49). The p-value (.0478) is also greater than the significance level (0.01). The mean amounts of money withdrawn are not different.

b. $$(82.5 - 38.2) \pm 1.703\sqrt{1{,}477.633\left(\frac{1}{10} + \frac{1}{10}\right)}$$

This reduces to 44.3 ± 29.3. So the endpoints of the confidence interval are 15.0 and 73.6. This pair of means do not differ.

31. **a.** H_0: $\mu_1 = \mu_2 = \mu_3 = \mu_4 = \mu_5 = \mu_6$; H_1: The treatment means are not equal. Reject H_0 if $F > 2.37$.

Source	SS	df	MS	F
Treatment	0.03478	5	0.00696	3.86
Error	0.10439	58	0.0018	
Total	0.13917	63		

H_0 is rejected. There is a difference in the mean weight of the colors.

33. Answers will vary.

35. **a.** H_0: $\sigma^2_{np} = \sigma^2_p$ H_1: $\sigma^2_{np} \neq \sigma^2_p$. Reject H_0 if $F > 2.05$ (estimated).
$df_1 = 67 - 1 = 66$; $df_2 = 38 - 1 = 37$.

$$F = \frac{(50.57)^2}{(33.71)^2} = 2.25$$

Reject H_0. There is a difference in the variance of the two selling prices.

b. H_0: $\sigma^2_g = \sigma^2_{ng}$ H_1: $\sigma^2_g \neq \sigma^2_{ng}$. Reject H_0 if $F > 2.21$ (estimated).

$$F = \frac{(44.88)^2}{(28.00)^2} = 2.57$$

Reject H_0. There is a difference in the variance of the two selling prices.

c. H_0: $\mu_1 = \mu_2 = \mu_3 = \mu_4 = \mu_5$; H_1: Not all treatment means are equal. Reject H_0 if $F > 2.46$.

Source	SS	df	MS	F
Treatment	13,263	4	3,316	1.52
Error	217,505	100	2,175	
Total	230,768	104		

Do not reject H_0. There is no difference in the mean selling prices in the five townships.

37. **a.** H_0: $\mu_1 = \mu_2 = \mu_3$; H_1: Treatment means are not equal. Reject H_0 if $F > 3.09$. The computed value of F is 1.30. We conclude there is no difference among the industries.

b. H_0: $\mu_1 = \mu_2 = \mu_3 = \mu_4 = \mu_5$; H_1: Treatment means are not equal.
Reject H_0 if $F > 2.31$. The computed value of F is 4.85. The treatment means differ. The MINITAB output follows.

```
Level     N     Mean    StDev
0        22    28921    14517
1        13    40074    22733
2         6    27228    16101
3        21    27619     9821
4        21    21510     6946
5        17    43002    22062

Pooled St Dev = 15507

Individual 95% CIs for Mean
Based on Pooled StDev
```

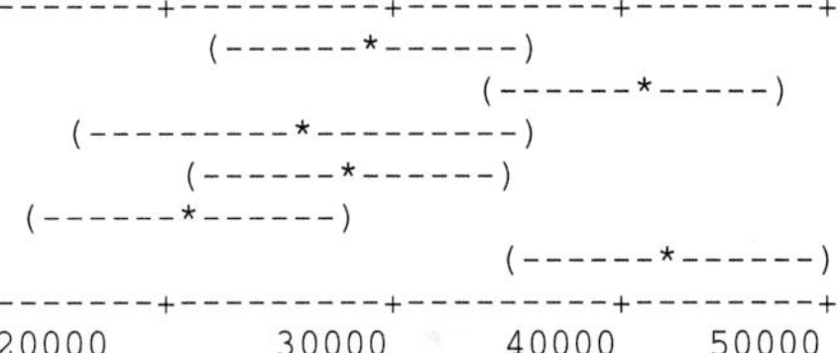

From this graph the following means differ: 0 and 5, 1 and 4, 3 and 5, and 4 and 5.

CHAPTER 13

1. $\Sigma(X - \bar{X})(Y - \bar{Y}) = 10.6$, $s_x = 2.7019$, $s_y = 1.3038$

$$r = \frac{10.6}{(5 - 1)(2.7019)(1.3038)} = 0.7522$$

The 0.7522 coefficient indicates a rather strong positive correlation between X and Y. The coefficient of determination is 0.5658, found by $(0.7522)^2$. More than 56 percent of the variation in Y is accounted for by X.

3. **a.** Sales.

b.

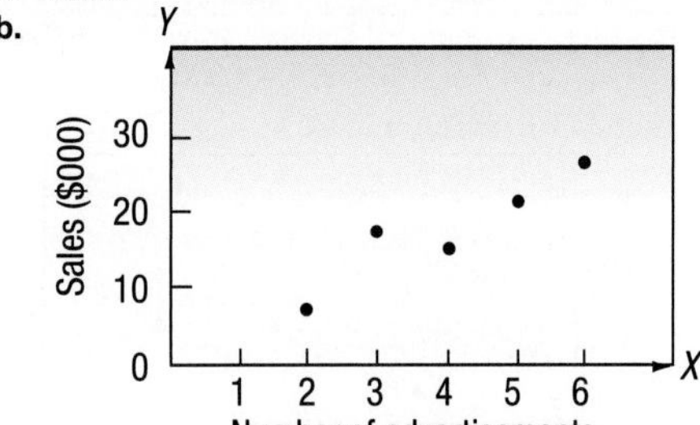

c. $\Sigma(X - \bar{X})(Y - \bar{Y}) = 36$, $n = 5$, $s_x = 1.5811$, $s_y = 6.1237$

$$r = \frac{36}{(5 - 1)(1.5811)(6.1237)} = 0.9295$$

d. The coefficient of determination is 0.8640, found by $(0.9295)^2$.

e. There is a strong positive association between the variables. About 86 percent of the variation in sales is explained by the number of airings.

5. a. Police is the independent variable, and crime is the dependent variable.

b.

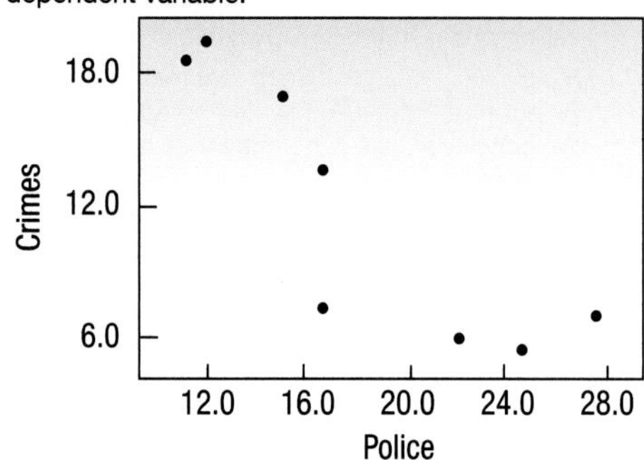

c. $n = 8$, $\Sigma(X - \bar{X})(Y - \bar{Y}) = -231.75$, $s_x = 5.8736$, $s_y = 6.4462$

$$r = \frac{-231.75}{(8 - 1)(5.8736)(6.4462)} = -0.8744$$

d. 0.7646, found by $(-0.8744)^2$

e. Strong inverse relationship. As the number of police increases, the crime decreases.

7. Reject H_0 if $t > 1.812$.

$$t = \frac{.32\sqrt{12 - 2}}{\sqrt{1 - (.32)^2}} = 1.07$$

Do not reject H_0.

9. H_0: $\rho \leq 0$; H_1: $\rho > 0$. Reject H_0 if $t > 2.552$. $df = 18$.

$$t = \frac{.78\sqrt{20 - 2}}{\sqrt{1 - (.78)^2}} = 5.288$$

Reject H_0. There is a positive correlation between gallons sold and the pump price.

11. a. $Y' = 3.7778 + 0.3630X$

$$b = 0.7522\left(\frac{1.3038}{2.7019}\right) = 0.3630$$

$$a = 5.8 - 0.3630(5.6) = 3.7671$$

b. 6.3081, found by $Y' = 3.7671 + 0.3630(7)$

13. a. $\Sigma(X - \bar{X})(Y - \bar{Y}) = 44.6$, $s_x = 2.726$, $s_y = 2.011$

$$r = \frac{44.6}{(10 - 1)(2.726)(2.011)} = .904$$

$$b = .904\left(\frac{2.011}{2.726}\right) = 0.667$$

$$a = 7.4 - .677(9.1) = 1.333$$

b. $Y' = 1.333 + .667(6) = 5.335$

15. a.

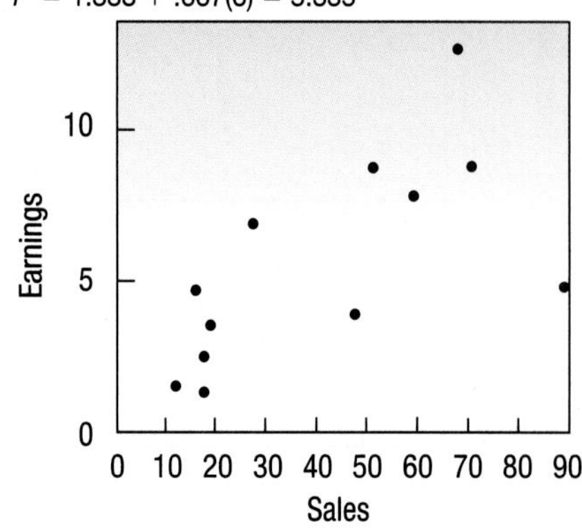

b. $\Sigma(X - \bar{X})(Y - \bar{Y}) = 629.64$, $s_x = 26.17$, $s_y = 3.248$

$$r = \frac{629.64}{(12 - 1)(26.17)(3.248)} = 0.673$$

c. $r^2 = (0.673)^2 = 0.4529$

d. A strong positive association between the variables. About 45 percent of the variation in earnings is accounted for by sales.

e. $b = .6734\left(\frac{3.248}{26.170}\right) = 0.0836$

$$a = \frac{64.1}{12} - 0.0836\left(\frac{501.10}{12}\right) = 1.8507$$

f. $Y' = 1.8507 + 0.0836(50.0) = 6.0307$ (\$millions)

17. a. $b = -.8744\left(\frac{6.4462}{5.8736}\right) = -0.9596$

$$a = \frac{95}{8} - (-0.9596)\left(\frac{146}{8}\right) = 29.3877$$

b. 10.1957, found by $29.3877 - 0.9596(20)$

c. For each policeman added, crime goes down by almost one.

19. a. $\sqrt{\frac{2.958}{5 - 2}} - 2 = .993$

b. $Y' \pm .993$

21. a. $\sqrt{\frac{6.452}{10 - 2}} = .898$

b. $Y' \pm 1.796$

23. $\sqrt{\frac{68.4877}{8 - 2}} = 3.379$

25. a. $6.308 \pm (3.182)(.993)\sqrt{.2 \pm \frac{(7 - 5.6)^2}{29.2}}$
$= 6.308 \pm 1.633$
$= [4.675, 7.941]$

b. $6.308 \pm (3.182)(.993)\sqrt{1 + 1/5 + .0671}$
$= [2.751, 9.865]$

27. a. [4.2939, 6.3721]

b. [2.9854, 7.6806]

29. $\bar{X} = 10$, $\bar{Y} = 6$, $\Sigma(X - \bar{X})(Y - \bar{Y}) = 40$, $s_y = 2.2361$, $s_x = 5.0$

$$r = \frac{40}{(5 - 1)(2.2361)(5.0)} = .8944$$

Then, $(.8944)^2 = .80$, the coefficient of determination.

31. a. $r^2 = 1{,}000/1{,}500 = .667$

b. .82, found by $\sqrt{.667}$

c. 6.20, found by $s_{y \cdot x} = \sqrt{\frac{500}{15 - 2}}$

33. a. Observe from the following scatter diagram that as the rates increase the number of housing starts declines.

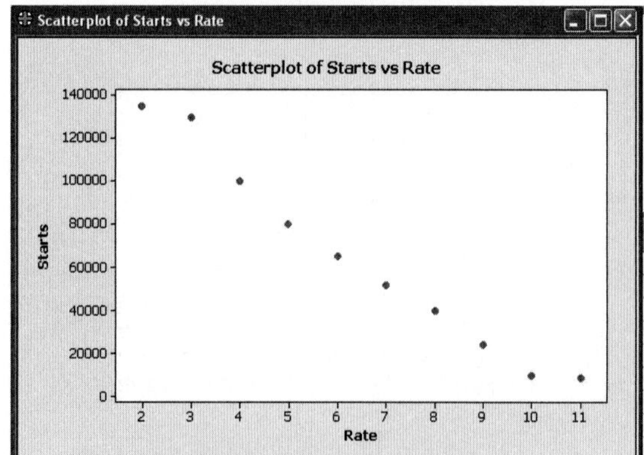

b. Below is the regression output from the MINITAB system.

```
The regression equation is
Starts = 162473 - 15073 Rate
```

```
Predictor        Coef   SE Coef       T      P
Constant       162473      5968   27.22  0.000
Rate         -15072.7     839.9  -17.95  0.000

S = 7628.59  R-Sq = 97.6%  R-Sq(adj) = 97.3%

Analysis of Variance

Source          DF           SS           MS       F      P
Regression       1  18742936364  18742936364  322.07  0.000
Residual Error   8    465563636     58195455
Total            9  19208500000
```

The independent variable Rate explains 97.6% of the variation in the number of housing starts. This is a very strong relationship.

c. The regression equation is:

$$Y' = 162{,}473 - 15072.7X$$

The estimate for a rate of 11% is

$$Y' = 162{,}473 - 15072.7X = 162{,}473 - 15072.7(11) = -3{,}326.7$$

An estimate of a negative number is not possible. This suggests that the relationship between the variables is not linear.

d. Below is the output when the number of housing starts is transformed to a log with a base of 10.

```
The regression equation is
Log-Starts = 5.55 - 0.136 Rate

Predictor       Coef   SE Coef       T      P
Constant     5.54691   0.09268   59.85  0.000
Rate        -0.13625   0.01304  -10.45  0.000

S = 0.118456      R-Sq = 93.2%      R-Sq(adj) = 92.3%

Analysis of Variance

Source          DF      SS      MS       F      P
Regression       1  1.5316  1.5316  109.15  0.000
Residual Error   8  0.1123  0.0140
Total            9  1.6438
```

The R-Square value is 93.2%, somewhat less than the value found using the actual variable. The regression equation is:

$$Y' = 5.54691 - 0.13625X$$

If we substitute the rate of 11%, the estimated number of housing starts is

$$Y' = 5.54691 - 0.13625X = 5.54691 - 0.13625(11) = 4.04816$$

The antilog of 4.04816 is 11,173. So the estimated number of housing starts is a positive number. The estimated number of housing starts for a rate of 12% is 8,164. Using the transformed variable seems more reasonable.

35. $H_0: \rho \le 0$; $H_1: \rho > 0$. Reject H_0 if $t > 1.714$.

$$t = \frac{.94\sqrt{25-2}}{\sqrt{1-(.94)^2}} = 13.213$$

Reject H_0. There is a positive correlation between passengers and weight of luggage.

37. $H_0: \rho \le 0$; $H_1: \rho > 0$. Reject H_0 if $t > 2.764$.

$$t = \frac{.47\sqrt{12-2}}{\sqrt{1-(.47)^2}} = 1.684$$

Do not reject H_0. There is not a positive correlation between engine size and performance. p-value is greater than .05, but less than .10.

39. **a.** Yes. Positive correlation between the variables.

b. $r^2 = (0.237)^2 = .056169$

c. $H_0: \rho \le 0$, $H_1: \rho > 0$
Reject H_0 if $t > 2.552$

$$t = \frac{.237\sqrt{20-2}}{\sqrt{1-(.237)^2}} = 1.035$$

Do not reject H_0. We cannot conclude there is correlation between the unemployment rate and the population.

41. **a.** $r = 0.589$

b. $r^2 = (0.589)^2 = 0.3469$

c. $H_0: \rho \le 0$; $H_1: \rho > 0$. Reject H_0 if $t > 1.860$.

$$t = \frac{0.589\sqrt{10-2}}{\sqrt{1-(.589)^2}} = 2.062$$

H_0 is rejected. There is a positive association between family size and the amount spent on food.

43. **a.**

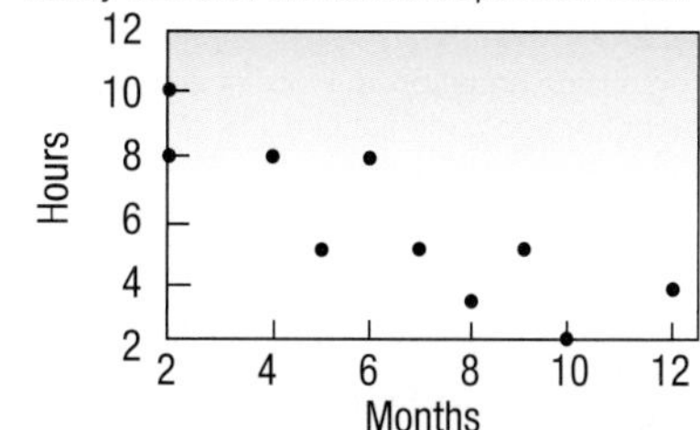

There is an inverse relationship between the variables. As the months owned increase, the number of hours exercised decreases.

b. $r = -0.827$

c. $H_0: \rho \ge 0$; $H_1: \rho < 0$. Reject H_0 if $t < -2.896$.

$$t = \frac{-0.827\sqrt{10-2}}{\sqrt{1-(-0.827)^2}} = -4.16$$

Reject H_0. There is a negative association between months owned and hours exercised.

45. **a.**

Source	SS	df	MS	F
Regression	50	1	50	2.5556
Error	450	23	19.5652	
Total	500	24		

b. $n = 25$

c. $s_{y \cdot x} = \sqrt{19.5652} = 4.4233$

d. $r^2 = \dfrac{50}{500} = 0.10$

47. **a.** $b = -0.4667$, $a = 11.2358$

b. $Y' = 11.2358 - 0.4667(7.0) = 7.9689$

c. $7.9689 \pm (2.160)(1.114)\sqrt{1 + \dfrac{1}{15} + \dfrac{(7-7.1333)^2}{73.7333}}$
$= 7.9689 \pm 2.4854$
$= [5.4835, 10.4543]$

d. $r^2 = 0.499$. Nearly 50 percent of the variation in the amount of the bid is explained by the number of bidders.

49. **a.**

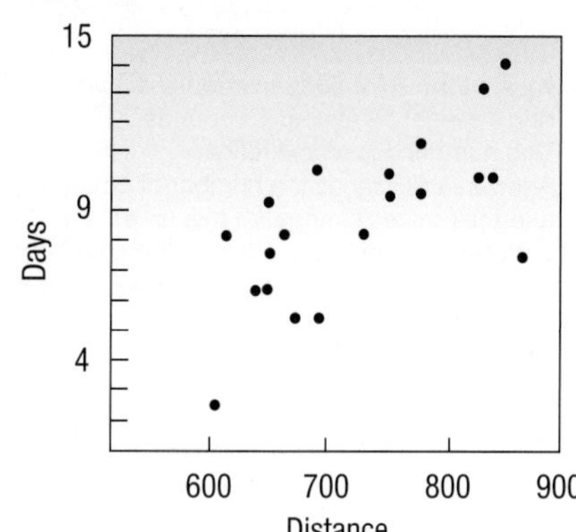

There appears to be a relationship between the two variables. As the distance increases, so does the shipping time.

b. $r = 0.692$
H_0: $\rho \leq 0$; H_1: $\rho > 0$. Reject H_0 if $t > 1.734$.

$$t = \frac{0.692\sqrt{20-2}}{\sqrt{1-(0.692)^3}} = 4.067$$

H_0 is rejected. There is a positive association between shipping distance and shipping time.

c. $r^2 = 0.479$. Nearly half of the variation in shipping time is explained by shipping distance.

d. $s_{y \cdot x} = 1.987$

51. a. $b = 2.41$
$a = 26.8$
The regression equation is: Price = 26.8 + 2.41 × dividend. For each additional dollar of dividend, the price increases by \$2.41.

b. $r^2 = \frac{5{,}057.65}{7{,}682.7} = 0.658$ Thus, 65.8 percent of the variation in price is explained by the dividend.

c. $r = \sqrt{.658} = 0.811$ H_0: $\rho \leq 0$ H_1: $\rho > 0$
At the 5 percent level, reject H_0 when $t > 1.701$.

$$t = \frac{0.811\sqrt{30-2}}{\sqrt{1-(0.811)^2}} = 7.34$$

Thus H_0 is rejected. The population correlation is positive.

53. a. 35

b. $s_{y \cdot x} = \sqrt{29{,}778{,}406} = 5456.96$

c. $r^2 = \frac{13{,}548{,}662{,}082}{14{,}531{,}349{,}474} = 0.932$

d. $r = \sqrt{0.932} = 0.966$

e. H_0: $\rho \leq 0$, H_1: $\rho > 0$; reject H_0 if $t > 1.697$.

$$t = \frac{.966\sqrt{35-2}}{\sqrt{1-(.966)^2}} = 21.46$$

Reject H_0. There is a direct relationship between size of the house and its market value.

55. a. $Y' = -1{,}031.0 + 1{,}877.3X$, $r^2 = .697$.

b. The second laptop (1.6, 1229) has a residual of −743.64. That is a noticeable "bargain price."

c. The correlation of Speed and Price is 0.835.
H_0: $\rho \leq 0$ H_1: $\rho > 0$ Reject H_0 if $t > 1.812$.

$$t = \frac{0.835\sqrt{12-2}}{\sqrt{1-(0.835)^2}} = 4.799$$

Reject H_0. It is reasonable to say the population correlation is positive.

57. a. $r = .987$, H_0: $\rho \leq 0$, H_1: $\rho > 0$. Reject H_0 if $t > 1.746$.

$$t = \frac{.987\sqrt{18-2}}{\sqrt{1-(.987)^2}} = 24.564$$

b. $Y' = -29.7 + 22.93X$; an additional cup increases the dog's weight by almost 23 pounds.

c. Dog number 4 is an overeater.

59. a. Answers will vary as the number of cottages available and their prices change. At this time there are 14 cottages that meet the criteria. The correlation between the number of baths and rental price is 0.668.
H_0: $\rho \leq 0$ H_1: $\rho > 0$
Reject H_0 if $t > 1.782$.

$$t = \frac{.0668\sqrt{14-2}}{\sqrt{1-(0.668)^2}} = 3.11$$

Reject H_0. There is a positive correlation between baths and cottage price.

b. The regression equation is $Y' = 758 + 347X$. The weekly price increases almost \$350 for each bathroom.

c. H_0: $\rho \leq 0$ H_1: $\rho > 0$
Reject H_0 if $t > 1.782$.

$$t = \frac{0.085\sqrt{14-2}}{\sqrt{1-(0.085)^2}} = .296$$

Do not reject H_0. We cannot conclude that there is an association between people and price.

61. a. The correlation between wins and salary is 0.417.
H_0: $\rho \leq 0$, H_1: $\rho > 0$, at .05 significance level, reject H_0 if $t > 1.701$.

$$t = \frac{.417\sqrt{30-2}}{\sqrt{1-(.417)^2}} = 2.428$$

Reject H_0: Wins and salary are related.
$Y' = 66.875 + .19864X$.
An additional \$5 million would increase wins by about .9932.

b. The correlation between wins and ERA is −0.672 and between wins and batting is 0.556. The correlation between ERA and wins is stronger. The critical values are −1.701 for ERA and 1.701 for batting.

$$t_{\text{ERA}} = \frac{-0.672\sqrt{30-2}}{\sqrt{1-(-0.672)^2}} = -4.802$$

$$t_{\text{wins}} = \frac{.556\sqrt{30-2}}{\sqrt{1-(.556)^2}} = 3.540$$

c. The correlation between wins and attendance is .512.

$$t = \frac{.512\sqrt{30-2}}{\sqrt{1-(.512)^2}} = 3.154$$

There is a significant correlation between wins and attendance.

63. a. The regression equation is: Unemployment = 9.558 + 0.0020 Labor force. The slope tells you one more person in the labor force will add 0.002 or 0.2% to unemployment. The predicted unemployment for UAE is 9.5608, found by 9.558 + 0.002(1.4).

b. Pearson correlation of Exports and Imports = 0.948
H_0: $\rho \leq 0$ H_1: $\rho > 0$
At the 5% level, reject H_0 when $t > 1.680$.

$$t = \frac{0.948\sqrt{46-2}}{\sqrt{1-(0.948)^2}} = 19.758$$

Reject H_0. The population correlation is positive.

c. Pearson correlation of 65 & over and Literacy % = 0.794
H_0: $\rho \leq 0$ H_1: $\rho > 0$
At the 5% level, reject H_0 when $t > 1.680$.

$$t = \frac{0.794\sqrt{46-2}}{\sqrt{1-(0.794)^2}} = 8.66$$

Reject H_0. The population correlation is positive.

CHAPTER 14

1. a. Multiple regression equation.

b. The Y-intercept.

c. $Y' = 64{,}100 + 0.394(796{,}000) + 9.6(6{,}940) - 11{,}600(6.0) = \$374{,}748$

3. a. 497.736, found by

$$Y' = 16.24 + 0.017(18) + 0.0028(26{,}500) + 42(3) + 0.0012(156{,}000) + 0.19(141) + 26.8(2.5)$$

b. Two more social activities. Income added only 28 to the index; social activities added 53.6.

5. a. 19

b. 3

c. .318, found by 21/66.

d. 1.732, found by $\sqrt{\dfrac{45}{[19 - (3 + 1)]}}$.

7. a.

Source	SS	df	MS	F
Regression	7,500.0	3	2,500	18
Error	2,500.0	18	138.89	
Total	10,000.0	21		

b. H_0: $\beta_1 = \beta_2 = \beta_3 = 0$; H_1: Not all βs are 0. Reject H_0 if $F > 3.16$.
$F = 18.0$, so reject H_0. Not all net regression coefficients equal zero.

c.

For X_1:	For X_2:	For X_3:
H_0: $\beta_1 = 0$	H_0: $\beta_2 = 0$	H_0: $\beta_3 = 0$
H_1: $\beta_1 \neq 0$	H_1: $\beta_2 \neq 0$	H_1: $\beta_3 \neq 0$
$t = -4.00$	$t = 1.50$	$t = -3.00$

Reject H_0 if $t > 2.101$ or $t < -2.101$.
Delete variable 2, keep 1 and 3.

9. a. $n = 40$

b. 4

c. $R^2 = \dfrac{750}{1250} = .60$

d. $s_{y \cdot 1234} = \sqrt{500/35} = 3.7796$

e. H_0: $\beta_1 = \beta_2 = \beta_3 = \beta_4 = 0$
H_1: Not all the βs equal zero.
H_0 is rejected if $F > 2.65$.

$$F = \frac{750/4}{500/35} = 13.125$$

H_0 is rejected. At least one β_i does not equal zero.

11. a. $n = 26$.

b. $R^2 = 100/140 = .7143$

c. 1.4142, found by $\sqrt{2}$.

d. H_0: $\beta_1 = \beta_2 = \beta_3 = \beta_4 = \beta_5 = 0$
H_1: Not all the βs are 0.
H_0 is rejected if $F > 2.71$.
Computed $F = 10.0$. Reject H_0. At least one regression coefficient is not zero.

e. H_0 is rejected in each case if $t < -2.086$ or $t > 2.086$.
X_1 and X_5 should be dropped.

13. a. $28,000

b. $R^2 = \dfrac{SSR}{SS\ total} = \dfrac{3{,}050}{5{,}250} = .5809$

c. 9.199, found by $\sqrt{84.62}$.

d. H_0 is rejected if $F > 2.97$ (approximately).

$$\text{Computed } F = \frac{1{,}016.67}{84.62} = 12.01$$

H_0 is rejected. At least one regression coefficient is not zero.

e. If computed t is to the left of -2.056 or to the right of 2.056, the null hypothesis in each of these cases is rejected. Computed t for X_2 and X_3 exceed the critical value. Thus, "population" and "advertising expenses" should be retained and "number of competitors," X_1, dropped.

15. a. The strongest correlation is between GPA and legal. No problem with multicollinearity.

b. $R^2 = \dfrac{4.3595}{5.0631} = .8610$

c. H_0 is rejected if $F > 5.41$.

$$F = \frac{1.4532}{0.1407} = 10.328$$

At least one coefficient is not zero.

d. Any H_0 is rejected if $t < -2.571$ or $t > 2.571$. It appears that only GPA is significant. Verbal and math could be eliminated.

e. $R^2 = \dfrac{4.2061}{5.0631} = .8307$.

R^2 has only been reduced .0303.

f. The residuals appear slightly skewed (positive), but acceptable.

g. The plots do not suggest a problem with homoscedasticity.

17. a. The correlation matrix is:

	cars	*adv*	*sales*
adv	0.808		
sales	0.872	0.537	
city	0.639	0.713	0.389

Size of sales force (0.872) has the strongest correlation with cars sold. Fairly strong relationship between location of dealership and advertising (0.713). Could be a problem.

b. The regression equation is:
$Y' = 31.1328 + 2.1516adv + 5.0140sales + 5.6651city$
$Y' = 31.1328 + 2.1516(15) + 5.0140(20) + 5.6651(1)$
$= 169.352$.

c. H_0: $\beta_1 = \beta_2 = \beta_3 = 0$; H_1: Not all β's are 0. Reject H_0 if computed $F > 4.07$.

Analysis of Variance			
Source	SS	df	MS
Regression	5,504.4	3	1,834.8
Error	420.2	8	52.5
Total	5,924.7	11	

$F = 1{,}834.8/52.5 = 34.95$.
Reject H_0. At least one regression coefficient is not 0.

d. H_0 is rejected in all cases if $t < -2.306$ or if $t > 2.306$. Advertising and sales force should be retained, city dropped. (Note that dropping city removes the problem with multicollinearity.)

Predictor	Coef	StDev	t-ratio	P
Constant	31.13	13.40	2.32	0.049
adv	2.1516	0.8049	2.67	0.028
sales	5.0140	0.9105	5.51	0.000
city	5.665	6.332	0.89	0.397

e. The new output is

$$Y' = 25.2952 + 2.6187adv + 5.0233sales$$

Predictor	Coef	StDev	t-ratio
Constant	25.30	11.57	2.19
adv	2.6187	0.6057	4.32
sales	5.0233	0.9003	5.58

Analysis of Variance			
Source	SS	df	MS
Regression	5,462.4	2	2,731.2
Error	462.3	9	51.4
Total	5,924.7	11	

f. Stem-and-leaf
Leaf unit = 1.0

1	−1	6
1	−1	
2	−0	5
5	−0	110
(5)	0	01224
2	0	58

The normality assumption is reasonable.

g.

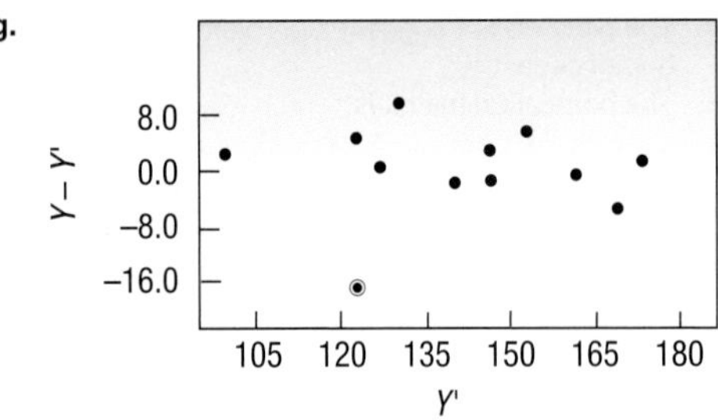

19. a. The correlation matrix is:

	Salary	GPA
GPA	0.902	
Business	0.911	0.851

The two independent variables are related. There may be multicollinearity.

b. The regression equation is: Salary = 23.447 + 2.775 GPA + 1.307 Business. As GPA increases by one point, salary increases by \$2,775. The average business school graduate makes \$1,307 more than a corresponding nonbusiness graduate. Estimated salary is \$33,079; found by \$23,447 + 2,775(3.00) + 1,307(1).

c. $R^2 = \dfrac{21.182}{23.857} = 0.888$

To conduct the global test: H_0: $\beta_1 = \beta_2 = 0$; H_1: Not all β_i's = 0

At the 0.05 significance level, H_0 is rejected if $F > 3.89$.

Source	SS	df	MS	F	p
Regression	21.182	2	10.591	47.50	0.000
Error	2.676	12	0.223		
Total	23.857	14			

The computed value of F is 47.50, so H_0 is rejected. Some of the regression coefficients and R^2 are not zero.

d. Since both the p-values are less than 0.05, there is no need to delete variables.

Predictor	Coef	SE Coef	T	P
Constant	23.447	3.490	6.72	0.000
GPA	2.775	1.107	2.51	0.028
Business	1.3071	0.4660	2.80	0.016

e. The residuals appear normally distributed.

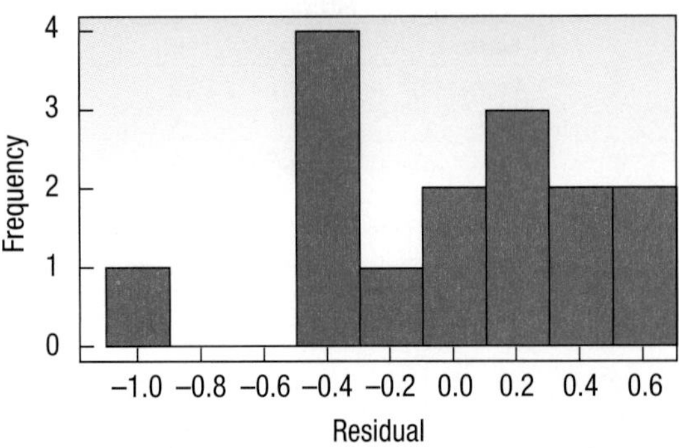

f. The variance is the same as we move from small values to large. So there is no homoscedasticity problem.

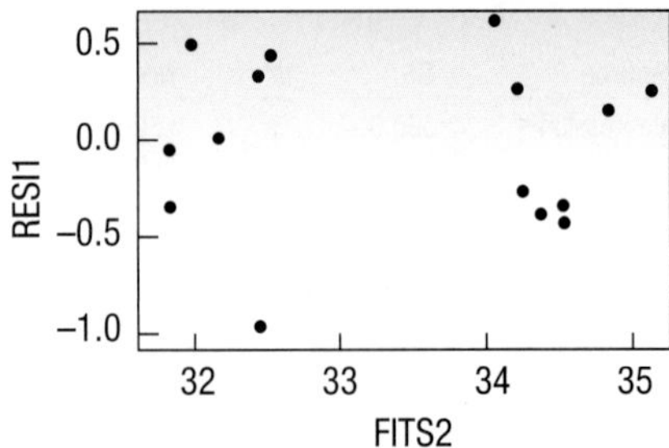

21. The computer output is:

```
Predictor     Coef    Stdev    t-ratio       p
Constant     651.9    345.3       1.89   0.071
Service     13.422    5.125       2.62   0.015
Age         -6.710    6.349      -1.06   0.301
Gender      205.65    90.27       2.28   0.032
Job         -33.45    89.55      -0.37   0.712

Analysis of Variance
SOURCE      DF        SS       MS        F      p
Regression   4   1066830   266708     4.77  0.005
Error       25   1398651    55946
Total       29   2465481
```

a. $Y' = 651.9 + 13.422X_1 - 6.710X_2 + 205.65X_3 - 33.45X_4$

b. $R^2 = .433$, which is somewhat low for this type of study.

c. H_0: $\beta_1 = \beta_2 = \beta_3 = \beta_4 = 0$; H_1: not all βs equal zero. Reject H_0 if $F > 2.76$.

$$F = \frac{1{,}066{,}830/4}{1{,}398{,}651/25} = 4.77$$

H_0 is rejected. Not all the β_is equal 0.

d. Using the .05 significance level, reject the hypothesis that the regression coefficient is 0 if $t < -2.060$ or $t > 2.060$. Service and gender should remain in the analyses; age and job should be dropped.

e. Following is the computer output using the independent variables service and gender.

```
Predictor     Coef    Stdev    t-ratio       p
Constant     784.2    316.8       2.48   0.020
Service      9.021    3.106       2.90   0.007
Gender      224.41    87.35       2.57   0.016

Analysis of Variance
SOURCE      DF        SS       MS        F      p
Regression   2    998779   499389     9.19  0.001
Error       27   1466703    54322
Total       29   2465481
```

A man earns \$224 more per month than a woman. The difference between technical and clerical jobs is not significant.

23. a. $Y' = 29.913 - 5.324X_1 + 1.449X_2$

b. EPS is ($t = -3.26$, p-value = .005). Yield is not ($t = 0.81$, p-value = .431).

c. An increase of 1 in EPS results in a decline of 5.324 in P/E.

d. Stock number 2 is undervalued, it is −18.43 below the fitted value. This is almost two standard errors.

e. Below is a residual plot. It does *not* appear to follow the normal distribution.

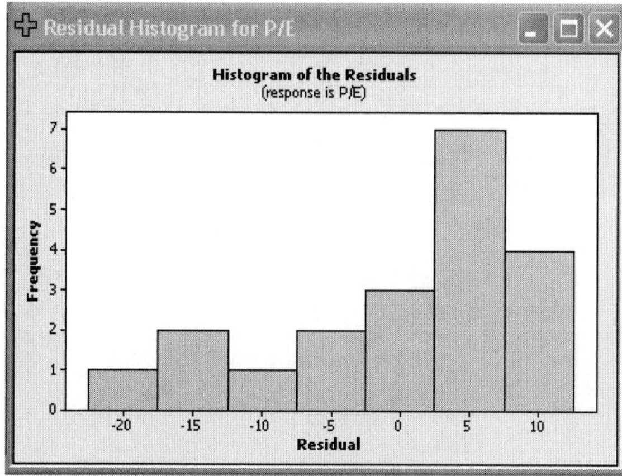

f. There does not seem to be a problem with the plot of the residuals versus the fitted values.

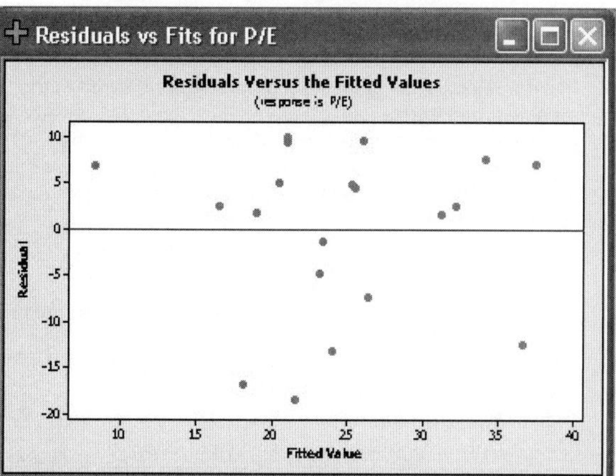

g.

	P/E	EPS
EPS	20.602	
Yield	.054	.162

The correlation between yield and EPS is not a problem.

25. Answers will vary.

27. The computer output is as follows:

```
Predictor        Coef    SE Coef        T       P
Constant        57.03      39.99     1.43   0.157
Bedrooms        7.118      2.551     2.79   0.006
Size          0.03800    0.01468     2.59   0.011
Pool          −18.321      6.999     2.62   0.010
Distance      −0.9295     0.7279    −1.28   0.205
Garage         35.810      7.638     4.69   0.000
Baths          23.315      9.025     2.58   0.011

S = 33.21  R-Sq = 53.2%  R-Sq(adj) = 50.3%

Analysis of Variance
SOURCE            DF      SS      MS      F      P
Regression         6  122676   20446  18.54  0.000
Residual Error    98  108092    1103
Total            104  230768
```

a. Each additional bedroom adds about $7,000 to the selling price, a pool adds $18,300, an attached garage $35,800, and each mile the home is from the center of the city reduces the selling price by $929.

b. The *R*-square value is 0.532.

c. The correlation matrix is as follows:

	Price	Bedrooms	Size	Pool	Distance	Garage
Bedrooms	0.467					
Size	0.371	0.383				
Pool	−0.294	0.005	−0.201			
Distance	−0.347	−0.153	−0.117	−0.139		
Garage	0.526	0.234	0.083	−0.114	−0.359	
Baths	0.382	0.329	0.024	−0.055	−0.195	0.221

The independent variable *garage* has the strongest correlation with price. Distance is inversely related, as expected, and there does not seem to be a problem with correlation among the independent variables.

d. The results of the global test suggest that some of the independent variables have net regression coefficients different from zero.

e. We can delete *distance*.

f. The new regression output follows.

```
Predictor        Coef    SE Coef       T       P
Constant        36.12      36.59    0.99   0.326
Bedrooms        7.169      2.559    2.80   0.006
Size          0.03919    0.01470    2.67   0.009
Pool          −19.110      6.994    2.73   0.007
Garage         38.847      7.281    5.34   0.000
Baths          24.624      8.995    2.74   0.007

S = 33.32  R-Sq = 52.4%  R-Sq(adj) = 50.0%

Analysis of Variance
SOURCE            DF      SS      MS      F      P
Regression         5  120877   24175  21.78  0.000
Residual Error    99  109890    1110
Total            104  230768
```

In reviewing the *p*-values for the various regression coefficients, all are less than .05. We leave all the independent variables.

g & h. Analysis of the residuals, not shown, indicates the normality assumption is reasonable. In addition, there is no pattern to the plots of the residuals and the fitted values of *Y*.

29. a. $Y' = -14{,}174 + 3{,}325X_1 - 11{,}675X_2 + 448X_3 - 5{,}355X_4$ Note age is dropped because of association with other variables. Women earn $11,675 less than men, and union members 5,355 less than nonunion workers. Wages increase $3,325 for each year of education and $448 for each year of experience.

b. $R^2 = .366$, which is not too good.

c. Education and gender have the strongest association with wages; age and experience have a nearly perfect association. Drop age.

d. The computed value of *F* is 13.69, so we conclude some of the regression coefficients are not equal to zero.

e. Drop the union variable, $t = -1.40$.

f. Deleting union decreases R^2 to .352.

g & h. Analysis of the residuals, not shown, indicates the normality assumption is reasonable. In addition, there is no pattern to the plots of the residuals and the fitted values of *Y*.

CHAPTER 15

1. a. 3

b. 7.815

3. **a.** Reject H_0 if $\chi^2 > 5.991$.

b. $$\chi^2 = \frac{(10-20)^2}{20} + \frac{(20-20)^2}{20} + \frac{(30-20)^2}{20} = 10.0$$

c. Reject H_0. The proportions are not equal.

5. H_0: The outcomes are the same; H_1: The outcomes are not the same. Reject H_0 if $\chi^2 > 9.236$

$$\chi^2 = \frac{(3-5)^2}{5} + \cdots + \frac{(7-5)^2}{5} = 7.60$$

Do not reject H_0. Cannot reject H_0 that outcomes are the same.

7. H_0: There is no difference in the proportions.
H_1: There is a difference in the proportions.
Reject H_0 if $\chi^2 > 15.086$.

$$\chi^2 = \frac{(47-40)^2}{40} + \cdots + \frac{(34-40)^2}{40} = 3.400$$

Do not reject H_0. There is no difference in the proportions.

9. **a.** Reject H_0 if $\chi^2 > 9.210$.

b. $$\chi^2 = \frac{(30-24)^2}{24} + \frac{(20-24)^2}{24} + \frac{(10-12)^2}{12} = 2.50$$

c. Do not reject H_0.

11. H_0: Proportions are as stated; H_1: Proportions are not as stated. Reject H_0 if $\chi^2 > 11.345$.

$$\chi^2 = \frac{(50-25)^2}{25} + \cdots + \frac{(160-275)^2}{275} = 115.22$$

Reject H_0. The proportions are not as stated.

13. H_0: There is no relationship between community size and section read. H_1: There is a relationship. Reject H_0 if $\chi^2 > 9.488$.

$$\chi^2 = \frac{(170-157.50)^2}{157.50} + \cdots + \frac{(88-83.62)^2}{83.62} = 7.340$$

Do not reject H_0. There is no relationship between community size and section read.

15. H_0: No relationship between error rates and item type. H_1: There is a relationship between error rates and item type. Reject H_0 if $\chi^2 > 9.21$.

$$\chi^2 = \frac{(20-14.1)^2}{14.1} + \cdots + \frac{(225-225.25)^2}{225.25} = 8.033$$

Do not reject H_0. There is not a relationship between error rates and item type.

17. H_0: $\pi_s = 0.50$, $\pi_r = \pi_e = 0.25$
H_1: Distribution is not as given above.
$df = 2$. Reject H_0 if $\chi^2 > 4.605$.

Turn	f_o	f_e	$f_o - f_e$	$(f_o - f_e)^2/f_e$
Straight	112	100	12	1.44
Right	48	50	−2	0.08
Left	40	50	−10	2.00
Total	200	200		3.52

H_0 is not rejected. The proportions are as given in the null hypothesis.

19. H_0: There is no preference with respect to TV stations.
H_1: There is a preference with respect to TV stations.
$df = 3 - 1 = 2$. H_0 is rejected if $\chi^2 > 5.991$.

TV Station	f_o	f_e	$f_o - f_e$	$(f_o - f_e)^2$	$(f_o - f_e)^2/f_e$
WNAE	53	50	3	9	0.18
WRRN	64	50	14	196	3.92
WSPD	33	50	−17	289	5.78
	150	150	0		9.88

H_0 is rejected. There is a preference for TV stations.

21. H_0: $\pi_n = 0.21$, $\pi_m = 0.24$, $\pi_s = 0.35$, $\pi_w = 0.20$.
H_1: The distribution is not as given.
Reject H_0 if $\chi^2 > 11.345$.

Region	f_o	f_e	$f_o - f_e$	$(f_o - f_e)^2/f_e$
Northeast	68	84	−16	3.0476
Midwest	104	96	8	0.6667
South	155	140	15	1.6071
West	73	80	−7	0.6125
Total	400	400	0	5.9339

H_0 is not rejected. The distribution of order destinations reflects the population.

23. H_0: $\pi_0 = 0.40$, $\pi_1 = 0.30$, $\pi_2 = 0.20$, $\pi_3 = 0.1$
H_1: The proportions are not as given. Reject H_0 if $\chi^2 > 7.815$.

Accidents	f_o	f_e	$(f_o - f_e)^2/f_e$
0	46	48	0.083
1	40	36	0.444
2	22	24	0.167
3	12	12	0.000
Total	120		0.694

Do not reject H_0. Evidence does not show a change in the accident distribution.

25. H_0: Levels of management and concern regarding the environment are not related. H_1: Levels of management and concern regarding the environment are related. Reject H_0 if $\chi^2 > 16.812$.

$$\chi^2 = \frac{(15-14)^2}{14} + \cdots + \frac{(31-28)^2}{28} = 1.550$$

Do not reject H_0. Levels of management and environmental concern are not related.

27. H_0: Whether a claim is filed and age are not related.
H_1: Whether a claim is filed and age are related.
Reject H_0 if $\chi^2 > 7.815$.

$$\chi^2 = \frac{(170-203.33)^2}{203.33} + \cdots + \frac{(24-35.67)^2}{35.67} = 53.639$$

Reject H_0. Age is related to whether a claim is filed.

29. H_0: $\pi_{Bl} = \pi_O = .23$, $\pi_Y = \pi_G = .15$, $\pi_{Br} = \pi_R = .12$
H_1: The proportions are not as given. Reject H_0 if $\chi^2 > 15.086$.

Color	Population	Expected f_e	Observed f_o	$(f_o - f_e)^2/f_e$
Blue	0.23	27.60	20	2.0928
Yellow	0.15	18.00	25	2.7222
Red	0.12	14.40	19	1.4694
Green	0.15	18.00	25	2.7222
Brown	0.12	14.40	10	1.3444
Orange	0.23	27.60	21	1.5783
Total	1	120.00	120	11.9293

Do not reject H_0. The color distribution in this bag agrees with the manufacturer's information.

31. **a.** H_0: There is no relationship between pool and township.
H_1: There is a relationship between pool and township.
Reject H_0 if $\chi^2 > 9.488$.

	Township					
Pool	1	2	3	4	5	Total
Yes	9	8	7	11	3	38
No	6	12	18	18	13	67
Total	15	20	25	29	16	105

$$\chi^2 = \frac{(9 - 5.43)^2}{5.43} + \cdots + \frac{(13 - 10.21)^2}{10.21} = 6.680$$

Do not reject H_0. There is no relationship between pool and township.

b. H_0: There is no relationship between attached garage and township. H_1: There is a relationship between attached garage and township. Reject H_0 if $\chi^2 > 9.488$.

	Township					
Garage	**1**	**2**	**3**	**4**	**5**	**Total**
No	6	5	10	9	4	34
Yes	9	15	15	20	12	71
Total	15	20	25	29	16	105

$$\chi^2 = \frac{(6 - 4.86)^2}{4.86} + \cdots + \frac{(12 - 10.82)^2}{10.82} = 1.980$$

Do not reject H_0. There is no relationship between attached garage and township.

33. H_0: Industry and gender are not related.
H_1: Industry and gender are related.
Note: There are only 3 observations in the industry coded 2; hence 1 and 2 are combined. There is one degree of freedom, so H_0 is rejected if $\chi^2 > 3.841$.

$$\chi^2 = \frac{(41 - 42.40)^2}{42.40} + \cdots + \frac{(8 - 9.40)^2}{9.40} = 0.492$$

Do not reject H_0. We cannot conclude gender and industry are related.

Photo Credits

Chapter 1
P1.1: Photo Courtesy of Wal-Mart Stores, Inc.; **P1.2:** PRNewsFoto/DreamWorks Home Entertainment/AP/Wide World Photos; **P1.3:** © elektraVision AG/PictureQuest; **P1.4:** © RF/Corbis

Chapter 2
P2.1: PhotoDisc/Getty Images; **P2.2:** PhotoDisc/Getty Images; **P2.3:** PhotoDisc/Getty Images

Chapter 3
P3.1: This image is reproduced with permission of United Parcel Service of America, Inc. © Copyright 2004 United Parcel Service of America, Inc. All rights reserved; **P3.2:** © RF/Corbis; **P3.3:** Photo by Stephen Chernin/Getty Images; **P3.4:** Courtesy of Dell Inc.

Chapter 4
P4.1: © RF/Corbis; **P4.2:** The Home Depot; **P4.3:** PhotoDisc/Getty Images; **P4.4:** © RF/Corbis

Chapter 5
P5.1: Photo Courtesy of Wendy's International, Inc.; **P5.2:** PRNewsFoto/AK Steel/AP/Wide World Photos; **P5.3:** © RF/Corbis; **P5.4:** © 2004 Busch Entertainment Corporation. All rights reserved

Chapter 6
P6.1: © RF/Corbis; **P6.2:** © RF/Corbis; **P6.3:** R.Sacha/Getty Images

Chapter 7
P7.1: PhotoDisc/Getty Images; **P7.2:** © RF/Corbis; **P7.3:** The Good Year Tire and Rubber Company

Chapter 8
P8.1: © RF/Corbis; **P8.2:** PhotoDisc/Getty Images; **P8.3:** PhotoDisc/Getty Images; **P8.4:** © BP p.l.c. 2002. All rights reserved

Chapter 9
P9.1: AP/Wide World Photos; **P9.2:** Best Buy Co., Inc; **P9.3:** PhotoDisc/Getty Images; **P9.4:** AP/Wide World Photos

Chapter 10
P10.1: Photo courtesy of NCR Corporation; **P10.2:** PhotoDisc/Getty Images; **P10.3:** PhotoDisc/Getty Images; **P10.4:** PRNewsFoto/The HON Company/AP/Wide World Photos

Chapter 11
P11.1: Digital Vision/Getty Images; **P11.2:** © RF/Corbis; **P11.3:** © RF/Corbis; **P11.4:** PhotoDisc/Getty Images

Chapter 12
P12.1: PhotoDisc/Getty Images; **P12.2:** PhotoDisc/Getty Images; **P12.3:** PhotoDisc/Getty Images

Chapter 13
P13.1: Tim Boyle/Getty Images; **P13.2:** © The Coca-Cola Company; **P13.3:** Feature Photo Service/Sharp/AP/Wide World Photos

Chapter 14
P14.1: © RF/Corbis; **P14.2:** PhotoDisc/Getty Images; **P14.3:** PhotoDisc/Getty Images

Chapter 15
P15.1: © Don Smetzer/Photo Edit; **P15.2:** PRNewsFoto/ING Americas/AP/WideWorld Photos; **P15.3:** © RF/Corbis

Index